METHODOLOGY AND FIELDWORK

Oxford in India Readings
in Sociology and Social Anthropology

GENERAL EDITOR
T.N. MADAN

METHODOLOGY
AND
FIELDWORK

Edited by

VINAY KUMAR SRIVASTAVA

OXFORD
UNIVERSITY PRESS

OXFORD
UNIVERSITY PRESS

YMCA Library Building, Jai Singh Road, New Delhi 110 001

Oxford University Press is a department of the University of Oxford. It furthers the
University's objective of excellence in research, scholarship, and education
by publishing worldwide in

Oxford   New York

Auckland   Bangkok   Buenos Aires   Cape Town   Chennai
Dar es Salaam   Delhi   Hong Kong   Istanbul   Karachi   Kolkata
Kuala Lumpur   Madrid   Melbourne   Mexico City   Mumbai   Nairobi
São Paulo   Shanghai   Taipei   Tokyo   Toronto

Oxford is a registered trade mark of Oxford University Press
in the UK and in certain other countries

Published in India
By Oxford University Press, New Delhi

© Oxford University Press 2004

The moral rights of the author have been asserted
Database right Oxford University Press (maker)

First published 2004

ISBN 0 19 566727 1

Typeset in Times New Roman 10 / 12 by Comprint, New Delhi 1100 29
Printed in India by Sai Printo Pack Pvt. Ltd., New Delhi 110 020
Published by Manzar Khan, Oxford University Press
YMCA Library Building, Jai Singh Road, New Delhi 110 001

Contents

Preface

Over the past two decades, qualitative research increased in importance as methods of social inquiry. These methods are no more considered 'inferior' to quantitative research as was the case earlier, when epithets such as 'journalists', 'soft scientists', and 'story tellers' were frequently used for qualitative researchers. Even in disciplines (such as economics and psychology) that are predominantly based on numbers and measurements, where training in statistics and mathematics, qualitative methods have now found a respectable place. These and other disciplines have been seeking the assistance of social anthropologists and sociologists, the forerunners in qualitative research and fieldwork, to develop their own traditions. Although some social scientists still regard qualitative researchers as 'second class' and whose work does not have quite so much explanatory power as, quantitative research, most studies on research methodology argue that the methods chosen for study depend upon the context and the researcer's goal. Furthermore, correlation between quantitative facts is explained in quantitative terms, often by resorting to imagination. It is, therefore, futile to argue in favour of the 'superiority' of one over the other. Rather, whenever possible, theoretical generalizations should be supported by counts. Each researcher learns that there are facts of society and culture, which cannot be quantified, and there are those that need to be counted and statistically treated. The readings assembled in this volume on methodology and fieldwork are mostly qualitative in nature, but the underlying idea is that qualitative and quantitative researches are complementary.

To undertake qualitative research, social anthropologists and sociologists make use of four methods: observation, interview, collection of texts and documents, and audio and video recordings of naturally occurring behaviour. Observation and interview may be relatively unstructured or may become increasingly structured. Questionnaires and interview schedules are used in survey research. Official statistics are also analyzed for understanding the macro-situation, its trends and directions.

In the second half of the twentieth century, several writings on the issues of research methodology by Indian scholars and on studies from India have appeared, therefore, the task of choosing readings for this volume was not easy. For each of its four sections, various articles and books were collected, and what seemed to me the most representative was included here. This volume is different from the standard books on research methodology, on the one hand, and the fieldwork accounts on the other, for it combines elements from both. The introduction gives a brief idea of the techniques and methods used in social research, some which have also been taken up in the introduction to each section.

I am extremely grateful to T.N. Madan for giving me the opportunity to edit this volume. He also advised me on articles and excerpts from books that I could consider. Alan Macfarlane, Christopher Pinney, and James Laidlaw obliged me with their original contributions. I am grateful to André Béteille for his painstaking perusal of my manuscript, and giving his apt and invaluable suggestions. Kulwinder Kaur and Sagar Preet Hooda read the introduction closely and critically. My wife, Kumkum, helped me with editing. And, for various acts of kindness, I am particularly thankful to Alka Malvankar, Vibha Joshi, Surinder Nath, Sukant K. Chaudhury, S.M. Patnaik, Subhadra Channa, and R.P. Mitra. I am especially appreciative of Sonal, Tushar, and Rohan, for providing me the happy moments of distraction. I dedicate this volume to the memory of my maternal grandparents, Suraj Mukhi, Ram Dulari, and Babu Brij Lal Srivastava.

New Delhi   VINAY KUMAR SRIVASTAVA
1 January 2004

Acknowledgement to Publishers

The publishers wish to thank the following for permission to include articles/extracts in this volume:

SAGE PUBLICATIONS for Satish Saberwal, 'On Reality, Its Perception and Construction', from Partha Nath Mukherji (ed), *Methodology in Social Research* (2000).

STATE UNIVERSITY OF NEW YORK PRESS for Ramkrishna Mukherjee, 'On Classification' from *Classification in Social Research* (1988).

UNIVERSITY OF CHICAGO PRESS for Gananath Obeyesekere, 'The First Intersubjectivity: The Anthropologist and the Native', from *The Work of Culture, Symbolic Transformation in Psychoanalysis and Anthropology* (1990).

GERALD D. BERREMAN for Gerald D. Berreman, 'Ethnography, Method and Product', from James A. Clifton (ed), *Introduction to Cultural Anthropology*. Boston: Houghton Mifflin Company (1968).

WENNER-GREN FOUNDATION for Anthropological Research for Joseph W. Elder, 'Caste and World View: The Application of Survey Research Methods', from Milton Singer and Bernard S. Cohn (eds), *Structure and Change in Indian Society*, Viking Fund Publications in Anthropology, No. 47, New York, 1968.

INSTITUTE OF ECONOMIC GROWTH for A.C. Mayer, 'Perceptions of Princely Rule: Perspectives from a Biography', from T.N. Madan (ed), *The Way of Life: Essays in Honour of Louis Dumont* (1986).

SAGE PUBLICATIONS for S.H. Rudolph and L.I. Rudolph, 'Becoming a Diarist: Amar Singh's Construction of an Indian Personal Document', *The Indian Economic and Social History Review*, Vol.25, No.2, 1988.

INDIAN INSTITUTE OF ADVANCED STUDY for A.M. Shah, 'Study of Changes in the Indian Family', from *Trends of Socio-Economic Change in India*, Vol. VII, Simla, 1969.

JOHN VAN WILLIGEN for John van Willigen and Narendra K. Chadha, 'Networks' from *Social Aging in a Delhi Neighbourbood*. Westport, Connecticut and London: Bergin and Garvey, 1999.

ECONOMIC AND POLITICAL WEEKLY for Malvika Karlekar, 'Search for Women's Voices: Reflections on Fieldwork, 1968-93', *Economic and Political Weekly*, Vol. XXX, No. 17 April 29, 1995.

MANOHAR PUBLISHERS for James M. Freeman, 'Collecting the Life History of an Indian Untouchable', from Sylvia Vatuk (ed), *American Studies in the Anthropology of India* (1978).

TAVISTOCK PUBLICATIONS for Stella Mascarenhas-Keyes, 'The Native Anthropologist: Constraints and Strategies in Research', from Anthony Jackson (ed), *Anthropology at Home* (1987).

RAI for Vinay Kumar Srivastava, 'On Payment to Respondents', *Anthropology Today*, Vol.8, No.6, December 1992.

Introduction

This introduction contains an account of the research methods used in social anthropology and sociology. The readings included in the volume are divided into four sections: the first is on the nature of social research, the second deals with fieldwork, the third with survey methods, and the last section takes up the issues of ethics in research, besides the problems of studying one's own society and undertaking field studies across class and gender.

The Idea of Social Research

Social research may be defined as a methodical and systematic study of a subject with the aim to generate new information, verify the existing knowledge in that subject, and reach a new understanding.[1] Sociology and social anthropology are empirical disciplines, and in them, like in other social sciences, facts are of crucial importance. Researchers know that for pursuing research they require specialized procedures that they learn before and during the process of conducting research. Given the optimum conditions, researchers believe that all areas and subjects can be researched. They are also aware that their findings are dependent upon, among other things, the methods they choose for study and their individual skills in manoeuvring them. Although commonality exists between research procedures investigating different areas of knowledge, each discipline has its distinct methodological apparatus to approach its specialized interest.[2] In today's world of interdisciplinary research, some elements of research methodology in a subject may be borrowed from another, but they will not make sense unless they are adapted to the study of the subject matter at hand.[3]

The process of planning a systematic study to seek probable answers to questions about social and cultural life is designated as social research. It begins with a set of questions about an event or a phenomenon in which the researcher is interested.[4] The questions are not just confined to researchers, for lay people also ask them. Not only that, both researchers and non-researchers formulate answers to the questions they have raised on the basis of their experience and understanding. But researchers consider their answers tentative, howsoever convincing they may appear at face value. They subscribe to the idea that one does not know a social fact unless one has conducted its systematic study.[5] Researchers know that all hypotheses, even the favoured ones, have to be tested. The literature they read may tell them that the cause of crime lies in society or that the number of latchkey children in the upper middle class is fast increasing but they demonstrate the relationship between crime and society by collecting and analysing the life history accounts of criminals and the cases of crime in a society. Similarly, they conduct household surveys to arrive at the percentage of children who are alone at home after school because their parents are at work. Researchers will base their conclusions on an analysis of empirical data that they themselves collect or that is collected under their close supervision. Lay explanations of phenomena, however brilliant and convincing, may at best help in formulating hypotheses, which are empirically tested through to determine their veracity.

Research of any type commences with a problem, the answers to which the investigator seeks to find out with an array of techniques, methods, and theoretical perspectives. In other words, the research process begins with the selection of the research question, followed by the selection of an appropriate methodology (Sarantakos 1998: 119). Following this are the steps pertaining to data collection—whether the data will come from libraries, archives, and museums, or from respondents belonging to a social group by adopting the methods of fieldwork or survey, or both, and whether the data will be quantitative or qualitative in character or a mix of both.

The sources an investigator taps will vary according to his interests, their accessibility, and the type of study (Whyte 1955: 356). Though there is a rough sketch in the investigator's mind of what he would look for, these sources (and/or informants) are not really decided in advance. The manner in which the investigation will be steered depends entirely on the actual unfolding of the research situation. What the research methodology literature contains is an account of the 'most frequently encountered techniques' of investigation (Pelto and Pelto 1978: 67). There are books and articles delineating the questions and topics that the researcher should keep in mind while investigating institutionalized modes of social behaviour.[6] But, in sociology and social anthropology, there is no specific tool kit that can be uniformly given to a researcher; rather, he chooses the appropriate tools from the available repertoire of methods and techniques and modifies them or supplements the standard procedures in light of the situation he encounters. In essence, he 'learns from the field' (Whyte 1984).

Each piece of finished research work, therefore, has its own story to tell; it is perhaps unique. This explains why accounts of how investigation was actually undertaken in a given context are enormously instructive to neophytes embarking on social research. Earlier when, apart from a few pieces, the practice of writing up the experiences of one's research had not come into vogue, we had literature on how research should be carried out and on the finished products of research.[7] Almost nothing was available on the intervening stage of the struggle of choosing the right methodology, adapting the gamut of methods and techniques to real-life situations, and learning newer modes of investigation from the frustrations encountered with textbook descriptions of the tools of research. Now we know the immense usefulness of the accounts of the real research process, the way in which a piece of research was accomplished.[8]

The Choice of a Research Problem

Many factors influence the choice of a research problem. A topic may be selected because it is assumed to be significant for scientific knowledge, ideas, and hypotheses. Or, it may be seen as important for ameliorating the living condition of human beings. Many researchers today work on health and hygiene, ecological and demographic issues, empowerment, and development in the hope of rendering a 'meaningful' and 'operational' solution to human problems. Contemporary fashions, fads, and foibles in research—the fields generally clinched for study at a particular time—also condition the choice (Sjoberg and Nett 1992). So do research guides and funding agencies. A topic is pursued because one is attached to a particular guide (or 'laboratory') that furthers a particular line and topic of research, or where grants are easily available. Also, the social background of investigators has implications for moulding their interests. And serendipity plays a definite role in taking up and navigating the research project. The researcher fortuitously 'stumbles upon' an area of investigation or a chance finding makes him change the original topic of enquiry.[9]

Whatever may be the reason(s) behind the formulation of a research problem, researchers should ask themselves the following five questions, originally asked by Bernard (1994: 103), before commencing their study:

1. Does the topic (the subject of study, the physical area where the enquiry will be carried out) really interest them?

2. Is this problem amenable to scientific investigation?
3. Do they have adequate resources to investigate this topic? (Here the questions of funding and time figure.)
4. Will the research questions, or the methods and techniques that are being used, lead to unreasonable ethical problems?
5. Does the topic have any theoretical interest?

It is possible that the researcher's interest may lie elsewhere, but he takes up a project because of convenience or other attractions. In anthropology departments of Indian universities, for example, it is common to find women doctoral students who are enthusiastic about conducting research among distant, isolated, pre-industrial communities, such as foragers and shifting cultivators, but, as they often fail to obtain permission from their families to go to remote areas for fieldwork, they compromise with a study of townspeople, or return to their own community for fieldwork.[10]

The researcher should think of more than one possible research topic and areas of fieldwork which may be closely related. If the chances of furthering one are bleak, the possibility of the other(s) should be explored. The following example may be considered. A researcher is interested in studying the social organization of the sufi tradition of Qalandars in South Asia (see de Tassy 1977: 176). For this, he should ideally carry out his fieldwork in the shrine of the most popular Qalandar saint, namely Lal Shahbaz of Sehwan (Sind, Pakistan), but in case he is denied permission to do fieldwork in Pakistan, he can always approach the other Qalander shrines, such as of Bu Ali Shah in Panipat (Haryana, India), for permission, or may decide to do his fieldwork in the shrine of Abu Bakar Tusi in New Delhi. For Lal Shahbaz, he may depend upon secondary sources—the already published materials— and interview people who had visited the saint's shrine in the past. When fieldwork was not possible in Japan during the period of the Pacific War, for example, Benedict (1946) interviewed the Japanese settled in America and those taken as prisoners of war, and analysed printed material (newspapers, broadcasts, and folklore) from Japan, to formulate certain observations about the Japanese personality and what inspired them to commit suicide for honour (*harakiri*). Similarly, when the Peoples' Republic of China did not permit a first-hand study of its communities, anthropologists conducted fieldwork with Chinese settled in Malaysia, Singapore, or Thailand. This research strategy is known as the 'study of a culture at distance'.[11]

Prospective researchers in social anthropology and sociology think in terms of the 'problem' they intend to investigate (for instance, whether it will be a study of an entire community or one of its institutions, groups, or typical persons) and the 'physical area' from where they will gather their data. In some cases, a research problem can only be pursued in a specific community; for example, for studying the highly elaborate procession of deities from their widely separated abodes in the hills to the town during a festival (such as Shivratri, Navaratri, and Dushera), one shall have to work in places like Mandi, Sundernagar, and Kullu, all located in Himachal Pradesh. By comparison, there are research problems that can be followed up at diverse research sites. For studying peoples' displacement due to development programmes, a researcher may choose to work in any of a number of states in India or, for local practices of eco-regeneration or water conservation, a village or community anywhere in traditional India may be suitable.

Researchers often delay the process of finalizing their research topic, or collecting data, or writing up, because they think they have not read enough and are not aware of an adequate number of references on the topic under study (see Wolcott 1990, 1995). One book or article leads to another; it is a snowball process, almost unending. No researcher (or author) can ever hope to have read all that has been written on a topic. One may be aware of the material available in a field of study in English, but there may be a parallel scholarship in that field in other languages, including the local. Therefore, while framing and finalizing a research topic, one should read closely the salient works available in that field, identify the ideas that interest him and need investigation. Each piece of research is built upon, and adds to, the work available in that domain, and no research work answers all questions. The final stage in the research process is of interpreting the results after coding and analysis of data. These interpretations raise many questions that guide further research.[12]

The Research Design

The research design is a systematic outline of the way in which a particular research will be carried out. In a research design, the investigator makes a distinction between the empirical phase and the interpretive phase. The former deals with the collection of data and the latter with the significance of the findings, which is conditioned by the nature of data and the theoretical approaches and conceptual models of the researcher. He decides 'how he will select certain facts (his data), how he will classify the facts, and how he will seek to uncover the order or pattern in which they actually occur' (Riley 1963: 5). As a part of this design, the researcher decides whether to gather new data rather than use available materials, take a larger rather than a smaller sample of cases, the way in which the techniques and methods will be administered, and which of them will be combined.

A research project begins with an identification of various concepts that pertain to the problem under study. Concepts such as income, rainfall, age, temperature, height, etc., 'that take on more than one value along a continuum are called variables' (Bailey 1978: 33). A concept having a single or fixed value is called a constant. Usually, the values or categories of a variable are signified by numbers (for instance, as in the case of income or rainfall), but there are variables that are designated qualitatively, by 'word labels rather than by numbers', for instance, gender is a variable (a 'qualitative variable') and its categories are designated by word labels—male and female. An important step in the research process is the formulation of the hypothesis, which may be defined as a testable proposition showing a tentative relationship between two or more variables, each having an empirical referent, meaning that each one is amenable to empirical investigation. A hypothesis should be conceptually clear, specific, operational, and related to the available techniques and methods of investigation.[13]

As stated, after the research problem has been selected, the researcher formulates its basic concepts that require to be studied independently or in a system of relationship. These concepts could be variables or constants; however, most social researchers, concerned with phenomena that vary, are concerned with variables. Then, the researcher constructs propositions (i.e., statements) about the variables (ibid.: 34). A proposition that discusses one variable is known as univariate; one showing relationship between two variables is a bivariate proposition. When in a proposition more than two variables are related it is called multivariate. These propositions may be illustrated with the aid of an example.

The following statement is an example of the univariate proposition: 'The practice of untouchability in Indian villages has declined in the second half of the twentieth century.' A bivariate relationship could be: 'The practice of untouchability in Indian villages has declined because of the legal prohibitions.' This relationship can be empirically investigated; it can be categorized as a hypothesis. A multivariate proposition could be: 'The practice of untouchability in Indian villages has declined because of the legal prohibitions against it, an improvement in the economic status of the ex-untouchable communities, and an increase in the level of education in villages.' This hypothesis will be termed multivariate. In this hypothesis, a decline in the practice of untouchability (the effect) is believed to be caused by legal prohibitions and an improvement in economic and educational levels among the people (the causes). The variable in which change occurs is known as 'dependent' (here, the practice of untouchability), whereas the variables that cause it (namely, law, economy, and education) are independent.[14] The relationship between these variables can be expressed in terms of the cause-and-effect relationship. For the purpose of testing, a multivariate relationship can be written down into several bivariate propositions, because, to follow the example given above, it is likely that legal prohibitions may cause a decline in the practice of untouchability but not economy or education. When the multivariate relationship is broken down, three hypotheses result, viz., the decline in untouchability practices is because of the legal prohibitions against it; the decline in untouchability practices is because of an improvement in the economic condition of ex-untouchable castes; and the decline in untouchability practices is because of an increase in the educational levels of people. And then each one of them can be empirically tested. With the help of multivariate analysis, the simultaneous relationship among three or more variables can be studied.

Furthermore, a hypothesis is not an opinion, a value judgement, or a normative statement. It may follow from a theory or ensue from experience or be inspired by reading or past research. But, even when it does not explicitly follow from a theory, it can always be related back to a theoretical orientation. A theory is viewed as a logical relationship between facts.[15] From this, relationships other than those stated in it can be deduced. These deduced propositions, which are hypotheses, are empirically tested. If substantiated, they become a part of the theory. The theoretical propositions the researcher carries in his mind guide the collection of data. When the data are collected without any biases, and the emerging relationship between facts, which may go contrary to the existing theory, is not suppressed, the theory and its propositions undergo change. In many cases, the link between the theory and the mode of investigation (data collection) is provided by the hypothesis.

For some sociologists, research without hypotheses may become unfocused and a random empirical wandering.[16] But, not all research is about establishing causality or other kinds of relations between variables. It may also be remembered that a hypothesis can be a liability.[17] The researcher must always guard against the Procrustean approach, in which the hypothesis is laid in advance and the empirical facts are tailored to prove it. Fashionable theories and enchanting hypotheses may inveigle us into looking for facts that lend them credence. The 'classical theory' of research methodology, as it is called, submits that a hypothesis is formulated in advance and then is empirically tested (Bailey 1978: 44–46). By contrast, 'grounded theory' suggests that one should begin with one's fieldwork without a hypothesis, describe what goes in the field, and offer explanations of the same. Instead of testing existing theories, grounded theory suggests that the best way to generate a theory is from the data itself (Glaser and Strauss 1967).[18]

There are advantages in beginning with the broad areas we wish to investigate without any hypotheses, but certain research topics may require clearly formulated hypotheses. The aim of a research design may be hypothesis-testing. One cannot, therefore, argue in favour of grounded theory (hypothesis-yielding approach) over the classical approach (hypothesis-testing or hypothesis-verification approach), or the other way round, because each one of them has its own merits. A preference of one over the other is determined by the aim of research.

Types of Social Research

Many types of social research can be profitably combined[19] in a given piece of research. Quantitative and qualitative researches are not opposed. There has been an almost inexhaustible debate about the scientific status of quantitative research in opposition to the so-called 'soft' (non-scientific and subjective) qualitative research. Today, it is well known that we use quantitative techniques if our subject matter and the materials we have collected demand that treatment. We switch on to qualitative research if we intend to describe the reality as our respondents experience it and when we are dealing with 'immeasurable' aspects of social and cultural life. In fact, quantitative and qualitative aspects of phenomena can be integrated in research.[20] It is relevant here to remember Myrdal's (1944: 1130) advice:

The ideal community study should start out from a careful *statistical analysis* of vital, social, and economic data concerning the individuals and families making up the community being studied. The less measurable data on attitudes, cultural traits, behaviour patterns in which social stratification is expressed, and the 'feeling' of social status or toward social status on the part of members of the various groups, should then be observed and the results *integrated into the framework* of statistical knowledge.

A research design is prepared according to the purpose of research. Research purposes may be categorized in the following terms:

1. The purpose may be to gain familiarity with a phenomenon or to obtain new insights into it. The phenomenon might hitherto be unexplored, or the material available on it might be unauthentic, heavily journalistic, or trying to capture its oddness.

2. The purpose may be to portray as accurately as possible the characteristics of a phenomenon about which some preliminary information is available. Or, one may be interested in testing a hypothesis in the field situation.

3. The purpose may be to test a hypothesis of a causal relationship between variables in a controlled situation.

These three are ideal types of research purpose, respectively known as exploratory (or formulative), descriptive, and experimental. The research design is also named after the specific purpose that it endeavours to accomplish; thus the design for exploratory work is termed exploratory research design, and so on.

Exploratory design intends to formulate a more precise research problem or to develop hypotheses. By comparison to other research designs, it is flexible, allowing researchers to navigate the area where they would later like to conduct a lengthy, more structured, study. It acquaints researchers with the possibilities and problems of studying real life situations and clarifying various concepts (Selltiz et al. 1959: 52–53). Insights gained from an exploratory study may provide a solid base for planning a descriptive study. As a matter of fact, most studies in sociology and social anthropology are descriptive in nature, offering detailed accounts of communities, their groups and institutions, events and material culture, and life histories of persons. Descriptive studies not only tell one what happens but also why and how it happens; the latter questions are sometimes subsumed under the head of explanatory studies. Events are also predicted in descriptive works. In comparison to exploratory studies, which are hypothesis-generating, descriptive studies are both hypothesis-testing and hypothesis-generating.

The experimental research design tests hypotheses in 'laboratory' conditions, i.e. the investigator systematically controls the independent variables as well as the external factors that may confound the result. Crucial to this design, in the words of J.S. Mill, is the method of difference.[21] The independent variable is introduced in one group and withheld from the other, where the two groups are identical in all respects. The recipient of the independent variable is called the experimental group whereas the one denied of it is the control group.[22] These two groups are compared after a lapse of time. The difference in their respective conditions supports or rejects the hypothesis.[23]

This design of experimentation, known as the 'classical' design, which is principally followed in natural and biological sciences, is however not amenable to social research because of the problems of creating experimental and control groups, and of keeping the external variables controlled for the entire duration of the experiment. Many aspects of social life cannot be brought into the laboratory. The experimental situation can also affect the responses of those studied.[24] And, the ethical problems of conducting experiments on human beings are equally important.

One may refer here to Richard Cabot's famous experiment of 1935 on the prevention of delinquency.[25] Popularly known as the Cambridge-Somerville Youth Study, it was here that for the first time in the history of social research, a carefully constructed control group was utilized. Cabot's hypothesis was that delinquency would come under control when trained social workers, using the case work techniques of their discipline, rendered regular friendly counselling to delinquents. The experimental group of delinquents received the benefits of counselling (the independent variable) that was denied to the control group. Upon a comparison of the two groups, it was found that besides a few success stories, counselling was not able to deflect the boys from committing to a delinquent career. The treatment programme seemed to be broadly ineffectual because besides spending some hours every week with the counselor, the delinquent boys spent their entire time with their community where were concentrated the social forces that lured these boys to antisocial acts. The external variables seated in the community nullified the positive outcomes of the counselling.

In certain other works on small group dynamism, the group members were temporarily insulated from the outside world, yet these 'experiments' did not have a control group.[26] They deviated considerably from the classical experimental design. The positivists—like Auguste Comte—had realized in the early nineteenth century that the faculty of experimentation in its true form was ruled out in sociology and they looked for its functional equivalent.[27] For some positivists, controlled comparison was an alternative to experimentation (Timasheff 1955). Moreover, experimentation is not central to the definition of science, for there are subjects (such as astronomy, geology, population genetics) that do not experiment but their scientific status is beyond doubt (Nadel 1951: 1).

The so-called 'before-and-after' studies are regarded as an alternative to the classical experimental design. In them, a phenomenon is studied before and after the introduction of the independent variable. A comparison of the two states will tell us about the change. F. Stuart Chapin's study (1963) of public housing in Minneapolis coined the term 'ex-post facto research' for such studies. Chapin studied the social life of the families which had been rehoused and compared it with those of the families that were still living in slums, waiting to be moved out. In Chapin's study, it is not the same group which is studied before and after the change, but there are two groups from the same stock, one portraying the 'before' and the other, the 'after'. In the Indian context, many researchers working on communities that have been displaced because of development projects (such as the construction of a dam, mining, or industry) have adopted this approach.[28] To know about the community before it was displaced, they have studied those families of the community that have yet to be displaced and compared them with those that have been displaced to a new setting.

The hypotheses emerging from an exploratory or a descriptive study can be empirically tested using an experimental design. The latter is primarily for hypothesis-verification, but we may come across serendipitous findings while conducting an experiment (or controlled comparison), whether it is in the natural and biological sciences or the social sciences.

Methods of Data Collection

Besides experimentation and 'before-and-after' research, sociologists use three other methods of data collection, viz., fieldwork, survey, and documentary research. The term 'field' refers to the place where the members of the community the investigator plans to study reside. It can also refer to the relatively enduring 'context' of modern institutions—such as the school, hospital, office, prison, hostel—which the researcher studies by staying there, if possible, or by spending a long time with people who do. The process of collecting data by living with people, having a first-hand experience of their lifestyle, is termed fieldwork.[29] Luhrmann (1989: 15) writes: 'Anthropology is the naturalist's trade: you sit and watch and learn from the species in its natural environment.' Compared to the other methods, fieldwork yields a lot of data about the lifestyles of people and the meanings they attribute to their actions. Fieldwork also teaches the distinction between 'what people think', 'what people say', 'what people do', and 'what people say they ought to have done'. The fieldworker can alter strategies and techniques of data collection, improvise newer methods, and follow up new leads that arise because fieldwork provides immense flexibility to the investigator. He can devise 'on-the-spot strategies to come to grips with unforeseen challenges of fieldwork' (Madan 1995: 112).

Survey research focuses on a large number of respondents, chosen through sampling procedures, who are systematically interviewed by the investigators or are requested to write down their answers on a questionnaire delivered to them. The answers thus received are numerically coded and analysed using statistical methods. Survey research allows for precise comparisons between the answers of respondents. Further, survey research may be cross-sectional, i.e., the respondents studied at one point of time represent a cross-section of the community, or longitudinal, where the same or different set of respondents are studied at different times. When the same individuals are studied at different times with respect to the same topic, the survey is called a panel study, and when each time there are different individuals for the same field of interest, it is a trend study. Beginning in the mid-1930s, survey research has expanded considerably in the second half of the twentieth century, constituting today one of the major industries in the developed world helping various organizations in obtaining feedback on their products and work.

Generally, research methodology books in sociology and social anthropology lay emphasis on fieldwork and survey methods, with the result that documentary research is pushed to the margins.[30] This is inevitable because documentary research is the special feature of history and not sociology and social anthropology, which have remained largely preoccupied with the observed present. The researcher has preferred to 'observe the behaviour' rather than relying solely on people's description of their behaviour. Moreover, social anthropologists (and also, many sociologists in India) worked with pre-literate societies where the possibility of finding documentary evidence in many of them was rather bleak. They relied on people's account of their actions when it was not possible, or permissible, for them to observe.

Some authors include both written and oral sources in documentary evidence (Burgess 1982: 131). However, a distinction should be made between the 'texts' that ethnographers prepare after several sessions of interviewing their respondents, and the written materials that are already in existence about people, such as personal documents, biographies, autobiographies, letters, diaries, sermons, poems, plays, novels, and newspapers. There is another category of documents that local people prepare under the guidance of anthropologists. For instance, fieldworkers often request the literate people of the society which they are studying to write up accounts of their lives and their cultural practices. This was the approach that Franz Boas adopted in his fieldwork; he engaged literate respondents to gather information from elders about tribal lore and also write up their own recollections (Lowie 1937). In his stay with the Nyoro, Beattie (1965: 27) employed ex-schoolboys as assistants to record the long statements of the illiterate people. These assistants, whom Beattie regarded as 'apprentice social anthropologists', also wrote detailed accounts of certain incidents in their own lives. As Nyoro found it 'easier to write than to talk', Beattie organized for them two essay competitions on subjects of local interest (ibid. 31). Even after Beattie had left the field, he could always write to his literate assistants for information or clarification by mail. Boas believed that the native's *ipsissima verba* (actual/identical words) represent an 'ultimate datum of reality', and there can be no substitute to the data that respondents write in their own words (Lowie 1937). The point to be stressed is that sociologists and social anthropologists do not privilege written records over oral, or vice versa. They not only collect oral episodes, but if conditions permit, they also make their respondents write up their memories, experiences, and views. This shows that with anthropological intervention respondents transform their oral sources into written records.

Calling written texts and artifacts 'mute evidence', Hodder (1998: 110–11), following Lincoln and Guba (1985), distinguishes records from documents. When a text is prepared to attest to some formal transaction, it is called a record. Marriage certificates, driving licences, building contracts, bank statements, examination transcripts, property papers, etc., are examples of records. Documents are prepared for 'personal rather than official reasons'; they include diaries, memos, letters, field notes, etc. Although the two terms—records and documents—may be used interchangeably, the difference between them is important. For Hodder, the distinction between them is like the distinction between writing and speech. He writes:

Documents, closer to speech, require more contextualized interpretation. Records. . . may have local uses that become very distant from officially sanctioned meanings. Documents involve a personal technology, and records a full state technology of power. . . [The] researcher may often be able to get access to documents, whereas access to records may be restricted by laws regarding privacy, confidentiality, and anonymity.

Records and documents are used for different purposes; records are used for the verification of facts and for understanding the system of administration, whereas documents give insight into personalized experiences. Newspapers also constitute an important source in documentary research.

In sociological and anthropological work, documentary evidence is used for strengthening observations or for attempting a brief historical sketch of people. Many fieldworkers spend time in archives looking for relevant materials to illuminate the local history.[31] Srinivas (1996: 94-101, 112) shows the importance of documents (like, partition deeds) in his study of disputes. He says that in those cases where documents exist, one may question the respondents on that basis and reconstruct the disputes and the dynamics of their settlement. However, there are situations of dispute about which documents do not exist, but the fieldworker comes to know that a number of people were involved in the dispute. In these cases, he can interview them individually to obtain an account that may be broadly true. In other words, documents may guide an empirical study of disputes, and the investigator may combine documentary evidence with the empirical.

There have also been full-fledged studies of documents, especially diaries. One may refer here to Alan Macfarlane's work (1970) on the family life of a seventeenth-century clergyman, Ralph Josselin. Subtitling his work as 'essay in historical anthropology', Macfarlane submits Josselin's diaries to anthropological examination, patiently analysing the entries and supplementing their evidence from other sources. One learns a lot about the society of Josselin's times from his diaries. Another work of profit is an analysis of the diaries of Subbalakshmi, written in the years 1924–26, by Visweswaran (1996: 143–65). Well known in diary research is the Rudolphs' work on Amar Singh's diaries, a Rajput prince from Rajasthan.[32]

Anthropologists are particularly interested in material culture. Even while pursuing the study of non-material culture, they find their study incomplete unless material culture is integrated with it. A study of the local patterns of music, for example, would require a study of the local musical instruments, the technology that creates them, the materials used in them and the ways in which they are acquired, and the people who make and use them. Anthropologists learn to draw material cultural objects to size. They also acquire them for their museums. In fact, the museum is one of the funding agencies of anthropological fieldwork in many universities. Besides integrating material culture with the study of non-material culture, it is also possible to focus on an aspect of material culture and through its study try to illuminate certain social and symbolic dimensions of people whose material culture is studied. One may begin with the study of jewellery, house types, clothes, or any other object. Using methods of interpretation, one may work out the principles of social structure that material culture illuminates.[33] The *vade mecum* of anthropological fieldwork, *Notes and Queries in Anthropology* (1874/1964), gives an inventory of questions one may keep in mind while collecting information on material culture.

Contesting Perspectives

An important aspect that research investigators should bear in mind is that members of a society may hold contesting, and conflicting, views about social reality, and each one of them is affected by the social position that the respondents occupy. Let me illustrate this with the help of an example from my own fieldwork.

In June 1985, a group of development workers, both men and women, arrived in a hamlet of western Rajasthan, where I was conducting fieldwork with a community of camel herders and shepherds, to assess and prioritize the local needs for developmental work. As the elaborate techniques of Rapid Rural Appraisal (RRA) and Participatory Rural Appraisal (PRA) were not fully known at that time, the development workers administered a group and focused interview to pastoralists from several adjacent hamlets, who were requested to assemble at a public place—a platform dedicated to a folk deity.[34]

More women than men came to the 'meeting', as the development workers defined the congregation. The able-bodied men and boys had gone on the daily routine of grazing their animals. As per the norm of sexual segregation, the womenfolk congregated in and around the house of the priest, near the deity's platform. Men squatted in the open. Although the meeting was scheduled for pastoralists, some men from non-herding castes had also walked in just to see what was going on and often they spoke more than those for whom the meeting was planned.

The group interview began with a development worker introducing his team members, their aim of a face-to-face meeting with the graziers, the type of development action they hoped for, and, on behalf of his colleagues, he sought the assembly's active cooperation. Then followed a torrent of questions that the development workers asked, whilst a couple of them took notes on congregants' replies, from which would evolve a guideline for appropriate action in the future.

One of the questions that evoked a good response concerned the causes of local poverty. The men drew attention to a gradual disappearance of pastures, the depletion of their herds, the emerging hostility between agriculturists and pastoralists after the double and triple cropping patterns had come into vogue, no development work being undertaken for animal keepers in contrast to peasants and farmers, and ecological changes, especially desertification of areas hitherto fertile. They were sharply critical of the stratagems and lip service of politicians, government officials, and even development workers. Unequivocally, the local men, more non-pastoral than pastoral, warned the interviewers to stay away from their hamlets and villages if no development work followed the meeting.

I suggested to the group interviewers to hold a separate meeting with women in which no men participated, for they tended to silence the women. I also told them that in the meeting for herdspersons, many uninvited males from other dominant non-pastoral castes had joined in and they often silenced the graziers. However, in meetings for pastoral women, women from other castes did not walk in because of normative restrictions on female mobility in the village. Pastoral men had non-pastoral friends and acquaintances, but not pastoral women, whose relatives and friends were mostly from their own caste. The female interviewers organized a meeting with pastoral women the same day in which males, including young boys who wanted to gatecrash, were requested not to walk by. I later learnt that the group interview with women was hugely successful and some of the findings were in sharp contrast to what the men had earlier said.

To the question on their poverty, the women did not discount the men's answers. Some of them had heard of the replies that their men had earlier given. Some of them knew the causes that their men thought were behind their poverty. But they emphasized that they were also poor because their men were addicted to opium, tobacco, and tea. Of these addictions, the principal was opium. Men spent a major portion of their meagre income on it, thus contributing virtually nothing to the running of the household. Women had to work as farm labourers to eke out their and their children's livelihood. Men acquired opium addiction in the prime of their life. By the time they grew older, they were habituated to opium to such an extent that they would not be able to do any work unless they consumed a 'tablet' of opium or its solution. The men did not think that their spending on opium (and on the other 'vices' such as tobacco and tea) did in any way contribute to their poverty and their leading an opium-dependent, vegetating existence, the life of a consumer rather than a producer.

An understanding of the gendered prioritization of needs and causes of poverty was insightful for my own fieldwork. While the men located the causes of their penury in external states—in the realm of politics and exploitation—the women pointed to internal states, in the reckless spending of their opium-habituated men, who because of their addiction had become 'physically hollow', and thus could not sustain arduous work or work for long hours. Opium addiction was a characteristic of being 'male', but women marked it as a curse on their households and children. The household and its welfare were central to the female discourse, which was not the case with men. Women tirelessly pleaded with the outsiders visiting or serving in their hamlets and villages (such as teachers, doctors, veterinarians, pharmacists, social workers, anthropologists) to help their men give up the nefarious practice, notwithstanding its centrality in the male ritual of greeting their male guests.[35]

Beginning with the sociology of opium in Rajasthan, I was able to delineate different, sometimes contrasting, viewpoints on virtually every aspect of social and cultural life within the same community. These perspectives were mediated by the social categories of gender, age, hierarchy, and power. The different perspectives did overlap and consensus prevailed on several issues, but on many others, sharp variations and contrasts were unmistakable. Each of them had its genesis in a social category—gender or stratum, for example—rather than in the idiosyncrasies of the respondents. The problem in fieldwork was to collate different, yet interrelated, perspectives that constituted the way of life of the animal breeders.

The methodological lesson is that the fieldworker should carefully separate the different points of view. He/she should not assume that one view would encompass the other. Thus, the male point of view, howsoever dominant, is not the society's point of view. A society may be conceptualized as a conglomeration of different, maybe contrasting, perspectives, some overwhelmingly dominating the others. The fieldworker's job is to document each of these perspectives, showing where people draw the boundaries, separating one from the others, and then to show the negotiations between these perspectives, stating the reasons that make a particular perspective dominate the others. This may be called the method of disaggregation, where the viewpoints of constituting social categories are separated out and then linked by focusing on the dynamic interaction between them.

The first principle of a social study is that each society is horizontally as well as vertically divided with several criss-cross patterns. When the observer takes an insider's position, what appears as homogeneous from an external vantage point is in fact multi-layered with contrasting and conflicting views and opinions. To describe and understand the multiplex reality as constructed by its different components is a daunting task. The vast literature concerned with social research and methodology endeavours to grapple with the issue of amorphous human behaviour and institutions that are perpetually changing.

Fieldwork

Fieldwork is central to anthropological work.[36] Library research, which is looked down upon by field anthropologists, is for 'lame ducks and rainy days' (Lewis 1986: 1). In Read's words (1986: 4), fieldwork is the 'crowning jewel' of anthropology. Seligman is reputed to have said that 'fieldwork was to anthropologists what the blood of the martyr was to church'.[37] Margaret Mead (1964: 5) writes: 'We still have no way to make an anthropologist except by sending him into the field: this contact with living material is our distinguishing mark.'

Reminiscing about his days as a graduate student in anthropology in Chicago, Rabinow (1977: 3) says that the world in the anthropology department was divided into two sets of people: those who had done fieldwork and those who had not. The latter were not considered 'anthropologists' in the true sense, notwithstanding their erudition on anthropological theory and other topics. The department of social anthropology at Cambridge, where I was a student in the late 1980s, had a pre-fieldwork class in which the techniques and methods of ethnographic investigation were taught and discussed, and another, post-fieldwork (or 'writing up') seminar wherein the doctoral candidates who had returned from their fieldwork presented their experiences as well as important chapters of their dissertation. Sometimes post-fieldwork students spoke to the pre-fieldwork class about their experiences of handling the anthropological tool kit, the ethical problems they confronted, and the solutions they improvised. The relation between the people in the pre- and the post-fieldwork stages was like the one between the 'uninitiated' and the 'initiated'. The symbolism of the rites of passage was apparent. The uninitiated ones were performing the rites of separation from their earlier status to plunge into the field. Fieldwork was structurally equivalent to the rites of transition. And the initiated ones had survived fieldwork and had performed the rites of incorporation to seek membership in the tribe of anthropologists.

Lewis (1986: 6) compares the fieldworker with the shaman. The fieldwork expedition is like the shamanic visit to unknown lands. While parachuting through the world of spirits and fairies, the shaman renders a description—often inchoate, sometimes gibberish—of all that he/she sees and endures, thus bringing home 'rich stores of exotic wisdom'. The fieldworker is the medium for alien cultures (and cultures treated as 'unfamiliar'), in the same way as the shaman acts as the medium for divine entities. The people the anthropologist studies 'possess' him, with the result that he calls them 'his people' and is ardently possessive of them. But as the shaman does not remain in his journey forever and returns to his social world to attend to his everyday chores, similarly the fieldwork, howsoever extensive and longitudinal, is time bound. Anthropologists return to their social milieus to write up their accounts of the people among an array of other roles they perform as private and public individuals.

Fieldworkers distinguish themselves from survey researchers. Sometimes using the term anthropology interchangeably with fieldwork, anthropologists consider their approach the most suitable for an insider's (emic) understanding of social and cultural life. For gaining such knowledge, the fieldworker is generally advised to spend not less than one year with a community of people, in their natural habitat, collecting information about all social and cultural aspects, so that in the end he has a fair idea of typical annual activities.[38] Evans-Pritchard's (1951) ideal anthropologist conducts his fieldwork with not less than two different societies, for this will make him think comparatively and not in terms of just one society. His first fieldwork is for at least two years, separated by a break of a few months in an anthropology department for collating the data collected on the first visit. His second fieldwork, with a different society, is usually of shorter duration because he can draw upon the trove of his first fieldwork's experience to provide solutions to various problems. He also has experience in recording field notes and writing up his work.

This suggestion of one or a couple of years' fieldwork needs to be critically examined. Evans-Pritchard's 'total residence' among the Nuer was for about a year, although he thought that a year was not really adequate for a 'sociological study of a people in adverse circumstances' (1940: 14). Yet, the amount and the quality of data that he collected working with a 'hostile people' was indeed praiseworthy, for it yielded his three books on the Nuer, besides a number of other articles.[39] Likewise, Dumont (1986: Chapter XVII) spent two years in Tamil Nadu and though his contact with Pramalai Kallar, the community he studied, was for eight months, the depth and quality of his ethnography was superb, 'comparable to Evans-Pritchard's Nuer'.[40] We may think of a number of similar examples, which help us conclude that the quality of data is not always a function of a long stay with the people. The time spent in carrying out fieldwork is in fact dependent upon the sociological problem the researcher has chosen for investigation. For a study of the ritual calendar or an agricultural cycle, he will be required to stay in the community for one year or more.

Further, the fieldwork tradition shows a great deal of variability. French and German anthropologists are well known for several successions of short fieldwork, sometimes visiting the same location every year for decades. Also included in the anthropology syllabi of many universities is short fieldwork to be conducted by students, under the supervision of their teachers, on the basis of which they write their respective dissertations.[41] When the field happens to be easily accessible, as is the case when the researchers study their own society, they can always go back to the field for a couple of weeks in the midst of writing up their work. A short spell of fieldwork follows a short spell of 'desk-work', and this may continue almost alternatively. This type of fieldwork has come to be known as 'extensive', in contrast to 'intensive' fieldwork. Béteille (1975: 12) has used this term—extensive fieldwork—for N.K. Bose's variety of fieldwork.

But the image that British social anthropology has popularized is of a solitary fieldworker, who, after having decided to study a particular community, goes to live with it for a lengthy period of time, the length of which he decides on the basis of the research problem under study. Because the field is located in a far-flung geographical area and short field visits are not easily possible, the researcher would like to spend as much time as possible with the people so that he has not to return to them with more queries. Throughout this period of intensive study, he immerses in the lifestyle of his hosts. Preferably, the fieldworker chooses a hitherto unstudied community.[42] The research design he prepares is exploratory and evolves into a descriptive one as the field probe continues. Earlier teachers of anthropology thought that the student would learn the art of fieldwork by practising it, by taking the plunge into the community selected for study.[43] Today, the beginners undergo training programmes in field methodology (in pre-fieldwork classes) and also self-learn from a host of books on research methods.

As one of the requirements of fieldwork is that it should be conducted in the vernacular, in many British and American universities, the student acquires the preliminary linguistic ability in the language laboratory of social anthropology departments before embarking upon the field.[44] If the facility for a particular language is not available, the fieldworker is advised to learn it by living with people, engaging an interpreter in the beginning, and then gradually using it himself.[45] Leach (1954: 311) wrote that he dispensed with the services of his interpreter very early in his fieldwork. This had its disadvantages, but it meant that he 'learnt to understand the Jinghpaw language very quickly.' Obeyesekere (1981: 11) observes that the field researchers should specify whether or not they engaged the interpreters, and if they did, they should give the full details of the social background of their interpreters. Against this background, the reader would be able 'to gauge the "interpreter effect" on the work as a whole'.

The fieldworker is a 'humble learner' of the cultures of other people (Evans-Pritchard 1951: 79); he is 'like a child and learns about the culture of the people in very much the same way as does a growing child in that culture' (Middleton 1970: 6). About the Indian anthropologist, A. Aiyappan, Kathleen Gough (1954: 54) wrote that he consciously took his respondent, the villager, 'as his *guru* (teacher)'. The fieldworker commits errors in learning the dialect, pronounces local words awkwardly, has difficulty in comprehending intricate details of social structure, and is admonished for transgressing boundaries or breaking rules. Finding him struggle, people laugh at him while he stands grinning oafishly; the local men and women become his tutors, rectify his errors, and teach him not only about themselves but aid his 'nativization'.[46] While teaching the anthropologist—both formally and informally—people also learn about their own cultures through their reflections and in attempting to answer anthropological questions systematically. Fieldwork, therefore, is a didactic experience for the investigator as well as his/her respondents.[47]

It may not be possible for the solitary anthropologist to observe everything that goes on in the community. Certain events may take place in a household when the ethnographer is busy interviewing someone else in the agricultural field. It is also possible that certain events may not take place during the time of fieldwork, or they may not form part of the annual ritual cycle.[48] When an event is taking place, the anthropologist cannot be present at all places of action. For instance, in a Raika wedding, the time when the auspicious wooden pole (*madā*) is erected to mark the beginning of marriage rituals is also the time when the earthen oven (*bhattī*) where cooking will take place is also set up, and around this time many activities take place in the women's quarter. Anthropologists may still manage to observe some rituals, but their presence in many others may be embarrassing to the hosts or they may be strictly advised to keep away from certain events and people. It is well known that male anthropologists working in sexually segregated societies have often been shut out from participating in or observing female activities.[49] Therefore, what they have reported is chiefly from the male perspective. Boas knew of this problem full well and thus encouraged women to take up a career in anthropology, carrying out fieldwork on those aspects that mainly concerned women.[50]

Gender bias (female or male) in reporting can be corrected if instead of a single anthropologist, two anthropologists, one male and the other female, can team up; the female anthropologist studying all those sectors of the community which are virtually closed to her male counterpart and vice versa. From that point of view, husband-wife teams of anthropologists (like that of Ruth and Stanley Freed) will fare better than solitary anthropologists.[51] But many anthropologists—such as Malinowski (1922), Evans-Pritchard (1951), Srinivas (1996)—think that loneliness in the field is a virtue, for it will drive the fieldworker to seek companionship among the people. It will also make him creative because he will write down in his diary these experiences of loneliness and the ways in which he mitigated them.[52] Apart from loneliness, fieldworkers pass through moments of frustrations when informants are not available. This is compounded by sickness and exhaustion. One of the experiences of fieldworkers consists of wading through these hours of inaction and ennui and keeping oneself optimistic and cheerful.[53]

A single researcher, maybe without an interpreter, can easily conduct a research investigation in a small society with a few hundred respondents.

But, for certain research problems, large research teams of fieldworkers, working under the guidance of a few experts, are required (Dube 1962: 250). Whether it is the first or the second type of study, there is, however, no compromise on the intensity of fieldwork and the quality of data. Furthermore, the type of group research (or 'field teams'), which is being discussed here, should be distinguished from surveys, because the members of the team primarily conduct fieldwork and not a survey. Also, it should be distinguished from fieldwork that students conduct together as a part of their curriculum. First, students' fieldwork is quite short, rarely for more than a month; and second, each student collects data for his individual topic, and generally, there is no research problem that the entire team investigates. The group research, by comparison, is long and intensive, and focuses on a research problem. All members of the group collect data pertaining to that, rather than getting engaged with their individual research projects.[54]

The people of an ethnographic investigation are treated as the other. When their moorings are different from those of the fieldworker, they constitute the other both in an empirical and a methodological sense. But even when the subjects of study are one's own people, the investigator does not assume that he knows them fully; rather he still considers them as the other, about whom he will only come to know during the course of his study. The otherness, therefore, is not an empirical quality but a methodological vantage point. There is a difference between the knowledge the investigator acquires by being a natural member of a society and the one he acquires by consciously undertaking its study. In the latter case, his society is the object of study, the other. Like the study of any other culture, the researchers excitedly discover many aspects of their societies that they did not know beforehand.

The otherness can be considered a frame of mind. One may extend here Levi-Strauss' idea of 'distantiation' to the study of one's own society.[55] Each anthropological study requires an observance of distance from the object of study, even when one may be a natural member of the society (by birth and socialization) which one selects for intensive work. Madan (1994: 136) expresses this idea eloquently:

One has to learn not only to *live intimately with strangers* but also to *live (behave) strangely with intimates.* One has to cultivate empathy for other cultures; contrariwise one has to create distance between oneself and one's culture and society in order to be able to see oneself in the round, as it were.

When one adopts this frame of mind, one's own society appears to be as distant and mysterious as are the other societies. The familiar is made unfamiliar (Madan 1994: 114); then with the help of the baggage of anthropological methodology, one makes the unfamiliar familiar.

The Fieldworker and the Field: Their Respective Impacts

The impact of the fieldworker may be tremendous in the society he studies. He may become the talk of the village. The people might like to identify with him, for it raises their status. They may give him preferential treatment or may volunteer help.[56] The fieldworker is not, to recapitulate Powdermaker's words (1967: 19), a 'faceless robot or a machinelike recorder of human activities', and, therefore, is likely to be involved with people. He may be approached to arbitrate a domestic dispute, intervene between external institutions (such as the police or the revenue department) and the people, or may become the spokesperson of the community's interests.[57] The fieldworker may have around him his own group of friends, admirers, and helpers, for which Madan (1989: XXI–XXII) has aptly used the term 'convoy', which helps him in a variety of ways and also expects several favours in return. This may happen even when the fieldworker is on neutral ground as Mayer (1975) points out that he stayed outside his field village but was often asked for his opinion on village matters and some of his remarks had value implications. The anthropologist may experience a sense of oneness with his people; for instance, Alan Macfarlane, well known for his fieldwork in Nepal, told an interviewer from a Cambridge magazine (Carter 2000: 7):

We [he and his wife] are regarded as wage earners temporarily over here [England], with our heart in Nepal, where it is really. When my (adopted) sister died, I had to return and perform the rituals for her death. I was one of the four who lit the funeral pyre. I felt more devastated than I have ever felt about anyone in my life. . . more so than my father.

A good example of the impact of the field on the fieldworker may be chosen from Crapanzano's portrait of Tuhami, who was a fatalist, believed in submitting himself to Allah's will, and had visions of supernatural entities. Of all the Moroccans Crapanzano met during his fieldwork, he found a few 'who were both interesting and likable' and Tuhami was one of them. As a consequence of the long interviews he carried out with Tuhami, Crapanzano often felt that he was not able to keep the 'ethnographic distance' that is required to be observed between the ethnographer and his/her respondent for the development of objective knowledge. Often, Crapanzano reacted against the repository of beliefs that Tuhami held.

In the process, Crapanzano adopted the role of a 'curer', endeavouring to explain to Tuhami the pitfalls created by his beliefs, and the interview with him developed into a 'therapeutic one'. The impact of the field (in this case, Tuhami) on the ethnographer was tremendous, as may be inferred from the following (1980: 141):

We [Crapanzano and his wife] were coming to know Tuhami as a person and beginning not only to sympathize with his condition but to empathize with him. Care had entered our relationship.

One of the lessons that Crapanzano learnt through his fieldwork, and so do other anthropologists, was that fieldwork teaches not only about the people (the other) under study, which in any case is its explicit aim. It is through fieldwork that the ethnographer 'discovers' himself, and is able to interpret his own culture and social milieu. Knowledge is created out of the constant struggle to come to terms with the self and the other. Crapanzano (ibid: 138–39) writes:

Fieldwork must be understood within its temporal dimension as a process of continual discovery and self-discovery. . . I learnt much about myself and my world through the detour of my comprehension of Tuhami.

But, in spite of the empathic involvement, the fieldworker does not become one with the people. Evans-Pritchard (1973: 3) writes:

One cannot really become a Zande or a Nuer or a Bedouin Arab, and the best compliment one can pay them is to remain apart from them in essentials. In any case one always remains oneself, inwardly a member of one's own society and a sojourner in strange land.

Nadel (1939) described the fieldworker as a 'freak member of the group'; and Middleton (1970: 14) wrote that since he was neither a missionary nor an official among the Lugbara, he was 'clearly an odd person'. In a perceptive ethnographic account, Briggs (1970) describes the roles that the Inuit Eskimos allocated to her chronologically. First, she was a stranger and guest, a white person, who was addressed by her personal name. Second, the family with which she stayed, treated her as a 'daughter', but the role of an adult woman was not given to her because neither did she excel in skin sewing nor had children. She was, therefore, a 'child'—i.e. educable. When the Inuit found her an 'incorrigible offender' (losing her temper, which was unacceptable to the Inuit, or her clumsy gestures), they termed her 'uneducable', and those who could not be educated were 'simple-minded'. Briggs alternated between the role of a 'child' and a 'simpleton'. She could never become a 'full' Inuit.

Not only does the anthropologist find a gulf between the people and himself, but also the former do not want the fieldworker to 'merge' with them. The Lugbara, who called Middleton (1970: 71–72) 'our European', insisted that he behaved as a European. They did not approve of him if he was not dressed formally and cleanly. When invited to Middleton's hut for drink, they expected some European beer to be served in glasses and some food laid out on a plate to be eaten with fork and spoon. In Middleton's words, the Lugbara 'did not like a slummer'. Although the fieldworkers try their best to 'interiorize' the local lifestyles, people do not really regard them as 'one of them' in all respects. As the fieldwork progresses, they become convinced that the fieldworker is different from them and will remain so in the future. They tolerate violations of norms by the fieldworker, for he is 'different'. Many ethnographers working in multicaste villages of India have told me that when they ate (or drank water) at the houses of lower castes, they did receive from upper castes comments strongly disapproving their behaviour but they were not excommunicated. In fact, the upper castes never denied them food and hospitality despite their close contacts with the lower castes. Emphasizing their differentness, my Raika respondents often said: 'You might have been a Raika in your last birth but in this, you are not and you will never become one. It will be our great luck if you are able to understand our problems.'

Not much has been written on what anthropologists do when leaving the field. Do they promise future visits to the community? A piece of advice to prospective fieldworkers is that they should refrain from promising to people what they would not be able to deliver. They should also communicate as clearly as possible that their work is time bound. One should take the role of the researcher immediately on reaching the field, so that people come to know from the first day of the arrival of the anthropologist among them that he/she is there to study their lifestyles and institutions. And that the study will culminate one day, after which the researcher will return to the place from where he/she came. Because of the empathy he develops for people, the ethnographer may overstay in the field, but he knows he will 'never become a native'. However, he may continue to nurture relations with some respondents through mail or telephone, or may periodically visit the field site, but it all varies with the researchers and the nature of their respective studies.[58] The letters one receives from the field also constitute an important source of data. Clarifications to information one has already collected may also be sought through letters.

A conclusion at this point is that the fieldworker occupies a marginal place in the society he visits in search of knowledge.[59] He may be treated honorifically because of his resources and power, yet it does not entitle him to become a part of the mainstream of society. Certain rituals and meetings may taboo the presence of outsiders. The native fieldworker may transcend these restrictions, but the fact that he treats the self as the other creates in him a kind of marginality. I may here refer to Edward Said's view that migration and marginality may cause creativity and intellectual ideas. The intellectual in Said's writings is an outsider, has multiple identities, and is not settled in any one place. He is involved in as well as detached from the affairs of the society in which he participates.[60] A close parallel exists between Said's intellectual and the anthropologist.[61] The latter migrates temporarily to a society—his own or the other—for the purpose of acquiring local knowledge. During the process of learning, he may be impressed by it, but at the same time he may be critical of certain local practices, especially those that contravene universal human values, such as female infanticide or human sacrifice.

The nature of fieldwork differs from one context to another. Fieldwork in a society where most of the social life is conducted outside the house—like in a typical Indian village—will be different from where people draw firm boundaries between the outside and the inside, and most of the social life is conducted inside the house, like in upper-middle-class neighbourhoods in metropolises.[62] Fieldwork in modern institutions—hospitals, banks, schools, and laboratories—poses its own problems, beginning with the finding of a 'community', and then selecting an appropriate toolkit for its study.[63] What distinguishes fieldwork from survey research is that it is flexible, spread out, and lengthy. Thus, the data collected in the first few weeks may turn out to be erroneous later (Béteille and Madan 1975: 9). It is after several months of interacting with one's respondents, and learning the local idioms and patois, that one starts collecting genuine information; therefore, it is unsurprising that most of the data are gathered during the final months of fieldwork (Middleton 1970: 6). As the time spent at the field site increases, the fieldwork 'funnel' narrows (Agar 1980). In the beginning, the enquiry has a wide focus, the questions are not clearly formulated, and the key respondents have yet not been chanced upon. As the work proceeds, the direction becomes clear, well defined, goals of study sharpen, questions emerge when one expands field jottings and reads one's field notes, and the enquiry is well steered. The fieldworker now knows the respondents who should be approached and the records which he should study. In the early period of fieldwork, the people control the topics about which the fieldworker can ask questions, but as the fieldwork continues, the researcher starts controlling the topics—he asks questions that interest

him. Towards the close of the field stay, the researcher may introduce schedules and, if the people are literate, questionnaires. He may also conduct, if
the research design requires, projective tests or transcribe oral texts (such
as folk epics). Fieldwork is a sensitive process. The relations the investigator
establishes with his respondents and the way in which they mature over
time govern its success.[64]

Observation and Interview

For data collection, first, the researcher observes the behaviour of people
in their natural habitat and place of work; second, he converses with them
wherever they are accessible (at tea stalls, in agricultural fields, offices, in
their houses) about why they do what they do, what they did which he
would never be able to observe, and their opinions on various social issues;
and third, he requests them to write up their answers to an inventory of
questions that he hands over to or mails them. These techniques can be
conveniently combined to yield life history accounts of respondents, detailed
descriptions of events and institutions, or kinship and affinal ties between
people. The first technique is called observation, the second, interview,
and a set of questions prepared to be filled in by respondents is a
questionnaire.

Observation should be distinguished from mere seeing and looking.
Observation may be defined as a systematic viewing, which is intentional
and planned. The observer is aware of the fact that he is systematically
viewing the unit under study. He records his observations and also, if conditions permit, films and photographs events that are later analysed. He
prepares an observation schedule that guides the data collection. Considered as a supreme technique for studying non-verbal behaviour, observation can be conducted in a 'laboratory' (as in psychology) or in a natural
setting. It can be structured or unstructured; in the former, we count the
frequency of the occurrence of peculiar features of a particular thing, whereas
in the latter, we merely record what occurs.

One of the main techniques—in some cases, the only technique—social
anthropologists and sociologists use is participant observation, which is
sustained, intensive, extended, day-after-day, and of a broad range. The
observer lives with people, eats the food they eat, gets closer to them, and
takes an active part in their activities; in other words, he participates in the
life of the people by adopting a role.[65] He has a first-hand experience of
sharing a people's culture in its natural habitat for a lengthy period of
time. The people's 'reactivity syndrome' is transcended as the investigator's

presence among them does not arouse suspicion or make them conscious of his presence.[66]

The term 'participant observation' is attributed to Edward Lindeman's publication, *Social Discovery* (1924). Frederic LePlay studied family budgets of people by living with them; Charles Booth wrote on labourers' lives and their problems by staying in their neighbourhood in London. But the clearest statement on participant observation was Malinowski's in his *Argonauts of the Western Pacific*. In the context of observing and recording the 'imponderabilia of actual life and of typical behaviour', Malinowski (1922: 21–22) wrote: '. . . it is good for the Ethnographer sometimes to put aside camera, note book and pencil, and to join in himself in what is going on.' From such plunges in the life of the Trobrianders, Malinowski found that their behaviour and their manner of being became more transparent and understandable.

Observation can be conducted without participation (non-participant observation) and it is possible to participate in the life of people without undertaking any 'intentional observations.' For the latter, sometimes the term 'complete participation' is used. These two may be regarded as the two ends of a continuum, and in between are placed different variants of observation. Participant observation creates role clashes—between the insider and the outsider, the stranger and the friend, and the pupil and the teacher. Earlier, it was pointed out that howsoever hard he may attempt, the fieldworker will never become an 'insider'. He may view himself as a 'humble learner' of other cultures, but in fact he has a lot to teach others. There are cases of anthropologists who imparted tuition to school-going children, apart from drafting several petitions and interceding with the authorities on behalf of the people. The fieldworker may become a 'good friend' but will still remain a 'stranger'. And this is true even when the anthropologists may claim to have 'gone completely native'. Some anthropologists suggest that the fieldworker, therefore, should strike a balance between the two roles mentioned earlier; with respect to those whom one is studying, one should choose the role of the stranger (Jarvie 1969: 505). Adopting of this role is also imperative for a scientific understanding of the community. When one 'goes native', there is a possibility that one might withhold the publication of certain details about the people or lose objectivity in analysis, think that one's publications might embarrass the people or betray the trust.

Non-participant observation is a successful technique in many situations, but its usefulness is questioned in simple societies where it may not be possible to keep a distance from the people or to explain to them the real purpose of one's visit. Hence, the adoption of this technique may retard the process of rapport establishment in such societies, which may not be the case in complex societies. Some anthropologists favour selective participation in the community and the choice of where to and where not to participate is conditioned by the context. This choice is also conditioned by the fieldworker's likes and dislikes, which should not be compromised, while maintaining humility and respect for the people. This type of observation is also known as quasi-participant observation.

Observation yields a treasure of data on non-verbal behaviour and what people's actions mean. But there is also a need to know why people do what they do, what they did in the past when the observer was not there, what they do in situations that are not accessible to the observer, and what their views are about various social issues. Therefore, the researcher has to talk to—interview—people. Participant observation in fact includes conversing with people. In many cases, 'participant observation is fieldwork', however not all fieldwork is participant observation (Barnard 1994: 137). In many cases, data come principally from interviews conducted with respondents, as Adrian Mayer's paper included in this volume shows.

Steiner Kvale (1996: 6) makes a distinction between 'everyday conversation' and 'interview'. The latter is not a 'conversation between equal partners'. Here, the 'researcher defines and controls the situation'. The characteristics of the interviewer—such as race and ethnicity, sex, social status, age, physical appearance, clothing and grooming, and demeanour—have an impact on the process of interviewing. For example, studies have found that white interviewers elicited responses significantly different from those obtained by black interviewers in similar situations (Bailey 1978: 164–65).

Interviews may be broadly divided into two types. In the first, the interviewer has a basic idea of the areas about which he would be interviewing the respondent. He carries with him a list of the topics—what may be technically called the 'interview guide'—that would guide him during the interview, but he does not structure specific questions in advance. In such situations, an interview is more or less a 'free-floating' conversation. Often, the interviewer begins with what seems interesting to him or what he thinks would be interesting to the respondent. The interview may cover a number of areas. Called unstructured, it is time consuming, but yields a lot of information apart from the topics in which the interviewer is particularly interested. Therefore, the fieldworker has to sluice away the grit to index what is especially relevant to him.

By comparison, the other kind of interview is structured, in which the investigator prepares a set of questions in advance and is specifically committed to seeking their answers. If the respondent deviates from the topic, the interviewer requests him to return to the point. Such an intervention might annoy the respondent, making him lose interest in the interview, but much depends on how the interviewer handles such situations. Unstructured and structured interviews may also be combined. The interviewer prepares an inventory of the topics of his interest in advance and then starts the interview in a conversational manner. Once rapport has been established, he may gradually funnel down his enquiry, making it structured. The way in which the interview develops depends greatly on the respondent's perception of the interviewer's role.

More elaborately, interviews have been classified into focused, depth, clinical, repeated, and group interviews (Young 1968: 219–22). The focused interview takes place with an individual known to have been involved in a particular situation. In a depth interview, the interviewee is encouraged free expression for an understanding about his/her subjective dimension. Clinical interviews are conducted for gauging the health and psychological status of a person. Social workers, counsellors, and prison workers carry out personal history interviews of the subjects with whom they deal. In a depth interview, the investigator may use projective techniques, such as picture interpretation and sentence and story completion. When the same respondent is interviewed again, it is known as a repeated interview, and when it is an interview with a group, rather than an individual, it is termed a group interview.

In her work on narrative analysis, Das (1999: 48–50) makes a distinction between three different techniques used for collecting verbal data. The first is the narrative technique in which the emphasis is on a sequence of events or a particular event that happened in the life of a person. In this case, the narrative is 'linear and oriented'. The narrative technique allows one to examine variations in the life histories of similarly placed persons in a society. The second is called the amplificatory technique, where the narrator is given the liberty to organize his life's story around the events which for him are the most significant. In the third type, which is called the elicitory interview, the emphasis is upon eliciting information rather than experience. It is used for testing a hypothesis.

Both observation and interview are techniques used for preparing case studies and genealogies. Aptly described as the 'social microscope' by E.W. Burgess (quoted in Young 1968: 247), the case study is a detailed account of the generic development of an individual, a group, an institution, an association, a community, or the total society. When it is an account of the life of a person, it is usually called life history.[67] An anthropologist may present an analysis of the total case in his monograph. In that sense, Malinowski's study of Trobrianders or Whyte's of the Italian slum are examples of the case study. The other possibility is that the researcher compares a number of cases pertaining to the same phenomenon aiming to arrive at certain propositions.[68] A case study can be made at a point of time and over time. After Gluckman (1961), the latter is known as the 'extended case study', which has proved to be valuable in the study of unwritten laws of simple societies, where the investigator follows a dispute between persons right from the time it takes place till it is laid to rest.[69] The study of the process of dispute settlement guides one to the anatomy of the legal system—the laws, their execution, and legal roles. Today, the extended case study method is also used in medical sociology and anthropology to study how people combine different, sometimes contradictory, medical practices. As in legal anthropology, where the dispute is followed to its settlement, in medical studies, the researcher follows the sick right from the time he announces the onset of his illness, collecting information on the specialists he consults, or is made to consult, the choice of medicines, the nursing care provided to him, and the case is followed till the time the sick is cured, or his illness becomes chronic, or he dies. The extended case study requires a long stay in the community and, therefore, in some cases, it may almost merge with participant observation.[70]

One method to study kinship, family, and marriage is by use of genealogies, which are prepared, as said earlier, using the techniques of observation and interview. W.H.R. Rivers (1910) showed the importance of genealogy in social and cultural studies and delineated the procedure of drawing up genealogical data. Malinowski (1922: 14–15) defined genealogy as a 'synoptic chart of a number of connected relations of kinship'. The investigator traces the genealogical chart of the respondent—the ego—by asking him questions, but it is likely that the respondent may not place all his relatives in the right birth order or his memory of them may be faulty; thus, the fieldworker comes to complete the genealogy seeking information from other egos. In this way the genealogical charts are also verified. But, one should not forget that in spite of the best efforts of the investigator, the genealogical charts might not be complete, because people may not remember their ancestors—their names and other details about them—beyond a certain number of generations even in societies where kinship may be the principle of social organization. The problem of remembering is bound to multiply in societies where descent is traced both from the sides of the father and the mother. Srinivas writes (1996: 78): 'Generally speaking, the remoter the past, the less reliable are the memories of informants.'

Not only do fieldworkers prepare genealogies, but the people whose charts they prepare may also keep an account of their kin and affines. The kinship chart, therefore, is an analytical tool as well as an ensemble of rules according to which the actors are expected to behave (Barnes 1978). As said earlier, people remember their relatives up to some ascending generations. In societies where writing technology has made inroads, kinship charts that hitherto existed as part of the oral tradition are now being written down. Some societies have specialized groups of genealogists, who derive their livelihood by charging their clients for keeping their kinship and marriage records. For instance, western Rajasthan has the caste of Ravs, the genealogists, and each one of their groups serves a particular caste in typical patron-client relations, what are called *jajmānī* ties, a characteristic of Indian villages. Once in two years or so, the Ravs visit their patrons (*jajmān*), note down in their books (*bahīs*) marriages, births, and deaths that have taken place since the time they last came. They may also record cases of excommunication from the caste, but essentially they will note down only those details that their patrons wish to have recorded for posterity. As the castes these genealogists serve are patrilineal, their books may have virtually no details about women. Also, some important demographic facts—such as infant mortality, reproductive history of women (details of still births, miscarriage, and abortion), age at marriage or delivery, serial monogamy—do not find a place in these books. In other words, these records may be partial and lack accuracy, for the information recorded in them, as noted earlier, is at the behest of the patrons of the genealogists.[71] In fact, the money and other gifts the genealogists receive from their patrons are also entered in the books.

In other words, the facts of kinship and marriage that are of relevance to the researcher may not hold the same importance for the people, thus the charts that people prepare for their purposes are different from those that fieldworkers prepare after sustained interviewing and observation, although some overlapping will definitely exist between the two charts. Following Fortes (quoted in Barnes 1978), the kinship chart that the actors prepare (diagrammatically, orally, or in writing) may be called pedigree, whilst the one the fieldworker prepares as part of his data, depending upon his research interests, may be known as genealogy.[72] This distinction is different from the one that physical anthropologists and human geneticists make between genealogy and pedigree—for them, pedigree includes only those relatives who have bio-genetic connections among them, thus the facts of adoption are not included here, which are taken care of in genealogy.

Genealogical data are used for a variety of purposes apart from that of studies of kinship. Demographers use genealogical statements. Migratory histories of people can also be studied through this method. Genealogy helps us know about the social structure of a community. Preparation of genealogies also facilitates the process of rapport establishment with people. Malinowski (1922: 15) writes that a genealogy 'allows the investigator to put questions which he formulates to himself *in abstracto*, but can put concretely to the native informant'.

Notes Taking

An extremely important aspect of fieldwork is 'notes taking', i.e., writing down details of observation, producing transcripts of conversational and interview sessions, describing the experiences of living in a different culture, and commenting on the usefulness of the techniques and methods in field situations and any improvisations made on them. Writing begins with the planning of research and should not be seen as the last phase (usually called 'writing up' or 'deskwork') that succeeds fieldwork.[73] In fact, many things written during the fieldwork are used verbatim in the texts that are finally produced. Monographs often carry chunks of field notes (as they were originally written) and leaves from the diary of the ethnographer.[74] A researcher produces a lot of written work during a lengthy field probe, besides the published and unpublished materials he/she collects from libraries, museums, archives, and from the personal collections of informants.[75] A suggestion made to fieldworkers is that they should begin with writing in the field in the presence of their respondents as soon as possible, so that they come to know that their 'guest' (or the 'intruder') has come to live with them with a particular mission—of understanding their society and later writing about it. It may be argued here that being cut off from the wider world, the hosts may not conceptualize the researcher's role, as perhaps was the case with 'primitive' societies at the beginning of the last century. But surely, if the fieldworker is seen noting down points from interview sessions or is seen writing up notes, people would know that his work is different from theirs and he has come to live with them with a specific aim.

Through the day's work, the fieldworker takes down jottings—certain crucial words and sentences from conversations or which describe a particular observation, or some ideas and comments—what Simon Ottenberg (quoted by Sanjek 1996: 197) terms 'scratch notes'. They constitute the basis for fuller written notes. The fieldworker is advised to schedule some

time each day for writing down a detailed account of his notes lest they
become 'cold' and he may find it onerous to remember details and nuances
(Mead, quoted by Sanjek 1996: 197). Goody (1995: 150) writes that
Malinowski was 'insistent on writing up fieldwork each evening, recommending various ways of categorizing and recording information. He also
wanted his students to send him back regular monthly reports'.

As these notes are written down, the investigator thinks about the relationship between different facts. Many aspects of the society become clearer,
for 'writing is a form of thinking' (Becker 1986: IX). Scratch notes make
sense to the fieldworker because he carries with him stored memories that
aid their understanding and interpretation. For these stored memories,
Ottenberg (quoted in Sanjek 1996: 197) uses the term 'head notes'. When
an anthropologist reads other ethnographers' notes he finds it difficult to
understand them because he lacks the head notes that facilitate understanding. Sometimes, while writing up a monograph, the ethnographer is
reminded of certain facts—head notes—that might have escaped being
penned in the field notes and diaries. In a lengthy fieldwork, the anthropologist learns so much about the people that he is able to write about them
without even consulting his notes or if he loses his field notes and diaries.[76] The major task after returning from the field is of indexing, classifying, and coding of notes. In many cases, the systematization of notes
begins right during the course of fieldwork. Anthropologists continue to
stay with people for some more time even after their stipulated period of
fieldwork is over, as they want to have a closer look at their notes so that
missing links can be filled in, certain dubious facts verified, and the half-
understood aspects fully understood. This is particularly important when
the field site happens to be far away, say, in a different continent.

Many factors affect the use of gadgets in fieldwork. First, the beliefs
people have with respect to these gadgets are important.[77] Second, people
may also know the probable use to which the output of these gadgets will
be put. They may refuse to be photographed, for they do not want to be
exhibited or printed in magazines and books. They may protest against the
use of tape recorders because they know their words may be used as evidence. Not only that, they may warn the interviewer not to note down
anything in his books while a conversation takes place. Or, they might like
to read the researcher's field notes or listen to the audiotapes. They might
dictate information about their institutions and cultural practices expecting the fieldworker not to deviate a bit from the text of their notes.[78] In the
contemporary age, the respondents will not only read what ethnographers
write about them but will also answer back. They may question the lazi-

ness of the fieldworker if he does not write up the accounts of their life with concern and interest after the fieldwork in which they had participated. The researcher has to be absolutely certain about the evidence; the quotes have to be accurate, as should be the references. Today, the researcher has to defend his thesis, as well as the photographs and other materials used in his work, against the comments and criticisms of the fraternity of anthropologists and sociologists and the general public, as well as the people of the study.

Survey Research

The first step in large-scale survey studies is to draw a sample.[79] Though traditionally associated with survey research, sampling is also used in field investigations.[80] The sum total of all the units of analysis is called the universe or population. Ideally one would like to study the entire universe, and such a study is called the census study, but when it is not possible to do so, the researcher draws a part of the universe that is viewed as an approximation of the whole. A good sample is adequate and representative of the universe.

In the words of Howard Wineberg (1995: 144), a census may be defined as 'an enumeration of population in a territory and the compilation of demographic, social, and economic information pertaining to that population at a given time'. The type of information which government authorities intend to collect, may remain the same with each census, conducted in a country after a certain number of years, maybe ten as is the case in India or in the United States of America. However, each census may have its own highlights. For instance, among other things, The Census of India—2001 collected information about types of ailments regarding physically challenged people and the age at which males got married. Earlier, the census had only counted the number of the physically challenged persons; and the data about the age at marriage pertained to women only. The inclusion of these items also shows, since the census, like any other social fact, is a reflection of society, the emerging social concerns of the government. For example, information about the age at which males got married was considered important for family planning programmes. Each census, therefore, is a 'snapshot of society at a single point of time' (Wineberg 1995: 145); it provides a 'national inventory, a picture of the situation existing at the time of the census' (Casley and Lury 1981: 30).

It is popularly believed that census and census data are associated with survey research, the research carried out in large societies by sociologists, economists, and demographers. But this is not really true as anthropologists and sociologists working in small-scale societies have devoted a lot of attention to census taking and then treating the data thus generated statistically.

Audrey Richards (1935) recommends that the anthropologist should take the village census, for this would check his impressions which are likely to be created from a few observations and interviews. Furthering this idea, Colson (1954) observes that since the anthropologist works within a restricted geographical area with a population numbering only a few hundred, he can afford to collect a census of his universe of study. As he stays in the community for a long time, as a result of which there is good rapport between him and the people, it will become easier for him to ask pointed, factual questions and seek people's cooperation. There will be less chances of rejection by comparison to a situation where an enumerator comes to the house with a long schedule and starts asking questions, a situation for which many respondents may be unprepared. Moreover, census work can be fruitfully combined with a close observation of the members of the society under study.

But not all societies that anthropologists study are small in scale. The individual populations of certain tribal societies in India (such as the Gonds, Santals, Bhils, Oraons) runs into millions, and each one of them is distributed in more than one state, because of which there is a lot of variation in styles of living and linguistic patterns within the same tribe. It will be difficult, almost impossible, for an individual researcher working with a large society (like any of the big tribes in India) to conduct its census-based study. However, what he can do is to artificially delimit a unit of the large society for study—a village or a couple of settlements of the people—that can be done by using the techniques of sampling. Then he can carry out a census study within it; in other words, there can be a census study of a sample. As a census of this kind is taken by the researcher, in collaboration with his assistants, if any, the chances of error are substantially minimal than in the national census in which thousands of enumerators are involved.

Census data may challenge the ethnographer's impressions and the statements of the respondents. Citing an example from her fieldwork with the Tonga, Colson (1954: 58) says that she was given to understand that the period of seclusion for pubertal girls had progressively diminished because of the impact of the school and the mission. When the census information on the length of seclusion was classified according to the decade in which a woman was born, it was found that instead of shortening, the period of seclusion had increased. When I started my work with the Raikas in Bikaner, in 1989, in a hamlet of the village known as Gadwala, which then had thirty-four households, I was given the impression that every Raika household kept camels, because the Raikas are traditional camel-breeders, and my respondents wanted to subscribe to the traditional image of their community. Later, the census conducted in their hamlet showed that there were only four camel herds, and many of the camels in them, which the Raikas grazed and looked after, belonged to other castes, particularly the peasants. Similarly, Beattie (1965: 36–7) observed that many propositions and correlations need substantiation; for instance, statements like 'most Nyoro marry their neighbours' or 'there is a correlation between bride wealth and marriage stability', need census data and quantification for their rejection or support.

Beattie introduced what he called methods of enumeration, i.e. collection of the data that could be quantified, after having been in Bunyoro for more than a year, when he knew the language of the people well. For filling the household survey form, he needed to spend nearly an hour in each house, and he tried to compensate them by paying an honorarium of one shilling to the head of each household surveyed (ibid.: 40). Köbben (1967: 49) spent one full year for conducting a census of 176 persons of the community of Djuka. During this time, he, however, carried out his other activities in the field. The long time spent on census taking was partly because the people became suspicious of why the information was being collected and the use to which it might be put. Although their scepticism diminished with the passage of time, certain questions, especially those concerned with infant mortality, did not evoke reliable answers, because high mortality was an indication of the existence of witchcraft in their community. Census taking requires exemplary patience, and should be supplemented with data collected through other techniques.

In survey research, the principal tool of data collection is the questionnaire, which may be defined as a set of questions (printed or typed) pertaining to a problem under study. It is usually mailed out to probable respondents or may be given to them personally, and it is self-administered by the respondent. Ideally, a questionnaire begins with a covering letter. The investigator knows in advance that the response to the questionnaire may be partial, incomplete, or false. The respondent may assume that the information he provides might be used against him. He may find the filling of the questionnaire a futile exercise, a waste of time, or an invasion into his privacy. To set things right, the investigator explains the nature of his research in the covering letter. He is candid about giving

details of the funding agency, the probable hypotheses, and any other research work he has previously undertaken. That complete anonymity would
be maintained is explicitly worded. The investigator may also advise the
respondent to contact him for more details in case he wishes. Some researchers also promise to send the respondents the findings of the study
they are undertaking. The contents of the covering letter show that research
is carried out not only in a literate context but also where people are sensitive to the meaning and implications of research activities, and are eager
to know what researchers find out about them.

The second part of the questionnaire consists of questions. Only relevant questions are asked since a long questionnaire may evoke a negative
response; therefore, the key word in the construction of a questionnaire is
'relevance' (Bailey 1978: 94). A distinction is made between close-ended
and open-ended questions. The former are multiple-choice questions,
whereas in the latter, the respondent is free to express himself. Unless
conditioned by the specific aims of the research, a questionnaire should
have a fair mix of close-ended and open-ended questions. In order to
measure the qualitative attitudes of people towards certain things, for example, normative statements, the questionnaire also consists of scales, in
accordance with which the respondents classify their opinions. Scaling
techniques are concerned with the methods of turning a 'series of *qualitative* facts (referred to as attributes) into a *quantitative* series (referred to as
a variable)' (Goode and Hatt 1981: 232). Survey researchers are expected
to know the methods of presenting the relations between people (i.e.,
sociometry, sociogram) and statistical techniques. Before administering a
questionnaire on a sample of populations, it is pre-tested to eliminate any
ambiguous questions. The final part of the questionnaire is a 'thank you
note'. Here, the investigator profusely thanks the respondent for his/her
cooperation, reiterating that the replies given in the questionnaire will only
be used for research purposes and their content will not be disclosed to
anyone.

Mailed questionnaires (in which the return postage is also provided)
have many advantages. There is a considerable saving of time and money.
It can include in its sample widely separated individuals, those who live in
different cities or even different continents. It thus saves travel costs. In
questionnaire research, the maximum effort of the investigator is directed
towards formulating relevant questions and pre-testing and revising them.
In so far as data collection is concerned, the surveyor does not run from one
respondent to another, striking rapport with each one of them, requesting
them for time to interview, and bearing their whims. He dispatches (now,

sometimes through emails) the questionnaires, sends some follow up mails and gentle reminders, and in case the filled up questionnaires are not returned, he draws another sample for his study, i.e., for mailing questionnaires. Another advantage of this tool is its greater assurance of anonymity; thus it can be used for highly personal topics of research (such as sexual behaviour, drug abuse, HIV/AIDS, domestic violence, embezzlement of public money). The questionnaire may be completed at the respondent's convenience. He may consult his records, confer with colleagues, or conduct minor research before handing in his replies. As the questionnaire is a standard tool, it is free from the biases that tend to plague interviews.

Although the questionnaire may be useful, one of its main drawbacks is the low response rate. The respondent may not return the questionnaire, and if he does, he may leave many questions unanswered, especially the open-ended ones. The investigator has no control over the respondent's environment. The respondent might ask some one else— say, his secretary or a family member—to fill up the questionnaire and send it back. Furthermore, the questionnaire lacks flexibility and records only verbal behaviour. It also cannot record spontaneous responses. The respondent may erase a hasty answer and write a contrived one. Survey researchers list several measures to combat the low response rate—from increasing the sample size, to making the format of the questionnaire more attractive, to giving material incentives to respondents.

When an investigator in an interview situation administers the questionnaire, it is called a schedule (or 'interview schedule'). The difference between interview and interview schedule is that the former is a 'specific conversational technique' with a lot of improvisations (Kvale 1996: 297). In the latter, the investigator simply reads out the questions as they have already been framed and records the responses *ad verbum*. The interview schedule does not have any scope for improvisation, but it assures a high response rate and answers to all questions. The respondent's environment is also controlled. It has been observed in many cultures that people find it onerous to write, however, they feel extremely comfortable in giving oral replies to the questions. This is particularly true of cultures where the oral tradition is valued. One of the greatest advantages of the interview schedule is that it can be used in non-literate societies, which is not the case with the questionnaire. But it may be noted that the interview schedule is an expensive technique, both in time and money, and does not ensure anonymity, therefore its use for the study of highly personal topics is limited.

Initially, fieldwork dominated social research, but later, especially after the Second World War, survey methods became quite popular in the social sciences, mainly because of their success in market studies and public opinion polls. Since then, the fieldworkers have led a debate of one-upmanship, professing the superiority of their deep and rich observational data as compared to the shallow nature of the survey, which is quite distanced from the complexities of the flesh-and-blood individuals.[81] Survey research finds out what people say about themselves whereas fieldwork's aim is to know not only what people say but also what they think and do.

Survey methodology has many advantages because it can cover a large number of people, quantify their responses, and aim towards generalizations.[82] The nature of the problem dictates the choice of methodology. Certain problems require survey methods for their investigation, certain others intensive fieldwork. The other point is that different techniques and methods can be easily combined.[83] One may apply the interview schedule in an intensive fieldwork and if it is being carried out in a literate society, one may use the questionnaire. We may use multi-techniques to yield rich data. Rather than subscribing to any one technique, for each has its inherent biases, we may draw upon plural research methods from our storehouse of methodology, depending upon the conditions in the research situation.

Writing Up Monographs

The main outcome of fieldwork and survey research is printed material—reports, articles and books—the quality and content of which varies in terms of the targeted readers. Fieldwork yields ethnographic accounts. Ethnography is a written account—it focuses on a particular community and describes analytically its way of life and institutions.[84] Its expected readers in the first half of the twentieth century and for some decades after were the literate populations in various parts of the world, particularly the West. The anthropologist could be distinguished from the field as he belonged to a distinct ethnic category and culture. As the erstwhile pre-literate populations are now fast getting educated and modernized, some of them have produced their own anthropologists, who study their own people. For these anthropologists and the type of ethnography they produce, sometimes the terms 'native anthropologists' and 'auto-ethnography' are respectively used, although some authors are sceptical of the claims of 'native anthropology' (Narayan 1993).

Writing is 'central to what anthropologists do both in the field and thereafter' (Clifford 1986: 2). As was noted earlier, it begins with the very act of planning research. The research proposal is written; the questions one would ask one's respondents and the observations one would make, are written down; the field jottings, scratched initially, are later fully developed into field notes and diaries; letters, and now emails, both written documents, are sent out to supervisors, project directors, friends, relatives, and they constitute an important part of one's data and may be quoted later in the text; and the analysis of data and its presentation in the form of a text, a monograph, is also an activity of writing. A fieldwork may not rise beyond the level of jottings or notes, because the fieldworker, after his return from the field, may get engaged in teaching and other activities, and, thus, not be able to schedule some of his time for writing up.[85]

The text that results from fieldwork is much more than a plain account of the facts observed. The facts that the fieldworker observes and the sense he makes out of them is conditioned by the theoretical perspectives he carries in his mind. The anthropologist, as the fieldworker, is at the centre of data collection—in the words of Geertz (1988: 130), 'I was there'—but he 'disappears from the text' (Rabinow 1986: 244), in which he seeks the authority of an impersonal scholarship. But the ethnographer needs to note that the text he produces blends his imagination, his literary consciousness, with facts that have become meaningful against the light of theoretical perspectives.

At one time, it was believed that an outsider, trained in methodology, could understand, write about, and represent the other, and to do so was his professional calling. But, in the last quarter of the last century, this view has been reversed. The monopoly claim of anthropologists to represent the other has come to be challenged, not by other anthropologists, but by the very people whom they study—the actors, the subjects, of their texts. Today, people in many communities believe that they alone can understand—and represent in a proper perspective—their own society. Some of the 'natives' make this claim after having read the writings of colonial anthropologists and others on them, which they find condescending, biased, incorrect, shallow, unsatisfactory, annoying, partial, unsympathetic, where several aspects of their culture have been distorted, some 'oddities' magnified out of proportion. They strongly feel the need to replace this genre of writings with reflexive accounts, which they would produce, sometimes after having done their higher studies in anthropology and sociology.[86] Against this background of the 'crisis of representation', to borrow an apt phrase from Marcus and Fischer (1986: 166), writing on and about cultures acquires a special meaning, and has become an act of great responsibility, because today, what ethnographers write is read, as was noted earlier, by other ethnographers, the general public, as well as the people of the text. The language and vocabulary that was used earlier to convey the exoticism of the other may no longer be the correct textual strategy, because the other is no more distanced, as it used to be when communication between different social worlds was far less than now, as an outcome of the processes of modernization, development, and globalization.[87]

The ethnographic text, therefore, is an account of the anthropologist's understanding of the people, a blend of facts, imagination, and creativity. The Trobrianders we know are 'Malinowski's Trobrianders'; the Balinese we know are 'Geertz's Balinese'; in other words, there cannot be an author-nascent ethnography. The anthropologist, to begin with, looks for facts and then he creates a text from them, by reconstructing and interpreting them, by delineating the meanings that the anthropologist thinks the people attribute to their life and their patterns of survival. In both cases, as Geertz says (1995: 167–68), the anthropologist is 'after the fact'—he looks for the fact and, then, he interprets it.

Ethnography is one of the most discussed topics in contemporary anthropology.[88] There are anthropologists who believe that each people comprehend and experience things, events, and behaviour according to their distinctive scheme. The ethnographer's task is to discover these schemes. Those who follow this approach of 'getting inside the head of the respondent' call themselves 'new ethnographers'.[89] Clifford Geertz (1973, 1983) disagrees with this approach, arguing that new ethnography does not pay attention to the central dimension of culture, i.e. meaning. Culture is a system of meanings.[90] For Geertz, ethnographic work is an exercise in 'thick description', trying to interpret meaning in terms of what people understand, think about, talk about, and how they describe their behaviour.[91] Cultures are like languages, which are translated into terms intelligible to members of other cultures. Therefore, interpreting a culture is like interpreting a 'text'; that is why, Geertz uses the term hermeneutics to describe the approach of ethnographers.[92]

Some anthropologists are roundly critical of these ideas. For them the aim of anthropology and sociology is to test ideas against empirical data, and therefore they prefer to follow the scientific approach. An understanding of these phenomena is especially important for initiating developmental work. Ethnography is one of the ways of learning about a community, but there are many cultural phenomena (such as financial institutions, bio-medical systems) that are not localized and for their study, one will have to move out of the confines of a microcosm. Certain studies, like of the tribal problems in India, require one to know about the impact of national and global factors on tribal communities and their resources. Therefore, investigators should expand their methods to include history and all those disciplines that help them in exploring the wider world. Nevertheless, the ethnographic approach remains crucial for an intensive understanding of the local situation, and from this, one spreads out to look at the relations the local communities have with the outside world.[93] The need to understand the local—the specific communities—because herein one can see the impact of the global has also gained importance in other social science disciplines, with the result that the fieldwork methodology and the ethnographic approach have become quite popular in them.

Against the background of these aspects of social research, one may now move to the sectional introductions and the readings classified in each one.

Notes

1. Here, I am not including the history of social research and fieldwork, for which see, Evans-Pritchard (1951), Kuper (1973), Payne et al. (1981), Stocking, Jr, (1983), Goody (1995). For a review of methodological works in India, see Madan (1972a: 282–315), Mukherjee (1979), Bose (1995); and for a detailed treatment of methodologies of social research, see Mukherji (2000).

2. Generally, the meaning attributed to methodology is a combination of the following aspects: techniques of data collection; tools of analysis, such as statistical methods; and theoretical perspectives that guide research and the logic of enquiry. See Mukherji (2000: 13–14). Also see Madan (1972: 283).

3. See Jain et al. (1983) for a volume on legal research methodology. Today, sociological techniques and methods are used in other social sciences as well—such as history, economics, psychology, geography, law, political science, linguistics, and several area study programmes—and each adapts them to its own specialized area (see Srivastava 2003). Bailey (1962: 262) writes: '. . . it is our technique of gathering information which commands respect from other disciplines'.

4. Singleton, Jr. and Straits (1999: 1–2) begin their work on research methods with certain observations and common questions that inspired the researchers to investigate the phenomena. The observations pertained to homelessness, witchcraft, evaluation in examination, domestic violence, or a brutal attack of a woman that was watched by thirty-eight people and none came forward to save her life.

5. See Durkheim (1966) on this point.

6. For instance, *Notes and Queries in Anthropology* (1874/1964). Those working on social mobility may see Saberwal's interview schedule (1976: 249-50); for economy, see Gregory and Altman (1989). Recently, some writers have compiled the questionnaires and interview guides they and other researchers have used. For one such dealing with social ecology and demography, see Bhasin and Bhasin (1997).

7. Some researchers did write on how they carried out their fieldwork and collected data. See Malinowski (1922, 1967), Evans-Pritchard (1940: 7–15), Whyte (1943: 279–358), Myrdal (1944: 1129–43).

8. For some detailed accounts of fieldwork, see Béteille and Madan (1975), Rabinow (1977), Srinivas et al. (1979); for some recent works, Srivastava (1991), Kumar (1992), Kulick and Wilson (1995), Caplan (1997), Thapan (1998), Hendry (1999).

9. See Whyte (1955). In other words, the progress of research methodology is directly related to the progress in investigation. What is not thought to be a tool of data collection, or the model of analysis in the beginning may become central as the study develops over time. In many cases, the community where the fieldwork is conducted determines the researcher's problem of study. Evans-Pritchard (1973: 2) writes: 'I had no interest in witchcraft when I went to Zandeland, but the Azande had; so I had to let myself be guided by them.' Similarly, he did not go to Nuerland to study pastoralism, but because the cattle complex was at the core of the Nuer society, he had to study it (Evans-Pritchard, 1940).

10. I know of female students whose parents (in many cases, the father) accompanied them for fieldwork and stayed for the entire duration. These parents also collected information on their own that was used by the researchers in their dissertations.

11. Freedman (1979: 378) cites the example of a French Sinologue, Jean Chesneaux, whose account of social change in China was based largely on the Chinese press and foreigners' reports. See pp. 398–406.

12. Bailey (1978: 4–5) views the research process as a circle. One begins with the problem, states hypotheses, formulates the research design, collects and analyses the data, and interprets the results, which lead to further research questions. An investigator may stop after interpreting the results, but the research process does not end as other researchers may take up for enquiry questions that emerge from the study.

13. For Goode and Hatt (1981: 57), a hypothesis should be 'good, definite, testable'. Also see Cohen and Nagel (1944) for a discussion of hypotheses.

14. Sociologists also speak of intervening variables. See the Glossary.

15. One may follow here Nadel's definition of theory (1956: 1): for him, a theory is 'a body of interconnected propositions (hypotheses, generalizations) concerned with a particular problem area and meant to account for the empirical facts in it'. In another, less ambitious sense, he says that a theory is a body of interconnected propositions that 'serve to *map out* the problem area and thus prepare the ground for its empirical investigation by appropriate methods'.

16. In this connection, see Fortes (1949), who regarded that one of the significant contributions of A.R. Radcliffe-Brown was to suggest researchers begin their work from a hypothesis.

17. Béteille (1965: 10–11) notes that he did enter the village he studied with a set of hypotheses, because he had a broad objective—i.e., to know the village and its social life—and an 'equipment' of hypotheses would have 'done more harm than good'. Madan (1989: 7–8) writes that he did not begin his study of Kashmiri Pandits with a hypothesis. His aim was to render 'intelligible in *sociological terms* the working of the Hindu kinship system in Kashmir'.

18. During my fieldwork with the Raikas of Rajasthan, it occurred to me that there existed a relationship between their modes of livelihood and their proclivity to ascetic and renunciatory ideology. I related this hypothesis to the 'elective affinity' that Max

Weber saw between the Protestant ethic and the spirit of capitalism (see Gerth and Mills, 1970: 302–22). See Srivastava (1997).

19. For instance, Sarantakos (1998: 6-8) offers a list of fifteen types of social research, which I have arranged in the following way: quantitative, qualitative, basic, applied, action, participatory action, exploratory, descriptive, classification, comparative, explanatory, causal, theory-testing, theory-building, and longitudinal. Rather than considering them as 'types', I shall view them as aspects of research activity that can be gainfully combined.

20. Refer to Durkheim's classic work on suicide (1951), where he shows that suicide rate—a social fact designated in numerical terms, for it is a cardinal number—is inversely related to another social fact, the degree of social integration, which is expressed qualitatively, in terms of the ordinal number.

21. In this context, see Durkheim (1966: Chapter VI) for his views on the relevance of 'experimental' and 'comparative' methods in sociology.

22. The experimental group is also known as the treatment group, the intervention group, or the stimulus group.

23. The state (or measurement) of the dependent variable (the group) before receiving the benefit of the independent variable is called 'pre-test', and after, 'post-test'. We calculate the difference between the 'pre-test' and the 'post-test'.

24. Changes might be caused by the fact that the subjects of experiments know that they are being studied. This is known as the 'Hawthorne effect', after the famous Hawthorne Experiment. It is also known as the 'reactivity syndrome' or 'reactivity effect' (see Singleton, Jr. and Straits, 1999: 29, 195).

25. For details of this 'experiment', see Powers (1963).

26. See Bales (1950) for experimental work on small groups.

27. See Durkheim (1966: Chapter VI).

28. See articles in the special issues of the *Economic and Political Weekly* (15 June 1996), *The Eastern Anthropologist*, 53 (1–2), 2000.

29. In common parlance, the term fieldwork, in contrast to laboratory work, is used for an outdoor activity of data collection. In this sense, biology students call their activities of plant and insect collection fieldwork.

30. In Indian universities, the most consulted books on research methods are by Madge (1953), Piddington (1957: 525–96), Moser (1958), Young (1966), Bailey (1978), Goode and Hatt (1981), Blalock and Blalock (1982), Ellen (1984), Bernard (1994). Two Indian authors (Wilkinson and Bhandarkar, 1984; Kothari, 1985) are also consulted.

31. For anthropological works that make use of archival materials, see Visvanathan (1993:xi), Cohn (1996), Smith (1996), Sundar (1997), Shah (2002). Some novelists also weave documentary evidence with fiction in their works; see, for instance, Ghosh (1992).

32. One of their papers is contained in this reader. Also see Rudolph and Rudolph with Kanota (2000).

33. See Marwah and Srivastava (1987).

34. See Chambers (1981, 1992), Mukherjee (1993). For focus group interview, see Greenbaum (1998).

35. The male guests are always welcomed (*manhvār karnā*) by offering them 'opium solution' (*amal*).

36. This, however, does not imply that the source of all data, information, and ideas is fieldwork. It should not be regarded as the end but a beginning in the vocation of anthropology. See Fox (1973: Introduction).

37. Quoted by Béteille and Madan (1975: 2).

38. Bailey (1962: 262) writes: '... our technique... rests on patience, on a willingness to wait and watch and allow the material to soak into us rather than to make quick samples out of the pool.'

39. Evans-Pritchard (1940: 13) writes about the difficult circumstances in which he worked with the Nuer, who were so hostile that one developed, 'if the pun be allowed, the most evident symptoms of "Nuerosis"'. See his other books on religion and kinship of the Nuer (1956, 1960).

40. See Moffat in his Foreword to Dumont (1986).

41. It has also happened that these short spells of fieldwork, carried out each year over a period of many years, have resulted in monographs. See Vidyarthi's (1963) book on the Malers of Rajmahal Hills, Jharkhand, India.

42. The desire to study a traditional community is also strong among anthropologists. Yalman (1967: 10) writes that he looked for a village 'which would be traditional, isolated and fairly large.'

43. Before starting for his fieldwork, Evans-Pritchard (1973: 1) went to his teacher, C.G. Seligman, for advice, and this was what he learnt: 'Seligman told me to take 10 grains of quinine every night and to keep off women.'

44. Obeyesekere (1981: 10–11) has emphasized the importance of having complete mastery over the native language for the study of symbolic systems. For his work, he had interviewed Tamil Hindus with the help of interpreters but since he did not know Tamil, he excluded all this information from his study of personal symbols.

45. See the section on field assistants in Pelto and Pelto (1978: 219–21).

46. During their training, fieldworkers are taught not to expect to find an idyllic society. Freed and Freed (1993: 18) write: 'When we sat in on [Margaret] Mead's fieldwork seminar..., she told about a student who went into the field with this idyllic concept. When he began his fieldwork, he suffered extreme culture shock and had to be hospitalized.' The contributors to Thapan's volume amply show that fieldwork is an 'arduous task' (1998:6).

47. Societies that have had a larger exposure to anthropological investigation have respondents who not only possess an idea of the mechanics of fieldwork but can also steer it, often suggesting relevant questions to the fieldworker. See Srivastava (1991).

48. I know of an anthropologist who had to wait in her field village for more than one year to actually observe death rituals. Herskovits (1954: 7) writes: '...in many societies there are certain rites that are performed only once every several years, and that even in a period which permits the observation of the ordinary annual round, especially in a small community, there may be no marriage or no death'.

49. Srinivas writes (1979: 26): '...I did not have a single conversation with any

young women during my stay in the village.' Another male anthropologist, Hans Buechler (1969: 13), who went to Bolivia for fieldwork, writes: '...the female view of society was practically closed to me.' Female fieldworkers are generally able to speak to male respondents of all age groups as compared to their male counterparts whose interaction is mostly confined to old women or those with whom they forge fictive kin ties. Not only gender, but also age differences are important. In her work with the Bakkarwals of Jammu and Kashmir, Rao (1998: 303) writes that probably because of her young age, she had 'relatively little intimate access to the elderly.'

50. Lowie (1937); also see Visweswaran (1996: Chapter 1) for female fieldworkers.

51. It is also possible that a male anthropologist, who was not able to interview women because of severe restrictions on the interaction between local women and male strangers, encourages his female students to study the same community that he had studied and focus on the women's world (T.N. Madan, personal communication, August 2002).

52. A husband-wife team, or any team for that matter, will form some kind of a closed group—an 'emotionally self-sufficient island' (Evans-Pritchard, quoted in Srinivas 1996: 217)—affecting the process of rapport establishment and reducing greatly the time one spends with one's respondents, who in fact become 'friends' when one is alone. An important observation in this context is from Crapanzano (1980: 141), who says that although his wife did not come to any of the interview sessions he conduced with an illiterate Moroccan Arab tilemaker named Tuhami, 'but the fact of her existence must have influenced Tuhami's relationship to me.' When the fieldworker is part of a team, his/her relations with the respondents are of a different quality.

53. See Malinowski (1967), Levi-Strauss (1976).

54. Some well known studies were the result of group research; for instance, see Dube (1955), Lewis (1958). Dube's study of a village in Hyderabad was an outcome of the Osmania University Social Service Extension Project, which he directed in 1951–52.

55. Levi-Strauss (1963: 378) himself suggested that the anthropologist can be called to analyse phenomena which exist in his society but are characterized by 'distantiation', either because they concern an unknown section of the society (like in prostitution) or because they are rooted in the unconscious (like resistance to food or health changes). But, here the argument is that 'distantiation' can be observed when a prostitute (trained in anthropology) studies other prostitutes, or when an anthropologist hailing from a conservative society studies resistance to change in his/her own society.

56. Nakane (1975: 19). Kantowsky (1995: 9–10) writes that almost all in his field village in Banaras tried to impress him and his wife—the 'white persons'. The temple priest offered them a good quantity of 'blessed food' (*prasād*); the renouncer (*sādhu*) demonstrated yogic exercises. The Kantowskys were the 'main attraction' in the village. Mayer (1975: 29) talks of the 'self-appointed young guides' who volunteered him help. Seymore (1999: 34) writes: '. . . my light skin and education gave me status.'

57. Some fieldworkers are reported to have married their respondents. Take the case of Kenneth Good (1991) who married a Yanomami woman, or of Verrier Elwin (see Guha 1998). Not much is available about sex in fieldwork. Rabinow (1977: 68–69) wrote that he spent a night with a prostitute to prove his affiliation with his male Moroccan friend.

58. One may have a look at the longitudinal research carried out in some communities. See Seymore (1999). Bennett (1983: XI) kept a steady contact of ten years with the families she initially studied. Wadley (1994: XIX) has been in constant touch with Karimpur for the last twenty-five years. Bernard (1994: 164) writes: '... no anthropologist really leaves the field.'

59. See Freilich, (1970).

60. Said has developed this argument in many of his writings. See one of his publications, *Out of Place, A Memoir* (1999).

61. This point has been fully developed by Grimshaw and Hart (1993).

62. Luhrmann (1996) writes that her fieldwork with Parsis in Mumbai was a kind of 'appointment' anthropology. She sought appointments with individuals and interviewed them. There was no small group that she could have joined.

63. In these institutions, one has to find a 'community'. Minocha (1979: 203-4), in her work in a Delhi hospital, describes the problem of looking within the hospital for a relatively large and stable community. She found such a community, with which she carried out extended contacts, in the medical ward of the hospital where the patients spent much more time than was the case in other wards. In his work on death and death rituals, Parry says that he could not find a stable community to work with in Banaras. He writes: 'For obvious reasons, intensive anthropological fieldwork amongst the huge number of transient and socially heterogeneous pilgrims who visit the city is not possible' (1994: 1). Similarly, Morinis writes that sociologists ignored the study of pilgrimage because of the 'sheer difficulty of defining and carrying out conventional fieldwork on sacred travel' (p. 358).

64. Regarding anthropological fieldwork as a 'form of conduct', Geertz (2000: 30) writes that here '[o]ne must find one's friends among one's informants and one's informants among one's friends'.

65. The role may also be imposed on the fieldworker. In my fieldwork with the Raikas, a woman, who did not have a brother of her own, 'adopted' me as her brother by tying a 'sacred thread' (*rākhī*) on my wrist in the presence of her affines. See Srivastava (1997: 231-2).

66. One of the best descriptions of participant observation is from John Madge (1953: 131). He writes: '...when the heart of the observer is made to beat as the heart of any other member of the group under observation, rather than as that of a detached emissary from some distant laboratory, then he has earned the title of participant observer.'

67. For life history method, see Langness (1965), Mandelbaum (1973), Watson (1976), Frank (1979), Shaw (1980), Ellen (1984: 247-57), Jean-Paul Dumont (1986), Srivastava (1990).

68. See, for example, Chakravarti's (1975) study of the impact of land reforms in an Indian village, in which he used the case study method.

69. Some scholars use the term 'extended case-history', which, to use Turner's words (1974: 43-44), is 'the history of a single group or community over a considerable length of time, collected as a sequence of processual units of different types'.

70. Refer to Srinivas' use (1996: 73-137; 2002) of case studies for studying disputes.

71. On the accuracy of genealogical records, see Shah and Shroff (1958: 40–70).

72. For genealogical method, also see Conklin (1964), Hackenberg (1997).

73. See Wolcott (1995: 198–221).

74. See, for instance, Parry (1994: 144–6).

75. Not many fieldworkers share with the readers of their works exactly how much they wrote during their fieldwork; however, Boissevain (1972: 31) writes that his notes ran into 1,500 pages, some 360,000 words. Fieldworkers may also collect other materials; for instance, fieldworkers collecting information on ethnomedicine and ecosystems collect plants and write about them (see Martin 1995).

76. Srinivas (2000) used the term 'memory ethnography' for an account written from memory. See also Leach (1954: 312) on this point; he had lost his field notes and photographs as a result of enemy action.

77. For instance, the Raikas made sure that the fieldworker had in his camera a colour film before he took the photographs of their married women. Photographing these colourfully dressed women in black and white was considered highly inauspicious because of the association of white and black with death and mourning. The Angami Naga girls believed that the camera was a 'diabolical contrivance for revealing their pudenda' (Hutton 1921: 251–52). The Bondo (of Orissa) also believed, Elwin told us, that the 'camera would extract a vital essence from their bodies' (Guha 1998: 172).

78. Sarah Harrison, with assistance from Penny Lang, translated Bernard Pignède's classic work on the Gurungs, a community of Nepal, among whom the movement to assert their identity has gained impetus. The leading Gurungs, including Pignède's own interpreter, C.B. Ghotane, wanted to scrutinize the text and, if necessary, modify the interpretation (Macfarlane 1997: 191).

79. The basic distinction in sampling is made between probability and non-probability sampling. In the first, the researcher can specify for each element of the universe the probability that it will be included in the sample. For the second, there is no assurance that each element has the same chance of being included. For details, see Moser and Kalton (1972), Pelto and Pelto (1976), Sarantakos (1998).

80. Anthropologists say that field researchers usually employ non-probability sampling. Mead (1953) points out the vital importance of identifying informants by the salient characteristics they possess that affect the validity of information they give. Also see Honigmann (1973).

81. Leach (1967) has been one of the ardent supporters of this position. In his recent biography, Tambiah (2002: x) writes: '...he [Leach] characterized the survey as an example of quantitative method, a statistical investigation predicated in taking individuals as units of population which misses out a wide range of sociological phenomena which are intrinsically inaccessible to statistical investigation of any kind, especially systems of relationship between persons. A social field does not consist of units of population but of persons in relation to one another.'

82. See Burton and White (1987).

83. The term ethnosurvey is used for a situation where ethnographic fieldwork is combined with survey techniques.

84. One of the satisfactory definitions of ethnography is from Marcus and Fischer (1986: 18). Ethnography is a 'research process in which the anthropologist closely observes, records, and engages in the daily life of another culture—an experience labeled as the fieldwork method—and then writes accounts of their culture, employing descriptive detail.' Also see Pelto and Pelto (1997).

85. Srinivas (1996: 194) notes: 'Anthropologists who, for one reason or another, do not publish at least some of the results of their fieldwork soon after leaving the field, live to rue their failure.'

86. Macfarlane (1997: 185) notes that the context in which anthropology is now produced has changed dramatically, because of which the gap between the anthropologist (the observer) and the people he studies (the observed) has broken down.

87. See Geertz (1988) on this point.

88. Aunger (1995) discusses the issue of ethnography as 'storytelling' and 'science'. Sanjek (1996) makes a distinction between ethnography as *process* and ethnography as *product*. Shweder (1996) places 'true ethnography' between solipsism and superficiality. Terms like analytical ethnography and critical ethnography are also popular in the literature. Jacobson (1991) discusses different styles of ethnographic writing.

89. This approach is called by different names, viz. new ethnography, cognitive anthropology, ethnoscience, and ethnosemantics. See Barnard (2000) for a succinct summary of cognitive and interpretive approaches.

90. Culture, for Geertz (1973: 144), is an 'ordered system of meanings and symbols, in terms of which social interaction takes place.' Also see Inglis (2000).

91. 'Thin description depicts behaviour in the sense of physical motions, as seen, for example, by the eyes of the camera; in contrast, thick description reveals its significance' (Jacobson 1991: 4). Geertz, in his famous article, 'Thick Description: Toward an Interpretive Theory of Culture' (1973), uses the example of 'twitches' and 'winks' to illustrate this point. Both entail the contraction of muscles of the eyelid, but a twitch is a physical movement whereas a wink conveys 'meaning', a message, within the framework of a 'socially established code'.

92. For Geertz (1973: 10): 'Doing ethnography is like trying to read (in the sense of "construct a reading of") a manuscript—foreign, faded, full of ellipses, incoherencies, suspicious emendations, and tendentious commentaries, but written not in conventionalized graphs of sound but in transient examples of shaped behaviour.' Appadurai (1981: 4) thinks that this view has a strong synchronic bias and may not be applicable to historical material.

93. See Mintz (2000) on this point.

I

Character of Social Research

Martin Bulmer (1977: 3) writes: 'The sociologist setting out to grasp the complexity of social interaction and social process is himself seeking both to *understand* and *explain* social phenomena (not merely to describe them), and is interpreting the world. . . through a frame of reference of some kind, even if this is based on the view that "the facts speak for themselves".' Some kind of a theory (or a set of theoretical propositions) guides research right from the time of the formulation of the problem to data collection and its analysis. Durkheim (1966) stressed that doing empirical research involved theory on the one hand, and the toolkit of enquiry, the strategies and techniques of empirical investigation, on the other. Social (or sociological) research aims to establish, as was stated in the introduction, a body of systematic, reliable, and valid knowledge about the social world, by undertaking empirical investigation of institutionalized human behaviour using research procedures and techniques.

Social anthropologists and sociologists use several theoretical perspectives, which may be broadly conceptualized as positivist, interpretive, and critical, with each one having many strains of its type (Sarantakos 1998: Chapter 2). For positivists, reality is 'out there' and can be perceived following scientific rules and canons that are fundamentally different from the practices of conjecture and common sense.[1] By comparison, interpretive approach believes that reality is in the minds of people. Not only is it internally experienced, it is also unceasingly constructed by people in their interactions with others. The task of the researcher is to understand it from the perspective of the people, the meaning they subscribe to their social world. For the critical perspective, which is represented by Marxists and feminists among many others, reality is imbued with conflict, tension, and contradiction, because those who occupy positions of dominance create structures (ideologies, value and norms, social sanctions) to keep others subservient. The researcher will not only expose these structures but also suggest strategies to change the order to one more equitable and just.

The perspective the researcher chooses depends upon many factors, one of which is the 'school' in which he receives training. The unremitting influence of research supervisors over their students as well as the dominant themes of a particular intellectual age also exercise tremendous impact over researchers.

This section includes articles that give one an idea of the nature of social research, taking up the concept of social reality and its dimensions; the importance of classification; the relevance of comparison and restudy in social research; and the possibility of arriving at the native's point of view. For the application of theoretical perspectives to empirical data, one may look at Srinivas (1952) for a functional analysis of rituals and religion; Desai (1959) for a Marxist understanding of the emergence of nationalism in India; and Das (1977) for the structuralist approach in sociology.[2] There are several other works that deal with the value of specific theories in the analysis of institutions, for instance, in social stratification, family, political sociology, inter-caste relations, religious experience, and life-cycle crises.[3]

The first article in this section, by Satish Saberwal, discusses the 'nature of reality' and how it should be understood. Saberwal begins by submitting that reality has many dimensions. Initially, we perceive a phenomenon subjectively—often, idiosyncratically—and this perception may be erroneous. For cooperative activity to become possible, the subjective character of our perception is transcended. An ordered social existence is made possible by, what Saberwal calls, 'intersubjective agreement', which is carried further in scholarship and scientific activity.

Saberwal then discusses the dimensions of reality. He considers three of them: the distinction between the physical and the cultural; the scale of things and the scale of representation of things; and the question of variability in phenomena. A point that Saberwal puts forward is that one is always concerned with reality, although one's level of abstraction changes from time to time. This leads him to have a look at the 'different rungs in the ladder of abstraction'. All these highly abstract ideas are illustrated with the help of 'ethnographic flesh', the case of a set of events in and around the campus of Jawaharlal Nehru University (New Delhi), where Saberwal used to teach, during the anti-Sikh riots in Delhi in November 1984. Later, Saberwal draws upon several historical examples to bring home his points concerning the nature of reality.

The perception of reality is mediated by material means—some created by nature, some fabricated by human beings—but the 'cultural resources' that we have interpret our perceptions. Therefore, there cannot be any interpretation, however scientific, independent of cultural intervention. The quality of our perception, Saberwal notes, depends upon our material means and relevant cultural resources. An interpretation of a phenomenon given in terms of a folk theory will differ from one where a scientific theory has been used. But then scientific explanations have to transcend specific cultural contexts, in the sense, they have to be 'culture-free'. This is possible when we concentrate on culture-free methods and replicable observations. Saberwal also says that when political factors start flouting scientific ethos, science turns into 'chicanery', rather than remaining a value-free enterprise in search of truth.

The second reading included here is from Ramkrishna Mukherjee's *Classification in Social Research*, dealing with the concept and importance of classification in social sciences. For Mukherjee, classification is 'concerned with the population of a schematically conceived universe'. Its role is to 'present in a consolidated manner our knowledge about the characteristics of variation in a population belonging to a specified universe'. Mukherjee also distinguishes the term 'societal' from 'social', and 'social science' from 'social sciences'. He argues that the procedure of classification should be flexible so that all possible variations in data could be accommodated.

One of the main aims of social anthropology and sociology is to arrive at a set of propositions that apply to human society and culture as a whole. Even when the universe of study is large, say, a region or state, social anthropologists and sociologists carry out what may be called, a 'micro-level and focused' study, and then, they compare their findings with other studies of the same type. Although today, rarely would scholars subscribe to the aim of social anthropology and sociology as the discovery of laws of human behaviour, comparable to those in natural and biological sciences, the concern with propositions about institutions in general exists in many intellectual circles. Radcliffe-Brown's description (1952) of social anthropology as a nomothetic (that is, generalizing) science echoes in several contemporary writings. The other idea popular from his writings is that social anthropology is a comparative science. Whether one speaks . of the early evolutionists (such as James Frazer), who compared institutions of different societies, or of '*the* comparative method', as did Radcliffe-Brown, or 'comparisons', as did Oscar Lewis (1966), a book on research methods is incomplete without some material on the comparative method. Keeping this in mind, two articles on comparative method, the first by Alan Macfarlane, and the second by André Béteille, have been included here.

Macfarlane begins his article by observing that social scientists should be aware that they indulge 'in comparison all the time'. When a sociologist conducts a micro-level study (for instance, of a band of twenty-five individuals of a foraging community or of a large urban neighbourhood), he knows that he is comparing the social categories of his own society with those of the one he studies. So, comparison is ubiquitous to every understanding. In this context, Béteille, in his article, observes: '...use of comparison may be natural to the processes of human thought', but this is not what one means by the 'conscious search for a comparative method with definite or at least defined rules of procedure'.

Building upon the works of both social anthropologists and sociologists, Béteille examines the comparative method from the perspective of the investigator. Disciplines such as economics and psychology focus largely on 'universal structures and processes common to all human beings everywhere', paying scant attention to differences between societies. Historians, by contrast, dwell more on the specific features of societies without attempting to generalize beyond their 'chosen boundaries in space and time'. Cardinal to social anthropology and sociology is the attempt to discover the general features of all societies and cultures and at the same time recognizing that each one of them has its distinctive characteristics. What characterizes human society and culture is its enormous diversity; underlying it is a set of common features. As a tool of investigation, comparative method deals with both similarities and differences of societies and cultures.

In addition to working in the ethnographic landscapes of England and Nepal, one of Macfarlane's recent interests is Japan. At places, he looks at the similarities and differences between Europe and Japan, and this illustrates the 'difference between the method of contrast and comparison'. He refers to E.L. Jones' observation that Japan provides a 'comparison' rather than a 'contrast' with Europe. The comparison of Europe and Japan inspires one to analyse the nature of capitalist development; this is something that the method of contrast would leave as 'unproblematic'. From this Macfarlane concludes that 'while Japan is different from England, it is not totally different'. Like Béteille, Macfarlane concludes that what lies behind the comparative method is the 'study of similarity and difference'.

Following this are excerpts from Gananath Obeyesekere's The Work of Culture, which deals with the nature of intersubjective relations, the claim of anthropology to represent the 'native's point of view', the 'emic' account of the other society and culture. Referring to the works of Peter Winch and Anthony Giddens, Obeyesekere notes that the respondent is like the social scientist in several regards. He carries certain conceptions of how his society functions in reality and provides answers to causality of institutions and practices. And like the social scientist, he too has controversies with his fellow members regarding all these things and sometimes these polemics turn acrimonious. Therefore, Obeyesekere writes that the respondent 'shares our own contentious natures as scholars'.

Barring certain 'rare' cases, Obeyesekere says, the native's point of view does not exist as a unified body, as a unanimous thought. Giving examples from his own area of specialization, Obeyesekere submits that there may be unanimity with respect to the key eschatological notions of Buddhism, but 'there is no uniformity in the discourse that expresses that unanimity'. When one comes to the spirit cults in Sri Lanka, there may be dissension in the opinions people hold about them and in their interpretations. In matters of economy, politics, kinship and marriage, and other aspects of culture, the differences of opinion are considerable. Obeyesekere concludes that because of 'internal controversy' and 'hidden debate', a native's point of view is almost impossible except for those parameters of history and society which transcend any controversy. Each society has a 'cacophony of voices' but this is unheard in an ethnographic account that seems to be obsessively engaged with portraying a native's point of view, which does not exist in reality.

Towards the end, Obeyesekere apprises us of his notion of 'good ethnography', which goes beyond the native's point of view and 'beyond the surface reality of everyday understandings'. This should be done through the use of a 'nomological theory', which endeavours to move away from the specificity of one culture or the other, and informs us about human life in general. Obeyesekere's contribution shows that the intersubjective relationship between the fieldworker and the people he studies is best highlighted by ethnography and with the aid of theory, he steps ahead towards the understanding of human society and culture in general terms.

The next reading kept here deals with the concept of 'restudy' in social anthropology and sociology. Whenever the discussion of restudy figures, one is reminded of the contrasting results that obtained from the study of Tepoztlán by Robert Redfield and then, twenty years later, by Oscar Lewis. Whilst Redfield found Tepoztlán relatively homogeneous, isolated, smoothly functioning and a well-integrated society, where peace and order prevailed, Lewis described it as individualistic, faction-ridden, with growing antagonism between landowners and landless people, and characterized by fear, envy, and distrust. The difference between the two monographs was caused partly by the techniques their authors respectively used. Redfield gave little attention to quantitative details, whereas Lewis gave a lot of information in numerical terms about the people of Tepoztlán and the surrounding villages—their demographic profile, changing occupational structures, marriage patterns, etc. On the basis of these details, Lewis reached certain conclusions about the changing nature of Tepoztlán. Reacting to Lewis' findings, Redfield (1960) said that the differences between the two investigators, their respective personalities, played an important role in contributing to two different reports on Tepoztlán life and character. He admitted that he was interested in certain aspects because he found them 'interesting and pleasing'. We are also reminded here of Raymond Firth's studies of Tikopians at two points of time, from which resulted the concept of 'dual synchronism', a comparison of two 'synchronic' ('here-and-now') studies of the same society at different time periods.

Peter Kloos' article, included here, suggests that the term 'restudy' is an 'unfortunate, time-bound, anthropological misnomer.' Instead, Kloos prefers to use the term 'replication' and observes that this is not a 'standard tool' in the anthropological kit. When Malinowski's book of 1922 titled *Argonauts of the Western Pacific* appeared, no one went to the Trobriand Islands to see if the inter-islandic exchange of 'valuables' (*vaygu'a*), called Kula, actually existed. Kloos rejects the methodology of dual synchronism, i.e., a comparison of two 'snapshots', and says that if one is 'interested in processes of continuity and change, it is these processes that should be studied'. A dual synchronic study may yield information on the products of change and not the processes that brought them about.

For Kloos, the concept of restudy is an 'anthropological accident'. It came into being when anthropologists developed interest in questions of change and history. For a study of continuity and change, we should combine the approaches from history and anthropology. Historians learn from anthropologists the 'principles of oral history' and they teach anthropologists the critical use of archival data. A combination of the approaches from history and anthropology is inevitable because 'every real society', to use Leach's words (1954: 5), is a 'process in time'.

Notes

1 See the glossary for the meaning of positivism.

2 The meaning of structuralism is given in the glossary.

3 See, Béteille (1965), Madan (1965), Pocock (1973), Gupta (1982), Fuller (1984), Gold (1988), Raheja (1988), Rao (1998), Robinson (1998), Ortner (1999).

On Reality:
Its Perception and Construction

SATISH SABERWAL

1. Introduction

Interpretations of reality may lie... of course, at several levels, ranging from a focus on epochs and civilizations to one on the passing moment. Furthermore, interpreting and understanding my own ongoing experience, academic and personal, has been a long-term preoccupation for me. I do this by:

1. bringing whatever little I know of the social sciences (and other fields) to bear upon my ongoing observations
2. isolating what appear to be the key operative processes in the field under observation, be these biological, psychic, social, political, or other; and
3. placing these operative processes in relation to the long-term historical context which gave rise to them.

Insofar as these operative processes, and their historical origins, are located accurately, one may claim to have recognised a little bit of 'reality'. One perceives more of its aspects, however, as this exploration stretches over diverse processes and historical contexts. These aspects are so varied that one has to lift one's focus to a more abstract level: to search for distinctions and conceptions which would enable us to talk intelligibly about the nature of reality in the round.

A category as encompassing as 'reality' has to have many dimensions, and a preliminary orientation to them is necessary (see Section 2). Our initial perception of any phenomenon is necessarily subjective, often idiosyncratic, and prone to error; yet, how we perceive it, what meaning we read into it, how we define it—on that basis alone can we act in relation to the phenomenon (see Section 3). The idiosyncrasy, the subjective character of our perception has to be transcended if cooperative activity is to become possible: that is to say, 'intersubjective agreement' is a precondition for orderly social existence (see Section 4).

This possibility of intersubjective agreement is carried further in scholarship and, especially, in scientific activity. Scholarship and science may be seen as specialized activities which may enable one to perceive reality in a more objective manner. This possibility rests on two bases: (*a*) a striving in the scientific community for intersubjective agreement spanning the whole of the concerned community of today and tomorrow—regardless of differences of culture, nationality, gender, or whatever; and (*b*) a search for shared methods, criteria, standards, and forms of interpretation which can underpin such allegiance to a common ethic across space and time (see Section 5).

Much of the expansive vigour of the West, in recent centuries, has emerged from secular, long-term improvements in its devices for perceiving reality; and this possibility germinated in Europe's historical experience, during and after the middle ages (see Section 6).[1]

A sociologist may legitimately duck the question: 'How are perceptions formed?—which properly belongs to psychology. The methods of individual and social psychology are experimental; their foci rest on the elementary processes which go into the formation of perceptions concerning simple objects, other persons, and the like. Social psychologists have been stretching towards comprehending more complex objects of perception, however, and have linked up with anthropologists in considering the implications of cultural difference for perception (Tajfel 1969 has reviewed the field).[2]

2. Dimensions of Reality

There are numerous dimensions along which the nature, and the perception, of reality may vary. I shall consider three:

1. The distinction between the *physical* and the *cultural*. A physical or biological phenomenon, say death, may carry a variety of meanings in different cultures. Each culture recognizes the meaning—the reality— of death in a distinctive way, though the underlying physical phenomenon is identical.
2. The twin issues of the scale of things, which concerns the phenomenal level, and that of the *scale of representation of things*, which concerns our manner of perceiving and representing a phenomenon. These two issues may be considered together.

3. The question of *variability* in phenomena. This is linked with the level of *abstraction* at which we conceptualize a phenomenon.

Physical/Cultural

To start with one kind of distinction, my father's death is a kind of reality; and if this leaves me polluted for a period, that 'pollution' too is real. In one case, however, the reality is physical; in the other, it is cultural. *Physical reality* is culture-free; fathers and others die in every society. *Cultural reality* refers to the terms of perception which are culturally specific: pollution at death of close kin is observed only in some societies, though the end of a life has implications serious enough for every society to take notice, and to have more or less patterned, shared form for responding to the occasion.

Many of the conceptions in the cultural realm take their cue from physical realities; but a conception formed in any one culture gets much of its form and content in the presuppositions generally prevalent in that culture. That is to say, apparently identical physical reality may carry vastly different meanings in different cultural contexts. To continue with our example of death, it may be an occasion for quiet mourning in one culture, for intense prayer in another, and for loud lamentation in yet another.

What is cultural, then, interprets, imputes one or another set of meanings to, the physical. On the other hand, whatever is 'cultural' at one level always has 'physical' aspects, even if wholly unconscious: minimally, thought is carried through neural processes.

The Scale of Things, and the Scale of Representation of Things

The difference of size or scale between the rock outside my house and a great mountain is obvious enough. Obvious, too, is the difference of scale between a person and a civilization. We should notice, however, that a qualitative change has been taking place in the world around us. In the social realm, it used to be that most lives were confined within spaces which could be traversed in a day's *walk*. In recent centuries, however, we have witnessed a manifold expansion of the scale of possible social activities and possible social influences. We owe this dramatic expansion of possible life space to such technology as the railways and the Internet, and to such institutions as general elections, widely read newspapers and stock exchanges.

To capture the outcome of these tendencies, it is common to use terms like the 'global village'. There is an irony to such terms. A scarcely literate traveller may indeed be borne across continents swiftly; yet (s)he may command the skills of the village only, being clueless at the global level.

The foregoing refers to differences in scales of phenomenal reality; but *any* phenomenon may be observed and represented on different scales. Illustratively, a map may represent a terrain on a scale of 1:1 or 1:1 million or whatever, incorporating different magnitudes of detail. Or, to take a different kind of example, the edge of a *blade*, used for shaving, has one kind of image to the naked eye; under a powerful microscope, the image would appear on a larger scale, it would be much more detailed. The different images—and levels of detail—refer to the same reality, and there are routines to observe in moving from one level to another. If you are doing research on blades, you would have to learn how to translate what you observe under the microscope into its likely feel against the face while shaving.

The point to remember is that the logic operative at one level of detail may not be the same as would apply at a different level. If one moves from one to another carelessly, the consequences may be as incongruous as those for mistaking a town map for a continental one, or historical time for geological time.[3]

Variability/Disembodiment/Abstraction/Durability

Phenomena observable in life are immensely variable. What we observe may change from one day to the next, one moment to the next: my friend's moods of elation, anger, or despair; a monsoon day changing from cloudy skies to torrential rain to bright sunshine; or the out-of-control truck hurtling towards me. A great novelist, or ethnographer, can indeed capture a palpable feel for such experienced situations: what piety is like in a great mosque; or what it felt like when disaster struck Bhopal that night. Such reportage is central to scientific activity (Runciman 1983: Chapter 4).

Scholarship commonly engages with social and other reality at another level too. One route to intellectual power is to begin with observable phenomena, and to try to climb a *ladder of abstraction*,[4] looking for, say, the physiochemical and psychological bases of changing moods; the physical principles of cloud formation, movement, and precipitation; the cultural bases of religious belief; and so on.

Such principles and theories must necessarily be abstracted out of their embedment in observable phenomena. Recourse to such disembedded formulations—or abstractions, generalizations—has consequences:

1. The *variability* gets abstracted away at successive rungs.
2. The abstract formulations—general principles, theories—conceive of phenomena at relatively invariant levels. A single theory, say, Newton's Laws of Motion, may account for particular categories of phenomena at an infinite variety of times and places.

The concern with 'reality' remains; the level of abstraction changes. Let us look at the different rungs in the ladder of abstraction. We have already noted the ground level of observation, with its high variability. Some aspects of what is observed may be part of a shared social tradition, set into relatively firm moulds—'institutionalized'—and therefore be subject to a relatively *slow* pace of change. Such patterns are relatively abstract.

A higher level of abstraction, in the social realm, carries such recognition as:

- every language has patterning in multiple layers (at the levels of sounds employed, *phonemes*; minimal units of meaning, *morphemes, lexemes*, etc.);
- one's cultural resources fashion, very largely, one's perceptions and one's interpretations of complex experience; and
- the dreams, myths, and religious beliefs generated in a society are projective systems explicable with reference to workaday personal and collective experiences in that society; and so forth.

Beyond this is the level of timeless realities which, once recognized, have a persistence amidst the enveloping flux: for example, the Periodic Table of Elements, or Newton's Laws of Motion. Now three centuries old, these latter, though subsumed in more complex formulations, remain valid within specified conditions.

Note that, as we move up the level of abstraction, and attain the more invariant levels, we get formulations which have greater durability. The validity of the basic laws of physics stretches beyond the emergence of human beings on the evolutionary scene. That is why an astrophysicist can lean on them to study distant galaxies confidently, and indeed make plausible guesses about the origins of our universe.

Concerning these several rungs of reality, I wish to make two points: (*a*) each rung has its own characteristic texture; and (*b*) the study of each rung needs techniques which have been shaped, through much trial and error, historically.

The foregoing hints at the great variety of levels of phenomenal reality, and the diverse modes of observing and conceptualizing that reality, which are available to us. These are important kinds of differences; these have strong implications and consequences. Attending to them directs us to firmer grounds for cognition and belief. Insofar as we recognize the physical or natural core of phenomena, separate from their cultural content, we can critique the latter, for the cultural is ultimately subject to our control in a manner that the natural is not: the fact of death may be inescapable, but do people have to be polluted as a consequence? And insofar as we achieve understandings which are disembedded, and invariant, these would be more durable—and therefore be a source of intellectual power.

Before proceeding further, I wish to narrate a set of events in and around the campus of Jawaharlal Nehru University during the widespread anti-Sikh riots in November 1984. This account will provide anchor for some of the later discussion.

3.Defining a Situation: An Account of Events in November 1984

On the last day of October 1984, Prime Minister Indira Gandhi was assassinated by her Sikh bodyguard. The next day, on 1 November, a busload of outsiders tried, unsuccessfully, to enter the Jawaharlal Nehru University (JNU) campus, presumably in search of Sikhs, and there were rumours of imminent attacks. For several days following, therefore, the campus was astir, with round-the-clock vigils to meet any possible attack from outside.

Much of this concern was focused on an urbanized 'village' which shares a border road with the campus. One night, I think on 3 November, a good deal of shouting was heard from the village side of the road, and hundreds of men and women assembled on the JNU side at the boundary wall, looking out on the village. Apprehension of an attack from the village was acute. In fact, nothing happened.

The next morning, a colleague and I thought of going to the village to enquire why there had been such a racket the previous night. Our first contact was a JNU staff member, who lived in the village and who led us to other inhabitants. Village elders, whom we had no reason to doubt, insisted that they had no hostile intent towards the university. The noise, they explained, had come from the village because the villagers themselves had feared an attack by Sikhs. Some of these fears, admittedly, rested on nothing more substantial than the sound of crackers which pranksters had saved over from the Diwali festival. Shouting had been part of their (the villagers) defensive preparation vis-à-vis the Sikhs. Note how this fear of Sikhs was part of at least some villagers' sense of reality even though no Sikh may have been in a position to attack the village. Subsequently, as the residents of the campus proceeded to formulate their own construct of reality, the sounds from the village were interpreted as being hostile.

A fair number of residents in the village find lower-level employment in the university, and sometimes persons working or studying in the university rent accommodation in the village. Many villagers collect wood and use pasturage in the campus routinely, and occasionally a student locates a minor field study in the village. Yet, significant contacts, and communication, between the university and the villagers have been scant. That is why, in November 1984, campus residents grossly misinterpreted the sounds coming from the village.

Defining a Situation

'Defining the situation' is a phrase sociologists often use, (e.g., Merton 1948, following W.I. Thomas). To define a situation is to interpret that situation, to read a particular meaning into it, at a given time.[5] The campus defined the situation on the premise of the villagers' hostile intent, the villagers on that of the Sikhs' hostile intent. Both these notions of reality—the villagers' and the campus'—were erroneous. Both suffered an acute sense of threat and insecurity when, on independent evidence, or, 'in reality', there was no threat 'out there'. Yet, until such error is recognized, the only available description of reality—on which we can base our intentions and actions—is the one given to us by our immediate perception and judgement, however faulty these may be. These perceptions and judgements go into shaping a certain mental state which influences what we choose to do.

The foregoing implies that, in defining a situation, we may have a certain choice, a certain room for manoeuvre. To take an instance from modern Indian history, Mohamed Ali could be a spokesman for 'Muslim interests' almost exclusively, *before* his incarceration during World War I, and again *after* Khilafat had collapsed. During the Khilafat phase, however, he was, along with Gandhi and others, a full-blooded Indian nationalist (Hasan 1979). Again, between 1937 and 1946, a good many Muslims in the subcontinent changed their definition of their political situation: they voted for the Muslim League and, implicitly, for the creation of Pakistan. Politically, the mid-forties were marked—as many periods are marked—by multiple, competing definitions of the situation in India, say, those associated with the Congress, the Muslim League, the RSS, the princes, the regional parties, the raj, etc. Now, if one definition of the situation comes to prevail over the other(s), it is because of the variety of elements which happen to buttress that way of looking at things (see Figure 1).

What all can go into your defining a situation in a particular way? Anything that counts in having you believe one thing rather than another: Figure 1 lists sentiments, symbols, interests, power and force. Furthermore, members of a group—a sect, a faction, a country at war—may persuade each other of the absolute truth of even their most arbitrary notions.[6]

FIGURE 1
Definition of a Situation

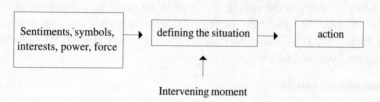

Intervening moment

There are two things to remember here:

1. In analysing an episode or a larger happening, when we say that X defined the situation as one of threat or opportunity or cordiality, giving it a particular meaning, we are recognizing an 'intervening moment' in our analysis: it specifies the mental state which later yielded a particular course of action.
2. When we say that an event or a social outcome resulted from a certain definition of the situation, this can only be a preliminary step in the analytic task. It remains then to ask: what produced that mental state? Why did that definition come to prevail over the alternative(s)?

Reality Testing

Insofar as my *definition* of a situation—physical or social—is consistent with 'what it really is like', this improves my capacity to 'deal' with it: that is, to anticipate the course it is likely to take, in order to avail of an opportunity, forestall a threat, or whatever. *Reality, we may say, is that which we have to take into account lest it surprise us with its consequences.* Hence, the importance of *reality testing*, of checking out my notion of what a particular slice of reality is like.

I may suspect that a crowd intends to attack me, when in fact its members are only testing me. I could check out my suspicion by making discreet enquiries, and observations, to see whether their intention is indeed hostile. In perceiving reality, however, we may err in two directions. On one side, we may assume that something exists when independent evidence would suggest that it does not, as in the instance just noted. The opposite error also is possible: we assume that something does not exist when independent evidence would suggest that it does. Surrounded by a crowd, I may be clueless about an undercurrent of antagonism, which may have grown without my being sensitive to it.[7]

A long-term advantage lies in defining reality in ways that take account, first, of how *others* define it and, second, of how it might be defined 'objectively'. We shall revert to 'objectivity' shortly.) This latter is a cultivated skill; it is a matter of learning to *face up to reality as it is.*

4. Perception and Construction of Reality

Perception

The reality I perceive may be social, as in my perception of my neighbour's intentions, or it may be physical, as in my perception of the imminence of monsoon rain. My perception of any particular phenomenon may be more or less accurate, depending upon my procedures; and these may be *naïve*, resting on the everyday categories and routines of my society, or these may be mediated, possibly, by my understanding of the principles of psychology, physics and the like.

Perception, in the first instance, is necessarily personal, subjective. It is *naïve*, in the sense that its own premises are not ordinarily subjected to critical appraisal. Yet, in a functioning society, everyday social practice rests crucially on agreement between different persons, on an *intersubjective agreement*, between participants in an activity, over what the phenomena at issue really are; such agreement defines the situation collectively. Such intersubjective agreement is necessary even though its premises would not ordinarily be examined critically; indeed, the participants would be aware of the *possibility* of such examination only rarely.

How I *perceive* reality becomes the basis for my actions and, therefore, goes into renewing and reconstituting—into constructing—the reality that you may perceive, and vice versa. We construct a large part of the reality which becomes an object for others to cope with—and to interpret. Perception and construction are, thus, successive moments in the social dialectic.

This intersubjective agreement rests commonly on the cultural assumptions which underlie the particular practice. If everyone in my community agrees that my father's death has indeed polluted me, this agreement arises from accepting the whole Brahminical ideology of purity and pollution. This has implications.

1. Defining a situation one way rather than another makes a difference. My state of pollution, following my father's death, imposes a range of obligations on me which would not apply in a society which does not recognize such a state.

2. Intersubjective agreement, here, is culturally specific; an ordinary Kenyan or a Dane would not find it easy to concur in this belief.

It is possible to push the search for agreement between observers—intersubjective agreement—beyond the limits of a specific culture; indeed such a drive underlies a great deal of science and scholarship. Section 5 below will return to these issues.

Construction

Although the particular ways of constructing—and transmitting—social reality are necessarily a social process, the process can scarcely proceed except through *particular persons*. We have to recognize two levels. First, we construct our image of reality with such materials as our perceptions make available to us: I propose to call these our *constructs* of reality. Social reality exists, that is to say, in the form of a multitude of *personal* constructs of that reality—even though the requisite materials be drawn from a shared cultural storehouse. To recall the incidents of November 1984, the villagers' perceptions led them to particular constructs of reality and then to certain actions; this latter provided the stimuli with which residents of the university campus constructed their image of reality, the stimuli around which the campus defined the situation at its perimeter. We shall return to the personal constructs of reality below.

Second, there is the *socially* constructed reality. Whatever the physical universe is like, a large part of the reality around us is constituted through human intentions, designs, and efforts: think of the telephone system; of the complex of doctors, drugs, chemists, and hospitals; of the universities; of the interlinked religious beliefs, practices, shrines, institutions; and so forth. What is constituted may itself be physical, or it may be a body of ideas.

These are realities which we humans make, remake, and sometimes modify as we go on our daily rounds. We make them not individually but collectively, in the course of our interactions; we make them not instantly but as part of a tradition or traditions which, in turn, we make, remake, and sometimes modify. What (reality) you perceive or experience is commonly what someone else has put together. For something like my experience of a musical tradition, that putting together may, of course, have been a long process, a long time ago, becoming available to me as part of my growing up.

These constructed structures of reality emerge in historical processes; and these processes may be swift, as in a revolution, or slow, as in the shaping of a language. These structures of a reality persist through patterned, institutionalized interactions and relationships—whose study lies at the heart of sociology, our discipline.

Embodied in institutions and in patterned forms of conduct, such realities make demands which are no less inexorable than the realities of nature: a monsoon shower and an income tax assessment can seem equally arbitrary and equally inescapable. These constructed structures of reality—traffic lights, the surgeon's orders, the pollution from someone's touch—can have a coercive potential that Newton's Laws of Motion and the like may not always have.[8] We flout them at our own risk.

Any consideration of the 'social construction of reality' reminds us of the terms of the dialectic which Berger and Luckmann (1966: 79) summed up pithily: *Society is a human product. Society is an objective reality. Man is a social product.* I have noted the 'manmade' character of social arrangements and institutions; and also the presence and the availability of these social arrangements as an external reality. There are these social arrangements as an external reality. These are available both to constrain us and to encourage and inspire us on occasion. To complete the dialectic needs the third element too; *society makes man.* That is to say, I would be like a feral child—a human child raised by a wolf mother—if I lacked the social matrices, and the cultural resources and traditions, to which I have had access, into which I have been inducted. Socialization with reference to ongoing arrangements, routines, and institutions enables the continuation of particular ways of constructing reality.

This socialization or, if you prefer, apprenticeship in particular ways of constructing reality, can achieve varying measures of success at best. The inadequacies of socialization, for some of which we may be thankful, may be traced to a variety of factors: there are intrinsic differences between *persons*; the *social structure* carries various alternatives, and these may be learned idiosyncratically; historical *circumstances* change, and what worked well for parents may work badly for children; and so forth.

Amidst all the variability, however, the *personal* construct of reality, which we mentioned earlier, does draw upon a received repertoire of meanings, of ideas concerning what that reality is or ought to be, of modes of visualizing the future, and so forth. One draws on these to construct a personal, individual, in some ways, unique ad idiosyncratic sense of the world around oneself. In order to cope with our life situations, we need to be able to give them meanings—definitions of situations—with reference to which we may act. These meanings are strengthened if others, whose opinions we value and whose judgements we respect, confirm them in word and deed.

It is a mark of situations of major 'social change' that such received, entrenched social forms decline during such periods. Even as the received social forms decline, however, some individuals may have the reputation of choosing well—of exercising good judgement—in situations of considerable uncertainty.[9] If such persons emerge as 'stable anchors', in relation to whom others learn to orient their own conduct (social psychologist Muzafer Sherif's phrase, quoted in Tajfel 1969: 357), the social process may continue in relatively stable ways. Particular actors may then continue to interpret—to make sense of—their own biographies satisfactorily.

It must be remembered, however, that the adequacy of these processes in a society can never be taken for granted. Whether these work, and how well these work, would depend on the adequacy of the society's educational system, that is, on how much care it routinely takes to equip its next generation to cope with the changing realities of existence.

5. Science, Intersubjective Agreement, and Error

We move now to a series of issues bearing directly on scientific activity. I begin with some observations on the ethos of science: in its commitment to transparency and to critical, recursive appraisals of its own activities laying the ground for intersubjective agreement—transcending particular localities and cultures. Searching for shared methods, criteria, standards, and interpretative forms is central to the scientific enterprise; and judgements of 'error'—in science or in everyday life—depend on the availability of reliable standards, independently of the particular situation at issue.

Intersubjective Agreement

It is imperative for scholars and scientists that, as part of their professional activity:

- they be willing to consider alternative formulations justly, and
- they routinely scrutinize, critically, the validity and adequacy of their own assumptions: in terms of internal consistency, in the light of empirical evidence, and in comparison with alternative formulations; it is imperative for them, that is, to be *recursive* in relation to their own work.

The better a scientist is able to objectively analyse his/her own ideas in relation to the ideas and results of other scientists, the better is this scientist likely to be.[10] Such recursive appraisal—and considering of alternatives—

cannot ever stop in sound scholarship; and therefore formulations in the social (and other) sciences may over time become less and less naïve. Importantly, however, these formulations can never shed this element of naivete altogether.

For scholarship, this recursive appraisal—and considering of alternatives—has a crucial consequence: professional scientists from varied institutional, religious, and national backgrounds are commonly able to agree on what is being observed, and on how to interpret it; hence the possibility of wide-ranging *intersubjective agreement*.[11] Indeed, scientific formulations seek, ideally, to be free from any particular cultural context, except that of science.[12] The Periodic Table of Elements, for example, emerged through the labours of physicists and chemists in many countries over several generations. Striving to achieve intersubjective agreement, across societies and over long periods of time, may then be one road to 'objectivity' (Pugh 1983: 47).

A body of knowledge like the Periodic Table of Elements may reasonably lay claim for its universal acceptance, and validity. We shall revert to this rather extraordinary cultural achievement: this collective ability to maintain wide-ranging intersubjective agreement, in shifting fields of knowledge, many of which are continually subject to thoroughgoing revision and reformulation.

It should be noted that vigorous disputation, over issues large and small, is part of the process. The point bears restating: wide-ranging agreement in the sciences, and in academia generally, is *not* despite the disputation. The agreements are a *consequence* of the disputation; and the orderly, purposive conduct of this disputation reinforces the participants' confidence in, and commitment to, the culture of science.

Quantification

At the heart of the scientific endeavour lies a search for generally applicable methods, criteria, standards, and interpretative forms. I wish to make two comments here:

1. This search for generally applicable methods, standards, and the like often seeks forms which can be repeated reliably; and the search commonly looks for aspects which can be quantified—and therefore measured by different scholars independently. A caveat is necessary, however. It cannot be the case that whatever can be quantified is significant. Quantification cannot confer significance; at best it can confer precision. If it should become possible, however, to quantify what is

judged, independently, to be significant, it would facilitate intersubjective agreement.
2. The shared search for alternative methods and standards, and the shared, higher order methods and standards for evaluating them: these are essential. These make it possible for the scholarly community to be able to transcend the limitations of particular localities and cultures. For the scientific community, these serve as 'levers of transcendence' (Schwartz 1985: 5 uses the phrase similarly).

Error in Everyday Life

The importance of such standards and criteria may be seen by reference to events in everyday life. My brother's extraordinary behaviour may persuade me that he has come to be possessed by a malignant spirit. If this belief is reasonable in the logic prevailing in the society in which I live, you may not be able to accuse me of error within that cultural logic. Indeed that 'possession' would be seen to be 'real' if you consider the statements made by my brother or, rather, by the identity claimed by the voice speaking through him.[13]

My belief in this case can be said to be an error only if a relatively context-free psychological criterion, or form of interpretation, concerning my brother's behaviour is ready to hand. Such a standard may not be available to me, or to you. Only *where a valid standard is available* can my *perception* of that slice of reality be judged to be false or illusory.

Error in Science

When scholars in the social (and other) sciences analyse, and make pronouncements regarding the nature of social (and other) reality, and others take them seriously, these pronouncements contribute to *defining* that reality. It is important to recognize that scholars and scientists make errors too. The ordinary risks of scholarship may be aggravated by partisan political backing—or by the impact of nationalist, religious, racist, or other prejudice. Such influence may trap a scholar into believing that (s)he need not consider alternative formulations justly; or one may merely fail in practice to do so. Such activity slides beyond the pale of scholarship proper, regardless of the eminence of the persons involved.

Insofar as such scholars abandon their recursive practice—whether consciously or not—their sterility grows with time. Backed by the Communist Parry, the Lysenko clique could impose its homespun notions of plant breeding techniques on the Soviet Union for a whole generation! Lysenko was

finally junked *because* of the higher order standards that elsewhere had
led to the discovery of the genetic bases of mutation in plants (Joravsky
1970). Academic sterility may, of course, have other antecedents too.

Ambition in Science

We may note that the methods of science give us a hold on only limited
segments of reality at any time. At any given moment, the sciences tend to
be *unambitious*—if you compare them with the knowledge claims of a
tantrik or a godman. Yet, the sciences' commitment to openness and
transparency, and a shared sense of method, gives their findings an
unparalleled cumulativity. Consequently, the sciences can be very ambitious
over the long term. The process of securing methods, criteria, standards,
and interpretative forms that transcend specific cultural contexts is a key
driving mechanism for the long-term achievements of the sciences; and it
provides the basis for intersubjective agreement over widening cognitive
fields.

6. Europe's Experience

One scarcely need say that the West has achieved secular, long-term
improvements in its devices, both material and mental, for perceiving reality.
I wish to ask, briefly, (*a*) wherein these improvements lay, and (*b*) how the
West came to take this tack during the medieval period.[14]

The Improvements

What is the nature of the improvements in these means for perceiving
reality? Commonly these bring to us *pictures of reality* at levels that are
inaccessible when using only the means with which nature has endowed
us. Telescopes, ultrasonic scanners, and the robots used for locating
fragments of Kanishka in the depths of the Atlantic—all illustrate these
devices. In the social sciences one thinks of the rise of anthropological and
psychoanalytic skills for plumbing the depths of the unfamiliar.

  Beyond particular techniques and instruments, there is the use of complex processes and routines, in and out of laboratories, for enlarging, and
making more reliable, our maps of reality which collectively constitute the
sciences of our time. Among these maps of reality are those drawn in the
social sciences, whether you consider interpretations of long-term
civilizational experience, say, by Michael Mann, or theoretical statements,
say, by Berger and Luckmann.

The History

Europe's skill in facing up to reality-as-it-is began to get sharper early in the second millennium. Accelerated by the experience of the Crusades between the late eleventh and the mid-thirteenth centuries, sailings of growing reach came gradually to connect the West Asian ports—in the Black Sea and the Mediterranean—with North European ports in the Baltic. Associated with this growth in shipping and commerce, one can identify a more general skill—that of the *accurate* recognition of external reality which facilitated wider agreement on the characteristics of that realty. There was a gradual recognition, furthermore, that action in terms of these accurate, agreed characteristics had a better chance of attaining its goal, avoiding mishap. The most dramatic expression of this orientation to reality was to be seen, of course, in Europe's mastery of the oceans and its ability, 1492 on, to penetrate every continent and island on this earth.

This orientation to reality included a growing capacity to organize information about that reality into usable form, and using it to advantage. Thus:

- sailing charts for jagged coastlines, and directions for sailing the oceans (Scammell 1981: 206–8);
- growing size of *ships* (up to 2,000 tons by the mid-fifteenth century, ibid.: 194) and an increased variety of sails for ships;
- *watermills* and *windmills*, harnessing inanimate energy (Thrupp 1972: 232ff; White 1972: 156f);
- papermills, from 1276 onwards, which made paper for writing on, at half the price of parchment, thereby making manuscript production, the book trade, and consequent activity faster and more efficient (Murray 1978: 301f);
- *reading glasses*, invented in Venice in the 1290s (ibid.: 302), often doubling a person's years of active reading; and
- *clocks*, in the fourteenth century, facilitating the organizing of one's own time, and coordinating with others (Le Goff 1972: 86ff; White 1972: 160); and so forth.[15]

Medieval Europe showed its sensitivity towards *social* reality too. In the mid-thirteenth century, the Mongols were knocking at the doors of Europe in the East. First the Pope, Innocent IV, and then the King of France, Louis IX, sent emissaries—Franciscan monks—to the court of the great Khan of the Mongols in Karakorum to ascertain what kind of society they had and what their intentions were towards the Muslims, the Christians, and so forth (Southern 1962: 44–51). (In contrast, during the seventeenth and eighteenth centuries, our ancestors made scant effort to judge what the long-term intentions of Europeans in India could be.)

The happenings in Europe may be seen as practical skills: sailing, harnessing inanimate energy, making paper and reading glasses and clocks, diplomacy, and so on. Alongside, there was also the level of ideas: ideas about the nature of the world, and how it works. Europeans in the middle ages brought the greatest seriousness to writing and arguing at this second level. By the early fourteenth century, in the universities, especially Oxford, and outside them, the premises being advanced, and the issues being discussed, were such that one may see in them intimations of the direction which led to men like Copernicus and Newton in later centuries.

These complex matters I can broach here only in unseemly brevity, referring to three issues:

1. The *context* in which, during the twelfth and thirteenth centuries, the stock of ideas in Europe took a quantal leap;
2. The *epistemic break* between the Scholastics (such as Thomas Aquinas, c.1225–74), whose scholarship leaned heavily on ancient authorities, such as Aristotle, in its search for truth; and a more empirically oriented scholarship (such as that of William of Ockham c. 1286–c. 1348), which privileged *experience* as the source from which to learn about the world we live in; and
3. The changing *societal conditions* wherein this empirical turn in medieval European thought could begin.

The Context

Late medieval European intellectual history features a signal event of unmatched significance. In its reduced circumstances following the subsidence of Rome, Europe had abandoned knowledge of the Greek language, and thereby lost access to the learning of ancient Greece. As part of the economic expansiveness of the eleventh and twelfth centuries, the West's contacts with the Arabs in Spain and elsewhere grew. The Arab philosophers' thought was stimulating enough; but this thought, and the Arabs' libraries, directed attention to the forgotten treasures of Greek thought. Europeans moved swiftly—from the twelfth century onwards—to translate this massive body of texts into Latin and to assimilate it into their thinking and their university curricula. The Greek corpus, and especially Aristotle, was the principal impetus, but Europeans were taking in the Arab masters' thought too. Further afield, the widening horizon of their experience was symbolized by Marco Polo's years in, and writings on, China.

The Epistemic Break

The history of ideas during these tumultuous centuries is intricate, immensely involuted;[16] out of that, I have space to make just one point. Different scholars dealt with a variety of issues, of course; but a dominant concern of European scholarship, during the thirteenth century, came to be to try to provide rational bases for key elements of faith: the nature of God and His working, His effect on man, the soul, the will, intelligence, truth, the possibility of knowledge, and so forth. The issues considered, and the arguments advanced, rested on hypothetical assumptions and distinctions. For this project, the Aristotelian apparatus of logic, and of directing error in argument, as well as his particular conceptions were seen to be an important resource, especially at the University of Paris.

The corpus of fresh writing grew, yet the increase in understanding was less than commensurate. On the contrary, numerous scholars were committed to the use of *reason* alone; and its play, unconstrained by doctrinal orthodoxy, could lead in directions which seemed perilously subversive of faith; so there was a good deal of conflict.

A way out of the impasse had already been taking shape at Oxford, led by Robert Grosseteste since the early thirteenth century. A distinction emerged between two kinds of knowledge: that concerning God, and that concerning experience. Truth about God is revealed; truth about the world of experience is an empirical matter, to be ascertained through observation and experiment. Positing this autonomy of empirical experience, a body of scholarship in the thirteenth and early fourteenth centuries ranged over fields which included mathematics, motion, optics, magnetism, astronomy, and linguistics. This new scholarship was distinctive in its empiricism, in recognizing the importance of *experience* for learning about the world we live in.

Compared with a priori knowledge, based purely on reason and speculation, that in the empirical mode has one advantage: its proponent can present his evidence publicly; and different observers may agree on the evidence of their senses the more easily. The empirical mode arose in a process internal to the course of medieval scholarship; but we may also refer to the societal conditions which proved hospitable to it. I mention two such conditions: first, the weakening grip of the Church, and second, the growing differentiation of society.

The Societal Conditions

By the fourteenth century, the Church was already in some difficulties: fleeing Rome, the Pope settled in Avignon in southern France in 1309, and stayed there until 1377, a dependant of the king of France. Under these conditions, William of Ockham, for instance, could defy the Church, finding shelter with a secular authority in 1328, and settling in Munich (Leff 1958: 280). The Church could do little to suppress the alternative perspectives being canvassed.

The ideological differentiation went with the continuing differentiation of society, with a growing specialization, or differentiation, of institutions. I have reviewed the historic trajectory of this institutional differentiation in medieval Europe elsewhere.[17]

There was the Church itself, which had long been the dominant institution. It had given rise to a wide variety of monasteries and other institutions which were substantially autonomous in relation to ecclesiastical authority. A thirteenth-century university was a centre of learning; it brought teachers of law, medicine, theology, and philosophy together in one institution—which would often be assertive of its own autonomy. The kingships had their consultative assemblies, their courts of justice, and their growing bureaucracies. The Italian cities' governmental arrangements rested on explicit, written, if frequently contested, constitutions. With growing commerce, there was the growing strength of merchants, bankers, and artisan guilds: interdependent categories, each of which, nevertheless, carried space for autonomous activity.

It is necessary to recognize the exceptional quality of these institutional realms. Though tending towards *autonomy*, these institutions were far from being *insulated* against each other socially. There was a good deal of seepage—of ideas and of people—across them, as through the Church, the monasteries, and the universities. We have here a differentiation of institutions, functioning autonomously, along with substantial mobility across them. Such a situation would have consequences.

On one side, this autonomy and differentiation provided institutional space for arguing out distinctive viewpoints, often subverting orthodoxies, despite recurring ecclesiastical efforts at stamping out ideas believed to undermine faith. On the other side, the frequent mobility across the institutions generated a pressure to search for a shared approach to things, for a shared sense of method, a shared world view, one that a person could carry even in transiting from one institutional realm to another.[18] It would be a shared, generalized view, one that would tend to transcend the specificities of world views associated with particular occupations or institutions. 'A crucial western property seems to be the interpenetration, both organisationally and ideologically, of the same general system wide culture,' notes the sociologist John Meyer (1989: 407).

7. In Conclusion

This essay has sought to explore a few aspects of the infinitely complex domain of reality. Our *perception* of reality is mediated by such material means as our eyes or telescopes, some means fabricated by nature, others by us. Furthermore, for interpreting—that is, for seeing the *meanings* of— our perceptions, we need devices of another kind. The significance of observations on telescope, which may be portentous for an astronomer or an astrophysicist, would be lost to the untrained eye. Alongside material means, then, we need cultural resources for interpreting our perceptions. Their overall quality depends on the quality both of our material means, our eyes or our telescopes, and of relevant cultural resources, whether folk belief or high-flown theory.

An important distinction about 'truth' is this: is the validity of a proposition limited to a specific cultural context, or is it general, culture free? The striving for a culture-free level of validity is central to the scientific enterprise; and such an aspiration can be sustained only through concentration on questions of method, which underpin replicable observations, and therefore the possibility of an expanding body of shared interpretations. Where the calculus of political advantage, or collective prejudice, leads to the flouting of this ethos, science gives way to chicanery. A recursive scepticism is central to this ethos, and it confers on the scientific enterprise the qualities of asymptotic approximation to truth. The possibility of intersubjective agreement in scientific work, furthermore, underlies the potential for an unrivalled cumulativity in science over the long term.

A caveat, in conclusion, concerning my insistence on the culture-free status of the scientific enterprise. For clear historical reasons, virtually all scientific knowledge, even that generated within India, comes to us in obviously Western cultural garb. The codes and notations it employs have drawn upon, and contributed to, everyday Western practices for centuries. When presented to an Indian child—or adult—who has not had much exposure to western cultural forms, such scientific knowledge is unmistakably alien. As social psychologist Tajfel (1969: 379) noted: 'Perceptual interpretations of notation systems are not "given"; they must be rooted in appropriate past experience. This points to difficulties that may be encountered in the introduction of systems of education using unfamiliar notation systems in new cultural contexts.' Science and scientific knowledge, then, can be 'culture free' only in principle; yet, at least potentially, these are more so than any other body of knowledge or activity.

I have argued that both the perception and the construction of reality are historically created and learned skills, outcomes of *social* processes. The shaping of these skills in Europe came to be funnelled into fields which we know as science and technology. We considered the processes propelling this course of events at some length. The waxing and waning of these skills are legitimate areas for sociological interest, though the philosophers' critique would help ensure that we do not jump rails in this project.

Notes

1. Anyone who relies excessively on Foucault might think my dating anachronistic. As late as the sixteenth century, Foucault tells us (1970: Chapter 2), European thought remained enchanted, imagining multitudes of resemblances in the universe, without worrying much about empirical validation. This may well have been the case in certain domains.

To be sure, Columbus was much given to reading signs in all manner of things (Todorov 1984). Yet, for men like Columbus and Vasco da Gama to push into uncharted oceans needed more than signs; it needed confidence in their ability to negotiate the physical and social terrains on their way.

2. Questions of 'reality' and 'perception', however defined, loomed large in the ancient Indian philosophical tradition. Indexes to the volumes of Dasgupta's *A History of Indian Philosophy* (1922–54) carry scores of references to these and related terms; and both terms appear in titles of B.K. Matilal's writings. Yet I lack the minimal orientation to this tradition needed for me to try to bring it into this discussion even marginally.

3. Some years ago I heard a lecture which drew wide-ranging parallels between the chronologies of national movements in several countries of Asia and Africa. A member of the audience insisted that the links between these countries were far older than these chronologies: Africa and Asia had once been *one* continent. To unify a geological process with a historical one in this manner was incongruous and wholly illegitimate—and therefore laughable.

4. A particular episode in science may also begin with a general theory—which directs attention to certain possible phenomena—and then the experimenter tries to create conditions for observing those phenomena. This possibility arises from a ladder of abstraction being already available.

5. Everyday use of language contributes to defining one's reality in some measure. Words, categories, serve to classify reality—and thereby to explain it: 'Why did the professor behave that way? 'Because he is *neurotic*'. Here the word 'neurotic' gives meaning to, defines the meaning of, an observation.

Words, categories, may *simplify* the reality which they define: a great variety of conducts and persons may be classified as neurotic, with or without reason. Such implicit, everyday simplification, in our constructs of reality, may serve either to illuminate key elements of that reality or to hide them from our awareness. Words and categories, by themselves, are neutral to such unwitting consequences.

6. See Section 5 ('Error in Science') for an arbitrary 'definition of situation' even in the domain of science, when it is backed by overweening political power and the like. Lysenko's dominance of Soviet plant breeding for a whole generation is a classic case in point.

7. The reader might notice the paraphrase here of the 'two types of error' in statistical hypothesis testing (Dixon and Massey 1957: 88).

8. Yet 'we do not jump out of aeroplanes without a parachute!' (Olaf Andersen, personal communication).

9. They may have learnt to work with such doctrines as Kant's categorical imperative: that the rational actor use one's autonomous reason, to define one's courses of action for oneself, such that the corresponding principles could be made universal laws too (Scruton 1982: 69–71).

10. I owe this sentence to Olaf Andersen (personal communication). He adds:

Many people may try to create different versions of the universe. Most of these individuals are 'crackpots' and will be forgotten; some are later proven right. If the latter individuals gave up trying to convince the sceptics that they indeed are right, there will be little progress. If the former individuals are too successful in convincing people that their picture of the world is correct, things may be even worse. The important point is that there is a subjective quality to all frontier science, which we [scientists] recognize as being part of the process; but which 'lay' people often are unaware of, and they mistake a scientist's personal opinions to be statements about reality.

11. I discuss 'intersubjective agreement' here in relation to perception and fields of knowledge. Section 4 ('Perception') noted its importance for everyday social practice too. Its significance for wide-ranging social action should be obvious enough.

12. Ramanujan's distinction between the context-bound and the context-free (1989: Sec. IV).

13. The implication of this position is clear: the 'spirit' which has taken possession of the patient *is* believed to be real within the patient's culture. The shaman who tries, and may be able, to effect a cure acts on the belief that the spirit is real. See Freed and Freed 1964.

True, a psychiatrist or psychoanalyst would interpret the phenomenon differently— and yet be able to cure the patient. We may see that the psychoanalyst's abstractions as well as the shaman's 'spirit' are hypothetical entities, yet both believe that these entities have real consequences. Kakar (1982) counterpoises culturally specific modes of therapy with those which seek to transcend the cultural specificities in this domain.

14. The latter question, of the sproutings of ideas and techniques in medieval Europe, raised here only briefly, is part of the larger issue, 'Why Europe?', reviewed at length in Saberwal 1995: Chapters 3–6.

15. These paras summarize Saberwal 1986: 15–17.

16. There are numerous writings on medieval European thought, addressed to the non-specialist: e.g., Piltz 1981 and Leff 1958. These paras rest principally on Leff.

17. Saberwal 1991a, worked into 1995: Chapter 4.

18. The insight here is probably from anthropologist Mary Douglas, though I have lost the reference. For such pressure to trigger such a search, the threshold was relatively modest in Europe's case: the Church had been promulgating a shared metaphysics for generations. Such pressure would be weaker, and the threshold higher, where the insulation between occupational realms was more thorough. For a related discussion, Saberwal 1991b, worked into 1995: Chapters 5–7.

On Classification

RAMKRISHNA MUKHERJEE

Classification is concerned with the population of a schematically conceived universe. The population may be human or any kind of inanimate or animate objects: for example, the population of Bengalis, bees, birch trees, bolt-making industries, banking institutions, brotherhoods (sacred or secular), and so on. We identify the universe of the population by space–time coordinates, for example, the Bengalis in the State of West Bengal in the Republic of India in the decade of the 1980s or the Bengalis in Bangladesh in the same decade. Now, if the characteristics of a population were the same (i.e., a constant), there would have been nothing to classify. For example, it is not a matter for classification that the Bengalis have one nose each, but the shape of the nose can be classified qualitatively as sharp or flat (narrow, medium, broad, etc.), and the process of classification will be precise and comprehensive when the shape of the nose is classified quantitatively according to the metric values of the nasal index. The Bengalis, or any other population, can thus be classified by a set of *variable* characteristics which may be developed from qualitative distinctions into quantitative measurements.

The role of classification is, therefore, to present in a consolidated manner our knowledge about the characteristics of variation in a population belonging to a specified universe. Hence, it is a perennial concern of scientific investigation, the task of which is to elicit the variable properties of the phenomena with which the populations are involved: the phenomena defined as things that are perceived but the constitution and the cause of which are not known—fully or partly, precisely or comprehensively. A scientist, accordingly, categorizes certain series of variation in such a manner as he or she considers suitable to (1) describe a phenomenon or a set of phenomena, (2) explain concomitance or causality regarding the phenomena, or (3) diagnose and predict, on a probability basis, the future possibilities regarding the phenomena.

Classification is thus seen to be inherent in any course of scientific investigation. At the same time, it does not seem on its own merit to require any specific attention by the scientist. Why should we therefore discuss classification as a subject in itself? This is the first question we must answer before proceeding with the methodology of classification.

The question is to be answered in the context of social research. Is it necessary, therefore, to elucidate what is 'social research'? Activities labelled as social research have been on the agenda of scientific investigation for a long time and have received academic recognition for more than a century. Social research is, however, seen to be distinguished from economic research, psychological research, historical research, and so on. It thus seems to be the specialized concern of the 'discipline' of sociology as the other kinds of research on society are distinguished by their 'disciplines'.

The field of social research, however, is also seen to cut across the social science 'disciplines' and, in that context a distinction is drawn by the terms *'societal'* and *'social'*. This brings us to the controversy on the formulation of the branch of knowledge dealt with by social research: is it to be characterized as 'social science' or as the 'social sciences'?

By the expression 'social sciences' we mean that there are different bodies of knowledge organized as different disciplines, i.e. distinctive branches of instruction on, and understanding of, society. The distinctions among such subjects as economics, political science, sociology, psychology, history, etc., can therefore be regarded as of crucial importance while their interrelations attain an auxiliary status as being helpful for developing a comprehensive understanding of society. *Thus the social science subjects would be considered as analogous to each other*, i.e., the subjects are parallel in origin and development out of the world of society they represent.

By the expression 'social science', on the other hand, we mean that there is one organized body of knowledge for understanding society and, therefore, there is one discipline. It follows that different aspects of society are examined as *specializations* in the discipline by means of the subject categorization according to economics, political science, sociology, psychology, history, etc. *Therefore, the social science subjects can be considered as homologous in character*; i.e., they have a common origin in the world of society although they are dealt with separately because of the inherent constraints on grasping the whole of society comprehensively as well as precisely. From this perspective, therefore, the interrelationship among the social science subjects would be of primary relevance, their distinctions secondary.

The difference between the two formulations may appear as quibbling. One may ask: Does it matter whether we regard subjects like economics, sociology, political science, etc., as different social science disciplines or as specializations within one discipline of social science? The answer would be that it matters because we should not be equivocal about the *generic* and the *specific* roles of these subjects for understanding society. In the present context, moreover, we must be clear on the scope of social research so as to discuss the role of classification in consolidating our knowledge of those characteristics of variation in the population relating to society as an organized whole; with which we shall be concerned.

In introducing classification as a subject, therefore, we should examine the following two issues: (1) whether the terms 'societal' and 'social' are to be equated or whether the two must be distinguished while at the same time being interrelated on substantive bases; and (2) how the solution of the first issue resolves the controversy on 'social science' or 'social sciences', which is reflected in contemporary developments in social research.

Beyond the demarcation of the field of social research in this manner, we should be clear on the focus of our attention in conducting research. Are we concerned with the *search* for information or data (i.e. information collected with a particular objective in view) or with *research* on the basis of all theoretically possible arrangements of the data space? The methodology of classification will be different according to whether we adopt one or the other mode of investigating social reality, that is, by searching for information or data, or by researching in the data space.

We should, therefore, discuss these two issues of search and research with reference to what we can conceive as (1) the information space, which is constituted of *any* item of information on the *enumerable* properties of all *possible* things constituting a phenomenon or a set of phenomena, and (2) the data space, which is constituted of particular *sets of information* considered as data with respect to the stated objective of examining a phenomenon or a set of phenomena. A data space is thus conceived of as emerging out of the information space in the light of a prior selection of things to represent a phenomenon or a set of phenomena and, correspondingly, the specifically chosen properties of these things.

Our interest may be restricted to a mere description of *what* are the structures and functions of a set of phenomena and *how* the phenomena operate within and among themselves. In that case, we collect and consolidate out of the available information space whatever information we consider relevant in these contexts. Theoretically, this space contains infinite but enumerable points of information. The collated information, therefore, may provide us with a description that would differ from other possible descriptions of the same set of phenomena according to the relevance one attributes to the sets of information collected. For example, Robert Redfield's (1956) portrayal of peasant society was different from that of Oscar Lewis (1951), although both were based on observations of life in a single Mexican village, Tepoztlan. All these variations, however, may emerge from mere search for information.

In addition to describing a phenomenon, we may wish to explain its causality with reference to an established theory or a hypothesis formulated on the basis of prior knowledge about the phenomenon. In that case, we must answer the *why* question about the phenomenon, which we do by collecting and consolidating the particular information necessary in the *context* of the theory or hypothesis adopted as the yardstick for explanation. We thus now attend to a data space, instead of the overall information space from which it emerges. As one adopts one or another established theory or previously formulated hypothesis as the yardstick for explanation, corresponding data spaces will, of course, emerge from the same information space. In all such cases, however, we are concerned with the search for a particular set of data in the given context.

Thus, so long as our focus of attention in conducting research is restricted to description or explanation on the basis of a theory or hypothesis, we are concerned with mere search for information or data. Each one of us, of course, may deal with different information sets in descriptive investigations, as illustrated by Robert Redfield and Oscar Lewis. We may also deal with different data sets in explanatory studies. In the latter event, the data sets may refer to the same data space for a set of homologous explanations, or to different data spaces (but all belonging to the same information space) for analogous sets of explanations. For example, Karl Marx's descriptions of the Asiatic mode of production vis-à-vis European feudalism refer to the same information space on the phenomenon of feudalism, but their explanations refer to analogous data spaces constituted of 'particular kinds of labour', its 'craft mastery and consequently property in the instrument of labour', and whether or not the respective kinds of labour equal 'property in the conditions of production' (Marx 1964: 101–2; R. Mukherjee 1974: 143ff). Marx's and Max Weber's explanations of the origin, development, and persistence of the Indian caste system, on the other hand, refer to the same data space but different data sets (R. Mukherjee

1979: 66–68). All the same, in all these cases our focus of attention is not research on data sets available from the same or different data spaces but the search for items of information which may be particularized as data.

If, on the other hand, we are interested in diagnosis and in answering the *what will be* question of prediction, we must arrange different explanations of a phenomenon in a series of alternate hypotheses. These hypotheses will include also those explanations which are not propagated as established theories but are formulated on the grounds of prior data as tentative hypotheses. All these hypotheses are to be tested in order to ascertain their relative efficiency in drawing an inference on the probable course of existence, change, or disappearance of the phenomenon in the immediate future. In this case, therefore, we proceed beyond the search for a particular set of data to explain the phenomenon. *We now undertake a course of research with reference to various ways of constructing data sets from the information space.* As noted, these data sets may belong to one or more data spaces, all of which emerge from the same information space with which the phenomena are concerned.

We are not concerned here with the scope, limitation, and the methodology of different modes of investigation, which are discussed elsewhere (R. Mukherjee, 1979). As we shall point out, contemporary developments in social research require us to deal with alternate explanations about a phenomenon or a set of phenomena. We should accordingly be engaged in diagnostic investigations on the relative efficiency of these explanations and, therefore, with various ways of constructing data sets. This means that the procedure of classification must be completely flexible, to accommodate all possible (and not merely all immediately available) variations in data sets. Such is not a necessary condition for merely explanatory investigations, which are restricted to search for data, and it is not even relevant to descriptive investigations, which are concerned with the search for information. The methodology of classification for dealing with alternate explanations will accordingly be different.

The First Intersubjectivity:
The Anthropologist and the Native

GANANATH OBEYESEKERE

Recent thought in the social sciences has attacked some of the fundamental assumptions anthropologists have entertained about the nature of intersubjective relations and consensual understandings in the cultures they study, including such fundamental notions as 'community' and 'culture'. I shall limit myself to the relevance of both anthropology and psychoanalysis in claiming to represent 'the native's point of view' that is, an 'emic' or a phenomenologically 'correct' account of the other culture. This task cannot be accomplished, however, without facing squarely the prejudices many anthropologists share regarding the applicability of psychoanalysis to the study of other cultures.

One of the commonest criticisms directed against psychoanalysis by anthropologists, both at the coffee table and in more formal settings, is that it is a theory of the mind developed in the West and is only applicable to Western man. Some would even argue that it at best tells us about neurotic Victorian people, especially female hysterics. I have much to say about this criticism in my discussions of metatheory, but here I want to pin down the more flagrant and absurd parts of this argument, and some of the hidden ones.

Let me start with the latter—the hidden part of this point of view. In ordinary discourse among anthropologists one constantly hears about Western culture and non-Western culture, as if they were opposed entities. This discourse is especially deep-rooted in Anglo-American thought but extends to other Europeans also. There might be some broad unity in European cultures, but the attempt to subsume the rest of the world as non-Western is as bad as the 'third world' label that is rapidly taking its place. I doubt that this is simply a manner of speaking through a useful, if crude, binary distinction. It is certainly the case that anthropologists, more than anyone else, would be the first to defend relativism, but nevertheless, this discourse is a reality and in my view contains implicit assumptions rooted in the Western anthropologists' cultural tradition. From the time of the earliest colonizations the Europeans felt themselves distinct, a superior race apart from the benighted savages who had neither civilization nor true religion. This is only too well known as the attitude taken by missionaries and colonial administrators everywhere and often justified by intellectuals like Macaulay. It is unlikely that anyone was exempt from them, the anthropologists included. The nineteenth-century theories of evolution were not only theories; they were also ideologies that placed the Europeans at the top of the evolutionary scale. Hence the well-known statement by Tylor (1958: 26):

The educated world of Europe and America practically settles a standard by simply placing its own nation at one end of the social scale and the savage tribes on the other, arranging the rest of mankind within these limits according as they correspond to savage or to cultured life.

It is difficult to assume that these recent and deep prejudices have simply withered away. While the grosser forms of ethnocentrism rarely prevail among anthropologists, I do think that the distinction they make regarding the uniqueness of Western man in opposition to the rest of mankind is the continuation of the same tradition and, one might add, the same arrogance. Indeed one cannot undertake to study the other culture without such arrogance, for it defies ordinary common sense that a young person with imperfect language skills could go into the field and study another culture to present the native's point of view during the period of a year or, at most, two. This defiance of common sense and this arrogance, to which all of us nowadays subscribe, have paid high dividends in our discipline for it is indeed likely that ordinary common sense might simply be wrong in this regard and arrogance pays off—some of the time.

The Sinhalas have a proverb to describe people in their own society who think they are special. They say, 'Have you emerged from an elephant's arse hole?'—as against ordinary people born from human wombs. It is the fact that we are born from human wombs, they say, that gives us our common humanity underlying formal differences. I think psychoanalysis tells us a similar message: Victorian neurotics did not come from an elephant's arse hole, but share instead a common humanity with us all. As early as

1924, Ernest Jones, in his address to the Royal Anthropological Institute, claimed that the cross-cultural use of psychoanalytic theory would 'humanize' the savage by showing the fundamental common nature that he shares with Western man (1924: 49). I think this is what any theory (metatheory) should do: it should exhibit enough nomological rigour to show the rules or principles that govern our common humanity while at the same time possessing enough flexibility to illuminate the different forms of life that spring from this common base. The problem of universality versus relativism then becomes a largely empty one.

Now from the hidden discourse to the flagrantly absurd. It is of course true that psychoanalysis is a Western science, but I am puzzled as to how contemporary history, anthropology, and practically every intellectual discipline are not. One could perhaps argue that insofar as ethnography presents the native's point of view it is exempt from this criticism, but this surely cannot be the case since, for the most part, the native's point of view is re-expressed in the language of the ethnography, which is generally English or some other European language. One does not have to subscribe to a Whorfian position to know that language is not a culture-free tool and that the description of another culture in a language that is different from the one being described must render any attempt to mirror the original entirely dubious. Ethnographic translation is a mode of appropriation of the culture, but not through a fusion of horizons; it incorporates the description of the other into the familiar grammatical and semantic categories of one's own language. This is of course over and above the fact that it is simply impossible anyway to present a native point of view since such a viewpoint does not exist—as I shall show presently.

Both Giddens (1976) and Winch (1974, 1958) make the point that the informant is like the social scientist in several regards; he also has theories of his society and other conceptions, ideal and real, of how the world should be organized.[1] But what further complicates this picture is that he too has controversies (or 'debates') with his own fellows regarding all of this. In this sense he shares our own contentious nature as scholars. In other words, a native point of view perhaps exists only in the rare case, let us say, of key eschatological notions, such as, for example, the nature of the Buddha and the meanings of karma and salvation in Sri Lankan Buddhism. But even here, while there can be unanimity, there is no uniformity in the discourse that expresses that unanimity. One area of the sociocultural life might be more subject to controversy than other areas. Thus Buddhism, owing to its scriptural tradition and its educated monks, who interpret the scriptures, may produce consensus on key eschatological meanings, but the spirit cults that have neither, permit greater leeway. And when it comes to things like politics, marriage, sexuality, and so forth, opinions begin to differ greatly. In other words, internal controversy and hidden discourse or debate render any notion of a native point of view a complete impossibility, except in certain areas where specific historical and sociological parameters render it less amenable to controversy. But this cacophony of voices is never heard in the ethnography; this work presents that which does not exist in reality—the natives' point of view.

Many ethnographers give primacy to the natives' point of view by constructing an 'emic picture' of the natives' society or culture. But an emic perspective is misleading for a variety of reasons. The very incorporation of the alien culture into the vocabulary and grammatical structure of the anthropologists' language makes nonsense of the emic claims of the investigation. Since, moreover, the natives' point of view is a misnomer, an emic presentation based on a misnomer must itself be a misnomer. The anthropologist never has a chance of sampling a range of native opinions, though ethnographies are peppered with pronouncements indicating that this is indeed the case—hence statements such as 'villagers say that. . .' 'according to my informants. . .'. In reality the anthropologist works with select or key informants who for the most part make themselves available to the investigator. An 'emic' perspective in this situation? The classic monographs that claim to present the natives' point of view in fact have constructed ideal types of X or Y culture, based on a point of view taken, implicitly or explicitly, by the ethnographer . What Weber (1969: 96) says of Christianity in the Middle Ages is as apposite to ethnography as it is to history and historical sociology:

Those elements of the spiritual life of the individuals living in a certain epoch of the Middle Ages, for example, which we may designate as the 'Christianity' of those individuals, would if they could be completely portrayed, naturally constitute a chaos of infinitely differentiated and highly contradictory complexes of ideas and feelings. This is true despite the fact that the medieval church was certainly able to bring about a unity of belief and conduct to a particularly high degree. If we raise the question as to what in this chaos was the 'Christianity' of the Middle Ages (which we must nonetheless use as a stable concept) and wherein lay those 'Christian' elements which we find in the institutions of the Middle Ages, we see that here too in every individual case, we are applying a purely analytical construct created by ourselves. It is a combination of articles of faith, norms from church law and custom, maxims of conduct, and countless concrete interrelationships which we have fused into an 'idea'. It is a synthesis which we could not succeed in attaining with consistency without the application of ideal-type concepts.

Weber recognized that an ideal type often requires analytical concepts, at the very least, of the sort Geertz calls 'mega-concepts'. And these concepts must be ordered logically and articulated systematically with the empirical data. This means 'they have to be fused into an idea', to use Weber's phrase for characterizing the overall conceptual unity manifest in the ideal type. Thus even a seemingly phenomenological description of reality is impossible without ideal types. The "natives' point of view" is an arbitrary construction, an ideal type. Ideal types, mega-concepts: these very words imply a rational understanding of reality that is the investigator's. In other words, one cannot understand the world without the mediation of abstract concepts, ideal types, metalanguages, distantiating discourses; consequently all rational interpretation of the first intersubjectivity is 'etic'.

Informants, however, cannot be dispensed with, except by those anthropologists who deal with historical texts. But even here one can imaginatively reconstruct the voices of informants, though few ever do so! One might argue that even if the voices of informants are disparate one might be able to work with a few key informants whose opinions have greater force. Let me deal with this problem using religious texts as examples. Obviously, I might get similar texts from different informants, but it is their interpretation that is important, because I must incorporate this into my work as the native point of view.

1. Even the best informant may not know the meaning of the texts he presents. Often texts come from a long tradition, and during this period the meanings of the texts may have been lost or forgotten. We assume the existence of a continuous tradition, but this is our fiction and might have little reference to reality. Let me give examples of what I mean.

Meanings are sometimes inaccessible or unknown even to the specialist. I have often interviewed priests and exorcists who were excellent *performers*, but I got no exegesis on the names of the deities, places, and so forth mentioned in some of their religious texts. I think this is a phenomenon of all ancient traditions: names of places, persons, and deities are mentioned, but they have ceased to have relevance for contemporary religion. They are mentioned in the text, and the text must be recited at religious rituals. But what is recited does not always make sense even to the specialist of the cult. In this situation the anthropologist is helpless except when he has independent historical evidence, in which case he is at an advantage: his very command of literary or historical material helps him to interpret the text that baffles the native specialist. A simple example: in a well-known Sinhala ritual for pregnant women known as *raṭa yākuma*, there is an important collectivity of female deities known as Riddhi Bisavu (that can be glossed nowadays as 'queens possessed with the power to fly'). I have not *yet* been able to get any informant to provide a gloss or exegesis or any reasonable account of these deities. Neither could I, until I found a reference to 'Riddhi' in the *Mahābhāratha* as the consort of Kuvera, the overlord of the demons. Now Kuvera appears in Sinhala ritual as Vessamuni (Vaiśravana), the god of the northern quarter and overlord of demons. It is his dread command that the exorcist uses to control demons. Thus it makes perfectly good sense that the Riddhi Bisavu are (or once were) consorts of Vessamuni-Kuvera in the Sinhala ritual also and incorporated into it from older sources traceable to as far back as the *Mahābhāratha*. From my superior historical knowledge and also from comparative material from other parts of the country, I can fill in the gaps that are left out or wrongly interpreted by the indigenous specialist.

The above is an example of a meaning hidden from the informant because it is buried in a tradition. To unravel a hidden meaning involves an archaeological thrust, a scholarly investigation into the past. But assume this tradition was inaccessible for scholarly investigation owing to the lack of historical or comparative data. The ethnographer must attempt an interpretation that is uniquely his. A great deal of ethnographic interpretation is of this quality. What then can mitigate the idiosyncratic nature of the ethnographer's interpretation in this situation? Comparison, search for family resemblances in other cultures, and above all, theoretical understanding of the sort that psychoanalysis provides in its metapsychology.

Hidden meanings are only too common in ethnographic texts, but their existence is rarely conceded by us. *We* tend to assume that the meaning of a text is accessible to informants or that informants provide the only valid exegeses. I wonder whether this strategy would work if I were to consult informants of various sorts for interpretations of poetry, art, or music in the Western cultural tradition, not to mention its religious texts?

2. Among the range of informants available to me, to whom shall I turn for exegesis of texts? Ordinary persons who come to worship, religious specialists, the wise old man, or combinations thereof, or whatever? This difficulty forces us to reckon with the 'open' nature of interpretation and exegeses (whether by natives or us); it also forces us to reckon with the arbitrary nature of what we make out of these levels of native interpretation in our descriptive presentation.

3. The puzzlement the anthropologist feels regarding whom to interview is compounded by the informants' puzzlement regarding whom the anthropologist *should* interview. Take a not too unusual scenario. The ethnographer asks an informant about the Christ, the Buddha, Siva, God, or

Whatever, and informant tells him, 'Go away, ask the priest.' The priest tells him, 'I do not know much about this but X priest in yonder village trained in the seminary knows, go see him'. What do I make of this? My informant is telling me that ordinary people do not know much about scripture, and therefore I should go see the priest, and the priest tells me I should consult a knowledgeable specialist. True enough; but then will I miss the viewpoint of the ordinary person? But suppose I do manage to talk to ordinary people, and they present views that are different from the scriptures; do I say that the scriptural religion is not Christianity? This is patently absurd, but I can certainly say that there are different life forms called Christianity, and these could be ideal-typically described on the basis of informant statements. But even this is not fully satisfactory, for some might say that the truth of the Truth cannot be articulated in words. They may be right, for the truth of the Truth exists in symbolic forms and rests on ambiguity, metaphor, overdetermination. It need not reside in a single place, but might be scattered in rites and myths, so scattered or so elusive that words cannot express its reality. Thus when one probes *nirvāṇa*, one encounters silence. In Christianity, words can only imperfectly capture the experience for the religiously musical of the *mysterium tremendum et fascinans*, the Eucharist. In this kind of situation the analyst must perforce move in with his (theoretical) interpretation to elucidate the hidden meaning.

4. Hidden meanings are different from unconscious meanings. For me unconscious processes are not problematic in the sense that I can believe in their existence, a belief supported by my personal experience, my literary and ethnographic experience, the texts of the Buddhist tradition, and my layman's knowledge of neurological structures. There are of course many intellectuals who deny this. But assume that unconscious processes do occur—the theory that explains them is irrelevant at this point—then it is likely that informant exegeses of cultural material that deal with deep motivation must be impaired, if not totally blocked, as Turner (1967: 24, 38) recognized. With respect to unconscious materials the anthropologist is in a particular dilemma. He must either deny that they exist; or he must adopt a comfortable sociologism that says that while they exist they do not manifest themselves in cultural form or social life; or he might ignore them and invoke his lack of training to handle them; or he must adopt a theory that helps him to understand them—whatever that theory might be. All but the last position would leave a large area of symbolic form and social life uninvestigated by the anthropologist and unexplained by his informant, or done badly on both levels, resulting in badly slanted descriptions of

cultural life. This naturally would be particularly serious in societies that give premium to states that seem to tap unconscious motivation—for example, those altered states of consciousness that I have labelled 'hypnomantic states'. Here the ethnographer has one rational choice if he is to deal directly with these processes: he must make his interpretations on the basis of a theory, a set of abstract rules, or a philosophical grammar or some such nomological set of concepts that can help grasp those phenomena that are elusive by their very definition.

All of the foregoing implies that a good descriptive ethnography of symbolic forms must go beyond the natives' point of view and beyond the surface reality of everyday understandings. Consequently good ethnography must disturb, shock, or jolt us into an awareness that we did not have before. This sense of surprise is quite different from the *offence* that bad ethnography so often exudes. For this reason, the generality of native informants may not comprehend or even sympathise with the ethnographic representation of their life-forms. I disagree with Taussig on this issue. Taussig takes his colleagues (Turner, Kapferer, Meyerhof, Moore) to task for their 'unstated rites of academic text making' and their creation of 'intellectual authority' (1987: 440–45). But Taussig, it seems to me, while escaping from a bourgeois world perspective, is as much locked into academia as anyone else who writes for a professional audience. His inspirations are Walter Benjamin, Gramsci, Marx, and surrealism; his megaconcepts are 'montage', 'epistemic murk'; his audience consists of bourgeois academics; his emulators are graduate students who will try (hopelessly, I am sure) to do what he is doing. Santiago, Taussig's informant, would not know what the hell all this is about. It is we who are jolted out of our complacency by Taussig's creation of a work of great power out of the mouths of shamans drunk on *yage*. Similarly, I feel that Rosaldo's paper (1987) is a good criticism of bad ethnography, or even ordinary ehnography, but a good ethnography need not necessarily be intelligible to the ordinary citizen in that society.[2] The reaction of the ordinary citizen cannot be a litmus test for ethnography, as it cannot be for history, philosophy, or fiction.

Thus good ethnography is an ideal typical description that probes beneath the surface reality through the use of a nomological theory. Theory then takes us away from the particularities of X or Y culture and tells us something about culture or life in general. Theory has an ontological thrust in the human sciences, since it is about human beings and being human that we are talking about. One can *ignore* the ontological problem in the physical sciences, but not in the *Geisteswissenschaften*. This is where I part company with Wittgenstein and move closer to critical theory, hermeneutics, and phenomenology. Wittgenstein seems to think that such ontological inquiries are useless or impossible to ask. But surely this cannot be predetermined philosophically; it must be investigated empirically. This *is* the anthropological quest. This quest, it seems to me, involves a circular procedure. We cannot ask the empirical question without an ontological assumption; but when we start answering the empirical questions, we begin to revise the ontological assumptions. Indeed the ontological *assumption* ceases to be an assumption but becomes an open ontological question or a theoretical proposition as a result of the empirical investigation. And so we go back and forth in this circular fashion, but it is not a vicious or closed circle. Thus the hermeneutical circle is not only a technique of interpretation of cultural forms in terms of the meaning between part and whole but also a technique of understanding man and culture through a circular logic of inquiry.

Notes

1. The idea of the subject as a self-reflective individual is, however, not Giddens's but is central to phenomenology and hermeneutics.

2. Rosaldo insightfully notes how a cultural encounter or argument between the anthropologist and the informant can lead to important insights: '. . . we ethnographers should be open to asking not only how our descriptions of others would read if applied to ourselves, but also how we can learn from other peoples' descriptions of ourselves' (1987: 91). His general point that objectivist anthropology has represented people as if they were emotionless robots is, I think, only too true.

Validation of the scholar's descriptions of his subjects' culture has evoked considerable methodological objectivization in sociology. For example, see Bloor 1978; Emerson and Pollner 1988. For similar 'emic' views in anthropology, see Frake 1964a, 1964b.

To Contrast and Compare

ALAN MACFARLANE

The Necessity of Comparison

Any social scientist should be aware that he is indulging in comparison all
the time. In the case of history, the comparisons are usually in time, in that
of other social sciences, predominantly in space. The most familiar method
of the historian is to take his own society as the norm and then to see how
far the past is similar or different from this. This is also what an
anthropologist, sociologist, or economist tends to do, in the dimension of
space rather than time. 'Informally, comparison is built into the method of
the subject, for even in his first piece of field-work the anthropologist is
comparing the categories of his own society with those of the society he
studies. . .' (Pocock 1961: 90).

De Tocqueville's work illustrates such a method of comparison, revealed
in his memoirs: 'In my work on America. . . though I seldom mentioned
France, I did not write a page without thinking of her, and placing her as it
were before me. And what I especially tried to draw out, and to explain in
the United States, was not the whole condition of that foreign society, but
the points in which it differs from our own, or resembles us. It is always by
noticing likenesses or contrasts that I succeeded in giving an interesting
and accurate description. . .' (1861, i: 359). He did this, ultimately, not to
understand America, but France itself; 'for no one, who has studied and
considered France alone, will ever I venture to say, understand the French
revolution' (1956: 21).

The necessity of comparison was stressed by the anthropologist Evans-
Pritchard: 'in the widest sense there is no other method. Comparison is,
of course, one of the essential procedures of all sciences and one of the

elementary processes of human thought' (1963: 3). He was here following his master Durkheim, who wrote that '. . .it is only possible to explain by making comparisons. Without this, even simple description is scarcely possible; one can scarcely describe a single fact, or one of which there are only rare examples, because one cannot see it well enough' (quoted in Lienhardt 1964: 30).

Hence a number of observers have noted that in order to understand one phenomenon, one must place it in perspective or comparison to others. As Robert Lowie put it, 'At the same time a phenomenon is understood only in relation to others: "He little knows of England who only England knows." Hence it is well to look at Western culture in perspective' (1950: 9).

The Purposes of Comparison

The comparative method is just one of many tools used by social scientists. As with all tools, it is necessary to consider both why one is using them, the purpose, and how best to use them.

Asking Questions

Distancing the overfamiliar

A first use of the comparative method is to act like a reverse telescope, pushing away things which are too close, so that a gap is created and one can see them. This might be termed, 'distancing the (over) familiar', or turning the obvious into the unobvious (or 'nature' into 'culture', in anthropological terms).

One difficulty for all analysts is the strong pressure to leave unquestioned (and hence unexplained) a great deal of behaviour in the past or in other societies because it is similar to our own and hence self-evidently 'normal'. As David Hume wrote, 'the views the most familiar to us are apt, for that very reason, to escape us' (quoted in Dumont 1977: 19), or, as Braudel put it, '. . .surprise and distance—those important aids to comprehension—are both equally necessary for an understanding of that which surrounds you— surrounds you so evidently that you can no longer see it clearly' (quoted in Burke 1972: 24). Likewise, Marx noted, 'Human history is like paleontology. Owing to a certain judicial blindness even the best intelligences absolutely fail to see the things which lie in front of their noses' (1964: 140). Or, as Kluckhohn observed, 'it would scarcely be a fish that discovered the existence of water' (quoted in Bohannan 1969: 14).[1] The difficulty was also alluded to by Sir Henry Maine, who wrote that one of the major problems for all of us is 'the difficulty of believing that ideas which form part of our everyday mental stock can really stand in need of analysis and examination' (1890: 171).

The problem is acute for the student of his own culture who needs some 'external fulcrum' in order to be aware of the central features of the society in which he lives. Such a fulcrum is automatically present for an anthropologist who works in an alien culture. Yet, even such an anthropologist may need support; as Homans argued, 'when a man describes a society which is not his own, he often leaves out those features which the society has in common with his own society. He takes them for granted, and so his description is distorted' (1960: 382).

This difficulty of studying 'the obvious', being too close to the subject, was alluded to by Peter Laslett. 'This feeling that it is all obvious is a curious and exasperating feature of the whole issue. . . the force of the contrast between our world and the world which the historian undertakes to describe has hitherto been somewhat indistinct. Without contrast there cannot be full comprehension' (1971: 7).

The benefits of a wider knowledge of alternative social structures through the comparative method acts as a 'distancer' of the familiar. This is probably what Bloch was referring to when he wrote that 'the comparative methods in the hand of ethnographers has restored to us with a kind of mental shock this sense of the difference, the exotic element, which is the indispensable condition for a balanced understanding of the past' (1967: 47). For, as he wrote elsewhere, 'to speak of discovery is also to speak of surprise and dissimilarity' (Bloch 1954: 120). Finally, to quote Dumont, 'To see our culture in its unity and specificity we must set it in perspective by contrasting it with other cultures. Only so can we gain an awareness of what otherwise goes without saying, the familiar and implicit basis of our common discourse' (in Carrithers 1985: 94).

Familiarizing the distant

Equally problematic is the fact that many of the things we encounter in our work are so unfamiliar and distant that we cannot get inside their logic or 'understand' them. In this difficulty, we need to use the method with the telescope in its normal position; in other words, to bring the phenomena closer. The difficulty was well described by David Hume: 'Let an object be presented to a man of never so strong natural reason and abilities; if that object be entirely new to him, he will not be able, by the most accurate examination of its sensible qualities, to discover any of its causes or effects,' (quoted in Winch 1958: 7). The usual temptation is either to avoid the subject altogether or to dismiss it as irrational nonsense.

How does the comparative approach help? One way is through providing hypotheses concerning how an unfamiliar system can work. This may be related to one of the two methods which the mathematician G. Polya suggests are used to solve complex problems: 'ransack our memory for any similar problem of which the solution is known' (quoted in Burgess 1982: 217). Now the solution may be 'known' in a sort of way through the studies of others in other societies. Examples would be the insights which anthropological studies of curious phenomena like the blood feud or witchcraft gave to historians studying the same phenomena in the West.

The comparative method provides possible alternative models of how things might be connected and what they might mean, it brings them within our range of comprehension, hence partly overcoming Hume's problem.

Making absences visible

A third important service the comparative method can provide is by revealing absences. In all societies, many of the most interesting things are the absences, and it is extremely difficult to be aware of these. What I mean is rather well illustrated by Robert Smith, who recounts how a Japanese scholar replied when he was asked why ancestor worship persists in modern Japan: 'That is not an interesting question. The real question is why it died out in the West' (1983: 152). Of course, both are interesting questions—but the absence is certainly just as curious.

To take two examples, many of the most important features in the English past were the absences; the weakness of kinship, the absence of religious intolerance and political absolutism, the lack of group pressure. The same is true in Japanese history. Many of the most significant facts have been things that did not happen; the absence of foreign invasions and the bubonic plague and the virtual absence of malaria and, in the late Tokugawa period, of domesticated animals. These gaps can only be detected if we have a strong positive image of what is 'normal' and then see that in certain cases the predicted did not happen. The failure to use comparative models is one of the reasons why there has been little success in explaining the origins of the various major changes which we collectively term 'modernity' or 'development'. A comparative framework provides a strong 'backcloth', against which the foreground can be seen. Without it much of the foreground is invisible.

There are, however, dangers with this approach, especially if the 'absences' are analysed at the level of whole societies or civilizations, rather than particular features. It is one thing to say that the domestic fly was largely absent in Japan, another to say, as some have, that the Japanese lack a sense of sin, the self, or principles in general. This is one of the reasons why labels like 'pre-industrial', 'pre-literate', 'pre-capitalist', with their evolutionary and negative connotations, can be both misleading and dangerous.

One strategy which was adopted to deal with the ethnocentric and often racist implications of the discovery of apparent absences was the development of 'functional equivalents'. For example, in the first half of the twentieth century it was shown that many features of Western societies were not 'absent' but 'disguised' and could be located by examining their functional equivalents. The State re-appeared in the form of segmentary lineage structures, the law as kinship reciprocities, Western philosophy and science as witchcraft cosmologies and complex mythical systems. The lessons were learnt but since then, as Peter Burke comments, there has been an inevitable reaction against too much relativism and an over-emphasis on deep similarities which ironed out differences. The problem now is to recognize both similarities and differences without returning to those arrogant assumptions whereby one's own solutions are seen as intrinsically 'natural' and 'better' than all others. I shall return to this problem.

Testing Answers

Another use for the comparative method is the possibility it gives us to test hypotheses. Let us look at this in relation to history. Although historians are aware that they are not trying to establish laws, their 'descriptions' always contain elements of causal connections of the form 'If this, then that'. They are constantly on the lookout for both necessary and sufficient causes, links of a specific and general kind. Starting with a problem such as 'What caused the English Civil War?', 'What were the effects of printing?', 'What caused the industrial revolution?', 'How did attitudes to childhood change in early modern France?', the search is for causal connections and covariations. Having formulated a hypothesis, it is necessary to move outside the particular instance to see if the connection holds more widely. For instance, if Calvinism is held to be a necessary precondition for 'capitalism', are there 'capitalist' societies that are not Calvinist?

Thus, as Nadel wrote, 'Even if we are initially concerned only with a single society and the appearance in it of a particular social fact (which we wish to 'explain'), our search for co-variations capable of illuminating our problem will often lead us beyond that society to others, similar or diverse, since the given society may not offer an adequate range of variations' (1951: 227).

It may be that social scientists will claim that they are not trying to make generalizations, but a brief glance at their work shows that they usually are; and any general statement has to be tested cross-comparatively. Evans-Pritchard rightly argued that 'It is also evident that if any general statements are to be made about social institutions they can only be made by comparison between the same type of institutions in a wide range of societies' (1963: 3).

The necessity for broad comparison has been recognized by most who have thought deeply about the origins of modern society and its likely future development. In discussing the 'European Miracle' and its causes, E.L. Jones wrote that 'Comparisons, or contrasts, with other civilizations are essential for an assessment of Europe's progress. Otherwise conjectures based on a winnowing of the European historical literature are uncontrolled' (1981: 153). In his equally ambitious 'The Unbound Prometheus', Landes declared that 'The method of inquiry is to seek out these factors of European development that seem to be both significant and different; that set Europe apart, in other words, from the rest of the world. By holding Europe up against the mirror of the most advanced non-European societies, we should be able to discern some . . . of the critical elements in her economic and technological precedence' (1972:14–15).

The general point is that one needs constantly to move back and forth between the minute examination of a single system and the comparison of whole systems. This was the method also advocated by the anthropologist Radcliffe-Brown. He pointed out that while 'the study of a single society may. . . afford occasion for hypotheses' these 'then need to be tested by reference to other societies', for the single case 'cannot give demonstrated results'. Nadel added that it is only 'if we include time perspective and cultural change in our enquiry' that 'the necessary co-variations will be available' (quoted in Nadel 1951: 240).

Methods of Comparison

Comparison can be undertaken in numerous ways, each appropriate to its task, and one cannot lay down in advance which will be the best. All one can do is to raise some of the alternatives. We may start by noting the three types of approach distinguished by Durkheim.

(1) We could consider a single society at a given time and analyse the broad variations in particular modes of action or relationships occurring in that society. (2) We could consider several societies of generally similar nature which differ in certain modes of action or relationships; more precisely, we could here compare either different and perhaps contemporaneous societies, or the same society at different periods, if these exhibit some limited cultural change. (3) We could compare several, perhaps numerous, societies of widely different nature yet sharing some identical feature; or different periods, showing radical change, in the life of the same society (quoted in ibid.: 226).

The Units of Comparison

The success of the comparative method will, of course, depend on the comparison of things that can be compared. This consists of several features. One is that the units compared are roughly of the same order of magnitude; for instance, it would not be particularly fruitful to compare the handshake in England with the family system in China.

Second, in order for comparison to be effective things must be of the same class or order in some way. Thus to compare, say, marriage in America with tea drinking in China would probably be fruitless. The selection of the comparisons is all-important. Yet even by choosing something that looks similar, one can be deceived. Words like 'city', 'marriage', 'family', 'law' are notoriously loaded with ethnocentric assumptions. Even such apparently obvious terms as 'house', 'meal', 'body' carry complex sets of assumptions within each culture. As Evans-Pritchard puts it, 'it was obvious that the method depended entirely on the units of comparison being of equivalent value. Are, for example, "monogamy" among the Veddahs of Ceylon and "monogamy" in Western Europe units of the same kind?' (1963: 9).

This is one of the reasons why anthropologists have tended to shy away from comparing 'things' in themselves, and stress the need to compare the *relations* of things. Pocock (1961: 114) argued that 'comparison can only be conducted in terms of relations, and not of items or isolated institutions; and this relational comparison begins from the moment that the research worker approaches his material'; or as Evans-Pritchard (1951: 57) wrote, 'what the modern anthropologist compares are not customs, but systems of relations'. Anthropologists have also reacted against what they take to be the Frazerian tendency to wrench bits of culture out of their context. They stress the need to compare a whole culture or social system; 'a solid and thorough comparison of values is possible only between two systems taken as wholes' (Dumont 1986: 243). This may be the reason why, as Peter Burke points out, the most famous, and successful examples of comparison are 'usually comparisons between examples of systems of social relations (feudalism, capitalism, mercantilism, absolutism, colonialism, etc.)'.

Some of the necessary precautions are summarized by Baechler (1988: 40): 'we must compare what is comparable. . . for example, it would be fruitless to compare the Europe of today with Africa South of the Sahara. . . Points of comparison of the same order of size must be selected—not pre-modern Europe on the one side and the rest of the world on the other, but Europe and a particular historical episode that occurred in a spatial and temporal framework of the same dimensions.'

Controlled and General Comparison

One might note two major forms of comparison—general comparison between, say, civilizations, and more limited comparisons, where the range of difference is limited. The latter method of controlled comparison is described by Louré: 'It is the method of intensively comparing groups of common derivation, or with a basically identical culture, yet differing in some specific factor, the point being to ascertain what other elements likewise differ' (1950: 47).

Contrast and Compare

There are two separate operations which need to take place in comparative work, the establishing of similarities and the establishing of differences. Rousseau recognized that different methods were required to establish each of these, and that one could not be done without the other. 'One needs to look near at hand if one wants to study men; but to study man one must learn to look from afar: one must first observe differences in order to discover attributes.'[2] Rousseau implies that the final aim is to reach the deeper similarities, the attributes, the 'psychic unity of man' as it was later to be called.

More recently, some anthropologists suggested the reverse, namely, that we are more concerned with differences than similarities. Evans-Pritchard wrote that 'I would like to place emphasis on the importance for social anthropology, as a comparative discipline, of differences, because it could be held that in the past the tendency has often been to place the stress on similarities. . . whereas it is the differences which would seem to invite sociological explanation. This is an involved question, for institutions have to be similar in some respects before they can be different in others. . .' (1963: 17). Pocock (1961: 90–91) echoed his views. 'More formal comparison is both possible and desirable, but here again the concern will be not with similarities only, for the sake of some pseudo-biological classification, but with differences also, for the sake of heightened understanding.' He put this even more strongly when he wrote that 'Comparison in this sense is concerned with similarities only to penetrate more profoundly into the differences' (ibid.: 114).

Of course it is possible to stress just the differences, to take cases which hardly overlap at all. This is the method of contrast. It can be fruitful in generating questions. This was recognized, for instance, by the sociologist Wright Mills, who advocated the study of extremes and opposites. 'Often you get the best insights by considering extremes—by thinking of the opposite of that with which you are directly concerned. If you think about despair, then also think about elation; if you study the miser, then also the spendthrift.' Or again, he writes that in order to stimulate mental activity, '. . . what you can do is to give the range and the major types of some phenomenon, and for that it is more economical to begin by constructing "polar types", opposites along various dimensions' (1970: 235). If the cases are not merely imaginary thought experiments, but real instances, the stimulus is even greater.

Yet, while the method of contrast is stimulating, in the long run it is probably not as fruitful as that of comparison; it only helps with posing questions. If we take seventeenth-century England as an example, the method of contrast might lead us to ask why cities did not have defended walls, unlike those in almost all other parts of the world, or why there were no 'castes' as De Tocqueville noted, or why there was hardly any concept of pollution or *mana*, or why the rate of interest was so low, or why there were no proper 'bandits', or why the English were so obsessed with pets, or why there was such a late age at first marriage for women, and so on. But while suggesting questions, the method of contrast gives little help in testing answers. Hence contrasts are only a start. Only through proper comparison can one begin to connect the threads and move towards some tentative explanations.

True comparison is based on the fact that there is simultaneously a good deal of overlap or similarity, but also considerable differences. This was recognized by Bloch, who wrote that 'there is no true understanding without a certain range of comparison; provided, of course, that comparison is based upon differing and, at the same time, related realities' (1954: 42). Nadel has explained the basis of the method of comparison. 'The study of co-variations is bound up, more specifically, with judgments on similarity and partial identity, the very concept of variations implying a sameness of facts which yet permits of some measure of difference' (Nadel 1951: 224–25). For him, the comparative approach 'means, in essence, the analysis of social situations which are at first sight already comparable, that is, which appear to share certain features (modes of action, relationships) while differing in others, or to share their common features with some degree of difference' (ibid.: 222).

Thus for true comparison we need cases where we can hold certain things constant, certain underlying similarities, and watch other factors vary. As we shall see, it is not easy to find such cases, at least at the global level.

How Many Poles of Comparison?

The degree of success of comparative work seem to lie to a large degree in the number and nature of the comparisons. The method of contrast involves a pair, a dyad—for example, the West and the rest, England and India, the present and the past. It is an example of binary thinking. This can be valuable, but almost inevitably, in practice, whatever the good intentions of the author, it leads to one of the pair being privileged as the 'normal', 'natural', the standard against which the 'other' is seen as a deviation or somehow inferior.

This is a danger noted by Peter Burke in his comments. He points out that, for example, in the famous case of 'feudalism' as an ideal type, there is a tendency to see French feudalism as the 'proper' form and all other forms of 'feudalism' as deviations. In fact, as he points out, there is no need to take the French form as the ideal type. Yet this tends to happen frequently because many of the central concepts in comparative sociology 'were invented by westerners who were thinking in the first place of their own societies'. How are we to escape from this danger?

The general nature and advantages of an approach which avoids binary thinking is outlined by Dipankar Gupta. As he puts it, the issue is 'whether we employ a dyadic or triadic mode of analysis'. In a triadic framework 'one can see peculiarities at both ends of the dyad and not just at one. To a great extent the triadic method takes care of both relativism and essential-ism, for the comparative eye can be turned inwards'. Gupta continues his important analysis as follows:

The triadic mode is the common ground in so much as it manifests itself in different ways in the dyads. No matter how many units we are comparing, at each point of com-parison there are two digits which are constrained by the triadic analytical common ground. The empirical similarities which allowed the units of comparison to be sum-moned up dissolves the moment a triadic comparative analysis is completed. This is because the analytical common ground, i.e., that which has to be explained, ceases to be relevant any longer, for in the process of comparison newer and fresh analytical problems emerge which require a new common ground, analytically and empirically. . . . As the common ground is pressured to dissolve, the initial dyadic distinctions cannot live on indefinitely either. . . . In this sense one can say that a triadic method of comparative analysis studies humankind and not social species (pace Durkheim), for ideal types and dyads keep getting out of date.

This seems to be an excellent account of what the answer to Burke's problem should be, and what we are aiming for. But how do we attain it? The answer was, in essence, given by Max Weber in his discussion of how one constructs ideal types, particularly in his essay '"Objectivity" in Social Science'. His account is so famous that all I need to do here is jog our memories by quoting one or two of his central passages.

An ideal type is formed by the one-sided accentuation of one or more points of view and by the synthesis of a great many diffuse, discrete, more or less present and occasionally absent concrete individual phenomena, which are arranged according to those one-sidedly emphasized viewpoints into a unified analytical construct (Gedankenbild). In its conceptual purity this mental construct (Gedankenbild) cannot be found empirically anywhere in reality. It is a utopia. Historical research faces the task of determining in each individual case, the extent to which this ideal-construct approximates to or diverges from reality, what extent for example, the economic structure of a certain city is to be classified as a 'city-economy' (Weber, 1949: 90).

Weber constantly stresses the fact that this is not a normative ideal. This is not a model of what 'ought' to exist, but only a logical construct. The construction of an abstract, ideal type 'recommends itself not as an end but as a means' (ibid.: 92). It does not exist in reality. 'It has the significance of a purely ideal limiting concept with which the real situation or action is compared and surveyed for the explication of certain of its significant components.' Thus it is 'an attempt to analyse historically unique configurations or their individual components by means of genetic concepts' ibid.: 93). An ideal type has 'no connection at all with value-judgments, and it has nothing to do with any type of perfection other than a purely logical one' (ibid.: 98–99). The aim is not to classify but to emphasize uniqueness. 'The goal of ideal-typical concept-construction is always to make clearly explicit not the class or average character but rather the unique individual character of cultural phenomena' (ibid.: 101). The ideal-type is a construct which is to be sharply distinguished from actual historical facts. Furthermore, as stipulated by Gupta, this is a dynamic process. Ideal types are constantly changing. Any set of ideas will fail to meet changing circumstances and the desire for new knowledge. 'The progress of cultural science occurs through this conflict. Its result is the perpetual reconstruction of those concepts through which we seek to comprehend reality' (ibid.: 105).

Weber and Gupta outline what we are striving for. The difficulty is in the practice. Max Weber himself was able to generate numerous highly suggestive and useful ideal types. Lesser mortals constantly find that their ideal types become too contaminated with the particular cases with which they are familiar. What is the way out of this?

Beyond stressing the need for some kind of triadic analysis which 'problematizes' particular cases and, as Weber says, makes each case unique, I can only offer one other practical suggestion here. This is a little different from Weber's and Gupta's third case lying in a 'common ground' or constructed ideal type. It is the suggestion that it is often extremely productive to study three, rather than two, cases.

Usually, when just two instances are considered, for instance 'holism' and 'individualism' or 'hot' and 'cold' or 'pre-industrial' and 'industrial', or 'India' and 'Europe' or 'The West' and 'The rest', then one is dealing with contrasts. More fruitful, because it gives the chance of deeper insights, is a three-way comparison, for instance, as De Tocqueville made of France, England and America, Norman Jacobs, of China, Japan, and Europe, or Baechler, of India, Europe, and Japan. It appears that the effect of choosing three rather than two poles of comparison is to increase the power of analysis by a very large factor.[3]

The method runs alongside that described above. There is a triangulation which makes each case equally unusual. It is no longer possible to 'side' with one against the others. In fact, this method is probably best combined with the Weberian one. In other words, one has an explicit three-way comparison of actual, concrete, historical cases, but they are set against a backcloth of the Weberian ideal types, which alone make the comparisons possible. In a way, this is a four-way comparison, with one part as common ground, as in the background of a painting. Each case comes into view because of that background and its peculiar and special features become more accentuated by a double process—both because a particular comparison is being 'constrained by the triadic analytical common ground' of the ideal type, but also by the tensions of the implied contrast to the third real case. By extending the triadic method of two cases and an ideal type to the more complex one of at least three cases and an ideal type, we move a long way away from those problems of relativism and essentialism which have plagued much social science for more than one hundred and fifty years. We can move towards a position where we simultaneously stress the similarities of peoples and rejoice in their uniqueness and differences. I will describe the start of an attempt to put this latter method into action in the final part of this paper.

The combination of these approaches also throws light on two other problems. The first concerns the question of universals. As the Rapporteurs commented, 'the comparative method tries, however imperfectly, to deal with universals: Prof. Kolff suggested that "gender", "time", "death", "order", "chaos", "individuality", "sociality" were certain universals present in all societies and the object of comparison is to isolate something which can be compared across boundaries of those units'. The problem is that one of the findings of anthropology is that these supposed 'universals' often dissolve when examined in detail. For example, the meaning of time or death is notoriously so varied in different societies that it is often better to consider them not as universals. Perhaps the best solution was summarized by Willem van Schendel (building on the remarks of Gupta), when asking me to comment on this. He noted that 'they are of course dealt with differently in different cultures. When we compare such categories, we may treat them as universals if we want to bring out the similarities, but we may just as legitimately focus on the differences, thereby deconstructing them as universals'. Just so. Behind any particular cultural treatment of 'death' or 'time' there are probably some universals but we do not need the progress of biology or physics to remind us that what these universals are is much contested.

The second problem is concerned with how comparative studies can deal with processes, with historical time. This was a point specifically noted by Majid Siddiqi in his discussant's paper, particularly in relation to the questions of colonialism and the difficulties of a practising historian. In theory, there should be no difficulty in applying the triadic method as much to variations over time, that is, process, as to variations over space. Weber himself clearly thought that this was possible. 'Developmental sequences too can be constructed into ideal types and these construct can have quite considerable heuristic value' (1949: 101). In fact, there is surprisingly little discussion of this and it might be worth very briefly considering what one or two ideal-typical developmental sequences might look like.

Let me give a few famous examples from the literature, confining myself merely to the period from the middle of the eighteenth century in the West. Adam Smith set up a model of the natural tendency towards wealth. Malthus set up an ideal type model of the tendency towards 'misery'. De Tocqueville saw a powerful tendency towards equality and individualism. Maine suggested the natural movement of 'progressive' societies from status to contract. Marx saw the natural tendency towards increasing class conflict and the final victory of communism. Tonnies saw an inevitable tendency from community towards association, Durkheim towards organic rather than mechanical solidarity. Weber himself saw the inevitable movements towards that simultaneous increase in rationality and irrationality. More recently, Wittfogel and Anderson have seen the natural tendency towards absolutism, and Fukuyama, towards democracy (1957, 1974, 1992).

The point about all these is that they are attempts to create dynamic models which apply over long periods of time, explaining both what normally happens and pointing to the deviations from the norm. They are, when treated with suitable caution, a valuable set of backdrops for a working historian, throwing up questions, exceptions, and some common, unifying, frameworks. Just to take one example, the Malthusian 'natural' tendencies towards increasing misery through the positive checks of war, famine, and disease as population builds up provides the backdrop against which the unlikely 'escape' of parts of the world into a new demographic regime in the eighteenth century can be appreciated more clearly.

A Short History of the Methods of Contrast and Comparison

The method of comparison has a very long history, as Peter Burke points out in his comments on my paper. He mentions Herodotus, Aristotle, Polybius, Plutarch, and Tacitus among the ancients and Bodin and Machiavelli from the Renaissance. It would not be difficult to add to the list, for instance, it would be a pity to miss out Montaigne, in many ways the founder of the comparative method at wider than Europe.

Yet in order to focus the discussion let us look at a number of these methods in action, when applied to perhaps the largest of all questions, namely the reasons for the emergence of that set of inter-linked phenomena which we call 'modernity', and in particular that aspect of it concerned with production and distribution, which we shall call industrial capitalism. In approaching such a problem, it would, of course, be possible to look at only one case, for instance, modern Europe. If one did this, there would be an implicit comparison between 'pre-industrial/pre-capitalist/pre-modern' and its opposite 'industrial/capitalist/modern'. Many people have approached the problem in this way and though some discussions are illuminating, in the end one goes away dissatisfied. There is a sort of inevitability about the account; we know it happened, therefore, it is difficult not to believe that it had to happen. It is impossible to test causal hypotheses. Factors which are stressed as necessary and sufficient causes seem to be so, but we cannot carry out a counter-factual thought experiment and wish them away. Are they really significant, or just coincidental?

Furthermore, we are left wondering whether there are other even more important and deeper pressures which are necessary, a sort of lowest common denominator, which can only be exposed by looking at other examples. Given this desirability for some explicit comparisons, what shall we compare, and how shall we compare them?

If we start with the assumption that the first case of the emergence of industrial capitalism is England, one strategy would be to compare it systematically with other parts of Europe. There is something to be gained by choosing areas where many of the factors could be held constant; within Europe we can assume an Indo-European language, a Graeco-Roman past, Christianity, a temperate climate, and so on. With such a strategy, we could compare England with almost anywhere in Europe—Ireland, Portugal, France, Italy. This procedure was the major one adopted by comparative thinkers until the middle of the nineteenth century, of whom Adam Smith, Millar, Kames, Voltaire, Montesquieu, and others are notable examples. Most of them also used a method of contrast, contrasting the 'West' with the 'rest'. For instance, Montesquieu's or Malthus' famous comparisons of Western Europe with China. The method was one of comparison within Europe, and contrast outside. We may roughly term this the Enlightenment approach. It was in many ways very fruitful and laid the grounds for the emergence of the social sciences as we know them.

It was modified and broadened in scope in the second half of the nineteenth century as the evidence available for the method of contrast became suddenly much richer. The work of the great classical parents of modern social science stretched the contrasts much further, contrasting 'Europe' with whole civilizations which had not 'escaped' into modernity. Sir Henry Maine contrasted India and Europe. Marx compared modern capitalist societies with the Asiatic and ancient modes of production. Later, the greatest of the comparative thinkers, Max Weber, compared parts of Europe (Protestant and Catholic) and contrasted 'Europe' with Islam, China, and India. With the developments of the hundred years which separate the Enlightenment from the later nineteenth century, the gap between the 'West' and the 'rest' in terms of technology, political power, social system, and so on had grown enormously. What struck the great founders were the contrasts, between status and contract, capitalism and pre-capitalism, between rational and traditional authority, and so on.

This seam of grand comparative work, later mined to good effect in the works of Perry Anderson, Fernand Braudel, Louis Dumont, Ernest Gellner, Jack Goody, E.L. Jones, David Landes, William McNeill, and others, continues to provide enriching insights. Yet it needs supplementing. Perhaps part of the problem is that the later nineteenth-century heritage and the huge gap that developed between the 'West' and the 'rest' tended to make the method too much one of 'contrast' rather than 'comparison'. One tends to be faced with those vast binary oppositions which are ultimately only of limited value. A sense of this difficulty was well described some time ago by Goody, when he criticized binary oppositions of all kinds (1977). Often the contrasts are so great, that there seems to be little overlap. Since there are so many and such great differences, one is left confused as to which are important and which subsidiary factors. For instance, is it the absence of caste and pollution, is it the absence of magical religion, is it the absence of corporate kin groups, is it the legacy of Greek science, is it the good water communications, or is it other factors, which explain the rapid economic development of certain parts of Europe? Furthermore, such a dichotomizing approach has the dangers inherent in 'Orientalism', that is, of creating mirror images, where everything is reversed.

In order to escape some of these difficulties, we need examples of countries which have some deep similarities with western Europe, but also very deep differences. In Weber's time, no such examples could be found. No country appeared to have achieved the kind of rapid economic growth which was then occurring in Europe. It was not at all clear that there was anywhere outside Europe with deep similarities to Europe.

One of the first to hint at a possible candidate for a true comparison was Marc Bloch. He noted that Europe and Japan shared one great blessing; they were each at the remote end of a continent, and hence shared protection from destructive invasion. 'It is surely not unreasonable to think that this extraordinary immunity, of which we have shared the privilege with scarcely any people but the Japanese, was one of the fundamental factors of European civilization, in the deepest sense, in the exact sense of the word' (Bloch 1962, i: 56). He does not explicitly make the connection, but he does notice that there is another deep structural similarity in the political foundations of Europe and Japan. He noted that despite differences, there was in Japan 'a regime which was nevertheless in many respects closely akin to the feudalism of the West' (1962, ii: 452). He argued that 'Feudalism was not "an event which happened once in the world". Like Europe—though with inevitable and deep-seated differences—Japan went through this phase' (ibid.: 447). Thus a deep political similarity seemed to exist. Later others were to notice other similarities. For instance, Robert Bellah noted the similarity between certain Buddhist sects in Japan and that ethic which Weber had distinguished as having an 'elective affinity' to capitalism (1957).

All this is made much more interesting as the pattern of economic development in Japan began to become obvious. If we concentrate on England and Japan, we find that they were the first to achieve sustained economic growth in their respective hemispheres, outdistancing their competitors by at least two generations in each case (Rostow 1962: 1). All of this only became obvious after Weber and Bloch could make use of the fact. Therefore, we are led to wonder whether there might be something in common in the two cases, assuming that there are some sets of structurally interlinked causes in each case. Thus a comparison of Europe with Japan, using the backdrop of the 'normal' situation where societies reach a 'high-level equilibrium trap', has considerable potential. On the other hand, the fact that Japan is in many respects so utterly different from England and Europe, means that we can conduct a kind of counter-intuitive experiment.

We can look at factors which seem to be necessary and those which seem to be sufficient.

A recognition of the value of Japan in this respect, and of the difference between the method of contrast and comparison, is provided by E.L. Jones when he wrote, 'Japan provides, intriguingly enough, a comparison rather than a contrast with Europe. . . remarkable for its outline similarity with late preindustrial Britain. Yet there was only the slenderest connection with Europe. . .' (1981: 157).

A comparison of Europe and Japan also forces one to rethink the nature of capitalist development, which the methods of contrast tended to leave as unproblematic. Japan has capitalism, but capitalism with a difference, and hence shows up the peculiarity of western capitalism itself, not only in comparison to preceding or non-capitalist societies, but also in relation to a very different form of equally successful industrial society.[4]

The approach depends on one major assumption. It assumes that while Japan is different from England, it is not totally different. We need a comparative case that has elements of both difference and overlap. Thus while recognizing, as Ravindra Jain in a written comment on this paper reminded me, that there are enormous cultural differences between England and Japan, in language, religion, history, philosophy, popular culture, and so on, there are some striking geographical, political, and demographic similarities. We also need to establish that there is not too much mutual contamination. The problems are well discussed by Jacobs (1958: 12–13) in relation to the problem of comparing England and Japan.

If every similarity was due to borrowing, sociological analysis would be limited to social history. The independent origins standpoint, on the other hand, prevents generalized analysis, limiting the validity of social analysis to one specific reference; the development of capitalism in both Japan and Western Europe would be attributed to coincidence. Following the principle of convergence, we see that the structures of Japan and western Europe show important underlying principles in common, despite variants in traits. . . .

There is not space here to develop this line of argument. The similarities and differences between England and Japan will be the subject of other work. All that I wish to illustrate are some of the dimensions involved in combining the study of similarity and difference. It is this combination which lies behind the comparative method. It is a method which will take on added importance as we witness the unprecedented economic growth of China, India, and parts of South East Asia, and wonder about the similarities and differences between what is happening there and what happened in the European, American, and Japanese cases in the past.

Notes

1. An old Chinese text, cited in Koestler (1960: 269) states that 'As the fish swims in the water but is unmindful of the water, the bird flies in the wind but knows not of the wind'.

2. I have been unable to locate the origin of this famous quotation and would be glad to hear from any reader who can point me to its origin.

3. Further discussion of the disadvantage of a binary approach (Dumont) and advantages of a triadic approach (Jacobs) is given in Macfarlane 1992/3 and Macfarlane 1994. For Baechler, see Baechler 1988.

4. For a similar kind of approach, but primarily comparing German-Swiss capitalism with Anglo-American capitalism, see Albert (1993).

The Comparative Method and the Standpoint of the Investigator

ANDRÉ BÉTEILLE

Comparison and contrast are so commonly used in the study of human society and culture that their utility seems hardly to require special emphasis. In a sceptical essay on the comparative method, one of Britain's leading social anthropologists had pointed out that comparison is 'one of the essential procedures of all science and one of the elementary processes of human thought' (Evans-Pritchard 1965: 13). Yet social scientists never seem to tire of criticizing the comparisons and contrasts made by their colleagues.

While the extensive, not to say automatic, use of comparison may be natural to the process of human thought, the same cannot be said about the conscious search for a comparative method with definite or at least defined rules of procedure. Here one will find characteristic differences among the various disciplines that together make up the social sciences. Some disciplines, such as economics and psychology, have focused largely on universal structures and processes common to all human beings everywhere, and paid little attention to characteristic and persistent differences between societies. Others, such as history in particular, have dwelt much more on the specific features of given societies without venturing too far across their chosen boundaries in space and time. The comparative method as a tool of investigation, designed consciously to discover the general features of all societies (or cultures) without losing sight of the distinctive features of each, has been a particular obsession of sociology and social anthropology, and more specially, as we shall see, of a particular stream within these two related disciplines.

As I wish to describe the comparative method in somewhat more specific terms than is usually done, I would like to ensure that not too much is claimed on its behalf. Here it may be useful to draw attention to the distinction made famous—or notorious—by Edmund Leach between 'comparison' and 'generalization'. As he put it, 'Comparison and generalization are both forms of scientific activity, but different' (Leach 1961: 2). He quickly declared his own preference for generalization, and dismissed comparison as 'a matter of butterfly collecting—of classification, of the arrangement of things according to their types and subtypes' (ibid.). But it must be noted that for Durkheim and Radcliffe-Brown (and many others), comparison itself was a step towards generalization, although such generalization was of a different kind from what Leach had in mind.

'Butterfly collecting' is a bad name for a great deal of what the naturalist does, and considerable insight into societies and cultures has emerged from the natural curiosity about the varieties of human life. At the same time, we must not lose sight of the differences of orientation between the different intellectual disciplines. In terms of Leach's distinction, a substantial part of the insights of sociology and social anthropology have come from systematic comparisons. Economics, by contrast, has been a generalizing rather than a comparative science in the strict sense. At the other end, history has been largely concerned with the distinctive features of human thought and action at specific times and places, although, no doubt, individual historians have also undertaken comparisons across space and time.

Cutting across the differences between disciplines, there have been differences between national intellectual traditions. In France, the appeal of the comparative method has been nourished by the stress on the unity of all the sciences, natural and social. In Germany, on the other hand, the division between the 'Naturwissenschaften' and the 'Geisteswissenschaften' has been a source of considerable disagreement among students of human society and culture. Those who maintained that the study of society and culture could not be incorporated into the natural sciences were on the whole sceptical about the comparative method, whose greatest successes had been in the biological sciences. For Dilthey, Rickert, and Windelband, the principal focus of attention in the Geisteswissenschaften was tradition, a tradition which they not only made the object of their enquiry and understanding, but one in which they in some sense participated. Hence they saw their task as being quite different from that of the Naturwissenschaften, which did not relate to tradition at all in the same way.

In Britain, Radcliffe-Brown followed closely the French sociologists, and in particular Durkheim. He drew attention to the difference in aim and purpose between nomothetic and ideographic enquiries, maintaining that the comparative method in the proper sense was central to the former and not the latter (1952: 1–14). At least in anthropology, there has been a tension, sometimes manifest but more often latent, between the comparative and the historical methods (Boas 1940; Evans-Pritchard 1965; Béteille 1990).

Nevertheless, it was the sociologists and anthropologists who took the lead in examining within a single framework of description and analysis, the usages, customs, and institutions observed and recorded among human beings in all parts of the world and at all times. It was they rather than the historians or the economists who made the first systematic attempts to understand and explain the practices and beliefs of the Australian Aborigines, the American Indians and the sub-Saharan Africans along with those associated with the more complex civilizations of Asia and Europe. This change of outlook was itself a major innovation, and it sometimes caused a scandal. Durkheim's argument that the study of totemism threw new light on all religions, including Christianity, appeared offensive to many believing Christians in France (Pickering 1975: 228–76).

The early sociologists—Herbert Spencer in England, Émile Durkheim in France, and Max Weber in Germany—were comparatists in a much stronger sense than the one implicit in the statement that comparison is one of the elementary processes of human thought. They believed that society, culture, religion, family, marriage, and so on gave shape to human life everywhere, and called for serious intellectual attention not only at home but also abroad. In this sense, the comparative method required in its practitioners a certain detachment from their own society and culture that was not required of the practitioners of the historical method. Many of the latter had been ardent nationalists. Since the comparative method does not admit, at least in principle, of privileged exceptions, it cannot as easily or as openly accommodate the spirit of nationalism.

The pioneers of the comparative method in sociology and social anthropology were all influenced to a greater or lesser extent by the theory of evolution.[1] Indeed, it was the search for the stages of evolution that largely shaped the comparative method of Spencer and Morgan. This imposed certain limits on the extent to which they did in fact assign equal value to all societies and cultures. It was tacitly accepted that western societies had reached the highest stage of evolution and that all other societies stood at graduated distances below them. This view seemed indisputable for technology and economic organization so that few would question the words of Marx (1959: 19): 'The country that is more developed industrially only shows, to the less developed, the image of its own future.' But the same view prevailed, with occasional and minor modifications, with regard to religion, family, marriage, and other institutions as well. It would not be difficult to show that the comparative method was extensively, if not always consciously, used by western sociologists in the late nineteenth and early twentieth centuries to reinforce their belief in the superiority of their own society and culture. There were hardly any voices outside the west to challenge these settled opinions. Thus a gulf existed from the very beginning between the aspirations of the comparative method and its achievements.

A hundred years ago, the practitioners of the comparative method in sociology and social anthropology were all Europeans or Americans. This is now no longer the case. Not only are many different societies being studied throughout the world, but they are being studied by a greater variety of persons from many different angles. There are more facts available and more ways of looking at the available facts. It is easy in the light of these developments to detect a clear Eurocentric bias in even the most successful users of comparison and contrast, including Durkheim and Weber. This bias may be detected not only in the earlier theories of evolution but also in the ... theories of development and underdevelopment (Arora 1968). Today, the comparative method has to come to terms not only with diverse facts but also with diverse perceptions of the same facts viewed from different angles.

In his essay on the comparative method written more than forty years ago, Evans-Pritchard (1965: 13–16) pointed out that its achievements fell far short of the claims made on its behalf. He was on the whole inclined to attribute this to the insufficiency of the facts at the disposal of students of human society and culture. We can see today that the problem may arise as much from an abundance as from a scarcity of data. In a sense, the more facts there are, the more acute appears to be the problem of reconciling different interpretations of them. However greatly the social sciences might benefit from the methods developed in the natural sciences, those methods cannot by themselves solve the problems of interpretation—or even of observation and description—that are fundamental to the understanding of human society and culture.

* * *

It is no longer possible for practitioners of the comparative method to evade the problems that arise in the social sciences from the complex relations between judgements of reality and judgements of value. Sociologists and social anthropologists have been aware of their importance, but they have dealt with them differently in their formulation and use of the comparative method. These differences become clear when we compare and contrast Durkheim and Weber, the two great comparative sociologists of their generation. Both Durkheim and Weber placed great emphasis on method—and not merely on comparison—but there were striking differences in their views of it.

Of the two, Durkheim's comparative method is easier to describe since it is formulated very clearly and applied systematically. Indeed, for Durkheim it was the comparative method that in some sense gave to sociology its distinctive character as a discipline as against such disciplines as history and philosophy. Moreover, the method was carefully developed within the workshop of the *Année sociologique* by a band of able and dedicated scholars, and it had great influence both within and outside France. In Britain its most forceful exponent was A.R. Radcliffe-Brown, who dominated anthropology in the late thirties and forties, and used social anthropology as another name for comparative sociology.

Perhaps I ought to state here itself that I believe Durkheim's (and Radcliffe-Brown's) attempt to formulate a canonically-valid comparative method that would provide the key to the scientific study of society was largely a failure. The failure, however, has many lessons to offer and, although the attempt failed to reach its goal, it generated many by-products of lasting value. In retrospect, Durkheim appears to have been too complacent about the scientific validity of his own standpoint to take sufficient note of the diversity of standpoints from which societies may be observed, described, and compared. Today, it is this diversity that forces itself on our attention and makes us realize that there simply may not exist any Archimedean point from which the comparative method may be applied by no matter which investigator.

Durkheim's ambition was to bring all human societies, simple and complex, within the purview of a single science having its own body of facts, its own concepts, and its own methods. He was greatly impressed by the success of the biological sciences, and the organic analogy featured prominently in his formulation of the comparative method. Although he recognized that social facts are at the same time 'things' and 'representations', he believed that they could be investigated, like the facts of nature, without any significant intrusion of the preconceptions acquired by the investigator as a member of his own society. This would be guaranteed once it was recognized that social facts, being things, were characterized by 'exteriority' and 'constraint'. In this view, there is no difference, at least in principle, between studies of one's own society and of other societies.

Durkheim regarded the comparative method as the counterpart in the social sciences of the experimental method pursued in the other sciences. He recognized that social facts could only be observed and not artificially produced under experimental conditions. 'When, on the contrary, the production of facts is not within our control and we can only bring them together in the way that they have been spontaneously produced, the method employed is that of indirect experiment or the comparative method' (Durkheim 1938: 125). What was essential to the success of the method thus conceived was the careful observation and arrangement of facts.[2]

We can see in this light how Durkheim came to regard his study of totemism among the Australian Aborigines as the 'one well-made experiment' that could lead to a proof that was 'valid universally' (Durkheim 1915: 415). Although Durkheim concentrated on one single religion, he did not confine himself to one single society, but examined facts selected from societies of a certain type. He compared the totemic practices of the different Australian tribes among themselves, and those in turn with corresponding practices among the tribes of North America. What I wish to stress is that these were not simple comparisons of the kind that the human mind automatically makes, but comparisons—and contrasts—systematically pursued in accordance with a definite plan.

Durkheim's plan in this 'experimental' study was to establish the presence everywhere of a particular form of religion in a particular type of society. But he was not satisfied with merely establishing a general correspondence between religion and social morphology with regard to totemism as a whole. He was interested in examining variation and change among subtypes within the type. Hence he compared different Australian tribes with each other, and those again with tribes outside Australia. The broader objective was to show that variation and change in religious beliefs and practices could always be related to variation and change in social morphology. In an earlier study of primitive classification, Durkheim and Mauss (1963) had used the comparative method to great effect in demonstrating the correspondence between social morphology and collective representations.

The systematic use of comparison and contrast as a method of enquiry became widely accepted among sociologists and social anthropologists in the first half of the twentieth century. Radclife-Brown (1952: 117–32) sought to extend Durkheim's sociological theory of totemism by comparing and contrasting the relationship between social structure and religious practice among the Australian Aborigines (who had totemism) and the Andaman Islanders (who did not have it). He also proposed that a relationship could be established through systematic comparative study between ancestor worship and lineage structure (ibid.: 153–77).

Durkheim's plan for the comparative study of societies was ambitious. He did not believe that comparisons should in principle be confined to societies of the same type, but only that they should be made according to a plan. The comparisons that he made in his study of totemism dealt by and large with societies of a single type; in his study of suicide (Durkheim 1951), he compared different types of European societies; and in *The Division of Labour in Society* (Durkheim 1933), he compared forms of solidarity among all human societies. As he put it in his book on method, comparisons 'can include facts borrowed either from a single and unique society, from several societies of the same species, or from several distinct social species' (Durkheim 1938: 136). Here, as in much of Durkheim's work, the concept of 'social species' is borrowed from the biological sciences.

It appears that the more Durkheim reflected on the diversity of social types, the more cautious he became about the feasible range of comparisons that could be fruitfully attempted. Reacting sharply against the work of Frazer and what he called 'the anthropological school' he wrote, 'The comparative method would be impossible if social types did not exist, and it cannot be usefully applied except within a single type' (Durkheim 1915: 94). This need to restrict comparisons within clear limits was forcefully expressed by Evans-Pritchard (1965: 13–36) in his critique of the practices of many of his colleagues. It was for a similar reason that Marc Bloch (1967: 47) favoured comparisons of 'societies that are at once neighbouring and contemporary'.

Among Durkheim's successors, Radcliffe-Brown took the lead in promoting the view that detailed empirical studies of particular societies must be combined with extensive and systematic comparisons. He argued his case in the Preface he contributed to an influential collection of papers on African political systems (Fortes and Evans-Pritchard 1940: xi–xxiii). His argument was that the systematic comparison of segmentary and centralized political systems in sub-Saharan Africa was a first and essential step towards a better understanding of all political systems, simple as well as complex.

The comparative method developed and employed by Durkheim and his successors was designed to free the investigation from the investigator's own biases and preconceptions. The first step was detailed and careful observation of facts. Durkheim specified the conditions for such observation. The development of intensive fieldwork on the one hand and of survey research on the other greatly extended the depth and range of observation. Not that ideas, beliefs, and values were to be excluded from observation, but they were to be treated as facts existing independently of the moral and political preferences of the observer. Once the techniques of observation had been perfected, one would need only patience and care, and it would not matter who made the observation.

A second major step, and one that was crucial to the success of the comparative method, as both Durkheim and Radcliffe-Brown saw it, was the classification of facts. Radcliffe-Brown had put it thus: 'But we cannot hope to pass directly from empirical observation to a knowledge of general scientific laws or principles. . . . The immense diversity of forms of human society must first be reduced to order by some sort of classification' (ibid.: xi). Some sort of classification is no doubt implied in the very use of general concepts, but what was being proposed here was a kind of master plan that would at once reveal basic similarities and differences among societies and their constituent parts.

Durkheim provided a sketch for such a master plan in his rules for the classification of social types. He believed that the concept of social type or social species was essential for avoiding the extremes of nominalism on the one hand and realism on the other.

But one escapes from this alternative once one has recognized that, between the confused multitude of historic societies and the single, but ideal, concept of humanity, there are intermediaries, namely, social species. In the latter are united both the unity that all truly scientific research demands and the diversity that is given in the facts, since the species is the same for all the individual units that make it up, and since, on the other hand, the species differ among themselves (Durkheim 1938: 77).

Radcliffe-Brown (1957) later used the concept of 'natural kind', which is a variant of Durkheim's concept of social species, as a basis for arguing the case for a natural science of society whose essential steps would be observation, description, classification, comparison, and generalization.

The comparative method developed by Durkheim and Radcliffe-Brown was based on a particular conception of society. A society had a life of its own that could be observed from outside and described objectively. Different societies could be easily distinguished from each other. They could be grouped together according to their similarities and differences in the same way in which plants and animals were grouped together by biologists. The comparative method could then be applied to arrive at general conclusions about the structure and functioning of societies, and to distinguish between the normal and the pathological according to objective criteria.

The approach to the comparative method through the classification of societies, though very widely used in the nineteenth century, faced problems from the very beginning. Various general schemes of classification were proposed, but each could be shown to have severe limitations. In the nineteenth century, it was common to attempt to classify societies in such a way that each *type* of society could also be seen as a *stage* of evolution.[3] Perhaps the most famous among these was the classification by Morgan (1964) into savagery, barbarism, and civilization, which fell into disrepute when evolutionary theories came under attack from British and American anthropologists from the twenties onwards (Lowie 1960; Radcliffe-Brown 1952).

One of the most extensively used schemes of classification, derived from Marx and Engels, was the one which grouped societies under primitive communism, ancient society, Asiatic society, feudal society, and bourgeois (or capitalist) society. This scheme, with minor variations, remained a part of the canon of Soviet social science for decades, but each of its major classes, with the possible exception of the last, was riddled with ambiguity. It is for specialists in the field to decide whether more good or harm was done by the efforts of a determined band of historians to fit pre-British India into the category of feudal society (Mukhia 1981, 1985; Sharma 1985; Habib 1985). In like manner, the discussion of the category of Asiatic society and its place in the general scheme of classification taxed the ingenuity of a long line of Soviet scholars, again, to what effect it is difficult to say today (Gellner 1980).

Durkheim's classification of societies is of special interest; first, because it was consciously linked to his comparative method, and, second, because it was in accordance with a set of rules. Although Durkheim maintained that 'one branch of sociology must be devoted to the constitution and classification of these [social] species' (1938: 76), his own effort in that branch did not proceed very far. His basic principle was first to identify the component elements of societies and then to arrange them according to '*the nature and number of the component elements and their mode of combination*' (ibid.: 81, emphasis in original). Perhaps the only thing of value that emerged from this effort was the concept of 'segmentary society' which in a modified form played an important part in the development of political anthropology. Beyond that, even the attempt to classify societies of the 'organized' type was not seriously pursued.

A problem that is bound to bedevil any attempt to pursue the approach described above is its presupposition that in dealing with societies we can easily distinguish the part from the whole, and one whole from another. It is not at all evident from the nature of things whether a certain unit which is conventionally called a society should count as a part or a whole. Not only do the parts of a society flow into each other—Durkheim recognized this for 'organized' societies—but whole societies are frequently, even typically, mutually interpenetrating.

The problem raised above did not escape the attention of Radcliffe-Brown even while he argued the case for comparisons between societies through their classification. In his Presidential Address to the Royal Anthropological Institute in 1940, he observed:

At the present moment of history, the network of social relations spreads over the whole world, without any absolute solution of continuity anywhere. This gives rise to a difficulty which I do not think sociologists have really faced, the difficulty of defining what is meant by the term 'a society'. They do commonly talk of societies as if they were distinguishable, discrete entities, as, for example, when we are told that society is an organism. Is the British Empire a society or a collection of societies? Is a Chinese village a society, or is it merely a fragment of the Republic of China? (Radcliffe-Brown 1952: 193).

There is no great harm done when the same author talks of 'Munda society' and again of 'Indian society', but it does create problems for the classification of societies.

Not only does the concept of societies as discrete and bounded units appear less tenable than before, but some anthropologists have begun to question the utility of the very concept of society (Ingold 1986: 1990). Arguments of different kinds have been made against the concept, particularly as it has been used in the scholarly literature of sociology and social anthropology: that it sets up false oppositions—as between 'individual' and 'society'; that it reifies an abstraction—as in the statement that society is a reality *sui generis*; and so on. Finally, it has been suggested that it is the uncritical use of the concept of society that has brought comparative anthropology to an impasse (Ingold 1990: 6).

* * *

'Max Weber,' it has been observed, 'was the one sociologist in the history of the discipline who saw beyond the boundaries of modern Western civilization' (Shils 1981: 292). But his approach to the comparative study of society was different from the approach of Durkheim and Radcliffe-Brown because he had a different conception of society and a different assessment of the limits and possibilities of sociological enquiry. Sociological enquiry in his view was concerned with causes and functions, but it was also concerned with meaning, and there the organic analogy was more a hindrance than a help: 'We can accomplish something which is never attainable in the natural sciences, namely the subjective understanding of the component individuals' (Weber 1978: 15).

What is lacking in the approach adopted by Durkhein and Radcliffe-Brown is focused reflection on the standpoint from which observation, description and comparison are made. Weber, on the other hand, was continually preoccupied by the standpoint of the scholar, acknowledging tacitly the legitimacy of a variety of standpoints. His work on the Protestant ethic has had enormous influence on the development of our subject, and comparisons have been made on its basis between western and other civilizations. But it must not be forgotten that Weber himself offered his work as a contribution from a particular standpoint. To be sure, he was thinking of the variety of standpoints available within the western intellectual milieu, but the observation may be generalized to include other intellectual and cultural milieus as well.

For Weber, even observation and description had to be different in the social as against the natural sciences since the investigator could not confine himself only to external characteristics. It was not enough to examine statistical tendencies in the course and consequences of social action, one had also to reach into its meaning and significance, since 'subjective understanding is the specific characteristic of sociological knowledge' (Weber 1978: 15). This no doubt opened up new possibilities for social and historical enquiry, but it also posed difficult, not to say intractable, problems for the comparative study of civilizations.

Weber made extensive use of historical (as against ethnographic) material and therefore had to confront more fully the questions raised by the historians of his time about the understanding of human society and culture. He was unwilling to accept the limits generally imposed on historical enquiry by its orthodox practitioners but eager to take advantage of the insights into the human condition revealed by their work (Weber 1950, 1988). He insisted that historical material threw light not only on events and personalities but also on structures and processes that could be compared and contrasted across both time and space. One required new tools for making those comparisons and contrasts, but Weber did not find it fruitful to turn to the biological sciences for aid in their construction.

Weber made wide and extensive comparisons among human societies in different places at different times, but those comparisons did not presuppose in either principle or practice any single scheme of classification covering all human societies. His principal strategy of comparison and contrast was through the construction of ideal types, which enabled the selection and use of facts to establish significant similarities and differences. The construction of ideal types (unlike Durkheim's social types or social species) is not necessarily linked to the comparative method as such, but Weber harnessed the device for making the most extensive historical and sociological comparisons and contrasts.

As is well known, Weber constructed ideal types of a great variety of phenomena, ranging from social action to whole institutional complexes such as bureaucracy and capitalism. He saw these ideal types as constructions of the mind rather than 'social species' or 'natural kinds' having some sort of independent existence outside the investigator's mind. As he himself put it, 'An ideal type is formed by the one-sided *accentuation* of one or more points of view.... In its conceptual purity, this mental construct (Gedankenbild) cannot be found empirically anywhere in reality' (Shils and Finch 1949: 90, emphasis in original). Further, he took pains to distinguish between 'ideal types' and 'average types', the former being designed to bring out qualitative differences rather than differences of degree (Weber 1978: 20–21).

In a trenchant critique of Weber's mode of procedure, Carl Friedrich (1952: 28–29) pointed out that Weber used, with a great deal of attendant confusion, ideal types in both an 'individualizing' and a 'generalizing' manner. The ideal types of social action were clearly designed for use in every kind of social and historical context. The ideal type of Calvinism, on the other hand, was used to focus on distinctions within a single historical context. Again, some ideal types may serve well simply as heuristic instruments whereas others appear to be designed to bring sharply into focus a particular historical object. They may then be used as labels for marking out one society or one type of society from another, such as 'Occidental' and 'Oriental' societies.

Weber's ideal types give priority to 'representations' over 'morphology'. In that way, he was able to bring differences into prominence, sometimes at the cost of important similarities. A contemporary critic of Weber has pointed out that 'his attention was focussed on the over-all tendencies *distinguishing* one civilization from another rather than on the extent to which accommodations of theology and popular practice might tend to *diminish* these distinctions' (Bendix 1968: 500, emphasis in original).

The comparisons made by Weber have a free-ranging character that make them quite different from those that aim systematically to arrive at laws of increasing generality. These comparisons have illuminated many dark corners of human activity and experience. But one must always remember that Weber's primary historical object was western civilization.

A recent commentator has noted: 'While Durkheim's main interest was in what all societies have in common, in what a society *is*, Weber's was in how societies differ' (Lockwood 1992: 15–16, emphasis in original). Much of Weber's work was animated by the desire to identify the unique characteristics of western civilization, and especially those characteristics that gave it its unusual dynamism and 'which (*as we like to think*) lie in a line of development having *universal* significance and value' (Weber 1976: 13, some emphasis added). In this sense, his comparative approach may be described as a 'typifying' rather than a 'classifying' approach. The ideal types used by him exaggerated, with a particular purpose, the contrasts between western and other civilizations. But the very act that brought into relief the defining features of the former often obscured significant differences among the latter.

One of the early attempts at a comparative study of civilizations by a scholar of non-western origin began with the observation: 'Max Weber helped to perpetuate a Western misconception that Hindus, as well as Egyptians and Arabs, are Orientals. Weber considered the civilization of India to be but one branch of the Oriental civilization, of which two other branches are the Chinese and the Japanese' (Hsu 1963: 1). As we have noted, Weber himself was very conscious of the importance of the standpoint from which historical or sociological investigations are made, and his own standpoint appears in review to be very much that of the European scholar at the turn of the century.

It may be plausibly argued that Weber's *interest* in Hinduism or Confucianism was different from his interest in Calvinism. In his famous critique of Eduard Meyer, he had argued that something may become of interest to the historian in at least three distinct senses: (1) as an 'historical object'; (2) as a 'historical cause'; and (3) as an 'heuristic instrument' (Shils and Finch 1949: 156). In terms of these distinctions, only Calvinism was of interest to Weber in all the three senses, whereas Oriental religious traditions were of interest to him primarily only in the third sense. One might then say that Weber's aim was not so much to devise a single comparative method that could be used by one and all irrespective of substantive interest, but to use comparisons extensively to sharpen his 'heuristic instruments' in the interest of particular substantive enquiries. The question of 'fair comparisons' between cultures is then left unsettled.

* * *

The comparative study of human societies must take into account not only their morphology or external characteristics but also the ideas and values characteristic of them or their self-representation. This much would be acknowledged even by Durkheim, for he observed, 'A society cannot be constituted without creating ideals. These ideals are simply the ideas in terms of which society sees itself and exists at a culminating point in its development' (1974: 93). In studying plants and animals, we are concerned only with how they appear to us; in studying societies and cultures, our concern has also to be with how they appear to themselves. Thus, similarities and differences have to be recorded on several registers, and not on just one register. This makes it difficult beyond a point to adapt to the social sciences the procedures for comparison and contrast used with such success in the biological sciences.

The differential evaluation of societies and cultures has been implicit to a greater or lesser extent in the use of the comparative method even when it has been presented as objective and neutral. As we have seen, where the method went hand in hand with theories of evolution, it inevitably placed some societies and cultures ahead of others. It is true that Durkheim maintained that all religions should be investigated by the same comparative method, but he also believed that Christianity was more evolved and exalted than other religions. Likewise, Weber believed that the elimination of magical components through the process of rationalization had progressed further in Protestant Christianity than in any other religion. The same kind of slant in favour of monogamous marriage and the nuclear family may be noted in the schemes of comparison freely used in the past.

Both Durkheim and Weber were aware of the problems that arise when ideas, beliefs, and values are made the objects of systematic enquiry, and each tried to solve them in his own way. Durkheim believed that objective evaluation became possible once the social basis of individual judgements was recognized, for, as he put it, 'Social judgement is objective as compared with individual judgement' (ibid.: 84). While this might provide some ground for identifying the arbitrary nature of individual judgements, it does not show how different social judgements—those held to be valid in Indonesia as against the Netherlands—may be compared in an objective way. Indeed, while Durkheim did seek to understand representations and judgements as social facts, the comparative method that he tried to adapt from the biological sciences proved less than adequate to the task he took on hand.

Weber's keen historical sense made him more aware than Durkheim of the difficulty of extracting standards of evaluation and judgement from an examination, no matter how systematic or scrupulous, of social facts. The dictum that the normal type is the average type would be as alien to Weber's sociology as the analogy of societies with organisms. While striving continuously to separate value judgements from judgements of reality, Weber rarely underestimated the magnitude of the problem involved. 'Nor need I discuss further whether the distinction between empirical statements of fact and value-judgements is "difficult" to make. It is' (Shils and Finch 1949: 9). He did not believe that the investigator could, or even should, free himself from his own values; but he did insist on self-awareness in the investigation of a problem and self-restraint in the expression of one's viewpoint.

One of the principal tasks of sociological enquiry, and most acutely of comparative sociology, is to devise a method for treating 'subjective' evaluation in an objective way (ibid.: 10–11). The problem is not confined to sociology. It is akin to that of dealing with what the famous jurist Hans Kelsen called 'norms in a descriptive sense' as against what may be called 'norms in a prescriptive sense'. How difficult it is to maintain the distinction consistently may be judged from the misrepresentation of the idea so lucidly explained by H.L.A. Hart (1983: 286–308). The problem becomes particularly acute when the values characteristic of different societies are being compared (or contrasted) by scholars from different standpoints and with different presuppositions.

Weber's observations on value judgements, ethical neutrality, and objectivity, no matter how acute or incisive, related largely to questions of policy or politics (in German, the same word serves for both) within one's own society rather than to comparisons between different societies. When he compared science and politics as vocations, he had in mind mainly western science and German politics. I have already referred to his concern for accommodating more than one standpoint. In a well-known intervention, Weber defended the appointment of anarchists as teachers of law on the ground that they can 'perceive problems in the fundamental postulates of legal theory which escape those who take them for granted' (Shils and Finch 1949: 7). But he nowhere discussed seriously the implications of examining the fundamental postulates of social theories prevalent in his time from standpoints outside the western intellectual tradition.

'To view history from the "standpoint" of a particular class,' it has been observed, 'is as damaging as viewing it from the "standpoint" of one's nationality or one's generation or one's village' (Shils 1981: 60). Weber was aware of the damage done by viewing history from the standpoint of a particular class, but it is doubtful that he reflected sufficiently on the implications of viewing it from the standpoint of a particular nationality.

The question that I am raising relates more specifically to comparisons, and to standards of judgement and evaluation that are consciously or unconsciously built into the comparative method itself. To what extent are the definitions, classifications, and ideal types employed in the comparative method coloured by the categories of one's own society, and to what extent do they, therefore, devalue or otherwise distort the representations of other societies? If, as Durkheim says, a society cannot be constituted without creating ideals, then the comparison of societies is in a sense the comparison of their ideals. Is it possible to make that comparison without injecting the ideals of one's own society into the very framework of comparison?

Every society is marked by conflicting aims and tendencies. The actual differences between societies, as we have seen from Bendix's observations, are accentuated by the method of contrast through ideal types. Much depends on what kinds of ideal types are used, how and by whom they are constructed, and with what ends in view. The accentuated contrast between societies might appear appealing from one point of view but invidious from another. There is sometimes only a thin line between the ideal type and the stereotype. Where human values are engaged, as they are in such comparisons and contrasts, it is difficult to remove allegations of misrepresentation and suspicions of bad faith.

The two features that strike us most about the comparative sociology practised by the generation of Durkheim and Weber are: (1) that they made a genuine effort to bring all human societies—simple and complex, past and present—under its scrutiny; and (2) that those who developed its concepts and methods all belonged within broadly the same social and cultural tradition. It is the second that is now changing before our eyes and calls for serious attention. It would be safe to say that neither Durkheim nor Weber gave much thought to the viewpoint of the investigator in sociological comparisons when that investigator belonged to a non-western society. They were aware that viewpoints might vary according to class or political affiliation, but they did not take much account of variations due to differences of national tradition. They took ideas and values in non-western societies into account, but only as objects of investigation and not as elements in the construction of method. This has become a source of some anxiety to scholars from Asian and African countries. It is seen, perhaps rightly, as a very serious limitation of the comparative method as it now stands; but the remedy for it cannot be found by recommending different methods for observation, description, and comparison to persons rooted in different geographical locations.

* * *

Whether or not he adopts the comparative method of Durkheim, or the approach of Weber, or some other approach, the sociologist is condemned to making comparisons, and he cannot dispense with the requirement of making them rigorously and systematically. Nor can he sweep under the carpet the 'value problem' that arises in every comparison. Cultural anthropologists have learnt to appreciate the virtue of 'reflexivity' (Rabinow 1977; Clifford and Marcus 1986) which calls upon us to recognize that what we write about societies and cultures tells us something not only about those societies and cultures but also about ourselves. This is certainly a good thing so long as it does not turn into self-indulgence, for sociology and anthropology cannot be used as covers for autobiography.

Sociologists are inclined to seek in their own or other societies the values to which they are committed as persons, as scholars, or as citizens. Individual and community, equality and hierarchy, the rational and the traditional are things about which most scholars care, one way or another; and if they are sociologists or social anthropologists, they discover or seek out societies that uphold, or disregard, or deny one or another of those values. Some sociological and much anthropological writing is about 'other' societies, but one's own society is always in the background, implicitly more often than explicitly, as a standard of comparison.

Today, some of these values have acquired a kind of universal significance in the sense that they are recognized and acknowledged, at least to some extent and by some individuals, in all parts of the world. Disagreements are bound to arise when societies are compared to determine the extent to which they embody, or fail to embody, one or another value, for those who make the comparisons are likely to care not only more about some values than others, but also, and perhaps inevitably, more about some societies than others. Scholarly disagreements over facts and their interpretations are sometimes underlain by suspicions that arbitrary and invidious moral judgements are introduced through the backdoor in the course of 'scientific' comparisons.

Suspicions of bad faith are bound to arise when comparisons that appear 'scientific' or 'objective' from one standpoint appear invidious from another. Such suspicions can never be eliminated, but they can at least be mitigated if there is willingness to moderate the claims made on behalf of not only one's favoured method but also one's favoured society. For it is a fact that the second kind of claim is occasionally introduced in the course of comparisons, albeit in a tacit or oblique way. It is not simply that sociologists might subscribe to the social values they seek to investigate comparatively, but they sometimes display a possessive attitude towards their own society in a way that jeopardizes their comparative method.

The set of ideas and values centering around 'individual', 'person', and 'self' has engaged the attention of many historians and sociologists with a marked interest in comparative studies. A very significant contribution to the understanding of the subject has been made by a succession of French scholars beginning with Alexis de Tocqueville (1956). The delicate balance of judgements required in comparisons involving such values may be seen in the opposition with which Tocqueville began between 'individualism' to which a positive value, and 'egoism' to which a negative value was attributed. Where societies are being compared, some bias in reading the evidence relating to them is likely to creep in where a prior judgement based on moral preference, conscious or unconscious, has been made about the basic qualities of the societies in question, so that similar facts are treated as evidence of 'individualism' in one case and of 'egoism' in another.

The ambivalent attitude towards the place of the individual or person in the plan of social life—wavering between scientific detachment and moral commitment—may be seen in the work of Durkheim. As a sociologist, he took the view—against both utilitarians and contract theorists—that the individual as an autonomous moral agent, enjoying respect and responsibility in his own right, was not the starting point of social evolution but its end product. Pre-modern societies were, in his view, based on mechanical solidarity in which the individual was subordinated to the group, legally and morally; modern societies, on the other hand, were based on the division of labour which assigned legal and moral primacy to the autonomy of the individual. By modern societies, Durkheim meant modern western societies with which he contrasted all other societies, past and present. In *The Division of Labour in Society* (1938), Durkheim traced with the methods of positive science the general demographic, occupational, and other social factors through whose operation the individual had assumed primacy in modern as against pre-modern—that is, primitive, ancient, and medieval—societies. The discussion of this transition included many comparisons but it gave no explicit account of his own value preferences for or against the individual.

Only a few years later, Durkheim wrote an essay on the significance of the individual in society and history. In that essay, which was written in support of those who were demanding the reinstatement of Alfred Dreyfus, he stated his value preference clearly and openly in support of the individual. But there he not only assigned great importance to Christianity (as against demographic and other material factors) as a source of individualism, but shifted its origin to a much earlier phase of history. 'It is thus a singular error to present individualist morality as antagonistic to Christian morality; quite the contrary, it is derived from it. By adhering to the former, we do not disown our past; we merely continue it' (Durkheim 1969: 124). This is a somewhat different story from the one presented earlier about the causes of the division of labour.

A similar argument was presented by Mauss in a comparative essay on the person delivered as the Huxley Memorial Lecture to the Royal Anthropological Institute in 1938. The essay was offered as a 'sample. . . of the achievements of the French school of sociology' (Mauss 1979; 59). It provided a survey of a whole range of societies—the Pueblo Indians, the Northwest Coast Indians, the Australian Aborigines, the Indians of India, the Chinese, and, of course, the modern Europeans. It is clear that only the last constituted, in Weber's terminology, the historical object for Mauss, all the others serving as heuristic instruments. The treatment of the ancient civilizations of India and China was cursory and superficial. The conclusion of the essay was that the 'category of the person' as an autonomous moral agent, as against a mere sense of the person, was acknowledged and valued only in modern western societies, and nowhere else.

Although the essay was offered as a sample of the work of the French school of sociology, one will find in it very little regard for the rules of sociological comparisons laid down by Durkheim. The objective of the essay appears to have been not so much to demonstrate a sociological approach as to assert a claim to an ideal and a value to which Mauss, like Durkheim before him, attached the highest moral significance. Hence the essay concludes with the following exhortation:

Who knows even if this 'category', which all of us believe to be well founded, will always be recognized as such? *It was formed only for us, among us.* Even its moral power—the sacred character of the human person—is questioned, not only everywhere in the East, where they have not attained our sciences, but even in some of the countries where the principle was discovered. We have a great wealth to defend; with us the Idea may disappear. Let us not moralize (ibid.: 90, emphasis added).

I may add that this essay, which some may regard as shallow and mawkish, has received the highest praise from anthropologists in Britain where two separate English translations of it were published within ten years (Mauss 1979; Carrithers, Collins, and Lukes 1985).

Do all scholars who make sociological comparisons involving fundamental values show themselves, like Marcel Mauss, to be good patriots in the end? When the occasion demanded, Max Weber showed himself to be as true a German patriot as anyone (Mommsen 1984), and who can say that his commitment to Germany and to Europe did not colour the many comparisons that he made? Patriotism is now out of fashion among the western intellectuals, but that does not mean that it has been laid to rest. It is still a great force in the countries of Asia and Africa among intellectuals and others, but perhaps we should all try to learn from the mistakes of Mauss and Weber instead of insisting on our right to repeat those mistakes in our turn.

Notes

1. Talcot Parsons (1966: 71) was perhaps the last great sociologist who attempted to unite the comparative approach with an evolutionary perspective.

2. The 'method of controlled comparisons', in one form or another, continued to be used for long by social and cultural anthropologists. Fred Eggan (1954) provides a useful account of the limits and possibilities of the method as used in social anthropology. It may be recalled that Eggan had been much influenced by Radcliffe-Brown.

3. This was continued until recent times by sociologists and anthropologists of the Marxist persuasion. See, for instance, Godelier 1977: 70–96.

Restudies in Anthropology

PETER KLOOS

Introduction

'Replication'—repeating an experiment or an observation in order to increase the reliability of a scientific statement—is not a standard tool from the anthropological tool-kit, unlike in the natural sciences. Indeed, one may even argue that in the case of the social sciences replication in the strict sense of the term is not really possible. However, anthropological fieldworkers use the term 'restudy'—and often on the basis of a restudy criticize particular facts as well as general insights of colleagues who have worked in the same place at an earlier date. Used in this way the term comes close to replication. And fieldworkers use the terms 'revisit' and 'resurvey' apparently to do something other than either replication or restudy. Evidently, conceptually and perhaps methodologically the issue is a little messy, and tidying up that mess may be useful. That is what I intend to do in this chapter. The basic question will be: what are the modalities, limitations, and alternatives of so-called restudies in anthropology? My conclusion will be that from the point of view of method, the term is an unfortunate, time-bound, anthropological misnomer that ought to be discarded. Because 'restudy' is a fairly vague concept compared to its apparent cognate 'replication', it is perhaps wise to begin with the latter.

One caveat should be entered here: being an anthropologist, I approach the issue of restudy primarily from the perspective of my own discipline, and it is from anthropology in a broad sense that I draw examples. I believe, however, that sociologists and economists carrying out village-based studies and restudies will find exactly the same obstacles as anthropologists.

Replication

In physics, replication and replicability are regarded as essential ingredients of research. Strategic experiments and observations in physics, chemistry, and astronomy are customarily *replicated*, that is, carried out again. This is not the case in anthropology....

For a variety of reasons replication in the technical, natural scientific meaning of the term, is not a basic element of anthropological methodology. Some of the reasons for this are practical. During the first decades of modern anthropology—when fieldwork by professionally trained anthropologists was becoming normal—the number of scholars was very low, and the feeling of urgency to capture what was felt to be fast disappearing was high. It seemed a waste of scarce resources to let two or more trained researchers go to the same place.

Other reasons are of socio-psychological nature. Fieldworkers tend to develop ownership feelings towards the community they have studied. Although the expression 'my village' is regarded as a joke, the joke is serious in its consequences. Feelings of ownership are often respected by other fieldworkers, who refrain from going to a place where a colleague has recently done fieldwork or is still carrying out fieldwork. The fieldwork sites of older and academically more powerful scholars in particular are not likely to be chosen by their younger colleagues.

Finally, there are methodological considerations to regard replication the way it is conceived in the natural sciences as impossible in the case of anthropology. Replication in scientific research is directly related to one of the basic features of scientific knowledge: reliability. Reliability defines the consistency between two or more scientific statements supposed to describe reality. Because reality can never be known other than through statements about reality, reliability is usually defined in an instrumental manner. The reliability of a statement about empirical reality increases in proportion to the number of independent observations that have led to the same statement. When a physicist does not believe the outcome of an experiment or an observation he repeats or *replicates* that experiment or observation.

Replication as the imperial road to reliable knowledge is based on a number of assumptions, and I shall mention two of them. First, it is assumed that empirical reality has not changed during the time that has elapsed between the first and the second observation, or, to put it differently, that the same reality is being observed. Second, it is assumed that the way in which reality is observed and measured is the same for both observations. In experiments in chemistry and physics, where reality itself can be controlled and the same instruments can be used, these conditions can indeed be met.

In non-experimental natural sciences, where reality cannot be controlled, a problem arises: differences between observations that have been made with the same instrument may, at least logically, be attributed to changes in reality that have taken place during the time elapsed between the two observations. As long as one can make the measurements with the same instrument, or with instruments that can be calibrated, this is a logically acceptable conclusion.

In anthropological research, however, the object, namely sociocultural reality, is not only beyond our control, we may also safely assume that it is continually changing. Moreover, we have to work with an instrument that cannot be calibrated and whose working is only partially known: human individuals, with their ears and eyes.

Given these fundamental uncertainties, one has to conclude that replication as carried out in experimental situations with instruments that can be controlled, or as carried out in natural situations but executed with instruments that can be calibrated, is impossible in anthropology. In fact, as far as I know, there is only one study which makes that claim to some extent, namely Holmes's study of Samoa (Holmes 1957, published in 1987).

Samoa is the subject of a famous study by Margaret Mead who went to this Polynesian island in 1925 to study adolescence. One of the intellectual issues of the 1920s was the so-called nature-nurture controversy. Was human behaviour basically determined by ultimately genetic, biological factors or was behaviour culturally determined, that is, learned? Mead's teacher, Franz Boas, was a staunch supporter of the idea that it was culture, not biology, that moulded human behaviour. A strategic phenomenon in this controversy was the problem of stress in adolescents....

According to Mead, there was among Samoan girls no question of the state of mind in Western society called 'Sturm und Drang'. The implication was that this psychological state is related to culture and is not the outcome of adolescent psychobiological changes.

In 1954, the American anthropologist Lowell Holmes went to Samoa. He went to the village where Mead had carried out her research, worked with many of her informants, and

systematically investigated and evaluated every word that Mead wrote in *Coming of Age in Samoa* (1928), *Social Organization of Manu'a* (1930) and several articles (Holmes 1983: 929).

Although every fieldworker comments on the reliability of data that is already available, Holmes's seems to be the first attempt (and as far as I know the only attempt) to systematically verify an earlier study in anthropology. Can it be regarded as replication in the strict sense of the term? I think not, even though Holmes comes quite close to it. From the point of view of logic there are two flaws in his 'replication' (whatever his conclusions: he judged that Mead's rendering of Samoa was basically correct). In the first place, his research took place twenty-nine years after Mead's original fieldwork. This period, which included the Pacific War, did not leave Samoa untouched. Logically, the differences which Holmes noted between Mead's work and his own may be due to change. Second, one should realize that as a young woman, Mead could enter into a relationship with Samoan girls in a way which was impossible for Holmes. This simply means that the research instrument used by Holmes was basically different from the one used by Mead. Because field workers as human beings always differ from one another in terms of age, sex, personality, and cultural background, and since sociocultural reality is always changing, replication in the strict sense is not possible in anthropological fieldwork.

Holmes himself uses the term 'restudy' for his research in Samoa, not the term 'replication'. What, then, is a restudy?

The first anthropologist to use the term restudy was, as far as I know, Oscar Lewis, when he called a book based on his Mexican fieldwork *Life in a Mexican Village: Tepoztlán Restudied* (1951). Tepoztlán is a village in the Mexican state of Morelos. Here, Robert Redfield had carried out research in 1926 and 1927. His book, *Tepoztlán: A Mexican Village* (1930) is one of the first studies of what came to be known as a 'peasant society'. Tepoztlán became famous only after Oscar Lewis' research in 1943–44. Lewis went to Mexico to assist in aid programmes aimed at improving Mexican Indian communities. It is in this context that he carried out research in Tepoztlán because the earlier work by Redfield offered him a base line from which to measure and analyse change (Lewis 1951: xiii). Yet, while working in Tepoztlán, Lewis became convinced that the picture which Redfield had painted was strongly biased. Redfield had described a harmonious community of people who worked collectively rather than individuality. Lewis stressed individuality and distrust in interpersonal relations as well as conflict.

This was not the first case in anthropology in which two fieldworkers arrived at radically different pictures of the same community. In 1937, for example, the Chinese student Li An-Che published an account of the Zuñi Indians in which he stressed elements of Zuñi thought and behaviour that were very different from Ruth Benedict's rendering of Zuñi culture and personality in her well-known *Patterns of Culture* (1934).

Today 'restudy' is an acknowledged term in anthropological jargon. However, it is not at all clear what it stands for. Of course it means what it literally says, that is, the study of a society and culture already studied, but it also has a special connotation. It often refers to those studies in which the second researcher arrives at quite a different picture of the 'same' society. Thus, there is an element of replication in a restudy!

As already stated, conscious efforts to systematically evaluate earlier studies are rare in anthropology since fieldworkers prefer to have their 'own' society (see Mead's 1972 autobiographical account for an inside view on what Brown in 1978 called the 'my-tribe' syndrome). In the case of restudy, however, a fieldworker deliberately turns to a society or even a village community that has already been studied. Does this mean that fieldwork practices have changed? What motivates a fieldworker to carry out a restudy?

Looking at studies of the same society there seem to be two categories of motivation. First, there is the restudy that deliberately wishes to use an earlier study as a point of departure to analyse processes of change. Second, there is the restudy which looks into hitherto neglected aspects of a society (purists will argue that neither is a *re*-study! I will return to this, because there is more involved than language purism only).

All this points to a change indeed in fieldwork practices. Two circumstances should be mentioned. The first is that as the number of professional anthropologists has risen enormously since the early years of modern fieldwork, the number of societies not yet studied has gone down. Apart from a few Amerindian groups in South America and perhaps a handful of New Guinean societies, there are no truly blank spots on the ethnographic map any longer. Furthermore, the absolute number of different societies and cultures has also gone down (at least, according to traditional, and nowadays rather old-fashioned anthropological conceptions). Due to rapid social change, especially since World War II, as well as to ethnocide and even genocide, many societies and cultures have disappeared. It is no longer possible for fieldworkers to find a society they can make their own; they simply have to work in a society that has already been the object of research.

The second is a change in perspective. The emphasis of the first generation of fieldworkers was on the uniqueness of sociocultural systems found on the spot. They were impressed by the complexity of sociocultural systems and the interdependence of sociocultural elements. Contrary to previous, strongly evolutionary approaches they tried to explain a sociocultural system not in terms of its history but rather in terms of how it functioned here and now. Malinowski in particular has been very influential here.

The historical perspective was re-introduced during the 1960s, although there are earlier examples as is evidenced by the work of Oscar Lewis (the historical perspective was never really absent in the case of American anthropology).The shift in perspective meant that older accounts, often written by the first generation of anthropological fieldworkers, acquired a new meaning: they offered the possibility of analysing change. After all, one of the problems of studying long-term processes confronting anthropological fieldworkers is the paucity or even absence of reliable historical data. The early monographs offered what Lewis called a 'base line' of change.

In a few cases, pupils of first-generation fieldworkers went back to the community where their teachers had done pioneering work (see, for instance, Gillin 1936 and Adams 1972 on the Barama River Caribs of Guyana). In other cases, fieldworkers restudied the peoples about whom interesting studies had been written (see Holmberg 1950 and Stearman 1987 on the Siriono in Bolivia). The third category consists of fieldworkers who revisited the place where they themselves had carried out research (the earliest examples being Raymond Firth in Tikopia—see Firth 1936 and 1959—and Margaret Mead in the Admiralties, see Mead 1930 and 1956). I use the term 'revisit' here on purpose, although it seems to be a neologism of the somewhat older term 'restudy'—with perhaps a slight difference. Many 'revisits' seem to be rather shorter than 'restudies' (cf. Wadley and Derr 1989: 79). The difference may therefore be one of modesty only.

Whatever the motivation of the restudy or revisit, in the relationship between first and second research there are as far as the results are concerned two possibilities. In a number, and perhaps the majority, of cases the results of both researches are largely *consistent* with each other. However, in a number of cases the results are so different that the restudy gives rise to a controversy over the question of who is right and who is wrong. The first controversy has already been referred to—the representation of Zuñi society and culture by Benedict (1934) and by Li An-che (1937). The latest one is the representation of a Boston street gang—here the reliability of Whyte's famous *Street Corner Society* (1943) has been challenged by Boelen (1992), who went so far as to accuse Whyte of having dabbled with basic facts. For instance, the famous and often-quoted account of Doc's bowling match, which Whyte used to demonstrate the relationship between rank and performance, was according to Boelen not based on observation at all, but on fantasy.

From the point of view of research results, the first possibility is the most useful. From the point of view of research methodology, the second should have our attention. Here the credibility of the discipline is at stake. In the next section of this essay I will concentrate on the second one.

Why Fieldworkers Disagree

Basically there are four possible reasons why ethnographers disagree (see Heider 1988, Kloos 1988 and 1944):

1. cultural variation within one and the same society
2. sociocultural change
3. errors of observation and fraud
4. differences in research perspective

The point of the first of these possibilities is that fieldworkers often too easily extrapolate the results of research in one village to a whole region. This gives rise to one or two ethnographic disagreements.

With regard to sociocultural change, the issues are more complex. Disagreements between fieldworkers may be attributed to sociocultural variations in time following from either cyclical or structural change. For self-evident reasons, a restudy takes place at a later moment and this means that processes of change may have substantially altered a society and its culture. The second fieldworker is usually quite aware of substantial change. Indeed, that is often what (s)he is investigating in an already known community. Still, there is a strange twist here, because the second fieldworker may become convinced that his or her colleague was wrong even with regard to the time (s)he did fieldwork. Still, the second researcher may overlook the effects of changes. Methodologically interesting is the Redfield-Lewis controversy. It is one of the rare examples in which the first fieldworker extensively comments on the discrepancies between his account and that by the second fieldworker. Discussing the discrepancies between Lewis' and his own account of Tepoztlán, Redfield stressed their complementarity. He saw in contrasting accounts of one and the same community a means to better understanding and pleaded in favour of the deliberate construction of complementary descriptions (Redfield 1960: 132–33. He argued that the difference in the case of Tepoztlán was due to a 'hidden question':

The hidden question behind my book, 'What do these people enjoy?' The hidden question behind Dr Lewis' book is, 'What do these people suffer from?' (ibid.: 136).

Lewis also seems to have believed that Redfield and he had studied the same village and that the differences between the results of their fieldwork were due to differences in research perspective. Such a difference undoubtedly existed. Lewis in particular did not want to present a 'neutral' picture of the village. Politically more committed than Redfield, he paid far more attention to what people suffered from.

But did they really describe the same village, albeit from a different perspective and for a different purpose? There is room for serious doubt here. Redfield arrived in Tepoztlán just after the atrocities of the Mexican revolution, when the inhabitants had had to flee from their village. Life in Tepoztlán was at the time of Redfield's fieldwork slowly returning to 'normal'. Between Redfield's stay there in 1926–27 and Lewis' fieldwork in 1943–44, Tepoztlán's population had grown rapidly. Lewis pays attention to the growth in population but gives little heed to its possible consequences. Many of the differences between Redfield's and Lewis' rendering of social relations can be explained in terms of population pressure resulting from rapid population growth (for example, the disappearance of communal land and of communal labour, the growing antagonism between landowners and landless people, the distrust in interpersonal relations). I therefore think that Coy was largely right when he concluded:

that both accounts were legitimate in the context of the situation ruling at the two periods of time [. . .] at some time between 1929 and 1935 economic and demographic changes in Tepoztlán favoured the expression of different behaviour patterns from that of the exhausted survivors of the revolution (Coy 1971: 56).

There is little doubt that Redfield did misrepresent Tepoztlán to some extent, but Lewis' account is biased too. Yet, the differences between the two accounts are in all likelihood also due to structural changes taking place during the intervening period of seventeen years.

There are also changes of a cyclical nature that may give rise to discrepancies. One should appreciate the fact that the structure of many societies is influenced by cyclical processes, sometimes requiring cycles up to thirty or forty years. This holds true, for example, for those New Guinean societies in which herds of pigs are slowly built up, to be collectively slaughtered in the context of huge socio-political rituals. Patterns of life before and after these events differ markedly. This can be seen in the different descriptions of one New Guinea society, the Tchambuli or Chambri (see Mead 1935 versus Gewertz 1983). In this case 'the facts' are not at stake, their interpretation, however, is. Gewertz shows that if the Chambri men, according to Mead, seemed to have been absorbed in political and ritual activities (in contrast with the more mundane involvements of the women), this was due to a response to circumstances coinciding with Mead's four-month visit, not to some basic Tchambuli ethos freeing the men from business-like behaviour characteristic of the women.

Still, reviewing the ethnographic controversies, time as an explanation of disagreement does not play an important role. Time is relative anyway. Annette Weiner, studying the Trobrianders fifty years after Malinowski's pioneering research, notes that despite her famous predecessor's gloomy predictions about the future of Trobriand culture, much had remained unchanged (Weiner 1976: 25).

Errors of observation, sometimes bordering on fraud, seem on first sight to be the easiest way to dispense with ethnographic disagreement. The question of who is wrong and who is right arises especially where widely differing images of the 'same' society have been put forward. When, in 1983, Freeman challenged virtually every statement ever made by Mead regarding Samoa, the one important single question seemed to be: whose Samoa was the right one. There is little doubt that a number of Mead's statements were wrong (but so are several of Freeman's statements, who repeatedly misquotes his sources and ignores information running counter to his own argument!). In other cases of ethnographic controversy, too, there is a fairly simple answer. When Redfield painted his rosy picture of Tepoztlán and ignored more than one hundred cases of crime reported to the police during his sojourn there, it is reasonable to call this an error.

Error borders on fraud. As already said, the accusation of fraud befell William F. Whyte. However, irony has it that in the few cases of probably deliberate (and known!) fraud that exist in ethnography there are very few factual differences between the fraudulent and the supposedly honest ethnography. A case in point is Donner's book containing her experiences with the Venezuelan Yanomamö. This book is, apart from fantasy, based on an account of a Venezuelan girl, Helena Valero, who had been kidnapped by the Yanomamö, and had lived with them for twenty-four years (Valero 1984). DeHolmes, who unmasked the fraud, could find numerous stylistic parallels between Donner's account and the book in which Helena Valero's autobiography was published. This strongly suggested plagiarism. However, she could find only one, minor, ethnographic mistake! (see Donner 1982, DeHolmes 1983).

Yet, in by far the majority of the cases of controversy, errors and fraud are not that simple to ascertain. Instead, one has to conclude that the differences in research results are due to differences in research perspective and in epistemological assumptions.

Sociocultural systems of even small-scale, pre-industrial, and pre-literate societies are complex. Although the ambition of anthropology, and of early fieldworkers in particular, is to comprehend a society and its culture in its totality, no fieldworker is really able to cover this complex totality. This inability necessitates selection. Research invariably means looking at reality from a specific point of view. The majority of ethnographic discrepancies are due to usually rather implicit differences in research perspective. Several kinds of perspective can be distinguished. In the first place, one should always remember that in anthropological fieldwork, the dominant instrument is a human individual. Human individuals differ, first of all, in their outlook in terms of *gender, age, and personality of the fieldworker*, and these differences affect their fieldwork possibilities, their ethnographic observations, and their interpretations. The big difference between Malinowski and Weiner, for instance, in their Trobriand fieldwork is that the first was a man, hailing from a patriarchal Central European culture (Poland), the second an American woman, working at a time when modern feminism was gaining momentum. Where Malinowski kept aloof from a number of women's activities, regarding them as unimportant, Weiner became inexorably involved in them. She was quite literally dragged into a women's ceremony, and although 'I had little notion of what was being enacted, the great amount of time, energy, and emotion involved made me sense the importance of the event' (Weiner 1976: 7). The consequences of gender are by now too well known to require much discussion here (see Bell et al. 1993). The consequences of age and personality are far less systematically studied but undoubtedly important.

In the second place, we should not forget the more or less explicit *political objectives* of the scholar. Lewis with regard to Tepoztlán was quite explicit about his aims when he wrote:

It seems to me that concern with what people suffer from is much more important than the study of enjoyment because it is more productive of insights about the human condition, about the dynamics of conflict and the forces of change [. . .]. To stress the enjoyment in peasant life [as Redfield did, PK] is to argue for its preservation (Lewis 1961: 179).

In the third place, one should take into account that ethnographic facts are constructs in which the *theoretical orientations* of the fieldworker are as important as the actual reality. And behind more or less explicit theoretical orientations more implicit cultural assumptions held by the fieldworker colour his or her observations. The most glaring ethnographic discrepancies seem to be related to differences in theoretical orientation rather than to anything else (see Kloos 1996). Materialist and idealist orientations in particular have given rise to very different monographs of 'the same' society (compare Beck's 1972 monograph of Konku with Den Ouden's monographs 1975, 1977).

How are such differences to be dealt with? Discussing the Zuñi controversy Bennett argued already in 1946 that what was needed was not so much an answer to the question whose description was right and whose was wrong. Necessary was 'a reflexive analysis of the meanings of the respective interpretations' (Bennett 1946: 374). It is my conviction that this reflexive analysis will be largely an analysis of implicit background assumptions and explicit theoretical orientations on ethnographic research. I will not pursue that argument here (I refer to Kloos 1996 for an attempt to formulate a kind of anthropological metatheory for such an analysis). In the present context another aspect of restudy is more important: restudy as a tool in historical research.

Anthropological Restudy or Historical Research?

So far I have focused on restudies, more or less assuming that two or more different scholars had been involved. In the cases of ethnographic discrepancies this is usually true. However, apart from the already noted shift in ethnographic emphasis towards a historical perspective resulting in restudying an already researched community, there is another important shift in ethnographic practice that should be referred to because it is highly relevant in the context of restudy.

To slightly exaggerate the point: the first generation of fieldworkers went to faraway places, stayed there preferably for a year or more, and spent a lifetime on writing about a people, a society, and a culture never to be visited again (see Evans-Pritchard's 1951 discussion of fieldwork). Malinowski never went back to the Trobriand Islands after he had left Australia. The same applies to the first batch of his students who went to West Africa (Meyer Fortes to the Tallensi, Sjoerd Hofstra to the Mendi, and Siegfried Nadel to Nupe) and to many others who followed. Travel difficulties are one explanation of this practice. This applied, for obvious reasons, far less to American anthropologists carrying out fieldwork among American Indians (the latter called the former 'summer-birds', because every academic holiday they flocked to the reservations). It also did not apply to a number of British scholars who worked in Africa and were attached to African research institutes, like the Rhodes-Livingstone Institute.

Still, there is a huge difference. Today, many fieldwork sites can be reached in a couple of days. For instance, if I take the night flight from Amsterdam to Colombo, Sri Lanka, this evening, I can be in the village in the northern Dry Zone where I have been doing research since 1977 before noon tomorrow (nowadays it is often research *permission* rather than travel that requires months of patience!). This means that for a fieldworker it has become fairly easy to revisit the place where (s)he carried out research. As I have already pointed out, the trend was set in the early 1950s, when Raymond Firth and Margaret Mead went back to Tikopia and Manus respectively, to study what had happened there since their earlier stay, in the late 1920s.

Given the shift in research interests (from synchronic to diachronic studies), given the number of scholars (necessitating research where research has already been carried out), and given the accessibility of research sites, the form of restudy initiated by Oscar Lewis is becoming dominant. The aim of this kind of research is to investigate change. Its main variants are the restudy either by the original researcher or by someone else.

In the remainder of this chapter I will concentrate on a number of practical and methodological problems arising from this way of studying change. A main theme will be the problematization of the original study.

The kind of restudy I am considering is inherently historical as well as comparative in its implications, entailing a comparison between two 'snapshots', so to say. From differences and similarities between the two snapshots conclusions are drawn regarding change. This comparison offers a number of problems. I will sum up some of them, paying attention to restudy carried out by the same scholar as well as a different scholar.

a. Physical Availability of Data

The second study usually departs from a published article or monograph if different scholars are involved, and from a published account augmented by unpublished data if the restudy is carried out by the scholar who also carried out the original study.

The possibilities for a restudy to a large extent depend on the precision of the published account. A technical problem here might be the anthropological usage which conceals not only the true names of persons dealt with in the published account, but often also the identity of the community. In many cases it is not too difficult to trace the true identity of the community (locally, the identity of key persons is usually even easier to find out). Still, moral reasons may have led an author to omit crucial data or even distort descriptions in order to avoid recognition.

The author of the account, if still alive and traceable, might help not only by identifying community and key figures, but also by making available unpublished and un-aggregated data. If no longer alive, data might be retrieved from research institutions or museums—if the fieldworker(s) concerned decided to preserve raw field data. As far as I know, this is not generally done. A quick survey in my own department taught me that many fieldworkers are not in favour of preserving their data, arguing that they alone can judge the value of them. Raw field data are usually destroyed after some time. Many also fear unauthorized use of their data if they are put at the disposal of a data bank.

This means that scholars who are doing the restudy themselves are clearly at an advantage, but the span of time between such a study and restudy is limited (as far as I know George Foster is an extreme but also extremely rare example of studying the same Mexican community for over fifty years (Foster 1979)). In many cases the time span is between twenty and thirty years (unless a scholar decides to return every year or so). The first study is often doctoral research.

b. Standardization

Comparison not only depends on the physical availability of data but also on their standardization. Social scientific reseach suffers from a lack of standardization. Even in the case of village studies—after all, a recognized *genre* in anthropology—standardization is not customary: anthropologists let themselves be guided by a highly idiosyncratic problem definition and generally shy away from standardization of vital data on the village as well as from defining basic concepts such as population size, village composition, and household. There are no generally accepted lists of core data that should be collected in any village study. Lack of standardization severely hampers comparison.

c. Problem Definition

Unlike 'the first research', a restudy implying a comparison between an earlier and a later study is restricted in its research questions. This comparison cannot go beyond things noted in the earlier study (unless the second researcher tries to go back in time, as Lewis did). This limiting effect of the earlier study has implications one should be aware of: it implies, for instance, that recent scientific interests are often absent in restudies, simply because they were not yet there when the first study was carried out. What strikes me in several restudies. . . is that two issues are hardly present: the consequences of gender specific perspectives and the effects of globalization on local ways of life. Twenty to thirty years ago the importance of the gender perspective had hardly entered the consciousness of the majority of male fieldworkers, and, consequently, their monographs. If one restricts the restudy to a strict comparison, gender does not play a role in the restudy. The same applies to globalization—a concept that was coined only in the 1980s (see Kloos and De Silva 1995).

This argument points to the necessity of problematizing the earlier study, but this has problems of its own.

d. Problematization

If a restudy is carried out by another scholar, the second should be cautious about the reliability of the source. After all, the monograph serving as a 'base line' is not reality itself. It is reality seen from certain perspectives. A village study is not a village. A village study can only be understood in terms of its historically-bound conceptualization. Cynthia Hewitt de Alcántara writes in her book on the study of rural life in post-revolutionary Mexico, that her original aim was a discussion of the changing levels of living and forms of livelihood in different regions of the Mexican countryside. After all, there were scores of village studies that ought to have made possible such an enterprise. She soon came to the conclusion that village studies could not be used in that way. They were 'an artefact of a changing anthropological or sociological imagination'. Therefore, it was

necessary to elucidate the nature of peasant studies in Mexico before one could hope to contribute substantially to the modern history of the [Mexican] peasantry (Hewitt de Alcántara 1982: iv).

However, to problematize the original study poses a dilemma: the more it is done, the more its contents are contextualized and criticized, the less its value is as base line for comparison!

For a scholar studying the same community twice, the problems are different. Here too, of course, one's earlier research result should not be taken for granted. This is probably quite difficult, especially for senior scholars whose career is usually built on their first research project.

I do not know many examples of scholars who carry out a restudy and who are basically critical of their own earlier work at the same time. An interesting example is Hein Streefkerk's 1991 assessment of his research in Bulsar in the late 1960s and the scientific climate in which he wrote his report. In his report he saw industrialization as not having much continuity. Due to the uncertain supply of raw materials and imperfect markets industrial entrepreneurs redirected their efforts as soon as profits went down. He concluded that betting on several horses is a rational entrepreneurial behaviour. Returning to Bulsar twenty years later the scene suggested that the course of events after he had left the field did not quite warrant his erstwhile pessimism. Bulsar had grown fast, industrial enterprise included, and there was more continuity than he had expected. This brought Streefkerk to reconsider his opinion of small-scale industrial enterprise. His conclusion is that the Amsterdam scientific climate of the late 1960s and early 1970s had led him to embrace an anti-capitalist perspective, in which entre-preneurial production could not be the solution to India's development problems because it would result in half-hearted modernization and ill-balanced progress. Looking back at his original data, Streefkerk found that among them are some that already in 1971 might have shown him that the reigning points of view were doubtful (Streefkerk 1993: 36). An-other example of scholars critically considering their earlier work is Wadley and Derr's (re)study of Karimpur, where the Wisers in the 1920s carried out their research resulting in *Behind Mud Walls* (1930).

e. Time

Given a comparison between two snapshots separated by two or more decades there is a general tendency to view the time span in between as linear. This is highly questionable. A comparison between two points in time cannot logically tell us about the process of continuity and change which historically speaking connects both points. *The only solution is to study the intervening process itself.* This, however, implies more than a restudy: it necessitates a historical investigation of the events making up the process of continuity and change, not as an assumed connection between two snapshots, but as an observable process.

Concluding Remarks

These considerations bring me to the conclusion that the concept of restudy as a tool to study process of continuity and change is misleading: if a scholar is interested in processes of continuity and change, it is these processes that should be studied, but not on the basis of a comparison between two 'snapshots'. This simplistic comparison is fraught with practical and methodological pitfalls and should be discarded.

The 'restudy' is a kind of anthropological accident. It probably came into being as a consequence of the fact that anthropologists habitually study *other* societies. Doing so, they created a physical distance between them and their home bases on the one hand, and 'the field' on the other. When historical interest returned to anthropology, the problem of the unavoidably brief fieldwork and the longer term interest was solved by the restudy comparing two or more studies.

From the point of view of travel this is no longer necessary, from the point of view of methodology it is not acceptable. As far as the study of continuity and change is concerned we should aim at a combination of anthropological and historical approaches. With regard to their subject matter the two disciplines hardly differ. Anthropologists can learn much from historians (with regard to the critical use of archival data, for instance). Historians can learn much from anthropologists (with regard to the principles of 'oral history', the use of time structures such as genealogies, etc).

II
Intensive Fieldwork and Ethnography

Margaret Mead (1970: 246) writes that the typical model of the fieldworker is of a 'single trained observer living for a specified period within and observing an ongoing community whose members share a single culture, different from his own, and organizing and integrating his observations and records of the behaviour of living identified individuals'. Central to anthropological and sociological research is the method of fieldwork, and it has been noted that today it has become truly cross-disciplinary, with specialists from other disciplines opting to combine fieldwork with the special methodologies of their respective subjects.

While Mead is right with respect to the typical meaning of fieldwork, many of its instances vary considerably. Instead of one, there may be two or more fieldworkers working together in the same community; there may be team or group research; the fieldworker may not actually live with the people but visit them during the day; one's own community may be opted for detailed observations rather than working on people belonging to a different culture. But, common to all cases of fieldwork is that the investigator collects information by spending as much time as possible with the people under study, using principally the techniques of observation and interview, and combining them with methods and techniques of survey or of any other discipline (such as projective techniques from psychology) as he deems fit. The fieldworker is also open to the idea that it is during the course of fieldwork that one can make many improvisations to its body of techniques and methods, and he also writes about these later. An important genre of writings in sociological and anthropological methodology concerns a first-hand account of how fieldwork was actually carried out. These accounts should not be regarded as instances of 'soft' literature, for they are of tremendous instructional value to other fieldworkers, especially those at the brink of initiating their first fieldwork.

The first reading in this section comprising articles on intensive field-work is from Gerald Berreman, whose 1962 publication titled *Behind Many*

Masks: Ethnography and Impression Management in a Himalayan Village
is still regarded as one of the best analytical accounts of fieldwork. I was
keen to include here excerpts from this publication but it was on Berreman's
advice that I decided to keep his article of 1968, which comprises relevant
portions from *Behind Many Masks* as well as several theoretical comments
on ethnography and fieldwork. Berreman carried out his fieldwork in
Sirkhanda, a village in the lower Himalayas, where strangers were few and
readily identified. Like in any other closed community, Sirkhanda peasants
were suspicious of outsiders—the strangers—and wanted them to leave
their area as soon as possible. An outsider could stay in a Himalayan village
if he bore a relationship with someone local. A non-Pahari wholesaler who
had acquired land in Sirkhanda introduced Berreman and his assistant, a
Brahmin of plains origin, to the village and they were able to stay there.

However, this introduction did not quell people's suspicion of and overt
opposition to what the ethnographer was doing in Sirkhanda. And then,
one day, a respondent publicly demanded from Berreman an explanation
of why he was in their village, the use to which he would put the information he was gathering, and his ulterior motives. This event was extremely
important for the fieldwork, for it gave the ethnographer an opportunity to
explain to all who were there—as comprehensively and precisely as was
possible—the purpose of his staying in the village. Berreman's speech,
stirring as it was, apparently laid to rest the fears of the local people regarding the presence of an outsider amidst them, and then the fieldwork
proceeded smoothly. When Berreman and his assistant brought their respective families to live with them in Sirkhanda, their degree of rapport
with the people further increased because unattached men were viewed as
a threat to the local women. Such fortuitous incidents change the course of
fieldwork and help it to continue without difficulty. They help the
fieldworkers to draw closer to people. One may recall here the incident
from Geertz's fieldwork (1973: 412–17) in Bali that singularly helped him
to gain access to the local community.

In 1958, Geertz and his wife arrived in a Balinese village, but the people
simply ignored them and it was quite frustrating. Ten days or so after their
arrival, a large cockfight was held in the public square of the village to
raise money for a new school. Cockfights were illegal in Bali because they
involved gambling, and that was the reason of their taking place secretly,
in secluded corners of villages, but the cockfight that Geertz described was
a big affair with hundreds of people watching it, including the fieldworkers.

In the midst of the third match of the cockfight, a 'truck full of policemen
armed with machine guns roared up'. People started racing down the road,

and so did Geertz and his wife, following a man, whom they did not know to the compound of his house. As the three of them reached the courtyard, the wife of the man, who knew what had happened, spread the table, and started serving them tea. After some time, when a policeman arrived in the house looking for the village chief and was curious to know what the 'White Men' were doing there, the hosts gave a convincing reply, telling him that their American guests were writing a book on Bali, and they had not seen the chief and knew nothing about the cockfight.

The following day in the village was a completely different world for the Geertzes, who were then the 'center of all attention', because they had 'fled like anyone else', and this demonstrated their solidarity with the villagers. They could have asserted their foreign status, showed the police their papers, but they did not do so, and instead chose to do what the people did: 'When in Rome, do as the Romans do.' Geertz writes: 'It was the turning point so far as our relationship to the community was concerned'. Incidents of this type work very well for fieldworkers, instantly helping them to establish rapport with the people.

An important aspect of Berreman's article is the set of characteristics he thinks an ethnographer should possess. He should be sceptical of the information he receives and should verify the facts from a cross-section of his respondents. A universal human characteristic is that people want to share certain facts of their lives and their views about varied matters with others. Once a rapport is established, the ethnographer is gradually flooded with information. Like a sponge, he keeps on absorbing it and in shorthand, keeps on noting down the details, but he has to be discreet about sharing it with others in general. In an attempt to verify certain facts, he speaks to several other respondents but refrains from divulging the source of his information, or its details, for this would be detrimental to the interpersonal relations in the community and also the relations of people with the ethnographer. What an ethnographer has to learn is to 'manage' his impression in the society; therefore, he has to be, following Paul Radin, Berreman says, 'honest, intelligent and humble'. The role with some kind of universality in the field is that of a 'student'. Each ethnographer adopts it—like a student, he has to be 'flexible, adaptive and open-minded'. In fact, one learns about fieldwork through its practice.

The factors conditioning the choice of field area constitute the focus of T.N. Madan's paper, the second in this section, which also shows the impact of research supervisors on young students, especially in the selection of research topics and the facts to be collected and analysed. In his article, Madan looks critically at the place of fieldwork in his career as an anthropologist.

His teacher, D.N. Majumdar, an anthropologist trained at Cambridge, believed that for a professional career in anthropology, one must have conducted intensive fieldwork with a tribal community. Madan decided to work with tribals in Ranchi (now the capital of the state of Jharkhand) and study the aspects of their rehabilitation, a topic that since the 1980s has acquired an important place in Indian anthropology. However, he became anxious with his fieldwork experience, for he thought that it was a 'violation of the privacy of the subject'. He also came to note his 'manifold incapacity for fieldwork among strangers'. This confession is admirable because anthropologists generally give the impression that they can carry out spells of 'successful' fieldwork in any type of society, at any point of time, which in fact may not be true. One's value commitments, the prevailing situation in a society, or restrictions imposed on research by local governments, may not permit one to conduct fieldwork with a particular community or institution.

Madan's solution to this problem lay in studying his own society, the Pandits of the Kashmir valley, but he did not return to his own family and kindred for fieldwork. At this point one is reminded of Srinivas' observation of 1966 that studying one's own society does not imply studying one's own social grouping. By consciously avoiding the study of one's kin group, one can at least be free from the obvious problems of value and subjectivity that are likely to surface. Madan rightly observes that the 'other' is in fact constituted by the anthropological method itself. One can transform the 'familiar' into the 'unfamiliar' and conduct its study in the same manner as one studies the so-called 'other culture'. By showing that one's own society can be successfully studied, Madan rejects the notion of defining anthropology as the study of the 'other cultures'. What is more important is the 'frame of mind' one adopts with respect to the social group under study. Madan's article also shows that the other disciplines of humanities (particularly, social history and literature) can be 'richer sources of inspiration' in anthropological and sociological works.

Madan also describes the respective influences of his teachers and supervisors on his research topic. This point is further developed in James Laidlaw's article, which discusses the role of informal collaborations with local respondents in fieldwork. It is one of the areas in the descriptions of fieldwork about which not many anthropologists have written.[1] Laidlaw chose to work on Jainism and Jain communities, not only because they had remained largely ignored, but also because of his close contacts with his teacher, Caroline Humphrey, and her doctoral student, Josephine Reynall, both of whom had earlier carried out their fieldwork with Jains in Rajasthan.

In his article, Laidlaw compares the nature of fieldwork in tribal and peasant villages with that in urban contexts, because he did his fieldwork with Jains in the city of Jaipur. In Indian villages, as several other observers have also noted, social life is conducted with a great deal of informality. Male respondents are easily available in public places and once minimal rapport has been struck, the ethnographer can unhesitatingly move about in their houses, ask questions, and live there as one of them. By contrast, urban neighbourhoods, however homogeneous, are characterized by a degree of anonymity and their networks are different from those in villages. The nature of one's fieldwork is considerably dependent upon the social milieu in which one works.

Villagers may not really be interested in what the anthropologist does amongst them. They may not, especially those in tribal villages, have any conception of research and pieces of writing based on fieldwork, and therefore, press the anthropologist much for the reason of his presence amidst them. They may share their knowledge with him out of courtesy, but as their rapport with him is built up, they find in him a potential sympathizer and in whom they can confide their inner feelings without ever being confronted with embarrassment. In addition to these roles that the anthropologist may perform in any society that he takes up for study, respondents in urban contexts are generally aware of the anthropological (or survey) work.[2] As a result, many of them become so involved with the work of the ethnographer that they start seeking information of their respective interests about their own community. Giving an account of his respondents, Laidlaw writes that although they worked 'jointly' with him, it did not imply that what resulted was his 'research project'. These respondents were engaged in their own 'intellectual exercise', independently of what the anthropologist was doing. Laidlaw provided the context in which his respondents formulated their 'research designs' and conducted their own enquiries.

Following Laidlaw's article is Meenakshi Thapan's paper on fieldwork in a school in Bangalore which experimented with J. Krishnamurti's ideology. At one time, Thapan had been a teacher at the school and this perhaps was one of the reasons for conducting an ethnographic study there. But it did not imply that fieldwork in any case was an easy venture for her. Like other sociologists who had conducted their fieldwork in modern society and its institutions, Thapan had to obtain permission to do fieldwork in the school from its authorities (the 'gatekeepers'), who decided about and controlled the flow of information, in the sense of what was to be shared and what concealed.[3] The management of the school had a critical look at the questionnaire that Thapan had prepared and deleted two questions from it. This may be contrasted to fieldwork in 'pre-literate' tribal and peasant societies, where there may not be 'gatekeepers' guarding information and if there are, they do not exercise the kind of surveillance on the fieldworker as is exercised in modern institutions.[4] Following Thapan, a distinction may be made between 'free knowledge' (one that is freely, easily accessible) and 'secret knowledge' (one that is confined to the management and they will try to guard it firmly). Fieldworkers endeavour to gather, as much as is possible in a stipulated time, both these types of knowledge.

Once, Thapan tells us, the ethnographer has gathered the information, the balance of power shifts from the respondents to the fieldworker, who may choose to use this knowledge in any desired manner. However, in reality, the fieldworker is caught on the horns of a dilemma. He may not reveal information that might harm the people in the long run. Or, he may receive a piece of information from a respondent with the explicit instruction of not using it ever in his writings. Thapan reads the diary of a teacher of the school that contains sensitive information, but decides not to use it in her work on the plea of the teacher. The respondents also request Thapan 'not to quote them', or tell her that the information they are giving her is 'off the records'. Therefore, the fieldworker does not have the kind of power that is generally assumed to exist because he will not use the information for any purpose that might harm the integrity, identity, and image of the people. If a fieldworker 'harms' the people in any way, he also jeopardizes the chances of future fieldworkers in that community. Besides the discussion of power in fieldwork, Thapan's piece is especially important for the use of techniques in fieldwork and her improvisations therein.

The final piece in this section is on visual anthropology. Although it has yet not emerged as an organized discipline in India, some scholars are devoting their attention to the analysis of calendar art, photographs, and films in the Indian context.[5] This, however, does not imply that there has not been a strong tradition of taking photographs in the field, using them in books and putting them up in exhibitions, and also of making films.[6] One of the main equipments that fieldworkers are expected to carry with them to the field, besides the tape recorder, is the camera. On some occasions, fieldworkers also seek the services of professional photographers in the field. For instance, Sunil Janah, the photographer, was Verrier Elwin's companion on many journeys through Bastar and Orissa (Guha 1999: 332–33; Janah 2003). Anthropology departments generally have a photographic laboratory and the position of a professional photographer and artist, who is expected to accompany field parties, take photographs, and, if need be, sketch material cultural equipments. Fieldworkers are also trained in both these activities—they should learn to sketch and the use of a camera, and the developing and printing of films. The courses on archaeology and material culture, which are viewed as essential to the curriculum of anthropology, provide enough training to students to learn to draw to size various material things which people use. However, the focus in visual anthropology is on film-making. Anthropological film-makers say that in films the actors speak for themselves, but this does not imply that tape recorders and cameras can replace anthropology. The visual material needs to be analysed with anthropological perspectives. One would agree here with Goody (1995: 150): 'Anthropology...is analytic or it is nothing.'

The article included here on visual materials is by Christopher Pinney, an English anthropologist, the author of *Camera Indicus: The Social Life of Indian Photographs* (1997). Pinney informs us that photography was first used in India in 1840, a few years after its discovery had been announced in Europe. Since then, there has been a lot of development of photography in India. In terms of technology, it had significant borrowings from Europe but the cultural milieu in which it was produced conditioned it greatly. The kind of photographs people preferred, the occasions on which they wished to be photographed, the types of dress they wore before the camera, the imagery they worked out in these photographs, were all culturally affected. Therefore, photographs and films are not just 'methodological supports to data collection'. Rather, Pinney observes, they are 'central aspects of South Asian cultural practice deserving of ethnographic study in their own right'. Some photographers—and Pinney cites their names—have left 'detailed bodies of work' that 'yield dense information of great ethno-historical value'. Pinney shows how photographs and films help us in understanding culture and its 'fragments'.

Notes

1. Carstairs (1983) gives an account of some of his informants but not on how they navigated his fieldwork.

2. They may also react by telling the fieldworker that they have chosen a wrong subject for study. See Humphrey and Laidlaw (1994: vii).

3. Taylor and Bogdan (1984) proposed the term 'gatekeepers'.

4. In a fieldwork, my colleague, I.S. Marwah, and I carried out with our students in 1985 in an Angami Naga village in Kohima (Nagaland), we were required to obtain formal permission from the village chairman before we started interacting with the people.

For this purpose, we gave in writing (in English) the aim of our visit to his village. He readily granted us permission. After that, he never bothered to ask us about the sort of information we were collecting. In fact, he greatly cooperated with us in data collection. Even sensitive questions did not make him raise his brows and he and his other colleagues, who occupied political offices in the village, answered our questions with the best of their knowledge.

    5. See *Contributions to Indian Sociology* (n.s.), 36: 1–2 (2002).

    6. See Roy and Jhala (1987: 1–19).

Ethnography: Method and Product

GERALD D. BERREMAN

Ethnography

Every science depends upon observed phenomena for its analytical and interpretative statements. In some cases the observation is aided by instruments such as microscopes, cloud-chambers, or seismographs, just as analysis may be facilitated by symbolic systems such as mathematics, and by data handling devices such as computers. These are simply aids to human observation and analysis—extensions of the person who uses them. No nonhuman device can make observations or analyses except by human design, manipulation, and interpretation.

Anthropology, in common with other social sciences, depends for its data upon observations of human behaviour, including verbal behaviour. The process of making such observations has been called 'ethnography'. 'An ethnography' is a written report summarizing the behaviours, and the beliefs, understandings, attitudes, and values they imply, of a group of interacting people. Thus, an ethnography is a description of the way of life, or culture, of a society. Everyone who does empirical research in cultural or social anthropology engages in ethnography as a process, though by no means does everyone report his research in the form of an ethnography. An ethnography is generally expected to give an overall view of the culture of the people about whom it is written, within the limits inherent in ethnographic research and in prose exposition. As such, it attempts to cover all aspects of the culture of a given society. In practice, it covers those aspects which the ethnographer considers relevant to an understanding of the main features of the culture he studied.

The manner and sequence of written presentation differ, of course, according to the outlook and style of the author and according to the nature of the culture being described. As we shall see, in recent years there has been increasing emphasis on organizing ethnographic descriptions along lines which represent the organization of the world as seen by the people who live the culture, rather than simply according to the preconceived notions and categories of the ethnographer. So far, however, there have not been whole ethnographies written in this fashion, chiefly because in the year or two available to most ethnographic researchers, it is not possible to accumulate the data necessary for acquiring a complete subjective view of a culture; and even if such data were collected, recording them would be a formidably massive undertaking. Therefore, to the present, most ethnographies comprise the scientist's description of a way of life he has observed in detail, described as it seems to him to be organized and to function. He combines indigenous concepts with his own analytical concepts in organizing his data.

Typically, the ethnographic account includes an introductory section on the geographical and historical setting of the people to be studied, their racial, linguistic, and cultural affinities. Following that are relatively detailed chapters on their means of making a living (often called economics), their political and legal organization, their religion, their social organization, (frequently the most detailed section of all, covering family and other kin-based groups, rules and terminology regarding kinship, social stratification, and various kinds of groups based on criteria other than kinship). There may perhaps be sections on such topics as how they rear their children, their values, 'expressive behaviour' such as folklore, art, and music, or special topics relevant to the society in question, followed by a closing section on the changes the people are undergoing as contacts with other groups or with urban centres and modern technology increase. Most often the account is written in the 'ethnographic present' which means that the present tense is used after the author has identified the time period for which the account is accurate. This is especially important to bear in mind for ethnographies describing former eras or 'memory cultures'. Often the accounts are written as though the culture being described were static—unchanging. Actually, of course, all cultures are dynamic and ever changing. The ethnographic account is like one frame of a motion picture, arbitrarily selected for display as a 'still', for continual change is impossible to convey in the stillness of the printed page.

Other sequences of presentation and of organization besides that described above have also been effectively used. For example, M.E. Opler approached Apache ethnography by focusing on the sequence of life events through which an individual typically passes, revealing the culture by unfolding a generalized Apache lifeway (Opler 1941), while Homer Barnett depicted the culture of the Palauans of Micronesia through the eyes of the people—by telling what it is to be a Palauan (Barnett 1960).

Whatever the method of presentation and analysis, the aim of ethnography is to report the culture studied in sufficient depth and breadth to enable one who has not experienced it to understand it. Understanding may be assumed to have been achieved if the reader learns how participants in the culture see themselves, others, and their environment, and how they deal with each. Ideally, this requires that the ethnographer convey information sufficient in quantity, variety, and quality, and so organized and analysed that it would enable the reader to understand events of the culture if he were to experience them, to anticipate the reactions of members of the society to the events they experience, and, ultimately, to behave appropriately in that society in a manner similar to that of a person who has lived the culture. In this respect, the ethnography is analogous to a linguist's description of a language. It may not enable the reader to speak the language easily, but it enables him to understand how it works. An ethnography comprises, essentially, a statement of a set of rules which describe how people act in their culture. Given time, the reader of an adequate ethnographic (or linguistic) description can understand what is done (or said), can act (or speak) correctly and meaningfully in the culture (or language), can anticipate the responses he will evoke in others, and can respond to them in ways they deem appropriate.

Ethnographic research often goes unreported in the form of an overall ethnography simply because the author preferred not to collect data on such a wide range of topics or was unable to do so, or because although he had such data, he preferred to present them in less inclusive form focussed on a particular and restricted problem or series of problems.

It is sometimes assumed that the broadly descriptive ethnographic report is not theoretical—that it represents the results of theoryless fact-collecting—and that while it may interest the reader who has a taste for esoterica, it is unlikely to lead to advances in the science of man. A reply to this position is that there can be no pure observation and no straight description without underlying assumptions—without a theory or theories—which determine what will be observed and what will be recorded. There is no day in the life of any people, family, or individual which could be observed or recorded in all its detail. The events and circumstances are simply too manifold.

The point here is that all observation is selective, all recording of observation is selective again, and the published account is selective of the recorded observations, since researchers rarely if ever publish all the records of their field research. Thus, between the event and the report there are at least three stages of selectivity on the part of the researcher. The underlying assumptions by which he selects what he will observe from the mass of stimuli with which he is confronted in his research, what he will record from the innumerable observations he has made, and what he will report from the multitudinous records he has kept, comprise his theory or theories. If he regards it as more important to record a ceremony than a bull session, a song than an epithet, how and where people eat rather than how and where they defecate, the rules by which they marry rather than the infractions of these rules, the circumstances in which they take grievances to court than the circumstances in which they become embarrassed, what they do when someone dies than when someone belches (or vice versa), it is because he has a set of understandings or assumptions about the nature of human society, how it works, and what is important in it. A theory is nothing more than a coherent set of assumptions.

There are wide differences, of course, in how aware individuals are of the theories upon which they base their research and in how explicit they are in conveying them to the readers of their reports. It is because they often do not realize or make explicit their assumptions that many authors of ethnographies are accused of being theoryless fact-collectors. Often the result of being theoretically unaware or inexplicit is that the account is incomplete, inconsistent, internally contradictory, or illogical. This does not mean that the researcher had no theories; merely that he was theoretically unsophisticated. If so, he is certainly as culpable as the oft-maligned theorists who do not relate their elaborately stated assumptions to empirically derived facts.

It is clear, therefore, that theory is inherent in ethnography and that good theory is essential to good ethnography. As theory becomes more explicit, observation becomes more perceptive, and as observation becomes more perceptive, theoretical formulation becomes more explicit. To evaluate a theory, one must know the observed facts which support it; to evaluate reported facts, one must know the assumptions of the observer. If these elements are made explicit in any particular study, it is even possible for either facts or theory to remain useful if one of the other is discredited. Facts may outlive the theory which led to their being recorded; a theory may prove to be valid even though the presumed facts on which it is based are discovered to be in error. But this can occur only if the theory and facts are known so that their limitations or defects can be assessed.

Ethnographers and their Craft

Ethnographic research differs from research in the nonsocial sciences in that it is above all a human undertaking. The ethnographer studies human beings from the point of view of a fellow human being. He is of the same order as the phenomenon he studies. Every scientist faces the problems of minimizing irrelevant external influences on the subject matter he studies and on his perception of that subject matter. Many also face the problem that the devices by which they study a phenomenon in some degree affect that phenomenon. But the social analyst faces the unique and acute problem that he is part of his own subject matter—of any social situation he attempts to study. His very presence alters the situation he studies, and alters it in ways and to an extent which cannot be fully anticipated, compensated for, or even known.

The method of study adopted by most ethnographers is loosely termed 'participant observation'. This refers to the practice of living among the people one studies, coming to know them, their language, and their lifeways through intense and nearly continuous interaction with them in their daily lives. This means that the ethnographer converses with people he studies, works with them, attends their social and ritual functions, visits their homes, invites them to his home—that he is present with them in as many situations as possible, learning to know them in as many settings and moods as he can. Sometimes he interviews for specific kinds of data; always he is alert to whatever information may come his way, ready to follow up and understand any event or fact which is unanticipated or seemingly inexplicable. The methods by which he derives his data are often subtle and difficult to define. He may have learned some of them by reading accounts of how research is or should be done or by talking with and being taught by experienced ethnographers. Often he has little advance preparation for the methodological and technical problems which will confront him in his field research. This is partly because of the subtlety of the ethnographic research process as it is usually carried out and partly because, until very recently, it was widely assumed that the process need not, and perhaps could not, be taught, that it was an ability or knack which came naturally or not at all. Recently, as we shall see, this view has been undergoing revision. Concerted efforts are now being made to explicate methods of research with the aim of communicating them so they can be taught, and so that any particular study can be put to the test of replication.

To describe the attributes of good ethnographers, one might refer to those factors which Gordon Allport (1937: 213ff) has identified as

characteristic of the mature personality, for maturity is essential to effective adult social interaction in any context. Of crucial importance is a sense
of perspective: the ability to distinguish the important from the unimportant, the inevitable from the results of choice, the part from the whole, the
self from society. This entails an ability to see oneself and one's society
with insight and a sense of objectivity or detachment. An aspect of this, I
think, is a kind of generic scepticism. A sense of perspective, objectivity,
and scepticism are associated closely with a genuine sense of humour. To
take oneself too seriously is unlikely to allow one to go through the trying
physical, psychological, and social circumstances which field research in
an alien culture entails. To take one's subjects too seriously is likely to
distort one's perspective on what they are doing and is apt to lead one to
become too caught up in the events of their lives to view them as subjects
of inquiry.

A crucial consequence of perspective and a crucial concomitant of
humour is empathy—the ability to put one's self in the place of others, to
experience the world as they experience it. Empathy is insurance against
narrow complacency, ethnocentrism, and sterile scientism. Only through
empathetic ability can the scientist hope to understand the phenomenal
world of the people he studies, to comprehend their motives, their hopes,
joys, and fears, and their reactions to himself.

In addition, an ethnographer must be flexible, adaptable, and open-
minded. In his work he will have to adjust to a variety of physical conditions and to a variety of people making diverse demands upon him. He will
have to adjust his research to the exigencies of the situation, which will
often be largely unanticipated. In the vast majority of cases he will have to
alter more or less drastically his research plan to accommodate to field
conditions and opportunities. He will also have to accommodate the social
conditions, personalities, and even the idiosyncrasies of his informants.

In personal relations the ethnographer will succeed best if he is straightforward, modest, tolerant, and adaptable. He must be liked and trusted as
an individual to win the trust and confidence of those with whom he works.
There are no shortcuts on this score.

All social interaction is reciprocal. The ethnographer must be prepared
to give as well as take in his relationships with those among whom he works.
He cannot expect them to give him their time and trust unless he is willing
to give of himself. Often material benefits are important. He may find it
necessary, appropriate, or advantageous to reimburse his informants for
their time in money or goods. Frequently, gifts will be acceptable and
appreciated where formal payment will not. Services of various sorts, such

as simple medical aid, instruction in English or in technical fields, and advice and help in dealing with official agencies, are often highly valued ways in which the ethnographer can reciprocate. Willingness to participate in an exchange of information—to tell about his own experiences and way of life—may greatly enhance his informants' willingness to provide information on themselves, for the situation is then defined as exchange rather than as prying. People are likely to be most appreciative of the simple fact that the ethnographer provides entertaining diversion by talking with them, demonstrating his possessions, showing his magazines, distributing photographs.

Closely related to this is a requisite ability to listen. The ethnographer must be an interested, sympathetic, and patient listener if he is to learn. If he is not willing to listen to his informants' opinions and information on subjects which he deems irrelevant to his research he will find it difficult to get them to talk on subjects in which he *is* interested. He will, of course, guide conversations in the direction of his research interests, but to win rapport he must not limit himself to such topics. To do so is indicative of lack of genuine involvement with the informants, or is likely to be so interpreted.

Energy, determination, and persistence are equally necessary to successful ethnography. One cannot learn about a culture unless one interacts with those who live it. Therefore, the ethnographer has to expose himself continually to social situations and project himself into them. He must keep talking to people, participating with them in their daily lives, and observing them. Even when he has no specific information in mind which he wishes to collect he must be on hand, talking, participating, and observing, for only by so doing can he hope to get new unanticipated, and sometimes crucial information. He never knows when or how such information will become available, but it will not unless he is there to obtain it. This may be exhausting psychically and physically, but it is the only way to learn what the ethnographer wants to know. In addition to awaiting the unpredictable information or insight, the fieldworker may spend months passively awaiting or engineering an opportunity to ask a crucial question or observe an important event. Earning the necessary confidence or acquiring the invitation may take great effort and cause considerable anxiety lest the effort be to no avail. Yet this is an important part of the ethnographic process. To ask too soon or in an inappropriate context may jeopardize further research.

An ethnographer must be inordinately curious about the human condition in its various manifestations and at the same time be sympathetic and empathic. Without these qualities, he would be unlikely to sustain himself over the long, often trying and lonely period of research.

Curiousity is not enough, obviously. To make anything of what one's curiosity leads one to learn, there must be a sense of the problematic—a fundamental creativity which leads the observer to seek and find relationships among his observed data, to see relationships between his observed data and other facts and ideas with which he is familiar, to see their relevance, and to weigh their importance. This is roughly what C. Wright Mills meant by the 'sociological imagination', which 'enables its possessor to understand the larger historical scene in terms of its meaning for the inner life and the external career of a variety of individuals' (Mills 1959: 5). He who possesses this imagination will see in specific behaviour and events indicators of structures, processes, and functions in the society at large, operative in significant historical context. It is 'the capacity to range from the most impersonal and remote transformations to the most intimate features of the human self—and to see the relations between the two (Mills 1959: 7). If one lacks this creative and synthesizing ability, one will be immobilized by the field experience simply because of the overwhelming number, immediacy, and variety of potential observations which confront one. One will either be unable to rise above the welter of facts to see their significance and relationships, or one will be unable to descend from one's theories and assumptions to relate them to events in the empirical world.

Finally, I think successful ethnography depends upon a thorough understanding of the nature of social structure and social interaction on the theoretical and practical planes, both in the culture being studied and in the most general human sense. The ethnographer needs an adequate theory of society. This is both the goal and the pre-requisite for good ethnography.

Ethnographic Research

Choice of a region and locality in which to work, like the ethnographer's theoretical orientation and his choice of research problem, is the product of a complex of factors which need not concern us here. Suffice it to say that availability of the prerequisite training in language and area studies and of financial assistance for field research are important limiting factors. Political considerations are also important. Some nations do not admit American scholars to study their people and the American government does not allow its scholars to study the people in some nations. Whole regions of the world are therefore closed to the ethnographer, and the number and extent of such areas seem to be increasing. Once in a country, the choice of locale may be limited by considerations of internal politics, by the availability of transportation, by health facilities, by housing, and many other conditions, as well as by the requirements of the research itself. The specific site for intensive study is often selected on the basis of such a variety of explicit and implicit factors that the researcher himself cannot fully explain his choice.

Time for research is never unlimited. Typically, the hopeful ethnographer spends a year—sometimes two—living with the people whose way of life he intends to learn. The duration of his or her stay is determined by many factors. The generosity of the foundation which supports the research must be considered. The academic calendar makes a year a convenient, often a maximum, period for research. Health and morale seem often to be capable of being sustained for a year under circumstances which would have telling effect over a longer period, and it is generally assumed to be possible to witness most things that happen in a society in the period of a year. There is also the assumption that it takes about a year to attain sufficient facility in the language, sufficient rapport with the people, sufficient familiarity with the culture, and sufficient notebooks full of information, to write a creditable account of the way of life of the people one has studied.

Because of limitations of time, the ethnographer must begin his research soon after his arrival in the field. To search for the ideal location might lead to endless delay. Therefore, after visiting a number of potential sites, the researcher usually settles on one which seems promising, and hopes for the best. If, of several comparable sites, one strikes him as intrinsically more interesting or attractive than the others, it is without doubt the one most often chosen and certainly is the one which should be chosen. Field research is sufficiently difficult, frustrating, and at times discouraging, that such subtle characteristics as interest or attractiveness can become important in sustaining the ethnographer's morale, attention, and energies. If, in addition to fulfilling his research requirements, the people he studies fascinate him, the ethnographer will find his work much easier and more rewarding.

At best the choice is an uncertain one. McKim Marriott (1957: 423) mentions that he was politely thrown out of three villages in which he attempted to work in India before he was allowed to settle in the one upon which he subsequently published his research results. Official permission, both from such national and regional agencies as the police and district offices and from the local authorities such as village headmen and elders, is important, but it may not be enough. Two anthropologists who had obtained permission from the chief of a village of Mexican Kickapoo Indians were formally ejected after only two weeks of work (Ritzenthaler and Peterson 1956: 9). This did not prevent them from publishing an account of their findings, but it certainly attenuated those findings.

Having chosen a place to work, the ethnographer is faced with two crucial and simultaneous problems: to account for himself to those among whom he plans to live; and to set himself up in housekeeping. The latter often seems to be the more pressing and the difficulties therein are not infrequently great, but the former is just important and may ultimately prove to be the more difficult. Local conditions and attitudes are vital to the success of both.

In some areas the ethnographer will have to live in a tent, build his own dwelling, or hire someone to build it for him. In others he will be able to stay in a guest house, borrow or rent an unused dwelling or portion thereof, or board in the home of a local resident. No general rule as to which is preferable can be adduced, except that the ethnographer should be prepared to do that which seems most likely to meet with the approval of the resident, consistent with his research aims.

Housekeeping can be a serious and time-consuming problem. It may take so much time as to preclude intensive research, in which case a housekeeper has to be sought. On the other hand, at least during the initial period when the ethnographer is seeking to establish understanding, trust, and friendship, housekeeping and associated endeavours may give him an invaluable opportunity to engage in understandable activity and to meet people in a natural way. It may be an excellent way to become a participant in local society.

Food itself can be an acute problem. In some areas there may be so little food available locally that the ethnographer will have to take his own. In others the local food may be insufficiently nutritious to maintain his health, or may be sufficiently unpalatable to him that, again, food must be imported. In many parts of the world considerable caution must be exercised in the preparation of food and drink to avoid acquiring the internal parasites and other ailments which, at best, may delay the research.

The researcher's morale is a palpable factor in all ethnographic research, and is vital to the success of the endeavour. Often the causes are obvious. Debilitating or dangerous illness or the threat thereof to oneself or one's dependants, hostile individuals or groups including officials as well as members of the society being studied, lack of easy-going, friendly, and understanding companionship, lack of respite from continual and stressful interaction in an unfamiliar context, inability to escape from the scrutiny of curious observers—these are factors which are not uncommon and cannot fail to have an effect on the ethnographer. He is, after all, only human. The effect may be to cause the ethnographer to fail in his work; more commonly, it is to restrict the scope or depth of his findings. Not infrequently such facts cause the ethnographer to have recourse to research methods other than participant observation. Stories of ethnographers who did their work by summoning informants to the resort hotel of the region, or by hiring assistants to report data back to the hotel, are rife, if perhaps most often apocryphal.

More frequently discussed in the literature, and no less difficult and important, is the problem of establishing one's role before the people with whom one wishes to work, and to establish good relations with them, once one has established one's physical presence among them. In some regions the role of an anthropologist is only too well known. The Zuni household of the American Southwest has been described as typically comprising a mother, a father, three children, and an anthropologist. The Nayar of the south-west coast of India, famous for their matrilineal kin groups, have been studied sufficiently that a Nayar youth is reported to have told an ethnographer recently, 'Please go away and do not bother us; we have no customs'. Occasionally an ethnographer in a well-studied society has been referred by his informants to the standard published ethnography on their way of life. The people of some nations or regions identify the anthropologist with the study of 'primitives' and therefore resent his presence. But more frequently, the role of the anthropologist is unknown—and therefore it is often suspect.

Few individuals are capable of such complete participation in an alien culture as to be able to act as if they were members of it. Participant observation does not imply or require that the anthropologist become one of those he studies. In the literal sense, this would be impossible in most cases, especially in the relatively short time available to most ethnographers. But circumstances vary widely; the relative proportions of participation and observation vary widely from one study to another. Some people urge the inquisitive outsider to emulate and interact with them in every possible way; others prohibit him from doing so. In the brief but insightful introduction to his account of research in the Sudan, the British ethnographer E.E. Evans-Pritchard compared two groups with whom he had worked: 'Azande would not allow me to live as one of themselves; Nuer would not allow me to live otherwise. Among Azande I was compelled to live outside the community; among Nuer I was compelled to be a member of it' (Evans-

Pritchard 1940: 15). Most peoples fall somewhere between these extremes. To become a member of the group one studied would doubtless inhibit the opportunity and perhaps the inclination to do research. There are cases on record of anthropologists who have become so closely identified with the people they studied that they have refused to divulge what they have learned, or even to come home.

Therefore, while some ethnographers pride themselves on having adopted the way of life of those they studied and having been accepted into their society, successful research is most often the result of being viewed and accepted as a trustworthy, interested, and sympathetic outsider. This has advantages in that an outsider can be naïve. He can ask blunt, embarrassing, trivial, or simple-minded questions, he can do or say the wrong thing, he can repeat his queries and pursue his interests ad nauseum, he can consort with people of every status and reputation. Such behaviour would not be tolerated in an insider, yet it may be crucial to the research. The outsider derives the benefit of an immunity borne of difference and ignorance.

A role which is known or at least understandable in many societies, and one which the ethnographer can legitimately claim, is that of the student. This role, broadly defined, is probably the most widely successful one for the ethnographic research. It is simply a special instance of the role of the interested person who wants to learn. It is not always easy to come by. People will suspect that other motives underlie those the ethnographer claims. Missionaries and government officials have often preceded the ethnographer with apparently similar interests or activities but with intentions which prove threatening to those who receive them. To avoid being identified as such, the ethnographer can only identify himself straightforwardly and behave in ways consistent with that claim and inconsistent with the suspected roles.

Having established his role, the ethnographer has to find people with whom to talk. They may be suspicious or hostile. They may consider even the most discreet inquiries to be not worthwhile, impertinent, or even threatening. Whole segments of potential informants may be unavailable to the ethnographer because of age, sex, social status, factional alignments, and so on. People may be too busy or too tired to talk at length after a hard day's work. In an absolute sense, these constitute obstacles to obtaining data. They also influence the kind of research that is possible, and the reliability and validity of the research results, by influencing or limiting the choice of informants.

There is a wide range in the representativeness of the sample of informants upon whose word published ethnographies have been based. Raymond

Firth derived information from all of the 1,300 living Tikopia (Firth 1956: 49). Cornelius Osgood, by contrast, worked some 500 hours with a single Inglalik Indian informant (Osgood 1940: 50–55). Circumstances may make a choice impossible, as when one is working with a culture which exists only in the memory of one or a few informants. Even in societies with large populations whose ongoing culture is the ethnographer's interest, it is likely that a few individuals will become the ethnographer's best friends and confidants because of their interests, capabilities, free time, alienation from their own society, hope for rewards from the outsider, or their position in the social structure (for instance, the 'old man' who is expected to talk, reminisce, and speculate at length). These people may become sources of extensive information, and often of information that could not be obtained from more casual and diffuse contacts.

The methodological question arising here is one of representativeness, reliability, and bias. Can one individual give reliable information on all phases of his culture? Can a man adequately observe and report women's culture, especially in a society such as that of India where the sexes are systematically segregated in many of their activities? One of the serious problems in ethnography is its heavy androcentric (male-centred) bias, since many ethnographers and informants are men. This may be unavoidable, but it should be recognized as a fact and as a problem. Can one occupational group, social stratum, or ethnic category suffice to give information on a multigroup society? Can a blacksmith know enough about the farmer's or priest's life to report it adequately? These and similar questions have led most ethnographers to conclude that a fairly representative selection of informants from different groups and strata within a society should be used wherever possible so as to minimize bias and error, and to bring out divergent viewpoints extant in the society, so they can be further investigated. A complete picture of the culture can be derived only by considering and collating the full range of views and experiences which comprise it.

Getting people to talk, once their confidence is won, is not as difficult as one might anticipate. It seems to be a universal human trait to like to talk about oneself to interested people one trusts—to tell one's accomplishments, misfortunes, and suspicions, to display one's knowledge, and to propound one's theories. It is almost as universal not to like to listen to the same kind of conversation by others, at least not by others whom one unavoidably hears often on the same topics. These traits are a boon to the ethnographer, especially if he is unafflicted with the second, or can suppress it in the research situation. If he has the trust of those with whom he works—

largely as a result of not repeating what he is told in confidence and not appearing overly interested in sensitive subjects—he is likely to be deluged with information, opinions, anecdotes, complaints, and gossip from people who have been unable to find an audience or whose audience has long since left them. It is as a sympathetic neutral confidant that the ethnographer receives much of his data.

There are always some things which individuals or groups consider private or secret and which are therefore not communicated to the ethnographer—at least not intentionally. By utilizing a variety of informants, and by being discreet, it is possible to learn much about even those aspects of a people's life about which they are sensitive (See Berreman 1962).

The Ethnographic Experience

In order to illustrate the nature of the ethnographic experience and factors relevant to that experience as it affects research results, I will briefly describe my own research in a tightly knit, socially closed, and highly stratified community.

This ethnographic research took place in and around Sirkanda, a peasant village of the lower Himalayas of north India. Its residents, like those of the entire lower Himalayan area from Kashmir through Nepal, are known as Paharis ('of the mountains'). The village is small, containing some 384 individuals during the year of my residence there in 1957–1958, and is relatively isolated, situated as it is in rugged hills accessible only on foot, nine miles from the nearest road and bus service.

Strangers in the area are few and readily identifiable by dress and speech. People so identified are avoided or discouraged from remaining long in the vicinity. To escape such a reception, a person must be able to identify himself as a member of a familiar group through kinship ties, caste ties, and/or community affiliation. Since the first two are ascribed characteristics, the only hope an outsider has of achieving acceptance is by establishing residence and, through social interaction, acquiring the status of a community-dweller, a slow process at best.

The reluctance of Sirkanda villagers and their neighbours to accept strangers is attested to by the experience of those outsiders who have dealt with them. In 1957 a new teacher was assigned to the Sirkanda school. He was a Pahari from an area about fifty miles distant. Despite his Pahari background and consequent familiarity with the language and customs of the local people, he complained after four months in the village that his reception had been less than cordial.

Among the forestry officers whose duty it is to make periodic rounds in these hills, the villagers' lack of hospitality is proverbial. The officers claim that here a man has to carry his own food, water, and bedroll because he cannot count on villagers to offer these necessities to him on his travels. Community development and establishment of credit cooperatives, two governmental programmes in the area, have been unsuccessful due largely to their advocates' inability to establish rapport with the people.

The reasons for such reticence are not far to seek. Contacts with outsiders have been limited largely to contacts with policemen and tax collectors—two of the lowest forms of life in the Pahari taxonomy. Such officials are despised and feared not only because they make trouble for the villagers in the line of duty, but because they also extort bribes on the threat of causing further trouble and often seem to take advantage of their official positions to vent their aggressions on these vulnerable people.

The villagers' fears on this score are not groundless. Aside from the unjust exploitation such agents are reputed to employ in their activities there are many illegal or semilegal activities carried on by villagers which could be grounds for punishment and are easily used as grounds for extortion. In Sirkanda, national forest lands and products have been illegally appropriated by the villagers, taxable land has been under-reported, liquor is illicitly brewed and sold, women have been illegally sold, guns have gone unlicensed, adulterated milk is sold to outside merchants, children are often married below the legal age, men have fled the army or escaped from jail, property has been illegally acquired from fleeing Muslims at the time of India's partition. Any of these and similar real and imagined infractions may be objects of a stranger's curiosity and therefore are reasons for discouraging his presence in the village.

Paharis are thought by people of the plains to be ritually, spiritually, and morally inferior. They are suspected of witchcraft and evil magic. In addition, they are considered naïve bumpkins—the hillbilly stereotype of other cultures is shared by Indians. Paharis try to avoid interactions with those who hold these stereotypes.

The only way to feel sure that such dangers do not inhere in a person is to know who he is, and to know this he must fit somewhere into the known social system. Only then is he subject to effective local controls so that he transgresses, or betrays a trust, he can be brought to account. The person who is beyond control is beyond trust, and is best hurried on his way. This is therefore a relatively closed society. Interaction with strangers is kept to a minimum; the information furnished to them is scanty and stereotyped. Access to such a society is difficult for an outsider.

Within this closed society there is rigid stratification into a number of hereditary, ranked, endogamous groups—castes—comprising two large divisions: the high or twice-born castes, and the low or 'untouchable' castes. The high castes, Rajputs and Brahmins, are landowning agriculturists who are dominant in numbers, comprising 90 per cent of the population. They are dominant in political power, for both traditional and new official means of control are in their hands. They dominate in ritual status as twice-born, ritually clean castes, while all other castes are 'untouchable'. In most villages, as in Sirkanda, Rajputs outnumber Brahmins and so are locally dominant, but the ritual and social distance between them is not great and the economic difference is usually nil.

The low castes, whose members are artisans, are disadvantaged in each respect that the high castes are advantaged. Ideally, their relationship to the high castes is one of respect, deference, and obedience. In return high-caste members are supposed to be paternalistic. In practice there is a good deal of tension in the relationship, and it is held stable largely by considerations of relative power.

In addition there are non-hierarchical cleavages within both the high and the low castes, cleavages based upon kinship ties (lineage and clan lines being paramount), and informal cliques and factions. As a result, the community is divided within itself. While there is consensus on some things there is disagreement on others. Acceptance by one element of the community does not imply acceptance by the whole community, and frequently, in fact, precludes it.

It was into this community that my interpreter-assistant and I walked, unannounced, one rainy day in September 1957, hoping to engage in ethnographic research. On our initial visit we asked only to camp there while we visited a number of surrounding villages. We were introduced by a note from a non-Pahari wholesaler of the nearest market town who had long bought the surplus agricultural produce of villagers and had, as it turned out, through sharp practices of an obscure nature, acquired land in the village. He asked that the villagers treat the strangers as 'our people' and extend all hospitality to them. As might have been expected, our benefactor was not beloved in the village and it was more in spite of his intercession than on account of it that we ultimately managed to do a year's research in the village.

The note was addressed to a high-caste man who proved to be one of the most suspicious people of the village. He was the head of a household recently victorious in a nine-year court battle over land brought against it by virtually the entire village, the leader of a much-resented but powerful minority faction. The he gave us an unenthusiastic reception was a blow to our morale but probably a boon to our chances of being tolerated in the village.

The interpreter-assistant who accompanied me was a young Brahmin of plains origin who had previously worked in a similar capacity for a large research project carried out in the plains village of Kalapur. I shall hereafter refer to him as Sharma.

For the first three months of our stay in the village, most of our time was spent keeping house and attempting to establish rapport, both of which were carried out under trying circumstances.

According to their later reports to us, villagers at first assumed that we were missionaries, a species which had not previously invaded this locality but which was well known. When we failed to meddle in religious matters or to show surprise at local rituals, this suspicion gradually faded. We had anticipated this interpretation of our motives and so were careful not to show undue interest in religion as a topic of conversation. We purposely used Hindu rather than areligious forms of greeting in our initial contacts to avoid being identified as missionaries. As a topic for polite and, we hoped, neutral conversation, we chose agriculture. It seemed timely too, as the fall harvest season began not long after our arrival in the village. Partly as a result of this choice of conversational fare, suspicion arose that we were government agents sent to reassess the land for taxation, based on the greater-than-previously-reported productivity of the land. Alternatively, we were suspected of being investigators seeking to find the extent of land use in unauthorized areas following the nationalization of the surrounding uncultivated lands. My physical appearance was little comfort to villagers harbouring these suspicions. One man commented: 'Anyone can look like a foreigner if he wears the right clothes'. Gradually these fears too disappeared, but others arose.

One person suggested that our genealogical inquiries might be preliminary to a military draft of the young men. The most steadfast opponent of our presence hinted darkly at the machinations of foreign spies—a vaguely understood but actively feared type of villain. Nearly four months passed before overt suspicion of this sort was substantially dissipated, although, of course, some people had been convinced of the innocence of our motives relatively early and others remained suspicious throughout our stay.

One incident nearly four months after our first visit to the village proved to be a turning point in quelling overt opposition to our activities in the village. We were talking one afternoon to the local Brahmin priest. He had proved to be a reluctant informant, apparently because of his fear of alienating powerful and suspicious Rajput farmers whose caste-fellows outnumbered his own by more than thirty to one in the villager (his was the only Brahmin household, as compared to thirty-seven Rajput households in Sirkanda) and in whose good graces it was necessary for him to remain for many reasons. However, he was basically friendly. Encouraged by our increasing rapport in the village at large, by his own feelings of affinity with the Brahmin interpreter, Sharma, and by the privacy of his secluded threshing platform as a talking place, he had volunteered to discuss his family tree with us. Midway in our discussion, one of the most influential and hostile of the Rajputs came upon us—probably intentionally—and sat down with us. The Brahmin immediately became self-conscious and uncommunicative, but it was too late to conceal the topic of our conversation. The Rajput soon interrupted, asking why the Brahmin was telling us these things and inquiring in a challenging way what possible use the information could be to an American scholar. He implied, with heavy irony, that we had ulterior motives. The interview was obviously ended and by this time a small crowd of onlookers had gathered. Since a satisfactory answer was evidently demanded and since most members of the audience were not among the people I knew best, I took the opportunity to answer fully.

I explained that prior to 1947, India had been a subject nation of little interest to the rest of the world. In the unlikely event that the United States or any other country wanted to negotiate regarding matters Indian its representatives had merely to deal with the British who spoke for India. Indians were of no importance to us, for they were a subject people. They, in turn, had no need to know that America existed, as, indeed, few did. Then in 1947, after a long struggle, India had become independent; a nation of proud people who handled their own affairs and participated in the United Nations and in all spheres of international relations on a par with Britain and the United States. Indians for the first time spoke for themselves. At once it became essential for Indians and Americans to know one another. Consequently India sent hundreds of students to America, among other places, and we sent students such as myself to India. We had worked at learning their language and we also wanted to learn their means of livelihood, social customs, religion, and so on, so that we could deal with them intelligently and justly, just as their students were similarly studying in and about America. Fortunately I had an Indian acquaintance then studying a rural community in Utah, whom I could cite as a case comparable to my own. I pointed out that Indian and American scholars had studied Indian cities, and villages of the plains so that their ways were well known, but that heretofore the five million Paharis—residents of some of the richest, most beautiful, historically and religiously most significant parts of India—had been overlooked. I emphasized that Paharis would play an increasing role in the development of India and that if they were to assume the responsibilities and derive the advantages available to them it was essential that they be better known to their countrymen and to the world. My research was billed as an effort in this direction.

I would like to be able to report that on the basis of this stirring speech I was borne aloft triumphantly through the village, thereafter being treated as a fellow villager by one and all. Needless to say, this did not happen. However, my questioner was evidently favourably impressed, or at least felt compelled to act as though he were before the audience of his village-mates. He responded by saying that he would welcome me in his house any time and would discuss fully any matters of interest to me. He also offered to supply me with a number of artefacts as exhibits of Pahari ingenuity to be taken to America. I might add, anticlimactically, that in fact he never gave me information beyond his reactions to the weather, and that the Brahmin, evidently shaken by the experience, was never again as informative as he had been immediately prior to this incident. This is partly attributable to the substitution, soon afterwards, of a low-status interpreter in place of Sharma, a circumstance to be described below.

The Rajput challenger, however, ceased to be hostile whereas formerly he had been a focus of opposition to my presence. General rapport in the village improved markedly and the stigma attached to talking with me and my interpreter almost disappeared. One notable aftereffect was that my photographic opportunities, theretofore restricted to scenery, small children, and adolescent boys in self-conscious poses, suddenly expanded to include a wide range of economic, ritual, and social occasions as well as people of all castes, ages, and both sexes. Photography itself soon became a valuable means of obtaining rapport as photographs came into demand.

The degree to which I was allowed or requested to take photographs, in fact, proved to be a fairly accurate indicator of rapport. One of the more gratifying incidents of my research in Sirkanda occurred at an annual regional fair about eight months after the research had begun. Soon after I arrived at the fair a group of gaily dressed young women of various villages had agreed to be photographed when a Brahmin man, a stranger to me, stormed up and ordered them to refuse. An elderly and highly respected Rajput woman of Sirkanda had been watching the proceedings and was obviously irritated by the fact and manner of the intervention. She stepped to the centre of the group of girls, eyeing the Brahmin evenly, and said, 'Please take my photograph'. I did so, the Brahmin left, and my photography was in demand exceeding the film supply throughout the fair.

The incident described above, in which the Rajput challenged my interviewing of the Brahmin priest, came out favourably partly because of the context in which it occurred. For one thing, it occurred late enough so that many people knew me and my interpreter. Having no specific cause for doubting our motives, they were ready to believe us if we made a convincing case. Also, there was a sizeable audience to the event. My explanation was a response to a challenge by a high-status villager and the challenger accepted it gracefully. It was the first time many of these people had been present when I talked at any length and my statement was put with a good deal of feeling, which fact they recognized. It was essentially an appeal for their confidence and cooperation in a task they knew was difficult and which I obviously considered important. They were not incapable of empathy. In fact, an effective appeal for accurate responses from villagers was to picture my academic examining committee in America as made up of relentless and omniscient taskmasters who would unerringly detect any inadequacies or inaccuracies in my report and perhaps fail me on that basis so that I could not pursue my chosen profession. This evoked empathy and cooperation from several informants, one of whom said he would assume personal responsibility for the accuracy of all information obtained from or checked through him.

One man had said, early in the research, 'You may be a foreigner and we only poor villagers, but when we get to know you we will judge you as a man among other men, not as a foreigner'. With time, most of the villagers demonstrated the validity of his comment by treating me as an individual on the basis of their experience with me, rather than as the stereotyped outsider or white man.

Most important, my statement placed the listeners in a position of accepting what I said or denying their own importance as people and as citizens—it appealed to their pride. They have inferiority feelings relative to non-Paharis which account in a large measure for their hostility, and my presence as defined in this statement counteracted these feelings. It was especially effective in response to the Rajput who put the challenge; a man with an acute, and to many, aggravating need for public recognition of his importance. He had gained some eminence by opposing my work; he now evidently gained some by eliciting a full explanation from me and magnanimously accepting it.

Although I remained an alien and was never made to feel that my presence in the village was actively desired by most of its members, I was thereafter tolerated with considerable indulgence. I became established as a resident of Sirkanda, albeit a peculiar one, and no one tried to get me to leave. I have heard strangers en route to or from further mountain areas inquire of Sirkanda villagers as to my identity, presuming that I was out of earshot or could not understand and be left to ponder the succinct reply, 'He lives here'.

Other, less spectacular rapport-including devices were employed. Unattached men in the village were considered, not unjustly in light of past experience and Pahari morality, a threat to village womanhood. This fear with regard to my interpreter and myself was appreciably diminished when our wives and children visited the village and when a few villagers had been guests at our house in town where our families normally resided. We won some goodwill by providing a few simple remedies for common village ailments. One of the most effective means of attracting villagers to our abode in the village during this period was a battery radio which we brought, the first to operate in this area. It was an endless source of diversion to villagers and attracted a regular audience, as well as being a focal attraction for visiting relatives and friends from other villages.

At first there had reportedly been considerable speculation as to why two people of such conspicuously different backgrounds as Sharma and myself had appeared on the scene as a team if, as we claimed, we were not sent by the government or a missionary organization. The plausibility of our story was enhanced when Sharma made it clear to villagers that he was my bona fide employee who received payment in cash for his services.

Villagers never ceased to wonder, as I sometimes did myself, why I had chosen this particular area and village for my research. I explained this in terms of its relative accessibility for a hill area, the hospitality and perspicacity of Sirkanda people, the reputation Sirkanda had acquired in the area for being a 'good village' and my own favourable impression of it based on familiarity with a number of similar villages. The most satisfactory explanation was that my presence there was largely chance, that is, fate. Everyone agreed that this was the real reason. Villagers pointed out that when the potter makes a thousand identical cups, each has a unique destiny. Similarly, each man has a predetermined course of life and it was my fate to come to Sirkanda. When I gave an American coin to a villager, similar comment was precipitated. Of all the American coins, only one was destined to rest in Sirkanda and this was it. What greater proof of the power of fate could there be than that the coin had, like myself, found its way to this small and remote village?

All our claims of motive and status were put to the test by villagers once they realized we planned to remain in Sirkanda and to associate with them. Sharma's claim to Brahmin status was carefully checked. Extensive inquiry was made about his family and their origins. His behaviour was closely watched. His family home was inspected by villagers on trips to town. Only then were villagers satisfied that he was what he claimed to be. When all the claims upon which they could check proved to be accurate, the villagers were evidently encouraged to believe also those claims which could not be verified.

That suspicions as to our motives were eventually allayed did not mean we therefore could learn what we wanted to learn in the village. It meant only that the villagers knew in a general way what they were willing to let us learn, what impressions they would like us to receive. The range of allowable knowledge was far greater than that granted a stranger, far less than that shared by villagers. Although at the time I did not realize it, we were told those things which would give a favourable impression to a trustworthy plains Brahmin. Other facts would be suppressed and if discovered would be discovered in spite of the villagers' best efforts at concealment, often as a result of conversation with some disaffected individual of low esteem in the village. Our informants were primarily high-caste villagers intent on impressing us with their near conformity to the standards of behaviour and belief of high-caste plainsmen. Low-caste people were respectful and reticent before us, primarily, as it turned out, because one of us was a Brahmin and we were closely identified with the powerful high-caste villagers.

Three months were spent almost exclusively in building rapport, in establishing ourselves as trustworthy, harmless, sympathetic, and interested observers of village life. In this time we held countless conversations, most of them dealing with the weather and other timely and innocuous topics. A good deal of useful ethnographic information was acquired in the process, but in many areas its accuracy proved to be wanting. Better information was acquired by observation than by inquiry in this period. We found cause for satisfaction during this frustrating and, from the point of view of research results, relatively fruitless time in the fact that we were winning the confidence of a good many people, which we hoped would pay off more tangibly later. When the last open opponent of our endeavour had evidently been convinced of our purity of motive in the incident described above, we felt we could begin our data collecting in earnest.

Until this time we had done all our own housekeeping, cooking, dishwashing, carrying of water and firewood. These activities gave us an opportunity to meet people in a natural setting and to be busy in a period when rapport was not good enough to allow us to devote full time to research. As rapport improved we found our household chores too time-consuming for optimal research. We attempted to find assistance in the village but, unable to do so, we added as a third member of our team a seventeen-year-old boy who was of low-caste plains origin but had lived most of his life in the hill station of Mussoorie and was conversant with Pahari ways and the Pahari language. His role was that of servant and he assumed full responsibility for our housekeeping in the village. His informal contacts with some of the younger villagers were a research asset and his low-caste origin was not overlooked, but otherwise he had little direct effect on our relations with villagers. His contribution to the research was primarily in the extreme reliability of his work and his circumspection in relations with the villagers.

At this point of apparent promise for productive research, Sharma, my interpreter-assistant, became ill and it was evident that he would be unable to return to our work in the village for some time. Under the circumstances this was a disheartening blow. It plunged my morale to its lowest ebb in the fifteen months of my stay in India, none of which could be described as exhilarating. I cannot here go into the details of the causes for this condition of morale: the pervasive health anxiety with which anyone is likely to be afflicted when he takes an eighteen-month-old child to the field in India, especially if, as in this case, he is away from and inaccessible to his family a good share of the time; the difficulties of maintaining a family household in town and carrying on research in an isolated village; the constant and frustrating parrying with petty officials who are in positions to cause all kinds of difficulty and delay; the virtual lack of social contact outside of one's family, employees, and the villagers among whom one works; the feeling of being merely tolerated by those among whom one works and upon whom one is dependent for most of one's social interaction. In such circumstances research is likely to become the primary motivating principle and its progress looms large in one's world view. Therefore, to lose an assistant whose presence I deemed essential to the research when I was on the threshold of tangible progress after a long period of preparation was a discouraging blow. I shall not soon forget the anxiety I felt during the five-hour trek to the village alone after learning of Sharma's illness and incapacity. To await his recovery would have been to waste the best months for research because his illness came at the beginning of the winter slack season when people would, for the first time since my arrival, have ample time to sit and talk. In two months the spring harvest and planting season would begin and many potential informants would be too busy and tired to talk.

After a period alone in the village, I realized that I could not work effectively without assistance due to my inadequate knowledge of the language. Although I dreaded the task of selecting and then introducing a new and inexperienced assistant into the village, this seemed to be a necessary step to preserve the continuity of the research. My hope and intention was to utilize a substitute only until Sharma would be able to work again. Not wishing to spend too much time looking for a substitute, and with qualified people extremely scarce, I employed with many misgivings and on a trial basis the first reasonably promising prospect who appeared. Happily, he proved to be an exceptionally able, willing, and interested worker. He differed from Sharma in at least three important respects: age, religion, and experience. Mohammed, as he will hereafter be called, was a middle-aged Muslim and a retired school teacher who had no familiarity with anthropological research.

These facts proved to have advantageous as well as disadvantageous aspects. I was able to guide him more easily in his work and to interact more directly with the villagers than had been the case with Sharma simply because he realized his inexperience, accepted suggestions readily, and was interested in helping me to know and communicate directly with the villagers rather than in demonstrating his efficiency as a researcher and his indispensability as an interpreter. As a result of his age he received a certain amount of respect. As a Muslim he was able to establish excellent rapport with the low castes but not with the high or twice-born castes. Perhaps most importantly, he had no ego involvement in the data. He was interested and objective in viewing the culture in which we were working, whereas Sharma had been self-conscious and anxious to avoid giving an unflattering view of Hinduism and of village life to an American in this unorthodox (to him often shockingly so) example of a Hindu village. Moreover, the Brahmin, almost inevitably, had his own status to maintain before the high castes who lived in the village, while the Muslim was under no such obligation.

Since it seemed probable that Sharma would return to work after a few weeks, I decided to make the best of the situation and utilize Mohammed in ways that would make most use of his advantages and minimize his disadvantages, for he was strong where Sharma had been weak, and vice versa. While high-caste people were suspicious of Mohammed on the basis of his religion, low-caste people were more at ease in his presence than they had been with Sharma. Further, low-caste people proved to be more informative than high-caste people on most subjects. I therefore planned to use this interpreter to get data about the low castes and from them to get as much general ethnographic data as possible. I was counting on Sharma's return to enable me to return to the high castes and my original endeavour to secure information from and about them. However, after several weeks it became evident that Sharma could not return to work in the village. By then we were beginning to get a good deal of ethnographic material with the promise of much more. In addition to remarkably good rapport with the low castes (greater than that Sharma and I had had with anyone in the village), we were also winning the confidence of some high-caste people. In view of these circumstances I felt encouraged to continue with Mohammed and to broaden our contacts in the village in the remaining months of research.

I had not anticipated the full implications for research of the differences in status of my associates, Sharma and Mohammed. For example, the villagers had early determined that Sharma neither ate meat nor drank liquor. As a result we were barely aware that these things were done by the villagers. Not long after Mohammed's arrival the villagers found that he indulged in both and that I could be induced to do so. Thereafter we became aware of frequent meat and liquor parties, often of an intercaste nature. We found that these were important social occasions, occasions from which outsiders were usually rigidly excluded. Rapport increased notably when it became known that locally distilled liquor was occasionally served at our house. As rapport improved, we were more frequently included in such informal occasions. Our access to information of many kinds increased proportionately.

Mohammed's age put him virtually above the suspicion Sharma had to overcome regarding possible interest in local women. Mohammed's association with me in my by then generally trusted status precluded undue suspicion of missionary intent or governmental affiliation. Probably his most important characteristic with regard to rapport was his religion. As a Muslim he was, like me, a ritually polluted individual, especially since he was suspected of having eaten beef. For most purposes he and I were untouchables, albeit respected for our presumed wealth and knowledge.

Lessons from the Ethnographic Experience

Had I been alone in the village I would have had a relatively free hand in attempting to determine with whom I associated, so long as I did not infringe too freely on the private life of the villagers or on matters of ritual purity.

However, since I was in almost constant association with an assistant whose behaviour was closely tied to my own, my status and his were interdependent. The definition of ourselves which we cooperated in projecting had to correspond to known and observable facts and clues about ourselves and our purposes. Since to the villagers my assistant was more conventional, hence more comprehensible as a person than I, it was largely from him that impressions were derived which determined our status. For this reason the characteristics of the interpreter-assistant were of crucial significance to the research effort.

In such a society as this the ethnographer is inevitably an outsider and never changes. He is judged by those among whom he works on the basis of his own characteristics and those of his associates. He becomes identified with those social groups among his subjects to which he gains access. The nature of his data is largely determined by his subjects. Polite acceptance and even friendship do not always mean that access will be granted to the confidential regions of the life of those who extend it. The stranger will be excluded from a large and vital area if he is seen as one who will not safeguard secrets, and especially if he is identified as a member of one of those groups from which the secrets are being kept.

Sharma was a high-caste plainsman and was consequently identified with very important groups outside the village—groups rigorously excluded from large areas of the life of both high-caste and low-caste villagers. As such he could possibly never have achieved the kind of relationship to the villagers which would have resulted in access to much of the life of Sirkanda. Access to that information was essential to the ethnographer because it constituted a large proportion of all village attitudes and behaviours in this closed group. Mohammed was able to gain substantial rapport with the low castes. In view of the attitudes of the villagers and the social composition and power structure of the village, the low castes were the only feasible source of information which high-caste villagers considered to be embarrassing, damaging, or secret. They were a reasonably satisfactory source of such information on the entire village because all castes were in such close contact that they had few secrets from one another and did not differ greatly in culture. This is not to say that the information obtained was complete or totally accurate, only to assert that it was much more so than would have been the case had Sharma been the assistant throughout the research.

In a highly stratified society the opinions and behaviours of one stratum are insufficient for an understanding of the whole society. An ethnographer coming into such a group inevitably becomes more closely identified with one or more strata than with others, a fact which largely determines the information he acquires, and therefore his analysis of the system. In choosing his employees and other associates he has to bear this in mind. In making his analysis he must be aware of the distortions in his data which result from the fact that he is identified by his subjects with certain groups or individuals and that the impressions and facts he perceives are largely determined by that fact.

Once one has been identified with a particular social group, it may be difficult or impossible to change this identification or to get information that is not coloured or determined by it. Early choice of the house in which one will live, of one's first acquaintances, one's associates and employees, are all crucial because they define one's role in the community. The first people one meets—the friendliest locals—are often the very ones who are marginal to their own culture and who therefore seek outside friends and allies. They may be excellent informants, but their probable biases and the effects of their friendship on further contacts in the community must be appreciated if the research is not to be seriously distorted by them. If, as is often the case, the community is riven with factions, rivalries, intrigue, and gossip, one can early and permanently become identified with a group of whose existence one is unaware but which has major effects on one's research. Generally, one will come to know of one's predicament eventually (often too late to do much good), but the extent of its effects is likely to remain indeterminate.

In the ethnographer's relations with those he studies, as in all human relations, there is some conscious effort on both sides to maintain a definition of the situation and of the individuals and groups within it which is socially acceptable and which is in fact advantageous to those involved. This is a crucial factor in research.

The ethnographer comes to his subjects as an unknown, generally unexpected, and often unwanted intruder. Their impressions of him will determine the kinds and validity of data to which he will be able to gain access, hence the degree of success of his work. The ethnographer and his subjects are both performers and audience to each other. They have to judge each other's motives and other attributes on the basis of short but intensive contact and then decide what definition of themselves and the surrounding situation they want to project—what they will reveal and what they will conceal and how best to do it. Each will attempt to convey to the other the impression that will best serve his interests as he sees them.

An ethnographer is usually evaluated by himself and his colleagues on the basis of his insights into the back region of the performance of his subjects. His subjects are evaluated by their fellows on the basis of the degree to which they protect the secrets of their team and successfully project the image of the team that is acceptable to the group for front region presentation. It is probably often thought this presentation will also satisfy the ethnographer. The ethnographer is likely to evaluate his subjects on the amount of back region information they reveal to him, while he is evaluated by them on his tact in not intruding unrecessarily into the back region and, as rapport improves, on his trustworthiness as one who will not reveal back region secrets. These tend to be mutually contradictory bases of evaluation. Rapport establishment is largely a matter of threading among them so as to win admittance to the back region of the subjects' performance without alienating them.

The impressions that ethnographers and subjects seek to project to each other are, therefore, those felt to be favourable to the accomplishment of their respective goals: the ethnographer seeks access to back region information; the subjects seek to protect their secrets since these represent a threat to the public image they wish to maintain. Neither can succeed perfectly.

If the ethnographer does not gain access to back region information he will have to content himself with an 'official' or public view of the culture he studies, derived from publicly accessible and approved sources. This, in any culture, is a limited view at best, which cannot result in accurate and thorough understanding of the culture.

Language and Interpreters

Language poses a problem in most ethnographic fieldwork for the obvious reason that the researcher works with people who speak a language which is foreign to him. Usually, now that training in many languages is available in universities and other institutions, the ethnographer tries to become at least minimally competent in a language known to the people he studies. His imperfect knowledge of the language introduces limitations to the research. The language he learns is sometimes a second language to his informants, known perhaps about as well by them as by him. In this case the limitations are even more severe. In any case, there are bound to be problems in translating ideas from one language to another. People of different cultures and different languages categorize their experiences and the world around them differently, and they verbalize them in different ways. Literal translation of words for objects, ideas, attitudes, and beliefs is often impossible. Even close approximations fail to communicate culturally specific connotations, and the consequent mistakes in communicating with informants, and in recording, interpreting, and analysing material can destroy research greatly.

Some anthropologists have made it a point to learn the language of their informants as well as they could, and then to rely entirely upon their knowledge for research purposes. Others have employed bilingual interpreters.

In a few instances, research has even been done via two interpreters where, for example, the people studied speak only language A and the ethnographer speaks only English, and where no one can be found who speaks both. Then one interpreter will be employed who knows English and language B, and another will be employed who knows language B and language A. All information must then be filtered though two intermediaries. Use of any interpreter inevitably results in cumbersome inquiry procedures, but does not preclude useful research.

Most fieldworkers agree that for effective use of an interpreter, the ethnographer himself must be able to follow much of what the interpreter and informant say. This enables him to check the accuracy of interpretation, to clarify points, to catch instances when, as inevitably happens, the interpreter simplifies, summarizes, or injects his own information, opinions, or impressions in his interpretation. If the ethnographer cannot understand any of the conversations between interpreter and the informant, he is completely at the mercy of the interpreter; what he learns is filtered and inevitably interpreted, and to an extent, distorted before he hears it.

Some ethnographers use an interpreter even when they are quite fluent in the language themselves, simply to enable them to probe deeply into meanings that otherwise might remain obscure, and also to guard against the natural tendency for informant to simplify answers for a foreigner. An interpreter can also keep a conversation going while the ethnographer makes notes, or he can follow up on side issues with some informants while the ethnographer continues the main conversation. While fluency is a goal for nearly every ethnographer, its lack has not prevented successful research. John Gumperz, a linguist, has mentioned that some kinds of inquiry and information became closed to him in his research in a village in north India when he achieved fluency in the colloquial language. Prior to that time, many naïve and trivial questions asked in his imperfect, foreigner's Hindi were indulgently answered. When he knew the language well and spoke it like a villager, he was no longer considered the naïve stranger, and his questions were dismissed as stupid or impertinent, as they would have been if asked by a local resident.

Communication between people occurs in many ways other than by verbal means, as Edward T. Hall has made abundantly clear in *The Silent Language* (1959). Human behaviour is largely symbolic; that is, arbitrary meanings are attached to it. Thus, many of the problems of nonunderstanding and misunderstanding which apply to problems of language apply to a wider range of behaviour and interaction as the ethnographer confronts those whose way of life he studies. As a stranger to that culture, he is likely initially to be unable to behave correctly—to convey, for example, politeness, to detect impatience, to identify sensitive subject matter, or to appreciate the significance of many social situations. He is likely to make blunders and he risks alienating those whose friendship and trust he most wants and needs. In this context, caution, circumspection, and sincerity are invaluable traits, and the role of stranger or neophyte is most useful, for it generally excuses mistakes, or at least gives their perpetrator another chance.

Special Techniques

The techniques used by anthropologists for obtaining data, as distinguished from the overall participant-observation method, vary according to the training and interests of the ethnographer, the problems he wishes to investigate, and the people he studies.

The bulk of field research is done by the simple but difficult method of living among the people one wants to learn to know, talking with them, observing them, and writing down that which seems significant. Various kinds of aids have been devised to facilitate this task (cf. Rowe 1953). Most notable among mechanical aids are the camera and the tape recorder. Neither substitutes for observation but both are aids to it.

In another sphere altogether are particular techniques of inquiry. These range from the census (Richards 1938) and the genealogical method (Rivers 1910) to a vast array of psychological tests including, prominently, projective tests (Henry and Spiro 1953; Henry 1961). Census-taking is simply a way of getting considerable information on a variety of topics in a systematic way in a short time. It involves finding out who lives in the society or group to be studied, where they live and with whom, their occupations, possessions, and many other kinds of information. It is a detailed listing of facts about the people who live in a locality. The genealogical method gathers similar information about people who are related to one another. It is acquired by asking people to remember their relatives as far into the past as possible and as remotely related as possible. This method focuses on the kin group rather than on the locality, and emphasizes antecedents as well as contemporaries. It affords information on a wide variety of topics, including kin groups, kinship terminology, marriage rules, residence rules, adoption, inheritance, history of the people, trends in culture change, and many others. Both the census and the genealogy are excellent means of initiating inquiries and of uncovering information which might otherwise go undetected. Thus, their value is as much in what is discovered incidentally in the process of their collection as in what is discovered intentionally as part of the formal collection of the data.

Psychological tests provide a wide variety of insights. Those which are projective in nature—which ask the informant to respond to an ambiguous stimulus (usually a visual image)—give the anthropologist an additional insight into the way his subjects see themselves and the world around them. Other ways to this end are the collection, on the individual level, of life histories (Dollard 1936), of dreams (Eggan 1961) and fantasies, and of folklore (Fischer 1963), art and other expressive forms on the group level. The aim in all these is to find out how people view their world.

Analysis of Data

The mode of analysis of ethnographic data, like the method of its collection, is dependent in large part upon the training and interests of the ethnographer and upon his research problem. It is also dependent upon the ways in which he collects his data (which in turn is determined partly by how he intends to analyse it).

Traditionally, ethnographic data have been presented so as to provide a picture of the way of life of the people studied which is as complete as possible. Obviously no account can be entirely complete. In presenting their reports, ethnographers have found it necessary to organize the data under subject headings. Even though culture does not occur in compartments, much less in handily labelled compartments, it is inherent in the nature of language and exposition that to describe a culture, it must be described sequentially according to some principle of organization. This means that, implicitly or explicitly, cultural facts must be categorized. G.P. Murdock (1950) published an indexed list of such headings thought to be useful to ethnographers and, if used consistently, believed to be capable of producing categorizations which are valid cross-culturally, that is, comparatively.

The Royal Anthropological Institute of Great Britain and Ireland has published frequently revised editions of *Notes and Queries on Anthropology* since 1874. This contains lists of topics to be investigated in any culture, and suggestions on how to derive the necessary information on each topic.

Categorizations such as these have been used with success by many ethnographers, more often as reminders of what to look for or what data to collect than as bases for organizing their ethnographic research or report. The question is often raised whether by using predefined categories, the ethnographer does not in fact force his data into inappropriate moulds, thereby distorting it. Is it possible, for example, to describe Hinduism, Christianity, and Eskimo religion under the same headings—according to the same categories? This is an argument we cannot go into here except to say that those who have used headings defend themselves on two grounds. First, they use the headings with insight and caution, so that distortion is absent or minimal. Wherever necessary they adopt novel categories derived from the data, and second, the headings are sufficiently abstract that cultural context and detail can be included under them, thereby preserving the nature of the phenomena as they occur in any particular culture, while maximizing the chances for comparison across cultural boundaries through the use of general criteria for categorization. Thus widespread and comparable phenomena are not obscured by their particular, unique manifestations. They point out that to refuse to use general categories is to focus upon the culturally specific, thereby eliminating comparison and generalization. There can be no science of the unique.

The desire to describe cultures in terms of their own structures and categories rather than in terms of imposed schemes has long been present in anthropology. An explicit technique of analysis has been devised for the purpose, adapted from linguistic analysis. Just as modern linguistics attempts to describe and analyse each language in terms of its own grammar, so culture can be analysed in this fashion. For this approach the terms 'componential analysis' and 'ethnoscience' have been coined (Frake 1962; Sturtevant 1964).

It is well known that people of different cultures construe their words in different ways. As the linguist Benjamin Lee Whorf has put it, 'We cut nature up, organize it into concepts, and ascribe significance as we do, largely because we are parties to an agreement to organize it in this way. . .' (Whorf 1956: 213). Ward Goodenough has made much the same point: 'Culture is not a material phenomenon; it does not consist of things, people, behaviour, or emotions. It is rather an organization of these things. It is the forms of things that people have in mind. . .' (Goodenough 1957: 167). Thus we know that people of different cultures categorize colours in different ways despite the fact that the visual stimuli they categorize are in all cases the same. Some name more colours than we do, some less. Other cultures do not place the boundaries between named colours exactly where we do. The componential analyst would seek to discover the colour terminologies and their referents in any culture he studied. He would attempt further to determine the rules or criteria by which the terminology is constructed and applied to the phenomena of the observed world. He would feel successful if he could devise a statement about rules or criteria for categorization of colours in terms of components such as hue, brightness, and so on, which would enable him or anyone else who knew them to categorize (that is, name) colours appearing in nature precisely as would a native of the culture he is analysing. Such rules or criteria are derived by collecting detailed data indicating how people group and distinguish the phenomena in their world. The analyst notes carefully not only the content of the categories, but the context in which distinctions are made. His aim is to find significant usage as distinguished from insignificant variation, just as does a linguist looking for phonemes and the structures of which they are constituent parts among all the phonetic variation which occurs in a language. The method is based directly upon linguistic methods.

Whether the rules the analyst devises are or should be the principles upon which the native actually bases his categorization, or whether the rules merely 'work' (and therefore may be only one of several alternative sets of adequate rules) is a point that has been much debated. Those who believe that a single, correct set of rules is immanent in any culture (and in any language), and that it merely awaits discovery, have been called the 'God's truth' analysts, while those who believe that the ethnographer's (or linguist's) task is to manufacture a workable set of rules (and that there may be any number of different rules which will work) have been called the 'hocus-pocus' analysts (Burling 1964).

What utility such analyses will have for ethnography in the long run remains to be seen. So far they have been applied only to extremely limited kinds of data—those data which are highly structured, and generally those which can be studied as terminological systems or taxonomies, for instance, colour categories, kinship terminologies, categories of disease, categories of plants, and so on. To study any one of these systems is painstaking, time-consuming work, which results in a detailed but very narrow description and analysis. Whether the procedure can be effectively applied to less obviously and formally structured data and to more subtle data (for instance, social interaction, attitudes, values) remains to be seen. Whether it can result in an overall ethnography is a question to be answered in the even more distant future. Its advocates would maintain that whatever it accomplishes analytically, it does so with a degree of validity which less formal analysis can never achieve. Therefore, it may not do much, as yet, but what it does, it does rigorously. Its aim, as stated by Frake, is 'eventually to provide the ethnographer with public, nonintuitive procedures for ordering his presentation of observed and elicited events according to the principles of the people he is studying' (1962: 85). Some would say that componential analysis is the only method adequate to the ethnographic aim of accurate description of a culture.

Its detractors and sceptics point out that they and their teachers and their teachers' teachers have been doing componential analysis inadvertently all their professional lives, simply as part of the ethnographic method, albeit in less rigorous fashion. They doubt that the added rigour pays off sufficiently well in insight or understanding or descriptive accuracy to make the restriction in scope worth the while. They express doubt that an ethnography will ever be written that is based on the method of componential analysis, simply because of the time required to gather the data and the space required to report it, for even one small segment of culture. It offers to many, at best, an unrealizable ideal. They suspect that in the process of componential analysis, the human understanding of the culture analysed is likely to be factored out, so that the product is sterile and in that sense untrue to life (Berremann 1965).

In Pursuit of Anthropology

T.N. MADAN

[T]he objective methods of investigation of cultural data have to be helped out, not only by historical imagination and a background of historical and geographical facts, but also by a subjective process of self-forgetting absorption or meditation (dhyana), and intuition born of sympathetic immersion in, and self-identification with, the society under investigation.

Sarat Chandra Ray (1938)

We might say then that both the relativist and his partner, the dogmatist, that is the 'true believer of science', lack the insight that their own form of life is always what it is not and that for this reason one does not become conscious of his own form of life until he leaves it....

But in some sense the researcher will always stay a bit 'between the worlds'. It is the price he has to pay for knowledge: to be forever excluded from the world of talking animals and from the world of talking anthropologists as well.

Hans Peter Duerr (1987)

The First Encounter

My 'engagement' with anthropology has now lasted forty years, which is long enough for some reflection on what it has come to mean to me. In this essay I will discuss some issues, which have had a significant place in my anthropological quest from the very beginning. These include the problem of 'objectivity' and the notion that anthropology is essentially the study of 'other cultures', defining otherness to refer to, narrowly, non-Western cultures, or broadly, cultures other than the anthropologist's own.

My first encounter with anthropology, as I now recall it, was almost fortuitous: I stumbled upon the word in a university prospectus! My way to a career in anthropology led through history, English literature, and economics. Although history emerged as the preferred subject when I first deliberated upon what to study after finishing high school, I was unable to make this choice. Instead I read natural sciences during the first two years in college and social sciences (economics and political science) during the next two. In the latter period, I chose English literature as my Honours subject, and found immense delight in it.

Yet, flowing with the stream, as it were, I opted for economics as the subject for my M.A. In the early 1950s, soon after Independence, while English language and literature seemed to harken to the past, economics via its connection with planning was the subject of the future. I decided to join Lucknow University, much against the advice of my economics professor at Amar Singh College (in Srinagar, Jammu and Kashmir). He warned me that one did not get good education in economics at Lucknow, but only a miscellany of courses, including sociology; one would thus earn only a 'hybrid degree'. I did not let this opinion deflect me from the journey I had planned to undertake, which was to become more than a journey from one city to another, and which was to lead to the choice of a vocation.

On enrolment in the Department of Economics and Sociology at Lucknow University, I found that, during the first year of the two-year M.A. course, I would have to study micro- and macro-economic analysis, with institutional economics thrown in, and also introductory sociology, including social ecology. Besides, I had to choose a 'paper' from among three optionals that included cultural anthropology. I did not know what anthropology was, and the dictionary I consulted defined it as the comparative study of races and cultures. The details of the course appeared interesting. On enquiry I found that it would be taught by one of the more popular teachers, D.N. Majumdar. The prospectus identified him as a Reader with a Ph.D. from Cambridge and the distinction of being a Fellow of the National Institute of Sciences. All this was impressive, and I opted for cultural anthropology, unmindful of my college teacher's warning. In the event, and not at all surprisingly, I learnt very little economics!

As for anthropology, in order to get us started, Majumdar asked us to read Robert Lowie's old classic, *Primitive Society* (1922), which had recently become available again. This book was supplemented by selected chapters from several others, including Majumdar's own works. Anthropology interested me, but I cannot really say that the engagement with it began then. The emphasis on the culturally specific datum recaptured for me something of the excitement of reading history. Ethnographic examples might have called to my mind aspects of the novel and the short story, but not only were we not required to read any monographs in the first year,

Majumdar's insistence that anthropology was a 'science' was also not conducive to such anticipations.

The way sociology and social ecology were taught to us (by Radhakamal Mukerjee and D.P. Mukerji) was more like anthropology rather than economics, in the interpretative rather than the analytical mode. Robert MacIver's *Society* and Radhakamal Mukerjee's *Social Ecology* were the introductory texts. The third teacher, A.K. Saran (who was a stern critic of positivism) began with the theory of symbolic interactionism a la G.H. Mead's *Mind, Self and Society*, which left me rather dazed. MacIver had a philosophical approach and a literary style, and I recall reading his discussion of themes like 'code and custom', 'the sociological significance of the family', and 'contrasts of urban and rural life' with enormous interest. D.P. Mukerji's exegesis of these and other themes was itself immensely absorbing. He introduced us to the Marxian perspective, but not at all in the high-handed manner of the copy-book Marxist intellectual. Together, anthropology and sociology seemed to me to be an invitation to consider everyday life worthy of serious study in a manner that economic analysis, with its graphs and curves and general concepts did not—concretely rather than in the abstract. (I will not say anything here about the economics courses and how they were taught.)

At the end of the first year a clear choice was offered to us in respect of the courses to be taken up in the second year: straight economics or a combined set of anthropology-sociology courses. I opted for the latter. Besides the history of social thought and theories of culture and civilization, we now had to study a broad-based anthropology course. Beginning with some lectures on palaeontology, Majumdar guided us through the monographic and theoretical works of Alfred Kroeber, Robert Lowie, Bronislaw Malinowski, Ruth Benedict, Margaret Mead, and Ralph Linton. He also often referred to his own fieldwork among Indian tribes such as the Ho, the Tharu, and the Khasa.

Anthropology, Majumdar taught us, was 'the science of man in totality'. Although the syllabus contained very little on biological anthropology and prehistoric archaeology, he always insisted that any anthropologist worth the name must know all three fields. He did not include anthropological linguistics in this 'core' or 'sacred bundle'. Besides its holistic character, Majumdar expounded at length on anthropology's scientific and applied character. Anthropology is a 'laboratory' science, he used to say, and a 'field' science. He considered the work that he did in his laboratory (serological classification, anthropometric analysis, etc.) continuous with what he did in the field (collecting blood samples, taking body measurements, etc). And he regarded the collection of data for his ethnographic work as an important aspect of the larger enterprise of fieldwork, guided above all by the ideal of objectivity.

The ways of life of the people being studied—their beliefs and behaviour—were as 'real' as their body weight, skin colour, and blood groups. There was, therefore, no more scope for spinning out tales in ethnography than there was in physical anthropological description. One had to ensure that ethnographic 'data' were reliable and their analysis was rigorous and guided by theory (which for him was functionalism informed by evolution). The ultimate test of 'scientific objectivity', which was his ideal, was that what one claimed to be the facts of the case, should be verifiable by another well-trained investigator. The model was the experiment in the laboratory.

D.P. Mukerji, who taught us the history of social thought, was rather disdainful of the conception of anthropology as narrative ethnography. He advocated an approach to the study of human cultures which was explicitly historical but not historicist—evolutionary but sensitive to cultural specificities. Without an interest in the general and the abstract, the study of the specific and the concrete, he used to say, would surely turn out to be an intellectual bog.

When he lectured on the theories of culture and civilization, the scholars whose contributions Mukerji discussed included sociologists such as Max Weber and Pitrim Sorokin, and historians like Jacob Burckhardt and Arnold Toynbee. The only contributions by anthropologists that he discussed were Bronislaw Malinowski's thesis on the mutual entailment of 'freedom and civilization' and Ruth Benedict's notion of the 'stubbornness of the core of a culture'. Although he did not find the ethnographic narrative particularly interesting, he acknowledged its value as a 'shock absorber'. He was a relativist, but not philosophically naïve. He considered the position of absolute value-neutrality wrong and also stressed the dangers of uncritical functionalism. Mukerji was committed to the notions of the unfolding of the possibilities inherent in every social formation and the arriving at the next, higher stage through the dialectical process. He maintained that anthropologists and sociologists would discover the true promise of their subjects only if they cultivated an interest in history and philosophy. Over the years, I myself have come to embrace this twin emphasis whole-heartedly, limited only by the elementary nature of my knowledge of philosophy.

The third professor, Radhakamal Mukerjee, lectured on 'the social structure of values' and 'the dynamics of morals', using his own books for the purpose. He was very eclectic in his approach. A prolific author, he had written on a wide range of themes in the fields of economics, sociology, psychology, and religious studies. He had a greater interest in ethnography than did D.P. Mukerji.

There was thus no single overall approach to the study of society, and to explicating the character of the social sciences, in the lectures and published work of the four professors who taught us. D.N. Majumdar, I should add, was not alone in his conception of the social sciences as essentially *scientific*: his approach found sympathetic echoes in the lectures and published work of practically all the economists in the department. None of them showed much concern for the role that personal preferences or ideological commitments play in the so-called sciences.

As for my own predilections, it was the courses on the theories of culture and civilization, taught by D.P. Mukerji, and on anthropological theories of culture, taught by D.N. Majumdar, that I found most interesting. I particularly enjoyed reading Toynbee's *A Study of History*, of which the first six volumes were then available. Also available was an excellent and helpful abridgement by D.C. Somerville. Reading Toynbee was for me a welcome return to history and comparative literature. The books of Malinowski and Ruth Benedict also interested me greatly: they were rich in ethnography and so also very readable.

By the time I finished my M.A. (in 1951), it was obvious that research and teaching were to be my vocation in life. Radhakamal Mukerjee and D.N. Majumdar both offered me scholarships for doctoral studies. Mukerjee suggested I work on the composition of the working class in Kanpur, but this did not attract me at all. Majumdar proposed fieldwork among a tribal community in the Almora (U.P.) area, with the focus on problems of rehabilitation. D.P. Mukerji, mindful of the interest I had evinced in Toynbee, suggested that I consider working on Toynbee's 'method' (or lack of it). After some vacillation I settled for a career in anthropology.

During the early years at Lucknow University, I had the opportunity to hear, besides my teachers, a number of distinguished scholars including A. Aiyappan, N.K. Bose, Louis Dumont, Irawati Karve, S.F. Nadel, and M.N. Srinivas. The subject of Srinivas's talk (winter 1954–55) was fieldwork and he spoke about the qualities of a good fieldworker, emphasizing, above all, total commitment. Not only must the fieldworker be a genuine participant observer, he must consider his relationship with the community he chooses to study as more than a strategy for data collection. He must recognize that there is a moral dimension to the relationship. He went so far as to suggest that the best fieldworkers are single individuals without family obligations. It is worth recalling here that Srinivas himself did his fieldwork among the Coorgs and in the village of Rampura in Karnataka before he got married.

Srinivas also stressed in his talk the importance of fidelity to facts. The importance of memory and imagination that are a distinguishing feature of his book, *The Remembered Village* (1976), were not, of course, anticipated in his talk. Actually, the discussion that followed his presentation was marked by a sharply stated difference of opinion between him and A.K. Saran on the issue of positivism in social sciences. For Srinivas, sociology was at its best when it was grounded in observable data in the manner of social anthropology. In fact, he considered a distinction between the two domains to be a colonial hangover. Saran's commitment was above all to a metaphysical perspective on social reality.

I would also like to mention the powerful impact N.K. Bose made upon some of us when he spent a day with the students in the winter of 1950. He lectured on caste in modern Bengal, on temple architecture in Orissa, and finally on Gandhi. The range of his interests seemed wide, like D.P. Mukerji's, but while the latter was a social theorist, Bose was, first and foremost, a fieldworker and a man interested in practical affairs. There was something earthy about him in the best possible sense of the term.

It was apparent from Bose's first and second talks that, for him, observation was a broad-based and wide-ranging engagement with a social phenomenon (caste, temple architecture), which was not to be bound by a narrowly conceived rule book. A great deal of what he told us about changes in the caste system was based on his own day-to-day interaction with people rather than on fieldwork in some village or hamlet. In contrast, his work in temples in Orissa was obviously based upon carefully planned and painstaking research, carried out practically single-handed. And when he spoke about Gandhi, he spoke more as a social activist with a deep moral concern for human suffering than as a social scientist interested in the form of social life, a subject on which he had written insightfully in Bengali (*Hindu Samajer Garan*, 1949). On our day with Bose, social anthropology was presented to us as a part of our own lives, not a study of primitive cultures. The objective and the subjective were both accommodated in his method.

The Quest for Objectivity

Anthropology, I had learnt from Majumdar, was the study of 'primitive societies', of cultures other than the literate and the industrial. The so-called tribes of India were what Indian anthropologists had studied. It was inexpensive and convenient to do fieldwork within the country, and there was no dearth of tribal people. He had done so himself, in Chota Nagpur (Bihar), Mirzapur (Uttar Pradesh), Jaunsar Bawar (Uttar Pradesh), and elsewhere, studying communities like the Ho, Tharu and Khasas.

Conscious of my inadequacy and even awkwardness in relating to strangers and cultivating social relationships, and also perhaps attracted to D.P. Mukerji's emphasis on the importance of general if not explicitly stated theoretical issues, I asked Majumdar if fieldwork among a tribal people was an essential requirement of a programme of doctoral studies. He said that, strictly speaking, it was not, for the limited purpose of preparing a dissertation, but one could not hope to make a professional career out of anthropology without it. Accordingly, it was agreed that the subject of my dissertation would be the 'rehabilitation' of Indian tribes. The data for it would be drawn from published sources of various kinds, including anthropological monographs and government reports. At that time the critique of development as a destroyer of cultural pluralism had not yet emerged, nor had the idea that the 'other' was in fact constituted by the anthropological method itself. Development from above was then considered a moral obligation rather than arrogance, and the 'other' cultures were considered essentially so.

About a year later, I joined a group of M.A. students who were being taken to Ranchi (Bihar) for a two-week 'field trip' as part of their training in anthropology. It turned out to be a depressing experience for me. Not that the Oraons appeared to be culturally very different from the Hindu villagers of the same area, what upset me was our behaviour.

Everybody in our group, I found, was asking the villagers questions about their family and economic life, religious beliefs, and similar matters of significance, without any regard for their feelings or convenience. My shyness crippled me, but I did manage to take photographs at an old woman's funeral and cremation, without first seeking anybody's permission to do so. As we came away from the village, I had the uncomfortable feeling that there was something indecent about such field trips. This feeling was accentuated by the fact that one of the girl students in our group had cried at the cremation, but no one else had shown any emotion. A year-long stay in the field by an anthropologist working on his own would be, I thought, far from the kind of 'assault' in which we had been engaged. Nevertheless, a strong feeling that anthropological fieldwork was in a certain sense degrading to the unwilling subject of observation, a violation of his personal life by strangers, took firm hold of me. This feeling was, perhaps, partly a cover for my own incapacity for fieldwork among strangers.

Gradually, almost imperceptibly, it occurred to me that a solution to the problem probably lay in studying my own community, the Pandits of the Kashmir valley, though perhaps not my own family circle and kindred, or any other such grouping in the city of Srinagar where I had grown up. Years later I wrote: 'It is clear to me now, though it was not then, that I was transforming the familiar into the unfamiliar by the decision to relate to it as an anthropologist' (1975: 134).

Early in 1955, the well-known anthropologist S.F. Nadel visited Lucknow. I took the opportunity to discuss my fieldwork problem with him. He told me that he could see no objection to an Indian studying aspects of the caste or community of his birth. He stressed the importance of training in formal anthropological research which, he thought, should help one to overcome the limitations of subjective bias. He also emphasized the importance and advantages of a good command over the 'native tongue' to anthropological research, particularly to the study of kinship and religion, and pointed out that being a native speaker would give one a head start in fieldwork. He had written about the importance of language competence in fieldwork in *The Foundations of Social Anthropology* (1952).

Soon afterwards, I discontinued work on my dissertation on the rehabilitation of Indian tribes. Majumdar, who had by then himself initiated a research project in a non-tribal village near Lucknow, agreed that I could write a dissertation on the basis of fieldwork among the Pandits of rural Kashmir. Accordingly I sent a proposal to Nadel at the Australian National University (ANU) for the study of 'kinship values': Radhakamal Mukerjee's lectures and book on the social structure of values may have had a deeper impact on me than I was conscious of at that time. He had laid considerable stress on family relationships and their underlying values of love, sharing and solidarity.

ANU awarded me a scholarship in the summer of 1955. I could never find out what Nadel actually thought of my research proposal, for he died early in 1956 before my arrival in Canberra. I had been apprehensive that he might not approve of the theme I had suggested. There was no evidence of such an interest in his own published work. My confidence had been somewhat shaken by A.K. Saran who had summarily rejected the idea of a study of values through fieldwork. My clarification that what I intended was to find out, through close observation, were the norms and values that were not merely verbalised by people, but which could be shown to have actually influenced choices and behaviour in real life situations, left him totally unconvinced. This was, of course, in tune with his known opposition to positivism and to the idea of a social science.

After my arrival in Canberra, the first person to discuss my proposal with me at considerable length was Edmund Leach, who was on a short visit to ANU. He told me in a typically forthright manner that, given his structural-functional approach, the focus of my proposed research worried him. He said that I would be making a very serious mistake if I got involved in a theme so vague and so difficult to handle as 'values'. He advised a focus on 'objective facts'. What mattered most in peasant kinship systems in South Asia was that 'people had land and they had maternal uncles'. This was obviously his way of saying that the 'two' most significant factors governing kinship relations and family life are the ownership and inheritance of property, notably land, and the disputes that arise over it among agnatically related kin who are the offspring of different mothers in an extended family. He advised me to collect case studies of family disputes and subject them to careful analysis, so that the existence of cultural norms may be demonstrated, and to avoid getting bogged down in 'an ideal, value-governed, mythical state of existence'.

Leach thus raised doubts about the study of kinship values, as had Saran earlier, but for the very opposite reasons. His advice, as I understood it, was to leave alone the people's notions of ideal behaviour, and to adopt a statistical concept of customary or normative behaviour: to study people's behaviour itself—that is, the objective reality—rather than their ideas about it, which are subjective formulations of objective reality, often no more than distortions and rationalisations. One could trace this distrust of what people say or affirm to the many excellent demonstrations of the gap between word and deed that abound in ethnographical literature, beginning with Malinowski's monographs on the Trobriand islanders.

Although rather disappointed by Leach's rejection of the proposed focus of my research, I was greatly relieved that he had not objected to my studying the Pandits, my own people. He had not raised a question which I had feared he might, namely how I could ensure that my research among my own people would be marked by scientific objectivity, as required by orthodoxy. I partially revised my research plan on the lines suggested by Leach.

The question of objectivity was not, however, absent in the discussions I had with various faculty members on my proposed fieldwork in Kashmir. One of them, Derek Freeman, cautioned me repeatedly to steer clear of Indological texts, and not get carried away by people's ideas about their culture and society. He called giving too much attention to such texts and ideas 'the besetting fault' of the work of Indian anthropologists on Hindu society. The anthropologist should, they all said or implied, draw his conclusions directly from observed behaviour, guided by well-established fieldwork techniques. (The department stocked copies of the venerable *Notes and Queries on Anthropology*, and I too equipped myself with one.)

We understand the import of such exhortations much better today than I was capable of doing then. They emphasized that, in today's language, Indians were not to be trusted to produce objective and reliable ethnography about themselves without the benefit of modern social science perspectives. Even when trained in them, they had to be careful about not losing their objectivity by being overwhelmed (beset) by native categories of thought. The few books that I carried with me to the Kashmir village where I went for fieldwork were what were then considered exemplary anthropological studies of kinship, notably the Nuer and Tallensi kinship books by E.E. Evans-Pritchard and Meyer Fortes respectively. Halfway through the fieldwork I felt the need for an authoritative work on Hindu law and obtained one (by mail), but that was as far as I went. Irawati Karve's *Kinship Organisation in India* (1953), which I had carefully read, was not in my kitbag in the field. On the whole, I thought I had the dangers of subjective bias and a book-view of society well under control, notwithstanding the fact that my Pandit villagers had lots of ideas about the character of their family life.

In fact, they had not merely stray ideas but a coherent and well-articulated ideology of the householder. I assembled this ideology from both statements, made directly by informants in reply to my questions, and observations on all sorts of topics which reflected the ideology. But eventually, on my return to Canberra, I did not include a discussion of this ideology in my dissertation. My focus was on observed behaviour, which would have been fine but for the fact that my notion of what constituted 'behaviour' was rather narrow. Thus I failed to collect sufficient material on Sanskritic rituals, such as initiation, marriage, and the rituals addressed to manes, because I believed that the quest would soon lead me to the forbidden texts. Caution about presuming that what is given in the texts is also to be found, and in the same form, in real life would have been in order. A total avoidance of the texts, however, was a mistake that I made, but nobody told me that I was doing so. I did not then realize that being objective requires paying attention to the subjective point of view—native 'texts', first-order interpretations, or whatever one may call them.

The Middle Position

Early in 1959, when I was nearing the end of writing my dissertation, I read the English translation of Louis Dumont's inaugural lecture, 'For a Sociology of India', which was delivered (in French) in Paris in 1955. The approach advocated by him, attaching equal importance to Indology and social anthropology in the making of the sociology of India, reopened for me the whole issue of the place of the ideas of the people in anthropological fieldwork and the ethnographic narrative.

Dumont's argument seemed clear and convincing to me. It is quite well-known for me to not need to go into it in great detail. It should suffice to recall here that, after affirming that the study of any civilization is ultimately inspired by 'the endeavour to constitute an adequate idea of mankind' (1957:9), he observed that 'modern social anthropology had made a significant contribution' to the definition of social facts as things and as collective representations through 'its insistence that the observer sees things from within (as integrated in the society which he studies) and from without'. Following Evans-Pritchard, Dumont described 'the movement from one point of view to the other as an effort of translation', but cautioned that 'in this task it is not sufficient to translate the indigenous words, for it frequently happens that the ideas which they express are related to each other by more fundamental ideas even though these are unexpressed' (ibid.: 11–12).

Dumont's perspective was welcome to me as it pointed to a seemingly satisfactory way out of the alleged conflict between anthropological and native understandings of the social reality: not by privileging the former and devaluing (and even excluding) the latter, but through a confrontation of the two. To the extent to which my dissertation had considerably relied on the Kashmiri Pandits' own conceptions of kinship, marriage, and the family (see Madan 1965), I felt vindicated. At the same time it was obvious that, in the absence of a solid theoretical position (such as I now found in Dumont's statement), I had not proceeded systematically, not far enough. I attempted to do so later in a number of essays (written between 1976 and 1985, see Madan 1987), which included one on the ideology of the Pandit householder. By then the role of ideas and ideologies in social life, and in anthropology, had begun to receive serious attention. Also, behaviouristic conceptions of culture were being replaced by symbolic ones that emphasized meaning and significance. In some of these essays I turned to notable works of fiction in various Indian languages for insights. With the arrival of the novel on my anthropological desk, I had finally put behind me an exclusive *social science* conception of the discipline.

Dumont's approach came under attack from F.G. Bailey soon after the publication of the English version of his 1955 lecture. Bailey restated the orthodox behaviourist position and advocated evasion of the ideas of the people, 'supposing they have any ideas which is not always the case' (1959:

90). He dismissed Dumont's approach as culturological and stuck in the intuitive understanding of the unique. This was gross distortion. There were a few others who joined the debate, including A.K Saran, who refused to grant Dumont the privilege of the ground he claimed to stand on. He wrote magisterially: 'social reality *qua* social reality has no "outside": ...the only outside is interpretation in terms of an alien culture' (1962:68). The conflict between 'scientific objectivity', so-called, and 'subjective understanding' was presented in a particularly uncompromising form in these criticisms.

Having followed the debate with interest, I tried to formulate my own response to it. I made the following two points, among others. While recognizing the significance of the dialectic of the views from within and without, I complained that Dumont weakened his argument by asserting that the sociologist shares the external point of view with the natural scientist. I wrote: 'I am not sure that such a point of view exists.... If it did, it should have been possible for us to study social life through observation unaided by communication with the observed people.... [W]hen the sociologist allows "the principles that people themselves give" ... to enter his analysis and explanation, he surrenders a truly external position' (1966: 12).

In response, Dumont argued that if the external point of view had not existed, there would have been no social anthropology, but conceded that the approach advocated by him 'might rather be called positive-cum-subjective' and reasserted: 'Duality, or tension is... the condition *sine qua non* of social anthropology or, if one likes, sociology of a deeper kind' (1966:22–23).

Although I may not have stated my position very clearly, what I was trying to suggest was that, beyond a point, a stark opposition between scientific objectivity (howsoever defined) and subjective understanding is sterile; it produces the kinds of negative extremism exemplified by Bailey's and Saran's comments cited above. As social anthropologists we were concerned with the 'concrete' and the 'particular'; to adequately describe and interpret the same, and provide causal explanations when doing so seems appropriate and possible, we need 'abstract' and 'general' concepts. It cannot be otherwise in the human sciences, and I am quite comfortable with this middle position.

Mutual Interpretation of Cultures

As my anthropological-sociological studies continued, I ceased to worry about the opposition between objectivity and subjectivity. I combined perspectives and methods in a self-conscious manner. I also dispensed with the notion of anthropology as the study of 'other cultures', and continued with the study of aspects of the society in which I lived.

In a paper written in 1974, I questioned the requirement of the personal study of an alien culture on the part of every anthropologist. Instead, I emphasized the importance of bridging the gap, or conversely, creating it, between the observer and the observed. I described fieldwork as the feat of 'living intimately with strangers' (Madan 1975). I might have added: 'or strangely with intimates', which was what I had done during my fieldwork among the Pandits of rural Kashmir. The anthropologist studying his own culture, I wrote, 'is an insider who takes up the posture of an outsider, by virtue of his training as an anthropologist or a sociologist, and looks at his own culture, hoping to be surprised. If he is, only then may he achieve new understandings' (ibid.: 149).

Subsequently, I moved a step further and argued that anthropology was best conceived, not as the study of other cultures but as 'the mutual interpretation of cultures' (Madan 1982). I mentioned the dual perspective of the views from within and without and added: 'we must adhere firmly to the notion that anthropology resides in this nexus, that it is a kind of knowledge—a form of consciousness—which arises from the encounter of cultures in the mind of the anthropologist. What an observer learns about an alien society's observable modes of behaviour will not yield anthropological understanding unless he is able to grasp, in the first place, the subjective purposes and meanings that make these modes of behaviour significant to the people concerned. But the knowledge about one's own beliefs and rituals which an informant may impart to the investigator is not anthropological either' (ibid.: 5). In other words, anthropological knowledge was not to be discovered, but generated by confronting, first, what people say with what they do, and, then, confronting the view from within with the view from without.

'What people believe in and do, and the relationship of belief and action, has first to be understood in the people's own terms—this is the first order interpretation of facts—before one may translate these understandings, into the language of anthropology. The anthropologist's task, then, is to establish a synthesis between the introversion of self-understanding and the extraversion of the scientific method' (ibid.: 7). It was thus that I arrived at the conclusion that anthropology was perhaps best defined as the mutual interpretation of cultures: learning about one's own culture from the other cultures one studied, just as one uses insights derived from one's cultural experience—one's personal anthropology—as well as knowledge of ethnography to make sense of the cultures one writes about.

Writing as a creative rather than merely recording activity, was soon going to attract a great deal of attention. Naïve realism and an uncritical mirror theory of knowledge were under attack. There was a great deal of overkill in some of these writings, but there was a hard core of genuine criticism of orthodoxy, which fitted well with my views developed over the years.

In a conference paper written in 1985, I briefly discussed the images of India in the work of American anthropologists, from Alfred Kroeber to Mckim Marriott. I identified several images or representations and concluded that all the representations seemed to be grounded in empirical reality; what distinguished them from one another was the perspective of each. Echoing James Clifford, I called these representations partial—committed and incomplete—and added: 'this does not mean though that someone has to piece them together and render them complete. Their utility lies in their being what they are and in their mutual contestation. The assessment of the truth value of anthropological images thus turns out to be not merely a question of information about the present situation or historical roots of institutions, or of future possibilities, but also a debate about appropriate perspectives. Such debates are, of course, notoriously inconclusive. One clear guideline though is that the perspective which enables us to understand more of the facts on the ground economically and in an internally consistent manner, and does not claim exhaustiveness, is to be preferred to those that lack coherence and lay claims to monopoly over truth' (1990:196).

I returned to this theme of the character of anthropological knowledge in the introductory essay to my book *Non-Renunciation: Themes and Interpretations of Hindu Culture* (1987). Writing about first order interpretations which a people provide when questioned about their culture, I suggested that while the interpretations fabricated by the people themselves may seem adequate and explicit to them, they usually are opaque to the outsider, which is what the social anthropologist is, in one sense or another: if not born in another society, his training as an anthropologist teaches him to turn a sceptical eye at everything that seems familiar. 'Interpretation thus involves the social anthropologist in a process of unfolding or unravelling what are at first riddles to him, by working out their implications: ... it is a search for significance and structure' (ibid.: 7–8).

Just as the internal interpreters one encounters in the course of fieldwork are several, I continued, the external interpreters also may be many, each capturing a particular facet of social reality, a particular cultural theme, and providing a comparative or general perspective on it. To say this is not to surrender to solipsism but to affirm the legitimacy and value of pluralism. The illusions of completeness and permanence that an ethnographic text creates are useful, each in its own way, but the interpretive endeavour knows no finality. As the questions change—and this happens for a variety of reasons ranging from on-going social change to changing theoretical orientations—so do the answers, and the completeness of description is inevitably deferred. I believe the positivists of yesterday knew this as well as do the grammatologists of today. The aims and the nature of the endeavour are, however, clear: namely, the effort to make sense of what the people we seek to understand think and do, and, as Max Weber put it, to grasp how they 'confer meaning and significance' on their lives. Our interpretations thus are not merely pictures of empirical reality. They are descriptive but they are not merely description. In our fieldwork and the subsequent writing, we not only *look* and *listen*, we also *think*. In other words, we inevitably, though not always self-consciously, put ourselves into our ethnographic accounts of others.

As I have reflected upon the nature of anthropological fieldwork and knowledge over the years, I have leaned more and more towards the humanities and found social history and literature richer sources of inspiration in my anthropological work than the natural or biological sciences. I have noted the need for immense caution implied by Karl Popper's admonition that 'the triumph of social anthropology' may have only been 'the triumph of a pseudo-observational, pseudo-descriptive, and pseudo-generalising methodology and above all marks the triumph of a pretended objectivity and hence an imitation of the methods of natural science' (quoted by Banton 1964: 99).

I have also become increasingly conscious of the significance of cultivating a philosophical perspective in the specific sense of comparative ethics. Ethnography merely as knowledge of how other people live their lives can be just baggage, a burden, unless it teaches one to live one's own life better—judged as such in terms of certain ultimate values that enjoy cross-cultural legitimacy. Whether this effort is described as 'the mutual interpretation of cultures', or as the cultivation of 'critical self-awareness' (see Madan 1994), the point being made is the same and obvious. It would be trite to try to illustrate such a world view by citing particular examples; it must inform all that one does and the way one thinks.

Anthropology and History

I began my discovery of anthropology in the light of what my teachers, first at the University of Lucknow and then at Australian National University, told me the subject was all about. They spoke to me in several voices in Lucknow, but the dominant voice at Canberra was that of positivism. As I have tried to describe in this essay, the need to choose between the different perspectives emerged fairly early in my research career. I had wanted to begin with a fieldwork-based study of kinship values, but ended up writing a structural-functional study of the family and the household. To be told by those whose opinions mattered in the profession that it was the first such study for north India, and a successful one, mattered a great deal to me. Besides, the question of what to do with the subjective understandings of the people being studied, what value to attach to them, seemed to me to move towards a satisfactory solution in the work of Louis Dumont rather than that of, say, Edmund Leach.

Doing fieldwork among the Pandits of rural Kashmir had meant dealing with a situation in which 'work' was an aspect of domestic life, even when it took place in the fields or the village shops. The idea of looking upon work on its own, which of course meant looking upon it in modern bureaucratized settings, interested me a great deal. Also, I was curious about the criticism voiced by economists, and by some sociologists too, that anthropological knowledge was of very limited practical value. Accordingly, I undertook studies of modern occupations and professions on the basis of secondary data, which involved statistical analysis at the state, national, and international levels. I supplemented these studies with personal observation of clinical medical practice and interviews with allopathic practitioners in an Indian city as well as interviews with the faculty of a major medical teaching and research and health care institution (see Madan 1972, 1980). I found this work, its concern with social development and its quantitative data and statistical analysis notwithstanding, intellectually less appealing and emotionally less satisfying than my earlier work. It had none of the interest of participant observation (in the real sense of the term), and I was sure that I never fully succeeded in finding what the doctors' work meant to them. Their world of subjective experience was not easily captured in interviews and quantified information.

While fieldwork thus remained an attraction, I looked elsewhere too for new perspectives. It seemed to me that besides 'kinship' and 'work', the third major area which the anthropologist should study, particularly in India, is religion. There are many excellent fieldwork-based studies of the meaning and significance of religion in the lives of village communities, or particular categories of people, such as pilgrims. But religion has become intertwined with politics in our times, and appears to us in the form of the 'ideologies' of secularism, communalism, and fundamentalism. It is these ideologies that have engaged my attention for much of the last decade.

While the anthropological method of comparison, with the focus on the particular, still guides me, the nature of the subject compels me to study it diachronically. I find, not a single ideology, but secularisms and fundamentalisms, each set of ideologies held together by a family resemblance. Thus, by a circuitous path, I find I have come back to history and, indeed, literature also. But when I turn to history today, I do so as an anthropologist. Actually, these labels and designations do not seem to me all that significant any more. What is significant is the social reality that we seek to know and understand, and what matters is whether our studies—our interpretations—illumine this reality more than the earlier explanations did. The critical question is, are we moving forward? The rest, it seems to me, is the vanity of intellectual fashions....

Informal Collaborations as an Aspect of Urban Anthropological Fieldwork: Experiences from Jaipur City

JAMES LAIDLAW

'Society is not a "thing"; it is a way of ordering experience.'

(Edmund Leach, 1961a: 304–5)

My first period of fieldwork among Shvetambar Jains in Jaipur was also my first visit to Jaipur city and indeed my first visit to India. I ended up there as a result of no serious deliberation or decision on my part. I was an undergraduate reading social anthropology at Cambridge, towards the end of my second year. For the finals—to be taken at the end of the following year—we had the option of writing a dissertation to substitute for one examination paper. This I knew was what all serious aspiring researchers did, so I asked my Director of Studies, Caroline Humphrey, if she had any suggestions about what I might do. Caroline had recently undertaken some research on Jainism in Rajasthan, and she had a graduate student, then on fieldwork in Jaipur, who she thought might be kind enough to look after me, and able to suggest something useful for me to do. She said she would write to her and enquire. This graduate student, Josephine Reynell, did indeed agree to take me under her wing and she introduced me to my first Jain contacts in the city.[1]

In the summer of 1983 I set about working in a Jain temple belonging to the Shvetambar Jain Khartar Gacch tradition in the suburbs of Jaipur. This temple is referred to as a Dadabari temple because its principal feature is a shrine to four patron saints of the Khartar Gacch, collectively known as the Dada Guru Devs. After six weeks, I came back, as I hoped I would, with material for a short undergraduate dissertation on the veneration of these saints in the Dadabari temple, but also with the outline of a project for my proposed Ph.D. research.[2] The striking counterpoint between the severity of Jain asceticism on the one hand, as exemplified especially by Jain renouncers but also in aspects of the lives of ordinary Jains, and the opulence of Jain collective life on the other hand—the splendour of their temples and luxuriance of some of their rituals—as well as the celebrated wealth of the community as a whole; all this raised for me a number of questions about the relation between religion and economic life, and about the form and nature of ethical ideals and values, and how they influence everyday conduct. And even a short acquaintance made clear that Jainism is a fascinating member of the family of Indic religious traditions which had, hitherto, largely escaped the notice of anthropologists.

Reflecting on the fieldwork I conducted on this project over the following years, one aspect stands out as important, and worth emphasizing in an account of ethnographic fieldwork in an urban setting. I frequently found that local people who helped me in various ways in collecting information were themselves intensely interested and often surprised by what I was finding out. In a few important cases I found myself engaged in quite sustained informal collaborations with local people who were consciously and purposively seeking what one can only call ethnographic knowledge. These relationships became quite an important part of my research, as well as important elements in my friendships with the people concerned. The salience of such informal collaborations, and the ease with which they seemed to have arisen, are related I think to the fact that my fieldwork was on the subject of collective life in a large and socially diverse urban setting. I do not think that it is only urban settings in which this may be the case, but they do powerfully exemplify the dispersal of knowledge which is likely to make informal collaborations an effective or even essential part of fieldwork. In my own case, the fluidity and non-formal character of the social realm I was moving in, and the importance of dispersed and complex cultural differences within it, both meant that these collaborations were not just instruments or methods for studying the forms of social life I was trying to understand, they also embodied important and characteristic elements of social relations within them.

The Fieldwork Setting of 'Fictive Villages'

By the time I completed 'the-book-of-the-thesis' in 1994, I had spent a total of about nineteen months working in Jaipur, spread over six separate visits. Most of my time on fieldwork was spent in two areas of Jaipur: the streets around Johari Bazaar in the walled city and a suburban area somewhat to the south of this, around Dadabari temple.

Not far from the Dadabari is a small colony of thatched mud houses. Although I never really got much closer than to cycle past, from the road it has a distinctly rural and pastoral look. Early in the morning, as smartly dressed Jains are making their way to the temple, the people who live here are bathing under taps by the side of the road, making tea in the open spaces between their houses, and tending to the buffalo whose milk and dung they sell. This scene served for me, especially in low moments when I didn't seem to be making progress, as an emblem of how much easier, I imagined, fieldwork would be in a village—the paradigm, preferred even over caste, of an anthropological object of study in India.

Over time, I got to know both of my fieldwork areas well. There were times when it seemed that whenever I went from place to place I would see or run into someone I knew, and as time went by the faces in the shops, the street stalls, and the temples became increasingly familiar to me. And evidently I did to them. Not far from where I lived was a large roundabout with a statue in the middle. One of my regular routes included a right turn here and I remember one occasion—just one—when I adopted the common local habit among cyclists of slipping round the outside edge of the road in a sort of illicit contra-flow lane, rather than going all the way round. I might have adopted the practice—in hot weather the proper method seemed a huge expense of energy—but the very next day one of my regular informants commented that someone had mentioned to him that they had seen me do this. It was clear that he felt this was a demotic practice which I ought to regard as beneath my dignity. In future I went round the roundabout. Thus both the Johari Bazaar and the Dadabari area could feel at times like villages, and there were times when I tried to imagine them as such. But the ways in which they are not like villages had a profound effect on how my fieldwork in fact proceeded. The details of the case are particular to Jaipur and the Jains, but the general characteristics of the public sphere are replicated elsewhere in urban India,[3] and the implications for how fieldwork on urban 'communities' might be conducted may apply still more widely than that.

Johari Bazaar, or Jewellery Market, is one of the busiest streets in Jaipur, and the centre of the city's gem business. The most obvious feature of the gem business is the many shops and showrooms on the Bazaar itself, selling jewellery of various kinds. But this is not the real gem business, which is a market co-ordinating the import, processing, trading, and export of large consignments of emeralds. Despite its size and importance, this business is largely hidden from public view, conducted as it mostly is from rooms in private houses in the alleyways off the Bazaar. The area is hot, noisy, and overcrowded, and the water supply is intermittent, but for those who engage in the gem trade it is a definite advantage to live here, because this is a face-to-face business in which deals are concluded on the spot, and so the rents are high.

A substantial community of Shvetambar Jains, in the order of a thousand families or so, lives, works, shops, and worships in this small area. They own many of the *havelis* (mansions), they dominate the emerald trade, and the area is also the centre of Shvetambar religious life. Within a few dozen yards of each other are five Shvetambar temples and a score of other religious buildings: offices, libraries, meeting halls, and renouncers' lodgings. The Jains who live in and around this area certainly think of it as 'their' district, but it is not exclusively theirs. The area is socially mixed, with a substantial sprinkling of non-Jain merchants also active in the gem market, and with rich merchants and their many non-Jain servants, tenants, and tradesmen all living on top of each other. There is no Jain monopoly on property ownership in the district, and no corporation or authority regulating sales, and while Jains are a higher proportion of the population here than elsewhere in the city, they are still not actually a majority, and the area of their concentration is not clearly bounded. Insofar as there is a Jain district, it is at best a matter of degree, and it shades off into other districts with different distinctive but similarly qualified identities.

In an urban neighbourhood such as this there may be many people one knows by sight and even to talk to, but this does not mean that the knowledge people have of each other is necessarily very comprehensive, or that their relations are necessarily very rounded. Unlike in a village, and despite the familiarity and apparent intimacy of the area, people who live here deal routinely in the streets, at stalls and shops, and even in religious forums such as temples and meeting halls, with people they do not know and whom they identify and assess according to their dress, speech, and bearing, matching them to impersonal social stereotypes.[4] Even people who buy regularly from the same shop year after year do not necessarily know more than the name and caste of the shopkeeper; or he more than the selective good news of their families which they may choose to tell him. In relations with their own tenants (or landlords), Jain families take an interest in the school careers of the children and so on, but their neighbours' tenants (or landlords) may be just names and faces.

Insofar, also, as the term 'village' has connotations of a settled and relatively stable community, it is inappropriate here. The Jains in this district appear very 'traditional' indeed. Almost all families are involved in the gem business, women observe quite strict purdah in many families, a high degree of social conformity is expected, gossip is rife, and sexual mores are strict. But none of this means that people are deeply rooted to place, or parochial in outlook, or that this is a community which is in any sense 'closed'. Although people are conscious that Jains have been present since the founding of Jaipur city, and it is easy to find a family which will claim to have been there since that time, on closer inspection it becomes clear that a large number of people, including many of the most venerable 'village elder' types, are first or second generation immigrants. They have come from all parts of Rajasthan and Gujarat, from Delhi, and from Bengal. And although most marriages are between Jaipur families, they are also regularly aranged with others in villages and towns throughout north-western India, and, among the rich, even further afield. This means, of course, that a very large number of the women living in Jaipur grew up and have families somewhere else. And many Jaipur families have one of their sons now established in some other important business centre such as Mumbai, Ahmedabad, or Bangalore. Even some of the most apparently 'traditional' people are widely travelled, and the gem business takes its more successful operator on regular trips to the United States, Europe, and the Far East. So swiftly changing is the Jain population—and, in this city of mushrooming suburbs, so increasingly dispersed—that in the mid-1980s a 'directory' was compiled (and since updated), the intention being to list all Shvetambar Jain families in the city, to help people in their search for suitable marriage partners, and to announce and affirm that despite appearances, something like a Shvetambar Jain 'community' exists.

My second 'fictive village' was around the Dadabari temple. The temple itself consists of a pleasant walled garden, with offices, kitchens, a meeting hall, a rest-house for renouncers, a Shvetambar temple, and, as its centrepiece, a shrine to the four Dada Guru Devs. Around the Dadabari there are shops and a successful private school, and even some light industry, but mostly, spacious bungalows, some of which are very luxurious indeed. As many Jains like to walk to a nearby temple for morning worship, the Dadabari has attracted a number of Jain families to this area, so that a highish proportion of the bungalows in this area are owned by Shvetambar Jains. As in Johari Bazaar, there is no boundary to this spatial clustering. The most one can say is that roughly, the nearer you get to the Dadabari, the more likely the houses are to belong to a Jain family. And also as in Johari

Bazaar, virtually all the Jains here are in the gem trade. There are a few professionals and academics, but in general this area is too expensive for anyone other than those in business.

In the same deceptive way that Johari Bazaar looks traditional, the colonies in this area look rather 'modern', with lots of smart cars, craft shops, fast-food restaurants, and bungalows being refaced in the latest New Delhi fashion. To sustain the comfortable bungalows set in gardens with neat lawns and flower-beds, Jain families here employ far more servants than those in the walled city, and almost all have a whole family lodged in little huts or an annexe at the back of the house. Overall, more of the women who live here work than do in the walled city, but for the great majority who do not (and this includes most Jains), life is more constrained and isolated, because they are more or less confined to the house and receive fewer visitors.

In fact, although these two areas of Jaipur do have certain different characteristics, there are many social connections which make them part of the same general picture. The Dadabari temple is linked organizationally to others in the Johari Bazaar area, and elsewhere. The families who live round the Dadabari frequently own property in Johari Bazaar, where other branches of the family may live, and from where their business is conducted. Some of the families who live near the Dadabari worship there regularly for convenience, but have closer links to other temples, perhaps in the walled city, and go there for the most important annual ceremonies. And the loose networks linking these two areas also extend to several other suburban localities, where relative concentrations of the Jain population have already or will soon give rise to a local Jain temple.

As that buffalo herders' *basti* (ghetto) reminded me, in a real village, one could count up all the people and make sure one had 'got' them all, whereas I was dealing with overlapping and open-ended categories of people and it just did not make sense to try to 'count them up'. In a real village, so much of life would take place in clearly identified open spaces, and would bear some legible relationship to the whole; whereas in Jaipur, much that I wanted to 'observe' was scattered across the whole city and tucked away in shuttered houses, and refused ever to be convincingly detached from people's disparate situations and projects. Of course, even in a village, social relations do not stop at the settlement boundary; but the fact that there is such a boundary makes possible the descriptive fiction that one is concerned with a social 'object': one which is linked to others, no doubt, but which has in itself a definite extent and an internal design and organization, and which can in principle be exhaustively described.

The people I knew did routinely talk about the 'Shvetambar Jain *samaj*' (community), as if it were such an object.[5] But it became clear to me that the phenomenon they were referring to had a highly problematical exist-ence. There are formal religious institutions, as we shall see, which play a part in the generation and reproduction of the Jain 'community', but they are not identical to it. And they are different from it in kind, because the 'community' is, in Hayek's (1982) terms, a *cosmos* rather than a *taxis*;[6] not, that is, a formal social entity constituted according to a knowable design, but rather the always evolving and unintended outcome of innu-merable individual actions.

It is intrinsic to an order of this kind that the knowledge participants have of it is radically dispersed among them, and in all cases partial and largely tacit. There is no implicit architectural plan. Participants' knowl-edge of and from their own particular circumstances is nowhere added together; but it is co-ordinated, because and insofar as it informs their several decisions and interactions. The fact that different people in differ-ent situations know different things is itself constitutive of this kind of social order. It is therefore not an obstacle for the anthropologist to over-come, in assembling an imaginary totality, of which each individual could be imagined as knowing a part. This dispersal is, rather, an intrinsic part of what the anthropologist must experience and convey. Social situations characterized by this kind of dispersal of knowledge—which certainly in-clude but are probably not restricted to urban settings—therefore present specific kinds of problem and challenge to the anthropological fieldworker.

The Processes of Local Community

The Dadabari temple is owned by the local Khartar Gacch Shrimal Sabha. The Shrimals are one of the two main castes represented among Shvetambar Jains in Jaipur, the other being the Oswals. Both are Baniya, or 'business', castes, and there are many members of both these castes who are not Jains but Vaishnava Hindus. Intra-religious marriage is preferred, but not strictly adhered to. Marriages between Jain and Hindu Oswals or Jain and Hindu Shrimals are not uncommon and attract no serious adverse comment (except from a few religious leaders in both cases); the general practice being for the bride, more or less rigorously depending on the particular family into which she is marrying, to adopt her husband's family's pattern of religious observance. In exactly the same way and on similar terms, marriages between Jain Oswals and Jain Shrimals are not uncommon in Jaipur.

'Khartar Gacch' on the other hand is not a caste label but a religious sectarian one. It refers to one of several lineages of Shvetambar Jain renouncers. Khartar Gacch lay people are followers of the renouncers of that tradition. All Jain religious property—temples, renouncers' rest houses, and preaching and fasting halls—are built, owned, and maintained by lay people who usually live nearby and use the property concerned, and are affiliated to a particular renouncer tradition.[7] Within the Shvetambar branch of Jainism the most important of these renouncer traditions are the Tapa Gacch, the Khartar Gacch, the Sthanakvasis, and the Terapanthis. The Terapanth is a special case, because that tradition forbids the erection of buildings dedicated to religious purposes, and is a single unified sectarian organization different in kind to the other Jain traditions, so I will leave it out of consideration here. (My own fieldwork was hardly concerned with it at all.) The Sthanakvasis do not maintain temples, being opposed to the worship of *murtis* (idols), but they do maintain rest houses and preaching halls in the same way as the Tapa and Kartar Gacch. Although a few temples are maintained at the expense of a single very rich family, the more usual situation is for a local association (or *sangha*), led by a committee of prominent laymen and women, to own and manage temples and other religious property. In Jaipur there is a Tapa Gacch Sangha which owns, among other properties, a large temple complex in the Johari Bazaar area, and a Khartar Gacch Sangha, which owns several temples and other buildings in the same locality. In new suburban colonies around the city, new Shvetambar Jain temples are being built, most of which are affiliated to one or the other of these corporations; but the degree of local autonomy they have, for instance, through the existence of a separate management committee, varies. This depends on the extent to which the funding of the temple has been a purely local initiative, or conducted through the older city-centre organization.

But the associations which own religious property may be defined not only by sect and locality but also by other criteria such as caste. The Khartar Gacch Sangha in Jaipur is dominated by Oswals, who are the most numerous Jain Baniya caste in the city, but also includes many families of other castes. The Dadabari temple is one of a number of properties, including a temple in the Johari Bazaar area, which are affiliated to the Khartar Gacch, but owned and run by an association only of Shrimals and not by the Khartar Gacch Sangha. Members of the Shrimal Sabha may also be members of the Khartar Gacch Sangha, and this includes the prominent committee members of the former. So the Shrimal Sabha in this case stands in sort of semi-detached relation to the larger Khartar Gacch Sangha. The situation varies locally between different towns and villages, depending in part on the mix of the local population. In some towns in southern India, for instance, there are temples run by groups of Jains from particular towns or regions, such as Bombayites or Gujaratis. The important point is that new associations can be formed by any group of people with the means to build and endow a religious building and the will to keep it running, and the constitutions of such organizations vary with local circumstances.

It is important to emphasize that the use as distinct from the ownership and management of temples and other religious buildings is generally very open. The use of the kitchens for entertaining guests and the privilege of sponsoring large religious ceremonies in the temple are usually reserved for subscribing members of the association, although the subscriptions are invariably only nominal sums of money; but anyone (even a non-Jain, provided they observe the normal proprieties) may come to worship in the temples or pay respects to visiting renouncers, and the same is true of attendance at the many religious festivals and gatherings throughout the year. Accordingly, many Jains worship regularly in their nearest temple, even if it is not specifically assigned to their caste or sect. But people who wish a more active participation in their local religious community will prefer to attend, and therefore to live close to, a temple to which they feel that they fully belong.

Participation admits of almost infinite degrees, from intermittent attendance for a quick *darshan* ('beholding') of renouncers or at the temple and maybe attending a few big annual religious gatherings; to daily performance of puja and regular attendance at sermons, calendrical fasts, ascetic rites, and other religious ceremonies. Those who live close by and participate in this latter way obviously become more securely and centrally part of what is imagined as a local Jain community than do those who appear only as names on a membership list. And at the extreme, at the effective centre of the local Jain community, are those who effectively fund its collective life through large donations.

The funding of local religious events is not separate from performance. All large rites of worship are sponsored by particular families, whose members thereupon take the leading roles in the ceremony. Annual ceremonies, periodic feasts, and special one-off events such as the consecration of a new temple idol or the ordination of a renouncer, are also sponsored by particular individuals, often as a result of an auction held at the event itself, at which rights to perform certain parts of the ceremonies are sold to the highest bidder. This is true of some of the most important gatherings in the whole religious year, which are attended by even quite marginal members of the community, and at which funds are raised by auction to cover the principal annual running costs of the temples and other property. Obviously this is where wealth comes into the picture. Rich families can place themselves at the centre of the local Jain community by making donations which materially reproduce the public sphere in which collective community life takes place, and which, at the same time, entitle them to prominent and dignified roles in that collective life. And in Jaipur, where Shvetambar Jains are both numerically concentrated in and symbolically identified with the emerald market, it is especially wealthy families involved in that market who act as patrons of the religious community.

So insofar as there is a Jain community—in Jaipur and in any other comparable settlement—this is not only a complicated cross-cutting cluster of groupings based on overlapping but different criteria of membership; it is also radically unequal and a matter of degree: some individuals and families are much more members of the community than are others. Therefore the way to think of the 'Jain community', which my informants all talked about naturally, is not as a group or an entity, with more or less definite boundaries and an ascertainable number of members; but rather as a set of activities—a public sphere—located in or around religious buildings (which is what makes it a specifically Jain community), but embracing also aspects of life which are not specifically religious, such as marriage and business connections; membership of the community being the highly variable and changeable matter of patronage of and participation in these activities. Thus, being at or near the centre of the community, and indeed membership in anything more than a merely token sense, is an effect of the ongoing decisions and actions of individuals and families.

To maintain membership is easier, more natural, and more important for some families than for others, as an example from my fieldwork may illustrate.

I got to know a family, which I shall here call the Porwals, early in my research. The husband was from a long-established family of Jaipur gem traders but he himself had gone into government service. His wife was from a different Shvetambar Jain tradition, but in accordance with custom she had effectively adopted his family's modes of religious practice. Their children were all academically able, and both sons and daughters were on course for professional occupations.

Although the first marriage among the younger generation had been arranged within caste and religious tradition, to a professional Jain family from another town in Rajasthan; the second, which occurred during my fieldwork, was a 'love marriage' to a Hindu of a Brahmin family. None of the family participated very much in public religious activities. The children's friends, drawn from the élite educational institutions they attended, were, for the most part, not Jain. None of them was looking to the gem market as a likely career, so contacts in the local Jain community were not important for that reason. The wife was never in strong health, so, rarely went out. In her way she was quite religious, but preferred to observe her private devotions at home. All in all, and over time, this family was drifting away from the local, business-centred Shvetambar Jain community. Already there were plans for the rest of the family to move from the Johari Bazaar area, which was likely to further advance this process.

The third child had reached the age for marriage proposals to be sought and the mother of the family, hoping to arrange a socially orthodox alliance, decided to take advantage of a grand religious feast being held at that time, to show off her attractive and accomplished daughter at this gathering of local Jain families. The feast was to embrace both her husband's and her natal religious tradition, and this breadth admirably suited the purpose. So she and her husband attended this feast, together with the daughter in question. If one had not already known, the reactions of others at the gathering would anyway have made clear that the Porwals' appearance at such an event was an unusual sight. The expressions of frank surprise from acquaintances who had clearly not seen the family for some time were of course followed immediately by looks of comprehension, as the carefully dressed and groomed young woman was introduced. Her mother carried off the operation with great aplomb. With broad smiles, and apparently finding genuine enjoyment in the unaccustomed social event, she strode up to old acquaintances in turn, and carrying in train her somewhat less enthusiastic husband and decorously embarrassed daughter, she chatted animatedly, regretted the interval since last they had met, and led the way in the exchange of family news and gossip.

Afterwards, the event was proclaimed a great success in the Porwal family. Acquaintances were renewed and matrimonial interest was expressed from some very acceptable quarters; but in the end, and putting a seal somewhat on the family's drift to the outer periphery of the Jain community, it happened that the daughter struck up a romance with a young man of her own choice and in due time—and very amicably—a second inter-religious and inter-caste marriage was concluded, this time with a Rajput family. It would have been open to the Porwals, and still is to some among them, to re-orient their activities firmly towards the local Jain community, and so to revive their participation and membership, but there were no compelling reasons for them to do so. Although economic and social capital was lost by the continuing drift away, it was not of great value to them, given their careers, plans, social ambitions, and interests, and the opportunities afforded elsewhere appealed more. The case is not unique, nor is the phenomenon new. It has always been the case, for instance, that for families at both the very top and the bottom of the economic scale, Jain communities have often been either excessively constricting or unattainable domains of activity; and in such cases there has been a tendency for the Jain identity of such families to be greatly attenuated, and over time forgotten. At the same time others have moved into the Jain fold, attracted if not by the religion itself then by the social, economic, and kinship opportunities that come with participation.

Where the 'object' of one's study is so thoroughly unlike an object—in being a loose collection of activities in which participation is a matter of variable and changeable degree—an ambition of descriptive *completeness* clearly would make no sense. My task was not to dissect and describe an order or entity conforming to a single design, but to understand and convey the complex and evolving interplay of individuals' dispersed decisions and activities. In such circumstances, the idea that the anthropological way to study social relations is by making social relations becomes more than usually applicable.

Routines and Improvisations

Anthropologists often talk rather loosely about how one goes about 'fitting in' and being 'accepted' among the people one works with, and some even talk about being accepted, 'as one of them'. Such talk might do, in a rough and ready sort of way, for a local community which is small and homogeneous enough to appear to think with one mind. (Doubtless this usually means in practice no more than that one agency effectively makes the decision for everyone else.) But in a situation such as this one, in a large city, and in a diverse, dispersed, and differentiated religious community which, whatever else it is, is not a bounded and even quasi-organic social entity, there were no grounds for thinking, even metaphorically, in terms of incorporation. No one, not even a Jain, is just 'accepted' *tout simple*. You are always accepted *as* someone in particular, and *by* particular social agents: most saliently, individuals and families. As it happens, I early on got to know some respected local figures: prominent business leaders and local savants, as well as some Jain renouncers who were in the city. No doubt appearing in public—at religious ceremonies or just in the temple precincts—in the company of such figures influenced how many others made

their own decision about how to respond to me. These influential figures
probably gave my presence a certain legitimacy. But this does not alter the
fact that individuals and families still made their own decisions; and my
work relied crucially on families opening themselves to me in ways which
occur only on a one-by-one basis. There is no point at which one could be
admitted or incorporated 'into the community' as such; all one could do
was to see—and if one was lucky, join in with—individuals and families
as they themselves took part in the activities and processes that are 'the
community' in this setting.

For most of my fieldwork I lived near the Dadabari, in a set of rooms in
the house of a university professor; not a Jain, but a Hindu Kayasth, called
Dr Mathur, who liked having foreign tenants and offered me rooms at a rent
so low that even a graduate student funded by the British government could
afford them. So I moved into his whitewashed bungalow, festooned in
bougainvillaea; and this became my home in Jaipur, off and on, for several
years. Dr Mathur was a fastidious man, and this was the cause of my only
major discomfort. He refused to install any air coolers in the house, although
he seemed to feel the heat of a Jaipur summer no less than anyone else, but
he hated the noise and unsightly appearance of the machines, and so,
honouring his principles though regretting their application, I was constrained like him to make do with ceiling fans. There were only two sources
of noise: a Hindu man, whom I never saw but who lived over the high wall
outside my bedroom and would come down to the bottom of his garden at
dawn to chant his morning prayers; and a gentle drumming in the after-
noons from the school for classical Indian dance next door.

Beginning with some contacts Caroline Humphrey had made on her
earlier field trip to Jaipur, the people to whom Josephine Reynell introduced me when I first arrived in Jaipur, and others whom I met simply by
hanging around in Jain temples, I quickly accumulated a number of regular 'informants'. It was easy to identify and meet the people I knew at the
outset I wanted to talk with: renouncers, temple committee members, ritual
specialists, local savants, or people of whom I had heard that they, or some
recently deceased member of their family, were notable either for their
ascetic practice or their religious knowledge. Some of these became regular
informants, so that I got to know their interests and concerns, their general
attitudes and points of view. For a few, my enquiries seemed a natural
recognition and corollary of their status as local experts, and at the end of
an interview they expected to know when I was coming next. Other regular informants had no particular reputation for religiosity or knowledge:
women who seemed to have an inexhaustible store of religious stories to

tell me; business men whom I saw every few weeks for an informal chat about how life was going and who would answer any questions I put to them, as well as checking that I knew about all upcoming religious events they felt I ought to attend.

As Paul Rabinow (1977) has observed, the people who naturally gravitate towards anthropologists include some whose positions and way of life is in some way or other anomalous, because it is they who find most congenial the anthropologist's requests to reflect on and imaginatively objectify the customs and conventions of the world they live in. Certainly I got to know rather well some members of the poorest Jain families I came across: people for whom being part of the 'Jain community' at all was an achievement they had constantly to work at and could not be taken for granted. I suppose I learned most directly from them that it was not merely an entity of which you are simply a part.

I soon came to love the oddly tranquil industriousness of Jain temples. Morning worship is particularly beautiful and I often began the day with a visit to a temple. Sometimes I would stop at the Dadabari, and sometimes cycle straight to one of the temples in the walled city, depending on whom I was to meet later on. From before dawn each morning, people arrive to perform puja, dressed in fresh, clean cotton and carrying offerings of flowers, fruits, and sweets. Most people come alone, but some others meet up at a fixed time each morning to perform puja together. Still others come for a shorter time, to pay their respects, say short prayers, and spend a quiet few minutes before getting on with their day. This is what I would often do. It was a good way to keep up contacts, as one often ran into people one knew and ended by chatting outside or drifting off to have tea or breakfast together. It was also a good way to meet new people, whom curiousity would drive to polite enquiries or questioning looks. Even when nothing else came of it, there was always the ritual itself to watch, and it was a pleasant way to start the day before going off to see the first of my regular interlocutors.

Generally, my fieldwork 'methods' were decidedly informal.[8] Although I always tried to collect certain basic facts—about occupation, caste, household size, etc.,—from everyone I met with, I early on abandoned the idea of conducting a survey or census.[9] In a situation of overlapping social categories and groupings, none of which had definite boundaries, when would such a survey ever be complete? Of course I prepared questions in advance of meeting people, and I also tried to ensure, where appropriate, that I asked the same questions of as many people as possible. But much more of the time I would change the way I approached a topic each time I did so with a different person, in a search for formulations that would elicit the most engaged and discursive responses. With my regular informants, who naturally included those who were most reliably discursive and who expected to be imparting definite information in fairly large quantities, I would prepare long, detailed, and logically constructed question schedules in order to work systematically through, for instance, what goes on in a certain religious festival, or dietary rules, or the prayers and songs they recited during puja.

For a period in the middle of my fieldwork I hardly arranged interviews in advance at all. Behind the crowded street scenes, where sheer numbers give an impression of frenetic activity, the pace of life and work in Johari Bazaar is really rather relaxed. I was never short of people who had time to sit and talk. I could set off in the morning confident that between dropping in on friends, meeting people in the street, running into someone at someone else's shop, and popping into one of the temples to see who was there or to talk with renouncers, I would be occupied until late in the evening.

When I first came to Jaipur I was still under twenty. People's reactions to me were conditioned by this, and I think that impressions and perceptions from that time continued to colour how people saw me for some time afterwards. I had a terror of being drawn into a ruinous business deal involving thousands of pounds worth of emeralds, so in most contexts I cultivated an ostentatious lack of interest in gem trading; at the expense, I suspect, of seeming even more naïve than I was, and also perhaps of being 'otherworldly', a description to which I had no valid claim at all. I tried to adjust to local circumstances and participate as much as possible, but largely for budgetary reasons, my ways of doing so clustered round the frugal and unsophisticated. I rode a bicycle, dressed mostly in *khadi*, and drank the tap water with what turned out to be regrettable alacrity.

It would be hard to exaggerate the generosity and hospitality I received. As I was living on my own, and had obviously no one to look after me, I was inexorably incorporated into three Jain households in Johari Bazaar (and one non-Jain household outside of it): places where I was expected to turn up whenever I liked, and where if too long passed without my coming for a meal, someone would be sent to look for me and check that I had not fallen ill again. And there were many others where I was made welcome and where time was always found for me. As the weather grew hotter and hotter in my first Rajasthan summer, I resisted for a while the practice of sleeping in the afternoon, and I remember more than one occasion from that time when a family I knew insisted on my staying to lunch after interviewing someone in the morning, and then insisted even more firmly that

I stayed and slept for an hour or two before they allowed me out into the day again.

Many people assumed I was going to become a Jain renouncer or at least go back and convert people to Jainism at home. My denials carried little weight. When I failed to explain satisfactorily what had brought me precisely to Jaipur to do precisely this research, the suspicion that I had probably been a Jain in a previous life became, for many, an apparently unshakeable conviction. I like to think, certainly, that as time went by what I was really doing became steadily better understood—beginning, of course, with the people I was working with regularly—and I remember a few occasions, at the time highly gratifying, when a recitation by a new acquaintance of the 'most important points' of Jain philosophy was stopped by one of my established friends with the declaration 'He knows all that!' and a succinct and forceful summary of what my current interests were. But I am fairly certain that this to me more congenial view of the direction and purpose of my research was, to them, perfectly compatible with their earlier, more comprehensively explanatory, and also more religiously creditable view of the underlying reason why I was there.

Fieldwork Collaborations

A few informants survived from the very beginning to the very end of my fieldwork. These included especially renouncers and others in more or less official religious positions, and locally recognized experts on Jain religion or local history, all of whom I would meet from time to time. But there was also a slow turnover as some more 'lay' informants came to feel they had done their duty to me—or rather, by the demands of religious merit or hospitality—or had got bored with answering questions, and as my relations with some others grew cool or in a very few cases turned sour. At the same time, a constant stream of new informants appeared, as I met people at temples or religious functions, or at the houses, offices, and shops of established friends and acquaintances. This continued until the very last days of my research.

Among all these people there were a few whose relationship to me and my fieldwork was quite distinctive and bears closer examination. They were more than 'informants' or 'respondents', although in all cases I certainly asked them a lot of questions. They are also different from the people I was sometimes able to pay for a while to act as 'fieldwork assistants'. Such assistants were invaluable, and not only in making up for my rather limited language skills. It usually smoothed things considerably in a first meeting to be accompanied either by a friend or assistant (or, as Gold (1988: 21) puts it, 'a blurred composite of the two'). This was especially true, as my assistants were all female, in meetings with women in their homes. It made it much less likely that a need would be felt for another, usually male, member of the family to be present, which almost invariably acted as a damper on the women's conversation. At the same time, interestingly, discussions between informant, assistant, and myself sometimes turned into three-way conversations in a very productive way, and I learned a great deal from observing the elaborate series of questions and answers by which informant and assistant located each other socially, established if they had acquaintances in common, and so on.

But even where it is the case, as it is in one example, that the people I shall describe did act as 'assistant' for a while, this is not the aspect of things I wish to discuss here. Each of these people, much more importantly, took an active part in what I was doing, so that they had a significant personal impact on how the research proceeded. They each became actively involved with me in what was in effect a joint inquiry which we conducted together. We formulated questions together, to which either I or we then set about finding answers; and we discussed together how to interpret the answers, and where they pointed us to next.

It is important to say at the outset that in no case was the inquiry we were jointly engaged in the same thing as my 'research project': it did not have the same form, the same scope, or the same *telos*. And in the case of each of my collaborators—I shall discuss four—our joint inquiries were different. From my point of view, each of these collaborations could be seen as a part (though not necessarily a central part) of my overall project. But from the point of view of my collaborators, each project made sense more or less without reference to my anthropological interests. Theirs was an intellectual exercise, certainly, but one whose rationale lay in their own individual circumstances.

It may be that relationships of this kind played a more important part in my research than in the fieldwork of many other anthropologists; but I suspect that something like them is almost never entirely absent. So it seems worth drawing attention to them, as a hitherto unremarked upon aspect (so far as I know) of 'participant observation'.

The first of my collaborators, whom I shall here call Seema, was not a Jain, but from a Hindu family of professionals and bureaucrats, originally from outside Rajasthan. Her immediate family had moved to Jaipur when Seema was a young school girl, and she had been educated in the city's most élite girls' school and then at Rajasthan University. We met on my first visit, through a friendly sociology professor at the univeristy to whom Josephine Reynell introduced me. He suggested that Seema might act as my assistant. I spoke no Hindi at all at this time, so I needed an assistant in order even to begin my work. Seema had recently completed a degree in sociology and was enjoying a summer holiday before deciding what to do next. She was clever, friendly, spoke impeccable English and fluent, though I later realized decidedly 'English-medium' Hindi, and we hit it off immediately. Apart from one much later episode, to which I shall return below, our work together lasted only for my first short visit. She went on soon afterwards to work in more policy-oriented research work in rural Rajasthan.

On a 'professional' level, although we were both completely inexperienced, things worked very smoothly. We conducted interviews together, my having prepared questions in advance. When the interviews were in Hindi, she would summarize the answers for me as they came, so that I could follow the general drift and ask supplementary and follow-up questions, and also decide when we needed to abandon our script. And afterwards we would go through the notes and tapes, and I would write out my notes in full. In this way we gathered most of the material for my undergraduate dissertation. This was all information on the basic teachings and most important religious practices of Jainism, the organization and liturgical routine of Dadabari temple, the lives and miraculous powers of the Guru Dev saints, and personal testimony from a variety of those who attended the temple regularly about how they worshipped the Guru Devs and why.

But I also learned from and with Seema in quite a different way. The first and most profoundly revealing lesson about the sociology of India which I derived from 'participant observation' came from the realization of how much of what I was learning that was new to me was just as utterly new or unexpected to Seema. She had learned about Jainism at school, of course. But what she had learned bore even less relation to reality than what I had been able to gather from English-language sources in Cambridge. Having been taught a pure, text-based, Orientalist version of Jainism as unremittingly austere and anti-Brahmanical asceticism, she was amazed by the opulence of the temples and by the colourful rituals, performed to the accompaniment of melodies from popular Hindu religious songs and even more popular Hindi film music, but with powerful and sensuous words which clearly conveyed a distinctive religious sensibility. And she was surprised too by a host of powerful deities and rather frightening protector spirits who were worshipped by Jains alongside the more expected renouncer figures. What was this rich and wholly unexpected culture? Our enquiries into the practice of Jainism as a lived religion were as much of a revelation to her as they were to me.

Of course, Seema had known a few Jains at school and college. Some of these were daughters of professional families—somewhat semi-detached in most cases from the centres of the local Jain community—and others were from business families. There were a couple of occasions, I remember, when on entering a Jain home it became clear that the demure and polite young woman who brought us water and tea turned out to have been at school or college with Seema, and was now living at home waiting for her marriage to be arranged. The conversation was awkward and embarrassed. The assumption, taken for granted in Seema's world, that the proper thing for a young woman at this stage in life to be doing would be work of some kind—if not actually a career then at least something artistic or vaguely intellectual, or some kind of 'social service'—was not even an option for these former school mates.

So my interest in learning about the social and domestic lives of the Jains we met together coalesced with Seema's amazed curiosity about this quite unfamiliar world, which she now realized existed right under her nose. She had grown up learning the stereotypes about 'the Baniyas' which are common to her class: they are rich, of course, and mean and money-grubbing, and personally austere; and also uneducated, uncultured and uncouth. We learned together that the Jains in Jaipur were by no means uniformly rich—some lived in severe, though none in abject poverty—and of course, we met generosity, grace, and profound and thoughtful religiosity among many of those we talked with.

Outside the specific lines of questioning we pursued in relation to the topic of the Guru Dev saints, we raised a range of other matters with our interlocutors and made our own observations. Anything that surprised or intrigued either one of us about the families we met with—meal times, apparent relations between family members, the furnishing of houses and the use of rooms—became a matter for further enquiry and observation and also for extensive discussion between us about how the matter in question stood in our own respective homes. But for the most part, our questions were prompted by Seema's expectations and reactions to what we were hearing and seeing. She was immediately struck by details, such as what people did with leftover food, which differed from what she had grown up to regard as normal. So on these matters our enquiries took as their point of comparison whatever was customary in our family, caste, class, and region of origin: an arbitrary starting point, as any is bound to be, but a considerably more productive one, for these purposes, than my own.

This collaboration was an important starting point for both of us. From Seema's point of view, even if it was the first conscious, sustained, and reflective enquiry into the 'otherness' of parts of the immediately neighbouring social world, it was only a minor prelude to much more extensive research work she was later to do in the villages of Rajasthan. But it was also the first practical realization of the distortions and blind spots of the modernist, secularist, Nehruite, middle-class world view she had grown up in. For me, less traumatically, it was an extremely fortunate opportunity, if not to see the Jains 'from an Indian point of view', at least to see them *being seen* from one particular Indian point of view.

When I returned to Jaipur in 1985 and in subsequent years to pursue my doctoral research, Seema was busy in her own work and although we saw each other regularly, we only talked about my work occasionally and very informally, except, that is, for a short period in 1990 when we went to visit Acharya Tulsi together. This celebrated Jain saint, who was leader of the Shvetambar Terapanth, was living at the time in Pali, in western Rajasthan. He was something of a public figure in India, known well beyond his own religious followers, partly because of his role in some conflict-resolution situations and his statements on some political issues. When Seema heard I was planning to go to meet him she expressed a desire to come too, and so we travelled to Pali together.

The situation was an interesting contrast to seven years before, since now, in our meeting with Acharya Tulsi, the relative proximity of our points of view was reversed, and therefore the main lesson I learned depended on an opposite dynamic from that which had been at work in our earlier collaboration. Seema saw him in general terms as a saintly religious teacher, with a spiritual message addressed to any interested listener, and with views on peace and non-violence and how public life in India might be improved through 'spiritual reform'. In the midst of fieldwork on a different Jain tradition, I much more naturally saw him in the context of sectarian disputes and doctrinal differences between Jain traditions. Some of his public pronouncements depended on fairly radical interpretations of key Jain teachings, although he tended not to acknowledge this, and some of his rhetoric was, if only implicitly, criticism of rival Jain traditions. All this I was able to explain to Seema; but in return she was able to make me see something that required one to stand back a bit from highly localized and contextual considerations. Because she responded to him simply as a religious teacher, speaking in a spiritual and symbolic vocabulary that is substantially common to all Indic religious traditions, she forced me to listen directly to what he was actually saying, and how, and so enabled me to see why he was so charismatic and convincing well beyond the specific sect of which he happened to be the leader.

My second collaborator was a Jain. Rajiv was a young man of about my age, serving an apprenticeship in the firm of one of the more prominent gem merchants in the city. He was a stranger in Jaipur himself, having been brought from his home town by the merchant he was attached to, and who thereby became his benefactor. Two aspects of Rajiv's situation helped shape our relationship. First, he was very much on probation. His benefactor's patronage—as well as the training he was receiving—were essential to his future chances of making a living in the gem trade, but they were not in themselves sufficient nor were they unconditional. The market is intensely personal. Trade is based on face-to-face relationships and un-secured credit, so that individual and family reputation are absolutely essential assets. Lacking family in Jaipur and beginning, as everyone knew, with very limited financial assets, Rajiv had his reputation to make.

It was generally accepted that for someone in his precarious position visible good conduct beyond that normally expected of a young man of his age was called for. So at public, especially religious, functions, Rajiv was always one of those who stepped forward to lend a helping hand: acting as a marshal at large gatherings and as a messenger between organizing bigwigs, and serving food and clearing away utensils at religious feasts. We struck up our friendship during a week-long religious festival held in the blistering heat of early May, at which both of us had to be on duty throughout. Spending time with me, while being less onerous than most of these other duties, was a visible 'good work' and therefore an acceptable substitute for some of them.[10]

Second, he was lonely and homesick and was having to work out who was friendly and who was not and generally what was going on in a complex and competitive environment. It was at this time that I was beginning to work in a concerted way beyond Dadabari temple and getting to know more of the Shvetambar Jain scene in Jaipur. We were thus in some respects in substantially similar predicaments, but at the same time we were never going to be in competition with each other, so I was a safe and 'non-combatant' person to compare notes and let off steam with. It was natural for us to pool intelligence.

We began to do so during long hours of sermons, speeches, *bhajan* singing, and puja at that week-long function. We both felt obliged for our different reasons to spend long sweltering days in densely packed crowds, sitting through very repetitive proceedings, but at least we could work out who was who. And I could get away with asking for information from those around us when Rajiv himself could not. He was not much interested in some of the religious minutiae which I was keen to detail, but his interest in the 'Who's Who' of local Jain society was every bit as keen as my own. Although he had only been in Jaipur for a few months, he already knew far more than I did, so it was hardly an equal partnership, but my contacts with local notables did enable me to contribute something here and there, and he enjoyed talking about it.

For a while afterwards he accompanied me on visits to interview people occasionally, and we had fun finding our way through some unfamiliar parts of town, into unmarked *havelis* and up unlit staircases, tracking down addresses that seemed to bear no relationship to streets and buildings. ('Just ask anyone, everyone knows where I live' was a reassurance I had already come to dread.) And I accompanied him on a, for me, instructive as well as enjoyable visit to his home town. But fairly soon our relationship turned much more purely friendly. The centre of my interests meant I spent too much time on religious matters to suit his tastes, and he was busy. But for a while our shared outsider status, and the need to be on our best behaviour in roughly similar ways, gave us both motive and opportunity to indulge in a shared project of inquiry.

In addition I saw, through Rajiv, what I otherwise might not have done: just how tough things were for those trying to work their way into the local community, and how the connection between business and orthodox religious practice, which seemed so flexible and negotiable a matter for most of those I knew, could be rather more coercive for those in a peripheral or insecure position. I remember arriving at his windowless room one day to find another young man sitting there—someone I had met before but knew only slightly. He was in a similar dependent situation to Rajiv, though attached to a different merchant firm. I could see at once that he was miserable. He was sitting propped against the wall on the mattress on the floor, hugging his knees, his features pinched and his eyes somewhat glazed. It turned out he was on a fast, and this was the third or fourth day.

This young man was not at all personally inclined to such austerities, and his thin build gave him only meagre reserves on which to draw, but he had no choice. His patron's wife had been heard complaining of his laxity and he felt sure that if he did not see it through his position would be in jeopardy. He had come here not to eat or drink secretly—I was interested to see that this did not seem to be considered as an option—but to take a break from work and the oppressive, supervised atmosphere there, where he had to give the appearance of religious motivation for his fast, and to enjoy the relief of vocalized complaint.

Vimal, my third collaborator, was rather more comfortably situated. In fact he was at the centre of things in a modest sort of way. His family was not rich but it was comfortable, with a nice *haveli* right in the centre of the business district. Vimal's father had retired early and his life was now dominated by his religious observations, but he had been a liked and respected businessman, so Vimal had entered the market on good terms, apprenticed to a close friend of his father. His life had had no real uncertainties. He had always lived in the same place and was still surrounded by the family and friends he had grown up with; he was always going to go into the gem business and his education had proceeded accordingly; and within a few years of our meeting a happy marriage would be arranged for him. Vimal was on easy terms with a wide acquaintance, some of whom were very much richer than he, but he behaved and was treated as an equal. His circle of close personal friends was large and, although mostly Jain, included a few Vaishnava Hindus of Baniya caste.

So Vimal had no reason to feel in any way marginal or detached, and in some ways he was perhaps fairly conventional. His expectations and ambitions as regards his business, his family, and his future wife were nothing out of the ordinary. But I soon learned that his easy, confident, and rather amused manner went along with a highly reflective and critical appraisal of the world in which he had grown up. Vimal was not altogether uninterested in spiritual or religious matters, and at a certain level is a sincere believing Jain, but he was personally austere and he had a keen eye and a sharp dislike for the superficiality and hypocrisy which he saw as being all too dominant in the public religious life of his community. Part of his reaction was at a general level of moral disapproval, but part of it was practical, a matter of everyday decision making and judgement. How trustworthy as a business partner should he take so-and-so to be? How should he weigh this or that fact about that man's religious observance against other things he knew about him? What inference should he draw about someone from news that they had made a big donation to fund a religious ceremony? How obliged should he himself feel to act in similar ways? Vimal was not convinced by the local establishment consensus on these questions.

Vimal never participated actively in any of my fieldwork activities: he never accompanied me, for instance, to meet other people or attended religious ceremonies with me. But in long conversations during our frequent meetings—typically in the evenings at the end of his working day—he would often question me on who I had been talking to and what I had been learning. At times it was almost like a debriefing, and with a fairly definite agenda. He would insist that I must not take verbal expressions of religious piety at face value, not mistake the empty forms of religious observance for real spirituality, and not miss the potential use of generosity to ostensibly religious causes as a front for personal aggrandisement. None of these things are unique to Jainism, of course, nor are they unknown to anthropology. But Vimal would guide me— alternating as he did so between ironical amusement and mild indignation—to the questions and the issues that would bring them out in the local context. And more importantly, he helped me to formulate questions that would get at how the very people he suspected of hypocrisy did actually think about how their religious actions and observations fitted together with their lives as traders, investors, money lenders, political operators, or arrangers of family alliances.

Perhaps someone had been telling me how religious actions and earning religious merit contribute to a person's success in business, because they would bring good *karma*; or perhaps they had been explaining the different kinds of religious gifts in Jainism and the effect they had on one's spiritual condition. After a few minutes' thought Vimal might say, 'I don't think so'; and then, with a laugh, 'Otherwise X would be a good man'. I would take up the position, as I understood it, of my interlocutor of earlier in the day, and Vimal would pick holes or cite counter examples. 'Maybe you should ask him what he would do in this situation', and he would outline some scenario of business or marriage arrangements. Or he would give me an example of a business practice that everyone engaged in but which definitely violated some Jain religious precept. 'Anyway,' he would add, 'next time you see him ask about so-and-so and why his business did not do well last year. Was that bad *karma*?' Sometimes, of course, Vimal's best weapon was gossip, but actually he hardly ever used it. Mostly the examples of individuals he cited were relatively well known or from some time ago; and most commonly he cited general situations, common practices or predicaments, or hypothetical examples as ways of thinking about how things worked.

Vimal was by no means the only person I knew who voiced an at least healthy scepticism about the pious self-presentation of some of the richest and most prominent of their co-religionists. He was singular, first of all, in seeing how this could be posed as a set of intellectual questions about the consistency of ethical thought, the role of ideals and values in people's actions and decisions, and so on; and secondly, in enjoying the fact that, generally more cynically disposed than I, he could use his knowledge of the frailties of human nature, as manifest in his particular local surroundings, to gain points for his overall view. The result, as I have said, is that conversations with him sometimes turned into combined debriefings and pep talks, in which he would encourage me to look in particular ways at some of the things I had learned, and furnish me with follow-up questions or topics in order to take the argument further.

These discussions were only occasional—we met much more often without our conversation taking this form—but they had a decisive effect on my fieldwork. I was anyway interested in how the local gem trade worked, in business practice and business ethics, in the funding and management of religious institutions, and in the workings of philanthropy and religious donations. Vimal's interest in these same matters sprang from different concerns, but we established ways of talking about them together in which they became objects of both theoretical interest and empirical investigation.

The interests of my fourth collaborator, whom I shall here call Kum Kum, ran in a very different direction. Kum Kum and I became friends about half-way through my fieldwork, and we shared a lively interest in the details of Jain ascetic religious practice, including the minutiae of how Jain renouncers live. She is a few years younger than me, and had recently finished education. She had suffered from poor health for most of her childhood and at that time there was no immediate prospect of marriage. It slowly became clear that Kum Kum had seriously thought about becoming a Jain renouncer herself. By the time we met she had decided firmly against this (her health would have made it a difficult and dangerous choice) but she retained a powerful attraction to the renouncer's life, and was on close and friendly terms with a number of *sadhvis*, including some who visited Jaipur regularly.

It was the more abstruse of the questions I was interested in that caught Kum Kum's attention. What happens to the hair that is cut from an initiate's head at ordination? What is inside the cloth bundles which renouncers put before them when they preach or pray? Why should ginger be a permitted food in dry, powdered form, when fresh ginger is forbidden? Why should it be that in puja one should use fresh well water rather than boiled water, which is recommended for all other religious purposes? Unlike Seema, Rajiv, and Vimal, Kum Kum had no overall interest or 'agenda' of her own, except perhaps to keep up and deepen her friendships with the *sadhvis* she knew; but she certainly did not need me for that. She found Jain renouncers fascinating and charismatic and she enjoyed being with them. And her interest in the renouncer's life and in the details of and rationales for aspects of Jain asceticism coincided with my curiosity about what for me were 'ethnographic details'.

In addition, Kum Kum felt that anyway as a Jain, she ought to be knowledgeable about her own religion. She had learned some fairly lengthy prayers
and passages of Prakrit to be recited in certain rituals, but was aware of
how much more there was that she did not know. My presence acted as a
spur to her here, and like many other Jains I met, she expressed the thought
that if I, a complete outsider, could be devoting my time to acquiring a
knowledge of Jainism, then surely Jains themselves should be doing at
least as much? The prevalence of this reaction has to do with the position
of Jainism as a relatively little understood minority religion in India, a
point to which I shall return. Kum Kum was unusual only in the extent to
which she acted upon this line of thought.

Kum Kum introduced me to the *sadhvis* she knew in Jaipur, and frequently accompanied me on visits to them; and I carried letters from her
when I travelled to meet others, in other towns and villages. She was on
close and friendly terms with many of them, and could converse easily and
in a light-hearted and joking way, without seeming disrespectful.
Renouncers' rest houses are public buildings and lay Jains come and go
throughout the day; at the same time renouncers' interactions with members of the opposite sex are strictly and elaborately controlled by highly
detailed rules. Kum Kum had a sure sense of which questions were
unproblematic, which had to be approached with care, and which were
best asked when no other laypeople were around, as well as being able to
ask some questions when I was out of the room which could not be
discussed in a man's hearing.

Being interested herself in the details of ascetic practice, and in trying
to discern a logic or rationale behind apparently arbitrary rules and restrictions, Kum Kum was never bored or impatient with even my most plodding
and mulish lines of questioning. Indeed we spent many happy hours going
through tape recorded interviews together, weighing the answers, deciding
if they really answered the questions or not, whether they were consistent
or not with answes we had been given previously, and whether they opened
up new questions to be taken up on future occasions; all this in addition to
Kum Kum explaining to me words or expressions that were beyond my
always inadequate Hindi.

These collaborators were not my 'most important informants', in the
sense that they were not those from whom I collected most 'ethnographic
data'. There were others whom I met regularly for long interviews, who
had special or remarkably detailed knowledge of some kind, or could tell
me of specific people or events unknown to anyone else. What is distinctive about them is that these were people who were themselves seeking

information, rather than merely giving it to me. It is this fact that explains, at base, why our inquiries were collaborative. There was in each case at least a significant overlap between information that I was seeking and their own interests or wonderings. In each case my fieldwork provided the context in which their inquiry could be formulated as such, and could take place; and as a consequence the inquiries in which they were interested thereby became a part of my own.

In each case the questions driving their 'research interests' derived from local situations and circumstances in a way that mine, of course, did not; but they were in each case local in entirely different ways. Seema's interest (to put these matters in my words) was in the differences of caste, class, and religion within the same locality; and how the realities of these are simultaneously hidden and exaggerated by conventional stereotypes and orthodoxies. Rajiv's was an incomer's inquiry into the basic facts about who ran what and what was what in the world he now had to get by in; though conducted under the specific constraint of having to play a certain role within it. Vimal's was an insider's sceptical reflection on the workings of wealth, prestige, and reputation in his own community; and was part, though in an unusually discursive form, of an ordinary self-reflective questioning of how one ought to live. Kum Kum, having made one important decision about how she was going to live, retained both an attachment and a reverential interest in the life of a Jain renouncer, and this fuelled a desire for detailed knowledge about it.

Of course, except in the context of my research project, there is nothing that united these different interests and in one sense putting them together is quite artificial. Each makes sense as part of the larger picture of the life of each of these individuals, of which I and my research project formed only a very minor part. On the other hand, this kind of loose, partial, and generally impermanent overlapping of interests and activities is, outside 'real villages', what human lives are largely composed of. Perhaps a better way to put the matter is to say that each of these collaborations was on a 'research project' (loosely defined) which in each case my collaborator and I invented together, by putting together and focusing on a set of interests we had in common, and which we could pursue together in the circumstances in which we jointly found outselves.[11] In each case, on both sides, this small joint enterprise was part of a set of interests and ambitions which for each of us was, of course, uniquely our own. It was only in my case that 'writing a book' figured in this larger picture; though the knowledge that a book would somehow result from our activities was important, at least, to Vimal and Kum Kum.

Self-consciousness and Dispersed Knowledge

I remarked above that collaborations of the sort just described are probably a part of almost all anthropological fieldwork. I suspect indeed that collaborators such as mine have often been the unsung heroes of anthropological research. But one can identify reasons why these informal collaborations played such an important part in my research, and these reasons point to the special contribution they make to anthropological research in certain kinds of complex social settings.

The first relevant fact is that the Jains are a religious minority in India. There is a widespread sense among them that their religion is little known and ill-understood by other Indians. Jains share a pride in the antiquity of the Jain tradition and a consciousness of its wider contribution to Indian civilization. For many, including Kum Kum, this view leads on to the thought that Jains themselves do not know enough about their own religion, in addition to not practising it rigorously enough. They are not worthy representatives of a long and distinguished tradition; not worthy embodiments of the truths that tradition contains. In any case, virtually all Jains are conscious of being part of a definite social minority—one in which, though many are well off, many others are poor, and which has been subject to persecution and victimization at times. In times of increasing polarization along religious lines in Indian politics, the whole question of Jainism's relation to Hinduism is a pressing one. Should one stress theological singularity, distinctive values, shared religious language and symbolism, social inclusion, shared differences from Islam? All this undoubtedly accounts for the extent to which the people I met were self-conscious about social differences, and had an unusual readiness and aptitude for articulating their knowledge about it. One of my common experiences, on visiting a Jain temple for the first time, was to be approached by someone who would begin carefully to explain, 'There are two kinds of Jainism, Digambar and Shvetambar...'.

Some other features of the Jain case, apart from religious diversity, can be related to the Indian context. One undoubted aspect of caste in India is that the fact of differences of lifestyle, customs, institutions, and values is explicitly recognized and structurally fundamental. However much caste ideology may 'naturalize' social and cultural conventions, awareness that others do in fact do things differently is everywhere consciously acknowledged. But as my collaboration with Seema illustrates, that such differences are known to exist does not guarantee reliable knowledge of what those differences are. This state of affairs means that in India, social or

cultural research makes remarkably direct and easily apprehensible sense
to people generally. Few people's lives are so restricted to their own caste,
religion, or whatever, that they do not have cause from time to time to use
the knowledge they have of the habits and mores of other communities.
Few cannot grasp that the distribution of such knowledge is an aspect of
the distribution of power. And few have not experienced simple curiosity
about how things are among some of the communities they come across
day after day.

In entering into informal collaboration with people in 'researching'
social and cultural arrangements, either their own and those of others around
them, the anthropologist is merely joining in with—though also in the
process no doubt heightening and giving his or her own twist to—an activity
that is always at least an implicit part of everyday social life. And the
anthropologist's ability to elicit engaged collaboration is at least an indication
that his or her ethnographic questions have some coherence with indigenous interests and concerns; that the ethnographic knowledge he or she is
seeking is recognizable as knowledge of how things are with them. In fact,
it seems worth taking a lead from potential collaborators even if their
interests diverge from one's original research plans.

If the facts of caste and religious diversity mean that all this is, perhaps,
easier to do in India than in some other parts of the world; it is also the
case that in India as much as anywhere else in the world, social knowledge
that is significant just because it is dispersed and unevenly distributed
relates also to matters other than caste and religion. The inquiries I
shared briefly with Rajiv related to wealth, reputation, power, and local
connections, and derived from the need we both felt to develop at least
a minimal acquaintance with the basic facts. Vimal's was a much more
sophisticated inquiry into these and other matters, and involved not
only discovering new information but in rendering some of his tacit
knowledge explicit, so that it could be used to challenge and guide my
enquiries.

It is important to emphasize that this kind of collaboration is important
not only because it enables one to grasp local ideas or 'perceptions' as
distinct from social realities. I have argued in the case of Jaipur that even
the experientially salient fact of there being a Jain 'community' at all
emerges from a range of partial and overlapping social processes; from the
way social knowledge, including and especially knowledge of others'
beliefs, attitudes, and expectations, is mobilized by social agents in the
pursuit of their own ends. Hannerz (1992) has plausibly suggested that the
importance of self-consciousness about social and cultural difference, of

the fact that people's perspectives on the world include what he calls "perspectives on others' perspectives" is a general characteristic of complex cultural situations in the contemporary world.

This kind of state of affairs is of course not specifically or exclusively urban. Cultural variation and charged self-consciousness about cultural difference can arise in many other contexts also. One thinks, for instance, of Edmund Leach's (1961b) classic description of relations between different cultural traditions and political entities in the huge highland region between the great civilizations of India and China. There, *mutatis mutandis*, similar factors would undoubtedly be found.

In the sections above I stressed that because community among Jains in Jaipur is an emergent and spontaneously changing order in public social space, and not a formal or institutional structure, it follows that to understand it is not to lay bare a single underlying design but rather to describe the terms on which and the forms through which individuals and families participate in it; and also to grasp in turn the ways in which their doing so generates and reproduces that public sphere. I linked this to the fact of an urban setting, as distinct from that of a village, not because structured institutions are found in villages and not in cities—obviously this is not the case—but because the size, spatial isolation, and relative simplicity of village social life allows it to be imagined as if it were a structure built to a single plan. It has always been a heuristic fiction, though it has not always been recognized as such, when anthropologists have described the 'social structure' of such a village. A village can be described as if it were a *taxis*. No doubt this has often been a useful fiction, but no such utility survives translation to a large and complex urban setting. The distinction between institutions and corporations on the one hand and unconstructed public realms on the other is essential to the understanding of how a complex urban social setting works. And in an anthropologist's attempts to understand the latter, in informal collaborations with informants—that is, joining them in mobilizing their local knowledge of the social order in order to extend that knowledge—he or she is seeing at close hand one of the most important of the dynamic processes of which that social order is composed.

Notes

1. Josephine Reynell was working on the religious lives of Jain women. See her, sadly unpublished, Cambridge Ph.D. thesis, 'Honour, Nurture, and Festivity: Aspects of Female Religiosity among Jain Women in Jaipur' (1985); and her 1991 article.

2. An abridged version of the undergraduate dissertation was published 1985. The PhD thesis, entitled, 'The Religion of Shvetambar Jain Merchants in Jaipur' (1990), was the basis, much modified and extended, of *Riches and Renunciation: Religion, Economy, and Society among the Jains* (1995).

3. See for instance Mattison Mines' (1994) excellent study of Madras (now Chennai). And for another Jain example, see Marcus Banks' fine comparative study of Jamnagar and Leicester (1992).

4. For some perceptive remarks on 'the myth of personalised, face-to-face contact in the traditional city' and on how she learned how far it can be from reality, even while it is affirmed by local residents, see Nita Kumar (1992).

5. On the question of whether and in what ways the Jains as a whole, or the Jains in various parts of India, may be regarded as constituting a community, see Michael Carrithers and Caroline Humphrey (1985).

6. There is an at least surface similarity between Hayek's taxis-cosmos distinction and Lévi-Strauss' (1949) distinction between elementary and complex structures. But one can do no more than note the similarity: Hayek's conception is worked out in a much more elaborate and sophisticated manner; and Lévi-Strauss' promised study of complex structures has never materialized, whereas Hayek's principal interest is in understanding how 'spontaneous' social orders work.

7. The case is slightly different with temples at pilgrimage sites located away from Jain populations large and wealthy enough to sustain them. These are owned and managed by one of a number of trust organizations, essentially very similar to local neighbourhood ones, except that they may draw their membership from among the most prominent Jains from a number of localities.

8. I should perhaps emphasize that although the remarks in this paragraph may sound like an opposition to quantitative methods in social research, this is not my position. I did not myself use any formal quantitative techniques in my Jaipur fieldwork but I can now see, in ways that I could not when I conducted the fieldwork, some ways in which they might be useful. But I remain convinced that it would have been nonsense to attempt to use the notion of a 'sample', when the phenomenon I was trying to understand was neither a group of people, an activity, nor an institution, and therefore could not, even in principle, be sampled.

9. I did not use written questionnaires for informants to fill in, or send research assistants to interview people without my taking part in the interaction.

10. I did wonder early on if Rajiv had been more or less explicitly instructed to befriend me and perhaps to keep me from getting too much in the way, but it became obvious that this was not so.

11. In the introduction to his remarkable ethnography of a Tamil village, E. Valentine Daniel (1984) expresses the thought that the object of his investigations was jointly invented by himself and his informants. The point Daniel is making here, which has no doubt influenced my own thinking in this paper (it is a brilliant book and has done so in many ways), nevertheless differs from the point made here in that (a) Daniel is concerned with a generic 'informant' and not only with those who stand in the relationship I have

here referred to as collaboration; and (b) in his view the 'thing' that was the joint invention of anthropologist and informant was 'a culture', which in some traditions (in Daniel's case that descended proximately from the work of David Schneider) is thought of as the proper object of anthropological research, but which is an entity I regard as, in the old fashioned pejorative sense of the term, 'imaginary'.

Fieldwork in Rishi Valley School

MEENAKSHI THAPAN

Fieldwork for me resulted from an attempt to render an educational institution intelligible in sociological terms. I was interested, specifically, in the implications of a particular ideology for the schooling process; in the nature of interaction between the participants in the school and between school processes and the wider society; and in the various dimensions of school life itself. In more general terms, I was interested in arriving at an understanding of the school through the process of observing and interacting with the ongoing reality and 'lifting the veils that obscure or hide what is going on' (Blumer 1976: 15).

In this process, the most crucial problems were raised by the seeking of information, both public and private, and the hiding of it by exercising control which created barriers between the ethnographer and the 'field'. The barriers I encountered raised some important questions of censorship and control: Who restricts information and thereby creates barriers? When is it considered appropriate for information to be freely given and when is it concealed? What constitutes free knowledge and restricted knowledge and what are the repercussions of this distinction on the ethnographer and her research? Here, I will present some of the problems generated in the field by the continuous interplay of the ethnographer's search for information and the participants' masking of it, and attempt to seek answers to some of the questions raised above.

I selected RVS (Rishi Valley School) as my fieldwork primarily because of the explicit presence of an underlying ideology. I carried out fieldwork in RVS for a period of nine months during 1981 and stayed on the school premises in accommodation provided by the school. This afforded me the necessary facilities and opportunities for sustained observation of school activities and for building intimate relations with teachers, pupils, and other school personnel

To begin with, I had no clearly formulated 'research design' as the basis for study, as I was not testing a hypothesis. A rounded case study was the aim. I was therefore not interested in any specific areas of school life to the exclusion of others and my focus on 'interaction' as the subject of study and as a method-ological device emerged during the course of my stay in the school.[1]

The first difficulty I encountered was in gaining 'entry' into the school. The school management are the 'gatekeepers', as it were, of the institution and wish to protect teachers and pupils as well as themselves from an outsider who seeks to observe school processes. I wrote several letters to the school which remained unanswered. I therefore approached a founda-tion member who readily granted me permission to study the school.[2] Her decision was based on the expectation that my work might serve as a feed-back to the foundation and school management on the functioning of RVS as seen by an interested but impartial observer. Her faith in my ability to undertake this task was not however shared by some other foundation members, who were apprehensive as to whether I, a doctoral student, had the 'maturity' and 'right understanding' to view the 'experiment in human education' which was going to be 'exposed' to me. What I did not realize at that time but which became evident later was that because I had come to the school through the foundation, I was viewed with even more suspicion and distrust than usual, as I was at first considered a stooge of the foundation by some teachers and the management.

It was with some trepidation combined with scholarly fervour that I arrived at RVS. My first few weeks there were fraught with tension and anxiety for the management and the teachers regarding the impact of my presence on the school, and this inevitably affected the nature of their relations with me. I briefly spoke to the teachers at a staff meeting about the nature of my work and sought their cooperation and assistance. At another meeting, however, from which I was absent, the teachers were told by the principal to consult the headmistress before speaking to me so that there would be 'no confusion or contradiction' in their statements to me. In this manner, the principal sought to control the flow of information by imposing an intermediary between the teachers and myself, who would determine what was appropriate for disclosure (free knowledge) and what was restricted to themselves (secret knowledge). The teachers were thus restricted in their relations with me in the beginning.

At this time some teachers did approach me for discussion but they were either those who were to shortly leave the school and had nothing to lose by talking to me freely, or those who were in general disgruntled with the school's mode of functioning. These teachers mainly complained about what they considered the management's misdirection, the pupils' preoccupation with themselves and lack of sensitivity to what was happening around them, parental disinterest in school goals, the foundation's 'interference' in school processes, and so on. Some of these teachers were identified by me as the 'ideologues' who were particularly critical of school processes and also dissatisfied with their own role at RVS. I was perhaps used as a sounding board by them and, while I listened carefully and took down notes later, I was all along aware I was hearing only one side of the story.

Some other teachers were antipathetic to my presence in the school. Their questions and comments, however, often reflected their own insecurities and fears. Thus a senior teacher who was unsure about how I would portray the school asked, 'Will you be writing what you are *told* to write or whatever you *feel* like writing?' I handled their rather derogatory comments as best as I could under the circumstances but I remember being embarrassed and upset by them.

The pupils were not quite clear about my position in the school. I spoke to them as I met them casually—individually and in groups—and told them about my work and made it clear to them that I was not a teacher in the school. It took me quite a while however to 'make friends' with them and to get them to be relaxed and comfortable in my presence.

It was evident to me from the outset that I had to first immerse myself in school life to the extent I could, and to the extent I would be allowed to, in order to penetrate the closed wall that stood between me and my 'understanding' of the school.[3] Before coming to RVS, I had decided not to participate in any teaching as I had felt that this would leave me with very little time for my own work. Nevertheless, had I participated in teaching, I might have gained a quicker understanding of school processes. As it was, I was left with the option of joining in activities—other than that of classroom and staffroom at first—such as the morning assembly, and accompanying pupils and teachers on hikes into the neighbouring countryside, interacting with them informally in the dining hall, and the houses. I also attended the yoga lessons, watched teachers and pupils at sport and gardening, and took part in co-curricular activities, such as music and drama.

During this time, I was engaging in what Berreman, following Goffman, call 'impression-management' in the field (1972: xvii–lvii). That is, I was trying to present myself in a manner that would be acceptable to teachers and pupils so that they could begin to trust me. I was behaving differently with teachers and with pupils, who had differing codes of conduct. Thus I presented an amiable but serious front to teachers and a more informal one to pupils. With teachers, I was genuinely interested in what the ideology was striving to achieve through school processes *as well as* in the problems that ideological expectations might pose for the practical tasks of running a school. This appeared to be the most crucial dilemma for the teachers and the management and by not taking sides for or against the ideology I was able to participate in discussions on related issues. By my participation I wished to make it clear that I was not merely an observer but also sufficiently interested in their problems so as to share and discuss them.

I realized that the only way in which I could interact with pupils was by being where they were, outside the classroom: at hikes and at sports and after-dinner activities. Slowly they began to accept my presence amongst them and soon began to invite me to accompany them on hikes or to visit them after dinner. After about three weeks of my stay at RVS, the principal invited me to attend the staff meetings as well as his meetings with the senior pupils. I thus began to take part in as much of school life as I could in the staffroom and the classroom—the two main arenas of school activity—and outside. This was done in an attempt to establish rapport with teachers and pupils and to get a picture of the community in the round, as it were.

Intimate and sustained observation helped in understanding the subtle and hidden as well as the manifest aspects of school life. I could thus perceive some of the ' "*imponderabilia of actual life*" which cannot possibly be recorded by questioning or computing documents, but have to be observed in their full actuality' (Malinowski, 1922: 18). While not participating as a teacher, I was very much 'involved' in the everyday life of the school.[4] I was not only attending and taking part in many of the activities but also developing close personal relations with teachers and pupils, and my role in the school gradually began to be viewed with less suspicion by everybody.

'Involved observation' was therefore an important research technique I used. I have emphasized the significant role of 'understanding through talk' which is necessary for obtaining the participants' view of themselves, of their relations with one another and of school processes.[5] I thus conducted interviews, discussions, and conversations with not only teachers and pupils but also with the founder, with foundation members, some parents, and other visitors to the school. I relied on formally structured interviews, informal discussions, and on what Woods calls 'naturalistic or behavioural talk' which is heard and noted by the observer in the 'ordinary course of events' (1979: 263).[6]

I conducted formal interviews with the key personnel in the school such as the principal, headmistress, junior school head, and others, in order to obtain answers to specific questions on school processes, namely, the official definition of school aims, the procedures for the recruitment of teachers and the selection of pupils, the structural organization of the school, and so on. I would begin the interview with questions from a prepared list and, apart from asking the interviewee to provide specific information, I also used the method of 'non-directive' questioning. This involves asking questions that are more open-ended than those which are formally phrased and are 'designed as triggers that stimulate the interviewee into talking about a particular broad area' (Hammersley and Atkinson 1983: 113).

In the course of informal conversations with teachers, I attempted to let them elaborate their formulations, perceptions, and meanings of school processes as well as their own roles and lives in the school. Through these interviews and conversations, observation of activities, discussion of topics unrelated to actual school processes, and listening to casual staffroom talk, I was able to construct the major ideologies of the teacher culture. This resulted in the formulation of a teacher typology based on the mode of recruitment, the teachers' perception of their roles, and the nature of their commitment. I then selected four teachers on grounds of their being either 'professional' teachers, who were primarily committed to teaching and a career, or 'ideologue' teachers, who were mainly committed to the elucidation, clarification, and propagation of the ideology. I interviewed them intensively on the course of their lives, careers, roles and their views on school processes. It is from these teachers that I derived the vital elements of the differing ideologies they subscribed to, which proved to be crucial to my understanding of the teacher culture.

It was in my conversations with teachers and the management that I became aware of the extent to which personal relations can either hinder or facilitate an interview. I rarely obtained any information from the principal, with whom I had a very reserved relationship. I also encountered resistance from some teachers who were clearly disinterested in expressing their views on any aspect of school life. They just did not trust me sufficiently, which was evident in their lack of response to my efforts to relate to them outside my role of ethnographer.

Good personal relations would, on the other hand, lead to an interview being transformed into a more informal encounter and I would often be supplied with rich and valuable information beyond what I had originally sought. Some teachers spent much of their 'free' time speaking to me at length about various aspects of school life. When they realized that they were sometimes saying more than they should, to someone who was really an ethnographer and therefore an 'outsider' in a very elementary sense, they would ask me not to quote them or say that a particular piece of information was 'off the record'. Here the teachers themselves sought to impose controls on the information which they could not however help sharing with me due to the rapport that had developed with time. Although the masks were removed at such moments, the distinction between ethnographer and participant nonetheless remained. This was evident to the extent the teachers were conscious of my role even while sharing confidences *and* I remembered to file away every bit of information I received whether or not I used it later.

With the passage of time, I established very close relations with some teachers who became my 'key informants'.[7] I did not select them as informants but in the course of time they entered into this role and provided me with not only important information but also with an overall perspective which might have been difficult to obtain otherwise. This was particularly in relation to the ideology and its association with school processes at both the manifest and the latent levels as this was not always easy to ascertain from observation. I was fortunate in finding informants with divergent attitudes and commitments to the ideology and their role in the school so that my understanding was not dependent on only one kind of perspective.

There were however two problems I encountered during the course of attempting to understand through talk. 'Talk' can readily turn into 'gossip' which is important as data but irrelevant beyond a point. It is important inasmuch as it plays a crucial role in the 'folklore' of a community and can lead to meaningful insights into interpersonal behaviour. Interaction in an institution is constituted by both formal and informal relations between participants, which are based on status and position, personal friendships, likes and dislikes, and so on. Gossip helps in understanding informal relations in themselves and the manner in which the participants view them and their more formal relationships. I was often compelled to listen to teachers gossiping about other teachers' private lives, pupils' relations across sexes, their relationships with their parents, the financial status of parents, the lives of the foundation members, and so on. The ethnographer is allowed to peep behind the mask of what is considered 'proper' social behaviour and thus deciphers some of the critical nuances characteristic of complex social interaction. I was however always conscious of the tenuous but important dividing line between fact and fiction in gossip and balanced data from gossip with other sources.

The other problem I encountered in my conversations with teachers and the management was when my opinion was sought on sensitive issues, such as the implementation of the ideology in the school, or the role performance of certain teachers, members of the management, and foundation members. It was even more embarrassing when I was expected to join in the gossip and asked to comment on a particular teacher's behaviour or activities even though this might have been viewed as a sign of inclusion in the community.[8] I had to use some tact, and at times I was circumspect, in my answers as I was always expected to respond and could in no way avoid such questions.

In this situation it is clear that controls on information are lifted by the participants themselves and the ethnographer is invited to participate in 'backstage' activity, as it were. This may be due to the fact that this activity is viewed by the participants as being irrelevant to the ethnographer's research and is therefore considered safe for exposure. The ethnographer however imposes her own controls, as I did at RVS, so as to steer clear of controversy as well as to direct talk into more relevant areas of interest.

Secret or restricted knowledge is shared not only as gossip which is not really private but external, as it were, to the speaker. More personal areas may be revealed depending on the rapport that has developed: one teacher, for example, showed me his diary and allowed me to read it over several days. It mainly contained an account of his experience of the ideology and attempts to implement it in RVS. While one may not use the 'confidential' material one is able to obtain in any direct manner, it cannot be denied that some of it is responsible for the insights one derives about the intricacies of everyday life that cannot be obtained in any concrete form. These insights inevitably find their way into the analysis although one may not refer to them or to the source so as to avoid revealing the personal or secret nature of the information received or the identity of the informant. Thus although mutual trust and rapport leads to the gain of vital information, the ethnographer then faces the ethical question of the *use* of the material obtained. This problem is a dilemma experienced by every ethnographer who has to first worry about breaking the barriers of suspicion and distance and, having done this, about how to use the sensitive information without betraying the informants.

While it was relatively easy to gain access to the teacher culture and understand it through talk and observation, it was more difficult to do so with pupils. It is simpler to identify with teachers and to relate to them than it is with pupils. At RVS, the difficulty in getting to know pupils did not lie with those who were younger and junior but with the older, senior pupils. My strategy in attempting to mingle with senior pupils, boys in particular, and thereby establish rapport with them was by gaining entry into a particular house and first forging links with them through informal visits and conversation. Once these pupils came to know me well enough, it was relatively easy to understand their perspectives through discussion. Through them, I came into contact with their friends outside the house and with other senior pupils in the school. My understanding of pupil views on different aspects of school life also developed in the course of my conversations with them in casual encounters and in watching and listening to them all over the school—in their interaction with teachers and amongst themselves.

A few pupils considered 'different' in both positive and negative terms by the teachers became particularly friendly with me. There were some who were viewed as having a special interest in the ideology and were therefore considered 'serious' and 'sensitive' in their attitude to both school work and the ideology. Such pupils, and others who were not very interested in the ideology but serious about school work in any case, provided me with an overall perspective of the dominant pupil culture.

There were some pupils who were disinterested in school work and in school goals in general. One boy who was considered definitely deviant and treated in a casual manner by the teachers due to his total lack of interest in school work used me as a 'relief agency' (Woods 1979: 261) in telling me at length about his personal problems and his apathetic relations with the teachers and other pupils. This pupil became an important informant in providing me with a 'peep-hole' view, as it were, of the 'underworld' of pupil culture (in this case, of senior boys) which appeared to consist largely of bawdy talk about girl pupils, the use of what was considered 'foul' language by the pupils themselves, smoking cigarettes surreptitiously, eating non-vegetarian food (which was not allowed at RVS), and so on. My only problem arose from the nature of information he sometimes supplied me. As he continuously broke school rules and told me about his exploits, I worried whether the teachers' trust in me would be undermined if they discovered that I was aware of his breach of rules but did not inform them. In order not to betray the pupil's trust in me, I censored my discussions with teachers by suppressing the information he made available to me. I was however always aware that I would lose the teachers' trust completely if they knew I was concealing 'deviant' forms of pupil activity from them. It therefore becomes the ethnographer's practical concern to hide some information obtained from one source from other participants in order not to lose credibility among different people. On the other hand, the sharing of some information may lead to the gain of further information. It is a situation of balancing one against the other in a continuous game of hide-and-seek with information.

Among the research methods I used to decipher school processes, class-room observation was particularly useful in understanding interaction in a situated setting. I did not use any of the conventional aids to classroom research such as the tape recorder, nor a predetermined set of categories into which I sought to 'fit' classroom behaviour. I wanted to remain open to everything that was taking place in the classroom to the extent that it was possible by being an unobtrusive observer sitting at the back of the room. My main task was to listen to and observe classroom talk and activity and take down detailed notes. By not using a recording device, which incidentally may have altered the 'normal' flow of activity, I am however aware I may have missed what was happening in different parts of the room.

I was primarily interested in observing the nature of teacher–pupil interaction in two different classroom settings: the junior and the senior schools. In the senior school, where I had selected a particular classroom for study, I faced no problems of entry. The teachers' permission was sought by the headmistress on my behalf at a meeting where I was not present and they agreed to my presence in the classroom. The teachers were, by and large, unconcerned by my presence as were also the pupils who would only sometimes glance at my notebook while passing by to see what I was writing. Some teachers however would later come up to me with explana-tions as to why they thought a particular lesson had not proceeded well. Only one teacher mentioned my presence as being responsible for the pupils' inattention in the classroom.

Apart from the evidence of the teachers' need to provide explanations to the observer so that their competence was not misjudged, they appeared to behave naturally in the classroom. Over a period of time, I observed almost every lesson taken by different teachers—some several times over—and faced non-cooperation in only one instance. I did not face 'withdrawal' or other tactics employed by teachers in the classroom to minimize observation as Hargreaves did (1967: 196). An important reason for the relaxation of such control in my case is that I sought to observe classrooms in my second term at RVS by which time most teachers had accepted me to the extent that they scarcely noted my presence as an observer at meetings and on other occasions.

It was in the classroom that I most directly experienced and shared pupil experience of school processes. For example, pupils had often told me that they found a particular teacher's lesson 'very boring'. I would invariably find them yawning their way through it, looking out of the window, participating half-heartedly in the discussion, and glancing at their watches several times waiting for the lesson to come to an end. Their description of the teacher as a 'bore' and their behaviour in the classroom enabled me to experience the situation as they did and I found this teacher's lessons boring myself.[9] I could also experience the pupils' enthusiasm for discussion when a teacher stimulated them into avid talk as well as their ability to listen in silence to a teacher who could hold their attention.

In the junior classroom, I faced some problems. I had selected the junior-most class, where an experiment in learning was conducted by three teachers. The class teacher was initially very apprehensive about my presence in the room and it was only with the intervention of the junior school head, and my assurance that I would only quietly observe and not disturb the lesson, that I was allowed to sit in the classroom. I was not however permitted to take notes during the lesson. I had to employ a strategy to circumvent the control that was being imposed: I began to attend every alternate lesson and took down detailed notes during the intervening period. Sometimes, in order to retail the immediacy of the situation, I would casually leave the classroom and quickly take down notes before coming in again. My experience in this classroom was however different from that in the senior classroom, not only because of the younger age of the pupils, who were easily distracted by my presence, but more importantly because the class was fraught with many difficulties due to the new curriculum.

The problems resulting from the attempts to implement the new curriculum escalated to such an extent that the junior school head had to intervene and the structure was reorganized. This was the only instance when I 'interfered' in school processes and the 'interventionist research strategy' unwittingly came into play.[10] My role in the process of change was triggered by a teacher seeking my advice as to what could be done, as she was finding it difficult to handle the situation. I asked her to speak to the head who until then was not aware of the deteriorating situation in the classroom. He first held a meeting with the three teachers concerned and also consulted me about possible changes and then took the necessary step of reorganization. An improvement in the situation however quelled my doubts about what I viewed as my lack of detachment from school processes.

In addition to observation and understanding through talk, I also distributed questionnaires to all the teachers and a section of the pupils in order to ascertain their socio-economic backgrounds, role perceptions, and views on the ideology, education, and various aspects of school life. The management sought to control the kind of information I was seeking from teachers by deleting two questions from the questionnaire, which had to pass the inspection and approval of the headmistress before distribution. The two very disparate questions, which I considered crucial to my questionnaire, were aimed at eliciting the teachers' views on the influence of the ideology on their lives and their description of a serious problem they had encountered in the classroom and how they had dealt with it. The reason given for their deletion was that the questions were 'personal' and probing too closely into the teachers' lives. This was the view of the management—the gatekeepers—who were protecting not only the teachers but also themselves, as the teachers' answers to these questions might reveal more than they would perhaps like the ethnographer to know. The teachers in general however remained unperturbed by these questions, which I raised in my conversations with them, thus evading the imposed control.

I examined school documents to obtain information on specific topics such as rules for teacher conduct, the criteria for pupil admission, reports on pupils, statements on finance, and annual reports. I also studied documents pertaining to the history of the school and to its relationship with the external order such as the council. Access to these documents was relatively simple: I was shown every document I asked for, including those that were considered 'sensitive' as they contained accounts of executive committee meetings. I saw some of these papers only in the last few weeks before I left the school. By then I was a completely trusted member of the community, which incidentally adds to the dilemma of the *uses* of the information obtained.

The various methods I used for the collection of data generated insights into school processes and thereby contributed to my understanding of the social reality of the school. The combination of different research methods resulted in what, following Lacey (1976), I may call the 'spiral of understanding'.[11] It is important to note that each level of understanding is associated with a particular mode of data collection but each level also contributes to an understanding of the whole. Thus, for example, classroom observation contributed as much to my understanding of the school and to my theoretical explanation of school processes as did understanding through talk. The latter was however my main research tool. It was partly imposed on me by the situation itself which necessitated intensive interaction with different kinds of participants. Initially, talk helped in establishing mutual trust and rapport and later led to the gain not only of detailed information on everyday life but an understanding of the complexities of school processes.

Although this has been discussed by almost every ethnographer, I would like to briefly comment upon the role and importance of 'subjectivity' in fieldwork, besides that of 'objectivity', which is generally acknowledged. For me, fieldwork has been not only an exercise in the collection of data but also a rich human experience to the extent to which I was completely immersed in and personally involved with the many dimensions of school life. I attained the status of a member of the community when my name appeared on the list of teachers put on the notice board in my second term at the school. This did not raise any objections from either teachers, pupils, or the administrative staff as it was assumed that I was one of them although I was clearly not a member of the teaching staff. Similarly, I was expected to participate at staff meetings and was invited to staff dinners and other occasions. I had established close relations with some pupils who would visit my room off and on and share their lives with me. I was also invited to attend their 'house functions' in the evenings and took part in as much of pupil activity as I could.

My involvement in school processes was such that I would be tense in sympathy with the pupils during examinations, fret over the problems being experienced by the teachers *vis-à-vis* the pupils such as indiscipline, experience the humiliation of a pupil when s/he was being ticked off by a teacher or was recounting such episodes to me, worry about the implementation of the ideology and try to examine ways by which it could be accomplished, and also feel perturbed about the professional teachers' role in such a school and the problems they faced apart from the limitations their presence imposed on ideological goals. I used to look forward to special events like 'moonlight dinners' and outings to a neighbouring city as other participants did. A 'tea party' with teachers or a 'gab session' with pupils became pleasurable occasions, as they were for the others.

All this while, I was also conducting fieldwork in what I hoped was an 'objective' manner. I was constantly aware of my role as ethnographer and worried about my involvement in school matters. It was in the process of taking down detailed notes and maintaining a field diary that I was able to sustain the 'detachment' that appeared to be necessary for 'objectivity'.[12] The significant role of subjectivity was however obvious to me all along in terms of 'trying the intimate experience of "the other" in oneself' (Levi-Strauss 1973: 9) in order to 'reach down into the "grammar" of the... culture, so as to establish a translation, not just of the words but of the poetic meaning' (Leach 1973: 12).[13]

In conclusion, I would like to draw attention to some of the problems that arose from the use of particular methods of data collection. I would also like to make some observations about the relations of power and control that exist between the ethnographer and the participants in the fieldwork situation and the problems these may pose for them.

In the study of complex organizations, like schools, the ethnographer engages in 'both explicit and implicit forms of sampling', which, following Ball (1984: 75), I use to refer mainly to 'problems of selectivity'. The first and most important point of selection is the choice of the field. Why did I choose RVS as my study school? My selection was influenced by a number of factors, including the lacuna in sociological studies of schools in India, my interest in Krishnamurti's work and my own experience as a teacher there several years earlier. Both academic and personal concerns thus motivated my decision. As stated earlier, I was interested in examining the relationship between ideology and education and the repercussions this had for schooling, based on the case study of a particular school. It could be argued that such a school is such a unique educational institution that the sociological findings would be insufficient for comparative purposes and have no bearing on wider social phenomena. It is however possible that while ideological discourse is explicit in one school, it may be hidden or underdeveloped in another. That is, in some schools there may be two forms of discourse: an official discourse, based on an ideology about education, that governs the functioning of the school, and an everyday discourse, as it were, that directs actual school processes and is shaped largely by the pressures and demands of the situation. In other schools, such forms of discourse may be muted in expression or may simply not exist. Such being the case, as well as the fact that private schools (both aided and unaided) constitute about 60 per cent of all schools in India, my understanding of the social reality of RVS is located in the overall context of schooling in India.

Apart from the general considerations regarding the selection of the field, there are the specific problems of sampling in the fieldwork situation. Thus, why does one choose to study two particular classrooms in preference to other classrooms? The reasons for this are related to the kind of information one is seeking. For example, I was interested in examining teacher–pupil interaction in the informal setting of a junior classroom where the pressures of school work and examinations did not exist, as well as in the more structured setting of a senior classroom where both teachers and pupils work under the pressure of imminent examinations. Although I made an arbitrary decision regarding exactly which classrooms I would observe, this did not in any way affect the kind of data I was able to obtain. What did happen was that in focussing on teacher–pupil interaction, I neglected a very important dimension of school life, viz., inter-pupil interaction in the classroom. Moreover, in my interaction with senior pupils outside the classroom, I was able to interact more closely with boys (who were more forthcoming) than with girls. I therefore had to supplement the data obtained through talk with other sources such as the questionnaire which was distributed to the three senior-most classes in the school.

Among teachers, the culture of the ideologue teachers emerged more predominantly than that of the professional teachers although the latter outnumbered the former. This is due to the encompassing nature of the ideology in school processes in terms of the superior value attributed to it by a dominant section of the participants although the focus of everyday life is educational transmission.

It is evident that the ethnographer *and* the participants censor and control the flow of information and thereby shape the nature of interaction between them. The ethnographer thus has little power over the participants as 'each works to place it (interaction) in particular social, emotional and political contexts' (Cassel 1980: 30–31). In this sense, power is distributed between them and interaction often involves negotiation rather than the stringent application of rules of procedure (Barnes 1979: 24). It is the ethnographer however who seeks to elicit the participants' cooperation and has thus to take the initiative to negotiate, cajole, and use alternative strategies to tease out, as it were, information which is secret and therefore restricted. This may include presenting different fronts to different kinds of participants, as I did, to make oneself acceptable to the entire community and thereby eligible for receiving secret information. Success with participants depends on the ethnographer's ability to handle interaction in a manner that engenders confidence and trust. Some participants may of course decline to enter into interaction and the ethnographer has no power to make them do so. Once the ethnographer has obtained information from others, who become friends and informants, the balance of power shifts from the participants to the ethnographer inasmuch as the latter may choose to use the information in any desired manner.

It is here that the ethnographer encounters one of the most thorny problems in fieldwork. This is primarily ethical in nature and, following Barnes (1979), may be succinctly phrased in terms of the question: 'Who should know what?' The dilemma of the use of the material obtained first occurs in the field itself. For example, I encountered situations in which I was censoring my conversations with different teachers and pupils to protect other teachers or pupils in the school. The ethnographer thus has to continuously be on guard so as not to betray participants and lose their goodwill and credibility in the field. Apart from this practical consideration, there is also the moral aspect in terms of the trust and confidence which has been placed in the ethnographer and which, in human terms, is not usually possible to betray.

The ethnographer also experiences the dilemma of the use of the material while providing an analysis of the acquired material. This can be overcome by not revealing the names of the participants who supplied controversial or sensitive information which is sometimes the most useful in revealing the underlying reality of the field. However, an extreme result of such a dilemma occurs when one has to drop the information altogether as any use of it would be completely unethical. This happened, for example, when I chose not to use the material from the teacher's personal diary although it would have helped in providing an interesting dimension to my understanding of the teacher culture from the viewpoint of one kind of teacher.

The crucial point that emerges is that the ethnographer does not really have the kind of power that is generally assumed to exist due to the acquisition of sensitive and important material. The ethnographer's use of the acquired material is generally governed by practical, moral and, most important, human considerations, and an attempt is made to protect the identity of the participants and the efforts of the particular community to achieve their goals. It is possible however that some ethnographers do misuse the information they acquire to further research in the area which has resulted in the extensive debate on ethics in social science research (see, for example, Barnes 1979).

Fieldwork thus implies not only the straightforward collection of data but the complex task of uncovering the masks or lifting the veils that lie between the façade and the reality within a framework that is guided by both practical (in terms of the ethnographer's objectives) and ethical considerations. To accomplish this task, the nature of interaction between the ethnographer and the participants is crucial to enable the ethnographer not only to gain information but to 'understand' the social reality of the field.

Notes

1. This procedure appears to be shared with others. For example, Béteille notes, 'When I went to Sripuram I did not have a definite preference for any particular aspect of its social life, and I certainly did not have a clearly formulated plan of investigation....

I did have an interest in the problem of social inequality, but this interest took shape only in the course of my stay in the village' (1975: 102). Becker *et al.* have also pointed out that their study had no research design: '... we had no well-worked-out set of hypotheses to be tested, no data-gathering instruments purposely designed to secure information relevant to these hypotheses, no set of analytic procedures specified in advance' (as quoted in Burgess 1982: 12).

2. This was one indication of the relations of power in the school—which were later revealed to me—in terms of who 'counted' in taking decisions.

3. I am using the term 'understanding', following Wax, to refer to 'a social phenomenon—a phenomenon of *shared* meanings' (1971: 11). That is, the ethnographer understands the field when she can interpret the words, gestures, and nuances of the participants' lives as they do.

4. I use the term 'involved' as it has been used by Woods, who defines his role in the field as that of an '*involved* rather than a participating observer'. He views his involvement in terms of 'the relationships entered into with staff and pupils, an identification with the educative process, and a willingness to go along with their perceptions of life' (Woods 1979: 261).

5. Woods has drawn my attention to the term 'understanding through talk', which he describes as a research style, concomitant with participant observation, and which consists essentially of conducting 'interviews, discussions, conversations: in short, some form of "talk"' (1979:263).

6. The 'ordinariness' of events has been identified by Woods (1981: 16) at three levels in relation to three levels of access. The first is the public image that is presented to the ethnographer in the initial few weeks at the school. With the passage of time, this front is relaxed and the ethnographer is allowed glimpses of life behind the mask. However, it is only with the building of rapport and trust that the participants begin to confide their feelings, experiences, attitudes which provide insights into the actual functioning of the school.

7. Some of my 'key informants' were among those at the school with whom I formed the closest and most lasting relationships. I could therefore never really view them *only* as informants, they were also friends and confidants with whom I shared my anxieties and problems, usually related to some aspect of fieldwork.

8. In this context, Gluckman notes that 'the right to gossip about certain people is a privilege which is only extended to a person when he or she is accepted as a member of a group or set' (1963: 313).

9. Woods notes a similar experience in his study suggesting that 'talk assumes an onomatopoeic quality' thereby enabling the observer to directly experience the situation (1979: 267).

10. The term 'interventionist research strategy' is used by Lacey to describe 'episodes of innovation and change (that) can occur through research...' (1976: 62) although in my case, it was not a planned episode but arose out of the circumstances.

11. Lacey states that what he did was to ' "escalate insights" through moving backwards and forwards between observation and analysis and understanding' using different methods of data collection (1976: 61).

12. It has been suggested that both 'involvement and detachment', or belonging and distantiation as Ricoeur (1981) puts it, are the essence of the ethnographer's experience in the field: 'Involvement is necessary to understand the psychological realities of a culture, that is, its meanings for the indigenous members. Detachment is necessary to construct the abstract reality: a network of social relations including the rules and how they function...' (Powdermaker 1966: 9).

13. Cf. Geertz (1983: 55–70) who scoffs at the anthropologist's attempt to get 'into some inner correspondence of spirit' with participants who, he suggests, would not welcome such an intrusion. He is emphatic that the ethnographer cannot 'perceive what his informants perceive' and 'whatever accurate or half-accurate sense one gets of what one's informants are... comes from the ability to construe their modes of expression,... their symbol systems...'. He thus concludes that 'Understanding the form and pressure of ... natives' inner lives is more like grasping a proverb, catching an allusion, seeing a joke—or, ... reading a poem—than it is like achieving communion'.

Sparks of Contingency:
Photography and Anthropology in India

CHRISTOPHER PINNEY

The relationship between photography and social enquiry has a particularly long history in South Asia. The earliest examples of this conjunction were ambitious official colonial attempts to document the physiognomy and costume of 'castes and tribes'. These fed into, but were then largely replaced by, an increasingly social documentary use of photography by anthropologists. More recently, anthropologists have started to become interested in photography and film not simply as methodological supports to data collection but as central aspects of South Asian cultural practice deserving of ethnographic study in their own right.

There is evidence that photography was in use in Calcutta (now Kolkata) by 1840, a few months after its discovery was announced in Europe. Some of the earliest anthropologically interesting images appeared from the mid-1850s onwards in a series of publications produced by William Johnson. Johnson's beautiful two-volume set *The Oriental Races and Tribes: Residents and Visitors of Bombay* (1863 and 1866) contained fifty-one exceptional studies of different communities in Bombay (now Mumbai). India was the locale of many of the most important official colonial documentation projects. Chief among these were Watson and Kaye's colossal *People of India* (8 vols, 1868–1875, which included 468 albumen prints) and M.V. Portman's Andaman project, which documented external physical form, and the production of material cultural items such as adzes (cf. Pinney 1990 for a more detailed account of these and other early official projects). If space permitted numerous other important projects might also be cited.

It would be easy to dismiss this early imagery as tainted and rendered useless by the colonial anxieties and obsessions which produced them. However, photography's filter is never complete, for no matter how painterly, how contrived the image, the indexicality of the photographic process will always ensure some small indeterminate element that eludes this desire to control. This resistance of the photographic image to the prejudice of the photographer has been most elegantly described by Walter Benjamin:

No matter how artful the photographer, no matter how carefully composed his subject, the beholder feels an irresistible urge to search such pictures for the tiny spark of contingency, of the Here and Now, with which reality has so to speak seared the subject, to find the inconspicuous spot where in the immediacy of that long-forgotten moment the future subsists so eloquently that we, looking back, may rediscover it (1985: 243).

This is an important revision of prevailing Foucauldian approaches to photography which assert that images produced as part of these state projects are interesting *only* as documents of this surveillance and for what they reveal of the colonizing mentality (cf. Tagg 1988). However, different photographs reveal sorts and degrees of 'sparks of contingency': some photographs *are* primarily interesting as evidential of the photographer's anxieties and intentions, whereas other photographers have left detailed bodies of work, only subtly inflected by the colonial episteme, which are far more willing to yield dense information of great ethnohistorical value. The work of E.H. Man in the Andaman and Nicobar Islands, for instance, constitutes a visual archive of great significance. Man's archive at the Royal Anthropological Institute (cf. Edwards 1992) is doubly important for its inclusion of one of the few images of the anthropologist/cameraperson at work. A drawing tipped into one of Man's albums transfers onto paper the style of a Nicobarese shamanaic *henta-koi* shield. The layered frames incorporate E.H. Man at work with his camera. An accompanying handwritten note by Man describes the uppermost scene as 'E.H.M. taking a photo of some Nicobarese. A Police orderly and servant holding an umbrella are in attendance'. The slip also gives Nicobarese words for the various aquatic creatures depicted in the centre, including a crocodile, a porpoise, a turtle, and a ray-fish. The lower panel 'represents the station St. Nancowry at anchor with Malacca village, Spiteful Bay and Leda Pt. in the background'.

South Asia's role in the history of anthropology has yet to be fully acknowledged. The earliest part of this history, with its unrivalled profusion of official colonial projects, has been alluded to here. The second part of this history sees the emergence of fieldwork practice in the first decade of the twentieth century through the endeavours of W.H.R. Rivers (among the Todas) and C.G. Seligman (among the Veddahs of Sri Lanka), who had both participated in Haddon's second Torres Straits Expedition.

A short monograph might easily be written concerning photography and the Todas. Both W.E. Marshall's *A Phrenologist amongst the Todas* (1873) and J.W. Breeks' *An Account of the Primitive Tribes and Monuments of the Nilagiris* (1873) are profusely illustrated with photographs and were to have a lasting impact through Rivers' later work. Whereas Marshall's work included anthropometric images of subjects photographed against a measured grid, Breeks' work was illustrated with pasted-in albumen prints of Toda material culture and ritual practice produced by a photographer from the Madras School of Arts 'whose performance' Breeks' widow notes in the preface, was 'by no means satisfactory' (Breeks 1873: iii). Although Rivers' work (five months' field research between 1901–02) is characterized by a 'lack' from a post-Malinowskian perspective (and hence characterized as part of the 'intermediate generation'), it is worth recalling that during the first decade of the twentieth century, Rivers played much the same messianic role among fellow academics that Malinowski was to later appropriate. Rivers was hailed as 'the apostle of the new approach to fieldwork, and as the greatest ethnographer who ever lived' (Langham 1981: 50). *The Todas*, Rivers' 1906 monograph, reproduced several prints by the anonymous Madras Art School photographer which had first appeared in Breeks (1873), together with commissioned images by the commercial Madras photographers Wiele and Klein, and Rivers' own variable photographs. Although the text of his monograph asserts a very muscular claim for a 'new' anthropological methodology that would dispel the earlier romanticism of a century's idealized distortion of the Todas, the photographic illustrations in the book relate a much more anxious and uncertain triumph. Many images literally reproduce the visual foundations of earlier analyses, and Wiele and Klein's images seem to strive for a noble classicism that undercuts Rivers' text with a very different argument (cf. Pinney 1992).

Elsewhere I have argued that the diminution of photographic activity that accompanies the emergence of what would now be recognized as 'modern' fieldwork is not paradoxical. Rather, it reflects a transference of authority from the indexical surface of the photograph onto the anthropologist's body. The post-Malinowskian anthropologist took onto his/her own person the functions of the photographic negative which, having been prepared to receive and record messages in a space of alterity during a moment of exposure in 'the field' is able, after suitable processing, to present them in a 'positive' state in the ethnographic monograph (ibid.: 82).

Twentieth-century anthropologists who made extensive use of photography became the exception, rather than the rule, and publishers' reluctance to reproduce photographic images further inscribed the hegemony of text. However, important figures such as Sarat Chandra Roy and Adrian Mayer continued to publish heavily illustrated monographs. Christoph von Fürer-Haimendorf, the prolific ethnographer of tribal India, was perhaps the most enthusiastic fieldwork photographer of the twentieth century, noting in the preface to *Himalayan Barbary*, his populist account of the Indo-Tibetan borderlands, that he took little equipment with him: 'the only exception was my Zeiss Contax III camera' (1955: ix).

The Chicago anthropologist, McKim Marriott, has produced one of the most remarkable bodies of fieldwork photographs which capture with tremendous warmth and subtlety the everyday routines of Uttar Pradesh and Maharashtrian villagers. Whereas Fürer-Haimendorf's images appear to owe much to nineteenth century representations in their concerns with normative bodies in appropriate environments, Marriott's focus intently on ritual and everyday sociality. Marriott's strategy of pursuing sequential action entails the inclusion of much extraneous detail and makes his archive one of enormous value for future historians of Indian rural society.

Although renowned for his textual ethnography, Marriott's photographic work is much less well known. In 1972, Marriott, in conjunction with the University of the State of New York Foreign Area Materials Center, produced an innovative slide pack containing 118 photographic images of Kishan Garhi village dating from 1951–52, and an equal number dating from the same village in 1968–69. The slides were matched thematically so that practices such as the positioning of castes during funeral feasts could be compared and contrasted across these two historical moments. The paired slides permit great insight into an enormous range of cultural practices and their historical contingency and change. Thus, a 1951 image records villagers' contentment with worshipping the *devi* (goddess) in 'simple homemade shrines in ordinary language', whereas in 1969, one schoolteacher has created a personal *devi* shrine 'at which he himself reads a Sanskrit text and does a 16-step routine of worship...' (Marriot 1972: 25). The 1951 mud house 'contained few but strictly utilitarian objects, most of them locally made or grown', while in 1969, 'Even a small cultivator's cupboard now contains dozens of imported items, notably lamps, cosmetics, books, prints of the Hindu gods that may ultimately replace homemade wall paintings' (ibid.: 21). Marriott's text and selection of images is aimed at an undergraduate audience and simplified accordingly, and like all texts, reflects the concerns of its own day. However, this little-known project is an object lesson in how visual images might be used as a more central part of anthropological teaching and research. Visuals are used in the pack to dramatize and embody historical change so that otherwise bland statements about (say) changes in costume ('women's drab clothing of 1951' contrasted with the 'colourful, and often boldly patterned' saris of 1969) assume a phenomenological vitality and reality (ibid.: 23).

We can imagine that many of the images that Marriott took in 1951 only subsequently became of particular interest because later events (for example, the disappearance of a practice or material feature evident in the 1950s) threw the content of the images into particular relief. Highly monological ethnographic texts would not permit this sort of recording because everything outside of the immediate concerns of the text would have been excluded: hence the frustration of many readers upon finding that the author of an earlier text 'was not interested' in a particular subject (or dimension of that subject) and that the text is consequently completely barren in that respect. Photographs, however, because they always ultimately resist the imposition of any systematic filter, will always as Benjamin noted, betray some spark of contingency. This will always ensure future audiences and future readings of photographs, although texts may crumble into dust because they may portray nothing other than the prejudices of a particular moment.

Perhaps the most controversial attempt, in recent years, to visually document India is Robert Gardner's narrationless movie, *Forest of Bliss* (1985). This characteristically brave and challenging attempt by Gardner to respond to the phenomenological dimensions of death in Banaras fuelled an enormous and futile debate. Jay Ruby's complaint that it comprised 'a jumble of incomprehensible vignettes' (cited in MacDougal 1998: 72) inaugurated a barrage of objections by filmmakers and anthropologists to Gardner's deliberate eschewal of explanation. David MacDougall, stepping back from the debate, has seen in the anxiety that the film produced, evidence of the threat of what Roland Barthes termed the 'third' or 'obtuse' 'meaning [that] appears to extend outside culture, knowledge, information' (ibid.) to anthropologists and others working within a discipline of words. Peter Loizos (1993) has also usefully commented on the fallaciousness of much of the debate which appears to operate on the assumption that *only one* form of representation of any subject (in this case, death in Banaras) is possible or appropriate. Loizos' pluralist conclusion is that many forms are possible, and indeed desirable: Gardner may provide one kind of experience, while (say) Jonathan Parry's highly analytic work (1994) will provide another. The two are not exclusive or incompatible.

Recent investigations of Indians' own popular photographic practices (MacDougall 1993, Pinney 1997) have begun to examine image-making practices as a central part of cultural practices, themselves deserving of analysis. In this later movement, the anthropologist's own camera primarily used to record what other people's cameras record of the world.

Anthropologists using photography as part of their fieldwork are likely to be quickly made aware of a divide between their own documentary aspirations and their photographic subjects' own desire for the presentation of an idealized self. These two distinct agendas might be made manifest in individuals' desire to always look at the camera, rather than be apparently engrossed in the activity that documentary photography seeks to 'document'. Equally likely is subjects' refusal to be represented in their everyday clothes and settings. My own experience of this during fieldwork in Madhya Pradesh sowed the seed of my interest in photography as cultural practice. Initially, however, villagers' frequent refusal to be photographed in their everyday-ness was a frustration, an intervention that I perceived as a failure, an obstruction preventing the visual record of a primary cultural reality that my anthropological training had made me privilege. Frequently, attempts to 'quickly' take a photograph as an adjunct to fieldnotes would produce a lengthy interruption: clothes had to be changed, hair to be brushed and oiled (and in the case of upper-caste women, talcum powder applied to lighten the skin). Thus challenged, agency was completely transferred to the putative subjects of the image who would then dictate their needs to the fieldworker/cameraperson who could be in no doubt that a completely different local aesthetic agenda was now directing events. This local aesthetic demands body images that are full length and symmetrical, and many anthropologists may see in the passive, expressionless faces and body poses the extinguishment of everything that they hoped to capture through photography.

Many anthropologists have experienced the force of this local aesthetic in the act of picture making during fieldwork. Additionally, most communities with whom anthropologists work in South Asia are likely to have their own family photographs, the result of itinerant commercial photographers, local studios, or (in the case of wealthier metropolitan individuals) images taken by a family member in possession of a camera. Studio produced images—which account for the majority of photographs circulating in most rural communities—reveal a great deal not only about the individuals and groups represented in them, but also about the wider 'interocular' (Appadurai and Breckenridge 1992: 52) visual culture in which they operate. Any early twenty-first–century ethnographic investigation in non-elite South Asia is likely to uncover a tradition of complex black and white imagery (often characterized by elaborate montage, collage, and composite printing), which has now been largely displaced by colour portraiture. These earlier images are often complex and intellectually witty constructions whose discussion with fieldwork subjects can be of enormous value in elucidating themes such as devotion, death, tradition, and modernity, and perhaps most frequently, the nature of love and marriage. More recent colour images have started to rediscover some of the earlier language of black and white photography, but technological constraints have involved a movement away from highly localized artisanal printing procedures to more centralized capital intensive colour processing.

Although a start has been made in the anthropological engagement with photography as a cultural practice, vast areas of investigation remain untouched. Ewald (1996) undertook an interesting 'self-photography' project in Gujarat, but she lacked any anthropological or linguistic skills. The potential of self-photography projects (either involving the distribution of cheap 'throw-away' cameras or tuition in basic camerawork and printing skills) remains to be fully explored in India. Recent Ford Foundation self-photography projects in China and Kenya have been funded because of their perceived social-uplift consequences, but one can envisage endless situations in which self-photography coupled with 'photo-elicitation' might provide extremely rich insights into such fieldwork environments as urban street dwellers' topography of place and value, pilgrims' experience of holy sites, and rural villagers' perception of 'modernity'. In all these cases, photographic images would play a strategic additional role in conventional fieldwork strategies rather than replacing those strategies, but one can imagine a phenomenologically rich dimension emerging that only self-photography would facilitate.

There is a further aspect of the photograph's inclusivity and inability to exclude that will increasingly make it of value. Walter Benjamin, so Adorno noted, had a 'preference for... everything that has slipped through the conventional conceptual net for... things which have been esteemed too trivial by the prevailing spirit for it to have left any traces other than those of hasty judgement' (Adorno, *Prisms*, cited in Bann 1989: 246). Echoing this, Siegfried Kracauer argued that 'The place which an epoch occupies in the historical process is determined more forcefully from the analysis of its insignificant superficial manifestations than from the judgements of the epoch upon itself.... The basic content of epoch and its unobserved impulses reciprocally illuminate one another (cited in Frisby 1985: 147).

As the grand narratives of modernist social theory increasingly fragment, anthropologists (taking a lead from South Asian historians such as
Partha Chatterjee 1993) are becoming increasingly concerned with culture
and its 'fragments'. Weariness with the systematizing 'hasty judgements' of
the past is increasingly producing a privileging of the margins, of those
key markers of significance that slip through the 'conventional conceptual
net'. Within this emergent paradigm, photography can help invoke an
'optical unconscious' (Benjamin 1985: 243) that will permit us to 'see'
what the burden of regional studies and its theoretical legacies no longer
permit us to hear.

III
Surveys and Documents

Catherine Marsh (1984: 9) defines the survey as 'an inquiry which involves the collection of systematic data across a sample of cases, and the statistical analysis of results'. Information is gathered in the survey through oral or written questioning. We have noted that the technique of oral questioning is called an interview; written questioning is accomplished through a questionnaire. Although not so easily acceptable, many authors think that if intensive fieldwork is a method of data collection in social anthropology—where its practitioners work mainly with small, pre-literate, and technologically simple societies—then the survey is the hallmark of research in sociology, a discipline mainly concerned with industrial, literate, differentiated, and technologically complex societies.

But one may note here that some anthropologists have used survey techniques in their lengthy spells of fieldwork and some sociologists have resorted to participant and non-participant observations in their studies. For instance, Oscar Lewis (1951: XXI) observes:

> Like the sociologist, the anthropologist must become skilled in the use of census data and comparative statistics to relate and compare population trends, standards of living, health and education, and types of agricultural problems.

Kroeber (1948) is reputed to have treated his data on fashions statistically. Although Leach (1967) expressed his uneasiness with the application of survey methodology in simple societies, many researchers have found that 'with respect to the standardized interview, there is no longer much difference in attitude between respondents in non-Western towns and those in Europe or North America' (Speckmann 1976: 59). Different techniques of data collection may be usefully combined; a fieldwork may begin with participant observation and towards its close the researcher may administer schedules on people. Today, investigators speak in terms of triangulation, i.e., they address 'social research questions with multiple methods or measures that do not share the same methodological weaknesses' (Singleton, Jr and Straits 1999: 569).

The first article in this section, by Joseph Elder, is an application of survey research to the understanding of the relationship between caste and world view, the latter in contemporary literature is also known as the 'cultural model' (Boyer 1990). This piece, thirty-five years old, is of a time when social researchers were uncertain about the usefulness of survey methods in India. They wondered if the individual in India could be a 'relevant unit of opinion'.[1] Elder shows in his paper that survey research can be successfully conducted in Indian villages. For seventeen months, Elder had conducted a typical anthropological fieldwork, using standardized techniques, in a village of Uttar Pradesh. Towards the last two months of his fieldwork, he administered a 'structured schedule' on over two hundred respondents drawn as a random sample from five groups.

The tabulations of the results of these interviews questioned some of Elder's tentative conclusions that were based on unstructured discussions with respondents. This convinced him of the 'advantages of supplementing standard fieldwork methods with systematic interviewing'. He also realized the value of a larger sample size and the heterogeneity of respondents, which could only be studied using sample methods. In this paper, he discusses the planning and outcome of his second piece of research based on survey methodology. One also learns here how Elder drew his sample, the interviews he conducted, and the results of his enquiry. One of the major advantages of the survey is that 'one typically deals with sufficiently large number of respondents... so that one can control for several variables'. Elder also notes a principal drawback of survey: it lacks the 'clarity of detail and the supplementary interpretive information' that one obtains from the use of participant observation.

As said earlier, the interview is one of the main techniques to gather information both in an intensive fieldwork and in a survey, but we shall keep a distinction between the nature of the interview in the two ways of data collection. Interviews take the shape of general, free-floating, unstructured, and everyday conversations in intensive fieldwork, whereas in a survey, they are focused on a topic and structured. The investigator prepares a set of questions in advance, which he asks his respondents, or keeps ready a list of topics and sub-topics (in the form of an interview guide) around which interactions take place. A respondent will be conscious of being *interviewed* and in most cases, the interview will be an interaction between individuals—occupying well-defined social positions of the interviewer and the interviewee—who have a secondary relation among them. This is in contrast to the primary ties that are gradually built up between the investigator and 'his people' in intensive fieldwork and the conversation that takes place between them is not viewed as an 'interview' as the term is understood in common parlance.

Researchers have also identified different types of interview situations while doing fieldwork. Middleton (1970: 63–66) describes four such situations in his fieldwork with the Lugbara. The first was when he would sit with a group of people who were engaged in drinking beer or in performing a ceremony or ritual. He would not interrupt the activities that were going on by asking questions. He would simply observe what was going on, listen to the conversation, ask a negligible number of questions, and later, note down the details. The second situation was when he sat with a few people, perhaps a family, and asked them carefully thought out questions, many of them emerging from his observational data. In such situations, he would take photographs and note down details in his diary, which he generally avoided in the first situation. The third situation was when he would have a long discussion with one person, his key respondent, who sometimes accompanied his confidant, and 'filled his notebook'. The last situation was when he would interview persons while filling schedules. For this work, he also engaged schoolboys and paid them in cash for helping him. Reflecting upon Middleton's work, one may say that all fieldworkers encounter these interview situations and in each one of them they have to decide the kind of interview they would like to conduct. In each interview, the respondent is given a 'voice', the capacity of self-representation.

To illustrate the use of the technique of interviewing, A.C. Mayer's article on the perspectives of princely rule has been included here. As princely states ceased to exist some decades ago, it is now too late for a fieldworker to study their actual working. One way to know about princely rule is to focus on the documents of that time, the materials available in archives and museums; the other is to interview people who were rulers of these states. Mayer adopts the latter method. He interviews the Prince of Dewas, whom he had known from the time of his first fieldwork in Dewas in 1954. In 1978 and 1979–80, Mayer interviewed the prince and his half-brother about their perceptions of princely rule. The interview with the prince was conducted in English and from the excerpts that have been quoted *ad verbatim*, it is clear that it was tape-recorded.

The question of what the difference would have been had the interview been conducted in the local language is not taken up in Mayer's article. Further, the prince not only provides information but also reads and comments upon the draft of the paper. We do not know of the changes made in the paper in light of the respondent's observations. In such cases, it is quite likely that the sociologist will be constrained to eliminate the interpreta-tions, remarks, comments, or even observations, which the literate respon-dent finds unsavoury or embarrassing if shared with a wider public. This type of sociological writing should be distinguished from the one where the informants provide the data but have no role to play in the final pro-duction of the text; neither do they read the draft nor, in many cases, see the final outcome, the book or the article. It may be submitted here that Mayer does not touch upon these issues of methodology, for his main con-cern is with the perception of princely rule and the implications this evi-dence has for Louis Dumont's views on kingship in India.

Undoubtedly, the respondent 'highlights himself' in these interviews, especially when he talks about touring in his territory, but Mayer makes it clear that his paper is not on how the prince actually ruled. It is on what the prince has to say about his rule. The difference between how he ruled, how he should have ruled, and how rulers should ideally rule, can be noted in several excerpts of the interview that Mayer presents, which is a great strength of this paper. The reader comes to know the questions the inter-viewer asked. In many other field reports, we learn the answers the respon-dents gave but not the questions the investigators asked and the words in which the questions were framed.

A study—such as Mayer's—can fruitfully combine individual percep-tions of a social phenomenon with whatever material is available on it. The historically informed anthropologists and sociologists follow this method: they interview the people who had witnessed an event and/or participated in it, and also look into the historical materials (or even archaeological, as the case may be). Because social anthropology and sociology are principally observational sciences, their first commitment is to the 'field view' of society, but it does not imply that the documents available with people or lodged in archives and museums should be set aside just because they do not constitute observational data. In fact, it shall be myopic to restrict anthropological and sociological works just to providing field views of societies, because more important than field views are the theoretical perspectives anthropology and sociology have on soci-ety, and these perspectives can be employed for analysing any kind of data—archaeological, historical, or the primary data collected in a fieldwork or survey. Anthropology and sociology are therefore ways of thinking about society and not just ways of collecting primary data. Moreover, in a literate civilization such as India, there is another corpus of materials—the religious texts—which contain an important source of knowledge about the society, namely what their authors thought should be the principles according to which people should live, what should be the ideal society, and what they thought was the nature of society at that time.[2]

The next article is by Rudolph and Rudolph, the couple well credited in sociological literature for their analysis of the diaries, running into ninety volumes, written by a Rajput named Amar Singh, and also for publishing excerpts from these diaries in the original. Among personal documents, diaries are an important source of information. The Rudolphs distinguish autobiographies, journals, and memoirs from diaries: the first three are meant for the public, the last is for the self. Diarists write for a variety of reasons—to improve upon their language, to record their daily happenings, to give vent to their emotions, to make sense of their contemporary life happenings. Ideally, whatever they write is only for their own consumption. Besides writing for personal fulfilment, the other important characteristic of the diarist is that he writes in the 'here-and-now'. He endeavours to interpret everyday life unlike the autobiographer who writes by the 'logic of hindsight', in a longitudinal frame of time. The diary 'reveals a person in the making', whilst autobiography is about a person who has 'mostly been made'. In this paper, the Rudolphs compare Amar Singh's diaries with those of others, especially that of a seventeenth-century religious leader, a man known as Banarsi, and therefore, from a comparative point of view, it is a significant contribution.

A similarity between religious texts, diaries (and other personal documents), and census data is that they are produced or collected by others—sages produce religious literature, some reflective persons write their diaries, census data are collected by 'enumerators' on already prepared schedules. Social anthropologists and sociologists subject these data to analysis, although they themselves do not collect them. The next reading we have included here, by A.M. Shah, is on the value of census data for sociological work. Census operations started in India with the advent of British rule and efforts were made to estimate India's population between 1820 and 1840. The census was conducted in the town of Allahabad in 1824 and in Banaras in 1827–28. Subsequently, census operations were carried out in different parts of India, and progressively, the information collected also diversified. The Bombay Presidency Census of 1872 took note of the occupational distribution, and, as Shah points out, the Census of India–1951 provided data on the household, however information on households was available in micro-level censuses, say, of a village or a town.

In this and his other works, Shah has looked at family patterns and household composition from the perspective of his fieldwork information (collected in rural Gujarat) as well as the census data. Basing his findings on census materials, in one of his papers (of 1996), Shah submits that while the joint household seems to have weakened in the urban, educated, and professional class, there has been an increase in joint households in the majority of the population in India. Shah's article included here refers to an analysis of the census data of 1820–30 on the household composition in a Gujarat village, which shows that it was rarely that the brothers shared the same household after the death of their father. The average size of the household was 4.5 persons and it was similar to that of a village in Maharashtra of the same period. Shah shows that the analysis of census data rebuts the commonly held assumption that people in traditional India lived in 'large and complex households of three or four generations'. By contrast to a typical anthropological study, which is of a minuscule unit, census data provide a macro picture. In this lies its relevance notwithstanding certain weaknesses the censuses and official statistics have (see Hindess, 1973).

In an intensive fieldwork in a small village, sociologists usually cover all the households rather than take a sample. It is likely that a census study guides to a random stratified sample—samples of different sizes drawn from different strata of the society depending upon the number of each one of them. Census enquiry preceding this helps us in determining the universe. Once we know the universe, we can draw a sample where each unit has an equal probability of being selected. The sampled households can then be subjected to intensive qualitative as well as quantitative study (see Epstein, 1979: 217).

Qualitative researchers may employ some methods that are used in quantitative research for presenting their data visually, such as tables, figures, and graphs. The structure of their presentation does not seem to conform to any strict rules and procedures because tables, figures, and graphs are 'always tailored to serve the needs of the particular study' (Sarantakos 1993: 359). The qualitative responses may be treated statistically. And quantitative data may certainly require a highly sophisticated statistical treatment.

The possibility of applying various statistical measures in sociological and anthropological researches has been explored.[3] Some authors—who popularized titles such as mathematical sociology or mathematical anthropology—predicted that future anthropologists and sociologists would use abstract algebra more than statistics, but these predictions have yet not been fulfilled (see Kay, 1971). What anthropologists and sociologists generally use is statistics, and not algebra, and within it, they rarely move beyond correlational analysis and tests of significance, and generally use the measures of central tendency (mean, mode, and median) and of dispersion (variance and standard deviation, range, and interquartile range). The measures of central tendency represent the average or typical value in a distribution, while those of dispersion represent the degree to which the data are spread around the mean. The reading we have included here to illustrate the use of statistics is from John van Willigen and N.K. Chadha's book on social ageing. They use mean and standard deviation in their analysis of the social networks of aged people in an upper-middle-class neighbourhood of Delhi. Some authors, in addition, use the tests of significance, which are used for assessing the likelihood that the results of a study would have occurred by chance. Elder, in his paper included in this section, uses the chi-square test.[4]

Notes

1. Refer to Rudolph and Rudolph (1958) for the problems of conducting social research in India through the survey. For its summary and comments, see Madan (1972: 293–94).
2. In this context, see Das (1977).
3. For a review of such efforts, see Köbben (1966), Mitchell (1967), Chibnik (1985).
4. Chi-square test is based on a comparison of the observed frequencies with the frequencies one would expect if there were no relationship between the variables.

Caste and World View: The Application of Survey Research Methods

JOSEPH W. ELDER

Those using survey methods in India have occasionally questioned whether the assumptions underlying the use of such techniques in the West apply in the Indian context. Lloyd and Susanne Rudolph, for example, have asked whether most people in India have opinions they can articulate on a broad range of issues and whether the individual in India is a relevant unit of opinion (1958: 235–44). Members of the Cornell Cross-Cultural Methodology Project in India, while not challenging the underlying assumptions of survey techniques, have shown that the interviewers' affiliations can markedly bias their results, even when they ask questions with identical wording (Ralis, Suchman, and Goldsen 1958: 245–60). The purpose of this paper is to describe certain limitations and problems, as well as advantages, which I have found in using survey research techniques in India.

Survey Research as a Supplement to Field Observations

From November 1956 to March 1958, I gathered data in a small village in Uttar Pradesh for my PhD dissertation on industrialism and Hinduism. The techniques I used were essentially those of anthropology: participant observation, interviews with the better-informed or at least more talkative members of the village, lineage-tracing, census-taking, map-making, and taking of copious field notes.

Two months before the end of my stay I added a type of data-gathering not generally included in an anthropologist's kit. With the aid of a structured schedule, I interviewed over 200 respondents selected as random samples of five groups I considered important for my research topic. The following are some of the main conclusions I drew from these interviews.

1. Such interviewing helps counteract the 'self-selection' of respondents so familiar to field workers. Before... the interviews, my best informants had been a tailor of the Dunha caste, a Bhangi boy, the Brahman village priest, and two or three of the younger Jat and Chamar farmers. My systematic interviews forced me to talk with categories of villagers I had missed in my less structured interviews; for example, village women (especially the new brides), men who were out of the village much of the time, and persons from some of the less numerous castes. From the respondents' point of view the fact that their name was 'on the list' appeared to justify their dropping what they were doing to talk with me.

2. An interview schedule that needs to be filled out can 'legitimize' quite a lengthy, far-ranging discussion. My questions included views on rein-carnation as well as attitudes toward urbanization and industrialism. The structured nature of the question, furthermore, permitted me to cover a wider range of topics in forty minutes than if I had been having a more informal conversation.

3. Asking the same questions from 200 people permits comparisons of their replies according to caste, age, income, religious belief, and other broad categories. For certain questions, such as 'How many *pakkā* houses were there in the village before the sugar mill was built?' or 'What happened to the Muslims in the village at the time of Partition?', three or four good informants are all one needs. But for other questions, such as, 'On the whole, would you say that the mill has brought more benefit or more harm to the village?', some people will say 'benefit' and others 'harm'. From the researcher's point of view, the relevant question is *who* says 'benefit' and *who* says 'harm' and what proportion of the total population each group represents.

As a matter of fact, the tabulations of my interview results forced me to change some of my tentative conclusions based on other discussions with respondents. For example, my general impression was that the poorer vil-lagers looked back with nostalgia on the days of the British; whereas the richer villagers were glad that India was independent. When I had totaled my interview returns, however, I saw that the rich–poor distinction was not as important as the caste distinction, with the highest and lowest castes feeling things had become better since Independence while the middle castes felt things had been better under the British. Unless I had systematically interviewed a sizeable sample of the population, I would not have been able to correct my initial error.

By the time I had completed my analysis of the interview data, I was convinced of the advantages of supplementing standard fieldwork methods with systematic interviewing. However, with only 200 people in my sample, there were all kinds of interesting questions that I was unable to pursue. For example, the nature of the group I interviewed was such that the higher castes were also highly educated and had spent a considerable length of time in cities, whereas the lower castes were largely illiterate and had lived most of their lives in the village. When the two groups differed in outlook, as they frequently did, there was no way in which I could attribute their attitude difference to caste, education, or urbanization. I could only note that, if my sample size had been larger and my respondents more heterogeneous, I could have separated caste from education and urbanization and have seen which of these factors correlated most closely with the attitude difference.

Survey Research as an Independent Data-Gathering Technique

Four years after completing my industrialism and Hinduism study, I was back in India on another project, this one dealing with changes in attitudes from 'traditional' to 'nontraditional'. Stimulated by the findings of my first study as well as the work of such writers as Everett E. Hagen, David McClelland, and W.W. Rostow, I had decided to conduct a large-scale study of such attitudes as mobility aspirations, universalistic versus particularistic identities, causality consciousness, empathy, authoritarianism, caste orthodoxy, and political awareness. I was concerned that writers describing the attitudes of persons in nonexpanding economies tended to lump all sorts of opinions under the general rubric of 'traditional attitudes' (see, for example, Hagen 1962: 83–84). They then occasionally concluded that, as one part of these 'traditional attitudes' changed, all other parts also changed.

My own experience in India suggested that the picture was more complex than this. I myself had met highly emancipated social reformers who were still orthodox, pure vegetarians. I had met religiously conservative and devout parents who insisted their children should have the highest university degrees possible. And I had met innovative farmers who still insisted that man proposes but God disposes. To my way of thinking, these people were full of contradictions. But, after meeting enough of them, I began to wonder how much of what I was seeing was contradiction and how much was merely different from some implicit notions of a priori western logic I was carrying about with me. One purpose of my research project was to determine the frames of reference being used by people themselves within a society undergoing change.

The Research Design

In order to be able to control for a sizeable number of variables (something I had been unable to do in my first study), I set up the following research design.

1. My sample would consist of a minimum of 600 11-year-old boys, plus their fathers, their mothers, and any resident grandparents. I chose 11-year-old boys hoping that they would be young enough to reconstruct the child-rearing patterns in their homes yet also old enough to answer the attitude questions. Generally this hope was realized. One reason for selecting boys, their parents, and their grandparents was that I would have three generations for comparison.

2. Half my sample would come from one section of India and the other half from another. This would make it possible to determine to what extent patterns of responses were regional and to what extent they might be the same throughout India. For example, do Harijans in all of India have the same attitude toward the caste system, or do Harijans in the south view the caste system differently from Harijans in the north?

3. My sample would be divided equally between villagers, townspeople, and city dwellers. This would allow comparisons of differences between relative degrees of urbanization. In order to make the towns roughly comparable, I decided that their populations would have to be approximately the same size and they would have to be tahsil (taluk) headquarters, similar to county seats in the United States. To make the cities more comparable, I decided that they would have to be political-administrative centres, either state capitals or large district headquarters.

4. In each of the designated areas, my sample would be a random cross section of the population. This would provide me with a variety of religions, castes, occupations, and levels of education, and would allow internal comparisons.

Selecting the Sites

Having set up my overall research design in terms of more or less carefully thought out criteria, I selected the actual sites according to conveniences of time, place, and previous acquaintance. My three north Indian sites and three south Indian sites were as follows:

Uttar Pradesh (north India)
  City: Lucknow, population 656,000, capital of the state of Uttar Pradesh.
  Town: Malihabad (15 miles west of Lucknow), population 8,000, headquarters for Malihabad tahsil.
  Villages: Utraitia and its vicinity (8–12 miles east of Lucknow), population of each less than 2,000.
Madras State (now Tamil Nadu, south India)
  City: Madurai, population 425,000, headquarters for Madurai district and partial headquarters for Ramanathapuram (Ramnad) district.
  Town: Melur (20 miles east of Madurai), population 15,000, headquarters for Melur taluk.
  Villages: Chittampatti and its vicinity (9–11 miles east of Madurai), population of each less than 1,000.

Drawing the Samples

In the towns and villages my teams of census-takers went from door to door finding 11-year-old boys. If the parents were not sure of the boys' age (as was often the case), the census-taker was instructed to guess. If the boy passed muster as being (more or less) 11 years old, and neither his father nor his mother proved to be dead or away on an extended trip, the census-taker recorded the boy's name, his father's name and some form of neighbourhood address. In the towns and villages we used as house addresses the orange malaria-control numbers the public health people had painted by each doorway. Despite these efforts to specify the location of given families, we still 'lost' a few of our respondents between the initial census-taking and the interviewing that took place a few weeks later.

In the originally enumerated villages in both north and south India we literally ran out of 11-year-old boys before the interviewers reached their quota of 100. In both cases we had to make a hasty additional census of several more villages to meet our quota.

In the cities we faced considerably greater difficulties. It was obvious from the size of both Lucknow and Madurai that a door-to-door census was out of the question. In Madurai I was able to obtain street maps of the thirty-three census zones plus information as to the percentage of total city population living in each zone. On the basis of this information I determined how many of my 100 Madurai families should come from each zone. Then I measured with a string the total street frontage on that zone's map, divided with knots the measured length of string into as many parts as there were to be families drawn from that zone, and measured the street frontage again, placing an 'x' on the map whenever I reached a knot. I then sent a census-taker to those x's and instructed him to obtain the name of the 11-year-old boy living closest to the x. Occasionally the census-taker found the x to be in the middle of a paddy field or a factory compound, but on the whole the system worked effectively in providing us with a random cross section of the Madurai population of 11-year-old boys. As for recording the addresses in Madurai, we often had street names and house numbers by which to go, although we were occasionally reduced to such addresses as 'house over grain shop beside water tap'.

Lucknow posed even more problems than Madurai. The recent Chinese invasion had swept most maps and census information out of public circulation for security reasons. In fact, the only way I was able to obtain a map of Lucknow district was to borrow the relevant district planning book from a local library and trace the map in the back of the book myself. At any rate, we were unable to carry out as reliable a system of randomization in Lucknow as we were able to carry out in Madurai.

Since Lucknow has a compulsory education bill, I decided to use school registers as my population source. After obtaining the names of as many primary and secondary schools as we could from the education offices, the Lucknow telephone directory, and general information of Lucknow residents, the census-takers went to the schools, perused the school registers, and recorded the names and addresses of every fifteenth boy born in 1952. By this method we obtained names and addresses for about 400 11 year-year-old boys in Lucknow. We were aware that our sampling procedure automatically ruled out any boys not enrolled in schools (despite the compulsory education bill) or enrolled in private tuition 'sidewalk schools' and probably skewed our sample toward the higher castes and occupations. Nevertheless, we could think of no better way of working it.

One of the most serious deficiencies in our Lucknow census concerned street addresses. The school register might carry something like 'Ram Lal son of Roshan Singh, Aminabad Park.' Several thousand people lived in the area known as Aminabad Park. How one was to find Ram Lal, son of Roshan Singh, was a neat problem. In the end we were forced to abandon nearly three-fourths of our Lucknow sample pool because we could not trace the addresses.

The Interview Schedule

The interview schedule presented unusual methodological problems. Certain English concepts do not translate into Hindi or Tamil. For example, one question asking whom people trusted more and providing paired alternatives had to be dropped after the schedule pretest because there was no well-known Hindi synonym for 'trust', and the roundabout explanation of 'trust' that I had devised simply confused the respondents. Because of translation problems, I almost dropped another question about adults 'standing together' or not, when one of them punished a child. The best I could do was to ask if all adults in the house should punish a guilty child with a 'common mind' or should one adult protect a child from the punishment of the others, which was hardly a smooth way of handling it.

Another wording problem arose regarding the three questions dealing with willingness to abandon caste orthodoxy. For example, should the question read, 'Would you be able to eat food prepared by someone from a *low caste*?' or 'Would you be able to eat food prepared by someone from a caste *lower than yours*?' A high-caste respondent might be willing to eat food cooked by some other relatively high-caste person while objecting to eating food cooked by a lower-caste person. If I held to the 'caste lower than yours' form, respondents were apt to ask 'which castes' and 'how much lower'. If I held to the 'low caste' form, a low-caste respondent might think, 'I'm a low-caste person, and I eat my own cooking; hence I should answer "yes".' In the end I chose the 'low caste' form of the question, hoping that the context would imply that the 'low caste' person was intended to be lower than the respondent.

In both the Hindi and the Tamil translations of the schedule, I went to considerable effort to have the questions put in normal, conversational language, so that a minimum of reinterpretation would be necessary in the field. Only those familiar with the gulf between the spoken and written languages in most of India can fully appreciate how difficult it was to convince both translation assistants and printers that I wanted to *write* the language *spoken* in normal conversations.

The final phrasing of the interview schedule brought a few additional problems. The lack of a generic term for 'you' in both Hindi and Tamil (see *'tum'* and *'ap'* in Hindi and *'ni'* and *'ningal'* in Tamil) meant that the same pronouns and verb endings could not be used in the parents' and sons' interview schedules. The difference in male and female forms meant that changes had to be made between the fathers' and the mothers' schedules.

Entire working days went into proof-reading the schedules in order to eliminate 'carryovers' from one schedule to another.

The Research Team

In order to observe the local proprieties, I had female interviewers talk to the boys, their mothers, and their grandmothers, while male interviewers talked to the fathers and grandfathers. In both north and south India my advertisements in the local papers and my inquiries in local colleges and universities brought a large enough pool of experienced candidates so that I could eliminate those with questionable talent, motivation, or energy. At the peak of operations, my north Indian team included nine females and five males (all of whom were high-caste Hindus except for one Muslim). My south Indian team contained five females and four males (who represented a range of Hindu castes and included one Christian).

After an initial training session, I required all candidates to complete two practice interviews with the trial interview schedule. These trial interviews served two purposes: they helped eliminate a few more candidates and they provided a pretest of the interview schedule. In neither north nor south India did I send the final schedule copy to the printer until I had added modifications recommended from the pretest.

To check against dishonest reporting in both north and south, I hired one person as 'back checker'. His job was to take completed interview schedules, return to the respondent, and find out if the respondent had really been interviewed and whether the date and length of interview time described by the respondent corresponded with the date and time recorded by the interviewer on the schedule. The 'back checker' also asked the respondent what questions he remembered and re-asked half a dozen questions to see if the respondent's answers the second time tallied with the answers he was reported to have given the first time.

I described in advance to all the interviewers how the process of 'back-checking' worked and informed them that they would be paid only for 'satisfactorily complete' interviews. On the whole, the knowledge that there was a 'back checker' discouraged dishonest reporting. However, in south India the 'back checker' uncovered one interviewer who had 'coffee-housed' two dozen interviews. The offender was promptly sacked, and the other members of the team completed the interviews he reported he had done.

The Field Operations

The field operations in the Lucknow area began in late May and continued
into early June. In Malihabad and the Utraitia village area we used public
works department and irrigation department inspection bungalows as our
base, the male interviewers remaining in the bungalows throughout the
period while the females commuted from Lucknow every day by hired taxi.
Public eating facilities were unavailable in these areas; so I had to hire
cooks and arrange for utensils and food supplies to be transported to the
bungalows. In both Malihabad and Utraitia the interviewers frequently
had to walk miles between interviews. Special arrangements for bicycles
and horse-drawn *ikkas* alleviated but did not solve the problem.

In south India, where we interviewed in July and August, the logistics
were considerably simpler. Melur contained numerous satisfactory 'hotels'
for meals, and buses were constantly plying between Melur, Chittampatti,
and Madurai. In the Chittampatti area there were still many miles between
villages, but even here the problem was easier to deal with than in the
north, since one could rent bicycles for a nominal sum near the bus stand.

The Interviews

Periodically, before going into the field, the interviewers received the names
of the respondents they were supposed to interview. Their instructions were
to locate the person at the given address and conduct the interview with as
much privacy as possible. As a mater of fact, from the moment they arrived
in the neighbourhood they were frequently surrounded by children eager
to tell them where the given respondent lived. Often after the interview
began the audience expanded to include relatives and neighbours. At times
the interviewers had to use considerable tact to discourage members of the
audience from interjecting their own answers to the questions being asked.

Occasionally the interviewers met with resistance. In Malihabad in north
India a Chamar neighbourhood insisted that after Independence they did
not have to perform favours for anyone; therefore they would not answer
questions unless they were paid. No amount of discussion or explanation
dissuaded the Chamars. In the end, we were forced to abandon their
neighbourhood. In the town of Melur in south India the rumour started
that the interviewing was part of a government programme to recruit 11-
year-old boys into the army to train them to fight the Chinese. In this case
the interviewer set an 11-year-old boy in the midst of the questioning townsmen and asked them if they seriously believed the government wanted

boys this size in the army. The townsmen had to agree it was unlikely, and there were no further objections to the study.

The field team was instructed to explain that the interviews were part of a large attitude study being done in two parts of India. However, it quickly turned out that people wanted answers about other aspects of the survey as well. Furthermore, upon checking one interviewer's answers against another's, they sometimes discovered discrepancies. For example, some of the interviewers, in their eagerness to elicit cooperation, promised that after the survey the neighbourhood would receive schools, roads, and electricity; other interviewers denied it. The static began almost immediately. I called the interviewers together and insisted that they make no promises of government largess. The survey had to sell itself on its own merits.

Even more touchy was the matter of the interviewers' salary. Early in the survey, some villagers overheard two interviewers totalling their day's interviews and figuring how much they had earned. The word was out. Respondents demanded that they receive part of the interviewers' pay. It took weeks for these demands to die down. In the meantime, I informed the interviewers that, if questioned, they were to state that they were receiving subsistence and expenses. Beyond that, they were never to discuss their salary while in the field.

The most effective way of eliciting support for the project was to describe it as an effort by university students to meet degree requirements. As most of the interviewers were university students, this explanation seemed plausible. We were surprised at how much sympathy there was for the plight of students trying to meet professors' demands and how much recognition there was of the neutrality of academic research. In a few places, especially in the south, we met respondents who had been polled as part of earlier biscuit and soap surveys. Such respondents seemed even more willing than others to be part of the survey.

In order to keep the morale high, in both north and south India I held periodic all-expenses-paid celebrations. These included such events as a special bus trip to a newly built dam, movies, dinners at a good restaurant, and mango and litchi feasts. Within the contexts of Madurai and Lucknow, this 'big daddy' approach seemed appreciated.

Three Examples of Results from the Survey

A major drawback of survey research methods is that one loses the clarity of detail and the supplementary interpretive information that one obtains in a case study. A major advantage of the survey research method is that one typically deals with sufficiently large numbers of respondents (in this case over 2,500) so that one can control for several variables. Below are three illustrations of how the use of such controls can radically alter the conclusions one draws from one's data. In the first illustration, an apparently significant association proves to be no association at all. In the second illustration, an apparent non-association proves to be 'hiding' some association. And in the third illustration an apparent association proves to apply only to a portion of the population.

1. *An Apparent Association.* Apparently a significantly greater proportion of lower-caste people believe that events occur because of fate; a significantly greater proportion of high-caste people believe that events occur because of discoverable reasons (see Table 1).

Question: One learned man says, 'Most things that happen like disease and poverty are caused by fate. As it is written, so must it happen'. Another learned man says, 'There are many other reasons besides fate for why these things happen. If we can discover the reasons, we can change what will happen.' Which of these learned men do you think is correct?

Table 1

	Mothers and Fathers		
	Twice-Born Castes	Intermediate Castes	Scheduled Castes
'Caused by Fate'	53%	64%	73%
'Caused by Discoverable Reason'	47%	36%	27%
	100%	100%	100%
	n=353	n=520	n=337

(Chi^2 for difference between 'Twice-Born Castes' and 'Intermediate Castes' = 10.4, significant at the 0.1 level. Chi^2 for difference between 'Intermediate Castes' and 'Scheduled Castes' = 6.03, significant at the 0.02 level. Chi^2 for difference between 'Twice-Born Castes' and 'Scheduled Castes' = 27.19, significant at the 0.001 level.)

With an association such as this, we might set out to discuss the 'fatalism' engendered by the caste system, the way in which this 'fatalism' is most thoroughly concentrated at the bottom of the system, how the stability of the system through time may have depended on this concentration of fatalism at the bottom, etc.

However, before starting off on a chain of plausible conclusions, it may be wise to control for other variables. Controlling for sex, we separate the fathers from the mothers. The association remains in both groups. Controlling further for north and south India, the association remains for north and south Indian fathers but disappears for all mothers. And finally, controlling for 'No Education' and 'Some Education', the pattern of caste association disappears entirely, to be replaced by a consistent pattern of association of 'Caused by Fate' with 'No Education' and 'Caused by Discoverable Reason' with 'Some Education'.

Had we plunged ahead with our initial statistically significant association, we might have come up with plausible explanations of why low status generates certain types of 'world view' fatalism. The only trouble would have been that our explanation would have been based on a spurious association.

2. *An Apparent Non-association:* Apparently there is no significant association between caste position and unwillingness to eat food cooked by a low-caste person (see Table 2).

Question: Would you be able to eat food prepared by someone from a low caste?

Table 2

	Mothers and Fathers		
	Twice-Born Castes	*Intermediate Castes*	*Scheduled Castes*
'Would be able to eat'	11%	12%	16%
'Would *not* be able to eat'	89%	88%	84%
	100%	100%	100%
	n=353	n=516	n=335

(Chi^2 for difference between 'Twice-Born Castes' and 'Intermediate Castes' is negligible. Chi^2 for difference between 'Intermediate Castes' and 'Scheduled Castes' is 2.75, not significant at the required 0.05 level. Chi^2 for difference between 'Twice-Born Castes' and 'Scheduled Castes' is 3.41, still not significant at the required 0.05 level.)

Although there is a tendency for lower-caste respondents to be more willing to eat such food than higher-caste respondents, the difference between the highest and lowest categories (5 per cent) is too small to be statistically significant. With this absence of any significant association, we might be tempted to write an essay on the equal penetration of pollution taboos at all caste levels. We might even be tempted to expand on this and describe how the equal support of caste-avoidance taboos on all levels reveals the strength of the present caste hierarchy. However, before starting off on this or some other chain of plausible conclusions, it may be useful to control for other variables.

Controlling for sex, we separate the fathers from the mothers. The slight trend of differences between the 'Twice-Born' and 'Scheduled Castes' appears on both tables, but continues not to be statistically significant. Controlling further for north and south India, two markedly different patterns suddenly emerge, each statistically significant (See Tables 3 and 4. To simplify the tables, I have again combined the fathers and mothers).

Table 3

| | Northern Mothers and Fathers | | |
	Twice-Born Castes	Intermediate Castes	Scheduled Castes
'Would be able to eat'	11%	3%	6%
'Would *not* be able to eat'	89%	97%	94%
	100%	100%	100%
	n=245	n=149	n=211

(Chi^2 for difference between 'Twice-Born Castes' and 'Intermediate Castes' is 6.3, significant at the 0.02 level. Chi^2 for difference between 'Intermediate Castes' and 'Scheduled Castes' is negligible. Chi^2 for difference between 'Twice-Born Castes' and 'Scheduled Castes' is 3.42, not significant at the 0.05 level.)

Table 4

| | - Southern Mothers and Fathers | | |
	Twice-Born Castes	Intermediate Castes	Scheduled Castes
'Would be able to eat'	10%	15%	33%
'Would *not* be able to eat'	90%	85%	67%
	100%	100%	100%
	n=108	n=367	n=124

(Chi^2 for difference between 'Twice-Born Castes' and 'Intermediate Castes' is 1.23, not significant at the 0.05 level. Chi^2 for difference between 'Intermediate Castes' and 'Scheduled Castes' is 17.23, significant at the required 0.001 level. Chi^2 for difference between 'Twice-Born Castes' and 'Scheduled Castes' is 16.06, also significant at the 0.001 level.)

Controlling for 'No Education' and 'Some Education', we discover that the above association pattern remains firm. Therefore, quite unlike our original conclusion that there is no association between caste position and unwillingness to eat food cooked by a low-caste person, it now appears that there *are* patterns of association by caste, but the patterns differ in north and south India.

Where in north India the most impressive break with tradition appears among the 'Twice-Born Castes' (a 'rebellion from above'), in south India the most impressive break appears among the 'Scheduled Castes' (a 'rebellion from below'). However, eating food cooked by a low-caste person is only one form of unorthodoxy. To see if the pattern is general, one needs to look at the other two caste orthodoxy questions in the schedule: 'Would you be able to be friends with someone from a low caste?' and 'Would you be able to marry your son or daughter to a boy or girl from a low caste?' Sure enough, the same pattern does appear to hold. One is then free to spin plausible links between the 'Twice-Born', Gandhianism, and the struggle against caste injustices in the north, and the Justice and Dravida Munnetra Kazhagam Parties and the struggle against caste injustices in the south. One is also free to look for parallels between the Indian data and other comparable data on the social and ideological correlates of 'rebellions from above' and 'rebellions from below'.

3. *An Apparent Association:* Apparently a significantly greater proportion of south Indians than north Indians feels that India needs an autocratic ruler.

Question: One man says, 'Our country needs a strong leader who will take over the government and make everybody obey him'. Another man says, 'Our country needs leaders who have been chosen by the people and who will act in accordance with the people's wishes'. Which of these men do you think is correct? (see Table 5).

Table 5

	Sons, Mothers, and Fathers	
	South India	*North India*
'Pro-autocracy'	46%	26%
Pro-democracy'	54%	74%
	100%	100%
	n = 1152	n = 1390

(Chi^2 for difference between 'South India' and 'North India' = 106.4, significant at the 0.001 level.)

With an association as high as this one, we might begin looking for roots of autocratic preference in the power structure of south India. Perhaps the long centuries of Brahman domination have produced a general pattern of subservience to power figures. Or perhaps the more recent anti-Brahman struggles in the south have generated pro-autocracy sentiment.

Before following these possible chains of reasoning, however, it may be useful to control for other variables.

Controlling for religion, caste and residence in city, town, or village, the difference between north and south India remains. Then, controlling for sons, mothers, and fathers, a different pattern suddenly emerges (See Table 6).

Table 6

	South India		
	Sons	Mothers	Fathers
'Pro-autocracy'	56%	54%	25%
'Pro-democracy'	44%	46%	75%
	100%	100%	100%
	n = 364	n = 360	n = 345

(Chi^2 for difference between 'Sons', 'Mothers' and 'Fathers' = 81.3, significant at the 0.001 level.)

Interestingly enough, the north Indian pattern does not change when controlled for sons, mothers and fathers (see Table 7).

Table 7

	North India		
	Sons	Mothers	Fathers
'Pro-autocracy'	25%	29%	22%
'Pro-democracy'	75%	71%	78%
	100%	100%	100%
	n = 431	n = 433	n = 403

(Chi^2 indicates no significant association between 'Sons', 'Mothers' and 'Fathers'.

As Table 6 shows, in south India the support for autocracy appears to come from the sons and mothers. The association that seemed to hold between north and south now needs to be refined, for the southern fathers are very similar to the north Indians in this response. To discover why this is so requires further questions: In south India what access to mass media do sons and mothers have, and does their access differ from that of the fathers? Does the sons' and mothers' pattern of political participation differ from the fathers'? In what other ways do the southern sons' and mothers' perceptions differ from those of the southern fathers? Can these help explain the association? To find answers to these questions, one turns to other questions on the schedule and one tries to control additional variables. Such steps do not necessarily provide explanatory hypotheses for phenomena; however, they do from time to time permit certain hypotheses to be discarded, such as the one suggesting that long centuries of Brahman domination in south India have produced a general pattern of submissiveness to power figures. If such were the case, one would hardly find such a dramatic difference between the mothers and fathers in south India.

Survey research methods, then, appear to have some use in the Indian context. I myself prefer to use them as one of several methods of gathering and analysing data so that the strengths of one might be supplemented by the strengths of another. Yet even by themselves, survey research methods can permit the identification of relevant associations and, depending on the nature of the questions asked, even permit a certain amount of checking of alternative explanations for a given finding. One of their greatest contributions comes from the fact that, by dealing with sufficiently large numbers of people to permit control, field survey methods help direct the search for explanations to focus on genuine, rather than spurious or accidental, associations.

Perceptions of Princely Rule: Perspectives from a Biography

ADRIAN C. MAYER

It is now some thirty-five years too late for me actually to study the working of a princely state. But there are a few men still living who were rulers before the independence of India and the subsequent merger of their states in the Indian Union in 1948–49. One of these is the present Chhatrapati Maharaja of Kolhapur, and what follows is an account of how this prince saw his rule. I have known the maharaja since the time of my first fieldwork in Dewas in 1954, and my material comes from several conversations[1] which I had with His Highness (HH) in December 1978 and December–January 1979–80. I also include a conversation I had with HH's half-brother Bhojsinharao Puar.

Shahaji Chhatrapati is perhaps unique in having ruled three states, two of them as their maharaja. Born in 1910 to Maharaja Tukojirao III of Dewas Senior State, he assumed the presidency of the Dewas Senior State Council when his father left his state (see, e.g., Forster 1953: 168 ff.), and ruled in this way from 26 July 1934 until his father's death, on 21 December 1937, when he succeeded to the throne as Vikramsinharao I, his coronation taking place on 18 March 1938. He ruled Dewas Senior until 23 March 1947, his reign being broken only by war service in 1941 (when the maharani acted as his regent). On that date he abdicated and was then adopted as the Maharaja of Kolhapur, ruling as Chhatrapati Shahaji II until the merger of the state in the Indian Union on 1 March 1949. In addition to these two reigns, he acted as president of the cabinet of Indore State for some six months in 1942–43 during Maharaja Yeshwantrao Holkar's absence abroad, though he was not of course installed as ruler of the state.

Since most of HH's 15-year rule took place in Dewas Senior, it is on this state that my account focuses, and to which his remarks mainly refer.

The administration of the State in HH's time consisted of a prime minister, ministers, and other heads of departments, and junior officers. By the time of HH's abdication there were some nineteen departments and twenty senior officers. Dewas was too small a state for a fully bureaucratic civil service. Rather, appointments to senior posts were made personally by HH after recommendatin and interview, and to junior posts by the *dewān* or head of the department. Personal qualities were sought which did not necessarily include professional qualifications except in technical posts. As HH observed, Dewas could not sustain the kind of competitive examination that occurred in Indore State: 'I knew who [the good people] were, that's all. Their background and everything.... If there is some good man among sardārs and mānkaris I'll pick him up from there and bring him [into the administration].'

Outside the state existed the British in the shape of a political agent (PA). Formal relations with the British varied between states according to the terms of their treaties. In Dewas Senior's case, the British considered the maharaja 'in every respect the Ruler of [his] present possessions' and engaged 'not to interfere in the internal administration of the country', although the maharaja on his part agreed to 'enter into no affair of any magnitude without the advice and concurrence of the said British government'.[2]

The British did in fact watch over the internal affairs of states and sometimes intervened. As HH put it:

HH: The PA came and watched whether you misruled or not; he didn't watch whether you ruled or not.

M: But misrule wasn't in the Treaty.[3]

HH: It's not in the Treaty, it became a usage. Treaty says 'full internal powers'.

M: Did any Maharaja object to that?

HH: What could he do? The whole of the British Empire's might, a small state in India can't fight it. In theory yes, but in practice it was impossible.... Anything that a Ruler was doing wrong, and the British authorities thought that it was not right, well over a cup of tea, as we are talking now, he'd say 'Your Highness, it might be better if you didn't do it'. Well, that was more than a hint, as I put it, that you'd better mend your ways.

Dewas Senior had had a somewhat chequered relationship with the British. During the rule of HH's grandfather, Krishnajirao II, the state had twice been put under the administration of a British-appointed superintendent as a result of the ruler's good-natured extravagance. And HH's father had

had a dispute with the PA, made famous by the accounts of Forster (1953) and Darling (1966), centred on the ruler's financial mismanagement, and which had resulted in his flight to Pondicherry. However, during HH's time there was little intervention. As HH put it: 'In the beginning [the PA] was careful just to see whether I had my head on my shoulders or not. Later on it became a mere formality.' However, British paramountcy was a factor in the ruler's situation, and one which both HH and his subjects recognized.

I should make it clear that what follows does not purport to be a re-construction of how HH actually ruled Dewas Senior. This would be an almost impossible task; for people's memories would, after thirty years, have tended to simplify into either a recollection of a 'golden age' of enlightened rule or a thankfully-superseded era of autocratic government. Rather, I centre on the ruler himself, outlining what HH saw as his role and how it should be carried out, and then on what HH considered to be the basis of his authority.

It may be objected that to ask a ruler about how he thought he ruled is merely to invite a refraction of a stereotype set by classical sources; of what value is a 'play back' of these, when the other side of the coin, the test of actual behaviour, is absent. I am well aware of this objection but I believe that HH was expressing the fruit of his own thinking and experience of rule, influenced though this naturally was by traditional concepts as well as by the actual nature of his state (its size, its administrative structure, etc.), rather than that he was simply repeating the outline of a cultural form that he had gleaned from the literature. Hence it is that one can take his observations as forming an immediate, rather than a literati model (Ward 1965).

A start can be made by considering the degree to which HH was an absolute ruler. Although his father had brought in a Constitution,[4] HH did not see his power as thus circumscribed. As he told me:

In 1944 or 1945 the Political Agent dropped in one day, very polite in typical way. He started off, 'Your Highness, you know Indore has given this Constitution, Narsingharh and Rajgarh have made this Constitution, Dewas Junior has been given a panchayat system' and this and that. 'Well', he said, 'What has Dewas Senior done?' At the end of it, suddenly he threw this question to me. I said nothing. So he turned round and said to me, 'But Your Highness, you must give *some* Constitution.' He said, 'What is your Constitution today?' I had a stick near me. I just turned round and lifted the stick. I said, 'My Constitution is this.'

By this, HH meant that the ruler was 'whole and sole' and that the governing of the State should rest on him. However, he was dramatizing his position here; for though Dewas Senior had no representative government, there was an administrative structure, much of which had grown up under HH's rule and which he fully accepted as necessary. The ruler's power could not be arbitrarily used, in fact; officials had to proceed according to laid-down rules, and the ruler was not to interfere with this: 'By the rules [the matter] goes. And until it is complete, don't interfere, because that would demoralise your officers.'

However, the ruler had the power to reverse decisions, though this power was to be used sparingly. Here the ruler acted by showing kindness (*meharbānī*) to a subject, this being done outside the administrative framework. Because the official could be said to have acted correctly, his position need not be impaired. 'According to the rules [the official] is right. But there's something called human in the approach to a problem. Now a Ruler must never forget that that is *his* prerogative.'

An example that HH gave was of a man whose land was to be auctioned, quite correctly, for non-payment of land revenue. HH ascertained the reason for non-payment (wedding expenses) and that the man only owned five acres, and decided that he should be allowed to pay the arrears in instalments over three years. The case suggests that by a 'human approach' HH meant that he saw the subject 'in the round', as an individual with other roles than that which was the direct subject of bureaucratic action (here, as father as well as landowner). This makes for a personal, dyadic link between ruler and subject which is good statecraft (the overruling of the 'hard' official by the 'sympathetic' ruler).

The question then arises, how to decide when an official's decision should be overruled, what case is genuine and exceptional? This, said HH, could only be a matter of judgement formed on the basis of an extensive knowledge of the people and their problems. And this could only be gained by the ruler mixing constantly and informally with the common people. In this way, also, the ruler could control his officials. Here, too, the difference between ruler and officialdom was pointed out. On the one hand, the ruler toured in a formal way with his officials: 'When I went on official tour all my officials went with me. Thus it was a made-up show that was put before me. The police and revenue officers will see that that particular man does not come into my presence.'

But what HH regarded as his real touring was quite different from 'the formal tour when you and officials and everybody go on tour, like the Governor's tours in the old days... that is where the Ruler did *not* end. The

ruler went one step further, that's what I call movement, movement in the
masses, mixing with the masses freely.'

The method employed by HH was to combine business with pleasure,
and turn his love of hunting (śikār) to good use.

I go on śikār. At the end of a beat I sit down tired under a tree. Some villagers come up,
they sit down. 'Maharaj, I have a difficulty.' 'What is your difficulty?' 'Maharaj, it is a
dispute about my land.' 'Did you go to the tehsīl [government officer] about this?' 'No,
I didn't.' 'The tehsīl is there, so you can go for that sort of thing. Are any of my officers
giving you trouble?' This is a point blank question I ask everyone when I go. 'No, Annadāta
[protector, lit. giver of food] there is no difficulty from them.' 'No? All right, is there
any other problem in your village?' 'Maharaj, we have difficulty with drinking water.'
'Is there a well in your village that gives copious water?' On the spot I make a decision.
'Right, this cold weather a well will be dug.' A note is made, an order is passed.

We see several points illustrated here: that villagers should go first to
the relevant official (i.e., HH did not short-circuit the process, but was only
prepared to take charge when it was not working properly); that HH is
signalling that any faults in the machine will be corrected; and finally that
on relevant matters, a quick decision can be taken. There is, it is true, a
rather large assumption behind the second point, namely that because the
officials are not present, villagers will speak out if they are being troubled
by them. For the officials are nearer to the villager than is the ruler, and
can retaliate at a later time when they learn what has been said about them.
HH's view was, first, that in such an informal atmosphere the villagers
would lose such apprehensions; and, second, that when they saw that their
complaints were effective, they would have the courage to speak up—for
HH was quite clear that he had dismissed officials found to have exceeded
their powers and to have harassed the people.

For this reason, as HH put it: 'Sikar in a way is a duty, I put it as a
duty... it is contact.'[5] Moreover, it was not used only for those villages
where game actually existed.

Raghogarh [village] has śikār, I made camp, then said, 'Today we'll go to these [other]
villages, get them together.' Then I ask them, 'Any problems? Is there any śikār?' I
know there is none. I sit for 5–10 minutes, then say, 'Well, my camp is over there, if you
have any problems, come over there.'

We can note from this that the ruler is not going incognito, he is not a
Haroun-al-Rashid in the bazaar,[6] but is rather explicitly and openly showing two things—his wish as a ruler to informally contact the people, and
his ability to communicate with them. This latter was seen by HH to be a

very important point. 'He must be free in his talk... make a joke with them, they're pleased, then they'll open, without free talk they won't open.' One is reminded here of Kautilya's listing of one of the 'best qualities of the king' as 'making jokes with no less of dignity or secrecy' (Kautilya: 287) though it is possible that this reference does not contain the instrumental aspect that HH gave to 'free talk'.

As I have pointed out, no officials are with the ruler on such occasions. This does not, however, mean that he is alone. He has his own staff with him, his ADCs and personal servants. 'My personal staff had no official positions. You are my personal staff; they work in the office. My personal staff is for my pleasure; officials are completely separate.'

These men and had other duties as well, however:

When I came back to the capital, I had in one of my staff. 'Take this down immediately.' In the Ruler's office, the department was addressed by the Ruler's secretary: 'HH visited so-and-so village, this was brought to HH's notice, please send a file up indicating'. The minister had to send the file up with his comments and prompt orders were passed.

And again: 'If I have a clever personal staff, he acts as a spy on the officials. He is not in the State, he is my personal staff. The Dewan can't hound him. He brings news to my ears; "Maharaj, it's like this". Then it's up to me: "Oh, it's like that, I'd better go there".'

The ruler, therefore, should be a person who must move about his kingdom to gain detailed knowledge of it and must be a man of action: 'If you really feel that a complaint is genuine you must take *quick* action, if it is delayed the effect of it is lost?' To consider further the nature of this action let us return to the statement of HH's with which I opened this section. In referring to his stick as his Constitution, HH was of course referring to the concept of *danda* of which 'stick' is the literal meaning, it being also translated as 'rod' and 'sceptre'. As Dumont points out, this word 'has a whole series of connotations' (1962: 64). At one end of the continuum, it simply means the use of force as punishment: moving towards the other end, it takes on successively stronger attributes of righteousness, so that one moves through the notions of the imposition of deserved punishment (Kautilya: 8) and hence danda as an instrument of justice to righteous rule as a whole, in which danda is the sustaining authority on which can be based an ordered society in which people and institutions are 'in their place.'

The reply by HH to my question, as to where danda enters into the rule of the prince, supports, by implication, the above schema. For he said:

Danda was in this. The Ruler's powers were not defined. The ministers' etc., powers

were defined. Rules, revenue code was drawn up. But a daṇḍa comes in that *my* powers
are not defined.... Now in the Constitution, a Ruler becomes part and parcel of the thing,
where he cannot go beyond specified reserved powers.

The point was made clearer:

Daṇḍa in that sense does not mean force, in the sense that I used it to the Political
Department. It meant overriding all other rules and regulations in the interests of my
people. I am not tied down by the Constitution, that this is the Revenue Minister's powers, he has taken the decision and you cannot intervene. That's all. I can say to the
Revenue Minister, 'I don't care, I think that in this case there is injustice, I am going to
do it.'

M: So that really means power, overriding power?
HH: That's it.
M: I thought that daṇḍa was force.
HH: That a Ruler should never use.
M: But sometimes you have to use force, no?
HH: If the people ask for it. Not of your will. If there's a small uprising, a report, you
      damn well come down very heavily on it.
M: Because the majority feel that you should?
HH: Yes.
M: But some used force as a substitute for solving problems?
HH: They used. That's where they got into trouble. Then the people used to go to the
      Political Agent, that we are oppressed. That is what you call zulum [tyranny],
      that is not daṇḍa.... Daṇḍa is both on officials and on my people.

It is clear that this view of daṇḍa focuses on power which is justifiably
used, and hence acceptable to the people. In its stress on 'overridingness'
it leaves the scope for action very much to the ruler, thus reflecting Bhisma's
view that 'the king makes the age'. On the nature of his decisions rests the
quality of his rule and hence the nature of his state. As the proverb in
Dewas went: 'As the king, so the populace' (*jaisa raja, vaisa praja*).

In later discussion, HH gave examples of this overriding power as he
had used it for the benefit of a subject:

I could overrule. I did overrule. When I thought that these lawyers were getting too
clever and, dammit, flagrant injustice is being done. You know, X [a prominent Dewas
lawyer] was turned out of my office. A peasant came and sat in my office, everybody
was allowed to. X came with him. He said, 'I am his lawyer'. I asked, 'Ask the peasant,
has he given him any money?' 'Yes.' 'Much money? Tell me why you didn't come to
me, why you gave him your money first?' Then I asked X, 'Did *your* land go, is this *your*
dispute?' He answered , 'No.' I said, 'You go out of my office, I am going to talk to my
peasant.'

The implications of doing this are, of course, serious in their effects on any body of regular rules and administration. As HH added, 'It's not a correct procedure, you can't do it today'. But such overruling could be justified because this expressed a higher value than that of orderly administration, i.e., that of the direct protection of the welfare of the people. In Lingat's terms (1973: 257f.) authority, rather than legality, underlay the system. Of course, this might involve punishment of anyone at all. The ruler 'should keep a watch on officers, so they think that if anyone goes and tells the Maharaja the truth [about them] the danda will fall from above'.

As HH said, '*Dandaniti* [proper policy of control] and *rājanūti* [proper policy of rule] go together'. In turn, the latter is closely linked to the appropriate duty of the ruler (*rājadharma*). Thus daṇḍaniti can be seen as rājadharma in action—as is suggested by the myth that Danda is the son of Dharma by his wife Krya (activity) (Prakash 1977: 26). Hence we are led to *rājadharma*. When I asked HH what he meant by this, he gave two answers. One was:

I could quote to you in Sanskrit [does so in a somewhat rusty fashion]: To protect the righteous/To destroy the wicked/And to establish the kingdom of god (*dharma*)/I [Krsna] am reborn/from age to age.[7]
M: That is one's duty?
HH: That is the king's duty.

Here, HH adhered closely to a classical view of the ruler by, quoting a celebrated verse from the *Gita* in his reply, though it should be noted that this stemmed not from a *sāstric* source, under which rājadharma protects *all* creatures,[8] but from a later source according to which the righteous ruler (dharmarāja) protects only the good. Note also that HH did not include any 'development' duties—e.g. to increase the wealth of his subjects or make their lives better. He did not see his role as primarily an initiatory one, though he was in fact responsible for such measures as the only pieces of town planning that took place in his capital. Nor did he see himself as a social reformer like his grandfather Shahu Chhatrapati, although he greatly admired him.

However, insofar as there was a demand for changes he would meet it, since his second answer was that a ruler's personal responsibility was to 'keep the people pleased and contented'.[9] The method by which this was accomplished was up to him. HH's conversation with the PA about the need for a Constitution had continued:

[I said:] 'The point is this. As far as you are the Political Agent concerned, I want to know, you are concerned whether my State is ruled well and my people are contented or

not. The method is immaterial as far as you are concerned?' He said, 'Yes, that's correct'. I said, 'That's the thermometer I use, the contentment of my people. Don't ask me
the Constitution. You can go on the street if you like, and ask the common man if he is
happy under my rule. If he is, I see no reason why I should give a Constitution'.

The pleasing of the people was not only part of the king's responsibility
and duty; it was also for his own benefit. As HH said: 'If I don't keep my
people happy, they're not going to follow me.' And when I asked him,
what would happen to a ruler who did not fulfil his responsibilities of protection and good rule, would he be superseded by a kinsman, he replied:

In the pre-British days you would get him murdered. That is where I have always been
of the view, the protection that the Princes got during the British days, the fear they lost
of their being displaced by their own people, has been the cause of the degeneration of
the Princes of India. They lost their sense of responsibility to *their* people. The Ruler is
responsible to *his* people.
M: And they lost this because they knew...
HH: They knew, British Treaty is mine, I can do as I please, drink, do anything.

HH's remarks bring out the double standard of the relation of the ruler
to the people. On the one hand, there was his personal responsibility, as
part of the divine purpose, the rājadharma that Derrett translates as being
'the way a king should comport himself in order to be righteous'; and on
the other, there exists the fact that, whether righteous or not, a king exists
at the sufferance of his subjects in the final analysis, and to avoid the fear
of replacement must look to his *rājnūti*, which Derrett translates as 'the
way a king should comport himself to be successful' (1969: 606). In both
those aims however, the ruler was operating in a context in which, though
in theory he and his people were 'partners' in a joint political enterprise,
in fact he had considerable power over them.

* * *

In considering HH's power, we have to take into account three factors. The
first is the actual position that a treaty state ruler had, the control he was
able to exercise over the jobs, lands, and the very lives of his subjects. The
second is the way in which this control was circumscribed by the above-
mentioned need to keep the people contented enough to prevent their
complaining to the British, as well as the need to conform closely enough
to British ideas about princely rule for the latter not to intervene. Together,
these produced what might be called the pragmatic basis for the ruler's
position. The third factor was the nature of the legitimacy of his position
and the authority it gave him, legitimacy in the eyes of his subjects.

As to the first factor, the treaty with the British gave HH a supreme position. He had absolute control of a major proportion of the state's lands; he was able to take back from his nobles the grants of village revenues as well as make grants to others; he had the power to appoint and dismiss all members of his administration from the dewān downwards; to ennoble any of his subjects or to banish them from the state; and to take the final decision on matters including sentences of capital punishment. As to the second factor, I have briefly indicated that people, if pushed too far, could go over his head to the British, and that the British themselves would take action over gross misrule. The third factor concerned the legitimacy given to the ruler by his ascension of the *gaddi*. That ascension both elevated him through his connection with the 'divine centre' of the state and could bring out in him the qualities appropriate to a ruler. I deal first with the nature of the gaddi, and then with the personal qualities of a ruler.

The gaddi is simply a cushionlike mattress stuffed with cotton, with bolsters at the back and sides. It stands in the hall in which the *darbār* is held, in the Old Palace of Dewas, being separate from but adjacent to the temple at which the royal rituals are held and where the lineage deity (Khandoba) and the ruler's special deity (Krsna) reside. The gaddi is established at the start of a dynasty and remains in the capital throughout. Even when a king was chased away, said HH, the gaddi could not be taken with him, though it might have to be reinstalled when he returned. The ascending of the gaddi is what makes a man a king, as HH recounts:

The day my father died, the PA motored into Dewas in the morning and suddenly handed over a letter to me from the Resident, addressed 'HH Maharaja Vikramsinharao Puar'. I opened it and found that my father was dead.

M: That was very sudden.

HH: I automatically asked that PA this question, 'Now, Sir, what is my position? I can't continue as President of Council, this letter says I'm Maharaja'. He said, 'Your Highness, you *are* Maharaja now... from today our supervision is finished'.

M: Then what did you do?

HH: I had to go into mourning immediately. There was no question of my getting on to the *gaddi*.

After the required fifteen days had elapsed, 'I assembled all the *sardārs* to the darbār and I ascended the gaddi'. Note that the occupancy of the gaddi took place with the minimum of ceremony. As HH said:

Now the first time that I go up to the gaddi, to sit on it, the priest is there... the ordinary, daily priest who comes to do the pūjā in our temple. He is there with his pūjā things. He will take the gulal (red powder), and all the other things necessary, and a few flowers.

You put it on to the gaddi, do your mujrā (obeisance) and get up. That's all. Nothing more. No vedic mantras and this and that at that time. This is just *my* showing reverence for the gaddi personally.... A Ruler also owes his allegiance to the gaddi.

M: Yes, he owes allegiance to the gaddi because that represents...
HH: It's from the gaddi that my power emanates.
M: So higher than that is nothing?
HH: Nothing. The rest is all custom, show, formality, whatever you may say.
M: But if you do obeisance to it, you are in a sense the servant of it?
HH: I am the servant of the gaddi. I accept it. I accept the position.

However, when I taxed him on this, HH replied:

Well, in another sense I am not servant, I am master of the gaddi. But I hold it in reverence.... You see, I am certainly on top of the gaddi, but at the same time I deeply respect. You may put it like husband and wife. It is mutual respect, but the husband is superior, according to all concepts. Now you put the gaddi in the position of the wife, the Ruler in the position of the husband.

The metaphor of husband and wife was not a chance one; for the gaddi was in fact seen as a feminine object (the Hindi noun is a feminine one), and the power that it held, a female power.[10] This was elaborated on by both HH and by his half-brother, Bhojsinharao Puar, when I asked further about HH's relation to the gaddi:

M: When you do obeisance [to the gaddi], is it pūjā [worship] or not?
HH: I do pūjā . Because it is not personal gaddi, it's my ancestral gaddi....
M: So when you do puja to it, do you think of asking for something in return?
HH: Blessings we ask, that we be given the strength to carry out our duty.
M: So you want something back? You want strength?
HH: Oh yes, we pray for that. The inspiration we get is from the gaddi....
M: Now, how would you call that strength? There are two words that I have heard. One is *śakti* and the other is *sattā*.
HH: Both, both combined. Because sattā is a power, śakti is the strength. Now if you're on the gaddi, either of them is missing, you are lost. You lose sattā, your strength has gone, and if you haven't got the strength you cannot impose your sattā.

In this, HH was referring to the fact that the raja is able to mount the gaddi in the first place because of his status as a conqueror or as an heir; but as soon as he does this, his dominion (sattā) is infused with the spiritual strength (śakti) derived from the gaddi itself. The following indicates this:

M: So strength is the spiritual thing that comes from the gaddi?
HH: Yes, comes from the gaddi. And this is a spiritual thing, the other is temporal.

Bhojsinharao developed the theme of the gaddi as a 'sacred institution' with 'the power of a benign deity'. He said that the gaddi was called 'Gaddi Mata' and thought of as a goddess; and HH, even though he did not go as far as saying that this was a general usage, agreed that villagers might think this and that town-people called the gaddi by the honorific term 'mājī' (mother) even if they did not consider it to be a deity. Bhojsinharao went on to say that people offered a rākhī (thread of protection) to the gaddi, out of love and sentiment. And again:

Commoners, many *sardār*, many people sometimes ask a favour from the *gaddi*. If a son is born in my house I shall tie *rākhī* to you, or I shall pay this kind of homage to you. So it is supposed to have attributes of divinity… rākhī means union, bond. So tying a rākhī to the gaddi, or presenting a rākhī to the gaddi means 'I am bound to', it is a binding.

That the gaddi was central to HH's position was shown in his view of its relation to his coronation[11] (*rājabhiṣeka*) and his court (darbār). The coronation consisted of a ritual which HH remembered[12] as centring on his and his wife's sitting on a 'chair' throne (*simhāsan*) made of special woods, where the priest[13] sprinkled them with the mixed waters of the sacred rivers, from golden jars held by the senior nobles of the realm, whilst Sanskrit verses were chanted. Traditionally, the royal consecration contained this unction as its major ritual, representing the birth of the king from the throne as the 'womb of kingly power' (Heesterman 1957: 17, 141), and being one of a class of consecration rituals, such as that which marks the assumption of a guru's status by a novitiate priest in the *ācārybhiseka* rite (Fuller 1979: 63). However, HH saw the ritual as less central to his status than this:

The gaddi we ascend immediately. This [the *abhiṣeka*] is just sanctifying the whole thing.
M: So the main thing is gaddi, not coronation?
HH: [Yes]. Coronation is a celebration of your having succeeded to the gaddi, as I put it, and giving it religious sanctity.
M: So if the Brahmans refused to give you coronation…?
HH: Would make no bloody difference. They would have lost their jobs at the most… nothing further would have happened. Others would have replaced them probably…. This is just a show to impress the people and to declare that I am here. Many a Ruler has passed without rājabhiṣeka.

In fact, though HH agreed with analysts of the classical ritual in seeing this as a sanctification (Gonda 1969: 87) he did not see in it a rebirth with a resulting inviolability; his changed status was the result, rather, of the ascension of the gaddi and consequent contact with its power; and it is perhaps significant that, as soon as the coronation ritual was ended, HH went from the hall in which the coronation had taken place to the chamber in which the gaddi lay, did obeisance to it, mounted it, and held a darbār; and it is also significant that the throne on which the coronation had taken place was not used again.[14]

In HH's view, then, the assumption of the gaddi was the action which made a ruler by giving him spiritual strength. In more general terms, there is perhaps a parallel in the position of the priest who cannot perform major temple rituals unless he has a living wife who gives him access to that śakti without which he cannot worship the goddess (Fuller 1979: 463f.). It is as if neither can fulfil his legitimate goal of life (*purusartha*) without access to that spiritual strength. As soon as HH ascends the gaddi, he can rule his subjects as well as becoming the object of their allegiance; both of these features are shown in the ceremonials of the court.

As I have said, the darbār was the occasion for nobles and other prominent citizens to gather in the presence of the ruler-on-the-gaddi. I link ruler and gaddi because, when I asked him 'what is the people's duty to the raja?', HH replied: 'loyalty to the person sitting on the gaddi, *and* to the gaddi. To the person sitting *on* the gaddi, remember. The privacy of the gaddi was brought home by Bhojsinharao:

If you are discontented with the Ruler, you will not vent your temper on the *gaddi*, because the *gaddi* is something in perpetuity, it's an idea. It has happened in several cases where nobles have fallen out with the Ruler and have not gone to visit him personally at his palace, but have always attended all the functions connected with the gaddi and the darbār.

M: They come to the darbār?

B: Yes, because they are servants of the gaddi....

M: So, if the gaddi is unoccupied, if for some reason there is no Ruler, still the kingdom will go on, the gaddi will protect, without a Maharaja?

B: Yes. Gaddi since its foundation has been, is, and shall be whether there is Ruler or no Ruler. The gaddi *is*.

One is reminded of Paul Mus's strikingly similar phrase '[le trône] *est* la royauté (quoted in Auboyer 1949: 190). The gathering at the darbār, then, 'symbolises the sovereignty of the ruler'.

HH: No business is transacted in the darbār. It is a formal show... of allegiance.

M: So that is the time when position...

HH: Position counts. Do a proper obeisance. You should take three steps back, you only took two, I am insulted.

For HH the darbār was all important; and even Bhojsinharao, who thought that a true darbār could only take place after the coronation (a view that HH disputed with precedents) had to admit: 'After all, the *abhiseka*

is merely something like dressing for dinner. The dinner is more important.' What then of the content of the 'dinner'? The main elements were
these. First, men entered the darbār hall in reverse order of precedence,
and left it in order of precedence, so that the structure of the court was
made manifest; then homage was made to the ruler-on-the-gaddi in the
form of obeisance (mujra); then a coin was circled clockwise in front of
HH in a movement known as *nichavar*, the aim being to keep the evil eye
away, such coins being accepted and distributed to HH's retainers; then a
further coin (*nazar*) was offered, this being accepted as token of homage
(and placed in the State treasury) on major occasions such as the darbār
following the abhiṣeka, but otherwise returned with the word 'excused'
(*māf*); and finally, there was a token of acknowledgement—or a return of
gift—by the ruler in the form of *pān-supārī* (betel and areca). There is a
similarity between *nazar-pān* and *bhog-prasād*, and between nichāvar and
arti[15] in the darbar ceremonial and in ordinary rituals of worship respectively. The situations are not homologous, however, because pan does not
appear to represent transformed and consecrated nazar, as does prasad of
bhog; this may be because the gaddi alone is not being worshipped, but
rather homage is being made to the ruler-and-gaddi. Nevertheless, the fact
that mujrā is made at the same time, and the HH saw this as being pūjā,
leads me to consider the question of the divinity of the ruler.

HH did not see himself as a 'divine king'. As he said, 'Though people
say he's a god (*deotar*) and so on, but personally, I do not believe in that'.
Nor should a ruler 'take advantage of that loyalty'. Nevertheless, he acknowledged the implication of his mounting the gaddi: 'It is sitting on the
gaddi that brings divinity. When we pronounce from the gaddi, it is divinity.
When we get off, we are only Rajas.'

Note that whilst on the gaddi HH was not actively ruling, but only
symbolizing the order of the kingdom through the allegiance of his court;
because of this he was not a 'divine ruler', in the sense of making divinely
inspired decisions, but only someone who was at times touched by divinity,
as might many of his subjects be when possessed by gods. Nevertheless,
the effect of sitting on the gaddi could not be entirely shed after he had
left the darbār. And so it was that 'divinity, a little part of it, comes into
the kingship part of it'.[16]

The place of the gaddi in other states has, to my knowledge, been little
discussed. The only relevant account of any detail that I have seen has
been that of the Mysore Maharaja's Dassara (Dasahara) celebrations (Rao
1936).[17] This is not entirely comparable, since the centre of the Dasara
rites and the attendant darbār is, in fact, a throne (simhasana), i.e., a chair-like

object. As we know from Auboyer's authoritative work, such thrones traditionally provided a rich symbolic statement by their iconographic details
(in the Mysore case, Rao mentions that the throne is 'lion-headed) of a
kind which the gaddi does not possess. Nevertheless, there are clear similarities between the Mysore and Dewas darbārs. Obeisance sand nazar are
offered by the nobles of the court as symbols of loyalty; and 'His Highness
not only blesses from his seat on the Throne, *the Seat of the Devī*, his
subjects, but also communicates individually to each of them her tender
goodwill towards them by offering a flower that had been placed at her feet
whilst he was in communion with her' (Rao 1936: 147f., my emphasis);
and he then gives (pān-supārī) to each darbāri as is done in Dewas. The
throne is therefore the abode of Devi, the divine mother who 'is the Sakti,
without which none can function (ibid.: 159); the Maharaja takes his seat
on it at this time alone, and the darbār is an essential part of the festival. So
far the parallels with Dewas are entire, but there also appear to be differences. For there is also a series of rituals—oil baths, worship of Ganeśa and
the nine Planets, etc.—which may well involve Brahman priests; and the
throne, by being assimilated to Durga, is 'universalised' in a way that the
Dewas gaddi does not appear to have been since it was simply the abode of
the 'spiritual strength' of the State.

I do not wish to push this comparison too far, because I do not have full
information about the Dewas situation, nor does Rao give great detail
on the Mysore festival. It is perhaps more interesting to emphasize the
similarities—the throne as the abode of śakti, the mounting of the throne
by the ruler,[18] and the 'worship' by the courtiers through their unmediated
homage to the ruler-on-the-gaddi. Of this latter duality, HH commented:

For the common man... it is Gaddi Mata, Ma-bap [mother–father] is *huzur* [lit. the
presence, hence the ruler].

M: So when you say 'Huzur is mā-bāp, ma is the gaddi and bāp is the Ruler?
HH: And the two go together. Huzur cannot be without the gaddi.

I had always taken the phrase 'mā-bāp' to mean that the government is,
in general, 'all in all' to its subjects, as are parents to children, rather than
that it referred to the specific combination of male and female principles in
royal rule. That this combination is a necessary one, however, is indicated
by the different status of a female ruler. As HH told me:

A woman Ruler will not sit on the gaddi in any Hindu states. Yes, Ahilyabai [celebrated
woman ruler of Indore State] sat on gaddi, but it was known as the *khāsagi* [i.e., private]
gaddi as against the Holkar [i.e., dynastic] gaddi. My wife never sat on [the Dewas
Senior] *gaddi* during her regency. Actually, no woman can sit on the *gaddi*.

We return to the 'true' gaddi as the source of power and of continuity, as an ancestral object which 'is'.

HH's account shows that the assumption of the throne and the coronation were independent, and that his assumption of the kingship, which bound him to protect and please the people and to fulfil his own destiny, was a religious act in being a union with the gaddi, yet one which required no Brahmans. The power of the ruler is neither purely secular nor is it religious in the conventional sense; it appears to contain an element of 'magico-religious kingship' (Dumont 1962: 61).

As for HH, his thoughts on mounting the gaddi for the first time were mainly directed to rājnīti rather than to his own translation. He had first suggested the latter by simply saying, 'I certainly felt a little exaltation, or whatever you may like to call it'. But the next day having thought it over, he told me:

Well, I didn't feel much, I certainly felt a little elevation. Not joy or anything like that, a little elevation. That I have now got what was so far accepted to be my word, my word was [now] law.

M: It's a very solemn moment?

HH: It's solemn, elevation.

M: All of a sudden, you feel that you're not like any one else?

HH: No. And a sense of responsibility came with it. Up till now, if I did anything wrong [as President of Council] the PA would come and put it right. Now it would be different. I would have to bear the consequences of it.

On the one hand, mounting the gaddi simply symbolized the granting of 'full powers' by the British; but it also, both to HH and to his subjects, meant that he was now a raja and had been given divine legitimacy as well as the potential for manifesting total responsibility and the appropriate qualities connected with it.

There are two questions to be considered in looking at the personal qualities of the ruler. One is, what did HH think were those qualities; the other is, were these qualities produced by his becoming the ruler or were they previously shown, though perhaps made more manifest in his new status?

As to the second question, an extreme position would be difficult to hold in the light of events. For who could maintain that a man was entirely born anew when he became a ruler; or who could, equally, maintain that to become a ruler made no difference to a man? The main factor in HH's reply was the difference between succession in pre- and post-British times. Before the British, a vacant gaddi invited claimants, both from among the late ruler's lineage and from others such as his successful generals. HH told me that a major reason why maharajas were not mourned for by their heirs was that the latter had to stay in the palace, rather than go to the cremation, lest an attempt was made to seize the gaddi. There were incidents ('not in Maratha but in Rajput history') where one of the lineage marshalled his supporters and sat on the gaddi. Were he to have come from outside the lineage 'you would call it a rebellion, he would be cut to pieces' but from inside, it was a question of capability:

HH: If he's got special courage (*pratāp*) he may succeed in it. That's a different thing.
M: So the qualities are individual?
HH: Yes, but the qualities are only sanctified by your sitting on the gaddi.

HH's last remark illustrates the difficulty in the matter; claimants were exceptional people, but nevertheless they were changed ('sanctified') by acceding to the gaddi. In pre-British times, then, actual rulers were more likely to have had the qualities I discuss, even before they ascended to the gaddi. After the British, as HH pointed out, not only were rulers protected by their treaties but so was the succession; hence a greater variation of personal ruling styles was made possible, and the question of the change in a man after accession was affected.

What, then, in HH's view should be the qualities of the ruler? In a general way, they were those attributes which contributed to operation of rājnīti and daṇḍaniti—those of a man of action. Rather than ask him about his own qualities, I focussed on two of the qualities which classical accounts attribute to the king. One is *tejas*, or *tej*, the 'radiant energy' (De Casparis 1979: 124) which a king traditionally exuded and through which he constituted a 'field of activity' which was his kingdom. The other was *pratāp*, translated as 'majesty, dignity, glory, valour, heat' (Lal 1949: 863). The two words have overlapping connotations, and together constitute a major part of the traditional ruler's face to the world.

When I asked HH whether he had *tej*, his reply was:

It adds to it. If you have got a personality, as you [could] put it in general terms, it adds and helps you a bit.
M: Tej would be personality?
HH: Tej would be personality.
M: It's not a spiritual thing? But it's heat, it's a power which comes...
HH: Tej means—very difficult, I'll give you a word for it in a minute [he never did!]. But as I said, it is more akin to personality. Now... your old ex-Kaiser, he had a personality, he had a *tej*. You can see it from his picture. Poor old Franz-Joseph of Austria–Hungary, he didn't have that. We have seen neither of them, but one had it.

It is perhaps not too much to infer from this than what is arguably the most striking difference between these two emperors is their gaze; for through his gaze the traditional ruler laid bare the justice of competing claims (Inden 1979) and through it he acquired the quality which produced that sense of fear and awe which HH said that a ruler should command. As De Casparis points out, a classical ruler's *tejas* had a stronger effect the closer one came to him—a remark which HH could have agreed with, since a person's personality is clearly something that can best be experienced in his presence. Hence, continues De Casparis, the king's tejas diminished towards the edges of his kingdom—a phenomenon that constant touring was designed to prevent. Thus the very existence of the kingdom depended on the activity of its rulers, being susceptible to the ability of the king to protect a tract of land, whether inherited or conquered.

When I asked HH whether the ruler possessed pratāp, which I did not translate, he at once commented:

Pratap means valour. . . if the Ruler went into action, well the people appreciate that—that is called pratāp. He is with his army, army meant his people, in those days there wasn't disciplined Army...

M: Could you, in modern times, say that the same quality is the raja going among his people in the same way he went among the army?

HH: No. I went to the War.[19] It was appreciated by the people. They are unaware of the change of techniques and all that now. But it gives them a sense that, if any calamity or anybody comes on them, our Ruler will protect us. He's got the guts... pratāp means, military man, military glory. You must be masculine, to put it bluntly. Now, even in śikār, pig sticking is a little more than killing with a gun [it is] spearing from a horse. Maharaja [i.e., himself] hunted tiger on foot. One incident occurred in Dewas, but it is still quoted in Raghogarh [where it occurred]. That is fearlessness.

In these replies, we have more than one obvious link between the ruler's dominating personality, his physical courage, and his martial activities, which maintain the kingdom and protect its inhabitants, if we recall HH's stress on his 'movement in the masses'. For though this may be a refraction of more modern ideas of leadership, it connects with the classical view of the king's more general essential quality as being made up of both the moral application of energy and the movement that this entails. A person's qualities (*guṇa*) are to do with movement, the quality of rajas being 'controlled movement, power that is encompassed', as distinct from the 'riotous movements and meaningless motion' of *tāmas* and the quality of statis (*sattva*), which transcends both (Das, Ms. 14f.). In this scheme of things it is the ruler who brings a controlled order and this, as HH saw it, was central to his *svadharma*, the 'inherent mode of behaviour proper to [a ruler]' (Weightman and Pandey 1978: 227)' and it was in this context that he quoted the verse from the *Gita* about 'establishing the kingdom of the dharma' (see above). In this, he saw his part as an active one, of making and enforcing policies—as he said, 'more of a Krsna ruler'. In his view:

Rāma was absolutely, you know, he stuck to his word, everything *has* to be done, what is said, what is written. Now, Krsna was a great diplomat, he was not only a king... I am not following as sacred and sanctified [a deity as] Rāma, I am a follower of Krsna, we adjust to things as they come.

HH, in fact, saw his duty not so much in terms of maintaining the general dharma (which he would have seen as over-philosophical), but rather in the use of his power to punish and provide succour. We have come full circle to the ruler's use of daṇḍa.

Notes

1. We talked in English. The excerpts given below have been edited for repetition and deviation. I thank His Highness most warmly for the many kindnesses he showed to me in discussing his rule and, later, for commenting on a draft of this paper. The responsibility for the statements and for interpretation is, of course, entirely mine.

2. See Articles 4 and 5 of the Treaty of 1818 (Aitchison 1909: 253). This compared with, for instance, the duty of other states to 'listen to advice' (Baroda), 'follow advice' (Kolhapur), 'pay at all times the utmost attention to such advice as the British Government shall occasionally judge it necessary to offer to him' (Travancore), and with states which could not introduce material changes in administration without 'advice' (Cochin) or 'consent' (Mysore), as Sastry points out (1941: 40f.).

3. The British saw an obligation to check gross misrule, rebellion, and inhuman practices; these they distinguished from the introduction of reforms (HH's 'whether you ruled or not') which was not a reason for explicit intervention (see Lee-Warner 1894: 291f.).

4. This was in 1922 (Malgonkar 1963: 275; Forster 1953: 159) but it proved to be a dead letter. HH himself was to draw up a further constitution, not put into operation (due to war) until after his abdication.

5. Not all rulers regarded śikār in this light; for some it appears to have resembled the official tour (see, e.g., Pillai 1976: 1–46).

6. Compare this with stories of other rulers who mingled in disguise, e.g., in Hyderabad (Lynton and Rajan 1974: 2–11).

7. HH, whilst quoting the whole verse from the *Gita* (chapter 4), did not translate more than the first two lines to me, giving this rendering: 'For good people a protector and for bad people a destroyer.' I have therefore given all four lines in the translation by Swami (1935: 33).

8. Though, see the qualification of this in some sources (Lingat 1973: 226).

9. See Basham (1954: 82) for what he terms the 'dubious etymology *raja-ranjayati*, he pleases', an etymology which Bhisma evidently accepts: 'And because he pleased all the people, therefore he was called Raja' (*Mahabharata*, Santiparva: LIX.125).

10. For a related discussion of the king's role as husband of his kingdom, see, for instance, Derrett 1959.

11. I use the term that HH used, although there was, of course, no crown, and a more accurate term would be 'consecration'.

12. I give only HH's memory of his coronation in Kolhapur, which was in fact much more complex than this. I have no reason to think that his Dewas coronation was essentially different, since both were held under the 'reformed rite' instituted by Chhatrapati Shahu Maharaja.

13. Under this form of the ritual the priest was a non-Brahmin, here a Maratha, and the verses were vedic. Maratha rulers were divided between those following the 'reformed rite' and using a non-Brahman Kshatrajagadguru (e.g., Indore) and those who continued with a Brahman Jagadguru and puranic verses (e.g., Gwalior, Dewas Junior).

14. In Kolhapur it was placed behind the gaddi, but HH told me that generally a new one was made for successive coronations. The Dewas Senior throne was no longer in existence.

15. The dictionary meanings of these latter two terms are given as 'propitiation' and 'adoration' respectively (Lal 1949: 147, 763).

16. Cf. 'The dominant idea of the *dharmasastra* writers seems to have been that it was not the king who had a divine nature, but the royal function itself' (Lingat 1973: 208).

17. I am indebted to Dr R. Burghart for drawing my attention to this work.

18. However, description by a visiting Portuguese in 1520 implies that the ruler at that time sat on a gaddi ('some cushions') because the throne was occupied by 'an idol' (Rao 1936: 174).

19. HH joined the Indian army as a second lieutenant and saw active service in the western Desert (see Malgonkar 1963: 294–303).

Becoming a Diarist:
Amar Singh's Construction of an Indian
Personal Document

SUSANNE HOEBER RUDOLPH
LLOYD I. RUDOLPH

This is an essay about a diarist and a diary. Amar Singh was a Rajput, Thakur of Kanota, a military officer in British and princely India. He wrote continuously for forty-four years, from 28 March 1898, when he was nineteen going on twenty, until 1 November 1942, the day before his death at sixty-four. The diary fills ninety volumes averaging 800 pages each. He missed one day when he lay unconscious after falling from a horse. Clearly, writing mattered; it was a lifelong commitment, central to his being and sense of self. It was a passion and a source of private recognition, but not a vocation, not a profession or public calling.[1] He wrote primarily for himself, initially for self-improvement and to master his liminal location between Rajput and English society, but for most of the forty-four years he wrote to keep himself 'amused'.

Because he wrote privately and confidentially, for his own amusement and not for public consumption, he escaped the literary, sociological, and economic determinations that, since the rise of the novel as a popular art form in the eighteenth century, shaped writers' careers. Amar Singh's diary was not subject to the influences and constraints of aesthetic or market forces, neither the anticipation of literary criticism nor what publishers thought would sell. A lone intellectual in a philistine sea, he communed with his own experience and the books he read.

About Diaries

A diary is a personal document. Written in the first person, its voice speaks for the self to the self. Journals, autobiographies, memoirs, and novels that fictionalize the author's first person voice are personal documents too. To a greater or lesser extent, personal documents live in the shadow of positivist assumptions about truth or reality, a presumption of factuality from which the novel and the poem are relieved. The decline of confidence in positive truth and its partial displacement by imaginative truth has affected all writing, history and social science as well as literature.

As the line dividing positive from imaginative truth has become feeble, imaginative truth's challenge to positive truth has led some to hold that all writing is a species of fiction. The imaginative truth of a Gabriel Garcia Marquez novel is said to surpass the positive truth of archival history. Here we are concerned with how the relation between imaginative and positive truth affects diaries.

We begin by distinguishing diaries from other kinds of personal documents, such as autobiographies, journals, and memoirs. Diaries are governed by different relationships to audience, historical time, and interpretation. The autobiography, journal, and memoir are meant for the public, the diary for the self. The public memoir depicts the self to a generalized other or to particular reference groups. The diary speaks privately, confidentially. In our time, blank diaries are offered for sale with little golden hasps and keys that promise secrecy.

The distinction between public and private that separates autobiographical and diary writing is, however, blurred. There is no purely private self. The social voice that has been incorporated in the self perches on the diarist's shoulder, a more or less obtrusive observer, sometimes even a scold. Amar Singh's pen periodically 'refuses to write'. He cannot tell even his diary certain unthinkable thoughts. The self constructed in a diary, like the self constructed in an autobiography, is mediated by the author's socialization.

Authors of diaries, like authors of autobiographies, are products of their time and place; both kinds of authors are social as well as self creations. Diarists may be more at liberty to dodge the social voice than authors of autobiography, but both live in the midst of a cultural context and a historical era that partially determine the self as author.

It was hard for Amar Singh to discern (much less to establish) the difference between a public and a private self that diary writing requires. Given the rigorously prescribed social roles characteristic of Jodhpur and Jaipur Rajput society in 1900, it was difficult for the diarist to distance himself from his place and time. Young men and women, even adult householders, were expected to speak and act in conformity with their family and social roles. There was no expectation of privacy in thought or action. At best, privacy was anomalous, at worst, illegitimate. A private consciousness that deviated from, much less criticized, conventional demands was unacceptable. To live with a private self was to be a deviant, a rebel, or a cultural sport.

The distinction between diaries and public personal documents can blur in another way. Confessional autobiographies—Augustine, Rousseau, Gandhi—engage in the private self-examination characteristic of diaries, but do so publicly. They live in a territory between the privacy of the diary and the public presentation of self that is autobiography. The result of self-conscious and deliberate self-examination, they mean to teach public audiences what has been learned in a private process.

Diaries differ from autobiographies with respect to time as well as privacy. Diarists write about their personal experience in the here and now. They account for and interpret the immediate, if not spontaneously, at least without the mediation of knowing the future. Willy-nilly, diarists write existentially. The diary is governed by the logic of its daily entry, the autobiography by the logic of hindsight. The diarist has less opportunity to historicize and mythologize the self, to rework experience in the light of the subsequent known outcome, to select evidence leading 'inevitably' to what one has become. The autobiographer, like the historian, can interpret and give meanings to acts and experiences which the diarist has neither the motive nor opportunity to interpret. Not that the diarist does not also select and omit, creating a particular and chosen self, a 'fiction' of his life and time. But the exigencies of daily entry preserve prior understandings of the self and of experience which the retrospective view of autobiography interprets or selectively suppresses.

Writing an autobiography makes it possible to construct a relatively coherent self based on a formed identity. Diary writing reveals a person in the making, potential identities, unfulfilled selves, inconsistencies and contradictions, abandoned paths, wrong turns, acts or events that proved embarrassing or shameful. While sharing in positive and imaginative truth, the diary adds another dimension: the truth of existentially recorded experience.

About the Amar Singh Diary

It is only since 1971 that scholars and a wider audience have come to know of the ninety-volume Amar Singh diary.[2] Amar Singh's military career as

Thakur of Kanota, cadet in the Imperial Cadet Corps, officer in the Indian Native Land Forces, Major in the British Indian Army, Commander of the Jaipur State Forces, and elder statesman of Jaipur state was important and distinguished. But Amar Singh's thirty-six-year military career was not so remarkable as to make him a historical figure. If he is known, it will be for the cultural value and historical significance of the diary he wrote, more than for his public career.

Amar Singh is an Indo-Anglian voice from his time and for his time that speaks to us today across the divide of postcolonial sensibility. His diary's voice and style engage us because they convey both a *temps perdu* and characters and events whose dramatic truth transcend Amar Singh's time and place. It is written with candour and insight in a direct, conversational style and in an English that is more authentic for its occasional Hindi syntax. Amar Singh interprets the politics of polo; the struggles for power at princely state courts; conflicts within the joint family; great 'cultural performances' such as marriages or a coronation durbar; the prices of dowry; the complexities of marriage negotiations; diet, dress, and 'etiquette' in Rajput and British society; and command and obedience among Indian and English officers.

Why did he write? For whom did he write? Why did he continue without interruption for forty-four years? At one level, there may be a rather straightforward narrative answer to the question. We imagine a simple conversation between Barath Ram Nathjee, Amar Singh's teacher, and the prospective diarist: 'Amar, you should keep a diary.' And why would Ram Nathjee have made such a suggestion? In order for Amar Singh to perfect his English; to offer him a vehicle for reflecting on his reading and experience; perhaps to fulfil Barath Ram Nathjee's own unrealized aspirations as a diarist. It seems likely that Barath Ram Nathjee, who had been a teacher and headmaster of the Jaipur Nobles School, gave his tutee an assignment he had used before. By 1898 diaries had become a known, even a common, pedagogic device in Anglo-Indian education. When Amar Singh joined the first class at the Imperial Cadet Corps four years later in 1902, he and his classmates were required to keep diaries.

This may indeed be the proximate cause of the diary. But it does not address the cultural and historical context of diary writing or the inner states of a diarist. Did writing autobiographically have to do with being a Rajput in princely India under British paramountcy? With literary models at home or abroad? With the liminality of living between two languages and their world views, simultaneously knowing and being 'the other'? Or did Amar Singh's disciplined and unrelenting passion for autobiographical writing reflect the influence of the austere, methodical Sir Pratap Singh, the Spartan prince regent of Jodhpur, who, for ten formative years was his guardian, mentor, and surrogate father?

Perhaps all these influences, the resort to exterior explanations, are beside the point. From a conventional social science perspective, the diary may be 'uncaused'. Amar Singh's commitment to autobiographical writing may defy the cultural and intellectual conventions of his time and place. Perhaps the diary is best understood as a social and cultural sport, a unique happening that expressed important aspects of Amar Singh's inner life and made it possible for him to be the kind of person he chose to be.

Cultural Warrants for Autobiographical Writing

Let us begin with Amar Singh the Rajput, an identity he frequently affirmed as much by criticism of Rajput failures to meet the community's own best standards as by repairing to its history and traditions. In the classical understanding, Rajputs as kshatriyas, the warrior-rulers among the four varnas, were called to the sword, not the pen, the robe, or the ledger. In Amar Singh's era, it was uncommon among Rajputs with landed estates and titles living under British paramountcy in the princely states of Rajasthan to write—and read—either 'vocationally' or as leisured amateurs. Neither scribes, nor priests, nor intellectuals, nor merchants, they were, as the British liked to put it, a 'martial race' who ruled, fought, and played for valour and honour. They were men on horseback—on the field of battle, at the hunt, and, in Amar Singh's day, on the polo field. They were at home with blood sports, with arms and horses in action, not with the life of the mind among inkpots and books. According to a Marwari proverb, 'A Rajput who reads will never ride a horse'.

However powerful this reading of the Rajput ethos is, it does not exhaust the possibilities available. Like all complex high cultures, Rajput culture was not of a piece. Rajput identity did not entail following a single path. Within certain limits, there were a variety of possibilities. Choices were available, some more conducive to the writer's calling than others.

Amar Singh, at a critical moment in his education, was exposed to the literate and literary component of Rajput culture. His much admired and respected teacher, Barath Ram Nathjee Ratnu, was a *charan*. Charans or *baraths* preserved, transmitted, and cultivated Rajput traditions and history. They were the guardians of Rajput codes of conduct whose poetry and history defined valour, loyalty, and honour. Charans told *charit*, biography, and reported on *charitra*, character and conduct. As court minstrels, they instructed by entertaining. They were the Rajputs' geneologists, historians, and teachers; sometimes they were leading state servants, sometimes guides and protectors of trade. Killing a charan, like killing a brahmin, was a mortal sin. It was the duty of powerful Rajput patrons to support and honour them.

Their pre-eminent medium was the *doha*, narrative poetry in couplets, whose composition and recitation was at once entertaining, informative, and moral. As minstrels at royal and noble courts, charan performances celebrated a lineage's glorious, tragic, and ignominious acts. The power of the charan lay in his poetic construction of Rajput history: chronology was subordinated to narration and narration to the identification of the heroes, cowards, and villains that mattered most for Rajput cosmology. Shyamaldas, a charan who became Rajasthan's first modern historian and served Udaipur maharanas as a *kaviraj* (poet laureate) and *pradhan* (first minister), called his monumental work *Vir Vinod* (Hero's Delight).

Amar Singh learned about dohas from Ram Nathjee; between 24 March 1898, when Amar Singh begins his notebook, until 3 September 1898, when it becomes the diary, Amar Singh fills its pages with dohas written or assigned by Ram Nathjee, who inducted him into the literary vocation. He continues to collect dohas for years thereafter; he and a friend at the Imperial Cadet Corps amuse themselves by recording dohas in their copy books.

The charan tradition of formulaic epic poetry provided a legitimate cultural option to Rajputs like Amar Singh, with literary as well as martial inclinations. While the standing of charan poetry in Rajput consciousness and culture sanctioned Amar Singh's literary bent as a *genre,* charan literature differed from first-person autobiographical and diary writing. Charan ballads about Rajput heroes addressed their conduct, not their private thoughts and feelings. Acquiring a taste for dohas, no doubt, helped Amar Singh to appreciate and respect literature but is not sufficient to explain why he became a diarist.

Amar Singh's liminal context provides another explanation why he wrote a diary. The liminal condition seems to be hospitable to dairy writing and journal keeping. Consider the coincidence in modern times between adolescence and diary beginnings, or that between travelling and journals, the *Reisebuch* from Marco Polo to Goethe. He was twenty when, in schoolboy fashion, he began his diary. He soon found himself living between English and Rajput societies. In 1900 he joins the allied expeditionary force sent to China to quell the Boxer rebellion. In 1902 he enters the Imperial Cadet Corps. In 1905 he joins General O'Moore Creagh's staff at Mhow. In all these social settings he comes in close contact with the manners and mores of British officers. For almost ten years he lives apart from his family, in an exclusively male society, as ward of the Prince Regent of Jodhpur. By contrast, in 1901, soon after returning from China, he marries, rejoins his joint family as a grandson, son, heir, and husband, and finds his way in Rajput court and civil society. Confronted by the contrast between English and male and Rajput and familial ways of life and world views, he learns to live with and in both.

Straddling cultural and intellectual boundaries, Amar Singh has to consider what manners, food, music, words, exchanges with men and women and responses to authority are morally right or instrumentally useful. His liminal state generates an intense internal dialogue and an effort to capture in words on paper what he knows and who he is.

Liminality can favour but not ensure diary writing. India's late nineteenth-century literary landscape would be crowded with diarists if liminality by itself was enough to ensure their creation. In Amar Singh's case, living between two worlds helped him to continue writing a diary. It was a vehicle for translating to himself and others the social and intellectual circumstances of the two worlds in which he moved.

Getting Beyond Iconography

We have suggested that Amar Singh's Rajput culture, with the exception of its charan literary influence, may have been a constraint on diary writing. Quentin Crewe's initial attempt to write T*he Last Maharaja: A Biography of Sawai Man Singh II* (1985) almost ran aground on the iconographic conventions of Rajput society. Those who knew Maharaja Man Singh, a socially sophisticated, mid-twentieth-century cosmopolitan, were anxious to help with so important and auspicious an enterprise. Yet they 'seemed never to have considered the Maharaja in a dispassionate light . . . . They surrounded him with a kind of mythical aura, telling what were obviously legendary anecdotes about him'. In keeping with the bardic style of charans, and observant of the divinity that rulers shared with the gods whom their public *personae* resembled, 'they remembered the royalty, not the man' (Crewe 1985: XIV).

The most difficult part,' Crewe found,

was to try to distinguish between fact and fiction. The Rajputs, being not much given to reading, have a style of conversational reporting which resembles bardic narration. What might have happened and what the speaker might wish had happened are given as much weight as what did happen—people drop dead on hearing bad news, they acquire untold riches as a reward for good deeds, their dreams came true, their horoscopes are neatly fulfilled (ibid.: XV).

It is a reflection of a cosmology—a world view—whose predicates entailed that what counts, what matters and is true, is found in a pluralistic universe of myth, legend, and manifestations of the divine.

The contrast between 'royalty' and 'the man' that troubled Quentin Crewe is reminiscent of the difference between Rajput and Mughal traditions in literature and miniature painting. Vishaka Desai has shown that paintings of Mughal emperors and eminent courtiers capture and reveal what is distinctive about the person being represented while Rajput court painting utilizes such highly stylized, standardized conventions, even stereotypes, in its treatment of rajas that it becomes difficult to distinguish one from another.[3] For the painter of Rajput courts and for those who spoke and wrote about kings, it was more important to convey royalty than to convey the man.

This difference between a patterned and formulaic truth and a more individualized and 'positive' truth is apparent in other aspects of Indian cultural traditions. Banarasi, a seventeenth-century religious leader, in describing Jaunpur where he spent most of his life, deserts the realism and intimacy that distinguishes his diary from the literature of his time. Instead, he resorts to a poetic convention that does for poetry what Vishaka Desai found formulae did for Rajput miniature painting. Mukund Lath explains this deviation in Banarasi's autobiography by telling us that in Banarasi's day it was an established practice among Hindi poets 'to follow certain fixed guidelines in describing a standard subject such as a city'. Such guidelines took the form of 'conventional formulae and set phrases' available in manuals of poetry or phrase books 'designed for the purpose' (Lath 1981: 129). 'Why,' Lath asks, 'did Banarasi insert a fanciful, stylised piece of description in a story avowedly meant to conform to real life?' Was this a 'grievous flaw,' a 'serious deviation' from his aim? The answer is no: his purpose in this passage was not descriptive but evocative and he used a standard technique for this purpose. In evoking rather than describing Jaunpur, Banarasi returns to deeply rooted conventions that define modes of thought and perception. He is reporting 'royalty' rather than 'the man'.

Amar Singh breaks with such powerfully entrenched literary and artistic conventions by speaking as an individual in a conversational, discursive voice that conveys the nuanced immediacy of everyday life. His accounts are particular, not formulaic, displaying a distinctly human view of eminent persons and their social contexts.

Literary Warrants for Autobiographical Writing

Perhaps Amar Singh became a diarist by reaching out beyond his Rajput heritage to autobiographical models in India's literary traditions. Were there exemplary works to which he might have turned, works that were available to educated persons because they were known, honoured, and read? The answer is, very few, and those that existed were not known to him. The only exemplary autobiographical writing in India to which he might have turned, the imperial memoirs and court histories of the Mughal era, were in Persian, a language that he, like most educated Indians of his time, did not command. English exemplars only entered his life well after he had become a committed diarist.

One might argue that the widely used and well known *roznamcha* (daily record) was—and is—a form of autobiographical writing. Kept by merchant and landed households, they provided descriptive accounts of persons, events, and finances—of comings and goings, weddings, births, and funerals; and money paid and money received. But their prescribed categories and terms pictured the surface of human behaviour, leaving motive and meaning untouched, to be inferred, deduced, or explained by 'independent variables'. Similarly, it might be argued that charitra (accounts of the character and conduct of deities, kings, and exemplary persons) provide models for autobiographical writing. But like charans' poetic accounts of Rajput heroes, they were alterbiography. They attributed formulaic motives to persons and stereotypical consequences to their deeds. Persons were constructed from honoured and familiar texts as social subjects playing roles.

'There is a widely-held view,' Mukund Lath writes, 'that Indians were deliberate anonymity-seekers.' Anonymity would seem to preclude autobiography. The authors and creators of India's most renowned and revered works of religion, literature, and art, works that 'virtually articulate the very spirit of Indian culture, *Ramayana, Mahabharata, Puranas*, the murals at Ajanta, the rock temple at Ellora, the *trimurti* Siva at Elephanta, remain nameless' (Lath 1981:X, XIV). Even though some probably had 'tangible authors' who might still be identified, they remain nameless because they are intended to bear an 'almost canonic superhuman authority'. No one cared to know who created them, because merely human authorship 'would render them fallible like all human utterances' and because, until modern times, 'little value was placed. . . . on the individual or his achievement'. If Indians held such views, Lath concludes, 'they obviously could not have produced autobiographically'.

Such a reading of the norms and practices of Indian culture neglects the considerable evidence of authorship that does exist and, more important, the deep concern for individual recognition articulated by playwrights (such as Kalidasa), writers in Sanskrit (such as Dandin and Bana) of *katha* (novels or romances) and *akhyanika* (realistic accounts of everyday experiences), song writers, painters, and architects.[4] If Indians did not write autobiography, it was not because writers respected the norm of anonymity. Yet there remains a discontinuity between the well-documented desire by writers and artists to assert and perpetuate their identity and the writing of autobiography. Given a manifest desire for recognition of individual creativity, the possibility for autobiography 'was not something entirely unthinkable'; indeed it was 'dimly discernible' (ibid.: XVI). Such a structural condition would have been impossible if anonymity was the 'completely overpowering ideal' that some allege. Autobiography that attends to motive and intention and reveals something of an individual's attitudes, judgements, and inner life stands as an unfulfilled possibility of India's traditional culture.

Two notable exceptions do exist: the autobiography of Banarasi, the learned seventeenth-century north Indian merchant and poet who became, toward the end of his life, the leader of an important heterodox Jain sect; and the eighteenth-century diary of Ananda Ranga Pillai, scion of the leading commercial family of the Carnatic and *dubash* (first minister) to Joseph Francis Dupleix, French governor of Pondicherry, in an era when trade, war, and diplomacy would determine whether India was to be dominated by Paris or London. Like Amar Singh's diary, neither Banarasi's or Pillai's autobiographical writing can be accounted for by reference to Indian literary traditions; they are *sui generis,* anomalies, cultural sports.

In his masterly introduction to *The Ardhakathanaka* (Half a Tale), the 1641 autobiography of Banarasi, Mukund Lath confronts the question of how, in the absence of literary models for autobiographical writing, Banarasi came to produce such a work, 'perhaps the only autobiography in the Indian tradition' (ibid.: I). According to Lath, 'true biography', in which a person reveals 'himself through his actions, aspirations and strivings, is completely missing' (ibid.: VIII). After reviewing the conventions of well-known literary texts from the seventh to the seventeenth century, Lath concludes that 'after long centuries almost totally devoid of meaningful autobiographical writing, the emergence of the *Ardhakathanaka*, a full-fledged autobiography, therefore, certainly occasions surprise' (ibid.: XX).

Lath recognizes a possible exception to his generalization about the absence of true autobiographical writing in India by considering its presence in the Persian literary writing that flourished during Banarasi's life-time (1586–1643). Babur, the first Mughal emperor, like his ancestors Timur and Changez, wrote autobiographically. So too did Jahangir, during whose reign Banarasi spent his youth in Agra. The great Mughal historians, Barni, Ibn Batuta, and Badauni, 'narrated the history of their own careers with sensitivity and appealing candour' (ibid.: XXI). Badauni, for example, conveys in his account of regional events aspects of his own inner life, personal misfortunes, triumphs, and love affairs. At a more general level, the kind of history that Persian men of letters wrote, like the paintings that court artists created, was strongly oriented toward individual lives and the importance of personal virtue.[5]

Banarasi could have written his autobiography as a result of exposure to Persian writing but did not because, according to Lath, 'even when opportunity presented itself he felt no attraction towards Persian learning'. The learned Mughal governor of Allahabad, Qiliji Khan, studied Hindi versification and poetic usage with Banarasi 'but the curiosity to learn was one-sided, no reciprocal interest was shown by Banarasi in Persian and its poetry. . . although knowing something of Persian poetry may well have been expected of him' (Lath 1981: XXIII).

Banarasi's life was a religious quest. He read mainly religious and particularly devotional literature. His community, his education, and his quest deterred him from responding to a vital cultural current of his era. If his autobiography cannot be connected with a cultural tradition, we are left with an unfulfilled possibility. Banarasi's decision to write an autobiography in the seventeenth century, like Ananda Ranga Pillai's in the eighteenth and Amar Singh's in the nineteenth, cannot be explained by his use or adaptation of literary models or traditions. All three seem to have taken to autobiographical writing sui generis.

Ananda Ranga Pillai's diary is the second of our cultural anomalies or sports. Written in Tamil, it spans the twenty-five years between 1736 and 1761. A fragment describing Admiral Boscaven's siege of Pondicherry in 1748 was translated into French and published in 1870 and, in 1892, extracts up to 1748 were published in Paris under the title *Les Francais dans l'Inde*. It was not until 1904, however, that the diary was fully translated, this time in English, and published in twelve volumes by the Government of Madras.

Rev. Price, one of the diary's editors and the author of the introduction, confirms its anomalous character. 'There is nothing to show,' he reports, 'what induced Ananda Ranga Pillai to keep a diary.' In this Pillai resembles Banarasi and Amar Singh; there is nothing in the literary traditions accessible to the Pillais, Jains, or Rajputs to induce autobiographical writing.

In the Rev. Price's estimate, Pillai's diary 'stands unique as a record
of the inmost thoughts of an extremely able, level-headed Oriental and of
his criticisms—which at times have the freest character—of his fellows,
and (French) masters.' 'It is a strange mixture,' Price continues, 'of things
trivial and important; of family matters and affairs of state, of business
transactions and social life of the day; interspersed with scraps of gossip,
all evidently recorded as they came to the mind of the diarist, who might
well be dubbed the "Indian Pepys".' Homely as is its diction, he continues, 'there are descriptions of men and things which are vividly life like,
and passages which are startling, some in their pathos, and others in
their shrewdness'. He concludes that 'the diary. . . is on the whole a
deeply interesting and valuable. . . account of things historical, political
and social pertaining to the period embracing the rise, zenith, and the
beginning of the decline of the French power in India' (Pillai 1904:
XI–XII).

Ananda Ranga Pillai and Amar Singh shared a condition that is independent of literary models and exemplars—liminality. It seems to have led
both men to write autobiographically. Each lived in two cultural worlds—
one 'oriental', the other 'occidental'. Pillai knew French and the French,
Amar Singh, English and the English. In the case of Ananda Ranga Pillai,
being a deeply rooted and well-established Tamil living for years among
French masters helps to account for what otherwise, in Rev. Price's words,
'stands unique'. By contrast, Banarasi's imperviousness to the Persian
literary world that surrounds him suggests that liminality has its limits as
an explanation for sui generis autobiographical writing in India.

Amar Singh was only slightly more determined than were Banarasi and
Ananda Ranga Pillai by surrounding literary modes. If he had lived within
the ambit of the presidency universities at Calcutta, Madras or Bombay,
rather than in princely Rajputana he might have entered the English literary world that Macaulay's educational policy helped to create. In Rajputana,
Mayo College and Government College, Ajmer, were the lonely outposts
of English medium school and higher education. Amar Singh attended
neither. His formal education was six years at the Powlett Nobles School
in Jodhpur. If Rajputs had a literary language it was Hindi or Marwari. A
few knew Urdu. Amar Singh began to learn Urdu after his grandfather,
Zorawar Singh, told him that if he hoped to become a princely state minister or *diwan* he would have to command Urdu as well as English. Given
Amar Singh's limited formal education and exposure to literary traditions,
we have little reason to believe that when he began his diary he had been
exposed to any autobiographical writing.

However, unlike Banarasi in the Hindi/Sanskrit literary world of the seventeenth century, and Ananda Ranga Pillai in the Tamil literary world of the eighteenth, Amar Singh in the nineteenth century could have encountered autobiographical writing by his compatriots. Although the subject awaits further systematic exploration, we think two worthy of mention. One is Mohan Lal's *Travels in the Punjab, Afghanistan and Turkestan to Balk, Bokhara, and Herat and a Visit to Great Britain and Germany*. First published in London in 1846,[6] it is a travel journal with striking autobiographical and introspective dimensions.

Another is the autobiography of a Maharashtrian woman married to an early Christian reformer. Lakshmi Bai Tilak's *I Follow After* is distinguished by its willingness to reveal the harshness of family relationships and to defy conventions that drew a protective veil of traditional duty, respect, and obedience over family life. Neither of these autobiographical works came to Amar Singh's attention.

If Amar Singh did not know about the few autobiographical efforts of his compatriots, it is plausible that he might have known about English diaries. Starting in the seventeenth century with the diaries of Samuel Pepys and John Evelyn, the English diary tradition continued into the eighteenth and nineteenth centuries. These did not come to Amar Singh's attention either. As we have seen, by the late nineteenth century, the diary in India had become *inter alia* a pedagogic device to instil discipline and teach English. When Amar Singh, four years after beginning his diary, was obliged to keep one at the Imperial Cadet Corps, he in fact kept two, one for his teachers and one for himself. The school diary was public, meant for inspection. Amar Singh kept *his* diary to himself. Routinized as a disciplinary and pedagogic device, the public diary was not likely to have influenced his literary sensibility.

If Amar Singh did not become a diarist because he read Indian autobiographies or English diaries, perhaps he did so through other literary influences. Autobiography is not far from the novel which, as a genre new to India, became a visible part of the literary landscape in the nineteenth century. As Philippe Lejeune (1971: 47) observes, 'The autobiographer came into his own only by imitating. . . novels' (cited in and translated by Fleishman 1982: 15). 'Most autobiographers,' adds Northrop Frye, ' are inspired by a creative, and therefore, fictional impulse to select only those events and experiences in a writer's life that go to build up an integrated person' (Frye 1957: 307). Perhaps Amar Singh continued his diary because he read novels.

Starting with the diary's first two years (1898–99), and for forty-two thereafter, Amar Singh appended a list, organized by month read, author, title, and brief comment, of the fifty or so books he managed to read each year in the midst of an extraordinarily active life. The list for 1898–99 is modest in length and literary merit. We learn that he read three books by that great proponent of self-help in the Victorian era, Samuel Smiles– *Character Duty*, and *Heroines of India;* books about London, *Round London* by Montagu Williams and the somewhat salacious four-volume account by G.W. Reynolds, *The Mysteries of London; Sports in Many Lands* by 'The Old Shikarry', three books in praise of the empire, W.H. Filchett's *Fights for the Flag* and *Deeds that Won the Empire*, and C.W. Stevens' *With Kitchener to Khartoum*; and, as befit a Jodhpur Lancer, General Sir Evelyn Wood's *Achievements of Cavalry*. There is not a proper much less a good novel among them.

It is only in 1900, after Amar Singh has kept his diary for almost two years, that he starts to read novels. His more extensive and better quality list of books read in 1900 includes Samuel Johnson's *Rasselas*, Alexander Dumas' *The Page of the Duke of Savoy*, and two novels by H. Rider Haggard— *Montezuma's Daughter* and *Nada, the Lily*. Those by Rider Haggard, the creator of romantic adventures set in exotic lands, like the stories and ballads of his friend, Rudyard Kipling, whose work Amar Singh was soon to read, helped to furnish British and Anglo-Indian literary and popular imagination with the images of the lands and peoples subject to imperial rule.

We can only speculate on the effect that exposure to the novel as a form of literature and of imaginative truth had on strengthening Amar Singh's commitment to diary writing. Perhaps exposure to the novel quickened his sense of self. More certain is the effect that reading novels had on his liminal condition; the novels he read were written by Europeans, mostly but not entirely English Europeans. The selves of the characters they depicted, like the contexts in which they moved, were alien to Amar Singh's Rajput and Indian heritage. At the same time, by enhancing his sense of the other he was coming to know and to become, they provided a spur to his diary writing.

More important to Amar Singh's commitment as a diarist than his exposure to novels was his reading of *Plutarch's Lives*. He acquired the Langhorne edition on 22 September 1898, three weeks after his notebook became 'the diary'.[7] He continued reading Plutarch throughout 1899, 1900, 1901, and into 1902. He marked passages, copied some into his diary and occasionally made comments on them. The intensity and duration of his interest in the initial years of the diary strongly suggest that his reading of *Plutarch's Lives* was more important for consolidating his commitment as a diarist than his extensive reading of fiction and non-fiction.

Plutarch created a classical world for the European renaissance imagination through contrasting biographical interpretations of eminent Greeks
and Romans—Theseus with Romulus, Lycurgus with Numa, Demosthenes
with Cicero, Demetrius with Antony, Dion with Brutus. We learn about
Greece and Rome through Plutarch's liminal constructions. The *Lives*, by
contrasting and translating the qualities and circumstances of prominent
Greeks and Romans, seem to have heightened Amar Singh's sense of
liminality, of living between the Indian variant of the Orient and the English version of the Occident.

The Self as Subject: Inner States as Warrants for Autobiography

So far we have looked to cultural determinants—literary conventions and
world views—and liminality in our search for explanations for
autobiographical writing. We concluded that from the cultural perspective
the three authors of autobiographical works—Banarasi, Ananda Ranga
Pillai and Amar Singh—were anomalies, cultural sports who wrote sui
generis. How then did this one of the three, Amar Singh, begin at nineteen
to write autobiographically and continue to do so for forty-four years? Were
there inner states to nurture the process?

A diary is written to someone, to a listener. At the most intimate level,
it is addressed to someone who embodies aspects of an ideal self, a benign
appreciator, a not too severe judge. At the more general level, it may be
addressed to future generations. A diary is an inner dialogue with the self
as subject.

The beginning lies, as we have said before, with the influence of Amar
Singh's teacher, Barath Ram Nathjee Ratnu. Amar Singh began his writing on a daily basis by starting a notebook of quotations from assignments
that Ram Nathjee gave him, interspersed with short accounts of daily events
and comments on texts he was reading. After five months, with the entry
of 18 September 1898, the notebook becomes 'The Diary'. Under Ram
Nathjee's guidance, Amar Singh's enthusiasm for reading and writing
noticeably quickened. Daily writing early on became a kind of benign addiction, rooted in conscience and self-estimate. If he began as a somewhat
overaged schoolboy trying to master a foreign language to please his teacher,
he soon internalized writing his diary. It became a necessary part of his
being, critical to his self-respect, an aspect of his life that made everything
else possible. Without writing and reading, life lost its *ras* (enjoyment;
literally, 'juice').

For Amar Singh amusement or pleasure is 'writing to my heart's content'. Boredom is being kept from writing, and reading. In December 1900, while Amar Singh is in China with the British Expeditionary Force as ADC to Sir Pratap Singh, the commander of the Imperial Service Troops, Amar Singh meets 'Sarkar' (ruler or government, a term that Amar Singh often uses to refer to Sir Pratap) on the parade ground. 'He asked me where I was during the whole of the day yesterday. . . . I explained that I went out for a walk in the evening and as for the noon time I was in mine own room reading books.' The purport of Sir Pratap's question, Amar Singh goes on to explain,

was that instead of sitting comfortably in our rooms we ought to loaf about after him doing nothing but staring at his face. Now this is too hard for me. I honestly say that this is the thing I hate most of all. He does no work that would occupy him. He cannot read, and cannot sleep the whole day through, and so naturally must pass his time somehow or other. It is quite different with me, who love reading as much as anything in the world.[8]

To be bored meant being trapped into mindless talk by empty-headed or philistine peers or being obliged to attend his patron, master, and military commander by standing silently in his presence when he could be reading or writing. 'I like Lichman Singh coming to me,' he wrote in July 1905, 'because he is not a bore. If I am busy I go on with my work and he does not mind.'[9] By contrast, two months earlier on 18 May 1905, as recorded in 'Notes About My Last Visit To Mount Abu'[10] he asks, 'how can a man enjoy his life when he has to go shut himself up in a bath room to escape the constant noise of the room and concentrate his mind on reading and writing.'[11]

The occasion of this macabre arrangement was a hot weather trip to the hill station at Mount Abu, to which the princes and British officers repaired in May and June to escape the intense heat of the plains. Amar Singh finds that 'the room where my father was put up is much too small for two men and so I. . .put myself up with . . . the rest of the crowd'.[12] He repairs to a bathroom where he devotes,

hours and hours writing my notes. . . . The room was a quite small one and the table was an awful thing. It was a small round rickety thing with room hardly enough to put my diary and an inkpot on. I had to put it against the wall to prevent it from moving up and down. . . . While I was. . . in the lower rooms I had to undergo all this bother. The others never would get me a table though I begged of them repeatedly to do so. They merely laughed. Even this table I brought against their will. They were an idle lot indeed. They never realised how much I wanted this piece of furniture.[13]

It was almost a month (12 June 1905) before Amar Singh was saved from these deplorable circumstances. 'Last night before dinner the durbar [Sir Pratap Singh] came to see us in our rooms and. . . said we were cramped up and that I can come up in the house and occupy the room' recently vacated by Captain Smith. 'The meal over, the durbar and my father went to talk in private and I went to bed in my new room.' 'I was very happy indeed. There was a fine table and I enjoyed writing to my heart's content.'[14]

A diary may be, among other things, a vehicle for self-discipline, for introducing regularity into one's life, for getting one's life under control. Not all diarists are methodical ascetics, but discipline seems to be essential to daily diary writing. Sir Pratap's ideological and characterological asceticism no doubt shaped Amar Singh's view of himself and of the world. Sir Pratap was his guardian and surrogate father from the age of ten when Amar Singh was sent from his home in Jaipur to live with and learn from the sometime prime minister or regent of Jodhpur state, the 'beau ideal' of the Rajput prince and favourite of Queen Victoria. As we have seen, Amar Singh refers to Sir Pratap in his diary as 'durbar' and 'sarkar'. He is not only his political master but also his patron, mentor, and military commander.

The diarist is clearly ambivalent about Sir Pratap. He affirms and incorporates much of what he is and stands for as a ruler, soldier, sportsman and reformer, but comes to reject his personal attitudes and values.

Amar Singh's account of his education under Sir Pratap's Spartan regime gives little indication that he found its demands difficult. Indeed, he becomes like Sir Pratap in a number of important respects. He shares Sir Pratap's Arya Samajist reform ideas and practices.[15] He rises regularly at 4 a.m., faithfully observes the routines of exercising and massaging horses and like chores; castigates himself for taking daytime naps; and exercises with Indian clubs regularly and at length. He plays polo and hunts well and often. Like Sir Pratap, he becomes an outstanding soldier, polo player and sportsman, an important state administrator; and an elder statesman. Like Sir Pratap, he tries to inculcate 'good habits' in those who are meant to learn from him; for instance, he gets three of his younger brothers and several of his military subordinates to keep diaries.

But starting in China, when in 1900 he accompanies Sir Pratap to fight against the Boxers, he begins to see his mentor and master's feet of clay. The diarist and unselfconscious intellectual that he has become under Barath Ram Nathjee Ratnu's guidance disapprove of the arbitrariness of Sir Pratap's relationship with his favourite, the harmful excesses of his asceticism, and his philistinism. It is the incorporation of Sir Pratap's disciplined habits, not his arbitrariness or philistinism, that help account for his becoming a diarist.

Who did Amar Singh think was listening to the diary's voice? Whom was he trying to inform and persuade? Beyond writing for his own amusement, whose approval did he seek? The answers to these questions change over time.

In the early years, the presence looking over his shoulder was quite tangible—Barath Ram Nathjee. For the first three years he read the diary as he might an assignment; his praise and criticism appear in the margins. Sometimes Amar Singh's restrained and reticent replies follow a Ram Nathjee stricture.

Even when Ram Nathjee stops reading and commenting on the diary, his presence blends into the significant others who hover over the writing. As a charan, Ram Nathjee knows and values Amar Singh's Rajput identity; as his guide to Indian and Western classics and to English literature, biography, and history his spirit helps the diarist to synthesize his diverse cultural experiences.

In time other figures enter. His father, Narain Singh, a distant, abstract figure until soon after the diary begins, becomes an active presence whom he quickly comes to know, admire, and address. Another is a sympathetic Englishman, an amalgam of several benign officers Amar Singh encounters in the early years of his military career. On the basis of mutual respect and admiration, they become friends, sometimes peers. Amar Singh communes with him in the context of his liminal location, such as, the marginal man in the English society of the officers' mess at the Mhow cantonment, the Indo-Anglian in a rather parochial Jaipur society. He is speaking to him as well as to Ram Nathjee, his father, and himself when he engages in cultural translations, long essays that seek to master and convey his family life and society's ways.

Ultimately, the diary is an exercise in self-communication, autopedagogy that aims at self-knowledge. Amar Singh composes manuals for himself to cope with his cultural heritage. He interprets and glosses the diary for Indian readers who need help with a cultural script whose meaning has begun to fade.

This becomes most apparent in connection with the long essays about Rajput marriages, seven in the first seven years of the diary, several of them more than fifty pages long, one more than a hundred. Mastering marriages involves mastery of the complex diplomacy associated with family and status, and the demanding logistics and economics of ritual events. All of these are requisite skills for a successful Rajput householder. Amar

Singh means to be like his father, respected and consulted on these and like matters. The diary entries help him to assimilate these experiences and appropriate them for later use and variation.

What does Amar Singh expect to be the fate of his diary? Amar, *a-mar* means non-death, without death. To what extent does Amar Singh expect the diary to transcend his own life, to speak to future generations? He seems to have no such awareness or ambition in the early years of the diary. It is in 1916, eighteen years after beginning his diary, when he is on a troop ship in the Mediterranean taking him from combat in Flanders to combat near Basra, that it occurs to him that the diary might have a public life after his own has ended. The occasion for this awareness is his reading of the multi-volumed diary of Samuel Pepys. Amar Singh forces himself to read to the end any book that he takes up even when, as in the case of Pepys, his interest flags. As usual, he perseveres, and at the end asks himself, 'I wonder whether anyone will ever read my diary as I am reading this one'.

Notes

1. Between 1909 and 1911, however, Amar Singh wrote publicly, in Hindi, for *Saraswati,* an early entrant in the creation of modern Hindi literature and style.

2. The original diary is preserved at Kanota fort, near Jaipur; microfilms are at the Nehru Memorial Museum and Library in New Delhi and at the University of Chicago.

In 1971 Amar Singh's youngest brother, the late Colonel Khesri Singh, noted as a shikari, author, and raconteur, whom we had known since 1956, suggested that some of our questions about the princely era in Rajasthan might be answered by his eldest brother's diary. It was then that we met Amar Singh's nephew and heir, Mohan Singh. He had already realized the importance of his uncle's diary and had begun to have selections typed. He welcomed our interest and collaboration. Since then Mohan Singh has been our collaborator in the tasks of selecting and interpreting the Amar Singh diary.

3. 'Images as Icons: Royal Portraits from Rajasthan, 17th–15th Centuries', in Karine Schomer et al., *The Idea of Rajasthan* (forthcoming).

4. Lath 1981: x–xxi for his evidence and interpretation.

5. See, for example, Harbans Mukhia's account in *History and Historiography During the Reign of Akbar,* 1976: 17ff, 126, 103–4.

6. We are grateful to Dirk Kolff for the reference to Lal's *Travels.*

7. John and Lawrence Langhorne, translators; published by Ward, Lock, Bowden and Co. His library also contains a 1910 printing of a ten-volume edition of the first (1577) English translation of Plutarch by Sir Thomas North, edited by W.H.D. Rouse and published by J.M. Dent at London. North's translation introduced Plutarch to the English speaking world of Shakespeare's time by translating Amyot's 1559 French rendering of the Greek text first published in 1517.

8. Ms. p. 216, Shanhai Kwan, 18 December 1900. Page references are to the unpublished selections.

9. Ms. p. 1400.

10. A hill station in Rajasthan on the border of Gujarat. Its 3,500 foot altitude made Mount Abu the highest point in Rajputana.

11. Ms. p. 1396.

12. Ms. p. 1346.

13. Ms. p. 1340.

14. Ms. pp. 1369–70.

15. Sir Pratap the ruler, soldier, and sportsman is better known than Sir Pratap the administrator and social reformer. Sir Pratap was an avowed follower of Swami Dayanand Saraswati, founder and leader of the Arya Samaj, the most important Hindu reform movement of the nineteenth century.

Study of Changes in the Indian Family

A.M. SHAH

'From joint family to elementary (or nuclear or individual) family'—this has been the slogan summarizing changes in the family in India during the modern time. Some sociologists have pointed out that the change implied by the slogan is not taking place; what is emerging, they say, is not the elementary family but a new form of the joint family. Even these sociologists, however, do not question the correctness of describing the traditional family system of India as the joint family system. This belief about the traditional Indian family subsumes a set of some other beliefs: (a) Traditional India was village India, and the joint family was therefore a characteristic of village India. (b) Contrariwise, urban areas are new and characterized by the elementary family. (c) Urbanization, therefore, leads to disintegration of the joint family. Some sociologists have pointed out that urbanization does not lead to disintegration but only to a transformation of the joint family. They do not, however, question the belief that the joint family was always a characteristic of village India. In this paper, I have made an attempt to examine these beliefs about the traditional Indian family. It is well known that a proper understanding of social change requires a proper understanding of the past. In the study of changes in the Indian family, therefore, the importance of an examination of ideas about its past can hardly be overemphasized.

It should be made clear that this paper is concerned with beliefs about the traditional family only in so far as they appertain to its household aspect. It has now become commonplace in sociology and social anthropology to distinguish between 'household' and 'family'. In common English parlance the word 'family' has several different meanings, including 'household'; the common Indian word for the family, viz. *kutumb*, has likewise several different meanings, but, for the sake of technical analysis, 'household' should be distinguished from the other referents of 'family'. For example, two brothers and their wives and children may live in two separate households, but they may be bound by a number of relationships of many kinds. For the sake of clarity, it is necessary to consider such inter-household relationships as distinct from relationships within the house-hold. Although the aim of the study of the family should be to study it in all its aspects, the beginning has to be made with the study of the household. An examination of ideas about the past of the Indian household is, there-fore, crucial in a comprehensive study of changes in the Indian family.

I shall examine ideas about the past of the Indian household in the light of the knowledge we have been able to gain about its dynamics from empirical researches carried out at the present time. A projection of sys-tematic knowledge about the present into the past is very helpful in an understanding of the past; at least it tells us what to look for in the past. However, it should be made clear that I describe here only the most essential characteristics of the dynamics of the Indian household, and that I describe them very briefly.

It we take a census of households in any section of Indian society, a village, town, or caste, and examine their numerical and kinship composi-tion, we find a number of types of composition, ranging from the most simple single member household to a very complex household of many members. A 'simple' household is composed of a complete elementary family or a part of an elementary family. A 'complex' or 'joint' household is composed of two or more elementary families, or of parts of two or more elementary families, or of one elementary family and parts of one or more other elementary families.[1]

One of the first tasks in an analysis of households is to formulate the types of composition. The structure of the household becomes more complex as more categories of relatives are included. In a one-member household there is no relationship; in a two-member household there is one relation-ship; but beyond this the addition of one relative means an addition of more than one relationship. For example, the addition of a son's wife to a household of father, mother, and son means the addition of relationships not only between the son and his wife but also between father-in-law and daughter-in-law and between mother-in-law and daughter-in-law. The ad-dition of relationships tends to create conflict between roles. For example, the conflict between a man's loyalty to his wife and loyalty to his parents is proverbial in Indian society. Each person in a household is involved in a complex pattern of behaviour with every other member. Everyone in a house-hold has his/her own likes and dislikes, habits, tastes, and idiosyncrasies. Life in a household is marked by sentiments and emotions, and coopera-tion as well as conflict. Therefore, if our aim is to understand household life in its entirety, the formulation of types of household composition should take into account all the various members of a household. After the types have been formulated, it is necessary to examine the frequencies of house-holds of the various types.

Classification of households according to types of composition is not, however, an end in itself. The types are not discrete and haphazard but are interrelated in a developmental process. This process may be in progression or in regression. Progressive development of a household takes place due to increase in membership, mainly by birth and marriage, while regressive development takes place due to decrease in membership, mainly by mar-riage, death, and partition. It may be mentioned in passing that there is always some pattern in the developmental process, but it is not cyclical in nature as considered by Professor Fortes and his associates (see Goody 1958).

One of the determinants of the developmental process is a set of explic-itly stated rules or norms governing the formation of households. In most sections of Indian society, at marriage, the bride leaves her parental home and goes to live in her conjugal home. A couple is required not only to start their married life in the man's parental home but also to continue to live there afterwards. This norm has a number of implications. For in-stance, if a man has more than one son, each of the junior sons and their wives will have to live not only with the parents but also with the other sons and their wives and children. In fact, frequently people state that a man and his wife should live with his brothers and their wives. Further-more, they say that brothers and their wives should live together not only during the lifetime of the (brothers') parents but also after their death, and the brothers' sons and their wives should also live in the same household. Sometimes the norm is extended still further. Taking all these norms together, the central idea is that while female patrilineal descendants of a male ancestor go away to live with their husbands, the male partrilineal descendants and their wives should live together. The wives should be so completely incorporated into their husbands' kin group that they should not be divorced and that even after their husbands' death they should stay on in the same household. Unmarried children should be with their par-ents; in the event of divorce or death of their mother, they should stay with their father or his male patri-kin. I would call the central idea behind these norms briefly the principle of residential unity of patri-kin and their wives. It is necessary to clarify that this principle is normative and that there are always deviations from it as in the case of all norms. The measurement of conformity to and deviations from the principle is, therefore, an important problem of inquiry.

While the principle is common to almost the entire Hindu society, there are differences between different sections of the society in the extent to which it is observed. First of all, there are differences in the maximum extent to which the developmental process goes in progression along the path set by the principle. For example, in a Gujarat village I have studied, there is no case of two or more married brothers living in a single household after the death of their parents. In a nearby village, on the other hand, there is a considerable number of households of this type. Such differences in the maximum extent may also exist between villages and towns, between one caste and another caste, and between one region and another region. Secondly, while the maximum extent of the developmental process may be the same in two sections of the society, there may be differences in the frequencies of the cases in which the norm is observed within this extent. For example, in the Gujarat village just cited, only about 5 per cent of the total number of households are composed of one or both parents and *two or more* married sons and their wives and children, while 19 per cent of the households are composed of one or both parents and *one* married son. This is mainly due to the fact that married sons tend to live separately from parents even before the death of the parents. Out of forty-one cases of parents having two or more married sons each, only in 12 cases (29.26%) all the sons live with the parents in a single household, while in 29 cases (70.73%) all or some of the sons live in separate households (in the village itself). And out of 50 cases of parents having one married son each, in 38 cases (76%) the parents and the son form a joint household, while in 12 cases (24%) the parents and the son live in separate households.

One of the factors affecting the degree of extension of the principle of residential unity of patri-kin and their wives appears to be the degree of Sanskritization of a caste. This is due to the great emphasis the Hindu scriptures lay on the high degree of observance of this principle. The ritually higher castes, who are under greater impact of the scriptures, tend to have a higher degree of extension of the principle. Another factor affecting the degree of extension of the principle appears to be the institution of cross-cousin and uncle-niece marriages.

Whatever be the maximum extent to which the principle goes in progression in a particular section of the society, it is important to note that the process of progressive and regressive developments go on simultaneously in the society taken as a whole; while one household may be undergoing progression, another may be undergoing regression. As a result, there are always households in the society which are small and simple in composition, along with households which are large and complex in composition.

When a complex household, say, of two or more married brothers, is partitioned, two or more separate households come into existence, but at the same time a number of other relationships continue to operate. They would cooperate in economic pursuits, hold and manage property jointly, help each other on many occasions, celebrate festivals, rituals and ceremonies jointly, and so on. This is also a normal process, which highlights the importance of the technical distinction between 'household' and 'family' mentioned at the outset. Thus, two or more households may be separate but they may constitute one family.

For a long time, students of the Indian family used ancient Indian literature for information about its past. This information is of two main kinds: (a) pertaining to the property aspect of the family, which is generally included in the study of Hindu Law, and (b) pertaining to certain family rituals, such as the *sraddha*.[2]

The Hindu legal text, *Mitaksara*, first defines a coparcenary; it comprises only those males who take by birth an interest in the joint or coparcenary property, i.e. a person himself and his sons, sons' sons and sons' grandsons. As each son acquires by birth an interest in coparcenary property, even a father and his unmarried son are sufficient to constitute a coparcenary. Under the *Dayabhaga*, there is no coparcenary between a man and his son(s), married or unmarried, even though they may be living in a single household. The legal definition of the joint family is based on that of the coparcenary; it consists of all males included in the coparcenary, plus their wives and unmarried daughters. The latter are not coparceners and have only a right to maintenance.

There are two main points here: (i) the legal definition of the joint family is a highly specialized one and has nothing to do with the sociological distinction between elementary family and joint family. A joint family of the legal conception can exist even within an elementary family of the sociological conception. For example, a father and unmarried son, or a widow and her unmarried son, are sufficient to constitute a joint family according to law. (ii) The law does not lay down the rule that the joint family of the legal conception should always be a joint household. A son may live separately from his father, and one brother from another, but they continue to be members of their respective joint property group. In brief, the law is concerned primarily with the rights of constituting a property-holding group and of maintenance therefrom, but not with the constitution of the household group.

In the *sastras* (Hindu sacred texts), the question as to who should hold and inherit property is discussed usually in relation to the question as to who should perform the sraddha ritual for whom. In other words, the legal definition of the constitution of the joint family tends to coincide with and is sanctioned by the definition of the circle of persons required to perform the sraddha. This circle of persons need not live in a single household, just as the persons constituting the joint property group need not live in a single household. It seems to me that it was because of the coincidence of the legal and the ritual definitions of the joint family that the definition given in the sastras came to be accepted as the general definition, of the Hindu joint family. I shall call it the Indological definition. As most of the early studies were carried out by Indologists (including historians, sanskritists, and orientalists) on the basis of sacred literature, and as both Indologists and lawyers were dominant in the academic field in India, the Indological idea of the joint family carried a lot of weight and gained popularity.

The Indological-cum-legal material on the Indian family was used by Sir Henry Maine in his general theory of the evolution of the family. He compared and contrasted the joint family of India with the individual family of the West, and considered the latter as later in evolution than the former. He thus laid the foundation of the sociological study of the Indian family, and through him the Indological view of the Indian family came to be accepted in sociology.

I just now pointed out the fact that the Indological definition is not concerned primarily with the composition of the household. In so far as it was concerned with the household, it laid down only the definition of the ideal household, or in my terms, only the maximum extent of progression of the developmental process of households. Indological literature does not provide any information on the various types of households, nor on the frequency of households of each type; obviously there was no census of households, in any section of Hindu society, at any period of time. Further-more, the literature provides information more about Brahmans and a few other higher castes, whose property relations and rituals were governed by the sacred texts. With regard to the household also, the ideal that the texts emphasized was high—a household of four generations—and it seems only the higher castes tried to emulate the ideal to a higher degree.[3] The texts do not provide any idea of differences in the family life of different sections of the society.[4]

We begin to get more precise data on the household only with the beginning of the British administration in India. The Office of the Census Commissioner of India planned to publish a series of volumes on population estimates for the period from the eighteenth century to 1871 on the basis of censuses conducted in different parts of India during the period. The first volume in this series, dealing with the decade 1820–30, was published in 1965 (Bhattacharya and Bhattacharya 1965). It seems to me that it will be extremely useful if attempts are made to find and then analyse the original schedules of all these censuses. My experience in Gujarat indicates that such attempts are likely to be fruitful. During my search for sources for the study of the social history of villages in central Gujarat, I found in the ta'luqa headquarters the original schedules of a census carried out by Captain Cruikshank and his associates,[5] the same schedules that he used in compiling general reports of different parts of Gujarat, which have in turn been used by Bhattacharya and Bhattacharya (1965) in their volume on population estimates for 1820–30. In this census of Gujarat, a Census Register was prepared for every village, in which were listed the names of heads of households in the village according to their religion and caste, and against each name were given the following details: (i) houses and huts, (ii) men, (iii) women, (iv) servants and slaves, and (v) total number of persons.

I have made a detailed analysis of the 1820–30 census data on the household composition in a Gujarat village.[6] It shows that (a) the average size of the household was 4.5, and (b) the progressive development of households rarely, if ever, went beyond the phase of co-residence of two or more married sons during the lifetime of their parents. It is significant that the census data of a village in Maharashtra of the same period, which Professor Ghurye (1960: 14) has presented, shows the same average size of the household as in the Gujarat village. The early nineteenth-century data thus indicate that we cannot start the study of changes in the family in India with the assumption that villagers in traditional India always lived in large and complex households of three or four generations. We need a more realistic base line, and the early nineteenth-century census data are a very useful source for reconstructing such a base line.

As regards differences in the family between rural and urban areas also, it is important to keep in view the position at the beginning of the nineteenth century. (It is hardly necessary to discuss the point that there

Study of Changes in the Indian Family

were towns in India before the modern processes of industrialization and urbanization began.) The early nineteenth-century census data indicate that there was a higher proportion of the population of higher and more Sanskritized castes in towns than in villages. The bulk of the population in villages consisted of lower and less Sanskritized castes. If this point is related to my earlier point that the higher castes were under the greater impact of scriptures and there was therefore a higher degree of observance of the principle of residential unity of patri-kin and their wives among higher castes, it follows that there was a higher degree of observance of this principle in towns than in villages. The reality was thus quite the reverse of the widely prevalent belief that there was a greater emphasis on joint households (i.e., on the principle of residential unity of patri-kin and their wives) in villages than in towns in traditional India.

Although the censuses upto 1871 had certain obvious drawbacks, they covered only small areas in the country, and even within a small area the census was not taken simultaneously in all the villages and towns; it is remarkable that they collected and recorded a great deal of information of demographic and sociological value. The later censuses covered wider areas and became uniform in techniques, terminology, and classification, but there was retrogression in the case of information concerning the household. In all the censuses from 1867 upto 1941, the distinction between 'household', and 'house', and 'building' was not followed uniformly in all the provinces and states and sometimes even in all the parts of a single province or state, and hardly any attempt was made to collect information either on the kinship or on the numerical composition of households. Nevertheless, even the meagre information they provided is highly *suggestive*. All of them show that the average size of the household was rather low—between 4.5 and 5. Sir E.A. Gait, the Census Commissioner for 1911, stated the position very succinctly: 'the average population per house is 4.9 or much the same as in European countries. In the British Islands it ranges from 4.8 in Scotland to 5.2 in England and Wales' (Census of India 1911: 47). This suggests that the people in India lived mostly in small and simple households. It is noteworthy, however, that almost all the census officials interpreted their figures unrealistically. They assumed that Indians in pre-British days always lived in large households, and therefore, they concluded from their figures that the traditional household system was disintegrating due to modernization. The assumption about the past was a great obstacle in a realistic interpretation of the figures before them.

Dr Henry Orenstein (1961) used the census data to examine the usual general idea about changes in the Indian household. He posed the problem as follows: If the widespread belief that the modern process of industrialization, westernization, etc., of traditional societies such as India lead to smaller households, then the increasing industrialization, westernization, etc., should be reflected in a decreasing average size of the household. He presents figures to show that the average size of the household has not only decreased from 1867 to the 1951 census, but there has been on the contrary a slight tendency—very slight indeed—towards increase. This suggests that the modern processes have not brought about the so-called disintegration of large and joint households. Dr Orenstein conjectures, I think quite rightly, that the belief about the wide prevalence of large and joint households in pre-British India is false.

During the last thirty years or so, professional sociologists and social anthropologists have studied the problem of changes in the family in India. Some of these studies are concerned only with the household and some with the household as well as other aspects of the family. I would refrain from commenting here upon those studies which are not concerned with the household, as well as upon those studies of the household which are not concerned with the problem of change. As far as the studies of changes in the household are concerned, I submit that most of them have suffered from the assumptions I have examined in this paper. It seems to me that we need a new and more sophsiticated framework for our study.

First of all, we have to distinguish the normal developmental process from change. This is a difficult task, but we have to face it. Studies of the early nineteenth-century data on the household seem to me to be very necessary for this purpose.

Secondly, there is no point in postulating a single line of change for the entire Indian society. I suggest that it would be profitable to bring into the study of the household Professor Srinivas's ideas on sanskritization and westernization. In this context it is worthwhile to recall the slight increase in the average size of the household indicated by Dr Orenstein. It is possible that this increase may be due to some demographic factor. Dr Orenstein himself suggested that it may be due to a rise in the average number of children or in the average number of adults per household. (If the latter is true, it strengthens the argument in favour of an increasing overall emphasis on large and joint households.) Notwithstanding the influence of demographic factors, it seems worth inquiring whether the sankritization of lower castes and *adivasi* tribes that has been going on on a massive scale in the country has contributed anything to an overall greater emphasis on the principle of residential unity of patri-kin and their wives. It cannot be denied that westernization of the higher castes has contributed to a lesser emphasis on the principle, but the countervailing influence of sanskritization might have led to an overall tendency in favour of greater emphasis on it. What I plead is that let us not assume that there has been an inevitable trend from large and complex (or joint) to small and simple households.

Finally, we need to have a fresh look at the problem of the impact of industrialization and urbanization on the household. It has already been pointed out that the situation in the past was possibly quite the reverse of what we have been assuming it to be. That is to say, there was greater emphasis on large and joint households in towns than in villages. Migration of rural people to towns, therefore, does not necessarily mean migration from a social environment of large and joint households to that of small and simple households. It seems to me that the study of the long-established population of older towns and cities is extremely important. I have in mind, for example, the walled cities of Delhi, Agra, and Ahmedabad, certain sections of the population of even Bombay, Calcutta, and Madras, and the large number of small towns. We should also examine the extent to which migrants to a town tend to be its permanent residents, and whether they practise the old norms when they are permanently settled. The whole question of the relation between migration and the household in India seems to be complicated. In any case, we begin to understand it better if we get rid of the old-established assumptions.

Notes

1. The terms 'simple household' and 'complex household' are not discussed here in detail for want of space. However, it may be noted that (i) 'elementary family' is not the same as 'simple household'; actually, a household composed of a complete elementary family is only one of the several types of 'simple households'; and (ii) 'joint household' is only a convenient alternative of 'complex household'. The background for discarding the usual dichotomy of elementary and joint family is provided in my paper 'Basic Terms and Concepts in the Study of Family in India', 1964.

2. For a fuller discussion of this literature as well as for citations, see Shah 1964: 10–14.

3. The definition of the household composition on the basis of generations is also confusing. For a discussion of this point, see Shah 1964: 5–6.

4. The indological literature is wider than the literature I have considered here, but I doubt if the other literature also provides the kind of data the sociologist needs for the study of the household.

5. For a detailed description of these records, see Shah et al. 1963.

6. See my Ph.D. dissertation, 'Social Structure and Change in a Gujarat Village', 1964, 76–86.

Networks[1]

JOHN VAN WILLIGEN & NARENDRA K. CHADHA

Composition of the Networks

We asked each [old] person we interviewed questions about the members of their network to find out more about their social identities. This resulted in asking questions to 3,623 persons.

The persons we interviewed reported that they interacted with 49.4 per cent of the people in their networks on a daily basis. A little over 21 per cent interacted with a few times a week, almost 13 per cent were interacted with weekly, and just over 16 per cent were interacted with monthly. It's probably true that if we would have asked about people that were interacted with once a year we would have gotten answers, thus increasing the size of networks to some extent. It may be a trivial point but compared to our earlier work in the United States (van Willigen, 1989), the percentage of people interacted with daily is very large. In the American sample about 16 per cent were in daily contact. In the American study the most frequently reported category was weekly. This probably reflects the weekly pattern of church attendance as much as anything else. The differences between the two places in regard to frequency of interaction is probably a function of differences in household size and residential density, that is, large households in a relatively dense urban setting in India and much smaller households in a rural setting in America. In Rana Pratap Bagh we were aware of the high level of daily interaction between friends and neighbours. Meeting and greeting people on the street was very common and from our observations, a pleasant byproduct of urban life.

We asked the persons in the sample to indicate whether the persons listed in their networks were men or women, neighbourhood residents, kin, neighbours, friends, service providers, coworkers, and/or fellow members of an organization.

We looked at the gender of the network members carefully. The majority of each person's network was made up of persons of the same sex. Sixty-four per cent of women's networks were made up of women. Seventy-seven per cent of men's networks were made up of men.

Across the sample about 24 per cent of network members were from the interviewees' households. The percentage of household members in the networks of men and women was different. For men 21.1 per cent of their networks were from their household. For women the percentage was 25.8.

In many cases we found that about 45 per cent of the persons in the networks were kin. Men and women had different percentages of kin in their networks. A higher percentage (58 per cent) of the networks of the men we interviewed were kin; 47 per cent of women's networks were kin.

We asked the men and women in the sample to rate their network members in terms of their importance to them using a one (least important)-to-five (most important) scale. The mean rating was 3.4. The most frequent rating category was five, accounting for 56.3 per cent of the total. The second most frequently used rating was 'least important' with 25.1 per cent of the total. The intermediate categories were used infrequently. The second category was used for 1.9 per cent of the alters, the third category was used for 4.2 per cent, and the fourth category was used for 10.1 per cent of the network. The general response of the Rana Pratap Bagh sample was similar to that of the American community. The mean rating in the American sample was 3.7. The Rana Pratap Bagh sample was much more willing than the Americans to use the 'least important' rating. Only 7 per cent of the people linked by the Americans were rated that way. The rating pattern of the Americans may be an indication of the small size of the households and the fact that there may be a tendency for relationships outside the household to be regarded as more important.

The stability of the neighbourhood and the age of the sample can be seen in the reported duration of the relationships between egos and alters. The mean duration of relationships with the 3,623 alters is 24.3 years. Twenty-five per cent of the relationships are for longer than forty years.

We looked at the changes in the percentage composition of the networks over the age groups. There are two basic patterns of change when we look at the differences in these categories from age to age. The first pattern is that as respondents age there is a small but perceptible increase in the percentages of all the kinds of relationships that would have a major affective component. The second pattern is that there is a decrease in the percentages of persons in more instrumental categories like coworker and service provider.

Our analysis was directed to identifying factors that are related to the size of a person's network as well as other qualities and characteristics. There is the risk of having this somewhat technical discussion be regarded as 'just a set of numbers'. It is important to keep in mind that the statistic that represents the size of a person's social network is a manifestation of social engagement on the one hand or social isolation on the other. We feel that understanding the causes of social engagement or isolation is one of the important justifications of social gerontology and an important consideration for the practice of social work.

The next question is, what is so problematic about social isolation? A person with a limited number of social relationships is up against a number of significant problems. It is true that some of these problems can be compensated for by somehow intensifying the quality of the remaining relationships. This happens frequently, of course, when a person's social network decreases in size, and household and kin relationships increase in importance. This is something that many of us have 'lived through' in the cases of our older loved ones.

The implications of social isolation, expressed, for example, as a reduction in network size include the following. First, the person to whom the person is linked will probably be a source of valued assistance, emotional support, information and economic assets. With isolation the older person will have less access to this kind of help. Second, the linkage with the network will help keep the community at large informed about the welfare of the older person. This is probably important for increasing the quality of the older person's care and to prevent abuse. The network link increases the exposure of the situation to the control by social pressure from the community. We feel that it is widely recognized that social isolation is often associated with abuses of various kinds. Third, linkages with the community through network ties help maintain social comprehension, by which we mean that a person and his or her history is known to the community (de Beauvoir 1972: 216–22). It is important that old persons be known to the communities within which they live, as a person with a history. The prototype for this is the parent–child relationship. Children will continue to relate to the aged parent as a once dynamic, robust, and sustained mother or father whereas others will see him or her in terms of relentless dependency.

That said, we need to look at the numbers. The mean network size of the population sample is 25.3 (SD 10.4) persons. This is essentially identical to what we found to be the mean network size of a similar population in the United States (van Willigen 1989). It is also consistent with the results of an attempt to determine network size norms through the study of a normal American population of various ages (Pattison et al. 1975).

To better understand the relationship between network size and age we divided the sample into different age groups and compared the mean network size of the different strata (see Table 1). We found very little variation in mean network size from strata to strata through the 70- to 74-year-old category. On average people in the sample maintain networks at about 25 persons up to 74 years of age. Starting with the 75–79 age strata there is a significant and cumulative decline in social engagement. The decline between 70–74-year-olds and 75–79-year-olds is about 9 per cent. The decline between 75–79-year-olds and those over 80 is 22 per cent. On average persons in the 80-plus age category have networks that are 27 per cent smaller than the sample mean.

Table 1
Network Size in Relation to Age Categories

Group's Age	Mean Network size	SD
55–59	24.1 persons	12.4
60–64	26.6 persons	9.5
65–69	25.8 persons	10.0
70–74	25.9 persons	11.2
75–79	23.7 persons	10.0
80 years plus	18.5 persons	8.8

This research was focused on factors that relate to social engagement as expressed in the size of social networks. Because of this we looked at a number of variables to see their relationships with the extent of social engagement. We found a significant difference in the size of the social networks of men and women. The mean network size of men is 27.6 while for women it is 22.8. That is, looking across the sample, women's networks are about 18 per cent smaller than those of men. This difference is very significant.[2]

When we looked at marital status, we found that married women's networks were much smaller than those of married men, as one would expect given the general male–female differences in the entire sample. The mean network size of married men was a robust 28.4 while the mean network size of married women was 22.9. While men and women who are widowed have very small networks, we found that the mean network size of widowed women was larger (22.7) than the mean network size of widowed men (21.0). The surprising aspect of this result is the similarity between widowed women and married women. Their networks were about the same size.[3] Men are more likely to remarry at the death of their wives. The men who remain widowed are usually older and less healthy as a consequence. They have smaller networks.

We found no significant differences between the mean network size of those living in joint families and those living in nuclear families. Those living in joint households have a mean network size of 25.3 (SD 10.1). The mean network size of persons living in nuclear households is larger, at 26.1 (SD 12.6). We were somewhat surprised with these results in that network rosters include people from within the household. Because of this one might expect that persons living in the more complex joint households would have significantly larger networks. In fact 25 per cent of network members of persons living in joint households were from the household itself across the sample. The comparable figure for nuclear families was 12 per cent. Persons living in nuclear households expand their network beyond the family. This may be done to compensate for the limitations on potential social interaction inherent in the small household. It may also be that they have additional time to develop and sustain relationships beyond the family. At least one person who lived in a nuclear family perceived that persons in joint families were unapproachable because they always seemed so busy. This in turn made the person feel that she was imposing. She also expressed the idea that because many of the joint families were of 'the business class' they were 'materialistic and always talking about how much they spent on this or that'. She felt that they were fine people but one hardly had anything interesting to talk to them about.

There may be a 'demographic' relationship that can be logically related to this pattern. There is, in fact, a very clear age-structure difference in the two types of households. We found that all persons in the sample seventy-five years and older live in joint households. Ninety-five per cent of the persons living in nuclear households are less than seventy years old. That is, the old-old live in joint family households and have smaller networks. The magic number argument would suggest that persons will attempt to establish a kind of optimal social world if their resources permit. This would suggest a psychological need that transcends mere opportunity.

[We] asked each person in the sample to describe their own health in relation to other persons their age. Their responses were analysed in terms of the categories poor, good, and excellent. We found that persons who rated their health in the poor category had significantly smaller social networks. The mean network size for persons in the good and excellent self-reported health categories were very similar. Those in the good self-reported categories have a mean network size of 26.8 persons. The persons that had reported their health was excellent had a slightly smaller mean network size of 26.7. The mean network size for persons who rated their health as poor was 22.2 persons.[4] Their networks, on average, were ·18 per cent smaller than for persons who rated their health as good. This difference is significant.

We found that persons with smaller networks did not report themselves as healthy as others, they had less income, and less control over their worlds. We also found that they were less satisfied with their lives. We found the life satisfaction variable clearly associated with the extent of their social engagement.[5] We divided the respondents in terms of their scores on the Life Scale. The persons below the sample mean are on the average socially isolated (see Table 2).

Table 2
Life Satisfaction and Network Size

Life Satisfaction Group	Mean Network Size	SD
Low Satisfaction	21.6	9.6
Medium Low Satisfaction	21.4	9.5
Medium High Satisfaction	25.7	10.3
High Satisfaction	30.7	7.7

These associations, however clear, have two plausible explanations. The first is that high levels of social engagement produce high levels of life satisfaction. The second posits the reverse. We feel that these relationships tend to support each other.

In this case we have shown that network size varies in significant ways in terms of age, gender, self-reported health status, and control of household resources. Analysis shows that control of household resources has an especially important relationship with network size. Material wealth and household type do not appear to be associated with network size. This analysis defines social ageing as primarily a process of acquiring and then losing power. Age itself is not that important. Because of the gender roles of the joint family, supported by the legal and cultural bias toward male control of family property, the social ageing processes of males and females will be very different.

This research is consistent with the following view of social ageing. People, as they age, will tend to maintain membership in a primary group of about 25 persons. If their economic or health resources are limited or they exist in a powerless condition their primary group will be smaller. We can postulate that people's networks (i.e., the persons with whom they regularly interact) will be this size unless there is some instrumental reason to invest in more relationships or unless their physical or economic resources preclude it. This research result in robust and can be demonstrated through the comparison of different kinds of communities, different kinds of people within samples, and through the life course. Small networks apparently are associated with some unattractive life circumstances such as poor subjective health and low life satisfaction, indicating that all of this may have important implications for individual men and women.

It is important to recall that the people who live in the neighbourhood that we studied are very well off. For the most part these people are from the upper middle class. Further, because of the way neighbourhoods are organized in Delhi, the residents tend to be relatively homogeneous. In the

Table 3
Income and Network size

Income Group	Mean Network Size	SD
Lower Income Group	24.5 persons	12.5
Middle Income Group	25.1 persons	9.7
Higher Income Group	27.8 persons	9.5

face of the homogeneity and relative wealth we still found variation in the income levels in the households of the people we interviewed. We divided the sample into three income categories, low, medium, and high. Our exchange theory orientation would suggest that the average network size of the persons in these categories would vary in the same direction. That is, persons living in households with less income would have smaller networks. While that is what we found, the differences we found were not significant.[6] We found that the mean network size of men was quite stable across the three income categories; they are all very close to the mean. Whereas for women there is a large increase in network size in the higher income category. The mean network size of the women from high income households is larger than all the male and female strata. Although this difference is not significant there is a trend (See Table 3). The value is 1.49.

Notes

1. Excerpts from Chapter six of John van Willigen and Narendra K. Chadha (1999). Data for this book were obtained by the authors from an upper-middle-class neighbourhood

of Delhi named Rana Pratap Bagh. The authors interviewed people aged between 55 and 90 years. About 53 per cent of the sample are male and 47 per cent female.

2. This difference was evaluated with the one-way analysis of variance procedure. The F probability value was .0059.

3. The difference in network size associated with marriage was not significant when examined through the one-way analysis of variance procedure.

4. The difference in network size associated with self-reported health status was evaluated with the one-way analysis of variance procedure. The F probability score was .0589.

5. The relationship between network size and life satisfaction was examined with the one-way analysis of variance procedure. The difference was highly significant. The F probability score was .0002. The correlation coefficient between life satisfaction and network size was .34, the P value = .000

6. We examined the differences in network size associated with household income with the one-way analysis of variance procedure and found that the differences were not significant. The F probability score was .5461.

IV
Ethical and Ideological Issues

John Barnes (1996: 180–81) writes: '…research has an ethical dimension whenever it impinges on creatures with whom we have moral relations.' The creatures could be from any species of the biosphere but at the centre of ethical research designs in social sciences are human beings, and each piece of research, however innocuous and non-controversial it may appear, should examine its ethical, social, and political consequences well in advance. Many universities and research funding organizations have set up committees to have a closer look at research projects, their goals and strategies of data collection, from the ethical perspective. Only after obtaining clearance from these committees shall a research proposal be valid and entitled for funds.

Ethical questions start surfacing as the research work begins. Should one inform the people about the true nature of one's study or should one resort to 'covert methods', or what has come to be known, after Douglas (1976), as 'investigative social research'? Is it possible to seek the 'informed consent' of people in all cases, even when they have no knowledge of social sciences or research activity, for instance in a pre-literate community? Should one publish one's findings notwithstanding the furore it may cause among the 'subjects' of the study? Or, should one deliberately suppress those pieces of information and practices that people find embarrassing? Should one hide people's identity under a pseudonym or should one be truthful to everything— the name of the community, the names of respondents, the exact transcriptions of their interviews?[1] Several other questions of this type are raised in every study, although there cannot be a set of pre-formulated answers. Each researcher has to address these issues and questions afresh with every research, keeping in view the contextual specifics.

This section opens with a contribution from John Barnes, a celebrated name in the sociology of ethics of research. From a number of his significant and popular writings on ethical issues, we have chosen the one where Barnes offers critical comments on six pieces of research, including two on

India, of which one is by an Indian studying his own community, and the other by an Indian studying the 'other culture' in a true sense.[2] Barnes notes at the outset that authors say little about how they collected the data and distance themselves from addressing ethical problems that arose in the course of their study and later, the publication of their conclusions. If the work is received well and its reviewers point out the author's silence on ethical matters, in subsequent issues of the work, it has been noted that the author may add a section or an appendix on them, otherwise the ethical concerns are invariably pushed to the margins.

From a comparative assessment of the six cases, Barnes concludes that the range of ethical issues addressed in the study of one's own society is different from a situation of a 'great cultural gap' between the investigator and the people he investigates, between him and his paymasters (or sponsors), between him and the 'gatekeepers' (those who control access to information). Therefore, even when there is a uniform code of ethics conditioning social research, the investigators will find it difficult to comply wholly with it. Each piece of research will bring forward its own ethical problems. The researcher has to reconcile the 'pursuit of knowledge'—conclusions backed by facts and good arguments—with the short-term and long-term interests of the people under study, the sponsors of the research, the wider public and the readers of research conclusions. Each research calls for arriving at a compromise between several polarities.

Ethical and fieldwork problems that precipitate in a study of women or a lower social stratum will be different from when the focus of study is on the entire society in which some perspectives may remain in a haze or some voices may simply not be heard. We have referred to the androcentric nature of the social sciences. It has also been pointed out that many sociologists erroneously believe that all castes, albeit their position in the hierarchy, equally share the Brahminical view of the caste system, the notions of purity and pollution. There are contesting perspectives of reality, as was discussed earlier. Extending this further, here are two papers, one concerning fieldwork with women and another with an Untouchable caste. Another paper included here, by Stella Mascarenhas-Keyes, also touches upon her experiences of doing fieldwork with Goanese women.

There is no dearth of literature on women in the field that amply supports the view that the experiences of female fieldworkers are different from their male counterparts. Mead (1970: 323) notes that in most cases fieldwork is 'lonelier for women than for men'. Mascarenhas-Keyes writes that the behaviour of female fieldworkers is more closely scrutinized than that of the males. Palriwala (1991: 34) says: 'A woman fieldworker stirs up contradictory currents in the society emanating from the conjunction of her role as a researcher and her identity as a woman in a male dominated society and she has to delicately balance them.' However, many fieldworkers think that in most situations, women are able to achieve good rapport with both male and female respondents in a short period of time, 'because of their less threatening quality, and better communication skills' (Warren, 1988: 44). They are 'better able to relate to people than men are' (Nader, 1986: 114). Further, in comparison to male fieldworkers, several papers in Peggy Golde's edited volume *Women in the Field* (1986) also show that the host communities (communities of people with whom fieldwork is carried out) are more likely to protect women fieldworkers. Nader (1986: 113–14) also notes that the success of women in fieldwork is perhaps because they are 'more person-oriented,' and maybe 'participant observation is more consonant with the traditional role of women'.

The article included here for fieldwork with women by a female sociologist, Malavika Karlekar, tells us about the problems of conducting a study with women. It also shows how the theoretical concerns of the fieldworker grew over time and crystallized. Karlekar relates her ethnographic discoveries with feminist and anthropological theories. Her article is particularly illuminating because of the contrasting social situations in her studies—her fieldwork with middle-class women (in Delhi and West Bengal) is juxtaposed to her work with an underprivileged sub-caste of sweepers and scavengers.

Biographies, autobiographies, and life history accounts of successful people (the 'achievers') are available in plenty. We do not have much information on the individuals from lower strata, those who have failed to improve upon their lot. Sociologists fill this gap by providing accounts of the lives of common people—the so-called 'typical' persons of a community. James Freeman is well known for the life-history account of an Indian Untouchable known as Muli, which is comparable in its details and depth to Oscar Lewis' account (1964) of a Mexican peasant, Pablo Martinez, and Marjorie Shostak's (1981) of a !Kung woman, Nisa. Here, we have included one of Freeman's articles that explicitly deals with the process of collecting Muli's life history. This article serves a dual purpose. Not only does it provide an insight into what it means to be working with a person of an Untouchable caste, but also on the technical aspects of collecting the life history. Muli's descriptive account, in original a document of 350,000 words, was the joint creation of the narrator, Muli, the anthropologist, Freeman, and the anthropologist's assistant, a Brahmin known as Hari. Because Muli knew that the co-translator of his narration was a Brahmin, he began with lavish praise for his Brahmin patrons. But he was more candid and forthcoming when he was told that he had to open his heart, conceal nothing, however unpleasant it might be, and state the truth, lest he offended his 'new patron' (the anthropologist) who was paying him, giving him food, buying medicines and paddy for him, apart from having a moral relation with him that was a natural outcome of a long fieldwork.

Freeman's account is really moving. It depicts the fear of the respondent that he may be cheated, for he and his caste folks have continuously been cheated in the past. It also documents in unambiguous terms the annoyance of the anthropologist when the respondent is mendacious. How frustrated the fieldworker feels on learning of the intermittent illnesses of his respondent![3] The alternating phases of likes and dislikes of the investigator for his respondent are clear in Freeman's article. At one point, Freeman exasperatingly wants to fire Muli but on the advice of Hari, his co-translator, he continues working with him. One may unmistakably note here the *power* the anthropologist has on people who are placed lowly in the hierarchy—he is the employer and therefore, can discontinue the services of his *workers*. This may be compared to a situation (like in Meenakshi Thapan's case) where the sponsors of the research and the 'gatekeepers' of the institution are powerful and the sociologist is at the receiving end. While preparing Muli's life history, Freeman compares himself with the 'photographic artist', whose job is to understand the society through the lived experiences of an individual. The greatest strength of life history, Freeman writes, is that it 'transforms the lifeless abstractions of behavioural science into vivid personal accounts'.

Another set of ethical and methodological problems come in the study of one's own society. Here, two papers have been presented—one by M.N. Srinivas and the other by Stella Mascarenhas-Keyes—that explore the dimensions of what has come to be known as 'native anthropology' or 'anthropology at home' (see Peirano, 1998). Srinivas has addressed the problems in the study of one's own society in several of his publications, the best known being his article of 1966. However, his paper included here is of 1996, where he begins registering his disagreement with Edmund Leach, who says that social anthropologists do not study their society well. Srinivas admits that the study of one's own society is a difficult venture, but it can be done well or badly, like any other study. Ideally, one should begin with the study of a culture different from one's own.[4] But fieldwork in a truly alien setting requires generous funds, which developing countries will not be able to afford, therefore they are likely to encourage the studies of their own communities. In a context such as India, well known for its diversity, a village would be a 'new world' (almost like the 'other culture') for a middle-class, city-based sociologist. When an Indian sociologist works in his own society, it is not his native village or neighbourhood where he goes for field-work, rather he selects a village, ethnic group, or town in a neighbouring region. Srinivas writes: '...it [the field site] is sufficiently different to stimu-late observation yet at the same time it is familiar.'

Whether it is one's own or a different society, much depends upon the 'frame of mind' that the sociologist adopts. One should look at one's own society as a stranger would, Srinivas notes, keeping aside one's pre-conceptions and the already-acquired understanding. In this context Mascarenhas-Keyes thinks that one should keep a split between the 'native self' and the 'professional self'. Being a Goan herself, but born and brought up in Kenya and England, Mascarenhas-Keyes went back to 'her people' in Goa for fieldwork. As she had to interact with different layers of Goanese society, she decided to adopt what she terms the 'multiple-native strategy with a chameleon-like virtuosity'. The dress she wore, the language she spoke, the kind of questions she asked, all differed with respect to the stratum with which she was interacting. By becoming a 'multiple native', she was able to achieve a 'high degree of empathy and respect to each social category'.

Srinivas writes in his article that the native anthropologist has a distinct advantage over the outsider-anthropologist: he has a mastery over the lan-guage.[5] Because of this, he does not need to engage a research assistant. Against this background we may note how important Hari, Freeman's field assistant, was in the preparation of Muli's life history. There are both ad-vantages and disadvantages of keeping a research assistant. Mascarenhas-Keyes thinks that the absence of a research assistant means that there is no 'psychological buffer' between the people and the fieldworker, leading to a 'heightened exposure of self to others'. In the face of stress and anxiety, one would run to the people rather than seeking solace in the company of one's assistant, thus turning one's 'anxiety' into 'method'. In the case of Muli's life-history account, Hari, an 'insider', is made an 'outsider' by the anthropologist, James Freeman. Hari provides the anthropologist with the cultural background of his village and of his own caste particularly, also the views of his caste about the Untouchables, apart from conducting the interviews and noting down sentences in the local language.

Another important ethical problem pertains to payments (and other favours) made to respondents during fieldwork. In this context, a short paper by Srivastava has been included here. Although not examined in great detail, the issue of payments and other favours has come up in a number of research methodology and ethnographic works. Supporting the idea that intensive fieldwork can be a lifetime commitment, Bernard (1994: 164) notes that many 'fieldwork friends' have approached their anthropologists—sometimes after twenty years of fieldwork—to help their children get into college or university. Whyte (1984: 108–9) writes that he never paid his respondents and as a general practice, making payment to informants for time and information should be avoided. However, in some cases, payment needs to be made, especially when the respondent is not wealthy and is constrained to make a 'financial sacrifice' to spend time with the researcher. When an informant is interviewed for several hours, perhaps cash payment may become an expected category.

In addition, the respondents might like to be photographed and the photographs be given to them in frames (Hayden 1999: 40–41). They might like the ethnographer who has a vehicle of his/her own to transport them from place to place.[6] Or, as Gutkind (1969: 30) writes: in Nigeria people 'aggressively demanded' that he provided them with work. Geertz (2000: 34–36) eloquently describes the behaviour of one of his respondents who had often been borrowing his typewriter for his own work. Once when Geertz refused to lend his machine, the respondent was so infuriated with him that not only did he refuse to help him but also stopped greeting him in the street. And, one of the respondents jokingly suggested to Carstairs (1983: 36) that he 'should serve all the young wives and leave them a legacy of young sahibs to enrich their breed.'[7]

The Ethical Guidelines for Good Practice issued by the Association of Social Anthropologists of the Commonwealth (1987) notes under the column 'Fair Return for Assistance' that individual respondents and research participants should not be exploited and should be given 'fair return' for their help. Each investigator will have to decide the nature of the 'fair return' and the informants who should be compensated. In addition to this, Srivastava submits in his paper that those who hold expertise over specialized knowledge (such as of ethno-veterinary medicine, epic singing) deserve to be 'paid' in a mode of reciprocity that the society values. But for knowledge that is fairly general, i.e., known to everyone (for instance, kin terms), one should refrain from making any payment, for this would create problems for the investigator as well as jeopardize the chances of future investigators who come to the field with meagre funds. Anthropologists have sometimes compensated the possessors of specialized knowledge so fabulously that their life style underwent a qualitative change. One such case is of a singer, known as Parbu Bhopa, of a local Rajasthani epic (the story of Pabu-ji) whose life chances increased manifold after he received payment for the work he did for a British author, John Smith, who later published the famous work, *The Epic of Pabu-ji*.[8]

Notes

1. Yalman called the village in Sri Lanka (Ceylon), which he had studied, by a fictional name, Terutenne, and he wrote: 'Whatever the material discussed might be offensive to persons concerned, fictional names have been used' (1967: XIII). This may be contrasted to Raheja's monograph on Pahansu, a village in Uttar Pradesh. She writes (1988: 257): 'The name of the village, Pahansu, is not a pseudonym. My friends and informants in the village insisted that I use its real name, confident that what I wrote on their way of life would never be used in anyway against them.' Whether the ethnographer uses the real name or not depends a lot on the trust people have reposed in him and the topic that he has studied.

2. See Barnes (1967a, 1977, 1980, 1984, 1996).

3. Fieldworkers want to collect a maximum amount of data in the shortest period of time. After all, they have an 'avariciousness' for data, to use an appropriate word from Crapanzano (1980: 134), and when they find that their respondents are not giving them enough, they feel frustrated, looking out for more respondents.

4. Srinivas (1966: 157) writes: 'The field study of an alien society, or of a different segment of his own society, prepares the sociologist for the more sophisticated task of studying his own society or that segment of it to which he belongs.'

5. There are other advantages that a native anthropologist has: he has privileged access to those aspects of his culture which may be closed to outsiders; he is able to 'feel' more easily the subtle interrelationships between different elements of his culture; he does not encounter the artificial and imaginative behaviour that a local people show to outsiders; he does not pass through the trials and tribulations of fieldwork associated with the exasperatingly slow period of rapport establishment when people may be looking through the 'outsider' fieldworker; and his fieldwork is not really 'time-bound' as would be the case when the field site, the 'other culture', is located thousands of miles away, and he can conveniently combine intensive with extensive fieldwork.

6. See Buechler (1969), Rabinow (1977); Saberwal (1969: 56–7) offered his car to the local people as an ambulance. Robinson (1998: 26) paid a small sum to the family with which she stayed during her fieldwork in Goa.

7. Some writers also believe that fieldwork relations do not have 'just exchanges' and often the local people exploit the fieldworkers (Hatfield, Jr., 1973).

8. In one of his emails (of 7 November 2001), Smith wrote to me: 'As a result of the money he [Parbu Bhopa] received directly from me and from film-work, foreign folk-festival tours, etc., in which I involved him, he became wealthy enough to be able to give up performing the epic; none of his children have learnt it either.' (Quoted with permission.) Perhaps, the commercialization of traditional arts and folklore also signals their slow demise.

Problems in Practice

J.A. BARNES

When a book or monograph appears reporting the results of an empirical inquiry in social science, the author often says little about how he collected his data and less still about the ethical problems, if any, that he had to face during the various stages of his research. In those instances where these matters are discussed, the reader is in a better position to assess the report, to interpret its retentions and omissions and to be alert to its likely biases. One of the last phases of the process of inquiry, the impact of the published report on the sponsors, gatekeepers, scientists and, above all, the citizens whose lives are described, is likely to raise ethical questions, but these can be discussed only if and when a second edition of the report, or some supplement to it, is published. In addition to research reports there are a few collections of essays in which social scientists who have completed empirical inquiries and published their findings turn to reflect on how they went about their task, what political, ethical, and technical problems they faced, where they went wrong, and what they learnt from carrying out the research. These retrospective essays cover only a very small subset of all the empirical inquiries carried out in social science, but it is only from them, from the even smaller set of studies where the second edition of a report includes a discussion of how the first edition was received, and from the very few instances where a piece of research has become the subject of public controversy, that my examples are necessarily drawn.

The Wichita Jury Study: Research and the Public Interest

My first case is taken from this last group of sources, where there has been public controversy. The preparation of a report and the repercussions of its publication often raise crucial ethical issues but in this inquiry the ethical and political issues were so acute that the study was never completed. The inquiry came to be known as the Wichita Jury study and was carried out in 1954 as one part of a University of Chicago Jury Project. Microphones were installed in a courthouse in Wichita, in the United States, in the room in which the jury met to consider its verdict. During six civil cases, the deliberations of the jury were recorded on tape. The study was carried out by a team of researchers from the University of Chicago Law School as part of a larger inquiry into the American jury system and into various aspects of law observance and infringement. The whole inquiry was supported by a grant of four lakh dollars from the Ford Foundation. The research proposal put to the Foundation in 1952 referred in broad terms to a study of the actual operations of the jury system; there was, however, no specific reference to any intention to record real jury deliberations, though the observation, under controlled conditions, of mock trials with selected juries was mentioned (cf. Broeder 1959). Indeed, the suggestion that real jury deliberations should be secretly recorded was first made in May 1953, nine months after the project had started, by a Wichita lawyer who had been circularized about the project. This lawyer proposed that recordings should be made only in civil and not in criminal cases, and that after the tapes of the deliberations had been transcribed they should be destroyed. The transcript should be edited to remove all personal names, geographical references, and other identifying statements. The recordings were to receive no publicity until after the project had been completed.

Negotiation between the lawyer and local judges eventually led to a judge granting permission in February 1954 for recordings to be made in a limited number of cases, provided the counsel for each party agreed. The recordings were made without the knowledge and consent of the jurors. After six cases, recordings stopped.

In July 1955, for reasons for which the evidence is contradictory, an edited version of the deliberations of one of the juries was presented at the annual conference of lawyers associated with the court circuit in which the cases had been heard. The existence of the recordings thus became publically known and led to a public hearing by the Internal Security Subcommittee of the Committee on the judiciary of the United States Senate. Following the hearings, the senators concerned introduced a Bill which passed both Houses and came into effect in 1956. Under this Act, recording the deliberations of any federal jury for any purpose whatsoever is prohibited.

Both political and ethical issues are raised by this study. The political wish of the senators to discredit the sponsor, the Ford Foundation, and to discredit social science as well, led them to ignore the serious ethical issues which the inquiry brought to the surface. Following to some extent the analysis of the incident made by Vaughan (1967), we may contrast two ethical positions. On the one hand are those who argue that the citizen has an inalienable right to trial by an impartial jury, and that any violation of the privacy of a jury's deliberations puts its impartiality in jeopardy. Even though something of scientific or practical value might emerge from a scientific investigation of the operation of a jury during its deliberations, this could not outweigh the wrong done by compromising the opportunity to reach an impartial and just verdict. On the other hand are those who hold that knowledge is inherently superior to ignorance and that, therefore, there should always be unrestricted freedom of inquiry. It is socially and scientifically important to understand how the jury system works, and this understanding can be achieved only by direct investigation and observation of how it does in fact operate in real instances. The inquiry does not threaten the integrity of the jury system, for the scientist is not concerned with the actions of individual jurors but only with patterns of behaviour.

Clearly there are many intermediate ethical positions that may reasonably be taken; my own would fall well between the two I have contrasted. Nevertheless the two positions indicate the views taken respectively by the senators and by some of the social scientists involved in the study.

In terms of our model, the citizens in this example are the members of the six juries, and their gatekeepers include the judges and counsel who gave permission for the deliberations to be recorded. The sponsor is the Ford Foundation and the scientists are a group drawn from the University of Chicago Law School, led by the Dean of the School, plus other lawyers who were drawn into the study. The two senators who conducted the hearings and later promoted the legislation that prevented any repetition of the inquiry do not fit easily into the model but may perhaps be regarded as additional self-appointed gatekeepers, anxious to shut the stable door even though six horses had already bolted.

First we should note that the gap between the two contrasted ethical positions is not simply a matter of conflicting ethical axioms, or of different orderings in a shared scale of values, but depends in part on a proposition that could be tested empirically, or at least in principle. It should be possible to discover, through mock trials, whether the verdicts reached by juries who are confident that their deliberations are not being recorded differ significantly from those reached by juries who know that they are being taped. If there is no difference, the social cost of the investigation is less, whereas if there is a significant difference the cost is greater. In my view, it would then be necessary for the scientists to provide stronger evidence that the information they seek is likely to lead to some improvement in the administration of justice, and that this information cannot be obtained by other means, for example, from mock trials. Those who believe that there should be unrestricted freedom of scientific inquiry presumably would not agree with me.

The interests of the sponsor were involved in this case, both politically and ethically. The political issue, arising out of the connection, at this immediate post-McCarthy period, between the Ford Foundation and the University of Chicago, does not concern us here but we do have to consider the ethical issue of whether the Ford Foundation was misled about the kind of investigation for which it was providing ample financial support. Should the scientists conducting the project have informed the Foundation that, although it had not been envisaged in their original research proposal, they now intended to make recordings of actual jury deliberations? When they made a request for additional funds in December 1954, should they have mentioned that they had already made recordings and were currently engaged in editing them? They did not do so. In fact the Foundation approved an extension of the grant and voted additional funds just after the existence of the recordings had been made public. It seems therefore that from the viewpoint of the scientists nothing would have been lost had they taken the Foundation into their confidence about the recordings. Yet many scientists hold that it is their task, and theirs alone, to decide on the technical procedures to be followed in an inquiry and that a sponsor has no right to intervene in their area of professional expertise. But is the secret recording of a real jury carrying out its deliberations just a technical procedure of data collection?

The ethical issues salient in this incident, as Vaughan sets them out in his analysis, emerges from the falsely presumed conflict between a public interest in maintaining the integrity of the jury system and a scientific interest in discovering more about how that system operates, both as a contribution to knowledge and as the only sound basis for maintaining and improving the system. I find it interesting that Vaughan largely ignores what is surely an equally important ethical matter—whether or not the interests of the jurors were affected by the secret recordings of their deliberations. The Dean of the Law School argued during the hearings that if a juror was conscious that there was a microphone in the jury room, 'this might result in some inhibitions' (Vaughan 1967: 62). The Dean presumably meant that the secret recording was somewhat similar to those procedures of inquiry... in which deception or secrecy is an intrinsic component for if the citizen knows what is happening he will behave differently. Here there are two questions to ask. First, is it ethically or morally justifiable to allow a juror to think that he is not being recorded when in fact his words are being taped? Second, is the scientist justified in exposing the juror to the danger that what he says in the jury room, despite elaborate precautions about security of tapes and thoroughness in editing, may still become public knowledge in some more or less identifiable form? After Watergate, even the most earnest advocate of the freedom of scientific inquiry may be allowed to hesitate before answering yes to the second question, even if he can dispose of the first more easily.

One final point can be made about the Wichita Jury Study. Even if everything had gone according to plan and there had not been a premature disclosure of the existence of the tapes, the book that was envisaged as an outcome of the inquiry would necessarily have revealed to the general public that somewhere in America, at some recent point in time, recordings had been made of actual jury deliberations. I cannot believe that the edited transcripts would have been used merely as background briefing for the scientists, and that their existence could have been kept secret permanently. Yet once it became known that recordings had been made, then any potential juror could expect that the experiment might be repeated on him. Indeed, given the competitive climate of research, and the methodological stress on the merits of replication, the pressure to repeat the inquiry would have been very strong. Thus a permanent change in the jury system would have been made, provided that, as both the senators and the Dean appeared to have believed, jurors who know that they are being taped do in fact behave differently from those who are confident that they are not. The social scientists seem to me to have acted irresponsibly in not considering the consequences of this inevitable change, and also in not trying to discover empirically whether the change would be beneficial or harmful or insignificant. As it happened, the only change that occurred was legislation that precluded any further inquiry of this kind. The legislation was prompted much more by political considerations, by the desire to discredit social science, and to protect traditional American social institutions from rational scrutiny, than from any consideration of ethical issues.

The Glacier Project: The Scientist as Clinician

The next inquiry is marked by the careful attention paid by the scientists to the interests of the citizens. In the Glacier Project a factory in north-west London was studied for several years by a team of research workers belonging to the Tavistock Institute of Human Relations. Relations between scientists and sponsor in this inquiry seem not to have been important; indeed it is not clear from the published reports who the sponsor was. We are told only that the grant was administered by the (United Kingdom) Medical Research Council, a body whom the author of the main report on the project describes as 'disinterested'. The study was endorsed by the Council for Industrial Productivity.

We are, however, told a good deal about relations between scientists and citizens. At the time of the study the Institute undertook consultancy work in addition to carrying out research on its own initiative. In both types of activity it was heavily committed to combining scientific inquiry with ameliorative action, and was popularly credited with the slogan: 'No research without therapy, no therapy without research.' Much of its work was carried out on industry. Requests for advice as consultants inevitably came from the managements of industrial enterprises rather than from, say, committees of shop stewards or individual employees. Nevertheless the Institute followed a policy of refusing on principle any request for consultation that did not have the agreement of representatives of the workers as well as of management. In the Glacier case, the initial approach was made by a research team of the Institute, rather than by the Glacier management. Three months of negotiations were needed before the quick positive response from the management was matched by an expression of approval from the committee of workers' representatives. This endorsement was secured only after the Trades Union Congress and the relevant trade union confederation had both been persuaded to give the proposed research their imprimatur. These bodies were, in our terms, invoked as protective gatekeepers by the workers' representatives who were initially suspicious of what appeared to them as merely the latest gimmick of management. Once the research team and its objective had been approved by management and workers, its members carefully specified what role they should play in the factory. An agreed statement of their position was pasted on notice boards in the factory, announcing that the team would act only in an advisory or interpretative capacity; that when an individual or group suggested a topic for study by the research team, it would be looked at only with the general approval of those likely to be affected by the results; and that nothing would be done behind anyone's back, that is, that no issue would be discussed unless representatives of the group were present or had agreed to the topic being raised.

Here then we have a striking instance of social scientists taking explicit steps to protect what they perceive as being the diverse interests of the citizens they are studying. The model they tried to follow was taken from clinical medicine, with its careful delineation of what constitutes professional conduct. In their efforts to avoid appearing to favour one group in the factory rather than another and, as they put it, to prevent themselves being captured by any particular group, they limited their contacts with members of the factory to strictly formal contexts and steadfastly refused to be drawn into any extra-professional ties. They refused invitations to play tennis or attend parties, or to do anything that, as it were, might involve them as ordinary human beings interested in fellow citizens, since such interaction would necessarily conflict with their impartial research role. Thus their mode of inquiry was as far removed as possible from participant observation, where the inquirer seeks to broaden the scope of his observations by participating in the various activities carried on by the citizens.

One other important consequence of the high value placed on professional impartiality is seen in the procedure adopted for publications. The research team undertook, apparently on its own initiative, not to make any public statement about the project except in collaboration with the firm or after due consultation. The book, *The Changing Culture of a Factory*, by Elliot Jaques (1951), which was the first major publication to emerge from the study, was treated as one of these public statements. Consequently each section of the book was circulated in draft to, and discussed in detail with, each of the groups particularly concerned. The book as a whole was then vetted by the Works Council, the main meeting place of management and workers.

Thus in this project explicit and almost self-conscious attention was paid to the interests of citizens. The study exposed strikingly the basic tenet of the human relations school of management (Baritz 1960), of which the Tavistock Institute is one of the chief supporters. The researchers recognized the existence of a diversity of interests among the citizens, in this case between management and workers, and between various groups of management and workers, and took elaborate measures to institutionalize this diversity. But at the same time they acted on the premise that conflicts arising from a divergence of interest could, in the end, be resolved by some quasi-clinical procedure of discussion and working through, as if the factory were a patient stretched on the couch of a psychoanalyst. It is, of course, just for this reason that the human relations school has been attacked by Marxists and others who hold that differences of interest between economic classes are too fundamental to be resolved by discussion with a clinically-clad member of a research team.

In the Glacier study we can see how an ethical stance taken by social scientists can determine how topics are selected for inquiry, how they are studied and how they are reported on to the public. It is easier for a research institute, with an ongoing programme of research extending over the years, to publicize and maintain a distinctive ethical code than it is for a single research worker to do so. Nevertheless, individual researchers each have their own ethical and political commitments and, though these may be harder to identify, they may have just as great an effect on research procedures, and on the unstated assumptions underlying their reports.

As far as I know, no information is available about what effect, if any, publication of *The Changing Culture of a Factory* had on the Glacier factory, even though reports on further studies carried out there by the institute have appeared.

Street Corner Society: The Limits of Participation

I have chosen for my next example a study in which, as in the Glacier project, a good deal of attention was paid to the wording of the final report but where the mode of data collection differed radically from that followed in the Glacier study, and where the range of ethical issues raised was greater.

Whyte's *Street Corner Society* (1955) is a study of a slum area of Boston inhabited mainly by Italian immigrants to the United States. The study was carried out just before the Second World War, and the book that emerged from it has become a classic. Here, just as in the Glacier project, the sponsor of the research was disinterested, for the Society of Fellows of Harvard University gave Whyte a very free hand. At several points in his study Whyte, rather than his sponsor, became concerned about his association with Harvard University, particularly when he feared that he might be arrested for illegal activities. He says that he resolved that if he was caught he would not mention his connection with the university. This device of protecting the fair name of a sponsor by concealing one's link with it is unlikely to apply in most contexts.

In this study there were no gatekeepers, though initially Whyte found it difficult to establish the personal relations he sought with the residents of the slum. He eventually made contact, through a social worker attached to a settlement house, with a man called Doc, who later became his principal informant and assistant. It is interesting that the only segment of the community that subsequently objected to Whyte's report was the social workers. They considered that Whyte had betrayed them, apparently because the book makes it clear that the 'corner boys', the groups of mainly unemployed young men who form the focus of Whyte's study, were scarcely being helped at all by the activities of social workers. In his fieldwork, once having met Doc, Whyte rapidly made contacts with members of the community and ceased to be associated with the settlement house. When he left Boston after three and a half years of fieldwork, a farewell beer party was held for him, organized not by the settlement house but by a recreational club he had joined. Some writers on field methods argue that a fieldworker ought to extricate himself from a field situation by the same route as he entered it, in this way making manifest his obligation to those who have facilitated his entry and at the same time indicating that the special status he has claimed for himself as a field investigator is being terminated. Such a procedure may well be appropriate, and even unavoidable, in studying a formally structured and protected community like a factory or a tribe living on a reserve, but seems less necessary where the community is an urban slum, open to anyone, and where the investigator is a fellow citizen from a university only two or three miles away. In any case, for reasons that Whyte sets out in his retrospective account of his fieldwork, social workers in the slum are likely to have been upset by his account of their shortcomings however carefully he might have tried to negotiate his withdrawal with them (cf. Whyte 1941).

In his book, Whyte disguises the identity of the individuals whose actions are recorded, and even disguises the location of the study. Boston appears in the book as 'Eastern City'. He says that he did this to avoid embarrassment to the individuals concerned. Although some of these individuals were engaged in illegal activities which are described, it is not the exposure of these that Whyte had in mind nor, indeed, what his informants disliked. The citizens with whom Whyte discussed the text of his book disliked being described in their true colours, warts and all, even under disguised names. 'The trouble is, Bill, you caught the people with their hair down. It's a true picture, yes; but people feel it's a bit too personal.' On the other hand his main informant, Doc, told him, 'This will embarrass me, but this is the way it was, so go ahead with it.' Whyte himself, however, seems to have been more concerned that those members of a gang who ranked low in the hierarchy of prestige and power would be embarrassed to see in print how low they ranked and the sorts of difficulties they got into because of this.

In stressing embarrassment at the documentation of low status and at the publication of acts done when, as it were, the citizens were not on their best behaviour, rather than at the exposure of illegal acts, Whyte adopts an attitude of moral relativism. This attitude may be easy to take when, for example, an anthropologist studies a tribal society with a code of moral and ethical values differing dramatically from his own, but it is harder to sustain when the citizens under study are indeed legally fellow citizens and near neighbours in the same urban conurbation. Whyte takes the ethical code of the slum as unproblematic for members of the slum, yet expresses a good deal of anxiety when, as a marginal member of the slum community, he himself is led to break the law. Part of this anxiety sprung from the fear of being caught, and of involving the repute of his academic sponsors, but part arises from the moral conflict he experienced. He describes vividly how he became involved in 'repeating', that is, voting several times in an election in other voters' names. Analysing this experience, he says that he was wrong to go against his conscience. He says, 'I had to learn that, in order to be accepted by the people in a district, you do not have to do everything just as they do it.... I also had to learn that the fieldworker cannot afford to think only of learning to live with others in the field. He has to continue living with himself.'

In my view, this is sound advice, but it raises the question of the extent to which a fieldworker's own code of ethics can diverge from that held by the citizens with whom he works. In Whyte's case not everyone indulged in repeating, and those who did 'were generally looked down upon as the fellows who did the dirty work'. It would therefore have been acceptable in the eyes of the slum community for Whyte to have refused to 'repeat'. On the other hand, Whyte felt no obligation to report to the police other instances of law-breaking that he saw going on around him. Indeed, it seems that under Massachusetts law, he had no legal liability to take the initiative in doing so (Broeder 1960: 71–72, 88; cf. Brymer and Farris 1967: 312–13). Had he considered it his duty to inform the police, he could scarcely have carried out his study. More serious dilemmas of the same kind arise whenever social scientists carry out field studies of juvenile delinquency and other forms of criminal activity, and are known to possess information about crimes that are still being investigated by the police.

Whyte's carefully analysed retrospective doubts about 'repeating' and his acquiescence in other instances of law-breaking, contrast strikingly with the attitude taken by another social scientist who, while working in a tribal area of his own country, was invited to agree that a senile woman should be buried alive. Several decades after the event, he baldly reports that 'Of course I agreed', though he excused himself from being present when the deed was done (Hart 1970: 154).

These reports suggest that, whether or not fieldworkers and their professional colleagues adhere to dogmas of cultural and ethical relativism, there has to be a fairly high degree of compatibility between the ethical codes held by social scientists and the citizens they select for study.

To some extent any scientist working in the field finds himself in the position described by Beteille (1975) in the context of his contacts with Harijans in a village in Tamil Nadu in which he deliberately chose to identify himself with the resident Brahmins. His hosts and neighbours objected to Harijans coming to visit him at his house and he therefore changed his mode of contact with them. He writes of his Brahmin neighbours: '...if I was to be given access to their homes and temples—to which access was not given easily to outsiders—I could not violate their sentiments at will.' These issues are, of course, partly matters of field tactics rather than of ethics but obviously the extent to which a fieldworker can bring himself to conform to the value system of the citizens, or maybe on occasion consciously to violate the tenets of that system, depends in part on the relation between the local value system and the system of values held by the fieldworker in his capacity as a citizen. I agree with Dube (1973: 20) when he says: 'The "social scientist" and the "citizen" cannot be compartmentalized; it is not possible for a citizen having personal values to bring about an instant role-switch, immunize himself to value-virus, and start functioning as an ethically neutral social scientist.'

In the same way there must be some compatibility between the views of the scientist and his sponsor. As Orlans (1967: 5) puts it bluntly: '...if you disagree with the objectives of an agency [i.e., sponsor] don't decry the morality of its staff, but try to change their objectives and, in the interim, don't take their money.'

Whyte raises another ethical point when he discusses his role as participant observer, and adopts a viewpoint that, rather surprisingly in view of the difference in their styles of work, matches that taken by the Glacier research team. Starting from the premise that the interests of the citizens must be respected, the Glacier investigators assert that 'any action for research purposes alone without regard to the needs of the client would be regarded as a breach of the professional role of the research worker' (Wilson 1951: xv). Whyte discusses how he spoke in support of a proposal at a political meeting merely in order to get himself into closer contact with a prominent racketeer. The manoeuvre failed for, feeling sure of Whyte's support, the racketeer ignored him. Whyte says, 'Here I violated a cardinal role of participant observation. I sought actively to influence events... it had... been a violation of professional ethics. It is not fair to the people who accept the participant observer for him to seek to manipulate them to their possible disadvantage, simply in order to seek to strengthen his social position in one area of participation.' If we adopt Whyte's view, then all field experimentation is ruled out, or at least all experimentation with significant consequences. Indeed, it is difficult to reconcile Whyte's assertion that a participant observer should never attempt to influence the course of events with his own action in connection with the public bathhouse in the slum. There was no hot water and Whyte decided that something should be done to improve matters. He says, 'I tried to tell myself that I was simply testing some of the things I had learned about the structure of corner gangs, but I knew really that this was not the main purpose.' Whyte then goes on to describe, with approval, how he organized a partially successful march on Boston city hall to demand hot water. The correct analysis is, I think, not that a professional ethic requires a participant observer never to intervene—something indeed which would conflict with the whole notion of participation. It is rather that intervention that does not lead to, or does not at least responsibly aim at, some enhancement of the interests of the citizens most directly affected by the intervention is necessarily suspect. The Tavistock formulation seems sounder to me than Whyte's.

Kashmiri Pandits: Scientist or Fellow Citizen?

Another good example of respect for the interests of citizens is provided by the work of T.N. Madan among Kashmiri Pandits. He (1975) has described how as a graduate student he was taken on a fieldwork training trip entailing two weeks of inquiry among Oraons living near Ranchi. For him this was a depressing and even traumatic experience, for he was upset by the behaviour of his fellow students. He says, 'Everyone was asking the people questions about their most intimate relationships and fondest beliefs, without any regard for their feelings or convenience... I had the uncomfortable feeling that there was something indecent about such a field trip.' Later, when he went to study citizens of his own community living in Kashmir, he was expected to abide by the basic rules of social, moral, and ritual conduct prevalent among the citizens. They accepted him as a rather wayward Pandit now engaged on a special task of social inquiry, and at the same time accepted the role of informants for themselves. Although the citizens were at first unwilling to talk to him about confidential matters, he was gradually able to gather information about a wide range of topics. Nevertheless many Pandits tried to shift this role allocation and attempted to absorb Madan into village life where, in their view, he properly belonged. After a while he was asked to intervene in family disputes over property and thus gained access to information about conflicts, a topic that he had hitherto found very difficult to investigate. He says that he was then faced with the ethical problem of what use he might make of information acquired in this way, and says that some of the information in his possession he decided not to publish, even though it was relevant to the theme of his book (Madan 1965: 12). Had the village he studied been hidden under a pseudonym, and its location obscured, Madan might have had to decide how impenetrable a disguise he should employ before he could justifiably make use of the information. The ethical issue was, I think, simplified for him by the citizens' insistence that the identity of their village should not be disguised at all.

Zuni: Passing on Information

Madan was himself a Pandit and it is therefore not surprising that the Pandits he studied should judge him by their own standards. Yet any fieldworker who 'lives intimately with strangers', to use Madan's vivid expression, will sooner or later be judged by the citizens in their own terms, however alien he may be to them. Thus, for example, Berreman, an American who worked in India, reports a citizen saying to him, 'You may be a foreigner and we only poor villagers, but when we get to know you we will judge you as a man among other men: not as a foreigner' (Berreman 1972: xxvi).

One aspect of being judged as a man among other men that every fieldworker has to come to terms with, whether he is working among citizens like himself or among people with radically different customs and values, is to what extent he should pass on to other members of the community the information he collects in the course of his inquiries. This may seem to be a straightforward matter but the available evidence shows that there is no simple formula that can be applied in all cases. Some field ethnographers have stated that they endeavoured to respect the confidence placed in them by their informants and therefore considered that they should not pass on to other members of the community any information collected in the ethnographer-informant context. Some have reported that only by being seen to be reticent in this way were they able to establish reputations as men of integrity. This has been my own experience in the field (cf. Berreman 1972: xlvi–lvi). Yet T.N. Pandey, whose account of fieldwork among the Zuni of the United States shows a sensitive awareness of the ethical issues in his relations with citizens, reports that he always told the old woman in whose house he lived what he had learned from different sources. He says, 'Zuni Indians resented their favourite anthropologists working with anyone outside the narrow family circle.' They were afraid of being suspected of disclosing tribal secrets, and felt unsafe if 'their' anthropologist went to talk to someone who might spread a rumour that they had done so. Therefore when Pandey talked to someone with whom his hosts were not on good terms, he was often asked on his return what had been said about them (Pandey 1975: 200, 210). The Zuni are well known for their highly developed sense of privacy, and for their sharp dichotomization of information into public and secret, and it would seem that Pandey was expected not to keep information secret from his hosts. Nevertheless, I find it surprising to learn that the topics in which Pandey was interested were factionalism and ingroup hostility, and attitudes towards envy, gossip, slander, and hate. Presumably it was information bearing on these topics that he recapitulated to his hostess, apparently on his own initiative. We may perhaps infer that at least in those areas of discourse with which Pandey was concerned, Zuni draw a socio-centred rather than an ego-centred dividing line between public and secret topics. Although the sanctions against disclosure of group secrets to non-members are stricter among the Zuni than in many other societies, in the public domain there is freedom to collect information for all approved inquirers.

But, however the notions of privacy, secrecy, and publicity may be defined and delimited in particular cultures, the onward transmission of information collected in the course of fieldwork is likely always to raise questions of ethics, whatever the culture and whether the information concerns illegal activities, political manoeuvres, marital intrigues, idle gossip, or even issues that are fully public knowledge. The social scientist, even if he shelters behind a clinical white coat as in the Glacier case, cannot be simply a sink or sponge, soaking up information and never transmitting any. He must have something to offer in return. Presumably in all cultures some kinds of information are public enough to be passed on with impunity. In the case of a scientist studying a community far removed from his own, he is the potential source of information about his own society that may be fresh and interesting to the citizens. I think that it is legitimate to avoid expatiating in this context on those aspects of one's own society that may be intellectually incomprehensible or morally offensive to the citizens, concerned—for example, the contemporary indifference to marriage in many Western societies. Yet it seems to me both unnecessary and wrong to convey false information, as has sometimes been done. For example, Bateson (1958: 232) explained a lunar eclipse, to an informant who had told him that the sun was a cannibal, by ascribing the redness of the moon to blood in the sun's excrement which had come between the earth and the moon.

Hindus of the Himalayas: Telling All or Only Some?

In my last example I take up the topic of deception with reference to inquiries carried out in the field rather than in the morally specialized environment of a psychological laboratory. In what circumstances and to what extent may a scientist mislead the citizens as to what he is really doing when he interacts with them?

This question arises inescapably where deception is achieved by some positive misleading act as in many laboratory experiments, but is also present, if not so salient, when the deception takes the form of an act of omission. Although the scientist may reasonably be expected to convey to the citizens his broad research goals, does he have to specify in detail what hypotheses he seeks to test, or what particular topics he would like to concentrate upon? He must be reasonably honest with the citizens; must he be absolutely honest? Positive acts of deception occur typically in psychological research, whereas in the course of intensive and extended field research typical of social anthropology and sociology, the scientists is more likely to find himself misleading the citizens by remaining silent about the main focus of his research interests. This happens not merely because of the intellectual or cognitive gap between him and them; it also arises particularly during that first traumatic period at the beginning of a field study, when the incoming scientist is still perceived as a potentially dangerous stranger and while the citizens are still very curious to discover whether he is a spy, missionary, policeman, or merely a harmless academic. To state bluntly at this early stage in the encounter that he has come to study, say, the mechanisms of factionalism, the sanctions against rate-busting, the incidence of adultery, or the extent of religious heterodoxy may be just as disastrous, from the point of view of achieving the objectives of the research, as it is to explain in advance the true aim of psychological tests. How honest, then, does the scientist have to be with the citizens?

The most perceptive analysis of this ethical question that I have seen is that provided by Berreman who, in effect, argues that the scientist does not need to be more open and honest with the citizens than they are with one another and with him. His analysis is based on the distinction made by Goffman (1969: 92–122) between back and front regions of social space. The back region is where the social actors prepare themselves in secret for the public performances they enact in the front region. The sociologist is, as Srinivas (1966: 156) says, 'like a novelist who must of necessity get under the skin of the different characters he is writing about'. Yet whereas he tries to find out what is really going on behind the scenes in the back region, the citizens are, at least initially, anxious that he should observe them only on the public performances of their social roles. In Whyte's terms, they don't like being seen with their hair down. In Berreman's view, the scientist, or the research team to which he belongs, likewise divide their activities between front and back regions. Writing of his work as an anthropologist in Uttar Pradesh, he says, 'the ethnographer will be presenting himself in certain ways to his informants during the research and concealing other aspects of himself from them. They will be doing the same. This is inherent in all social interaction'. Given this interpretation of what happens in practice, he says, 'I believe it to be ethically unnecessary and methodologically unsound to make known his specific hypotheses and in many cases his area of interest. To take his informants into his confidence regarding these may well preclude the possibility of acquiring much information essential to the main goal of understanding their way of life' (Berreman 1972: xxxiv). In Berreman's case one of his main foci of interest was intercaste relations, yet his initial presentation of his interests to the citizens was in terms of America's need to learn more about India following her achievement of independence, and of the increasing role that the inhabitants of the Himalayan region would play in the independent nation (ibid.: xxv).

I accept the validity of Berreman's model of social interaction but I think that he does not entirely settle the ethical question. Indeed, he seems to put forward his answer as appropriate merely in those contexts, like the one in which he worked, where ascription, i.e., caste membership by birth, is the only criterion for full acceptance in the society. He leaves unstated whether or not his normative pronouncement applies to other situations where the relation between scientist and citizens is not constrained in this way. My own view is that the extent to which the scientist should take the citizens into his confidence depends at any time on the extent to which he has established relations of mutual trust and sympathy with them, and on the degree of congruence between their cognitive and affective views of the world and his. It may be harmless enough to begin an inquiry into some controversial topic like wife-swapping or illegal distilling by professing to be interested only in a general understanding of how the citizens live. Nevertheless the scientist should try to communicate to the citizens a deeper and constructive appreciation of what his research is really aimed at. The sooner he does this the better, and the more likely that trouble will be avoided when he publishes his report on the research.

Yet perhaps this pious advice is unnecessary. Berreman's book describes how Brahmins and Rajputs sacrifice animals, eat meat, drink alcohol, ignore the great Hindu gods, marry widows, marry across caste lines, are polygynous and polyandrous, and sell women to men from the plains (ibid.: xxxviii–xxxix). Despite this catalogue of enormities, his book was apparently perceived by the citizens as not disparaging their mountain village, and its publication did not result in any attention being paid to their village by policeman, government agents, or missionaries. Accordingly, when Berreman returned ten years later, they were glad to welcome him back (ibid.: 367). Hence it appears that not only was it tactically expedient for Berreman to remain initially silent about his research objectives, but that no deleterious consequences for the citizens or for him resulted from his silence. Thus again we see that the distinctive features of a field situation may play havoc with standardized ethical prescriptions.

Conclusions

The examples used in this [paper] do not display the full range of ethical issues that arise in connection with empirical inquiry in social science. In particular little has been said about relations with sponsors and gatekeepers, and about the consequences of publication. But these examples, which, as we should expect, all come from pluralist societies, should be sufficient to give some indication of how wide this range is. Though I have indicated some of the likely ethical questions, I have done little to supply correct answers to them. Indeed it should be clear that these issues cannot be resolved easily by reference to any detailed standard code. Part of the difficulty that many professional bodies have experienced in trying to draw up a code of ethics (cf. Unnithan et al. 1967: 185–89) springs from the diversity of ethical positions held by their members, but part comes from the great variety of social and cultural contexts in which empirical research is carried out. The counsels of perfection that may be appropriate and applicable when a social scientist studies citizens similar to himself, with the same values and assumptions, and similarly placed in relation to power and resources, may be inappropriate and inapplicable when there is a great cultural gap between the parties or where there is a great disparity, one way or the other, between them in terms of power to articulate and defend their interests. In each case we can go back to first principles and endeavour to see what extent the commitment to the pursuit of knowledge, which is the diacritical mark of the scientist, can be reconciled with the short-term and long-term interests of the sponsors, citizens, and the wider public who may benefit or be harmed by the outcome of the inquiry.

Search for Women's Voices: Reflections on Fieldwork, 1968–93

MALAVIKA KARLEKAR

I

I shall attempt to understand and analyse what happens to a fieldworker before, during, and after fieldwork. I have, to date, completed fieldwork for four different studies, three of them focusing on women. What I find particularly interesting at both personal and intellectual levels is that my perceptions of women and of what is of concern to them changed radically between 1968 and 1992. Today, when in the field, I ask for a lot more directly as well as indirectly, and try to see beneath the apparent much more than I did in the early years. In part, of course, this is due to the process of 'growing up' and maturing in the disciplines as well as in a fast changing world. Equally importantly, this development owes much to the emergence of women's studies and the women's movement. Their impact on individual lives as well as on collective judgements has not been inconsequential. Here, I shall try a rather complex exercise of relating changes in my orientation to developments in theory. In order to do so I shall trace briefly these developments viewed in the context of my work.

II

When in 1968 I enrolled for an M. Litt. Degree at the Department of Sociology, Delhi School of Economics, I spent considerable time training myself in research methods; an Oxford degree in philosophy, politics, and economics with two special papers in sociology had not much on methodology and research techniques. My specialization in the sociology of education oriented me towards a research topic which would reflect my interest. In those days there was a growing body of literature on the sociology of professions, the school as an institution, socialization processes, education as an agent of mobility, and so on. I read Myrdal and Klein on working women and their dual roles (Klein 1965; Myrdal and Klein 1956), and in keeping with the current emphasis on role theory decided to study women school teachers and their commitment to a profession and to professionalism [Karlekar 1970; 1975]. Based on a study of fifty-six teachers in both government and private schools in Delhi I concluded that only a few in my sample were 'positively motivated' towards teaching. Respectablility of the occupation was more important than job satisfaction. Further, 'investigations into the background of those committed to teaching show that they come from the economically privileged strata of society' (Karlekar 1975: 53).

I noted that 'more than 30 per cent of the sample chose teaching because they perceived it as a respectable occupation for educated women' (ibid.: 55). Thus, social respectability—which meant working in the safe environment of the school, mostly with women colleagues, going to work by a school or chartered bus, and limited working hours—were important factors in determining choice of profession. I found that the economic motive was very important for over a third of the sample. While for a quarter, their entire income was spent on household expenses, a majority of the rest said that their earnings helped improve the general standard of living of their families. As over 90 per cent were first-generation women earners, I analysed in some detail the social change brought by increasing female employment.

My thesis was an analysis of growing employment among middle-class women, contrasts between government and private jobs, and motivations for working outside the home. The emphasis was primarily on professionalism and then on women as a category of analysis. Thus, I concluded, women in private schools who did not need to work for a wage were more professionally committed and involved with their students. Most of those in government schools, on the other hand, did not think that being a teacher meant a special responsibility; in fact, as their students often came from underprivileged sections of society, middle-class school teachers were keen on maintaining a distance from them. A few also felt that a lower-caste background meant a limited capacity to learn.

What I did not do was to question too closely or enter into heated discussions on any issue, be it determinants of student capabilities, gender differences in achievement, parental roles, or relations with the school administration. Nevertheless, I observed interactions with students, parents, and the administration and discussed these in the thesis. Nor did I question respondents on role-sharing at home—what is now known as the sexual division of labour—and whether they found the dual, if not triple, burden situation onerous. I remember myself as an eager young woman, anxious to succeed and to please. But I also remember being aware of my privileged position: I had a good education, a secure and well-placed family background, and above all, the freedom to make choices and ask questions of myself and of my family. I was acutely conscious of these factors, which I am sure also held me back from questioning too intensely those with few choices. On the other hand, I listened carefully to the teachers' observations and value judgements and noted them down, almost verbatim. These were then included as long quotations in the text. The women's voices came through clearly here and in the case studies of eight teachers.

I enrolled for a Ph.D. in 1971 but did not think of expanding my M. Litt. dissertation, a not uncommon option for many doctoral theses. In part my decision was governed by the fact that marriage took me to Kolkata and to a different social and political world. Also, I was clearly not sufficiently interested in women teachers or professionalism among women to pursue the theme in West Bengal. Work on my thesis introduced me to a completely different life situation, that of *realpolitik* violence, coping strategies, both fair and foul. I studied the Chhatra Parishad, a student association affiliated to the Congress Party, and its role in the party's resuscitation between 1970 and 1972. I found most useful F.G. Bailey's *Stratagems and Spoils* and William Foote Whyte's *Street Corner Society*. Bailey's typification of 'public face' and 'private wisdom' were extremely appropriate in trying to understand individual and group behaviour. Whyte's fascinating work on street corner boys in Cornerville provided many insights into methods of observation, both participant and non-participant.

I remember wondering why the Chhatra Parishad did not have more women cadre or leaders. In fact, of my eighty-one respondents only two were women. While one of these girls was included as a case study, and hence interviewed in detail, I was more concerned with her political socialization or if she was trying to get other women friends to join the Chhatra Parishad. In other words, as with M. Litt. dissertation, my interest was with social change and mobility. Though the M. Litt. had an all-women sample, the emphasis was clearly on the growth of a profession. For my Ph.D. I was fascinated by the evolution of a movement, the creation of first-generation leaders and their socialization. Both theses then straddled current interests of the time in agents of mobility, overall change and political development; collective processes were of greater importance than individual dilemmas.

A common thread, however, which linked my later work with these two theses was my consistent emphasis on case studies, long quotations, and detailed descriptions of the physical environment. Clearly, through all my fieldwork experiences, how I should represent another's life situation, opinions, and views was a cause of great concern and as far as possible, I was being 'true' to them. This was of course during the high point of positivism and structural functionalism in Indian sociology, when it seemed enough to be aware of one's role as an outsider, an interpreter, while doing an academically sound piece of research. Ideas on plurivocality, polyphony, the neo-imperialism of the fieldworker, and so on, had yet to assault the post-Independence Indian in the field.

III

In 1974, the report by the Committee on the Status of Women in India, *Towards Equality*, was published. Its many startling findings indicated the need for much greater investigation into the issues before women. Accordingly, the Indian Council of Social Science Research funded several studies, many of which were available in mimeo form by 1979. The shift in emphasis to case studies and the micro level was significant. By 1975 I had developed a certain sensitivity to the inequalities in Indian society: some interviews in the early 1970s with members of the scheduled castes (mainly men) made me acutely aware of the need to study the roots of oppression and inequality. I also acknowledged the gender dimensions of this inequality. Thus I applied for an ICSSR fellowship to work on the socio-economic status of *balmiki* women, a sub-caste of the north Indian caste of *bhangis*, or sweepers and scavengers.

Balmiki women are underprivileged *vis-à-vis* their menfolk, and further, as members of a stigmatized group they share with other caste fellows a general sense of discrimination and rejection. Apart from a socio-economic profile of eighty women, I hoped to examine two generalizations about third-world working-class women which had by then started appearing with some regularity in western literature. First, it was felt that the spread of mechanization would prove a threat to the employment of women of the labouring classes; second, deprived of an income and relative economic independence, women's position and status would deteriorate even further. While not wholly without basis, nonetheless I felt that these propositions were considerably constrained by cultural perspectives on the meaning of work, employment, independence, and so on.

The balmikis are substantially affected by the urbanization. Together with other categories of the urban poor, they live dispersed in the various slum and tenement colonies of the capital. When I chose to study Sau Quarters, a west-Delhi colony constructed originally by the Delhi Municipal Corporation for its sweepers, I was aware of some of the problems I was likely to encounter. My fieldwork came in the wake of the Congress government's sterilization drive as well as its slum demolition campaign. Consequently, it would have been impossible for me to talk to the women before my bona fides had been established; this was achieved through my introduction to an important informant in the area by a local social worker. After an initial trip to the field with this lady, I subsequently visited Sau Quarters with my two research assistants. It was not too difficult to allay the women's suspicions about our motives, and we soon found that our respondents were more than willing to talk to us.

A limited sample has its disadvantages but some advantages as well. We found that with fewer people it was easier for us to extend our conversations beyond the framework of the formal interview schedule. More than merely filling up a form, my primary aim was to initiate a dialogue with the women involving perceptions of themselves and their situation. I had already learned that the respondent has to be understood within his or her own frame of reference and not that of the investigator. At times, it is not easy to accept widely differing views and attitudes, and the fieldworker is tempted to intervene. However, in 1975 I believed that if the danger of 'taking sides' is internalized, it was possible to reduce intervention to a minimum. To overcome some of these problems, my research assistants and I encouraged respondents to speak at length on a range of subjects. Wherever relevant, these views were incorporated in the text as instances of attitudes and views. Finally, suggestions on the possible nature of slum reform were based on extended conversations with the women. It was significant that several conventional strategies were rejected as being irrelevant to 'the lives of us poor women'. My formal fieldwork techniques remained the same as those used in 1968; yet, now I was asking a few more questions on what was soon to gain currency as the sexual division of labour and women's multiple roles.

On the basis of my data, primary as well as secondary, I found that rather than being deprived of employment, poor women in certain caste- and occupation-based jobs remain in traditional fields of employment, while their men tend to move to new opportunities brought about by development of mechanization. When traditional jobs become unavailable due to a number of factors, women are forced to seek employment in other areas which may have no relationship with their original expertise. The machine can rarely succeed in keeping working-class women unemployed. The sample of balmiki women corroborated these trends; further, it was clear that the notion of economic independence, popular among western feminists as a panacea for gender inequality, was severely class-bound, being of relevance only to a small minority of upper-middle-class women, who were in a position to retain control over their earnings. At the end of my fieldwork, I felt that I had enough material for a study of a section of working-class women, which included questioning certain prevailing views about them, and in 1982, *Poverty and Women's Work—A Study of Sweeper Women in Delhi* was published.

What, however, did not come through in my work was the dilemma I faced while in the field and the consequent mental and conceptual adjustments I had to hastily perform. It is too many years down the road for me to try and recollect whether I faced similar problems in my earlier fieldwork situations: in retrospect, I feel that it was only during the balmiki study that I was beset by a sense of unease about my role. Of course, by this time, women's studies was making its early beginnings, probing the conceptual and methodological assumptions of the social sciences. Problems arose primarily because of my construction of a different reality on the basis of certain presuppositions; though I had pre-tested my interview schedule, obviously what I considered relevant and important, were not always similarly viewed by my respondents. Here I shall mention only a few instances from which it became clear to me that we were operating on different wavelengths. To start with, there was a basic difference of opinion on what was meant by a job or *naukri*: when I spoke to the fifty-eight respondents in private employment, most said that they did not have a job or naukri. As I persisted, it became clear that by naukri they meant employment in the municipal corporation, offices, schools, and hospitals. A naukri had definite implications and implied work focused around a single location, permanent or semi-permanent in nature, higher and more stable wages, and a fairly institutionalized employer-employee relationship. While to me both categories of women were employed because they worked for a salary, for my respondents there was a vital difference between a naukri and, as they called it, 'privatee'. Underlying this distinction was the association of a naukri with security of tenure as well as access to certain safeguards, both of which were of considerable importance to women living on the verge of poverty. In addition, a naukri had much more status than '*aisey he, kaam kartey hain*' (I just do some kind of work), and it was the aim of privately employed women to move to naukris.

Another important area of enquiry in which I found myself having to rethink my preconceived ideas related to decision-making. Women's studies scholars had started—and of course continue—to be greatly interested in this sphere of women's lives, as they feel that an analysis of it gives a good understanding of the division of responsibility within the family. I wanted to have answers to questions such as when women were equal contributors with men to the family kitty, did they have an equal say in decision-making? What were the areas in which their wives prevailed? However, the answers I got belied a few of my previously held notions. The women in my sample had a marginal role in decision-making, and were held primarily responsible for keeping the hearth going. While they may have been occasionally consulted on marriage negotiations, they had practically no role in major financial decisions such as whether to buy a bicycle, land in the village or take a loan. It may of course be argued that across classes, decision-making is by and large a male domain. However, in this case, I had assumed that the answers may be somewhat different because women contributed substantially to the family income. My research indicated that there was in fact no correlation between the degree of economic contribution and decision-making.

I had also assumed that there was likely to be some interest in education. While only a third of the daughters were in school, more than twice the number of boys were being educated; generationally, this reflected a vast improvement in enrolment. What I was not altogether prepared for, however, were the sardonic comments of many mothers on what they expected from school or in fact why they were educating their children. Caste discrimination and a feeling that middle-class upper-caste teachers would not help their children made many cynical about the likely long-term benefits of education. Most mothers felt that it would have been more useful if their sons were able to have access to some form of job-oriented training rather than waste their time in school. Schooling was viewed as a convenience, not as a likely solution to a life of poverty. The only reason why girls were sent to school was to enable them to communicate with their families after marriage. As Shyamo wryly remarked, 'at least if my daughter's being beaten to death she'll be able to write and tell us'. Mothers scoffed at the suggestion that with a school education their daughters might have access to occupations other than sweeping. Similarly, they made it amply clear that my questions on leisure-time activities as well as the assumption that they their visited natal homes regularly were incredibly naïve.

A further issue brought home to me poignantly how middle-class notions of what the poor require are based on inadequate and incorrect perceptions of their needs and expectations. The women were extremely agitated over the slum demolition plan and did not find the government's reason of providing better living conditions in any way convincing. It meant giving up existing jobs, taking children out of school, and forming new networks. They also resented the idea of being evicted from their homes. As Rani said to me, *'Bibiji, ghar chodna aap ko kaisa lagtha? Aap hamara dukh kya samjhenge!'* (Bibiji, how would you like leaving your home? What will you understand of our suffering?) Domestic violence, drunkenness among the menfolk and their illicit relationships were accepted as a matter of course. Unless things got really out of control, these were clearly not areas where intervention by outside agencies like the ubiquitous social workers would be appreciated. I asked no detailed questions on these sensitive issues, a fact which I find interesting as well as intriguing—two decades down the road. In part, my rectitude in these areas was on the advice of the social worker; in part also, it is clear to me today that I did not really understand the need to study domestic violence—or indeed appreciate the everydayness of its incidence.

When, at the end of fieldwork I told my respondents that they had been of considerable help to me, Shanta, who had become quite a friend, said, *'Bibiji, aap to apni kitab likhengey, pur hamara kya hoga?'* (Bibiji, you will write your book, but what will happen to us?) I had no honest answer to give her, just as I had not really been able to deal with the persistent question of many women: *'Bibiji, hamey issay kya milega? (Bibiji, what will we get out of this?)* Today I realize that my dilemma is of course not something unique; many a fieldworker has been faced with similar situations where questions of one's role keep cropping up. Such questions inevitably set up a chain of thought, a process of introspection: is one in fact exploiting one's respondents by taking up their time? Does not the process of questioning sooner or later sow the seeds of doubt in the minds of one's informants? For instance, how did my constant harping on the issue of how much work men actually did within the home affect women who had internalized exploitation as their fate? Or for that matter, what impact did my surprise at the fact of rare visits to the natal home have on an unhappy girl longing for a bit of motherly love? I rarely allowed myself to think too much about these uncomfortable questions during my visits to the colony.

When I sat down to write my report, however, many images continued to flit through my mind. I felt Bimla's anguish and Mayavati's cynicism regarding education as well as little Sharada's excitement as she prepared for a longed-for day in school. I was not always sure of how I should write about the lives of the women I had spent days with. While I knew any act of telling to be interpretative in nature, I was nonetheless anxious to be as 'true' to my respondent's reality as was possible. I also knew that when those under study are physically and mentally subjugated by society and by men, the moral overtones of a fieldworker's intervention and probing have implications of a different order. Inadvertently, one may be initiating a process of self-analysis, of consciousness-raising, among a group which has little hope of escaping from the bondage of daily life. The resultant frustration and anger are in this case the direct responsibility of the fieldworker, who becomes an agent of exploitation. As already described, my intellectual apparatus—be it categories of analysis, vocabulary, as well as questions which I regarded as important, and so on—were, in a few situations, not relevant. Consequently, my pre-fieldwork construction of what a typical oppressed balmiki woman was like had to be constantly amended; the conversion of experience into expression was not an easy process. I took the easy uncomplicated way out and wrote a monograph on the women I had studied. Not unexpectedly, it did not capture much conflict or the sense of latent aggression and power inherent in my role as privileged researcher.

IV

This study convinced me of the growing validity of women's studies in understanding inequality (Karlekar 1982a). It also made me aware of my inability to face the field again for a while. A number of reasons, one of which was a definite nagging feeling that I could not enter into another exploitative relationship, took me to a completely different area of study. As a middle-class Bengali woman with an interest in her roots, I was curious to find what role education had played in the lives of early pioneers, that is, nineteenth-century women. I felt that archival research in this area would help me to understand better the socio-historical genesis of unequal gender relations. For this, as the point of view of historians and social chroniclers was clearly not enough, I decided to read women's commentaries on their lives and times.

I was now moving into a field of another kind: that I had to read, analyse, and interpret the words of others meant once more a dialogic relationship, this time with the text. While writing my first draft I was acutely aware of the fact that I was treading on difficult terrain. Nonetheless, I persisted in a manner which I felt best represented my understanding of the texts. At the same time, I experienced several moments when I wondered whether I was not imposing my late-twentieth-century views on a group of women who no longer defend themselves. While contemporary developments in literary criticism which speak of 'an interpretation of work... to be an account of what happens to the reader' (Poovey 1988) are attractive, they are also enchanting. They put the onus of representation in writing and reading on the individual and not on the originator of the work, be it speech, a folk tale, or a book. How then could I be sure that my understanding was more valid than that of my neighbour? How could the very real issue of multiple readings and interpretations and perhaps subsequent chaos be tackled? I concluded that how I read a text was shaped by class, gender, and educational background. After all, I do belong to a distinct intellectual tradition and am a member of what Stanley Fish (1980) has called an 'interpretive community'. At some point then, I came to terms with myself and decided to go ahead and write. I decided that I was justified in choosing *a* framework rather than *the* framework (Stivers 1993). In fact, I had by then started thinking some more about the '*the* framework' worldview and its limitations. That *Voices from Within* emerged out of two very different drafts is proof enough of the fact that it has not been easy to work out where one belonged.

I concluded that advocacy of women's education in the last century had two aims: first, to inculcate in upper- and middle-class Bengali society and its women suitable Victorian values; and second, it was the beginning of a process by which women were to be introduced to the male world of formalized learning. For many women who emerged from the confines of the female world, their first teachers were their fathers, brothers, and husbands. Taking advantage of their new experience, Bengali women started writing about themselves as well as noting down their responses to the changing environment. In many cases, their points of view were quite different from those of men, or the ideas put forth of them by men. Though the middle class educated Bengali 'bhadramahila', or gentlewoman, was in absolute terms privileged, she was clearly underprivileged *vis-a-vis* the *bhadralok*, or gentleman. In part, her inferior position arose because of her sex; however, of equal importance was the subordinate role assigned to her within the family. Further, with the incorporation of women in the man's world of learning, where they are denied access to equal years of schooling and the same curriculum, inequality at home was matched by inequality in the public sphere. In most accounts written of the period, women are mentioned fleetingly, if at all, the assumption being that they benefited greatly from the changes being introduced in their lives. Though privileged in comparison to the majority of women, the bhadramahila was bhadralok's, or genteel society's, subaltern.

With growing industrialization and a cut-throat market economy it suited the British middle class to reinforce, through various sources, the image of the female homemaker *par excellence*. By the middle of the nineteenth-century, the Bengali middle class too fast realized the merit of a sympathetic home environment based on the willing cooperation of its women. In order to create this compliant and understanding woman and wean her away from the *antahpur* or culture of the women's world, it was essential for her to have the right kind of education. Thus, learning and writing for women were primarily introduced for the creation of accomplished house-wives and daughters. The word was viewed as an instrument of power and control over women and their development within the parameters of a prescribed model. However, though men may have been the 'owners' of what they wrote, they could neither control interpretations of their work or fully monitor women's access to and use of literacy. While most women were duly grateful for being granted access (however limited) to the pre-serve of male power, a few used their skills to express their resentment against prevailing social injustices. They wrote novels, essays, as well as about themselves, providing valuable insights into women's lives. The articulation of such views often acted as a catharsis, triggered by the unequal encounter between the sexes and between cultures.

Autobiographical writing is a literary genre of considerable importance to students of literature as well as to society. In recent years there has been a growing interest in women's autobiographies, which only tell stories of individual lives but also reflect on society. An autobiography is read differently by a literary critic who may look more keenly at the authorial voice and its implications, the structure of the text, and so on. As a social scientist, I looked at women's writings from the point of view of what I could glean about processes of learning, the evolution of relationships, the exercise of power and authority, and so on. My data helped me understand a particular phase in the evolution of Bengali society. The desire as well as the ability to express oneself often coincides with a specific phase in the life cycle when the sense of personal identity and awareness of the self is heightened. Some autobiographies more than others give expression to the feelings and personalized responses of the authors to a particular situation or course of events; others are primarily a chronicle of events.

Whatever its aim, writing about oneself results in soul-searching, a quest for the right phrase, the 'correct' sentences, and so on. For many Bengali women who felt the urge to write or talk about themselves, the desire came at a time when external factors were affecting family life; old tensions were giving way to new ones as many traditional relationships started changing, or they simply had more time, as in widowhood and old age. In particular, with access to learning and writing women started examining hierarchical family relations and their own roles. They were helped by an ambience which increasingly stressed the need for social, physical, and occupational mobility. The East India Company, and later, the British empire, provided substantial scope for ambitious and adventurous men who wanted to be freed of the feudal frame of reference and complex family obligations.

In some cases, and this is particularly true of the autobiographical writings of women, the act of putting pen to paper or recounting one's experiences is like a cry of anguish against a life of oppression. For instance, the dictated life of Sharadasundari Debi, mother of the eminent social reformer, Keshub Chander Sen, is a long and sad narration of ill-treatment by her in-laws after her widowhood at the age of nineteen. (Sharadasundari Debi 1881). I found that between 1876 and the 1970s, there is a record of at least fifty autobiographies and autobiographical sketches having been written by Bengali women. The earliest was by Rassundari Debi, the wife of an East Bengal zamindar, who was born in 1811; unlike many of those who followed her, the self-taught Rassundari received little encouragement from her family, and recounted how she used to hide pages, removed from her son's books, within the folds of her sari. Rassundari wrote her autobiography in two parts: the earlier part, which was written in the late 1870s, gives a more comprehensive account of her life. She felt strongly about being denied education and reflected, 'women were indeed unfortunate, and could be counted as being like animals'. But 'my mind would not accept this, and it was always restless with the urge to learn'. Rassundari evoked the image of a strong-minded woman who was not afraid to question existing unequal gender relations (Rassundari Debi 1881). She anticipated in many ways the questions of present-day feminist researchers, for the desire to learn also implies the desire to be heard— as well as the right to reject.

V

To hear those voices and that protest, the methodological tools of literary and autobiographical analysis become vital. For me it is particularly interesting that women's studies has much to share with fieldwork-based traditions in sociology and social anthropology. As already mentioned notions of objectivity versus subjectivity, of taking sides and yet trying to remain 'intact', and ultimately, questions on the space occupied by the fieldworker, are those which have concerned sociologists and social anthropologists for some decades now. In a provocative essay, James Clifford (1992) brings home relentlessly the inherent contradictions of contemporary ethnography: the flirting between cultures, the many masks facilitated by the jet age which raise questions of boundary/local, insider/outsider, and articulation. Clifford goes on to describe convincingly the dilemma of those studying diasporic communities. He asks, who is the true Cambodian? What of the boat people? How is an immigrant woman's identity transformed? Above all, who is to define this identity?

Such doubts are of great interest to feminist scholars who are well aware of their, at times, ambivalent position. They acquire particular poignancy for women from the south. The emphasis of women's studies on reflexivity, on knowledge as shared experience, finds an echo in contemporary theoretical traditions, particularly post-modernism and post-structuralism. Critics of the reigning canons in western culture point to the dominance of the enlightenment and universalizing principles, objectivity and positivism. These belong to 'a specific historical time and geographic region... associated with certain political baggage' (Nicholson 1990: 4) such as the legitimacy of science, the distinction between high art and mass culture, and so on.

Post-modernism believes that legitimacy—and hence discourse—is plural, and therefore local. At the same time, the inherent danger of shifting foci and many legitimations implies that the truth lies in no fixed place— or rather it is in many places. There are many truths, to be created and recreated by the reader and the text, the fieldworker and the observed, and so on. Women's studies scholars find attractive the belief that the observer and the observed, the teacher and the taught, the reader and the text, collaborate in the act of interpretation and creation. A dialogue and a mutuality characterize these relationships; but, caution anthropologists, these must be within the parameters of location and context. A recognition of different locations and of different power matrices does not mean a denial of location altogether. Feminist anthropologists Marilyn Strathern, Micaela di Leonardo, and Susan Gal point to the lack of 'parity between the authorship of the anthropologist and the informant' (Strathern 1987: 281). In other words, my authorship of a piece of writing is the product of my specific context, my background, my experience.

While writing about balmiki women's lives I was aware that the quest for common creations often overlooks the fact that the one initiating the processes is often a woman from an advantaged social, educational, and sometimes racial background. She comes with a specific intellectual and social baggage which may hinder her best attempts at incorporating 'the other' into the discourse. For, her world-view, categories of analysis, dialogic tools, modes of translation are determined by her culture and training. Thus the new reality—or the one the researcher/teacher hopes to have created through the involved participation of her respondents/students—may in fact reflect a privileged view, her understanding of another's world. While this dilemma characterizes any situation where one attempts to represent the other, it is particularly significant when a vast divide separates those in an essentially hierarchical relationship. This dilemma need not be limited to contexts of first-world researcher and third-world researcher alone. Equally, the differences and inequalities within what is characterized loosely as a culture can pose a moral dilemma for the one involved in the act of creating a new reality. This is precisely what I faced when I wrote about balmiki women while trying to blot out their searching questions on my role, my inquisitiveness and the authority which went with my socio-economic background.

Recently, in an interesting interface with anthropologist Clifford Geertz, writer Ngugi Wa Thiong'o, and others, Jack Goody was concerned with the loss of context and 'a wider frame' (Goody 1992). In short, not only is not enough thought given to the situated observer and where she has come from, but also giving space to essentialism and the narrowly local can ultimately be limiting and inward-looking. In some senses, these are inevitable developments of an intellectual freedom of a very special kind. At the same time, it is necessary to be aware of the dangers of extreme relativism. Here anthropologist Edward Bruner's idea of 'a basic story' is useful. When read in conjunction with the belief in many stories, and alternative truths, it helps the researcher to situate herself better. Bruner (1983: 5) points out that each time a story is read, referred to, or studied, 'it is placed in a particular context and given meaning by a reader.' However, this does not get away from the fact that there is a basic story which has to be understood. For, if interpretation is of the essence, it is dependent on the existence of a story. No anthropologist will quibble over the issue that certain kinds of data such as factual information on respondents or their milieu such as age, household size, children in school, number of castewise households, and so on will appear the same to all investigators: they are the backbone of the 'basic story'. Interestingly, over the last couple of decades innovations in data-gathering techniques, particularly for grassroots-level workers, have responded to the need to develop the basic story from more 'authentic' sources: the technique of rapid rural appraisal (RRA) which was developed in the 1980s was oriented mainly to obtain 'quick field-oriented results' (Mukherjee 1993: 2) in agricultural development (Chambers 1981). Soon it was evident that with paradigm shifts in development strategies, it was important to involve the people concerned in an analysis of their situation. Thus participatory rural appraisal (PRA), which built on RRA, 'is a methodology for interaction with villagers, understanding them and learning from them' (Mukherjee 1993: 30). The emphasis, then, is on hearing the people's voices not only on felt needs but also their perceptions of the context of their lives (Chambers 1992).

While the fieldwork NGO activist/interpreter does often become an involved actor, there have to be in-built mechanisms for crawling out, for distancing oneself somewhat from the scene of action. Nor should the distancing be a mere physical act but also an intellectual one in which the anthropologist dons the garb of the professional. Here, Max Weber's insistence on stating one's position is extremely instructive. For him, it is a 'straightforward requirement of intellectual integrity' to make clear to the audience as well as to the teacher the distinction between 'logically demonstrable or empirically observable facts' and 'practical value judgements' (Runciman 1978: 70). Yet, each resolution of the observer-observed, teacher-taught situation is a highly personalized one. As a South Asian woman trained in the western academic tradition, I was well aware of my intellectual baggage. Nor was I skilled or trained enough to 'nativize' my tools; at the same time, I felt that an articulation of my position whenever possible helped in contextualizing where one has come from and perhaps how far one can go. The context, I felt, was vital. The gruelling process of interaction in the field can well result in situations where the researcher may mediate for a common perspective, decide to abandon her intellectual baggage or choose a completely different area of research the next time round.

After my study among the balmikis, I chose the last option because I felt that I could not enter into another potentially exploitative interactive situation. For, at the end of fieldwork I had the distinct feeling that a process of questioning which can either raise hopes or cause deep resentment is violative of another's privacy and sense of self; the interaction is potentially hierarchical and exploitative in nature. Even if we accept that a piece of writing is the result of collaboration between the author and the respondent, the problem of an unequal relationship exists. Looking back now, I think that it was perhaps a subconscious awareness of this inequality which kept me away from too much probing in my early work. Thus, by the 1980s I was greatly interested in the question of inequality (Karlekar 1983) and its relationship with established institutions. In particular, I wanted to trace the historical roots of gender inequality in the educational system. Here, of course, I was moving into a field of another kind; that I had to read, analyse, interpret the words of others meant again a dialogic relationship. The difference of course was that the author could not question what I was staying. In the process of this study I became involved in the contemporary issue of the highly personalized relationship between the reader and the text. As a woman, I identified with much of what was being written; at times I felt that I was entering into a conspiracy with the writers, empathizing with them, sharing their joys and their pain. I used their voices as much as I could as I wrote about their life experiences.

Hearing and including the voices of my respondents has consistently been of vital importance to me. Today, a range of theories and ideological positions stress the importance of heteroglossia. In the present context of my work and choice of research methods, I have found it particularly interesting that despite many differences in ideology and belief, the expanding women-and-development or, the more recent gender-in-development areas, share a few vital points of convergence with feminist theory and postmodernism; all celebrate the legitimacy of competing voices—which question the notion of a single truth. Plurivocality influences developments strategies as well as how one reads a text. This brief oversimplification of highly sophisticated intellectual debates is merely to emphasize the legitimization of different and disparate realities. While development strategies stress the need to involve women in decision-making processes and thereby empower them, postmodernism also speaks of giving a voice to the hitherto mute and oppressed. Discovering these convergences and accepting the differences is a fascinating exercise.

VI

Since 1975,the Indian women's movement has gone a long way in identifying problems, agitating for solutions and getting them implemented. Coincidentally, these were also the years when I withdrew from fieldwork into the reassuring portals of libraries and the homes of the nineteenth-century elite. Yet, by 1990, I felt a restlessness to go back to the field once more. In part, this restlessness was an anthropologist's craving to be with 'real' people—but only in part. If the last fifteen years had not been so rich in methodological and conceptual debates, I am not sure that I would have felt confident to do so. My choice of research methods had, over all these twenty-five years, been pointing me in a definite, unbroken direction. While the naivete of a twenty-three-year-old later gave way to a more systematic mode of enquiry, the emphasis has consistently remained on hearing many voices. I have not been alone in my dilemma, nor in my search for an appropriate methodology. When one's private anxieties find a reflection in public discourse, clearly there is scope for articulating and moving back to the field again. A novice's apprehensions at encountering an uncharted terrain, which led me to seek legitimacy in the words of respondents, are today viewed as vital in the construction of new realities. No matter what adjective one may use thinking, interpreting, representing or writing about another's life is tricky business. It is useful and reassuring then to share with others that the 'actual expertise and language of women is the central agenda for feminist social science and scholarship' (Du Bois 1983: 108). Feminist researchers have over the last decade been increasingly emphasizing the need to hear the voices of women.

My confidence also grew in large part because of the ease with which women are today willing to share, to speak, and to rethink their lives again. Before I ventured back to the field, I had many encounters of mutual sharing and trust which assured me that a context is not impossible to create and even recreate anew. For the fieldworker has to tell the story of many lives, one of which is surely her own, and when those voices she wishes to hear speak to her with a poignancy and an almost crystal-clear honesty, she works hard to suppress too many questions on her role and the problems of interpretation, understanding, and so on. Twenty years ago I felt threatened, pained, inadequate, by that honesty and the reaching out for answers. Today, I find it easier to cope with the expectations of respondents not only within myself but also because the scope of childcare, employment, domestic conflict resolution mechanisms, and so on, have increased and been legitimized. I can at least try and work towards some solutions to the age-old problem of wife abuse with a battered woman: with the balmikis I did not even have the courage to ask the question not only because I felt that it would be an invasion of privacy but also because I did not know how to approach it.

My present work on violence against women has led me to listen to women under severe tension and stress. As they speak, they are defining and redefining themselves and their psycho-physical boundaries. For it is clear that aggression and violence, physical or otherwise, is an all-pervasive phenomena in most heterosexual relationships. It is there in wife and child abuse, in the process which persuades a young woman to be a respectable school teacher rather than a surgeon, as well as in tension-ridden inter-caste relationships in villages and slums. Its ubiquity makes it an important area for research and debate as it underpins social and personal constructions of femininity, masculinity, and identity. Thus as I continue with my present project, I feel a drawing together of the threads from my earlier work.

It is an exciting time to be a social anthropologist with a commitment to women's studies. I have found it particularly challenging to map the trajectories of feminist theory and anthropology with that of post-modernism. Feminists claim the right to contribute to knowledge creation often by 'deposing' reigning canons. So do postmodernists. But for the former—as for anthropologists—the context is of vital importance. Anthropologists in the field are talking to and writing about human beings in a variety of situations. Feminist theorists base many of their sensibilities and observations on the lives of other women in poverty, in struggle, in situations of oppression and exploitation, and in joy and victory. It is in these contexts that the stories lie and give strength to those who reach out. The quest for new realities is firmly rooted in women's experiences, their knowledge of these experiences, and the capacity to reflect, articulate, and share.

Despite a partial resolution of my dilemma as field worker, I am still at times bewildered and overwhelmed by the entire process of giving expression to and creating another reality. At the same time, I am conscious of the 'freer spirit' in anthropology which allows us to be 'more honest with ourselves and acknowledge the force of our emotions' (Bruner 1983: 15). Over twenty years ago I would have baulked at any suggestion that I had to probe beneath the surface. Today, I am not only asking the unaskable of my respondents but also of myself. As I question academic concepts, research methods, official policies, and programmes, I tell myself that as long as I am aware of my life situation and my intellectual baggage, I should be fairly sure of keeping a basic story intact. At the same time, I grow more and more aware of the many stories which surround a single event in a single life. This feeling, however, does not contradict a commitment to the basic story: it only heightens one's perceptions and sensitivity to a plurality of voices and points of view which privilege that basic story.

Collecting the Life History
of an Indian Untouchable

JAMES M. FREEMAN

During my last visit to India, I came to know an Indian Untouchable named Muli well enough to have him confide the story of his life to me.[1] The first time I saw him, he was sitting on the dusty road in front of one of the small thatch-roofed tea shops in the village with his glass and saucer placed conspicuously beside him—a silent signal to the shopkeeper that an Untouchable wanted to buy some tea. Muli was a gaunt forty-year-old with betel-blackened teeth who wore his long hair swept back. His once handsome face was pain-lined, his cheeks were sunken, but his eyes were bold and piercing, not submissive.

Above Muli, sitting on benches in the shop, three men sipped tea, and I heard them gossiping about the marriage feast they had attended the night before. A ten-year-old boy dressed in shorts leisurely refilled their glasses while he studiously ignored the silent man outside. I stopped and watched. After several minutes the boy glanced at Muli, then, in language that deliberately and offensively signalled that he was addressing a social inferior, he called harshly, 'Hey there, brother-in-law Bauri boy! What'll you take?'[2] Muli pointed to his glass. From a proper distance, Muli dropped two coins into the boy's outstretched palm. As the boy bounded up the steps of the shop, Muli poured his tea into the saucer, then blew on it, and slurped it. Suddenly he stood up and shuffled off, crouching to show respect, so that as he passed by the men in the tea shop his right hand trailed in the dust.

Because I was impressed by the Untouchable's control, I asked the tea-stall boy if he knew the man's name and address. The boy spoke contemptuously, 'His name is Muli. What do you want with him? He's dirty, like all his people. He lives over there.' He pointed to a cluster of tiny mud and thatch huts set apart from the rest of the village—one of five such segregated wards for the people of Muli's caste.

Nearly 16 per cent of India's population, or about 100,000,000 people, are Untouchables.[3] Most of them, despite legislation and two and a half decades of government efforts to improve their economic and social position, remain desperately poor, semiliterate or illiterate, subject to brutal discrimination and economic exploitation, with no realistic prospects for economic or social gain. Stigmatized from birth as spiritually defiling and therefore as potential polluters of 'clean' high-caste people, India's Untouchables lived for centuries in segregated hamlets and villages. High castes denied them the use of public wells, as well as entry to schools, shops, and high-caste shrines, and forced them to perform the most despised and degrading jobs of the society: exhausting unskilled physical labour, scavenging, cleaning out latrines, and carrying off dead animals.

Untouchability is officially 'abolished' in India. Contemporary Indian laws, as well as the Constitution of India, prohibit discrimination against Untouchables. Although Indian federal and state governments have spent millions of rupees and made a great many efforts to improve the economic and social status of the Untouchables, a wide gap remains between the law and successful social reform; the gains of Untouchables are sparse and uneven. Muli lives three miles from Bhubaneswar, the capital of the eastern coastal state of Orissa. In Bhubaneswar, as in other Indian cities, Untouchables experience no obvious public discrimination. But in Muli's village, the old ways persist: although legally permitted to do so, Untouchables enter neither shops nor village temples, because they fear high-caste reprisals.

The memory of Muli's humiliation stayed with me. I recalled similar incidents in my own country, and I wondered if the responses of Untouchables to discrimination paralleled those of minorities in other countries. Was Muli indifferent to the insults he bore in silence? I hardly thought so, but I wondered how an ordinary Untouchable like Muli survived economically, socially, and psychologically as a member of a despised group at the bottom of society. What were his joys, aspirations, and triumphs, as well as his humiliations? What would provoke someone like Muli to question the treatment he received from upper-caste people, to fight back?

I was aware that although many books, novels, articles, and short stories depicted the lifestyles of India's Untouchables, only a handful of Untouchables had been the subject of biographies. Fewer still had described their own life experiences in a narrated autobiography or 'life history'. Of the few available biographies and life histories, every one had been the story of extraordinary achievers, well-educated, economically successful persons, most of whom had held high government and professional positions.[4] As far as I knew, at that time not a single biography or life history had examined the lifestyles of the vast majority of India's Untouchables who, like Muli, had failed to improve their lot. In short, no one had bothered to find out about the life of an ordinary Untouchable from the Untouchable's own point of view.

I determined that as part of my two-year anthropological study of Muli's village, I would collect the first detailed life history of an ordinary Indian Untouchable, perhaps Muli's if he were willing. On a gusty March morning in 1971, Hari, my friend and research assistant, who was a native resident of Muli's village, led me along a stony path to the small clearing where Muli's house stood: a windowless irregular hut of low red mud walls, with a roof of mousegray thatch bleached of its once golden colour by wind, rain, and scorching sun. At the open well in the clearing, a woman was laboriously pulling up a bucket of water, while six girls sitting on the dusty road were throwing dice. Two men stepped from their houses with pickaxes on their shoulders. Most adults had already left for their daily work of dry-season cultivation, stone quarrying, and road building. Except for quarrying and plowing, the women of this caste work alongside the men.

Muli sat on the narrow veranda of his house. Hari introduced me and then said, 'Oh, Muli, we are doing a census of different wards of the village. Could you tell us about your household?' Since he trusted Hari, he described his daily activities. Muli had lived all of his life in his home village, working, like most people of his caste, as a landless, unskilled agricultural labourer, earning one-twelfth of the paddy he harvested for his landowning masters, unable to save any money, frequently without food when work was unavailable or when he was ill and unable to work. He pointed to his right foot, wrapped in a dirty cloth. He had sliced it with a pickaxe in the quarries. Since he had been unable to walk for a week, his wife had kept him and their son from starving by cutting and selling grass for cattle.

Muli was articulate, detailed, voluble. I asked him if he would tell me the story of his life. He looked puzzled. 'What does "the story of my life" mean?'

'Oh, about what you did when you were a child, the games you played, how you became married, the work you do, your friends, things like that.'

'Sure, why not?'

Hari and I finished the census. Then we began collecting life histories of high-caste villagers. Five months later, Muli suddenly appeared at my doorstep, unshaven, wearing a dirty loincloth. 'My father just died,' he said, 'Would you take his photograph?'

I grabbed my camera and we ran to his house. Muli and his brothers propped their father's frail, still-warm body on an armchair and posed beside him; the women of the house wailed. I took several photographs; then some men of the ward placed Muli's father on a hastily constructed bamboo and cloth stretcher, carried him at a fast walk to the cremation grounds, and placed him on the caste-segregated stones reserved for the cremation of Untouchables. Muli, the eldest son, lit the funeral pyre.

Two weeks later, Hari and I returned to Muli's house and gave him the photos of his father. Muli was pale, haggard, and thin. 'Something is wrong with me,' he said. 'I went to my uncle's house to work for a week. I became ill there.' Although it was nearly midday, Muli had not eaten since the previous night; his house contained no food. He was dizzy and unable to walk. We carried him by bicycle to the town hospital. 'It's his lungs,' the doctor said to me. Medical care is free, but medicines are not; lacking money for food, let alone medicine, most of the people of Muli's caste neglect going to the hospital for treatment. I bought Muli the medicine he needed, plus oranges, eggplants, and rice. In gratitude, he offered to tell us whatever he could remember about his life. Harvesting would soon begin. Realizing that Muli could hardly afford to spend days at my house discussing his life without remuneration, I offered him meals, money for marketing, and as much paddy as he would have earned had he laboured in the fields. Little did I realize what he would offer in return. Muli, a masterful storyteller, narrated his life history to me in his native language, Oriya, during a series of almost daily interviews for six more months. His account, which Hari and I later translated into English, comes to some 350,000 words.

Muli's life history is one of thirteen that I collected that describe from different perspectives the rapidly urbanizing village in which Muli lived. Many Westerners have written about India's problems of modernization, urbanization, poverty, population growth, and political stability, usually from Western points of view or from those of high Indian administrators and politicians. Few studies of change probe deeply to reveal what ordinary Indians think about their transition to modernity. Surveys and questionnaires without other supporting data often provide little more than biased, shallow responses. When investigators ask about change, they receive answers that focus on change. To be polite, Indian villagers often provide the answers that they think the investigator wants to hear. Their replies usually bear little relation to the way they live their lives or view the world. Many excellent biographies and autobiographies describe the lives of extraordinary, urbanized, highly educated high-caste Indians involved with change, but their views and concerns differ significantly from those of ordinary Indians (Karve and McDonald 1963; Erikson 1969; Chaudhuri 1968; Tandon 1968). When not prodded to answer leading questions by technological missionaries and elites who want to change them, ordinary Indians provide distinctly different views of the problems that they consider vital, shattering many stereotypes about the joint family, women's roles, attitudes towards the elderly, religious lifestyles, sexual mores, caste rules and rankings, as well as strategies of adaptation to poverty, new opportunities, and urbanization.

A detailed life history like Muli's provides a way to reach behind the surface answers outsiders often receive, grasping from the insider's perspectives what he really values, and how he interprets his experiences. Muli does not necessarily represent a typical Untouchable or villager; he makes his own distinctive choices and adaptations; others of his caste choose differently. What Muli shares with the other men of his caste is a limited range of choices of lifestyles, determined by a common physical, economic, and social environment.

Collecting Muli's Life History

Muli began narrating his life history at my house in early November 1971, and continued intermittently through April 1972. When I first chose the house I would live in for the two years of my anthropological study of Muli's village, I anticipated both the need for privacy in interviews and ready accessibility to the village. Accordingly, I chose a house located in a secluded spot just outside the village limits. About mid-morning, Muli would come to my house. After taking tea and breakfast, he would narrate episodes from two to five hours, with a break for lunch, which we provided. At first Hari, my assistant and translator, wrote down each sentence in Oriya while Muli spoke. Every few minutes, when Muli reached a stopping point, Hari and I worked out the English translation, which I wrote down. Then Muli would begin again.

I could follow ordinary spoken Oriya, as well as read high-school-level Oriya texts. Muli's use of Oriya, however, differed from the cultured, high-caste Oriya that I knew. He used conventional words in unconventional ways, Bauri dialect words, feminine expressions, proverbs, obscenities, and curses. I insisted from the first day that both Muli and Hari explain in detail the meanings and uses of any words and phrases that were unfamiliar to me. At times we spent as much as one hour examining a single word, phrase, or concept. After Muli left, Hari and I reread the Oriya and English narratives, looking for discrepancies, unclear passages, and topics that needed further development. Muli soon became restless during the periods that Hari and I were translating his narratives. To keep his interest, we let him narrate his story and we translated it after he had left.

I had originally planned to interfere as little as possible with Muli's narrative, letting him choose the topics, so that he would reveal his ways of thinking rather than mine. Muli, however, said that he did not know where to begin. I told him to start by describing his daily activities as a child and his relationship to his parents, relatives, and friends. Muli narrated a brief and altogether inadequate sketch of his childhood, and then turned to elaborate descriptions of his life as a youth. At this point I again tried unsuccessfully to direct the interviews. Despite my numerous requests, Muli never again discussed his childhood, which held no interest for him. Similarly, he omitted describing his own wedding. When Hari and I reminded him of this, he dutifully catalogued a number of dry, lifeless rituals as if he were an outsider to the event. He gave no description of his wife during the ceremony except when we prompted him. He wished to forget the ceremony that had marked the beginning of his unhappy marriage.

Muli was clearly at his best, not when directed, but when allowed to develop his story in his own way. Muli's spontaneously selected episodes are the liveliest and most poignant of his life history. Once he began such stories, he never ran out of words. Our problem was the reverse: he would narrate with repetitious detail how, when, and where each day he defecated, bathed, brushed his teeth, ate breakfast, and to whom he spoke while performing these activities.[5] Complicated plots unfolded; stories developed within stories as Muli plodded literal-mindedly through chronological sequences of the day's events. I soon realized that, valuable as his descriptions of minutiae might be, at this pace Muli would require years, not months, to complete his narrative.

I told him to skip those events, previously described, that remained unchanged day by day or those that were less important for his story. Puzzled, Muli said that he was unable to select what was important or to depart from narrating each detail, although he was willing to try. We worked for several days showing him what we considered important; he tried to follow our directions, but with little success. At this point, we told him simply to narrate his story, forgetting our directions. To save time as Muli spoke, I told Hari what to write down and what to leave unwritten. I interrupted Muli's narratives only to ask him to clarify obscure points and inconsistencies, and to expand his descriptions of customs or rituals and their meanings.

As I had expected, Muli at first described events from the conventional viewpoints that he thought high-status people, non-Untouchables, would prefer to hear. He praised his Brahman employer, as well as other Brahmans of the village. I told Hari in English that I did not believe Muli's statements. Hari, himself a man of high caste, nodded in agreement.

Looking worried, Muli, who understood no English, asked Hari, 'What did James *babu* [mister] say?'

Hari replied in Oriya, 'He wants you to tell us what is in your heart. You speak respectfully of the Brahman who hired you to work as his farm servant, but throughout our village that man is renowned as a great miser who cheats all of his employees. Has he never cheated you? Tell us frankly.'

Surprised but obviously delighted by this unexpected question, Muli smiled and described an episode in which he ridiculed the Brahman in most unflattering terms. Later that harvest season, Muli narrated the unfolding drama that led to his great quarrel with his Brahman employer.

Muli hinted about topics such as prostitution that he said he thought Hari and I might find offensive. He was testing us, hoping that we would be interested. We assured him that he should tell us what he truly believed as well as the true incidents of his life, and that we would be offended only if he failed to tell us the truth. Emboldened by these words, Muli began describing his life as a pimp, in which he supplied Bauri women to high-caste men. I found out later that he had hoped to draw us into his net as customers of his prostitutes. As he became more comfortable in my presence, Muli revealed not only his life as a pimp, but also his attraction to transvestite men. Dropping his initial reserve and pretences, he shifted into Bauri dialect and the feminine expressions of women and transvestites.

We had scheduled our interview session daily, but one week after we began, Muli failed to show up. After waiting an hour, Hari and I walked to Muli's house. He limped out. I asked, 'What happened to you?'

'It's my leg. Look, boils.' He had a huge boil on his left leg. 'I can't walk. I have to wait until the boil goes down. Then I'll continue my work with you.'

I said, 'Go to the hospital; otherwise the infection may spread.'

His face showed fear. 'No! no! They'll cut the boil. It will hurt! I can't stand the pain!'

'The pain will be a lot worse if you don't get treated,' I said.

Hari said soothingly, 'They won't hurt you, but just give you medicine. Then you'll be all right'.

For five days Hari and I took Muli to the hospital for treatment and medicine. When the boils cleared, Muli resumed narrating his story. A few days later, he had dysentery; after that, a deep cough; then a gashed hand from harvesting paddy—a continuous line of minor ailments and injuries that interrupted our interviews. At first I was annoyed with these delays, but soon I realized that his low resistance to disease, weak stamina, fear of pain and injury, and injury-proneness accounted in great measure for his willingness to narrate his life history: instead of starving while recuperating from his injuries, he earned money by sitting and talking at my house. Furthermore, I realized that his weakness and ill health accounted in part for his having become a pimp rather than a stone quarry worker.

The interviews with Muli proceeded unevenly. At first Muli was shy and avoided saying directly what he wanted. Instead, he would pout like Orissan women do, sitting silently, looking unhappy.

During one of his pouts I asked, 'What's wrong, Muli?'

'Nothing'.

'Come on now—you have a long face. Why?'

'Nothing's wrong. I'm quite all right.' He lapsed into silence, occasionally looking up mournfully, otherwise looking downward. He sat motionless.

'If you don't tell us, how can we do anything about it?'

Looking up, he said without conviction, 'I am not unhappy, Babu, but if I come here to tell you the story of my life, well, how will I eat?'

Hari replied, annoyed, 'We already settled that. We'll pay you your daily wage and we'll pay a shopkeeper in the village to supply you with bread, milk and snacks every day, just as you asked. The shopkeeper won't overcharge you since we are paying him. You told us you were happy with our agreement, so what's the problem?' Since Bauris have little money, they buy oil, spices, and rice in small quantities at much higher rates than do the wealthier villagers, who buy in larger quantities.

Muli replied, 'Well, how am I to be paid?'

Hari reminded him of our agreement. 'We'll pay you in paddy, which is what you asked for, since the daily wage in paddy is worth more than money wages. I bought you some paddy which I stored at my father's threshing floor. We'll give it to you when you finish your life history.' At that time, we did not realize that Muli would be narrating his story for six months. We later paid him in instalments as he finished parts of his life history.

Muli looked frightened. He wanted more money but feared to ask us. He also wanted assurance that we would pay him. People had often cheated him when he had tried easy or short-cut schemes to acquire money or influence. He said, 'But Babu, how do I know that I'll really get the paddy? Look how the Brahman miser has cheated me. If you don't give me that paddy after I work for you rather than harvesting in the fields, what will happen to me and my family? That paddy will feed us for three months. If I don't get it...'

I interrupted, 'You'll have to trust us, Muli. Take it or leave it. If you prefer to work all day in the fields for a lower wage than I give you, then feel free to do so. I don't want to make you do something you don't want to do.'

'Oh, no,' he replied quickly. 'I'll work for you, except on those days when I must work as a farm servant. On those days I must gather my crop.'

I replied, 'Yes, of course. We agreed on that several days ago. Between December and the end of January you may miss up to 20 days. On the days you are not in the fields, you work for us. Also, we'll give you money on market days.'

Muli's city friends were customers for his prostitutes. Hoping still to attract Hari and me to his prostitutes, he described several stories about them. His stories became repetitious; we told him to discuss other topics.

He asked softly, 'Wouldn't you like to try one of these women?' He laughed shyly and covered his face with his shoulder cloth.

I replied, 'I have a wife; Hari has a wife; we don't need your women.'

He peered out over the cloth. 'Once you try them, you can never leave them.'

'I've got pure gold at home,' I replied, 'so why should I look elsewhere?'

I had wondered what sort of Untouchable would tell his story I now realized with dismay that not only had I selected him, but he had selected me as a way to earn easy money and possibly involve me with his prostitutes. Clearly, by his own account, he was a deviant in his culture, a weak, sickly man unable to do men's work, often living entirely off of his wife's earnings, constantly embroiled in scandals, a self-confessed liar and scoundrel whose schemes often brought disaster not only to himself but to everybody associated with him.

This was hardly the sort of person I had planned to interview. I had expected to collect several life histories of high-caste and Untouchable males and females representing different lifestyles and ages, and illustrating various adaptations to rapid urbanization. I had expected to find villagers who might describe their participation at some of the numerous

local religious festivals, and might discuss religious values and beliefs.
Muli went to festivals only to solicit customers. I had hoped to collect the
life history of a Bauri who would refute the stereotyped images that high
castes had of them. A well-educated Brahman woman spoke for many of
her caste when she assured me that, 'The Bauris are lazy and ignorant
people. All my life we have hired them to work on my father's estate. They
are unreliable. You never know when they will come to work. They never
work hard. That's why they are so poor'. I now realized that I had inadvertently selected a person who reinforced these very stereotypes. I told
Hari that I thought we should pay Muli what we had promised him but
terminate the interviews and seek a normal working Bauri male or female.

Hari said, 'You won't find anybody else at this time of year. All Bauris
who can work are in the field harvesting paddy. No one else can give you
as much time as Muli does. Also, he speaks well, his stories are interesting, and he has given you a lot of information that you cannot get easily
from other Bauris. I know that many things he says are true, and we can
check the accuracy of any statements that we doubt. I think that you should
keep interviewing him.'

I accepted Hari's judgement. I had known him since 1962, when as a
fifteen-year-old youth he had helped me collect census data during my first
study of his village. Now, nine years later, he had offered his services again
and I had hired him. I needed a translator-assistant; no Untouchables spoke
English. Hari, a robust athlete, was the college-educated married son of a
leader of a high-status, landowning caste that hired and often exploited Bauri
labourers. Hari himself was a popular youth leader who all his life had received deference from villagers of all castes. While I expected that I could
train Hari to work well among the people of his own caste, I was unsure if he
could effectively interview Untouchables, who understandably might resent
high-caste persons. Other high-caste youths and men were totally unsuited
to the task. Despite frequently claiming no caste prejudices, Hari's well-
educated high-caste friends conspicuously avoided Untouchable youths and
never invited them to their social functions. Hari, by contrast, was the only
high-caste villager who by his actions had demonstrated a genuine friendship and concern for the Untouchables of his community, speaking respectfully to them instead of down at them, eating with them, helping them
organize a political group, establishing and running an adult night school
for Bauris, and interceding for them when high-caste landowners and shop-
keepers cheated them. Although many Untouchables nevertheless distrusted
Hari, a few, like Muli, accepted him enough to crack jokes with him about
the high castes and to reveal their deep resentment of high-caste people.

I thought that Hari had the potential to do the job I needed. Accordingly, for several months I carefully trained him to conduct interviews among the people of his own caste, most of whom trusted him and readily confided to him in my presence. We conducted all interviews jointly. He became sensitive to the kinds of questions I asked. He learned to translate literally, to self-consciously examine ways in which he might have selectively screened or omitted information. He learned to explain to the villagers carefully and in detail what we intended to do with the information we collected, and to inform me about those households from which he could not gather information.[7] By narrating his own life history to me, Hari learned how to collect the life histories of others.

Hari's most difficult adjustment came when I told him that he had to abandon his accustomed role as a leader, because such a person often prompted people to give answers that they thought would please the authority figure. Hari had at first enthusiastically tried to extract information from the people of his caste whether or not they were willing. 'They are my neighbours,' he said, 'they must tell you the truth.' Later, when Muli omitted details, Hari said, 'we are paying him; he must tell what he knows.' I insisted that Hari never order people to divulge information but rather respect their right to offer or withhold it as they pleased. With practice he learned to do this, as well as to ask questions unexpected of persons in authority roles, such as his questioning of Muli's praise of Brahmans.

I came to rely on Hari's judgement. He could spot inconsistencies or errors in responses that escaped me. Using his detailed knowledge of the villagers and their lifestyles, he followed up leads about topics that I never knew existed. He became a skilled interviewer, and, most importantly, as a trusted insider he elicited information that an outsider like myself working alone might never have received.

Muli's motivations in confiding to us were more complex than I had at first realized. He narrated his life history not simply for money, but also to strike back at his neighbours, who disliked him, and also at his parents and brothers, who had thrown him out of the house. He used his life history to recall nostalgically his happy youth, which he contrasted with his unhappy life as a married man. By narrating his life history, Muli also vented his resentment against high-caste men. 'To keep their prestige, they avoid us in public, but in private they screw our women, "hu, hu", panting like dogs.' Finally, he wanted people to know what it meant to live like a Bauri: 'Who has ever cared about us? People should know how we live.'

Because Muli was dissatisfied with his lot, he dreamed of ways to break away from his starvation-poverty, from his position as a despised Untouchable. Although resenting high-caste gentlemen for their double standard, he admired them for their wealth, easy jobs, fine clothes, and jewellery. He wanted to associate with and emulate them, to be *accepted* by them. He imagined that if he provided a service for which a high-caste man became dependent or compromised, such as supplying him with male or female prostitutes, he would become that man's friend. Prostitution temporarily brought men of wealth and social status to his door, but as customers, not friends. Acting out his hopeless fantasy of friendship, Muli refused to admit the true basis of his relationship with high-caste men, and thus often entangled himself in difficulties he never anticipated.

The frustration of Muli's life was that he wanted his customers to treat him as their friend rather than as the pimp who supplied them with prostitutes. Outwardly he was proud, but inwardly he coveted the money from prostitution. He went to devious lengths to deny to himself that he was a pimp, even while earning money from that work. Usually he refused to accept direct payment from a customer-'friend'. The women gave him the money, which he interpreted not as a payment, but as a donation. Muli construed any attention from gentlemen as 'friendship', although their sole aim was to sleep with his prostitutes. Muli's relationships with high-caste men never lasted. He was forty years old, and most of the women he knew intimately were of his age or older. He was unable to mix freely with the younger women of his caste without arousing suspicion. Wanting fresh young women, the men of the city soon lost interest in Muli. While he dreamed, and his futile schemes failed, Muli's hardworking wife supported their family by cutting grass and harvesting paddy. Increasingly impatient with Muli's introspections, she often quarrelled with him and called him lazy.

On those days during the harvest that Muli worked in the fields, Hari and I accompanied him. The miser had hired Muli as a farm servant; Muli in turn was supposed to hire day-labourers to help harvest the crop and then pay them one-twelfth of the paddy they cut. To keep all the earnings among his relatives, Muli selected his wife, son, mother, youngest brother, and brother's wife. Since he was the overseer for the day, Muli came to the field attired in a fine dhoti and fancy shirt, while the others came in their working clothes of old saris for the women, a short loincloth for his brother, and short pants for his seventeen-year-old schoolboy son. Muli, the supervisor, sat on the raised bank of a paddy field and watched. The group was supposed to finish cutting the crop of that field in one day. Muli's wife cut a wide path; the others moved slowly cutting narrow paths. Although she was working faster than they were, her path was shorter because it was wider. Her son helped her a little, but most of the time he sat and watched, like his father.

Muli's wife talked loudly to herself, making remarks that would embarrass others. 'Yesterday I said that we should hire three to four outsiders, but the head of our household said, "Why get others when all of us in the family can do the work?" So I brought my family out here, but nobody is working hard. This plot of land is small; we should be able to cut it in one day. But the way they work, it will take them two days. Where will the wages come from to pay for two days? If you hire five people to work for two days on such a small piece of land, how much will they take as wages, and how much will remain for us?'

Her son, sitting nearby, said irritably, 'Why are you opening your big mouth, shouting falsely?'

She shouted, 'What, shouting falsely? I'll throw this sickle at your face so that half of it flies away!'

Muli became angry. 'Why are you showing off your work? I don't know what work you do except for my sexual work.'

She replied, 'What, you don't know what work I do? Sitting, sitting, speaking big things.'

Muli stood up and shouted, 'What are you saying?... Characterless! Younger brother's wife! [she who has sexual intercourse with one's younger brother]... Adulteress! Will you bring their wage from your father's house? Why are you shouting like this? Shut up!'

Lapsing into Bauri dialect, she replied, 'Why shut up? For this you are my husband?' Her term for 'husband' was disrespectful. A wife should refer to her husband as 'son's father' or 'respected master'. Men, in turn, when showing respect to their wives, call them not by name, but by the name of their first child.

Muli raised his fists to beat her. Hari pulled him away, saying, 'Why are you scolding your wife? She is right in her way; she is justified.'

Muli calmed down. 'Yes, she's a very hard worker, and she earns a lot of money. She doesn't depend on my income. But her mouth is very sharp. Nobody can tolerate her language. She's expert in all work. She has been ill for three days, so she is quite angry when my son and younger brother stand around like they have been doing. She can scold my son, but she must not scold my younger brother. He lives in a different household. She has no control over him. That's why she's angry, and that's why she criticized him indirectly.'

In his stories, Muli prided himself on being clever and dishonest, an inveterate liar who thought up quick-witted ruses to escape from tight predicaments. Although he also described with ironic detachment how his devious schemes invariably backfired, I became sceptical of the reliability of the life history of a man who claimed to be a liar. Furthermore, some of Muli's stories, like his quarrel with the Brahman miser, sounded so out of character that I believed none of them. Muli claimed that while standing before a tea shop full of patrons he had quarrelled with and insulted his Brahman employer. To our knowledge, no Bauri from Muli's village had ever publicly insulted a Brahman.

Unknown to Muli, Hari and I quietly investigated his incident with the miser, which had occurred during the period that Muli was narrating his life history. Several eyewitnesses, including Bauris, Brahmans, and even the miser's own cousin, not only confirmed Muli's description of his confrontation with the miser, but claimed that the miser had truly provoked Muli by cheating him. Both the betel-seller and the youth selling vegetables at the market confrimed the incidents involving the miser at the market.

Next we checked Muli's stories about his grandfather, Dharma, by questioning Muli's paternal uncle, a son of Dharma but no admirer of Muli. He confirmed all of Muli's stories but one. Another Bauri confirmed Muli's scandal involving his second wife. While collecting the texts of religious songs, Hari and I asked several Bauris, not about Muli, but about the history of drama and singing troupes. These persons again confirmed several of Muli's stories about his grandfather, Dharma, as well as some of the drama-troupe incidents.

Muli's descriptions of Bauri rituals and other activities paralleled those I witnessed, and my own observations of Muli with his prostitutes, customers, transvestite friends, brothers, and wife matched his descriptions of his behaviour with them. Whatever his motivations might have been, Muli narrated a life history that was accurate for the most part in its portrayal of Bauri life, including lifestyles that differed from his.

Muli saw himself as a deviant in his own culture, but far from claiming that all Bauris act and think like he did, he contrasted other lifestyles with his own without condemning or praising either. Of the thirteen life histories that I collected, Muli's was the most pitilessly self-critical. He often described himself in unflattering terms, but with neither remorse nor pride. To be sure, in telling his story, Muli selectively omitted some topics and exaggerated when relating others. Muli was a middle-aged failure with a bleak future. His youthful dreams had failed to materialize. No wonder, then, that he dwelled at length on his idyllic days as an unmarried youth, a time of hopes and dreams, the happiest days of his life. While he avoided speaking about his childhood, he would sit for hours with his eyes closed, speaking in a low monotone, recalling those days of his youth when high-caste men came to his door, flattered him, and gave him gifts so that he would supply them with women.

Faced with perpetual poverty and frequent starvation, Muli quite un-derstandably overstated the amounts of food, gifts of cloth, and expenses that his family supplied at feasts and ceremonies. Similarly, he stated that his family paid for the expensive 'sin of the fly larvae pollution' ceremony, an unlikely expenditure for an impoverished family.

To enhance his prestige, Muli exaggerated not only about feasts, but about the leadership activities and skills of his grandfather and his brothers. According to Muli, his grandfather learned wrestling from high-caste villagers, but in fact these persons never allowed Bauris to practise with them. Muli also embellished the details of his many quarrels with his family and with other families. He claimed that his parents made no preparations for their youngest son's fourth-night-after-the-wedding ceremony, which is hard to believe, as is Muli's claim that he and his wife paid all the expenses of his brother's ceremony.

Aside from neglecting his childhood, Muli's greatest omission was his refusal to admit that he worked as a pimp for the women of his own ward. Despite much evidence to the contrary, he insisted that, except for one woman, all came from other wards and villages, because to use women from his own ward would have been very disgraceful. However, he fre-quently associated with the prostitute women of his ward, one of whom, not knowing that I understood Oriya, asked him in my presence if I was a potential customer whom he could send to her. One of Muli's sisters earned money as a prostitute. In Muli's stories, many wealthy high-caste custom-ers unaccountably showed great interest in Muli's family, particularly his sisters, whom Muli probably drew into his prostitution business. No won-der Muli's parents constantly quarrelled with him and finally threw him out of the house permanently. For months Muli insisted that he could not understand why they had done this, and denied that his activities as a pimp might have embarrassed his family. By April 1972, Hari and I had col-lected 350,000 words of Muli's text. We had paid him his paddy, as well as other things we had promised him. The harvest was over. Muli frequently failed to show up for interviews; he was not working but wandering about the market with his transvestite friends. We began other life histories. One day Muli appeared at the door; he needed some money, so he had come for another interview. I agreed to hold one final session. We doubted that he had anything new to tell us, and indeed that day his stories covered the familiar topic of family quarrels. Suddenly, however, the interview took an unexpected turn. Muli described how he had quarrelled for the first time with his favourite uncle, Satyabadi, his mother's brother, who criticized him for neglecting his ill father: 'What kind of son are you, not looking after your father? You are young, you earn well, yet you neglect him. Who will count you as the son of your father? It is better for this kind of son to die before his father dies!'

Muli had replied, 'Don't tell me about my father. Whenever my father and mother have bad times, they call me for help, but when I am in trouble, they say they aren't my parents. So why does he wait for me now? He's got other sons. Why don't my brothers look after him? I don't like my father. He and his wife are nothing to me; I am nothing to them. I know what kind of people they are. What haven't I done for them when they needed it? But they never looked after me nor ever talked to me. Rather, they complained to other people that I don't take care of them. I don't need a father like that; I don't want to hear any more about him.'

At that point, my assistant Hari interrupted Muli. 'Why was your father displeased with you and not with your brothers? You always helped your father and they didn't, so why did he dislike you?'

Muli replied, 'My father was displeased with me not once but many times. At first my father and mother liked me, but after my marriage, when I didn't work but spent most of my time with Buli and her lovers, Mother became angry with me and quarrelled with me.'

Hari asked, 'Do you remember the first time your parents threw you out?'

'Yes, it was when my infant son, wife, and myself became covered with boils, and my wife and I couldn't earn any money.'

Hari asked, 'You separated many times because of quarrels over lack of food. Many families do this. But why was your father displeased with you even after driving you out of the house? Did he have other reasons?'

Muli replied, 'I don't know why. I always tried to make my father happy whether or not we were separated. I don't know why my father looked at me with a bad eye.'

Hari said, 'How can you fail to understand? You see, Muli, it is very rare and painful to see a father dislike his son. Even if a son is bad, his father helps him. Did you ever do anything against your father's wishes, something that everybody would dislike?'

'You may ask questions from any side. I am unable to understand anything. You are an educated man. You please point out my faults. Where were they?'

'Did you father ever scold you because people insulted him or complained about your badness? Think about your secret work. Did people find out that you had taken their daughters for bad work? Did they publicly scold you? This would have insulted and humiliated your father. Did this happen?

'Why not?' admitted Muli. 'People insulted Father and me many times because I did things that made everyone hate me. Not only the people of my own ward, but also my mother, father, wife and brothers found out that I had sold the services of the girls.'

Muli then described the first time he was caught. The angry elders called a meeting at which they fined Muli's father and forced him to give the people of the ward a feast. They said that Muli's father had caused Muli's bad behaviour by being lax with him. After this public humiliation, Muli's father scolded him: 'A man who does these things—no father should have to look upon a son like you.'

Muli's life history was the creation not of one man, but of three: Muli the storyteller; Hari, the native cotranslator and interviewer; and myself, the outside cotranslator, interviewer, editor, and analyst. Our combined efforts created something new that none of us anticipated. I never expected to collect a 350,000-word life history on the topics covered. Hari never realized how little he had known about Bauri lifestyles and values. Muli by himself would never have narrated his story, for such oral histories were not part of his tradition; he simply took for granted the details of his existence.

How representative of Bauris is Muli's life history? The details and the manner of telling the stories reflect Muli's distinctive style, but the environment of extreme poverty, social stigma, economic exploitation, and discrimination against Untouchables is a reality shared by all of the Bauris of Muli's community and most Bauris elsewhere. Muli's own lifestyle represents one of only three possible adaptations ordinarily available to Bauri men and women: the life of unskilled labourers; the life of shamanistic faith healers; and the life of transvestites, pimps, and prostitutes. These lifestyles are neither incompatible nor mutually exclusive, but like Muli most Bauris emphasize one of them more than the others.

Muli was neither my friend nor a person whom I particularly admired. But his life history taught me to understand why, given the limited opportunities available to him, he chose to live his life the way he did.

The Editor's Role in Muli's Life History

In biographical accounts of semiliterate or nonliterate people, the distinction between biography and autobiography is often difficult to make, given problems of editing, translation, and direction of narrations. Consequently, as Langness had observed, some anthropologists prefer to use the term 'life history' to cover the extensive account of a person's life, whether written or narrated by that person, or by others, or by both (Langness 1965: 4–5).[9]

If the life histories of semiliterate and nonliterate people are the result of the combined efforts of narrator and translator-editor, then how much of a completed life history reflects the narrator's efforts, and how much reflects the editor's contributions? What aspects of a life history are independent of the investigator who collects it?

Allport, recognizing this problem in 1942, cautioned against excessive editing, while at the same time he claimed that personal documents take their meaning from the investigator's comments and interpretations (Allport 1942: 83–86, 142; also see Blumer 1939: 77–81). More recently, Devereux has argued that, '... a rat experiment, an anthropological field trip or a psychoanalysis contribute more to the understanding of behaviour when viewed as a source of information about the animal psychologist, the anthropologist or the psychoanalyst, than when it is considered only as a source of information about rats, primitives or patients' (1967: xix). The data of behavioural science, according to Devereux, is threefold: '1. The behaviour of the subject; 2. The "disturbances" produced by the existence and observational activities of the observer; 3. The behaviour of the observer: his anxieties, his defence manoeuvres, his research strategies, his "decisions" (= his attribution of a meaning to his observations) (ibid.). The data of the observer that needs study, says Devereux, include not only the observer's cultural and social background, but also the process of 'countertransference', that is, how an observer reacts as a person to his own observations (ibid.: xvi–xx, 41–47, 83–126). In summary, to quote La Barre's comments about Devereux's perspective, '... field ethnography (and indeed all social science) as presently practiced, may be a species of autobiography' (La Barre 1967: viii). I do believe that Devereux's insight on the observer as a datum of behaviour is an important one. However, I also believe that La Barre's evaluation of its importance, if taken literally rather than metaphorically, would carry it to such an extreme as to reduce it to an absurdity. For example, I am quite convinced that Muli's life history is not the autobiography of James Freeman.

I have no doubt that in certain subtle and significant respects, Muli's account of his life history, as elicited by my promptings and as affected by my translations and editing, constitutes a rearrangement if not an actual alteration of the raw data of the facts of his life. However, I believe that the portrait of Muli which emerges is a faithful one in all essential respects. My own contributions can be compared with those of the photographic artist who produces a portrait of his subject by controlling the lighting and background in his studio and modifying the composition of the portrait in the darkroom by selective cropping, that is editing. I would grant that Muli's life history might well have been recognizably different had it been collected by a different person with a different personal background and different categories of reference guiding his direction of Muli's narration and the editing of Muli's account. Nevertheless, I am convinced that Muli would have been *recognizable* as the subject of the life history, just as he would be recognized as the same subject had he sat for a photographic portrait by two different photographic artists with their own distinctive styles. Thus, to elaborate the example, Karsh's famous portrait of Churchill, while instantly recognizable as a Karsh photograph, is nevertheless a portrait of Churchill and not of Karsh.

A life history like Muli's does not exist as an external datum, independent of time, place and person, waiting to be written down or recorded. Rather it is the joint production of two or more persons with the right combination of personalities, interests, and biases, who happen to come together at the right time and place for creating a life history. The role of the observer thus is a crucial component of a life history. No comparison of life histories is possible without knowledge of the editor's perspectives and values that influenced the final form of the life history. Failure to assess, or at least recognize, the observer's or editor's role leads to an image of a life history that is distorted and incomplete, since each editor, even though not consciously, is necessarily influenced by his perspectives. In describing my relationship with Muli and my influence on him, I have also deliberately discussed my own values and my reactions both to Muli's behaviour and to my own behaviour. Since I may well be unconscious of the extent to which my own frame of reference and biases influenced my editing of Muli's narration, the reader must himself consider more fully what in the narrative appears to be more a reflection of the observer than the narrator. If I were to attempt to trace out in detail my own unconscious biases, I would need to write an entire volume, as indeed Devereux has done—a Herculean task that could not be included in the limited space of this study.

Nevertheless, to the reader who might wonder not only about my conscious biases, but about their origin—the extent to which my own background might need to be taken into account in separating my contribution from Muli's in the production of his life history—I offer the following brief summary of the personal background which I brought to the study and which led me to do it. Any self-analysis may be simply self-delusion, but as I see it now, besides collecting information on social change, my motivations for collecting Muli's life history were twofold: first, to describe the world of meaning of a person from a culture other than my own; and second, to document a life history of oppression.

While my interest in other cultures and world views originated in my early childhood, my focus on India, Untouchables, and life histories was inspired by accident rather than by choice. When I entered graduate school at Harvard in 1958 I had no narrowly focused interest, but rather several interdisciplinary ones concerning focused interest, but rather several interdisciplinary ones concerning symbols, ritual, and myth. My selection of a geographical area came, as it does for many anthropology graduate students, because I had to choose a thesis topic and do field research in a culture other than my own. What initially drew me to India was not its village life or its social problems, but rather its philosophy and religion, and indeed my first publication, which appeared in a journal of philosophy, dealt with the distinction between myth and metaphysics in Indian thought (Freeman 1966: 517–29). I soon learned, however, that philosophical speculations were not the stuff of Harvard doctoral dissertations in anthropology. One professor told me to quit dabbling; another asked me what my philosophical bubble-blowing had to do with anthropology; and a third suggested that I transfer to the Divinity School.

I felt, however, that what I was doing belonged in anthropology, for my focus in that article on metaphysics was on how people attribute meaning to their universe, and what consequences follow from losing the belief in a meaningful universe. In retrospect, the study of meaning in worldviews is the main thread that connects my early philosophical writing, my subsequent studies of Hinduism, including firewalking, my study of Muli's life and worldview, and my current ongoing life-history studies of other Indians. But why was I fascinated with questions about meaning, and why in particular with meaning in a culture other than my own? What was there about such questions that absorbed my attention, that made them interesting to me?

Of the many possible influences that led me to my present studies, surely those exerted by my mother and father were particularly formative. My mother, uprooted as a child from her native village in Hungary, an immigrant to the USA, where she became an academic editor, idealizes family and village life from her childhood recollections, but at the same time has developed an acute sense of the relativity of different social settings. She sees herself not as attached to a particular place, but as an outsider ready to move on, an inhabitant of two cultural worlds. My father, an American-born citizen whose parents came from the same village as my mother's, actively rebelled in his youth against the religious and cultural traditions of his parents, to which he has remained a hostile critic. He became a university professor of philosophy, a Peircean pragmatist impatient with social and religious customs that he considers nonrational nonsense. From my mother, I developed my curiosity about other cultures, my desire to experience living in a close-knit social group with a meaningful worldview, and also my empathy and respect for village lifestyles without committing myself to those lifestyles. Thus I was particularly attracted to Muli's description of his drama troupe because of the sense of community that it revealed. From my father, I developed an outsider's sceptical attitude towards people's explanations of their own behaviour, and a penchant for scrutinizing such statements critically. Muli's life history intrigued me intellectually because it tested my ability to wrestle with the paradox of what statements were 'true' in the narrative of a man who proudly proclaimed himself a liar.

As members of a minority religious group, my parents (and I to a much lesser extent) experienced various forms of discrimination that heightened my sensitivity to the emotional plight of people like Muli, and motivated me to seek an oppressed person and portray his sufferings. I recognized in Muli's accounts of discrimination, exploitation, and stigma a common bond that Muli shared with me and my own relatives. While my personal experiences may not be a necessary prerequisite to taking the life history of an oppressed person, they undoubtedly guided my decision to highlight the psychological effects of discrimination in Muli's life.

In 1962 I selected Bhubaneswar, Orissa, as a research site because one of my professors, Cora DuBois, had begun a long-term study there. The site interested her because it featured an old Hindu pilgrimage centre adjacent to a newly built administrative town. The new town, squat, ugly, traditionless, and bureaucratic, turned me off immediately. By contrast, the village where Muli lived, a minor pilgrimage centre, intrigued me with its distinctive caste of temple priests and their strong sense of identity and rootedness in this one community, that reminded me in many ways of the village of my mother and grandparents. My doctoral dissertation (1968) focused on certain aspects of the religious lifestyle of those priests, while my subsequent book (1977) described many contrasting lifestyles within the same village. While I included life history materials in these two studies, I focused mainly on the broad features of village, caste, economic, and religious organization rather than on the personal experiences of the villagers. With this material as necessary background, I then turned to what had become over the years my primary interest, a focus on the villagers as persons, on their recollections of the events and experiences that gave meaning to their lives or forced them to question the meaning of their existence. By recording the lives and sufferings of Muli and his people, I hope that I have helped to hasten the day when such sufferings cease, not only for Indian Untouchables, but for all victims of social inequality.

Significance of Muli's Life History

The story of Muli's life may move others, as it did me, to ponder their own experiences in ways that they had previously neglected. An authentic life history confronts us with an immediacy and concreteness that compels our involvement, that causes us to discover within ourselves something about human predicaments everywhere in the face of which our cultural differences become insignificant. Muli presents such a life history. The cultural idiom in which he operates may be foreign to us, but his aims are not: he strives for dignity; he seeks to be respected by the people around him; he questions why fate has brought him to his present circumstances; he wants a good life for himself. As he approaches what he thinks of as old age, Muli sees his dream of achieving a good life slipping by; a bleak end awaits him. He expresses no hopes of salvation or of a better existence in a future life. His particular beliefs are guided by his cultural setting, but his predicament is not.

The unique contribution made by a life history is that it helps the reader to understand the abstract principles of behavioural science as reflected in the lived experience of the narrator. A life history at its best transforms the lifeless abstractions of behavioural science into vivid personal accounts. Abstract discussions of the concept of stigma provide a necessary basis for generalization, but the high-caste tea-stall boy's humiliating caste insults of Muli bring the concept of stigma to life in a way that no abstraction can convey.

The life history of Muli also gives us an insight into the nature of oppression in any caste society. Muli's life history stands as an indictment, not merely of the caste system as an Indian phenomenon, but rather as an indictment of stratified systems of inherited inequality everywhere, which invariably produce effects similar to those described by Muli. In his comparison of stratified societies, Berreman contends that, 'The Black in America and in South Africa, the Burakumin of Japan, the Harijan of India, the barber or washermen of Swat, the Hutu or Twa of Ruanda, have all faced similar conditions as individuals and they have responded to them in similar ways' (1972: 405).[10] On the basis of evidence from many stratified societies, Berreman concludes that, '... no group of people is content to be low in caste hierarchy—to live a life of inherited deprivation and subjection—regardless of the apparent stability of the system and regardless of the rationalizations offered by their superiors or constructed by themselves' (1973: 17).

Berreman's words are particularly apt when applied to India. Untouchables throughout India rarely claim to be proud of their place in society; instead, individually or in groups, many attempt to pass as 'clean' high castes by changing their names, customs, occupations, and dress to those of the 'clean' castes. Others deny their caste by converting to anticaste religions such as Buddhism, Islam, or Christianity. Still others join political groups that cut across caste lines. In the anonymity of cities, Untouchables usually can blot out more of their past than those who reside in villages, but the process, slow and painful, often takes generations. In Muli's village, where Untouchables depend for their livelihood on higher-caste employers, denials of Untouchability provoke severe high-caste economic retaliation, if not physical violence. Thus external conditions have doomed Muli and most of the people of his caste to failure no matter what they choose to do, and Muli's adaptations reflect this situation. Muli and other Bauris have failed, not because they embody expectations of failure or accept their lot, but rather because the Bauris face social and economic disabilities that they are presently powerless to change.

Notes

1. 'Muli' is a pseudonym, as are all Indian names used in the narrative, except Hari's.

2. The people of Muli's caste consider most of the words used by the tea-stall boy to be insulting, and they greatly resent the people who use these insults: 'hey there', a particular term used to call Untouchable people; 'brother-in-law', connoting that one has had sexual relations with a sister of the man being addressed; 'Bauri', in the context of this sentence, a derogatory use of the name of Muli's caste; 'lad' or 'boy', an insult when used to address an Untouchable adult male; 'you will take', the intimate personal pronoun and the corresponding verbal form used for children and inferiors.

3. The figure is an extrapolation from the estimated figure of eighty million in 1971.

4. The best known autobiography of an Untouchable is that by Hazari (1969), a remarkable document written by an educated man who converted to Islam. Zelliot's fifty-page bibliography on Untouchability (1972) additionally lists only a few short of biographies of Dr B.R. Ambedkar, the most famous Untouchable leader, and only one of another prominent leader, Jagjivan Ram. Isaacs (1974) uses brief selections of life histories of Untouchables. All of the Untouchables mentioned above are highly educated.

5. Wallace Chafe, after reading a preliminary version of this chapter, told me that he doubted that a person remembers over long periods details such as the food eaten at dinner or the details of complex anecdotes. Instead, based on the results of his present

research on remembering, as well as on Bartlett's classic investigations (1967), Chafe argues that what Muli remembered was more a process of reconstruction than an exact recollection, that Muli imposed an organizational framework on the details he had stored. See Bartlett 1967: 197–214. Similarly, in his article on the life history of Tukbaw, a Llongot leader in the Philippines, Renato Rosaldo observes that Tukbaw described experiences from his early childhood that appeared to be based not on memory but on reconstruction from observing the behaviour of his children (1976: 121–51). Norman notes, however, that some persons appear to have a better memory than other people, although he questions how much is true memory, and how much is reconstruction. Experts in tasks, he notes, often can reconstruct complex events from very little information, in part because they can rule out implausible happenings (Norman 1969: 138). Food plays an important part in Muli's life. Since feasts are great and memorable events in his life, Muli may well have better recollection of such details than do persons for whom feasts are not central events.

6. Most older Bauris call high-status people and employers *sāānta* [master], which is a term of higher respect than *bābū*. Muli conspicuously avoids using the term 'master' when he addresses high-status people.

7. One household unavailable to him was his father-in-law's household, where Hari had to observe respect-avoidance relationships; another was that of his father's cousin, who was feuding with Hari's household.

8. For details on the economic plight of the Bauris, see Freeman 1977.

9. For reviews of life history studies in anthropology, see the following: Kluckhohn (1945) provides a comprehensive review of life history studies in anthropology up to 1945, and gives a brilliant analysis of their defects, as well as of some of the problems involved in collecting life histories. Langness (1965) reviews developments in the study of life histories up to 1965, and outlines the uses of life histories, particularly in studies of psychological anthropology and social change. Mandelbaum (1973) reviews the study of life histories and formulates a comprehensive perspective for the analysis of life histories. In my book on Muli I have used Mandelbaum's perspective for interpreting Muli's life history, and I have included all of the topics that Kluckhohn considered necessary for an adequate life history: (1) a comprehensive narrative; (2) a discussion of the conditions and ways in which a person collects a life history; (3) an indication of how a person's life history integrates with information about his group; (4) use of a coherent conceptual scheme for interpretation of a life history.

10. Many incidents in Muli's life history show striking similarities with events recorded in other cultures. For example, Muli often quotes himself as saying to his masters that he is dark, dirty, and polluting, but his tone suggests that, like the slaves of the antebellum southern USA, he plays up to his masters by telling them what he thinks they believe or want to hear. He often pretends loyalty to high-caste masters, while privately ridiculing his master's ideals (see Osofsky 1969: 9, 21–4; also see Meier and Rudwick 1976: 75–86). Muli's description of the double standard of high-caste men who treat him familiarly in private and disavow him publically, finds its exact parallel in a passage describing a high-status Japanese woman's treatment of her low-status friend (see Norbeck 1972: 195–6).

The Insider Versus the Outsider in the Study of Cultures

M.N. SRINIVAS

There is a marked tendency among Western cultural and social anthropologists to define the discipline as concerned with the study of 'other cultures/societies', together with frequent mention of the difficulties involved in studying one's own society. According to Leach, for instance, the 'justification for studying "others" than "ourselves" is that, although we first perceive others as exotic, we end up by recognizing in their "peculiarities" a mirror of our own' (1982: 127). Leach also adds, 'Despite my negative attitude towards the direct anthropological study of one's society, I still hold that all the anthropologist's most important insights stem from introspection' (ibid.).

That fieldwork in one's own society is far more difficult than fieldwork in an alien society, may be conceded readily, and also, that the neophyte should not be encouraged to begin his career by studying his own society. I am in basic agreement with this recommendation of Leach's. But his other conclusion, that though social anthropologists have been studying their own society for a long time, they 'mostly do not do it very well' (ibid.: 124), is much more disputable, to say the least. For, as a matter of actual fact, the study of 'others' has gone on for a longer time than the study of one's own society. Also, Leach's conclusion is based on four studies carried out by Chinese anthropologists who did their work between 1934 and 1949. Three of the four seem to have been clear failures. The first one was Lin Yueh Lwa's study of his native village, but Lin, instead of writing it up as a proper anthropological study, wrote it as a novel as it enabled him to 'evade the problems posed by autobiographical honesty' (ibid.). But that 'artifice did not really work.'

The next instance cited by Leach is Martin Yang's study of his natal village: 'but he wrote about it at a distance when resident in New York. In the outcome the characters in his study were completely depersonalized. Indeed, Yang's self-imposed anonymity reduces his book to a kind of caricature of a European ethnological description of a primitive tribe written around 1900' (ibid.: 125).

The third study was by Francis L.K. Hsu.

His book is about ancestor worship in West Town which is presented as prototypical of that which prevails in Chinese culture as a whole. Hsu himself grew up in eastern China but his account is evidently a syncretic blend of what he learned as a child from personal experience and what he learned as an adult, several thousand miles away to the west, during fourteen months' fieldwork in the Yunnanese city of Tali-fu, where he was employed for a while as a teacher in a local missionary college (ibid.).

The inhabitants of Tali-fu are mostly Min Chia, a population with a distinctive language of their own, and to Hsu's personal dismay he was treated as a stranger.... But Hsu was so anxious that 'West Town' should typify China as a whole that the Min Chia peculiarities of the local culture are hardly ever mentioned. This is a palpable distortion but the resulting stereotype picture is curiously static. The fieldwork was conducted during the period July 1941–September 1943 but the book is written as if the culture of 'West Town' was timeless and entirely unaffected by the chaos of the surrounding political situation (ibid.: 125–26).

Leach characterizes Hsu's study as not a study of one's own society: '...the author expressly claimed that he was studying members of his own society, but by the ordinary criteria used by social anthropologists he was not doing anything of the sort' (ibid.: 125, emphasis mine). On the basis of three unsuccessful studies, of which one was not even a study of one's own society, Leach comes to the conclusion '. . . that the understandable, and indeed laudable, desire on the part of some social anthropologists to study their own society is beset with hazards. Initial preconceptions are liable to prejudice the research in a way that does not affect the work of the naïve stranger' (ibid.: 126). Granted the existence of 'initial preconceptions', are they such as to be insurmountable? Leach obviously thinks they are: 'when anthropologists study facets of their own society their vision seems to become distorted by prejudices which derive from private rather than public experience' (ibid.: 124). Not only does Leach not tell us how to distinguish between prejudices stemming from private and public experience respectively, but he is also silent on the question—why are prejudices stemming from private experience an insurmountable obstacle to fieldwork?

But, as a matter of actual fact, whatever the prejudices and other shortcomings from which the anthropologist wanting to study his own society may be suffering they have not been such as to prevent him from carrying out successful studies. For Leach's fourth example is of a successful study of one's own society: Fei Hsiao Tung made a study of a village in the Yangtze Delta, about 125 miles south-west of Shanghai. He was not a native of the village,

... but he had grown up in the same district so that he was familiar with the nuances of the local dialect. Also it is clearly relevant that his sister, who was in charge of a local, government-sponsored, silk development project, was well-known to all the villagers. But when one learns that the whole project involved only two months of actual field research (July-August 1936), it becomes obvious that, in this case, the success of the enterprise must have been heavily dependent upon Fei's prior local knowledge....

However, the merit of Fei's book lies in its functionalist style. Like all the best work by social anthropologists it has at its core the very detailed study of the network of relationships operating within a single very small-scale community. Such studies do not or should not, claim to be 'typical' of anything in particular. They are not intended to serve as illustrations of something more general. They are interesting in themselves. And yet the best of such monographs despite the concentration upon a tiny range of human activity, will tell us more about the ordinary social behaviour of mankind than a whole shelfful of general textbooks labelled *Introduction to Cultural Anthropology'* (ibid.: 127).

The success of Fei's work offers convincing evidence that one's own society can be studied successfully, provided the anthropologist is well trained, and in addition exercises abundant caution in his choice of the field-community and generally, in his fieldwork. It also needs to be stressed that the insider enjoys immense advantages denied to the outsider, to mention but one of them, mastery over the local language. The study which Fei took two months to carry out might have taken a foreigner several years and even then, he might not have made an equally good study. The insider and outsider have each advantages as well as disadvantages, and it is dogmatism to assert that one or the other is bound to fail.

Leach also states, *en passant,* a few difficulties faced by anthropologists studying communities in remote areas of the tropics. Long travel, and the hardships of living in the primitive tropics, are expectably the principal difficulties. Leach urges anthropologists to treat the indigenes as equals. He does not, however, comment as Evans-Pritchard has done in his short book, *Social Anthropology* (1951), on the moral and intellectual qualities required of anthropologists who want to make a study, using the method of participant observation, of an alien community in a faraway country. Evans-Pritchard thought that it was essential for the anthropologist to regard himself as inferior to the natives, as he had gone to them to study their culture and society. He also wanted the anthropologist to make friends locally, and to this end, he had to be single. A wife (or husband) would come in the way of seeking such friendships.

The very potent method of participant observation which Malinowski forged for the study of exotic communities, calls for a combination of such unusual qualities that one wonders how many of those who have carried out fieldwork really meet the requirements. For instance, how many Western anthropologists feel that the indigenes are their genuine equals and not inferiors? And even if they did not regard themselves as superiors, unless the anthropologists lived, as far as possible, as did the indigenes, their relative affluence, and easy access to the powerful, were likely to create feelings of inferiority in the local community.

How many anthropologists master the language sufficiently to be able to read a novel in it, or are capable of dispensing with their interpreters and talk directly to the people? During the last thirty-five years or so I have come across a good many Western anthropologists who did fieldwork in India but the number of those who had some mastery over the local tongue was very few. A few scholars even stayed in nearby towns with their families and commuted to the field while their Indian assistants did much of the work of collecting the data. Frequently, the fact has to be faced that the final picture of the culture and society drawn by the Western anthropologist is heavily based on information supplied by interpreters, themselves not always equipped with a deep knowledge of, or respect for, their culture.

Leach has spoken of the absence of 'initial preconceptions' on the part of the outside stranger as contrasted with the insider. But the absence of initial preconceptions, however, offers no guarantee that they will not develop later. I have come across a few Western specialists on India who hated the people of the country and their culture but a grim purposefulness enabled them to write up accounts of their fieldwork and publish them. My own hunch is that anthropologists working in alien cultures frequently develop a deep ambivalence towards the cultures they study but this is not articulated widely enough. It is only mentioned in confidence to a few friends. It would be interesting to find out if such ambivalence is widespread, and if so, why.

Many, if not most, Western anthropologists are rationalists who have scant respect for the religious beliefs and practices of the members of their own culture or that of any other. A large segment of the culture of the primitives, or peasants in the non-Western world, must appear nonsensical to them. Given this basic situation, how can Western anthropologists have respect for the non-Western cultures that they study? Attempts to justify religion on the basis of its contribution to political or social stability, does not really answer the question.

Sociology and social anthropology became increasingly popular in a large number of Third World countries during the years following the end of World War II. However, as between the two disciplines, sociology was able to spread more easily, as it did not have the taint of an exclusive, or even dominant, association with the study of primitives. Among the educated people in the former colonies, there was a strong feeling that to be studied by anthropologists was enough to label them as primitives. In nationalist circles, there was even a suspicion that European anthropologists were employed by colonial governments to drive a wedge between the tribal and non-tribal populations of the country. The point which I am making is that given the historic suspicions against social anthropology in Third World countries any attempt to confine it now to the study of 'others', particularly tribals, will not only narrow its scope but prejudice the non-Western intelligentsia against it. But Western anthropologists might see this phenomenon differently; as facilitating concentration on the study of 'fundamental' problems in such areas as social structure, particularly kinship, mythology, religion, cognitive anthropology, etc. The study of social change and development, apart from being very messy, tends to get entangled in ideological disputation, for which not everyone has the appetite.

Many former colonial countries, including India, observe, though not strictly, a division of labour between anthropology and sociology, the former concentrating on tribal groups and the latter on rural and urban ones. Anthropologists concentrate on the method of participant observation while the sociologists tend to undertake surveys using questionnaires and sampling techniques. By and large, the two go for ideas to different intellectual traditions in Europe and America. Communication between anthropologists and sociologists is minimal. Anyone who tried to argue that social anthropology and sociology should both form a single discipline as they are both engaged in the study of human societies, would not get a serious hearing. The less imaginative scholars seem to think that out there in the external world there are two distinct entities called 'sociology' and 'social anthropology'.

The crucial point, however, is that sociologists and social anthropologists are now both an integral part of the academic milieu in many Third World countries. In some of these countries at least modest funds are available for research which was *not* generally the situation during the colonial era. But funds are available only for research within the country, and more rarely, for research in neighbouring countries. There are usually priorities in the matter of themes for research, the study of change, planned as well as unplanned, the condition of the 'weaker sections', etc., enjoying preference over other themes which some scholars might regard as more fundamental. As a result of the encouragement given, it is not unlikely that in the near future, information about cultural and social phenomena and their analysis and interpretation, at least in a few Third World countries, is likely to come mostly from the indigenes. This is different from the situation that prevailed before World War II when not only the basic theoretical frame but even ethnographic information about Third World countries came very largely from Western anthropologists. This is an important phenomenon though many seem to be unaware of it and its implications.

The phrase 'studying one's own society' needs some clarification: very few are ill-advised enough to take up their natal village or town or quarter for study. It is more generally a village, ethnic group or town in a neighbouring region that is selected. And in a country like India where linguistic, regional, religious, caste, sect, class and other differences are quite acute, the selection of a group or category outside one's natal region, has a dual advantage. It is sufficiently different to stimulate observation yet at the same time it is familiar. But the familiarity might prove to be misleading and closer examination might reveal subtle differences underlying the familiar mask. For instance, village or other goddesses are an all-India phenomenon but there are significant differences between the goddess-cults of different regions. Sometimes the differences are so radical that one wonders whether it is right to put them all into a single rubric. Similarly, caste is best studied, at least initially, as a regional system, for there are interregional differences which tend to be lost sight of when viewed only as an all-India system.

India has a large tribal population, and the tribes not only differ from the non-tribal population but from each other. An urban middle-class Indian can select a tribe in the confident expectation that its culture will be very different from his own. While tribals and non-tribals form a single political community, culturally they are very different.

In the circumstances described above, the 'outsider', then, becomes more a question of degree than kind. But such a situation is not confined to India. For instance, William Whyte's classic study of an Italian slum near Boston, *Street Corner Society* (1943), gives a first-rate insight into grassroots politics and culture in a corner of America during the years immediately following the depression. Studies of one's own society, admittedly difficult, can be done well or badly just as studies of other societies.

Fei and Whyte did it well, and they eloquently disproved the notion that it cannot be done well at all.

A crucial difficulty confronting the anthropologist who wants to study a segment of his own society is the imperative need to achieve some distance from it. Not only is the anthropologist a part of his own society but he carries it along with him as well. Over a period of years, it should be possible to train him to observe his own society, to try and see it as a stranger would. As part of his training, he should study, in his country, a community other than his own, and preferably located in a different region. The differences between his own group, and the community selected for study, should stimulate his powers of observation. If the community is sufficiently different, he might experience a 'culture shock' much as the anthropologist studying a faraway and exotic community experiences it.

The involvement of the anthropologist with his own society may be so deep that he might fail to recognize the presence of disruptive forces around him. But, on the other hand, the alien anthropologist, coming from a more tidy and homogeneous society, might see disruption in a noisy procession or strike. But the very depth of the involvement of the insider in his society is likely to invest his work with a relevance and urgency which the outsider's work is not likely to possess. It may be worthwhile reiterating here that in anthropological understanding, as distinct from some other forms of understanding, the entire psyche of the anthropologist is involved and not only his cognitive faculties. Such involvement is more generally characteristic of insiders rather than outsiders.

There is a view, not very popular, I admit, that it is not possible for a member of one culture to really understand another. It is a truism that the method of participant observation, when practised fully, in letter and spirit, does give the anthropologist the feeling that he understands, not only intellectually but emotionally, the community he is studying. Malinowski went so far as to say that the anthropologist's aim was to understand the society from the inside. While the anthropologist can reconstruct the logic of the culture of studies, and the statements of the indigenes do give him clues to how they think and feel, but he cannot totally put himself in the position of the indigene without ceasing to be an anthropologist. A gulf does exist between the anthropologist and the community he studies, and at best it can be reduced greatly. It can never be totally annihilated. The only point with the insider is that he shares, as a member of the culture—the larger culture—some of the values, beliefs, and attitudes of the people he studies, and this gives him—or ought to give him—greater insight into their behaviour.

I must hasten to add that I am not only not against studies of a culture by outsiders but on the contrary *I am positively for them*. I would prefer the outsiders to come from diverse cultures because there would then be multiple views of a culture. In the kind of universe that anthropologists study, all that we can have are multiple views of the same culture. There cannot be a single correct or all-embracing view. One of the views ought to be that of the insider and various views can be complementary even when—or especially when—they differ from that of each other.

The Native Anthropologist: Constraints and Strategies in Research

STELLA MASCARENHAS-KEYES

Introduction

British social anthropologists, at home as well as abroad, usually do fieldwork in 'exotic cultures' (Sarsby 1984: 130). However, for the 'native anthropologist',[1] research occurs within the 'non-exotic' sociocultural context of primary socialization and requires, as will be shown, a professionally induced schizophrenia between the 'native self' and 'professional self'. This paper addresses itself primarily to the problems of professional access to information and role definition in a context where 'my people' 'do not perceive the investigator as special, exotic or powerful' (Cassell 1977: 413). Section I discusses the factors leading to the adoption and the implementation of a multiple-native strategy. Section II examines the ways that permanent kinship and associational links affected the legitimation of research, and required strategies to overcome constraints on access to information. In Section III, I demonstrate the value of using self as informant, borrowing the concepts of transference and counter transference developed by psychoanalysts. Since anthropological praxis involves not only fieldwork, but also writing texts, in the final section of this paper I examine some of the issues involved in producing texts destined for both native and academic audiences.

I. On Becoming a Multiple Native

Outsiders attempt during fieldwork to become 'marginal natives' (Freilich 1977) and to negotiate a temporary 'social space' within the society.

However, the problem is reversed for the native anthropologist who has to transcend an *a priori* ascribed social position in the society in order, like the Outsider, professionally to relate to the whole spectrum of native social categories. The problem is compounded when the native anthropologist is located in a very complex society, such as is found in Goa.

Goa, a tiny region situated on the west coast of India, had been under Portuguese rule for 450 years, with the result that the indigenous population comprises both Catholics, and Hindus. Since the mid-nineteenth century, large numbers of Catholics, in comparison to Hindus, have migrated and established globally dispersed satellite communities, with the result that the majority of Catholics in Goa are part of an international Catholic Goan community which transcends geographical boundaries.[2] I was born and brought up within the confines of the Catholic Goan community in Kenya and, on subsequent settlement in Britain fifteen years ago, became an integral member of the Catholic Goan community in London (see Mascarenhas-Keyes 1979). My two previous month-long visits to Goa as a child and teenager had not sensitized me to its social and cultural diversity which was richly manifested in Amora,[3] my focal village, with its population of just under 3,000 persons. From 1979 to 1981 I set up an independent household in the heart of Amora with my European husband, in a bungalow rented from a Catholic Goan living in Bombay (now Mumbai).

Apart from a few tribal Kunbis, Amora consisted of equal proportions of indigenous Hindus and Catholics, and there was some residential segregation. The Hindus, who had begun to settle in Amora thirty years previously, were mainly poor low-caste farmers and casual labourers employed by Catholics. The Catholics, who had ancestral links with Amora, were predominantly Brahmins, moderately educated, with good cash incomes derived mainly from current remittances or pensions from technical and white-collar employment outside Goa. They lived in large, moderately furnished houses, usually dressed in Western clothes, ate meat, and drank alcohol, while the Hindus lived in small huts, wore Indian-style clothes, and were largely vegetarian and teetotallers. Konkani (the local vernacular), English, Portuguese, and some Swahili were spoken by different sectors of the society.

Within this heterogeneous society, I was identified by natives in terms of a complement of immutable characteristics: international Catholic, Brahmin, female, married, educated, middle class (but of recent peasant origins). However, I was extremely reluctant to conform to behavioural patterns and modes of thought culturally expected of my ascribed position because of my respect for cultural diversity cultivated through anthropological training, and my intention to operate as an anthropologist. Although there were some continuing difficulties, described in greater detail below, in legitimizing my research interests and methodological approach, initial verbal acceptance encouraged me to venture into non-stereotypical forays across multiple boundaries. However, I was dismayed to find that I courted considerable criticism and ridicule and it became apparent that, as a neophyte, I was unprepared 'for the more sophisticated task of studying (his) own society' (Srinivas 1966:157). I longed for an outward sign, such as a large badge, saying 'I am an anthropologist' and therefore should be granted 'diplomatic immunity'. Furthermore, various categories were responding to my overtures with confusion because, although I initially made some cultural concessions, such as sitting cross-legged on the floor eating vegetarian food with Hindus, my specific native identity was still transparent.

The situation was compounded because the nature of the research required periodic visits to other parts of Goa and interviews with government officials and other 'big men'. My first interview with a 'big man' proved fruitless; on greeting me he exclaimed, 'You're so young. I expected a man or an older woman,' and then proceeded summarily to dismiss all my questions. Furthermore, I did not acquire, as outsiders usually do, someone to sponsor me or mediate between self and natives. I had decided against engaging a native research assistant because his/her socio-economic characteristics would circumscribe access to sources of data (see Berreman 1962). I was also reluctant to use key informants (see Casagrande 1960) because of my belief in the necessity of obtaining first-hand rather than socially and personally 'percolated' information. Trapped in a multiple-bind situation, my intuition suggested I wholeheartedly adopt a multiple-native strategy with a chameleon-like virtuosity, in the hope of achieving a higher degree of cultural consonance in different contexts than I had previously managed. This strategy generated different sorts of problems and considerable personal anxiety and anger, which I discuss later in this paper, but for the moment I shall briefly describe how I became a multiple native.

The 'props' used in what was, to a large extent, a 'dramaturgical exercise' (cf. Goffman 1982) were language and the large wardrobe of Western and Indian clothes, footwear, ornaments, and other accessories I felt compelled to acquire. As Pelto points out, because styles of clothing are important signals of social status and role, the 'fieldworker can *always* influence local attitudes towards him by adopting particular habits of costume' (1970: 227). When visiting 'elites' and 'big men' I wore 'executive' London-style clothes, high-heeled shoes, fashionable accessories, lipstick, a hairstyle that added a few years; I presented my visiting-card and spoke English in

'elaborated code' (see Bernstein 1971). A broadly similar 'scholarly' image was essential when I went to interview sailors in the tavern, which
respectable Goan women never enter. With lower-status Catholics, I dressed
in clothes tailored in local materials and fashions. I reserved loose
sun-dresses, slacks, and other casual wear for research sessions spent with
international returnees living in a city beach-side residential area. For
periods spent with Hindus, particularly when attending rituals and ceremonies both in Amora and their distant ancestral villages, I dressed in a
sari, plastic sandals, smothered my face with white talcum powder,
adopted the oiled plaited hairstyle adorned with flowers, and wore gold
jewellery and a 'clip-on' nose ring. This evoked favourable comments
from Hindus—'You look like one of us' and derisive ones from Catholics:
'You look just like a Hindu'.

Outsiders inevitably have to deal with the native language problem and,
to some extent, I was confronted by a similar one. Like most international
Catholics of my generation, I spoke English, not Konkani, as a first
language. However, I did not wish to engage a Konkani-speaking interpreter because, professionally, I was aware of epistemological limitations
(Owusu 1978) and, personally, I wanted to redress the effects of cultural
imperialism. Consequently, I took an intensive language course in Goa,
which considerably improved my previous minimal facility in Konkani.[4]
With the overwhelming majority of Hindus, Kunbis, and a smaller number
of Catholics, who spoke only Konkani, I conversed in this language, and
gradually learned to switch to the dialect of the specific group I was with.
Among those who spoke both English and Konkani, I acquiesced in their
preference for using English. With traditional Catholic elites, who were
multilingual but preferred to speak Portuguese in social gatherings of peers,
my limited fluency in Portuguese enabled me to intersperse conversations
with token words which often elicited approval. I colluded with Africa
returnees by conversing in Swahili, the language they resorted to when
transmitting confidential information in mixed company. Language was
called on to play a predominant rather than a complementary role when
natives dropped in unexpectedly to visit me. Caught, so to speak, in my
'home clothes', usually a plain frock and casual hairstyle, I had to rely on
my linguistic repertoire to articulate the multiple-native strategy.

The operation of the multiple-native strategy was considerably facilitated by my residence in an independent household; hence I was exempt
from the patronage of a resident native which would probably have circumscribed my autonomy (see Beteille and Madan 1975; Srinivas 1976).
Furthermore, by working alone not only did I have the freedom to be

psychologically mobile (Powdermaker 1966: 291) but socially mobile too. I did not have to ensure that a 'team performance' was maintained (Goffman 1982: 85–108), and I could consciously and intuitively refine impression management through heightened sensitivity to verbal and non-verbal behavioural nuances. Gender served as a further advantage as cultural elaboration of dress and demeanour was articulated by females. I feel certain that it was only by becoming a multiple native that I was able to achieve a high degree of empathy with respect to each social category. Furthermore, unlike at the beginning of fieldwork, when different natives tended either to 'put on a show' or remain reticent, when my ascribed identity was opaque they relaxed and interacted in a far more 'natural' manner, thus improving the quality of data obtained.

II. The Significance of Permanent Kinship and Associational Links

The outsider is usually incorporated into native society by acquiring a temporary fictive kinship position (Middleton 1970). However, like a few other anthropologists (Nakleh 1979; Loizos 1981; Stephen and Greer 1981) I was already a permanent component of a web of kinship and associational relationships. These were continually reinforced by visits from my parents (Africa returnees who lived in a nearby town), close kin from my ancestral village, overseas siblings, and international Goan friends holidaying in Goa. Hence Catholics located me within an international kinship and associational network. In contrast to this, Hindus and Kunbis identified me in terms of my husband's foreign status, referring to me as 'hippie's wife'.[5] Both identifications served to obscure the fact that my presence in Goa was for professional purposes. For instance, I was expected by 'relations' as well as villagers to fulfil a host of kinship obligations and I suffered rebuke when I declined. At first I used to regard such visits, particularly to dispersed geographical locations, as a waste of time for anthropological training had socialized me into the 'single village mentality'. To make virtue of necessity I resolved to regard the information gleaned at such events as 'grist to the mill', which facilitated the cultivation of an all-Goa perspective to serve as a backdrop to my focal village.

Kinship and associational links ensured that my past was not a closed book, as is often the case with the Outsider, since many Catholics knew that I had previously held the reputable jobs of secondary school teacher in Kenya and secretary in London. Although educational standards are high, there is little familiarity with the aims and practices of the social sciences.

However, a few who 'knew about anthropology' strongly suggested I should study the tribal Kunbis who, because of their different dress, diet, and customs, were regarded as 'exotic' and hence, unlike themselves, the appropriate objects of anthropological study. It was considered strange that an educated, married woman would return from 'modern, advanced Britain' to the 'primitive village' to find out how 'ordinary', let alone 'exotic', people lived. Initially many thought that it was my foreign husband who had come to do research and, at the beginning, invitations were always extended to him to 'show you Goa and how we live'. Not only was I not studying 'exotic' people but the subject of my research was not 'exotic' either, since it focused on the patterns and consequences of international migration, and Catholics saw themselves as much a part of the process as I was. I was made acutely conscious of Agar's comment that 'Ethnography is really quite an arrogant enterprise' (1980: 41) as there were many remarks from Catholics to challenge my claim to special expertise, the implication being that any Goan with time on their hands and the ability to inveigle funds from an agency could do the 'research'.

With the Hindus, the conventional Outsider's excuse of ignorance and curiosity about an alien culture was more acceptable, although perplexing, in gaining entry because the cultural segregation between the two communities was acutely evident. My research interest in the Hindus derived from the fact that their recent settlement in Amora and the agricultural labour force they constituted were directly correlated with the international migration of Catholics. However, Hindus perceived that it was my ignorance of Hinduism typical of Catholics, which was the basis of my interest in them. Consequently they always invited me to any religious ceremony taking place in Amora or their distant ancestral homes. They admonished me when I did not take copious notes of their descriptions of deities and explanations of religious events, saying, 'Why aren't you writing that in your book?' My real research interest was perceived as tangential to what they discerned as my 'research', and while I was able to broach the issues I was interested in, conspicuous note-taking of such information had to be avoided.

Unlike the Outsider who can become a 'neutral confidant' (Berreman 1962: 11, 19; Goffman 1982: 159), kinship and associational links made it credible that the information I was seeking was not for innocuous 'research' purposes but for personal motives. The Outsider usually has potentially greater access to information because asymmetrical power relations and his ignorance are conspicuous. As Jarvie points out, 'The fieldworker as humble supplicant is obviously not often the case. Many people would not tolerate the white stranger snooping around were it not that he belongs, as far as they are concerned, to the powerful white society which they hesitate to brush with' (1969: 508). While I had considerable success in asking direct questions about migration patterns, the need for extensive questioning on a variety of topics was rarely understood. Even my parents and siblings found such questions exasperating, and often said 'but what has *this* got to do with your research?', and beseeched me not to 'cross-examine our friends'. Questions perceived as peripheral and tangential to my 'research' indicated an unwarranted inquisitiveness, and indeed epitomized the type of Goan who is most feared: the one 'who becomes your friend to get all your news', the one who 'minds everybody's business and not just their own'. Further, even if I could be trusted to keep my promise of confidentiality, there were some fears that other literate natives who dropped in casually at my home would have access to privileged information. I do not wish to imply that 'my people' were excessively paranoid, but intimate knowledge has an ominous and indefinable potency in an environment to which international migration has contributed to making competitiveness, insecurity, and anxiety endemic.

To depersonalize information and alleviate anxiety, I resorted to techniques gained outside anthropological training. I pre-coded quantifiable data in a format suitable for computer analysis, and in the presence of natives recorded data numerically on computer sheets. The significance of the numbers could only be discerned in conjunction with a master sheet specifying what the figures represented. With qualitative information I conspicuously made notes in my personal version of (Pitmans) shorthand, and the nature of the symbolic system employed made it virtually impossible for anyone else but myself to decipher notes.

Like the outsider, but to a greater degree, I had to resort to covert investigation to get 'back-stage' information. I often had to be seen consciously to be discarding my professional role and operating as an ordinary native. 'Chatting' was invaluable here, and once the art had been mastered, I had access to various arenas of 'private' information. Since I prepared and cooked our own meals, and was genuinely interested in learning to cook traditional dishes, there were numerous occasions when 'cookery lessons' surreptitiously covered a multitude of topics. Cooking and related activities were perceived as legitimate concerns because they attested to my being a 'good Goan wife' who made considerable efforts to provide her foreign husband with the full flavour of Goan cuisine. It also became essential to participate in numerous 'innocuous' activities such as various religious services. Such regular and frequent attendance by an Outsider would have been perceived by natives as conspicuous evidence of professional status

and interest in learning 'native ways', but in my case it was seen to testify
to my being, unlike most young people, a very 'devout Catholic'. Attendance at novenas at the numerous village chapels and wayside crosses was
perceived as a pious measure to remedy my childless condition. Of course,
not all natives were 'fooled' and a young teacher remarked, 'You are not
concerned about praying; you are going to everything because of your research'.

For the outsider, as well as the native anthropologist, fieldwork entails
the 'balanced reciprocity of relationships and information' (Mayer 1975:
28). However, the demands for reciprocity were different with respect to
different social categories. With Hindus, as well as Kunbis and poor Catholics, reciprocity approximated the measures an outsider would resort to: I
wrote official letters, acceded to requests to take photographs, lent money
and foodstuffs, paid bus fares, etc. However, with middle- and upper-class
Catholics, the fact that I was native, young, and female removed any reticence that older Catholics, and women in particular, had of questioning
me about the minutiae of my life. Ablon, who studied middle-class Americans
with whom she was culturally identified, points out that the 'diminution of
cultural barriers leads to increased personal visibility of the anthropologist' and demands for intimate information (1977: 70). Like the natives, I
had little hesitation in divulging impersonal information but was wary of
disclosing personal details. Furthermore, since it was obvious that through
'gallivanting around the village', as my behaviour was referred to, I had
undoubtedly gathered 'salacious information' and there were many attempts
to prise it out of me. Hence, with most Catholics, reciprocity led to a heightened vulnerability of Self, and I generally circumvented questions by
resorting to evasive answers, lightning and subtle changes of conversation, partial answers, half-truths and so forth—the very strategies I tried to
steer 'my people' from. While everyday native social interaction, particularly for women, was articulated in the exchange of 'personalized'
information, I could only engage partially and cautiously in this activity
because had I acceded to their excessive demands, not only would I have
epitomized the 'bad native' but also breached professional ethics.

III. Self as Informant

A belief in naive empiricism has led anthropologists 'to turn the fieldworker
into a self-effacing creature without any reaction other than those of a
recording machine' (Nash and Wintrop 1972: 527). However, recent
publications have compelled us to recognize the existence of the 'personal

equation' (e.g. Malinowski 1967; Beteille and Madan 1975; Okely 1975; Rabinow 1977; Cesara 1982) and that, in a world of already constituted meaning (Rabinow and Sullivan 1979), anthropologists are interpreters, not mere recorders of cultures (Agar 1982; Hammersley and Atkinson 1983; Ellen 1984). Devereux, in his book *From Anxiety to Method in the Behavioural Sciences*, recommends that we must use 'the subjectivity inherent in all observations as the royal road to an authentic, rather than fictitious, objectivity' (1967: xvii). I would further argue that we should incorporate the creative use of emotional reactions of Self and Other as methodological tools in fieldwork. Like Okely (1975: 182) I think social anthropologists should explore analogous methods to psychoanalysts, as I found during fieldwork that I intuitively made methodological use of the concepts 'transference' and 'counter-transference'.[6] Earlier in this paper I described the strategies used in becoming a multiple native and alluded to the hostility directed at me, and the self-anxiety and anger it generated. In the absence of a research assistant and key informants who would have served as social and psychological buffers (Wintrop 1969:68–69), there was not only a heightened exposure of self to others, but correlatively a greater psychological retreat into self. In the face of stressful experiences in the field, I began to turn 'anxiety to method' but this was an intuitive response, not dictated by any prior training.

Anthropologists continually invite diverse comments as natives try to make sense of their behaviour. However, more so than the outsider, I became an enduring topic of village comment precisely because I was a native who, by my activities, was constantly challenging multiple norms and values. The most conspicuous areas were non-conventional relations with low-status Catholics and with Hindus, and inappropriate behaviour for a married woman. Women anthropologists (e.g.,Golde 1970: 8; Dube 1975: 175) have noted that the behaviour of a female fieldworker is more closely scrutinized than that of a male. Although Catholic Goan women enjoy a considerable degree of autonomy and independence (Mascarenhas-Keyes 1985), nevertheless, my absence from the home and widespread research contact with men provoked numerous snide remarks and jokes from all sectors of society. My husband's Anglo-Saxon reserve and confinement to the private domain of the home engrossed in philosophy books conformed to local expectations of a scholar and served to magnify my enigmatic and public behaviour.

The constant barrage of criticism made me initially very angry and demoralized, and I would self-righteously defend myself by proclaiming my professional status: 'I am an anthropologist; it is my job to mix with all sorts of people; my husband is capable of looking after himself.' Further-more, initially I told my critics the truth and said I found walking around the village alone and familiar relationships with low-status people very stimulating and enjoyable; not surprisingly, this only served to increase my ostracization. I experienced a great deal of coldness and withholding of information and this in turn increased my anxiety as, by losing rapport with certain sectors of society, my investigation was suffering. Consequently, I adopted a number of strategies.

First of all, I began to regard all comments on self as valuable sources of information about the society. I recorded the transference reactions (not as systematically as I now wish I had done), analysed them, and used them as methodological tools to indicate areas for investigation. For instance, I would constantly ask myself 'why is criticism made of this aspect of my behaviour and not that; why do some criticize/praise my actions and others do not; when I mention the criticism or comment to another social group, or members of the same social group, why do they respond in the way they do?'

Second, in order to ensure that I maintained rapport with different crit-ics, and was not seen to be unequivocally identified with particular sec-tions, I discreetly and selectively resorted to the manipulation of reality. Hence, for instance, I would return from a few days spent with Hindus in their ancestral villages, and tell Catholics what I had begun to realize they wanted to hear: it was very uncomfortable sleeping on a cowdung floor; toilet facilities were abysmal; I was weak from living on a vegetarian diet; and that to my horror I had discovered nits in my hair. Furthermore, no longer did I rationalize my involvement with Hindus because I had chosen to do such research but because 'my European professor in London would be angry with me if I did not obtain real information on how Hindus lived'. This strategy evoked sympathy and commiseration and, equally impor-tantly, provided a focus for extensive discussions on the nature of Catholic–Hindu relationships. Hence, with various social categories I periodically tried to take the role of other and this served not only as a diplomatic exercise but also allowed me to get into the native's skin' and see things from multiple perspectives.

It was not only criticism of my behaviour which used to anger me but also the views expressed by natives on a variety of topics. The anger stemmed from a conflict of values, and I would agree with Ablon when she states 'the potential of actual value conflicts with our informants becomes more real when we deal with persons who live and interact within our own cul-tural world' (1977: 70). Initially I would give vent to my anger and argue vehemently, but I was acquiring the reputation of a 'fishwife', particularly because women, even educated ones, do not challenge male views on politics, economics, and religion. Women took me aside and told me to 'stop fighting with the men', and accused me of being inebriated. Consequently, I decided to adopt an approach used by psychoanalysts with respect to counter-transference. I allowed myself to experience the anger but controlled its expression by the adoption of a 'professional attitude' (Winnicott 1960). I noted and analysed my reactions and attempted to use them with equanimity to stimulate further discussion and hence generate data.

Of course, psychoanalysts use transference and counter-transference as therapeutic methods, but I did not see my role during fieldwork as akin to that of a therapist. While I agree with Huizer (1979) and Kielstra (1979) that anthropologists can operate effectively as social activists, my interest in Goa was in 'pure' research rather than research in 'the service of humankind' (Spradley 1980: 16–20). Hence it was important not deliberately to try to change native behaviour, and to adopt strategies that would not prevent access to the whole cross-section of the population. The stresses of fieldwork are legion (see Henry and Saberwal 1969) and anthropologists have resorted to various measures to alleviate stress such as short vacations, excessive eating, social isolation of Self (see Pelto 1970: 223–25). However, since stress seems to be the *sine qua non* of fieldwork (Kobben 1967: 46), rather than escape from it I suggest that we could usefully integrate it into fieldwork methodology. Simultaneously, the strategy helps to maintain emotional balance as it reduces the vulnerability of Self and increases resilience to adverse comments.

IV. The Implications of Writing Texts for a Native and Academic Audience

'A reflexive awareness of ethnographic writing should also take into account the potential audience for the finished product' (Hammersley and Atkinson 1983: 227). For the native anthropologist, it is the academic as well as the native context which significantly affects the writing of anthropological texts. For most Outsiders' post-fieldwork contact consists of sporadic correspondence with a few natives, while for the native anthropologist interaction with 'my people' is a life-long engagement. Since my return to London and the Goan community here, letters and personal enquiries have always included the questions 'When will the thesis be finished?' 'When will we be able to read it?' Some have even raised provocative questions about academic verification: 'Who will examine your thesis? Do they know about Goa? If they don't know about Goa, how will they know that you are right?' In producing an anthropological text for an audience which includes natives, the native anthropologist shares the concerns of the Outsider about respecting confidentiality, protecting individuals, and keeping the field open for further research (Barnes 1967: 205–12). However, there are additional issues. Natives, like everyone else, want to be portrayed in the most advantageous light and will feel betrayed if this is not done. Furthermore, the demands of science must be finely weighed against those of humanity (Kloos 1969: 511) as publication of certain material may lead to long-term disruption of the anthropologist's personal relationships (Nakleh 1979: 349) as well as those of his kin with other natives (Stephen and Greer 1981: 129).

During the writing up of the thesis, I found myself being somehow compelled, in comparison to other students, to devote a disproportionate amount of time to history. Reflecting on this recently, I have identified three main reasons, apart from a theoretical attraction to a diachronic perspective. First of all, despite the fact that I have always emphasized to natives that I am a social anthropologist whose concern is with contemporary society, it is the minimal historical material contained in my previous writings (Mascarenhas-Keyes 1979, and short articles in the Goan Association (UK) Newsletter), that has aroused greatest interest. Indeed, I am sometimes publicly referred to as 'our *historian'*, and Amora natives enquire, 'Have you finished writing the *history* of our village yet?'

Second, my personal reasons for undertaking the research involved a desire to locate an autobiography within a cultural biography. The decision to read social anthropology after graduating in psychology, the choice of ethnographic area and research problem were determined primarily by a quest for self-knowledge. Perhaps anthropological research is inherently autobiographical (Crick 1982: 16) and all academic research is 'really all about the perfection of one's own soul' (Barley 1983: 10). Given this emotional involvement, there is the danger of egocentricism referred to by the native anthropologist, Delmos J. Jones: 'the insider may depend too much on his own background, his own sentiments, his desires for what is good for his people' (1970: 256). However, as Aguilar points out, such dangers 'can be mitigated with relative ease once one is aware of them' (1981: 23).

Third, I have been responding to the demands of the profession, which socializes anthropologists to look for 'exotica'. For a native anthropologist, the 'exoticism' of one's own society is less apparent, and hence I have been beset by an unconscious need to look for 'extraordinariness'. Conscious recognition of this was facilitated by introspection and recent participation in outsider research. By delving into historical material, particularly Goa's unusual colonial experience, I have sought to draw out its 'uniqueness' and 'exoticism'. 1 felt compelled to explore the 'exotic' through history in order to highlight the 'exotic' of the ordinary, contemporary situation. Hence the native anthropologist, in order to operate within the conventional model of knowledge generation, has to 'discover' or 'uncover' the exotic by utilizing a different level of reality than that given by the ethnographic situation. Furthermore, the Eurocentric bias persists in the academic pressure to highlight certain features, such as caste, which have 'exotic' appeal to European audiences (Asad 1973).

'When we publish, our eye is more often to our colleagues than on our informants' noted Barnes (1967: 205). However, academic feedback takes place mainly in an ethnographic and methodological vacuum (Crick 1982: 17–18). In addition, the culture of Academia, about which we know only a little (Caplow and McGee 1965; Boissevain 1974; Bailey 1977; Platt 1976), influences the various stages of research, including script production and promotion, in ways which have so far remained invisible, particularly to neophytes. The pursuit of 'objective ethnographic accounts' or the 'definitive ethnography' is illusory (Nash and Wintrop 1972: *531;* Agar 1982: 784; Devereux 1967: 207) as evidenced by contrasting accounts of the same culture (e.g., Mead 1935 and Fortune 1939; Redfield 1930 and Lewis 1951). Furthermore, professional natives have criticized a number of texts produced by Outsiders for inaccuracies in the translation of cultures and have suggested a dialogue between native and foreign professionals (Owusu 1978).

However, since cultural phenomena are differently interpreted by anthropologists, native or outsider, as well as natives, I would go further than Owusu and suggest a continuing dialogue between anthropologists and 'my people', a dialogue which has so far begun and terminated with fieldwork. Although texts have found their way to the field (Barnes 1967: 205), this has been haphazard, and furthermore the asymmetrical power relations that pertained, particularly during the colonial era, probably militated against natives contesting the point of view developed by the powerful outsider (Nash and Wintrop 1972: 531). I propose that we take seriously Parkin's tentative suggestion that a commitment to reflexivity include native reflection on anthropological texts (1982: xii–xiv). Such reflection should be from a cross-section of natives, not a selected few. In cases where the level of literacy precludes appraisals of written texts, native feedback can be obtained to other mediums of discourse, such as oral accounts

(Josselin de Jong 1967) and ethnographic films, whose potential has yet to be exploited (see MacDougall 1978; Henley 1985). I suggest that native feedback be used to complement academic feedback in order to advance our knowledge and understanding of culture and society. Such 'multiple triangulation' (Denzin 1978) would also reduce the dangers of ethnocentricism of Outsiders and egocentricism of native anthropologists.

Conclusion

This paper has provided a case illustration of the conduct of fieldwork and script production by a native anthropologist. Unlike the outsider, who becomes a marginal native in order to gain access to natives, I have shown that for me it was necessary to become a multiple native in order to transcend the limitations of an *a priori* ascribed position and to deal with the cultural complexities of the field situation. Furthermore, since the native anthropologist, unlike the outsider, is an intrinsic and permanent part of a complex web of kinship and associational relationships, I have indicated the strategies used to legitimize research, and provide assurance that information collected during fieldwork is for professional and not personal interests. I have shown that fieldwork exposed me to a considerable degree of stress, and argued that anxiety can be turned to method. By using Self as Informant the culturally induced sources of stress can be subjected to systematic analysis and used as a methodological tool in fieldwork. Finally, I have shown that because the dialogue with natives does not terminate with fieldwork for the native anthropologist, as it does for most outsiders, their demands, as well as those of the profession, influence the production of anthropological texts. I have concluded by suggesting that anthropologists should not only welcome academic feedback, but also systematically solicit and analyse native feedback from a cross-section of natives in order to obtain a more penetrating insight into culture and society.

Notes

1. A plethora of names has emerged to label anthropology at home (see Messerschmidt 1981: 13). There are also different categories of native anthropologists (Stephen and Greer 1981: 124). I use the term to refer to an anthropologist, who through and from birth, is an active and integral member of the society studied.

2. Since Goa was until 1961 a Portuguese enclave within India, the term 'international migration' is used here to refer to migration from Goa to elsewhere in India as well as overseas.

3. Pseudonym.

4. No facilities for learning Konkani are available in London, either at universities or within the Goan community.

5. Goa is the current mecca of Western 'hippies' and while international Catholic Goans differentiate between different categories of Europeans, the Hindus and Kunbis use the generic term 'hippie' to apply to any white person, irrespective of age.

6. The two terms have been defined in a number of ways by psychoanalysts and I am using the inroad definitions where transference refers to the patient's emotional attitude to the analyst, while counter-transference refers to the analyst's emotional attitude to the patient (see Heimann 1950; Winnicott 1956; 1960; Rycroft 1968) and by extension of these terms to anthropology, we can substitute anthropologist for psychoanalyst, and native for patient.

On Payments to Respondents

VINAY KUMAR SRIVASTAVA

I

I began thinking of the issue of payment to respondents in the initial phases of a fieldwork with the Raikas— the caste of traditional camel-breeders— of western Rajasthan in north-west India.

My stay in their hamlet, which I had first studied in Bikaner, was facilitated by a local Raika school teacher, He mostly lived in Bikaner town, and on weekends he visited the hamlet where he owned one of three cemented (*pacca*) houses. He not only introduced me to his extended family but also provided me with an outhouse to live.

After a few days of fieldwork I discovered that the others in this hamlet apart from his family were not particularly friendly. Whenever I went to their male gatherings they would all turn quiet, and if I stayed, one by one they would leave. Frustrated and dismayed, I would return to my outhouse. A couple of weeks elapsed. I was unable to break the barrier.

I might have been able to think of a strategy to befriend them had I known why I was being treated in such a manner. Having conducted fieldwork in other parts of India, I intuitively knew that it was not the usual lukewarm response anthropologists receive at the beginning of their research. My salutations (*Ramashama, namaskara*) to them did not go unanswered: however, they lacked the warmth I expected after having been there for weeks. My interaction was painfully confined to the teacher's family, and I was sensitive to being labelled as 'the teacher's friend from Delhi' (*master-ji ra Dilliwala bhaila*). I knew that this reputation would destroy my chances of becoming familiar with the rest of the hamlet.

I quickly learned that there were two factions in this hamlet—the teacher's and the rest—although it was an extended kin group. Whenever

I asked the teacher and his family members why they did not have cordial relations with the rest of the hamlet, their reply consisted of stories of nasty and evil deeds their neighbours had relentlessly executed against them. These stories ranged from stealing to witchcraft, from argument to fight. I was also assured that whatever information I needed would be available from them, so I should stop worrying about the others.

To understand this situation and, more particularly, to conduct peaceful and unrestricted fieldwork, I knew that I had to move into a neutral space. On the pretext of being accustomed to working at night when there was no electricity, I shifted from the teacher's outhouse. With difficulty, I eventually learned to manage both factions, and could move freely from one part of the hamlet to another without receiving frowns from either group. I gave the impression of a person who was keen to speak to all, and not one interested in interpersonal squabbles.

As time went by, the reasons for factional enmity became clear. Many events, one related to another, were responsible, but an important one was the payment made to some and not to others by an outside agency. It could be argued that this selective payment served to underline and aggravate pre-existing conflicts, Even today both parties talk about this issue, although the facts are tailored according to each one's stand-point.

II

Some years before my arrival (1989), a team of filmmakers came to this hamlet. They got in touch with the teacher, as I did, because he happened to be at that time, as today, the only educated person in this hamlet. The film centred around the travel of Raikas with their camels from the hamlet to the cattle fair at Pushkar, a pilgrimage town near Ajmer. Once in Pushkar, the filmmakers focused on the Raikas' visit to their caste temple, the rituals they performed, the fair deals and their return to the hamlet. Although the film producer was told of camel herds (*tolas*) in neighbouring hamlets, he was keen to hire a group of Raika herders with their camels from this hamlet. As expected, the teacher was assured of handsome payment for liasing with them as well as for use of the herd. The people hired for managing the *tola* were also promised good money.

There were four camel herds in this hamlet. The teacher's and his brothers' nuclear families did have a couple of camels each, but they did not have a herd. His cousin was a well known ethno-veterinarian of camel diseases in Bikaner tehsil, but had sold off his herd a long time ago.

The teacher and his cousin decided to ask one of their 'brothers' to loan his herd so that they could help the visitors in their film. Except for the core group of the teacher, his real brothers, and the cousin, it seemed no one else knew about the promise of money. Since the teacher's cousin not only wore the typical, and pristine, Raika dress, but was also a handsome man, the film producer was pleased to take him as the main character in the film.

Although the film producer and his assistants visited the hamlet many times and took interest in other camel herders, they uncritically accepted the teacher's advice and the plan he charted out for them. The payment was made clandestinely, but soon after the film crew had left it came to the knowledge of others. In a small community, it is difficult to guard secrets, as well as keep new wealth concealed. When the Raika who had made his herd available for the film came to know about the payment, he was furious. He gave his herd to his 'brother' following the 'ethic of brotherhood' (*bhaicara*). He was unhappy with the teacher's 'artfulness' (*calaki*).

I pursued the story of this event from the perspective of each faction. The teacher explained that the film producer entrusted him with making all the necessary arrangements. Thus whatever he did was his personal decision. As he did a lot of running around in this connection, he deserved the payment. The others said that they were as experienced in taking out the camel herd as was the teacher's cousin. Then why were they left out?

When I told them that the entire hamlet could not have possibly been accommodated by the film producer, they argued that the matter could have been placed before the council of elders (panchayat), and its decision would have been all-binding. They were referring to a centralized process of allocating opportunities, even if they came to particular individuals. This case brings out some interesting features of individualism in simple, largely undifferentiated, societies but I shall reserve their discussion for some other occasion.

III

Was the film producer responsible for the ill will caused in the hamlet? All of my respondents agreed that the film producer should have paid them for their services. However, they added, they can work for others without expecting any returns; in fact, self-sacrifice is seen as central to their dharma (religious duty) and charitra (character). Since the film producer was 'rich' (*gharon amir*) and offered to pay, there was nothing immoral about accepting his money. But the film producer's fault lay in being naïve. Instead of placing his request before all—all being represented by elders—he fell into the hands of an unscrupulous few. No one would have felt bad or envious had the charge of organizing the work for him been given to the teacher and his cousin by the elders.

The teacher was criticized for being selfish. He acted as an 'individual' in a community which did not sanction the 'value of the individual', thus monopolizing the benefits without thinking of anyone but himself. Since the film was on the community, I was told, everyone should have been informed about it and taken into confidence. When I asked how they knew that the film was on the entire community as no one had seen it (it could have just focussed on one family), they said that even then it was the teacher's responsibility to inform everyone. Furthermore, the man who loaned his camel herd should have been told of the money involved. The matter could have been placed before the council of elders by the owner of the camel herd, but it did not happen. From the perspective of the aggrieved faction, boycott seemed to be the only viable means of protest.

In the process of gaining information on this case, two things became clear. First, the people expected a return for their help. Second, returning favours to some but not others was not only jeopardizing amicable relations, it also caused deep, sometimes unbridgeable, cleavages in the local community. And related to these two points were several ethical questions. Should the respondents be paid? If they are to be paid, what should be the mode of payment? Who should be paid, and who should not be? Which services require payment, and which do not?

To my mind these are important questions, and have a considerable bearing on ethnography. But unfortunately, they have been little discussed. Ethnographers do let others know that they hired research assistants, but never tell us if they ever made any payment to selected respondents for information.

IV

Let me begin with two opinions on the issue of payment. First, one of the 'ethical guidelines for good practice' laid down in 1987 by the Association of Social Anthropologists of the Commonwealth is that ethncgraphers should make 'fair return' to respondents for assistance. Note that the term used is 'fair return' and not 'payment'. The guideline, however, does not elaborate on the fairness of return and the judgement on this is left to the fieldworker.

Second, in a short letter to *Man* (1983), Veena Das and Jonathan Parry are critical of those ethnographers who receive 'their information very largely through direct payment to selected respondents'. Besides being suspicious of the prejudiced nature of such information, they rightly submit that obtaining information in exchange for payment 'spoil(s) the field', thus making it very difficult for future ethnographers, especially poorly-funded ones, to conduct what I call a 'peaceful fieldwork'.

Das and Parry raise another very crucial point. They observe that contemporary south Asian anthropology is in large measure dependent upon the 'mutual critique which local and foreign anthropologists make of one another's work'. But with a practice of paying respondents, the local, meagrely-funded anthropologists stand disadvantaged as the 'hired respondents' would be more generous towards their employers. As a consequence, local anthropology will suffer, and so would the prospect of 'mutual critique.'

It is difficult to reconcile the first opinion with the second, because Das and Parry do not touch the issue of 'fair return'. Their concern is with the practice of obtaining information through 'direct payment to selected informants'. They do not tell us who these 'selected informants' are. For what type of information is the payment made? And also, they do not define the content of payment. Though it may not be easy for me to guess the 'selected informants', I assume that by 'payment' they mean 'payment in terms of money and/or valuable gifts'.

Das and Parry's context is South Asia. Although they are unsure if ethnographic landscapes in other parts of the world are being spoiled through payment to respondents, I think this issue concerns all anthropologists irrespective of the area they investigate. Put another way, the issue of payment is neither confined to a particular ethnographic zone nor to potential dangers to the theme of 'mutual critique'. 'Should anthropologists pay their respondents?' is a question that needs to be discussed by all of us. Also, the ethnographers should not be shamefaced in telling their readers the payment or favours, if any, they made to their respondents, and for what sort of information. They should also reflect upon the moral categories in which the dilemma posed by payment is resolved. The general question (of which payment to respondents is a part) is: what are 'fair returns'?

Although I see a point in Das and Parry's letter, I think the assistance our respondents give us must be properly reciprocated. I shall devote the rest of this paper to the idea of 'fair return' keeping my fieldwork experiences in perspective.

V

We can reciprocate for our respondents' help in the following ways:

1. Providing assistance to the household members with whom we live during our fieldwork. I lived with a Raika family in the second hamlet I chose for their study. During this time I occasionally herded the sheep of my family and regularly bought food and other goods such as kerosene oil, lentils, sugar, and vegetables. Whenever I went to the nearby towns, I brought gifts for my kin and friends. Sometimes I paid the school fees of the children, and helped two boys in their study. In other words, by sharing household chores and augmenting the resources, I tried my best to reciprocate all that I received from my Raika family.

2. Suppose the anthropologist lives in a neutral space, as I did in the first hamlet, he is largely free from such obligations as he is not bound to a particular household. In this case—and it also applies to other fieldwork cases— he might think of making a 'gift' to the entire community.

   Let me give an example here. Around the same time when I was doing my fieldwork in Rajasthan, a veterinarian-cum-anthropologist arrived in the area. She was attached to the National Research Centre on Camel (Bikaner), and her project mainly dealt with the traditional aspects of camel management. Now I have learnt that in collaboration with a local Raika veterinarian she has founded what they have termed the Raika Fund (Kohler-Rollefson & Dewasi 1991). This fund, to be locally managed, will grant scholarships to deserving Raika students. In addition it will be used for animal health care programmes, documentation of indigenous knowledge of animal breeding and medicine, and providing legal help.

   Under the idea of a 'gift' to the entire community we can also include the financial help anthropologists provide to up-and-coming local institutions. For instance, the Secretary of the Raika Mahasabha ('association') edited a caste-periodical titled *Raika Jagriti*, and in 1989, he also started a primary school. I made a small donation towards both these local efforts.

3. This brings me to the last aspect of 'fair return', that is reciprocating the specialists of local knowledge. If, for example, I am working on religion, I must know the exact spells used for pacifying deities and exorcising evil spirits, and this knowledge is only available from specialists. For social history, I must look into the genealogical records that may be, as is the case in Rajasthan, the sole source of earning of the

Rav (the traditional genealogists). The collection of a folk epic (for example, the sort of work undertaken by Smith, 1991) would require many of hours with their narrators. The same applies to a work on astrology and society (for instance, Perinbanayagam 1982) for which the ethnographer has to spend countless hours with specialists and diviners. Similarly, a project on ethnomedicine, like the one envisaged in the Raika Fund, would demand a survey of local herbs, their medicinal properties, the methods of preparing drugs, and for these the local medicine men would have to spend months with the ethnographer. Do not these specialists deserve 'fair return' for their time and energy they spend on us?

VI

Expanding this final aspect—of a fair return to the specialists—let me draw a tentative distinction between 'general' and 'specific' knowledge. By 'general' knowledge, I mean the knowledge that is shared by most members of a society. Everyone knows about it, although age and gender distinctions affect it. The Raika women, for example, have more complete knowledge of household rituals than their men. And all adult men are adept in grazing practices. The point is that the knowledge of household rituals or grazing techniques is not confined to any one woman or man.

By contrast the specific knowledge is the repository of fewer individuals who are its specialists. I may learn grazing practices by living with any group of herdsmen, but for a project on ethnoveterinary aspects, I shall have to depend on their specialists. This knowledge, to reiterate, is available with particular individuals rather than being generally distributed in a community.

When it is a question of general knowledge, all the community members speak. The ethnographer collects information from all: however, he may cite the households he knows well. For this knowledge, he is committed to the entire community, and should refrain from paying any particular individual. Thus, paying a respondent for collecting, for instance, kin terms could well invite discord. Obviously, if one is paid for 'general' information, the others have a reason to feel left out because they are all equally competent in giving this. To recapitulate the case with which this paper began, the members of the other faction felt neglected because they thought that they were as competent as the teacher's cousin in taking the camel herd from Bikaner to Pushkar. Had the film been on indigenous medicines for camel diseases, I think everyone in the Raika hamlet, notwithstanding their interpersonal scrimmages, would have recommended the teacher's cousin because of his knowledge and fame.

Specific knowledge is that which is a part of the community's heritage at large, but guarded and transmitted by a select few. The Raikas themselves recognized this: while they admitted that they are the 'ethnoveterinarians' of repute, some problems had to be treated by specialists. In the Bikaner hamlet, those opposed to the teacher's cousin did not consult him when their animals were ill. Instead, they sought the service of specialists in other hamlets. But, this was not a reflection on the ability of the teacher's cousin. He was well respected although his loyalty was to the opposite group.

The specialists with whom I worked confided to me their fears regarding publication of their knowledge. They thought that with this they may not only lose their moral authority but also the source of their livelihood. An epic singer told me, 'If the story of Devanarayan-ji is freely available in audio cassettes, who would call me to narrate it?' A genealogist was reluctant to show his books (*bahi*) to me because he thought that I might then take up the task of narrating (*banchna*) the genealogies, thus jeopardizing his occupation. On both occasions, I tried to dispel their fear by convincing them that the nature of my work was certainly not to compete with them.

VII

I tried to compensate all the specialists who helped me in my study. I worked almost like an apprentice with the ethnoveterinarian of the first hamlet. When I was leaving Bikaner to join a migratory herd, I presented him with a woollen coat, a turban, a transistor and Rs 51. The genealogist at Pali, who spent many days helping me to record the story of Raika origin and other mythical and quasi-historical details, did not want to accept any gift from me: however, he had no objections to such gifts from his clients, the Raikas. So I gave Rs 101 to my Raika friend who offered it to the genealogist. I spent some days with a singer of one of the local epics (of a Rathore Rajput warrior, Pabu-ji), and to him I made an offering of Rs 51 and a blanket.

None of these gifts were clandestinely made. When I gave gifts to the teacher's cousin, almost everyone in the hamlet, including those of the other faction, approved of the gesture. Some praised me for being a 'good man' (*bhala admi*) who recognized the actual worth of local specialists, whereas others thought the specialists deserved more for their knowledge.

On these occasions, I honestly confessed that my grant was limited. As I see it, the opinion that I overpaid or underpaid the specialists provoked only minor disagreements among a few scattered individuals. In contrast, the selective payments made by the film producer created a deep-seated and long-lasting enmity in the community.

VIII

All exchanges in the field occur and are perceived in terms of the local moral code. As my examples make clear the gifts I offered to the specialists were not only in kind but also in cash.

My first submission is that gifts in cash should not be classed as 'amoral' and 'inferior'. True, exchange in kind is an exclusive principle in non-monetized economy. But, are there communities in present times untouched by cash economy? Contemporary societies in all parts of the world, irrespective of their dominant modes of economy, are linked in one way or the other with the monetized national and international economic system. Relations based on exchange of kind or labour have been gradually replaced by cash. In such a dynamic environment when local communities have not only realized the enormous purchasing power of money but also *respect* it, it may be incorrect to regard a 'fair return' in money as amoral. The people we now study are aware of the value of money, and they also understand the value of their time and labour. Return in money is thus both expected and valued. My submission is not that every return in field-work should be in money. But if money is an expected category in the local exchange system, the ethnographer should have no moral hesitation in using it.

Second, the nature of payment made to field assistants is different from that made to the specialists of local knowledge. Payment to the former is a salary determined by the number of hours worked and the quality of that work. No such indices apply when deciding gifts for the local specialists.

In what moral terms, then, should one see these gifts? My field experience informs me that these gifts are seen in two contradictory, yet coexisting, perspectives—the ethnographer's and the specialists'. From the ethnographer's perspective, these gifts can be seen in the paradigm of *guru daksina* ('offering to the teacher'). But, when looked at from the perspective of the specialists (and also the local people) the paradigm of patronage is inescapable: put in another way, the local specialists and people seek patronage from anthropologists just as anthropologists seek patronage from the specialists.

Let me first take up the model of guru daksina. True, my preference for this is linked not only to my field experiences in India; but also to my moorings as an Indian, born and brought up in a traditional north Indian family. However, from the ethnographer's perspective, the premises of the guru daksina model apply equally to the relations between ethnographers and specialists: in other words, the model is generally applicable.

What are the premises of the guru daksina model? In traditional terms, it is an offering (daksina) a would-be disciple makes to his teacher (guru). If the guru accepts it, it means that he has consented to take the 'gift-giver' as his disciple. The meaning of this gift is not that the gift-giver is compensating for what he will receive from his teacher: and it is erroneous to see this relationship as an example of balanced reciprocity. Through this offering the disciple expresses his gratitude to his teacher, and the teacher and his disciple are bound in some sort of a permanent relationship.

Perhaps, the same happens in the ethnographer's relation with the specialists of local knowledge. The latter are his 'teachers': and the ethnographer is expected to spend a long time with them to properly understand their lore. Here it is not suggested that the ethnographer learns to practise the lore as do the local disciples of these specialists. But insofar as he learns the content of local knowledge and how it is practised, he steps into the role of a pupil. The ethnographer does not pretend to be a disciple: he becomes a disciple because he can only learn through the framework of this relationship. For all the time and attention these specialists give him, he can express his gratitude by offering them some gifts in the moral ethic of daksina. The point to be stressed is that the local specialized knowledge can only be understood if it is approached in terms of the role of the disciple and the accompanying ethic of humility and gratitude expressed in gifts of cash and/or kind.

Coming to the second point, how do these specialists view their relationship to the ethnographer? For most of them, their specialized knowledge or skills is how they earn a living. They may not haggle, but it is known to all in a local community that they must be compensated for the services they provide. The teacher's cousin, for instance, never charged for his veterinary services, he was nevertheless offered food, and given some milk, clarified butter, seasonal vegetables, grains etc., for his household. Similarly, the singers of folk epics never haggled for their service. When engaged for a performance, they only advised their patrons to arrange for ritual ingredients to be provided. But each patron knew that they should be paid in money; the more he offered, the more was the respect (*sakh*) he earned in the local community.

Similarly, ethnographers are seen as patrons, perhaps more influential and affluent than their local counterparts. And thus it is not surprising that when specialists agree to impart their knowledge to anthropologists they do so with total commitment, putting their soul into explaining their lore and skills. Expectation of 'fair return' is at the heart of this relation.

Like the 'gift' to the entire community on the part of the anthropologist, one way to reciprocate the help specialists give is to plan a 'gift' for them. Local governments may be approached to provide financial support themselves for the specialists and to help in the preservation of indigenous lore and knowledge.

Glossary

ANONYMITY. A condition wherein researchers do not identify their data with particular respondents. Pseudonyms are used for the respondents and locations of study in order to conceal their identity and save them from possible persecution, embarrassment, and stigma.

ASSOCIATION. The strength of the observed relationship between two variables (or dimensions or factors).

ASYMMETRICAL RELATIONSHIP. A relationship in which a change in one variable leads to a change in the other, but not vice versa. When change in either variable results in change in the other variable (for instance, A affects B and in turn is affected by B), the relationship is known as symmetrical.

AUTHENTICITY. The state of being original, natural, and not influenced. This concept is of particular significance in qualitative research.

BIAS. A systematic error in data collection, presentation, and interpretation.

BIVARIATE. Two variables. A statement of relationship between two variables is called bivariate relationship.

CASE STUDY. An in-depth and comprehensive study of a social unit—be that unit a person, a group, a social institution, a district, a community, or a society.

CAUSAL RELATIONSHIP. A relationship where one variable affects changes in another. A 'cause and effect' relationship is deemed to exist whenever a particular event or condition (the effect) is produced by another (the cause).

CHI-SQUARE TESTS. Statistical tests which provide information about whether the collected data are close to the value considered to be typical and generally expected, and whether two variables are related to each other.

CLOSED-ENDED QUESTIONS. Also known as 'forced-choice', 'fixed-response', and 'fixed-choice' questions, they are survey questions (quite like multiple-choice questions) that limit (or force) the respondent to choose responses from the categories already provided.

CODING. Assigning symbols (usually numbers) for each category of each answer. It creates categories and sorts out raw data in them.

CONCEPT. A mental image or perception, communicated by words or other signs, referring to common properties among phenomena. A concept is an abstract idea. Concepts (such as culture, society, role, institution) which researchers develop for analysis are also termed 'constructs'.

CONTENT ANALYSIS. A method of analysing the content of communication using a quantitative coding scheme. The contents of documents or visual materials are classified with an aim to bring out their basic structure. Some investigators apply this method to the analysis of answers to open-ended questions in survey research.

CONTROL GROUP. A group selected to be identical to the experimental group in terms of all characteristics but is not exposed to the experimental stimulus (the independent variable).

CONVERSATION. Verbal communication between two or more individuals. The term conversation analysis is used for the empirical study of conversations using techniques drawn from ethnomethodology. (See ethnomethodology.)

CORRELATION. A statistical measure of relationship between variables. It describes the direction and strength of relationship between two variables—how one is related to the other. When the values of the two variables tend to increase or decrease together, the correlation is described as positive. When the value of one variable increases while that of the other decreases, the correlation is negative.

COVER LETTER (or COVERING LETTER). The letter aimed to obtain cooperation from prospective respondents. It identifies the sponsors of study, succinctly describes its importance, and in general, is designed to encourage response. In cases of interviews and administration of schedules, the cover letter is sent before the interviewer calls on the respondent. In mail survey, it accompanies the questionnaire and is regarded as the first part of the questionnaire.

CROSS-CULTURAL SURVEYS. Surveys conducted in different cultures based on equivalent samples.

DEPENDENT VARIABLE. In an asymmetrical relationship, the variable causally influenced by another, which is called the independent variable.

DESCRIPTIVE RESEARCH. Studies undertaken to collect facts about a specified group of people. A public opinion poll is an example of descriptive research.

DIRECT QUESTION. In survey research, a question in which there is a direct, clear relationship between the question that is asked and what the researcher wants to know. When the link between the researcher's objectives and the question asked is less obvious, it is called an indirect question, and is commonly used in the psychological techniques of projection. (See projective techniques.)

DIRECT RELATIONSHIP. Also termed 'positive relationship', it is one where an increase (or decrease) in the value of one variable accompanies an increase (or decrease) in the value of the other variable.

DISCOURSE. A set of ideas, concepts and beliefs, and common assumptions which become established as knowledge about a phenomenon or as an accepted world view. The discourse thus created becomes a powerful framework for understanding and carrying out action in social life.

DISPERSION. A statistical measure to determine how far the elements of the sample are spread away from the mean. The statistical tool to study dispersion is standard deviation. Often, the two terms—dispersion and standard deviation – are used interchangeably.

DOCUMENTARY RESEARCH. Research based on evidence drawn from the study of documents, printed or otherwise.

EMPIRICAL RESEARCH. A way of knowing or understanding the world relying directly or indirectly on our experiences through the five senses. The term empirical investigation is used for a factual enquiry. An inductively derived generalization about empirical occurrences is called an empirical generalization.

ETHICAL NEUTRALITY. The perspective that a social researcher should remain neutral and not be swayed by moral issues or values. A concept closely related to it is of value-free sociology, which submits that sociological research can and should be conducted with the values of the investigator kept in abeyance so that they do not conflict with the research process and bias conclusions.

ETHICS. A body of guidelines or standards for moral conduct. In research, ethical principles (or codes of ethics) are enunciated for upholding the rigours and objectivity of science and resolving the conflicts that occur between scientific ideals and social values.

ETHNOGRAPHY. Literally, 'writing on people'. Based on direct observation of the ways of living of members of a particular community, ethnography is the description and analysis of people's activities. This term was earlier used for first-hand anthropological studies of what were called 'primitive societies', but is now applied to writings based on observational studies in any social context.

ETHNOMETHODOLOGY. Literally meaning 'people's methods', the term introduced by Harold Garfinkel, it is a method proposing to investigate how people construct their world, that is, make sense of what others say and do in the course of day-to-day social interaction.

ETHNOSURVEY. A research design that combines ethnographic methods with survey research.

EXPERIMENT. Testing of hypotheses in controlled situations where extraneous variables do not confound the results.

EXPERIMENTAL GROUP. Identical to the control group in all respects, it receives the experimental stimulus (or the independent variable), which is denied to the control group. The term *ex-post facto* experiment (also called 'before and after' research) is used for a study conducted after the independent variable has already been introduced. In this, the investigator does not introduce the test stimulus, but claims to control the other extraneous factors.

EXPLORATORY RESEARCH. Studies carried out to explore a phenomenon or topic about which almost nothing or scanty knowledge is available. An exploratory research design helps in gaining familiarity with the field of study, besides generating hypotheses for further testing.

FIELD STUDY. A study conducted in the natural habitat (the 'field') of the people, as opposed to an artificial experimental laboratory.

FUNCTIONALISM. A theoretical perspective according to which a society should be studied from the point of view of the contribution its parts (groups, organizations, institutions, etc.) make towards its orderly persistence. Functionalism is chiefly concerned with the issues of consensus, order, and equilibrium.

FUNNEL TECHNIQUE. Also known as 'funnel sequence', it refers to a sequence of survey questions that progresses with general questions to put the respondent at ease, and then gradually becomes more specific and focused (the process of 'funneling down').

GATEKEEPERS. Authorities whose permission, sometimes written, is required to conduct research in their settings.

GROUNDED THEORY. Theory derived inductively from first-hand observations. It is distinguished from theory logically derived from a priori assumptions (i.e., a theory formulated in an 'ivory tower').

HERMENEUTICS. The theory and method of interpreting texts.

HYPOTHESIS. A proposition or set of propositions about two or more variables stating unconfirmed relationships between them, put forward for empirical testing.

HYPOTHETICO-DEDUCTIVE METHOD. A method of enquiry in which a theory is verified or refuted by empirically testing hypotheses derived from it.

IDEAL TYPE. Also called 'pure type', it is constituted by emphasizing certain traits of a given social concept which do not necessarily exist anywhere in reality. Developed by Max Weber, the ideal type is an analytical tool.

INDEPENDENT VARIABLE. The variable that can bring about changes in the other variable (dependent variable), but is not affected by changes in the dependent variable.

IN-DEPTH INTERVIEW. Intensive, long-term, less structured interview in fieldwork, which requires many sessions for completion. It is in contrast to structured interviews of survey research.

INDUCTION. A process of reasoning in which the researcher arrives at conclusions that go beyond the information contained in the premises. The researcher formulates general propositions on the basis of particular findings, which are then subjected to testing and falsification. The term inductive generalization is used for the reasoning process in which statements are made about the entire category of objects on the basis of the study of only part of the category. Deduction, by contrast, is the reasoning process, where particular statements are derived from general premises. It is, therefore, a movement from general to particular. Sociological arguments are rarely deductive in form; they are largely inductive.

INFORMED CONSENT. An ethical practice in which research participants (or respondents) are supplied with enough information about the study, particularly its potential risks, so that they make up their mind about participation after having judged the different aspects and consequences of their proposed participation.

INTERQUARTILE RANGE. A version of the range but it excludes the lower and upper quarter of the distribution.

INTERVENING VARIABLE. A variable intermediate between two other variables in a causal chain. Suppose, A affects B which in turn affects C, thus A causes C through B. In this causal relationship, B is the intervening variable.

INTERVIEW. A method of data collection where information is gathered through oral questioning.

INTERVIEW GUIDE. A list of topics or areas which the interviewer prepares in advance and consults while asking questions. Questions are framed around the topics that have been identified earlier.

INTERVIEW SCHEDULE. In terms of its structure, a schedule is identical to a questionnaire, but in this, the interviewer asks the questions and notes down the respondent's answers verbatim. A questionnaire, in contrast, is self-administered by the respondent.

INVERSE RELATIONSHIP. Also termed 'negative relationship', in this case, when the value of one variable increases, the value of the other decreases.

KEY INFORMANT. A local respondent who helps a fieldworker gain access to and acceptance within his community. He provides maximum information about his social setting and introduces the ethnographer to other important and knowledgeable people, who in course of time become key respondents.

LONGITUDINAL STUDY. A study in which data are collected over an extended period of time. By comparison, a cross-sectional study is conducted at one point of time. Generally, fieldwork tends to be longitudinal while survey tends to be cross-sectional.

MEAN. The average value. Along with mode and median, a measure of central tendency. It is obtained by dividing the sum total of all values by the number of cases.

MEDIAN. The mid-point of the sample. Along with mean and mode, a measure of central tendency. It indicates the point below and above which fifty per cent of the values fall.

MICRO-ANALYSIS. Small-scale analysis. It focuses on a small group (or even a single individual) as the unit of study. By contrast, macro-analysis uses a large aggregate (such as a nation) as the unit of analysis.

MODE. The most frequent (and typical) value in the sample. Along with mean and median, a measure of central tendency.

MODEL. An abstract presentation of a phenomenon that describes relations between its parts. The model of a phenomenon differs from the same phenomenon in reality; however, it is accurate enough to provide sufficient information about that phenomenon. The model is an analytical device.

MULTIPLE REGRESSION. A statistical measure that analyses the simultaneous effects of several independent variables on a dependent variable.

MULTIVARIATE ANALYSIS. A statistical method to study the simultaneous relationships among more than two variables.

NON-PARTICIPANT OBSERVATION. A type of observation wherein the investigator conducts observation without participating in the social setting, and without the knowledge of the people who are being observed.

NON-PROBABILITY SAMPLING. A type of sampling procedure in which the probability of the selection of an item is not known or cannot be determined.

OBJECTIVITY. The notion that the investigator should exclude subjective influences on the research process and endeavour to eliminate or reduce bias in the collection, analysis, presentation, and interpretation of data.

OPEN-ENDED QUESTIONS. Also termed 'free-response questions', they are survey questions in which no response options are given. The respondent is given sufficient space on the schedule to write (or dictate) his/her answer to the question.

OPERATIONAL DEFINITION. Meaning 'measurement of concept', it implies the empirical measurement of a verbal concept. If a concept is not amenable to empirical measurement, it is not operational.

PARADIGM. A set of questions, practices, and institutions which characterizes scientific activity in a particular historical context.

PARTICIPANT OBSERVATION. A technique of observation in which the investigator participates in the social life and organizational activities of the people he/she studies.

PARTICIPATORY RURAL ASSESSMENT (PRA). A technique used in applied and evaluation research where the focus is on involving people (the proposed beneficiaries) right from the time of the conception of the project to its execution and impact assessment.

POPULATION. Also termed 'universe' in survey research, it refers to the total group (or community) under study. If it is not possible to study the entire group, then a sample is drawn from it with the belief that what is true for the sample may also be true for the entire group.

POSITIVISM. A doctrine, associated with Auguste Comte, which submits that social life should be analysed and explained in the same way that scientists study the natural world.

PRETESTING. A trial run of a questionnaire with a small number of respondents with the aim to evaluate, detect errors and confusions, and modify it. The term pretesting is also used in experimental research designs for the trial run of an experiment and its evaluation.

PROBABILITY SAMPLING. A sampling procedure in which each unit of the population has an equal chance of being selected for study.

PROJECTIVE TECHNIQUES. A term used for techniques (such as the Rorschach test) employed by psychologists that provide the respondent with a stimulus situation in which he freely and directly reveals knowledge about himself and his social milieu.

PROPOSITION. The generic name for any statement which discusses a single variable or logically describes the interrelationship between variables.

QUALITATIVE ANALYSIS. Deals with information that is not quantified.

QUANTITATIVE ANALYSIS. Analysis based on precise measurement.

QUALITATIVE VARIABLE. Variable designated by words or labels.

QUANTITATIVE VARIABLE. Variable which has numerical distinctions.

QUASI-PARTICIPANT OBSERVATION. A type of observation in which the observer decides where to participate and where not to. It is a kind of selective participation.

QUESTIONNAIRE. A survey tool consisting of a set of questions which is self-administered by the respondent. An interviewer-completed instrument is known as interview schedule.

RANDOM SAMPLE. A probabilistic sample in which each unit of the population has an equal chance of being included in the sample. The procedure is also known as 'simple random sampling'.

RANDOM SELECTION. A process that gives each unit of the population an equal chance of being included in the sample. Here, the probability of the selection of each unit can be statistically determined.

RANGE. A measure of dispersion. It describes the distance from the lowest to the highest value of the distribution.

RAPID RURAL ASSESSMENT (RRA). A technique used in applied and evaluation research where the focus is on collecting relevant information in the shortest period of time so that the developmental action can begin.

RATIONALITY. A term used to indicate coherent, non-contradictory beliefs which are compatible with experience. Science involves the systematic testing of hypotheses by methods of observation, experimentation, and logical reasoning, and therefore, it is an outstanding example of rationality.

REFLEXIVITY. A process of examining and questioning the behaviour of the self and others.

REGRESSION ANALYSIS. A statistical method for studying bivariate (simple-regression) and multivariate (multiple-regression) relationships between variables.

RELATIVISM. An approach which denies the existence of absolute truths and states that beliefs, theories, values, or lifestyles of people are relative to time and place. In other words, things are meaningful in their respective cultural contexts.

RELIABILITY. A term used to indicate the extent to which repeated measurements under the same conditions produce the same, consistent results.

REPLICATION. The process of repeating an earlier study with the same research questions but with a different sample of cases. The aim is to find out whether the conditions of research and the personality of the researcher exercised any impact, thereby affecting the results. Some scholars prefer the term 'restudy' to 'replication'.

RESPONDENT. The person who answers questions in an interview session or in a survey.

RESPONSE RATE. The proportion of people in a sample who provide complete information on the questions listed in a questionnaire or asked by the investigator while filling the schedule.

SAMPLE. A part of the universe that one desires to study. A sample should be adequate and representative of the universe.

SAMPLING FRAME. An accurate list of the units of the total population under study. The sample is subsequently randomly selected from this list.

SCALE. An item or set of items for measuring certain characteristics or property, such as attitude, opinions, etc. The process of the construction of scales is called scaling.

SEMI-STRUCTURED INTERVIEW. Although the interview questions have a structure, the interviewer is free to formulate questions, determining their order and presentation. If this happens, the interview is called semi-structured.

SERENDIPITY. Unanticipated findings, for the study of which the researcher has to look into some other theories and explanations.

SOCIAL CONSTRUCTION OF REALITY. The view that some sociological concepts are mentally constructed or defined rather than existing as empirical entities.

SOCIOGRAM. A graphical representation of the relationship of every individual to every other individual in the group studied.

SOCIOMETRY. Formally proposed in 1937 by Jacob Moreno, this technique provides the means of presenting simply and graphically the structure of relations existing at a given time among members of a group.

STRATIFIED RANDOM SAMPLING. A probability sampling in which the universe is divided into strata and independent random samples are drawn from each one of them depending upon the size of each stratum.

STRUCTURALISM. A theoretical perspective derived from the study of language that holds that there are a set of unobservable, underlying structures that generate observable social phenomena. Structuralists try to identify such structures in social and cultural systems.

SURVEY. Systematic gathering of information about a large number of individuals and their communities using oral and written questioning, administering tools such as questionnaire and interview schedules and then interpreting the data by applying statistical methods.

TEST OF STATISTICAL SIGNIFICANCE. A statistical procedure for assessing the likelihood that the results of a study could have occurred by chance.

TRIANGULATION. An approach employing more than one method of data collection and analysis.

T-TEST. A test of significance. It is an interval/ratio test, employed when one or two samples are considered.

UNIT OF ANALYSIS. The basic unit about which the investigator gathers information. That unit may be an individual, social roles and relationships, groups, communities, organizations, nations, or any other social artifact.

UNIVARIATE ANALYSIS. Univariate means 'one variable'. Statistical analysis of one variable at a time.

VALIDITY. A term used to indicate a situation where the findings are in agreement with theoretical or conceptual values.

VARIABLE. A concept that contains two or more values along a continuum that vary over time or over a given sample, for example, temperature, income, age, etc. When the value of a concept is never-changing, it is called a constant. Usually the values of a variable are designated quantitatively, but some variables have categories which are stated by word labels rather than numerically, for instance, gender.

VARIANCE. A measure of dispersion. It is defined as the average of the distances of the individual scores from the mean.

WORKING HYPOTHESIS. A tentative hypothesis formulated in the initial stages of research but subjected to revision after preliminary data have been collected and analysed. Often, the working hypothesis is revised during the course of fieldwork.

References Cited

Ablon, J., 1977. 'Field Method in Working with Middle-Class Americans', *Human Organization*, 36: 69–72.

Adams, Kathleen, 1972. *'The Barama River Caribs of Guiana Restudied: Forty Years of Cultural Adaptation and Population Change'*, Ph.D. thesis, Case Western University.

Agar, Michael, 1980. *The Professional Stranger: An Informal Introduction to Ethnography*. New York: Academic Press.

————, 1982. 'Towards an Ethnographic Language', *American Anthropologist*, 84: 779–95.

Aguilar, J., 1981. 'Insider Research: An Ethnography of a Debate', in D. Messerschmidt (ed.), *Anthropologists at Home in North America: Methods and Issues in the Study of One's Own Society*. Cambridge: Cambridge University Press.

Aitchison, C.U.,1909. *A Collection of Treatises, Engagements and Sanads Relating to India and Neighbouring Countries*, Volume 4. Calcutta: Superintendent, Government Press, India.

Albert, Michel, 1993. *Capitalism Against Capitalism*. London: Whurr Publications.

Allport, G.W., 1937. *Personality: A Psychological Interpretation*. London: Constable and Co. Ltd.

————, 1942. *The Use of Personal Documents in Psychological Science*. Social Science Research Council Bulletin, 49.

Anderson, Perry, 1974. *Lineages of the Absolutist State*. London: New Left Books.

Anonymous, 1973. Dalit Literature. *Times Weekly, Bombay,* 4 (17), November 25.

Appadurai, Arjun, 1981. *Worship and Conflict under Colonial Rule: A South Indian Case*. Cambridge: Cambridge University Press.

Appadurai, Arjun and Carol A. Breckenridge, 1982. 'Museums are Good to Think: Heritage on View in India', in Ivan Karp (ed.), *Museums and Communications: The Politics of Public Culture*. Washington: Smithsonian Press.

Arora, S.K., 1968. 'Pre-empted Future? Notes on Theories of Political Development', *Behavioural Sciences and Community Development,* 2 (2): 85–120.

Asad, T. (ed.), 1973. 'Introduction', in *Anthropology and the Colonial Encounter*. London: Ithaca.

Auboyer, J., 1949. *Le trone et son symbolisme dans l'Inde ancienne*. Paris: Presses Universitaires de France.

Aunger, Robert, 1995. 'On Ethnography: Storytelling or Science?' *Current Anthropology,* 36 (1): 97–129.

Baechler, Jean, John A. Hall and Michael Mann, (eds), 1988. *Europe and the Rise of Capitalism.* Oxford: Blackwell.

Bailey, F.G., 1959. 'For a Sociology of India?', *Contributions to Indian Sociology,* III: 88–101.

_____, 1962. 'The Scope of Social Anthropology in the Study of Indian Society', in T.N. Madan and G. Sarana (eds), *Indian Anthropology.* Mumbai: Asia Publishing House.

_____, 1967. *Stratagems and Spoils.* Oxford: Basil Blackwell.

_____, 1977. *Morality and Expediency: The Folklore of Academic Politics.* Oxford: Blackwell.

Bailey, Kenneth D.,1978. *Methods of Social Research.* New York: The Free Press, and London: Collier Macmillan Publishers.

Bales, Robert F., 1950. *Interactive Process Analysis: A Method for the Study of Small Groups.* Cambridge, Mass: Addison-Wesley Publishing Company, Inc.

Ball, S., 1984. 'Beachside Reconsidered: Reflections on a Methodological Apprenticeship', in R.G. Burgess (ed.), *The Research Process in Educational Settings: Ten Case Studies.* London: Falmer Press.

Banks, Marcus, 1992. *Organizing Jainism in India and England.* Oxford: Clarendon Press.

Bann, Stephan, 1989. *The True Vine: On Visual Representation in the Western Tradition.* Cambridge: Cambridge University Press.

Banton, Michael, 1964. 'Anthropological Perspectives in Sociology,' *British Journal of Sociology,* 15: 95–112.

Baritz, L. 1960. *The Servants of Power: A History of the Use of Social Science in American Industry.* Middletown, Conn.: Wesleyan University Press.

Barley, N. 1983. *The Innocent Anthropologist.* London: British Museum.

Barnard, Alan, 2000. *History and Theory in Anthropology.* Cambridge: Cambridge University Press.

Barnes, J.A., 1967. 'On Genealogies', in A.L. Epstein (ed.), *The Craft of Social Anthropology.* London: Tavistock.

_____, 1967. 'Some Ethical Problems in Modern Field Work', in D.G. Jongmans and P.C.W. Gutkind (eds), *Anthropologists in the Field.* Assen: Van Goreum.

_____, 1977. *The Ethics of Inquiry in Social Science.* Delhi: Oxford University Press.

_____, 1980. *Who Should Know What? Social Science, Privacy and Ethics.* Cambridge: Cambridge University Press.

_____, 1984. 'Ethical and Political Compromises in Social Research', *Sociological Imagination,* 21: 100–11.

_____, 1996. 'Unavoidable Compromises in Social Research', in A.M. Shah, B.S. Baviskar, and E.A. Ramaswamy (eds), *Social Structure and Change (Vol. 1: Theory and Method—Evaluation of the Work of M.N. Srinivas).* New Delhi: Sage.

Barnett, H.G., 1960. *Being a Palauan.* New York: Henry Holt.

Bartlett, F.C., 1967. *Remembering: A Study in Experimental and Social Psychology.* Cambridge: Cambridge University Press.

Basham, A.L., 1954. *The Wonder That Was India*. London: Sidgwick and Jackson.

Bateson, Gregory, 1958. *Naven*. Stanford: University Press.

Beattie, John, 1965. *Understanding an African Kingdom: Bunyoro,* London: Holt, Rinehart and Winston.

Beck, Brenda E.F., 1972. *Peasant Society in Konku: A Study of Right and Left Subenstes in South India.* Vancouver: University of British Columbia Press.

Becker, Howard S., 1986. *Writing for Social Scientists.* Chicago: Chicago University Press.

Bell, Diana, Pat Caplan, and Wazir Jahan Karim (eds), 1993. *Gendered Fields: Women, Men and Ethnography.* London: Routledge.

Bellah, Robert, 1957. *Tokugawa Religion.* Glencoe, Illinois: Free Press.

Bendix R., 1968. 'Weber, Max', in D.L. Sils (ed.) *International Encyclopaedia of the Social Sciences.* New York: Macmillan, Vol. 16: 493–502.

Benedict, Ruth, 1934. *Patterns of Culture.* New York: Houghton Mifflin.

_____, 1946. *The Chrysanthemum and the Sword.* Boston: Houghton Mifflin.

Benjamin, Walter, 1985. 'A Small History of Photography', in *One Way Street and Other Writings.* London: Verso.

Bennett, John W.,1946. 'The Interpretation of Pueblo Culture: A Question of Values', *Southwestern Journal of Anthropology,* 2: 361–74.

Bennett, Lynn, 1983. *Dangerous Wives and Sacred Sisters: Social and Symbolic Roles of High-Caste Women in Nepal.* New York: Columbia University Press.

Berger, Peter, and Thomas Luckmann, 1966. *Social Construction of Reality.* Harmondsworth: Penguin.

Bernard, H. Russell, 1994. *Research Methods in Anthropology: Qualitative and Quantitative Approaches.* Sage.

Bernstein, B., 1971. *Class, Codes and Control: Theoretical Studies Towards a Sociology of Language.* London: Routledge and Kegan Paul.

Berreman, Gerald D., 1962. *Behind Many Masks: Ethnography and Impression Management in a Himalayan Village.* Ithaca: Society for Applied Anthropology (Monograph No. 4).

_____, 1963. (1972). *Hindus of the Himalayas.* Berkeley: University of California Press.

_____, 1965. 'Anemic and Emetic Analyses in Social Anthropology', *American Anthropologist,* 68: 346–54.

_____, 1972. 'Race, Caste, and Other Invidious Distinctions in Social Stratification', *Race,* 13: 385–414.

_____, 1973. *Caste in the Modern World.* Morristown, New Jersey: General Learning Press.

Béteille, André, 1965. *Caste, Class and Power: Changing Patterns of Stratification in a Tanjore Village.* Berkeley: University of California Press.

_____, 1975. 'The Tribulations of Fieldwork', in A. Béteille and T.N. Madan (eds), *Encounter and Experience: Personal Accounts of Fieldwork.* Delhi: Vikas.

_____, 1975a. 'Introduction', in N.K. Bose, *The Structure of Hindu Society.* Delhi: Orient-Longman.

_____, 1990. *Some Observations on the Comparative Method.* Amsterdam: CASA.

Béteille, André and T.N. Madan (eds), 1975. *Encounter and Experience: Personal Accounts of Fieldwork.* Delhi: Vikas.

Bhattacharya, D. and B. Bhattacharya (eds), 1965. *Census of India 1961: Report on the Population Estimates of India (1820–30).* Delhi: Office of Registrar General.

Bhasin, M.K. and Veena Bhasin, 1997. *Human Ecological Studies, Schedules and Proformas.* Delhi: Kamla-Raj.

Blalock, A.B. and H.M. Blalock, 1982. *Introduction to Social Research.* New Jersey, Englewood Cliffs: Prentice-Hall, Inc.

Bloch, Marc, 1954. *The Historians' Craft.* Manchester: Manchester University Press.

———, 1962. *Feudal Society.* London: Routledge and Kegan Paul.

———, 1967. *Land and Work in Medieval Europe.* London: Routledge and Kegan Paul.

Bloor, M., 1978. 'On the Analysis of Observational Data: A Discussion of the Worth and Uses of Inductive Technique and Respondent Validation', *Sociology,* 12: 545–52.

Blumer H., 1939. *Critiques of Research in the Social Sciences: 1. An Appraisal of Thomas and Znaniecki's The Polish Peasant in Europe and America.* Social Science Research Council, Bulletin, 44.

———, 1976. 'The Methodological Position of Symbolic Interactionism', in M. Hammersley and P. Woods, (eds), *The Process of Schooling: A Sociological Reader.* London: Routledge and Kegan Paul.

Boas, Franz, 1940. (1896). 'The Limitations of the Comparative Method in Anthropology', in *Race, Language and Culture.* New York: Macmillan.

Boelen, W.A., Marianne, 1992. 'Cornerville Revisited', *Journal of Contemporary Ethnography,* 21 (1): 11–51.

Bohannan, Paul, 1969. *Social Anthropology.* London: Holt, Rinehart and Winston.

Boissevain, Jeremy, 1972. 'Fieldwork in Malta', in J.D. Jennings and E.A. Hoebel (eds), *Readings in Anthropology.* New York: Mcgraw-Hill Book Company.

———, 1974. 'Towards a Sociology of Social Anthropology', *Theory and Society,* 1: 211–30.

Bose, P.K., 1995. *Research Methodology.* New Delhi: ICSSR.

Bovenkerk, Frank, 1992. 'Street Corner Society: een geval van wetenschappelije fraude?' in H. Moerland et al. (eds), *De menselijke maat. Opstellen ter gelegenheid van het afscheid van Prof. dr. G.P. Hoefnagels.* Arnhem: Gouda Quint.

Boyer, Pascal, 1990. *Tradition as Truth and Communication: A Cognitive Description of Traditional Discourse.* Cambridge: Cambridge University Press.

Breeks, J.W., 1873. *An Account of the Primitive Tribes and Monuments of the Nilagiris.* London: India Museum & W.H. Allen and Co.

Briggs, Jean, 1970. 'Kapluna Daughter', in Peggy Golde (ed.), *Women in the Field: Anthropological Experiences.* Berkeley: University of California Press.

Broeder, Dale W., 1959. 'The University of Chicago Jury Project', *Nebraska Law Review,* 38: 744–60.

———, 1960. 'Silence and Perjury before Police Officers: An Examination of the Criminal Law Risks', *Nebraska Law Review,* 40: 63–103.

Brown, P.J., 1978. 'Field-site Duplication: Case-studies and Comments on the "My-Tribe" Syndrome', *Current Anthropology*, 22: 413–4.

Bruner, E., 1983. *Text Play and Story: The Construction and Reconstruction of Self and Society*. Washington: American Ethnological Society.

Brymer, R.A., and B. Farris, 1967. 'Ethical and Political Dilemmas in the Investigation of Deviance: A Study of Juvenile Delinquency', in G. Sjoberg (ed.), *Ethics, Politics and Social Research*. Cambridge, Mass.: Schenkman.

Buechler, Hans C., 1969, 'The Social Position of the Ethnographer in the Field', in F. Henry and S. Saberwal (eds), *Stress and Response in Fieldwork*. New York: Holt, Rinehart & Winston.

Bulmer, Martin (ed.), 1977. *Sociological Research: An Introduction*. London: The Macmillan Press Ltd.

Burgess, Robert G. (ed.), 1982. *Field Research: A Sourcebook and Field Manual*. London: Unwin Hyman.

Burke, Peter (ed.), 1972. *Economy and Society in Early Modern Europe*. London: Routledge and Kegan Paul.

Burling, Robbins, 1962. 'Cognition and Componential Analysis: God's Truth or Hocus-Pocus?', *American Anthropologist*, 66: 20–28.

Burton, Michael L., and Douglas R. White, 1987. 'Cross-cultural Surveys Today', *Annual Review of Anthropology*, 16: 143–60.

Caplan, Pat, 1997. *African Voices, African Lives: Personal Narratives from a Swahili Village*. London: Routledge.

Caplow, T., and R.J. Mcgee, 1965. *The Academic Marketplace*. New York: Anchor Books.

Carrithers, M. and Caroline Humphrey (eds), 1991. *The Assembly of Listeners, Jains in Society*. Cambridge: Cambridge University Press.

Carrithers, Michael, Steven Collins, and Steven Lukes, (eds), 1985. *The Category of the Person*. Cambridge: Cambridge University Press.

Carstairs, G.M., 1983. *Death of a Witch: A Village in North India 1950–1981*. London: Hutchinson.

Carter, Alison, 2000. 'Parade Profile: Alan Macfarlane', *King's Parade*. Autumn Issue: 6–7.

Casagrande, J.B. (ed.), 1960. *In the Company of Man*. New York: Harper & Brothers.

Casley, D.J., and D.A. Lury, 1981. *Data Collection in Developing Countries*. Oxford: English Language Book Society and Clarendon Press.

Cassel, J., 1980. 'Ethical Problems for Conducting Fieldwork', *American Anthropologist*, 82 (1): 28–41.

Cassell, J., 1977. 'Relationship of Observer to Observed in Peer Group Research', *Human Organization*, 36: 412–16.

Cesara, M.,1982. *Reflections of a Woman Anthropologist: No Hiding Place*. London: Academic Press.

Chakravarti, Anand, 1975. *Contradiction and Change*. Delhi: Oxford University Press.

Chambers, R., 1981. *Rapid Rural Appraisal: Rationale and Repertoire*. Discussion Paper No. 155. Sussex: Institute of Development Studies.

Chambers, R., 1992. *Rapid Appraisal: Rapid Relaxed and Participatory.* Discussion Paper No. 311. Sussex: Institute of Development Studies.

Chapin, F. Stuart, 1963. 'The Social Effects of Public Housing in Minneapolis', in Matilda White Riley (ed.), *Sociological Research, Volume 1: A Case Approach.* New York and Burlingame: Harcourt, Brace & World, Inc.

Chatterjee, Partha, 1993. *The Nation and Its Fragments: Colonial and Postcolonial Histories.* Princeton: Princeton University Press.

Chaudhuri, N.C., 1968. *The Autobiography of an Unknown Indian.* Berkeley: University of California Press.

Chibnik, M., 1985. 'The Use of Statistics in Sociocultural Anthropology', *Annual Review of Anthropology,* 14: 135–57.

Cipolla, C.M (ed.) 1972. *The Fontana Economic History of Europe: The Middle Ages.* Collins/Fontana Books.

Clifford, James, 1986. 'Introduction: Partial Truths', in James Clifford and George E. Marcus (eds), *Writing Culture: The Poetics and Politics of Ethnography.* Berkeley: University of California Press.

————, 1992. 'Travelling Cultures', in L. Grossberg et al. (eds), *Cultural Studies.* New York: Routledge.

Clifford, James, and George Marcus (eds), 1986. *Writing Culture: The Poetics and Politics of Ethnography.* Berkeley: University of California Press.

Cohen, M.R., and E. Nagel, 1944. *An Introduction to Logic and Scientific Method.* New York: Harcourt, Brace & World, Inc.

Cohn, Bernard S., 1996. *An Anthropologist among the Historians and Other Essays.* Delhi: Oxford University Press.

Colson, Elizabeth, 1954. 'The Intensive Study of Small Sample Communities', in Robert F. Spencer (ed.), *Method and Perspective in Anthropology: Papers in Honour of Willson D. Wallis.* Minneapolis: The University of Minnesota Press.

Conklin, H.C., 1964. 'Ethnogenealogical Method', in W.H. Goodenough (ed.), *Explorations in Cultural Anthropology.* New York: McGraw-Hill.

Coy, Peter, 1971. 'A Watershed in Mexican Rural History: Some Thoughts on the Reconciliation of Conflicting Interpretations', *Journal of Latin American Studies*, 3: 39–57.

Crapanzano, Vincent, 1980. *Tuhami: Portrait of a Moroccan.* Chicago: Chicago University Press.

Crewe, Quentin, 1985. *The Last Maharaja: A Biography of Sawai Man Singh II, Maharaja of Jaipur.* London: Michael Joseph.

Crick, M., 1982. 'Anthropological Field Research: Meaning Creation and Knowledge Construction' in D. Parkin (ed.), *Semantic Anthropology.* London: Academic Press.

Daniel, E. Valentine. 1984. *Fluid Signs: Being a Person the Tamil Way.* Berkeley: University of California Press.

Darling, M.L., 1966. *Apprentice to Power.* London: Hogarth Press.

Das, Veena, 1977. *Structure and Cognition: Aspects of Hindu Caste and Ritual.* Delhi: Oxford University Press.

Das, Veena, l999. 'Contemporary Methods in Narrative Analysis', in R.L. Kapur (ed.), *Qualitative Methods in Mental Health Research*. Bangalore: National Institute of Advanced Study.

—————, n.d. *Paradigms of Body Symbolism*. Manuscript.

Das, Veena, and Jonathan Parry, 1983. 'Fieldwork in South Asia', *Man*, 18: 790–1.

Dasgupta, Surendranath, 1988. *A History of Indian Philosophy*. Five Volumes. New Delhi: Motilal Banarsidass.

De Beauvoir, Simone, 1972. *The Coming of Age*. New York: Putnam and Sons.

De Casparis, J.G., 1979. 'Inscriptions and South Asian Dynastic Traditions', in R.J. Moore (ed.), *Tradition and Politics in South Asia*. New Delhi: Vikas.

DeHolmes, Rebecca, 1983. 'Shabono: Scandal or Superb Social Science?', *American Anthropologist*, 85: 664–67.

Denzin, N.K., 1978. *The Research Act: A Theoretical Introduction to Social Research*. New York: McGraw-Hill.

Derrett, J.D.M., 1959. 'Bhū-bharana, Bhū-palana, Bhū-bhojana: An Indian Conundrum', *Bulletin of the School of Oriental and African Studies*, 22: 108–23.

—————, 1976. 'Rājadharma', *Journal of Asian Studies*, 35: 108–23.

Desai, A.R., 1948. *The Social Background of Indian Nationalism*. Mumbai: Popular Prakashan.

De Tassy, Garcin, 1997. *Muslim Festivals in India and Other Essays*. Delhi: Oxford University Press.

de Tocqueville, Alexis, 1861. *Memoir, Letters and Remains*. London: Macmillan.

—————, 1956. *L'Ancien Regime*. Oxford: Blackwell.

—————, 1956 (1840). *Democracy in America*. New York: Mentor Books.

Devereux, G., 1967. *From Anxiety to Method in the Behavioural Sciences*. The Hague: Mouton.

Dixon, W.J., and F.J. Massey, Jr. 1957. *Introduction to Statistical Analysis*. New York: McGraw Hill.

Donner, Florinda, 1982. *Shabono: A Visit to a Remote and Magical World in the Heart of the South American Jungle*. New York: Delacorte.

Douglas, J.D., 1976. *Investigative Social Research: Individual and Team Research*. Beverly Hills, Calif.: Sage.

Dube, Leela, 1975. 'Women's World—Three Encounters', in A. Béteille and T.N. Madan (eds), *Encounter and Experience: Personal Accounts of Fieldwork*. Delhi: Vikas.

Dube, S.C., 1955. *Indian Village*. London: Routledge & Kegan Paul.

—————, 1962. 'Social Anthropology in India', in T.N. Madan and G. Sarana (eds), *Indian Anthropology*. Mumbai: Asia Publishing House.

—————, 1973. *Social Sciences in Changing Society: D.N. Majumdar Lectures 1972*. Lucknow: Ethnographic and Folk Culture Society.

Du Bois B., 1983. 'Passionate Scholarship: Notes on Values, Knowing and Method in Feminist Social Science', in G. Bowles and R. Duelli-Klein (ed.), *Theories of Women's Studies*. London: Routledge & Kegan Paul.

Duerr, Hans Peter, 1987. *Dreamtime: Concerning the Boundary Between Wilderness and Civilization.* Oxford: Basil Blackwell.

Dumont, Jean-Paul, 1986. 'Prologue to Ethnography or Prolegomena to Anthropology', *Ethos,* 14 (4): 344–67.

Dumont, Louis, 1957. 'For a Sociology of India', *Contributions to Indian Sociology,* I: 7–22.

————, 1962. 'The Conception of Kingship in Ancient India', *Contributions to Indian Sociology,* 6: 48–77.

————, 1966. 'A Fundamental Problem in the Sociology of Caste', *Contributions to Indian Sociology,* IX: 17–32.

————, 1977. *From Mandeville to Marx.* Chicago: Chicago University Press.

————, 1986. *Essays in Individualism.* Chicago: Chicago University Press.

Durkheim, Émile, 1915 (1912). *The Elementary Forms of the Religious Life.* London: Allen and Unwin.

————, 1933 (1893). *The Division of Labour in Society.* Glencoe: The Free Press.

————, 1951 (1897). *Suicide.* Glencoe: The Free Press.

————, 1966 (1938, 1895). *The Rules of Sociological Method.* New York: The Free Press and London: Collier-Macmillan Limited.

————, 1969 (1898). 'Individualism and the Intellectuals', *Political Studies,* 17: 114–30.

————, 1974 (1924). *Sociology and Philosophy.* New York: The Free Press.

————, and Marcel Mauss, 1963 (1903). *Primitive Classification.* London: Cohen and West.

Edwards, Elizabeth, 1992. 'Science Visualized: E.H. Man in the Andaman Islands', in Elizabeth Edwards (ed.), *Anthropology and Photography.* New Haven: Yale.

Eggan, Fred, 1954. 'Social Anthropology and the Method of Controlled Comparison', *American Anthropologist,* 56 (5): 743–63.

Ellen, R. F. (ed.) 1984. *Ethnographic Research: A Guide to General Conduct.* London: Academic Press.

Emerson, R. and M. Pollner, 1988. 'On the Uses of Members' Responses to Researchers' Accounts', *Human Organization,* 47 (3): 189–98.

Erikson, Erik H., 1969. *Gandhi's Truth: On the Origins of Militant Non-Violence.* New York: Norton.

Evans-Pritchard, E.E., 1940. *The Nuer.* Oxford: Clarendon Press.

————, 1951. *Social Anthropology.* London: Routledge & Kegan Paul.

————, 1963. 'The Comparative Method in Social Anthropology', *L.T. Hobhouse Memorial Trust Lecture,* 33.

————, 1956. *Nuer Religion.* Oxford: Clarendon Press.

————, 1960. *Kinship and Marriage among the Nuer.* Oxford: Clarendon Press.

————, 1965. *The Position of Women in Primitive Societies and Other Essays.* London: Faber and Faber.

————, 1973. 'Some Reminiscences and Reflections on Fieldwork', *Journal of the Anthropological Society of Oxford,* IV (1): 1–12.

Firth, Raymond, 1936. *We, the Tikopia: A Sociological Analysis of Kinship in Primitive Polynesia.* London: G. Allen.

Firth, Raymond, 1956. *Elements of Social Organization*. London: Watts & Co.
_____, 1959. *Social Change in Tikopia*. London: George Allen and Unwin.
Fish, S., 1980. 'Introduction: How I Stopped Worrying and Learned to Love Interpretation', in *Is There a Text in the Class?* Cambridge: Harvard University Press.
Fleishman, A.., 1982. Figures of Autobiography: *The Language of Self Writing in Victorian and Modern England*. Berkeley: University of California Press.
Fortes M., 1949. 'Preface', in M. Fortes (ed.), *Social Structure: Studies Presented to Radcliffe-Brown*. Oxford: Clarendon Press.
Fortes, M., and E.E. Evans-Pritchard (eds), 1940. *African Political Systems*. London: Oxford University Press.
Fortune, R., 1939. 'Arapesh Warfare', *American Anthropologist*, 41: 22–41.
Foster, G.M., T. Scudder, E. Colson, and R.V. Kemper (eds), 1979. *Longterm Field Research in Anthropology*. New York: Academic Press.
Foucault, Michel, 1970. *The Order of Things: An Archaeology of the Human Sciences*. Vintage Books.
Fox, Robin, 1973. *Encounter with Anthropology*. Penguin Books.
Frake, C., 1964. 'A Structural Description of Subanum Religious Behaviour', in Ward Goodenough (ed.), *Explorations in Cultural Anthropology*. New York: McGraw Hill.
_____, 1964a. 'How to Ask for a Drink in Subanum', *American Anthropologist*, 66: 127–32.
Frank, Gelya, 1979. 'Finding the Common Denominator: A Phenomenological Critique of Life History Method', *Ethos*, 7: 68–94.
Freed, Ruth S., and Stanley A. Freed, 1993. *Ghosts: Life and Death in North India*, New York: The American Museum of Natural History.
Freed, Stanley A., and Ruth S. Freed, 1964. 'Spirit Possession as Illness in a North Indian Village, *Ethnology* 3: 152–71.
Freedman, Maurice, 1979. *The Study of Chinese Society: Essays by Maurice Freedman*. Stanford, Cali.: Stanford University Press.
Freeman, Derek, 1983. *Margaret Mead and Samoa: The Making and Unmaking of an Anthropological Myth*. Cambridge, Mass.: Harvard University Press.
Freeman, James M. 1966. 'Myth and Metaphysics in Indian Thought', *The Monist*, 50: 517–29.
_____, 1968. 'Power and Leadership in a Changing Temple Village of India', Ph.D. Dissertation, Harvard University.
_____, 1977. *Scarcity and Opportunity in an Indian Village*. Menlo Park, California: Cummings.
Freilich, N. (ed.), 1970. *Marginal Natives at Work: Anthropologists in the Field*. New York: Schenkman.
Friedrich, C.J., 1952. 'Some Observations on Weber's Analysis of Bureaucracy', in R.K. Merton, et al. (eds), *Reader in Bureaucracy*. Glencoe: The Free Press.
Frisby, David, 1985. *Fragments of Modernity: Theories of Modernity in the Work of Simmel, Kracauer and Benjamin*. Oxford: Polity.
Frye, N. 1957. *Anatomy of Criticism: Four Essays*. New York: Routledge.

Fukuyama, Francis, 1992. *The End of History and the Last Man*. London: Hamish Hamilton.

Fuller, C.J., 1979. 'Gods, Priests and Purity', *Man* (n.s.), 14: 459–76.

_____, 1984. *Servants of the Goddess: The Priests of a South Indian Temple*. Cambridge: Cambridge University Press.

Fürer-Haimendorf, Christoph von, 1955. *Himalayan Barbary*. London: John Murray.

Gait, E.A., 1911. *Census of India, 1911, Vol. 1 (India), Part 1 (Report)*. Calcutta: Government Press.

Gardner, Robert, 1985. *Forest of Bliss* (Film). Harvard University: Film Study Center.

Geertz, Clifford, 1973. *The Interpretation of Cultures*. London: Hutchinson.

_____, 1983. *Local Knowledge: Further Essays in Interpretative Sociology*. New York: Basic Books.

_____, 1988. *Works and Lives: The Anthropologist as Author*. Cambridge: Polity Press.

_____, 1995. *After the Fact: Two Countries, Four Decades, One Anthropologist*. Cambridge, Mass.: Harvard University Press.

_____, 2000. *Available Light: Anthropological Reflections on Philosophical Topics*. New Jersey: Princeton University Press.

Gellner, E. (ed.), 1980. *Soviet and Western Anthropology*. London: Duckworth.

Gerth, H.H., and C. Wright Mills (ed.), 1970. *From Max Weber: Essays in Sociology*. London: Routledge & Kegan Paul.

Gewertz, Deborah B., 1983. *Sepik River Societies: A Historical Ethnography of the Chambri and Their Neighbors*. New Haven: Yale University Press.

Ghosh, Amitav, 1992. *In an Antique Land*. Delhi: Ravi Dayal Publisher.

Ghurye, G.S., 1960. *After a Century and a Quarter*. Bombay: Popular Book Depot.

Giddens, Anthony, 1976. *New Rules for Sociological Method*. New York: Basic Books.

Gillin, John, 1936. *The Barama River Caribs of British Guiana*. Cambridge, Mass. Papers of the Peabody Museum, No. 14.

Glaser, B.G., and A.L. Strauss, 1967. *The Discovery of Grounded Theory: Strategies for Qualitative Research*. Chicago: Aldine.

Gluckman, M., 1961. 'Ethnographic Data in British Social Anthropology', *Sociological Review*, 9: 5–17.

_____, 1963. 'Gossip and Scandal: Papers in Honour of M.J. Herskovits', *Current Anthropology*, IV (3): 307–16.

Godelier, M., 1977. *Perspectives in Marxist Anthropology*. Cambridge: Cambridge University Press.

Goffman, Erving, 1982 (1969). *The Presentation of Self in Everyday Life*. Penguin Books.

Gold, Ann G.A, 1988. *Fruitful Journeys: The Ways of Rajasthani Pilgrims*. Berkeley: University of California Press.

Golde, Peggy, (ed.), 1986 (1970). *Women in the Field: Anthropological Experiences*. Berkeley: University of California Press.

Gonda, J., 1969. *Ancient Indian Kingship from the Religious Point of View*. Leiden: E.J. Brill.

Good, Kenneth, 1991. *Into the Heart*. New York: Simon and Schuster.

Goode, William J. and P.K. Hatt, 1981. *Methods in Social Research*. McGraw-Hill Book Company.

Goody, Jack, 1977. *The Domestication of the Savage Mind*. Cambridge: Cambridge University Press.

———, 1992. 'Local Knowledge and·Knowledge of Locality: The Desirability of Frames', *Yale Journal of Criticism*, 5 (2).

Goody, Jack, 1995. *The Expansive Moment: The Rise of Social Anthropology in Britain and Africa, 1918–1970*. Cambridge: Cambridge University Press.

———, (ed.), 1958. The Developmental Cycle in Domestic Groups. Cambridge: Cambridge University Press.

Gough, Kathleen, 1974. 'Dr. A. Aiyappan as an Ethnographer' in B.K. Nair (ed.), *Culture and Society*. Mumbai: Popular Prakashan.

Greenbaum, Thomas L., 1998. *The Handbook for Focus Group Research*. Sage.

Gregory, C.A. and J.C. Altman, 1989. *Observing the Economy*. London: Routledge.

Grimshaw A., and K. Hart, 1993. *Anthropology and the Crisis of the Intellectuals*. Cambridge: The Prickly Pear Press.

Guha, Ramachandra, 1999. *Savaging the Civilized Verrier Elwin, His Tribals, and India*. New Delhi: Oxford University Press.

Gupta, Dipankar, 1982. *Nativism in a Metropolis: The Shiv Sena in Bombay*. Delhi: Manohar Books.

Gutkind, Peter C.W., 1969. 'The Social Researcher in the Context of African National Development: Reflections on an Encounter', in F. Henry and S. Saberwal (eds), *Stress and Response in Fieldwork*. New York: Holt, Rinehart & Winston.

Habib, Irfan, 1985. 'Classifying Pre-colonial India', *The Journal of Peasant Studies*, 12 (2 & 3): 44–53.

Hackenberg, R.A., 1997. 'Genealogical Method in Social Anthropology: The Foundations of Structural Demography', in J.J. Honigmann (ed.), *Handbook of Social and Cultural Anthropology*. Vol. 1. Jaipur and New Delhi: Rawat.

Hagen, Everett E., 1962. *On the Theory of Social Change*. Homewood, Ill.: Dorsey Press.

Hammersley, M., and P. Atkinson, 1983. *Ethnography: Principles in Practice*. London: Tavistock Publications.

Hannerz, Ulf, 1992. *Cultural Complexity: Studies in the Social Organization of Meaning*. New York: Columbia University Press.

Hargreaves, D.H., 1967. *Social Relations in a Secondary School*. London: Routledge & Kegan Paul.

Hart, C.W.M., 1970. 'Fieldwork among the Tiwi, 1928–1929', in George D. Spindler (ed.), *Being an Anthropologist*. New York: Holt, Rinehart & Winston.

Hart, H.L.A., 1983. *Essays in Jurisprudence and Philosophy*. Oxford: Oxford University Press.

Hasan, Mushirul, 1979. *Nationalism and Communal Politics in India*. New Delhi: Manohar.

Hatfield, Jr, C.R., 1975. 'Fieldwork: Toward a Model of Mutual Exploitation', in P.B. Hammond (ed.), *Cultural and Social Anthropology, Introductory Readings in Ethnology*. New York: Macmillan, and London: Collier.

Hayden, R.M., 1999. *Disputes and Arguments Amongst Nomads: A Caste Council in India.* Delhi: Oxford University Press.

Hayek F.A., 1982. *Law, Legislation and Liberty,* Vol. 1. London: Routledge.

Hazari, 1969 (1951). *Untouchable.* New York: Praeger.

Heesterman, J.C., 1957. *The Ancient Indian Royal Consecration.* Gravenhagen: Mouton.

Heider, Karl, 1988. 'The Rashomon Effect: When Ethnographers Disagree', *American Anthropologist,* 90 (1): 73–81.

Heimann, P. 1950. 'On Counter Transference' *International Journal of Psychoanalysis,* xxxi: 81–4.

Hendry, Joy, 1999. *An Anthropologist in Japan: Glimpses of Life in the Field.* London: Routledge.

Henley, P., 1985. 'British Ethnographic Film: Some Recent Developments', *Anthropology Today* 1: 5–17.

Henry, F., and S. Saberwal (eds), 1969. *Stress and Response in Fieldwork.* New York: Holt, Rinehart & Winston.

Herskovits, M.J., 1954. 'Some Problems of Method in Ethnography', in Robert F. Spencer (ed.), *Method and Perspective in Anthropology: Papers in Honour of Willson D. Wallis.* Minneapolis: The University of Minnesota Press.

Hewitt de Alcántara, Cynthia, 1982. *Boundaries and Paradigms: The Anthropological Study of Rural Life in Postrevolutionary Mexico.* Leiden: Leiden Development Studies, No. 4.

Hindess, Barry, 1973. *The Use of Official Statistics in Sociology: A Critique of Positivism and Epistemology.* London: Macmillan.

Hodder, Ian,,1998. 'The Interpretation of Documents and Material Culture', in N.K. Denzin and Y.S. Lincoln (eds), *Collecting and Interpreting Qualitative Materials.* Sage.

Holmberg, A.R., 1950. *Nomads of the Long Bow: The Siriono of Eastern Bolivia.* Washington: Smithsonian Institution.

Holmes, Lowell D., 1957. *The Restudy of Manu'an Culture: A Problem in Methodology.* Northwestern University Ph.D. thesis, Ann Arbor Microfilms, No. 23.514.

_____, 1983. 'A Tale of Two Studies', *American Anthropologist,* 85: 929–35.

_____, 1987. *Quest for the Real Samoan: The Mead/Freeman Controversy and Beyond.* South Hadley, MA: Bergin and Garvey.

Homans, George C., 1960. *English Villagers of the Thirteenth Century.* New York: Russell and Russell.

Honigmann, J.J., 1973. 'Sampling in Ethnographic Field Work', in R. Naroll and R. Cohen (eds), A *Handbook of Method in Cultural Anthropology.* New York: Columbia University Press.

Hsu, F.L.K., 1963. *Clan, Caste and Club.* Princeton: Van Nostrand.

Huizer, G., 1979. 'Research-through-Action: Some Practical Experiences with Peasant Organizations' in G. Huizer and B. Mannheim (eds), *The Politics of Anthropology.* The Hague: Mouton.

Humphrey, Caroline, and James Laidlaw, 1994. *The Archetypal Actions of Ritual: A Theory of Ritual Illustrated by the Jain Rite of Worship.* Oxford: Clarendon Press.

Hutton, J.H., 1921. *The Angami Nagas*. Oxford: Clarendon Press.

Inden, R., 1979. Seminar Paper delivered at the School of Oriental and African Studies. June 1979.

Inglis, Fred, 2000. *Clifford Geertz: Culture, Custom and Ethics*. Cambridge: Polity Press.

Ingold, Tim, 1986. *Evolution and Social Life*. Cambridge: Cambridge University Press.

_____, (ed.), 1990. *The Concept of Society is Theoretically Obsolete*. Manchester: Department of Social Anthropology, University of Manchester.

Jacobs, Norman, 1958. *The Origin of Modern Capitalism and Eastern Asia*. Hong Kong: Hong Kong University Press.

Jacobson, David, 1991. *Reading Ethnography*. Albany: State University of New York Press.

Jacques, Elliott, 1951. *The Changing Culture of a Factory*. London: Tavistock.

Jain, S.N. et al. (eds), 1983. *Legal Research and Methodology*. Mumbai: N.M. Tripathi Pvt Ltd.

Janah, Sunil, 2003. *The Tribals of India*. New Delhi: Oxford University Press.

Jarvie, I.C., 1969. 'The Problem of Ethical Integrity in Participant Observation', *Current Anthropology,* 10 (3): 505–8.

Jones, Delmos J., 1970. 'Towards a Native Anthropology', *Human Organization*, 29: 251–59.

Jones, E., 1924. 'Psychoanalysis and Anthropology', *Journal of the Royal Anthropological Institute*, 54.

Jones, E.L., 1981. *The European Miracle*. Cambridge: Cambridge University Press.

Jongmans, D.G., and P.C.W. Gutkind (eds), 1967. *Anthropologists in the Field*. Assen: Van Gorcum & Comp. N.V.

Joravsky, David, 1970. *The Lysenko Affair*. Cambridge, MA: Harvard University Press.

Josselin De Jong, P.E., 1967. 'The Participants' View of Their Culture', in D.G. Jongmans and P.C.W. Gutkind (eds), *Anthropologists in the Field*. Assen: Van Gorcum.

Kakar, Sudhir, 1982. *Shamans, Mystics and Doctors: A Psychological Enquiry into India and its Healing Traditions*. New Delhi: Oxford University Press.

Kantowsky, Detlef, 1995. *An Indian Village Through Letters and Pictures*. Delhi: Oxford University Press.

Karlekar, M., 1970. *Career Orientation and Commitment of School Teachers: A Study in the Sociology of Profession amongst Women Teachers in Six Delhi Schools*. Unpublished M.Litt. dissertation, University of Delhi.

_____, 1975. 'Professionalization of Women School Teachers', *Indian Journal of Industrial Relations*, July issue.

_____, 1982a. 'Women's Studies in the Eighties: State of the Discipline in USA and India', *Samya Shakti: A Journal of Women's Studies*, 1(1).

Karlekar, M., 1982b. *Poverty and Women's Work—A Study of Sweeper Women in Delhi*. New Delhi: Vikas.

_____, 1983. 'Education and Inequality', in André Béteille (ed.), *Equality and Inequality—Theory and Practice*. New Delhi: Oxford University Press.

_____, 1990. 'Construction of Feminity in Nineteenth Century Bengal: Readings from *Janaika* Grhabadhur Diary', *Samya Shakti: A Journal of Women's Studies,* IV and V.

Karlekar, M., 1991. *Voices from Within—Early Personal Narratives of Bengali Women.* New Delhi: Oxford University Press.

Karve, D.D., and E. McDonald, 1963. *The New Brahmans: Five Maharashtrian Families.* Berkeley: University of California Press.

Kautilya, 1915. *Kautilya's Artharaśāstra.* Mysore: Mysore Printing and Publishing House.

Kay, P. (ed.), 1971. *Explorations in Mathematical Anthropology.* Cambridge, Mass. MIT Press.

Kielstra, N., 1979. 'Is Useful Action Research Possible?', in G. Huizer and B. Mannheim (eds), *The Politics of Anthropology.* The Hague: Mouton.

Klein, V., 1965. *Britain's Married Women Workers.* London: Routledge & Kegan Paul.

Kloos, Peter, 1969. 'Role Conflicts in Social Fieldwork', *Current Anthropology,* 10: 509–12.

_____, 1988. *Door het oog van de antropoloog: Botsende visies bij heronderzoek.* Muiderberg: D. Coutinho.

_____, 1994. 'Replication, Restudy, and the Nature of Anthropological Fieldwork', in Van der Veer, Van Ijzendoorn and Valsiner (eds), *Reconstructing the Mind: Replicability in Research on Human Development.* Norwood: Ablex Publishing Corporation.

_____, 1996. 'Multiple Images of Ethnic Reality: Beyond Disagreement', in A. van Harskamp (ed.), *Conflicts in Social Science.* London: Routledge.

Kloos, Peter, and Purnaka L. deSilva, 1995. *Globalization, Localization and Violence: An Annotated Bibliography.* Amsterdam: VU University Press.

Kluckhohn, Clyde, 1945. 'The Personal Document in Anthropological Science' in *The Use of Personal Documents in History, Anthropology, and Sociology.* Social Science Research Council, Bulletin, 53.

Köbben, A.J.F., 1966. 'New Ways of Presenting an Old Idea: The Statistical Method in Social Anthropology', in F.W. Moore (ed.), *Readings in Cross-Cultural Methodology.* New Haven: Hraf Press.

_____, 1967. 'Participation and Quantification: Fieldwork among the Djuka (Bush Negroes of Surinam)', in D.G. Jongmans and P.C.W. Gutkind (eds), *Anthropologists in the Field.* Assen: Van Goreum.

Koestler, Arthur, 1960. *The Lotus and the Robot.* London: Hutchinson.

Kohler-Rollefson, Ilse, and Dewa Ram Dewasi, 1991. 'The Raikas of Western Rajasthan (India): A Pastoral Caste Under Pressure', Unpublished Paper.

Kothari, C.R., 1985. *Research Methodology.* New Delhi: Wishwa Prakashan.

Kroeber, A.L., 1948. *Anthropology.* New York: Harcourt Brace and World.

Kulick, Don, and Margaret Wilson (eds), 1995. *Taboo: Sex, Identity and Erotic Subjectivity in Anthropological Fieldwork.* London: Routledge.

Kumar, Nita, 1992. *Friends, Brothers, and Informants: Fieldwork Memoirs of Banaras.* Berkeley: University of California Press.

Kuper, Adam, 1996 (1973). *Anthropologists and Anthropology: The Modern British School.* London: Routledge.

Kvale, Steiner, 1996. *InterViews: An Introduction to Qualitative Research. Interviewing*. Sage.

La Barre, Weston, 1967. 'Preface', in G. Devereux, *From Anxiety to Method in the Behavioural Sciences*. The Hague: Mouton.

Lacey, C., 1976. 'Problems of Sociological Framework: A Review of the Methodology of "Hightown Grammer" in M. Hammersley and P. Woods (eds), *The Process of Schooling: A Sociological Reader*. London: Routledge and Kegan Paul.

Laidlaw, James, 1985. 'Profit, Soluation, and Profitable Saints', *Cambridge Anthropology*, 9 (3).

Lal, Ram Narain, 1949. *The Student's Practical Dictionary*. Allahabad: Ram Narain Lal.

Landes, David, 1972. *The Unbound Prometheus*. Cambridge: Cambridge University Press.

Langham, Ian, 1981. *The Building of British Social Anthropology*. Dordrecht.

Langness, L.L. 1965. *The Life History in Anthropological Science*. New York: Holt, Rinehart and Winston.

Lath, Mukund, 1981. *Ardhakathanaka: Half a Tale, A Study in the Relationship between Autobigraphy and History*. Jaipur: Rajasthan Prakrit Bharata Sansthan.

Laslett, Peter, 1971. *The World We Have Lost*. London: Methuen.

Leach, E.R., 1954. *Political Systems of Highland Burma: A Study of Kachin Social Structure*. Boston: Beacon Press.

_____, 1961. *Rethinking Anthropology*. London: Athlone Press.

_____, 1961a. *Pul Eliya, A Village in Ceylon*. Cambridge: Cambridge University Press.

_____, 1961b. 'The Frontiers of "Burma"', *Comparative Studies in Society and History*, 3(1).

_____, 1967. 'An Anthropologist's Reflection on a Social Survey', in D.G. Jongmans and P.C.W. Gutkind (eds), *Anthropologists in the Field*. Assen: Van Goreum.

_____, 1982. *Social Anthropology*. Oxford: Oxford University Press.

Lee-Warner, W., 1894. *The Protected Princes of India*. London: Macmillan.

Leff, Gordon, 1958. *Medieval Thought: St. Augustine to Ockham*. Penguin.

LeGoff, Jacques, 1972. 'The Town as an Agent of Civilization, 1200–1500', in C.M. Cipolla (ed.), *The Fontana Economic History of Europe: The Middle Ages*. Collins/Fontana Books.

Lévi-Strauss, Claude. 1949. *Les Structures Élémentaires de La Parenté*. Paris: Presses Universitaires de France.

Lévi-Strauss, 1963. *Structural Anthropology*. Penguin.

_____, 1976. *Tristes Tropiques*. Penguin.

Lewis, I.M., 1986. *Religion in Context: Cults and Charisma*. Cambridge: Cambridge University Press.

Lewis, Oscar, 1951. *Life in a Mexican Village: Tepoztlan Restudied*. Urbana, Illinois: University of Illinois Press.

_____, 1955. 'Comparisons in Cultural Anthropology', in W.L. Thomas, Jr (ed.), *Current Anthropology*. Chicago: University of Chicago Press.

_____, 1958. *Village Life in Northern India*. Urbana: Urbana University Press.

Lewis, Oscar, 1959. *Five Families: Mexican Case Studies in the Culture of Poverty.* New York: Basic Books.

————, 1961. 'Some of My Best Friends are Peasants', *Human Organization*, 19 (4): 179–80.

————, 1964. *Pedro Martinez: A Mexican Peasant and His Family.* Vintage Books.

Li, An-Che, 1937. 'Zuñi: Some Observations and Queries', *American Anthropologist*, 39: 62–76.

Lienhardt, Godfrey, 1964. *Social Anthropology.* Oxford: Oxford University Press.

Lincoln, Y.S., and E.G. Guba, 1985. *Naturalistic Inquiry.* Beverly Hills, CA: Sage.

Lingat, R., 1973. *The Classical Law of India.* Berkeley: University of California Press.

Lockwood, David, 1992. *Solidarity and Schism.* Oxford: Clarendon Press.

Loizos, Peter, 1981. *The Heart Grown Bitter: A Chronicle of Cypriot War Refugees.* London: Cambridge University Press.

————, 1993. *Innovation in Ethnographic Film: From Innocence to Self-Consciousness.* Manchester: Manchester University Press.

Lowie, Robert H., 1937. *History of Ethnological Theory.* New York: Farrar and Rinehart.

————, 1950. *Social Organization.* London: Routledge & Kegan Paul.

————, 1960 (1921). *Primitive Society.* London: Routledge & Kegan Paul.

Luhrmann, T.M., 1989. *Persuasions of the Witch's Craft: Ritual Magic and Witchcraft in Present-day England.* Oxford: Basil Blackwell.

————, 1996. *The Good Parsi: The Fate of a Colonial Elite in a Postcolonial Society.* Delhi: Oxford University Press.

Lynton, H.R., and M. Rajan, 1974. *The Days of Beloved.* Berkeley: University of California Press.

MacDougall, David, 1978. 'Ethnographic Film: Failure and Promise', *American Rev. Anthropology*, 7(4): 5–25.

————, 1998. *Transcultural Cinema.* Princeton: Princeton University Press.

MacDougall, David, and Judith MacDougall, 1991. *Photo Wallahs* (film). Fieldwork Films, Australia.

Macfarlane, Alan, 1992–93, 'Louis Dumont and the Origins of Individualism', *Cambridge Anthropology*, 16 (1).

————, 1994. 'The Origins of Capitalism in Japan, China and the West: The Work of Norman Jacobs', *Cambridge Anthropology*, 17 (3).

Macfarlane, Alan, 1997, 'Identity and Change among the Gurungs (Tamumai) of Central Nepal', in David N. Gellner et al. (eds), *Nationalism and Ethnicity in a Hindu Kingdom, The Politics of Culture in Contempoary Nepal.* The Netherlands: Harwood Academic Publishers.

Madan, T.N., 1965. *Family and Kinship: A Study in the Pandits of Rural Kashmir.* Mumbai: Asia.

————, 1966. 'For a Sociology of India', *Contributions to Indian Sociology*, IX: 9–16.

————, 1972. 'Doctors in a North Indian City: Recruitment, Role Perception, and Role Performance', in Satish Saberwal (ed.), *Beyond the Village.* Simla: Indian Institute of Advanced Study.

Madan, T.N., 1972a. 'Research Methodology: A Trend Report', in *A Survey of Research in Sociology and Social Anthropology.* Mumbai: Popular Prakashan.

————, 1975. 'On Living Intimately with Strangers', in André Béteille and T.N. Madan (eds), *Encounter and Experience: Personal Accounts of Fieldwork.* New Delhi: Vikas.

Madan, T.N., et al. 1980. *Doctors and Society.* New Delhi: Vikas.

————, 1982. 'Anthropology as the Mutual Interpretation of Cultures', in Hussein Fahim (ed.), *Indigenous Anthropology in Non-Western Countries.* Durham, N.C.: Carolina Academic Press.

————, 1987. *Non-Renunciation: Themes and Interpretations of Hindu Culture.* Delhi: Oxford University Press.

————, 1989. *Family and Kinship: A Study in the Pandits of Rural Kashmir.* Delhi: Oxford University Press.

————, 1990. 'India in American Anthropology', in S. Glazer and N. Glazer (eds), *Conflicting Images: India and the United States.* Glendale, Maryland: Riverdale.

————, 1995 (1994). *Pathways: Approaches to the Study of Society in India.* Delhi: Oxford University Press.

Madge, John, 1953. *The Tools of Social Research.* London: Longman, Green & Co.

Maine, Henry, 1890. *Ancient Law.* London: John Murray.

Malgaonkar, M., 1963. *The Puars of Dewas Senior.* Mumbai: Orient Longman.

Malinowski, Bronislaw, 1922. *Argonauts of the Western Pacific.* London: Routledge & Kegan Paul.

————, 1967. *A Diary in the Strict Sense of the Term.* New York: Harcourt, Brace.

Mamdani, M., 1972. *The Myth of Population Control.* New York: Monthly Review Press.

Mandelbaum, D.G., 1973. 'The Story of Life History: Gandhi', *Current Anthropology,* 14: 177–96.

Maquet, J.J., 1964. 'Objectivity in Anthropology', *Current Anthropology,* 5 (1): 47–55.

Marcus, George, and Michael Fischer, 1986. *Anthropology as Cultural Critique.* Chicago: University of Chicago Press.

Marriott, McKim, 1972. *Kishan Garhi Village: A Generation of Change—Technology, Society and Culture.* New York: University of the State of New York, Foreign Area Materials Center, Mimeograph.

Marsh, Catherine, 1982. *The Survey Method: The Contribution of Surveys to Sociological Explanation.* London: George Allen & Unwin.

Marshall, W.E., 1873. *A Phrenologist amongst the Todas or the Study of a Primitive Tribe in South India: History, Character, Customs, Religion, Infanticide, Polyandry, Language.* London: Longmans Green and Co.

Martin, Gary J., 1995. *Ethnobotany,* London: P. Chapman & Hall.

Marwah, I.S. and V.K. Srivastava, 1987. 'Khel Gate and Social Structure: A Study of their Relationship and a Note on the Place of Material Culture in Anthropology', *Indian Anthropologist,* 17 (2): 63–99.

Marx, Karl, 1959 (1867). *Capital.* Moscow: Progress Publishers, Vol. 1.

————, 1964. *Pre-capitalist Economic Formations.* London: Lawrence and Wishart.

Mascarenhas-Keyes, S., 1979. *Goans in London: Portrait of a Catholic Asian Community*, London: Goan Association (UK).

_____, 1985. 'The Changing Role of Women in a Migration Oriented Society', Paper Presented to Conference on Women and the Household, New Delhi.

Mauss, Marcel, 1979 (1950). *Sociology and Psychology*. London: Routledge & Kegan Paul.

Mayer, A.C., 1975. 'Becoming a Participant Observer', in A. Béteille and T.N. Madan (eds), *Encounter and Experience: Personal Accounts of Fieldwork*. Delhi: Vikas.

Mead, Margaret, 1928. *Coming of Age in Samoa*. New York: William Morrow.

_____, 1930. *Growing Up in New Guinea*. New York: William Morrow.

_____, 1935. *Sex and Temperament in Three Primitive Societies*. New York: William Morrow.

_____, 1935a. *The Mountain Arapesh. V: The Record of Unabelin and Rorschach Analysis*. Anthropological Papers of the American Museum of Natural History, 41, Part 3.

_____, 1953. 'National Character', in A.L. Kroeber (ed.), *Anthropology Today*. Chicago: University of Chicago Press.

_____, 1956. *New Lives for Old: Cultural Transformation,—Manus 1928–1953*. New York: William Morrow.

_____, 1964. *Anthropology: A Human Science*. New York: D. Van Nostrand Co., Inc.

_____, 1970. 'The Art and Technology of Field Work', in R. Naroll and R. Cohen (eds), *A Handbook of Method in Cultural Anthropology*. Garden City, New York: The Natural History Press.

_____, 1970a. 'Field Work in the Pacific Islands, 1925–1967', in Peggy Golde (ed.), *Women in the Field: Anthropological Experiences*. Berkeley: University of California Press.

_____, 1972. *Blackberry Winter: My Earlier Days*. New York: William Morrow.

Meier, A., and E. Rudwick, 1976. *From Plantation to Ghetto*. New York: Hill and Wang.

Merton, R.K., 1948. 'The Self-fulfilling Prophesy', in *Social Theory and Social Structure* (1968). New Delhi: Amerind.

_____, 1968. *Social Theory and Social Structure*. New Delhi: Amerind.

Messerschmidt, D., 1981. 'On Anthropology "at home"', in D. Messerschmidt (ed.), *Anthropologists at Home in North America: Methods and Issues in the Study of One's Own Society*. Cambridge: Cambridge University Press.

Meyer, John, W., 1989. 'Conceptions of Christendom: Notes on the Distinctiveness of the West', in Melvin L. Kohn (ed.), *Cross-National Research in Sociology*. Sage.

Middleton, J., 1970. *The Study of the Lugbara: Expectation and Paradox in Anthropological Research*. New York: Holt, Rinehart & Winston.

Mills, C. Wright, 1970 (1959). *The Sociological Imagination*. London: Penguin.

Mines, Mattison, 1994. *Public Faces, Private Voices: Community and Individuality in South India*. Berkeley: University of California Press.

Minocha, Aneeta A.,1979. 'Varied Roles in the Field: A Hospital in Delhi', in M.N. Srinivas, A.M. Shah, and E.A. Ramaswamy (eds), *The Fieldworker and the Field:*

Problems and Challenges in Sociological Investigation. Delhi: Oxford University Press.

Mintz, Sidney W., 2000. 'Sows' Ears and Silver Linings: A Backward Look at Ethnography', *Current Anthropology,* 41 (2): 169–89.

Mitchell, J. Clyde,1967. 'On Quantification in South Anthropology', in A.L. Epstein (ed.), *The Craft of Social Anthropology.* London: Tavistock.

Mommsen, W., 1984. *Max Weber and German Politics.* Chicago: University of Chicago Press.

Morgan, L.H., 1964 (1877). *Ancient Society.* Cambridge, Mass. The Belknap Press.

Moser, C.A., 1958. *Survey Methods in Social Investigation.* New York: The Macmillan Co.

Moser, C.A. and G. Kalton, 1972. *Survey Methods in Social Investigation.* London: Heinemann.

Mukherjee, N., 1993. *Participatory Rural Appraisal—Methodology and Applications.* New Delhi: Concept.

Mukherjee, R., 1974. *The Rise and Fall of the East India Company.* New York: Monthly Review Press.

————, 1979. *What Will it Be? Explorations in Inductive Sociology.* New Delhi: Allied Publishers.

————, 1979a. *Sociology of Indian Sociology.* Mumbai: Allied Publishers.

Mukherji, Partha Nath, 2000. 'Introduction', in Partha Nath Mukherji (ed.), *Methodology in Social Research: Dilemmas and Perspectives.* Sage.

Mukhia, H., 1976. *History and Historiography during the Reign of Akbar.* New Delhi: Vikas.

————, 1981. 'Was there Feudalism in Indian History', *The Journal of Peasant Studies,* 8 (3): 273–310.

————, 1985. 'Peasant Production and Medieval Indian History', *The Journal of Peasant Studies,* 12 (2 & 3): 228–51.

Murray, Alexander, 1978. *Reason and Society in the Middle Ages.* Oxford: Clarendon Press.

Myrdal, A. and V. Klein, 1956. *Women's Two Roles: Home and Work.* London: Routledge & Kegan Paul.

Myrdal, Gunnar, 1944. *An American Dilemma: The Negro Problem and Modern Democracy* (Vols 1 & 2). New York: Harper.

Nadel, S.F., 1939. 'The Interview Technique in Social Anthropology' in F. Bartlett, M. Ginsberg, E.J. Lindgren, and R.H. Thouless (eds), *The Study of Society: Methods and Problems.* London: Routledge & Kegan Paul.

————, 1951. *The Foundations of Social Anthropology.* London: Cohen & West.

————, 1957. *The Theory of Social Structure.* New York: Free Press.

Nader, Laura, 1970. 'From Anguish to Exultation', in Peggy Golde (ed.), *Women in the Field: Anthropological Experiences.* Berkeley: University of California Press.

Nakane, Chie, 1975. 'Fieldwork in India: A Japanese Experience', in A. Béteille and T.N. Madan (eds), *Encounter and Experience: Personal Accounts of Fieldwork.* Delhi: Vikas.

Nakleh, K., 1979. 'On being a Native Anthropologist', in G. Huizer and B. Mannheim (eds), *The Politics of Anthropology*. The Hague: Mouton.

Narayan, Kirin, 1993. 'How Native is a "Native" Anthropologist', *American Anthropologist*, 95 (3): 671–86.

Naroll, R., 1962. *Data Quality Control: A New Research Technique*. New York: Free Press of Glencoe.

Nash, D. and R. Wintrop, 1972. 'The Emergence of Self-Consciousness in Ethnography', *Current Anthropology*, 13: 527–42.

Nicholson, L., 1990. 'Introduction' in L. Nicholson (ed.), *Feminism/Postmodernism*. New York: Routledge.

Norbeck, Edward, 1972. 'Little-Known Minority Groups of Japan', in G. DeVos and H. Wagatsuma (eds), *Japan's Invisible Race: Caste in Culture and Personality*. Berkeley: University of California Press.

Norman, Donald A., 1969. *Memory and Attention: An Introduction to Human Information Processing*. New York: John Wiley & Sons.

Notes and Queries in Anthropology. 1964 (1874). London: Royal Anthropological Institute.

Obeyesekere, Gananath, 1981. *Medusa's Hair*. Chicago: Chicago University Press.

Okely, J., 1975. 'The Self and Scientism', *Journal of the Anthropological Society of Oxford*, 6: 171–88.

Opler, Morris, 1941. *An Apache Life-way: The Economic, Social and Religious Institutions of the Chiricahua Indians*. Chicago: Chicago University Press.

Orenstein, Henry, 1961. The Recent History of the Extended Family in India. *Social Problems*, 8(4): 41–50.

Orlans, Harold, 1967. 'Ethical ,Problems in the Relations of Research Sponsors and Investigators', in G. Sjoberg (ed.), *Ethics, Politics and Social Research*. Cambridge, Mass. Schenkman.

Ortner, Sherry B., 1999. *Life and Death on Mt. Everest: Sherpas and Himalayan Mountaineering*. Delhi: Oxford University Press.

Osgood, Cornelius, 1940. 'Informants', in *Ingalik Material Culture*. London: Oxford University Press.

Osofsky, G. (ed.), 1969. *Puttin' on Ole Massa: The Slave Narratives of Henry Bibb, William Wells Brown and Solomon Northrup*. New York: Harper & Row.

Ouden, Jan H.B. den, 1975. *De onaanraakbaren van Konkunad: Een onderzoek naar veranderingen in de sociale positie van de Scheduled Castes in een dorp van het district Coimbatore, India*. Wageningen: H. Veenman.

———, 1977. *De onaanraakbaren van Konkunad: Een onderzoek naar de positieverandering van de Scheduled Castes in een dorp van het district Coimbatore, India*. Deel II. Wageningen: Vakgroep Agrarische Sociologie van de niet-westerse gebieden.

Owusu, M., 1978. 'The Ethnography of Africa: The Usefulness of the Useless', *American Anthropologist*, 80: 310–34.

Palriwala, Rajni, 1991. 'Researcher and Woman: Dilemmas of a Fieldworker in a

Rajasthan Village', in M.N. Panini (ed.), *From the Female Eye: Accounts of Women Fieldworkers studying their Own Communities*. Delhi: Hindustan Publishing House.

Pandey, T.N., 1975. ' "India Man" among American Indians' in André Béteille and T.N. Madan (eds), *Encounter and Experience: Personal Accounts of Fieldwork*. New Delhi: Vikas.

Parkin, D. (ed.), 1982. *Semantic Anthropology*. London: Academic Press.

Parry, Jonathan P., 1994. *Death in Banaras*. Cambridge: Cambridge University Press.

Parsons, Talcott, 1966. *Societies: Evolutionary and Comparative Perspectives*. Englewood Cliffs: Prentice-Hall.

_____, 1971. *The System of Modern Societies*. Englewood Cliffs: Prentice-Hall.

Pattison, E.M., D. Francisco and P. Wood, 1975. 'A Psychosocial Kinship Model for Family Therapy', *American Journal of Psychiatry*, 132 (12): 1246–51.

Paul, Benjamin D., 1953. 'Interview Techniques and Field Relations', in A.L. Kroeber (ed.), *Anthropology Today*. Chicago: University of Chicago Press.

Payne, Geoff et al. 1981. *Sociology and Social Research*. London: Routledge & Kegan Paul.

Peirano, M.G.S., 1998. 'When Anthropology is at Home: The Different Contexts of a Single Discipline', *Annual Review of Anthropology*, 27: 105–28.

Pelto, Pertti J., 1970. *Anthropological Research: The Structure of Inquiry*. New York: Harper & Row.

Pelto, Pertti J., and Gretel H. Pelto, 1978. *Anthropological Research: The Structure of Inquiry*. Cambridge: Cambridge University Press.

_____,1997. 'Ethnography: The Fieldwork Enterprise', in J.J. Honigmann (ed.), *Handbook of Social and Cultural Anthropology*, Vol. 1. Jaipur & New Delhi: Rawat.

Pelto, Pertti J., and G.D. Spindler, 1965. *The Nature of Anthropology*. Columbus, Ohio: Charles E. Merrill Books, Inc.

Perinbanayagam, R.S., 1982. *The Karmic Theatre: Self, Society and Astrology in Jaffna*. Amherst: Massachusetts University Press.

Pickering, W.E.S., 1975. *Durkheim on Religion*. London: Routledge & Kegan Paul.

Piddington, Ralph, 1957. *An Introduction to Social Anthropology*, vol. 2. Edinburgh: Oliver and Boyd.

Pillai, Ananda Ranga, 1904. *The Private Diary of Ananda Ranga Pillai, 12 Volumes*. Madras: Superintendent, Government Press.

Pillai, S.D., 1976. *Rajahs and Prajas*. Mumbai: Popular Prakashan.

Piltz, Anders, 1981. *The World of Medieval Learning*. Oxford: Blackwell.

Pinney, Christopher, 1990. 'Anthropology and the Colonial Image', in C.A. Bayly (ed.), *The Raj: India and the British, 1600–1947*. London: National Portrait Gallery.

_____, 1992. 'The Parallel Histories of Anthropology and Photography', in E. Edwards (ed.), *Anthropology and Photography*. New Haven: Yale.

_____, 1997. *Camera Indica: The Social Life of Indian Photographs*, London: Reaktion Books, and Chicago: University of Chicago Press.

Platt, J., 1976. *Realities of Social Research: An Empirical Study of British Sociologists*. Brighton: University of Sussex.

Pocock, D.F., 1961. *Social Anthropology.* London: Sheed and Ward.

_____, 1973. *Mind, Body and Wealth: A Study of Belief and Practice in an Indian Village.* Oxford: Basil Blackwell.

Poovey, M., 1988. 'Feminism and Deconstruction', *Feminist Studies,* 14(1).

Powdermaker, H., 1966. *Stranger and Friend: The Way of an Anthropologist.* London: Secker and Warburg.

Powers, Edwin, 1963. 'An Experiment in Prevention of Delinquency', in Matilda White Riley (ed.) *Sociological Research: A Case Approach.* New York and Burlingame: Harcourt, Brace & World, Inc.

Prakash, O., 1977. *Political Ideas in the Puranas.* Allahabad: Panchanada.

Pugh, Derek, 1983. 'Studying Organizational Structure and Process', in Gereth Morgan (ed.) *Beyond Method: Strategies for Social Research.* Sage.

Rabinow, Paul, 1977. *Reflections on Fieldwork in Morocco.* Berkeley: University of California Press.

_____, 1986. 'Representations are Social Facts: Modernity and Post-Modernity in Anthropology', in James Clifford and George E. Marcus (eds), *Writing Culture: The Poetics and Politics of Ethnography.* Berkeley: University of California Press.

Rabinow, Paul, and W. Sullivan, 1979. 'Introduction—The Interpretative Turn: Emergence of an Approach', in *Interpretative Social Science: A Reader.* Berkeley: University of California Press.

Radcliffe-Brown, A.R., 1952. *Structure and Function in Primitive Society.* London: Cohen and West.

_____, 1957. *A Natural Science of Society.* Glencoe: The Free Press.

Raheja, Gloria Goodwin, 1988. *The Poison in the Gift: Ritual, Prestation, and the Dominant Caste in a North Indian Village.* Chicago and London: The University of Chicago Press.

Ralis, Max, et al., 1958. 'Applicability of Survey Techniques in Northern India', *Public Opinion Quarterly,* 22: 245–60.

Ramanujan, A.K., 1989.'Is there an Indian Way of Thinking? An Informal Essay', *Contributions to Indian Sociology* (n.s.) 23: 41–58.

Rao, Aparna, 1998. *Autonomy: Life Cycle, Gender and Status Among Himalayan Pastoralists.* New York, Oxford: Berghahn Books.

Rao, C.H., 1936. *The Dasara in Mysore.* Bangalore: Bangalore Printing and Publishing Co.

Rassundari Debi, 1981. 'Amar Jiban', in N.C. Jana et al. (eds), *Atmakatha,* vol. 1. Kolkata: Annanya Publications.

Read, Kenneth E., 1986. *Return to the High Valley: Coming Full Circle.* Berkeley: University of California Press.

Redfield, Robert, 1930. *Tepoztlán: A Mexican Village.* Chicago: University of Chicago Press.

_____, 1955. 'A Combination of Opposites, and Whole and Parts', in *The Little Community.* Chicago: University of Chicago Press.

_____, 1956. *Peasant Society and Culture.* Chicago: The University of Chicago Press.

_____, 1960. *The Little Community and Peasant Society and Culture.* Chicago: The University of Chicago Press.

Reynell Josephine, 1985. Honour, Nurture and Festivity: Aspects of Female Religiosity amongst Jain Women in Jaipur. Unpublished Ph.D. thesis: Cambridge University.

_____, 1991. 'Women and the Reproduction of the Jain Community', in Michael Carrithers and Caroline Humphrey (eds), *The Assembly of Listeners, Jains in Society*. Cambridge: Cambridge University Press.

Richards, Audrey I., 1938. 'The Village Census in the Study of Culture Contact', in B. Malinowski (ed.), *Methods of Study of Culture Contact in Africa*. New York: Oxford University Press.

Ricoeur, P., 1981. *Hermeneutics and the Human Sciences*. Paris: Maison des Sciences de L' Homme and Cambridge University Press.

Riley, Matilda White, (ed.), 1963. *Sociological Research: A Case Approach*. New York and Burlingame: Harcourt, Brace & World, Inc.

Rivers, W.H.R., 1906. *The Todas*. London: Macmillan.

_____, 1910. 'The Genealogical Method of Anthropological Inquiry', *Sociological Review*, 3: 1–12.

Robinson, Rowena, 1998. *Conversion, Continuity and Change: Lived Christianity in Southern Goa*. Sage.

Rosaldo, Renato, 1976. 'The Story of Tukbaw: They Listen as He Orates', in F.E. Reynolds and D. Capps (eds), *The Biographical Process: Studies in the History and Psychology of Religion*. The Hague: Mouton.

_____, 1987. 'Where Objectivity Lies: The Rhetoric of Anthropology', in John S. Nelson, Allan Megill, and Donald N. McCloskey (eds), *The Rhetoric of the Human Sciences*. Madison: University of Wisconsin Press.

Rostow, W.W., 1962. *The Stages of Economic Growth*. Cambridge: Cambridge University Press.

Roy, Rakhi, and Jayasinhji Jhala, 1987. 'An Examination of the Need and Potential for visual Anthropology in India', in *A Portrayal of People: Essays on Visual Anthropology in India*. New Delhi: Anthropological Survey of India and Indian National Trust for Art and Cultural Heritage.

Ray, S.C., 1938. 'An Indian Outlook on Anthropology.' *Man* (Article 172), pp. 146–50.

Rudolph, L., and S. Rudolph, 1958. 'Surveys in India: Field Experience in Madras States, *Public Opinion Quarterly*, 22: 235–44.

_____, with Mohan Singh Kanota, 2000. *Reversing the Gaze: Amar Singh's Diary A Colonial Subject's Narrative of Imperial India*. Delhi: Oxford University Press.

Runciman, W.G., 1978. *Weber—Selections in Translation*. Cambridge: Cambridge University Press.

_____, 1983. *A Treatise on Social Theory (Volume 1: The Methodology of Social Theory)*. Cambridge: Cambridge University Press.

Rycroft, C., 1968. *A Critical Dictionary of Psychoanalysis*. Penguin.

Saberwal, Satish, 1969. 'Rapport and Resistance among the Embu of Central Kenya (1963–1964)', in F. Henry and S. Saberwal (eds), *Stress and Response in Fieldwork*. New York: Holt, Rinehart & Winston

_____, 1976. *Mobile Men: Limits to Social Change in Urban Punjab*. Delhi: Vikas.

Saberwal, Satish, 1986. *India: The Roots of Crisis.* Delhi: Oxford University Press.

———, 1991. 'On the Rise of Institutions, or, the Church and Kingship in Medieval Europe', *Studies in History* 7: 107–34.

———, 1991a. 'Segmentation and Literacy', *Economic and Political Weekly,* Annual Number, 26: 723–38.

———, 1995. *Wages of Segmentation: Comparative Historical Studies on Europe and India.* New Delhi: Orient Longman.

Said, Edward W., 1999. *Out of Place: A Memoir.* Viking.

Sanjek, Roger, 'Ethnography', in Alan Barnard and Jonathan Spencer (eds), *Encyclopedia of Social and Cultural Anthropology.* London: Routledge.

Saran, A.K., 1962. 'Review of *Contributions to Indian Sociology*', No. IV', *The Eastern Anthropologist,* XV (1): 53–68.

Sarantakos, S., 1998 (1993). *Social Research.* London: Macmillan.

Sarsby, J.G., 1984. 'Special Problems of Fieldwork in Familiar Settings', in R.F. Ellen (ed.) *Ethnographic Research: A Guide to General Conduct.* London: Academic Press.

Sastry, K.R.R., 1941. *Indian States.* Allahabad: Kitabistan.

Scammell, G.V., 1981. *The World Encompassed: The First European Maritime Empires c. 800–1650.* London: Methuen.

Schwartz, Benjamin I., 1985. *The World of Thought in Ancient China.* Cambridge, MA: Harvard University Press.

Scruton, Roger, 1982. *Kant.* Oxford: Oxford University Press.

Selltiz, Claire, Marie Jahoda, Morton Deutsch, and Stuart W. Cook, 1959. *Research Methods in Social Relations.* New York: Holt, Rinehart & Winston.

Seymore, Susan C., 1999. *Women, Family and Child Care in India: A World in Transition.* Cambridge: Cambridge University Press.

Shah, A.M., 1964. 'Basic Terms and Concepts in the Study of Family in India', Indian Economic and Social History Review, 1(3): 1–36.

———, 1964a. Social Structure and Change in a Gujarat Village. Ph.D. Thesis. Baroda: University of Baroda.

———, 1996. 'Is the Joint Household Disintegrating', *Economic and Political Weekly,* 31 (9): 537–42.

———, 2002. *Exploring India's Rural Past: A Gujarat Village in the Early Nineteenth Century.* New Delhi: Oxford University Press.

Shah, A.M., and R.G. Shroff, 1958. 'The Vahivancha Barots of Gujarat: A Caste of Genealogists and Mythographers', in M. Singer (ed.), *Traditional India: Structure and Change.* Philadelphia: American Folklore Society.

———, and A.R. Shah, 1963. 'Early Nineteenth Century Village Records in Gujarat,' in Tapan Raychaudhuri (ed.), Contributions to Indian Economic History, Vol. II. Calcutta: Firma K.L. Mukhopadhyay (pp. 89–100).

Sharadasundari Debi, 1981. 'Amarkatha' in N.C. Jana et al. (eds), *Atmakatha,* Kolkata: Annanya Publications.

Sharma, R.S., 1985. 'How Feudal was Indian Feudalism?', *The Journal of Peasant Studies,* 12 (2 & 3): 19–43.

Shaw, Bruce, 1980. 'Life, History Writing in Anthropology: A Methodological Review', *Mankind,* 12 (3): 226–33.

Shils, Edward, 1981. *Tradition.* Chicago: University of Chicago Press.

Shils, Edward, and H.A. Finch (eds), 1949. *Max Weber on the Methodology of Social Sciences.* New York: The Free Press.

Shostak, Marjorie, 1981. *Nisa: The Life and Words of a !Kung Woman.* Cambridge, Mass. Harvard University Press.

Shweder, Richard A., 1996.'True Ethnography: The Lore, the Law, and the Lure', in Richard Jessor et al. (eds), *Ethnography and Human Development: Context and Meaning in Social Inquiry.* Chicago: University of Chicago Press.

Singleton. Jr, Royce A., and Bruce C. Straits, 1999. *Approaches to Social Research.* New York: Oxford University Press.

Sjoberg, Gideon and Roger Nett, 1992. *A Methodology for Social Research.* Jaipur and New Delhi: Rawat.

Smith, John D., 1991. *The Epic of Pabu-ji.* Cambridge: Cambridge University Press.

Smith, Robert, 1983. *Japanese Society.* Cambridge: Cambridge University Press.

Smith, R.S., 1996. *Rule by Record: Land Registration and Village Census in Early British Punjab.* Delhi: Oxford University Press.

Southern, R.W., 1962. *Western Views of Islam in the Middle Ages.* Cambridge, MA: Harvard University Press.

Speckmann, J.D., 1967. 'Social Surveys in Non-Western Areas', in D.G. Jongmans and P.C.W. Gutkind (eds), *Anthropologists in the Field.* Assen: Van goreum.

Spradley, J.P., 1980. *Participant Observation.* New York: Holt, Rinehart and Winston.

Srinivas, M.N.,1952. *Religion and Society among the Coorgs of South India.* Oxford: Clarendon Press.

————, 1966. *Social Change in Modern India.* Berkeley: University of California Press.

————, 1976. *The Remembered Village.* Berkeley: University of California Press.

————, 1979. 'The Fieldworker and the Field: A Village in Karnataka', in M.N. Srinivas, A.M. Shah, and E.A. Ramaswamy (eds), *The Fieldworker and the Field: Problems and Challenges in Sociological Investigation.* Delhi: Oxford University Press.

————, 1996. *Village, Caste, Gender and Method: Essays in Indian Social Anthropology.* Delhi: Oxford University Press.

————, 2000. 'Ex Igni Renascimur, *The Remembered Village* and Some Thoughts on Memory Ethnography', *Current Anthropology,* 41 (2): 163–68.

————, 2002. *Collected Essays.* Delhi: Oxford University Press.

Srinivas, M.N., A.M. Shah, and E.A. Ramaswamy (eds), *The Fieldworker and the Field: Problems and Challenges in Sociological Investigation.* Delhi: Oxford University Press.

Srivastava, V.K., 1990. 'A Note on Life-History Method', *Guru Nanak Journal of Sociology,* 11 (2): 1–9.

————, 1991. 'The Ethnographer and the People: Reflections on Field Work', *Eco-*

nomic and Political Weekly, XXVI (22 & 23): 1408–11, 1413–14; and XXVI(24): 1475–81.

Srivastava, V.K., 1997. *Religious Renunciation of a Pastoral People.* New Delhi: Oxford.

_____, 2003. 'Some Aspects of Indian Anthropology', Dr. K.S. Mathur Memorial Lecture', (delivered at Lucknow on 1 March).

Stearman, A.M., 1987. *No Longer Nomads: The Sirionó Revisited.* Lanham: Hamilton Press.

Stephen, J.B and L.S. Greer, 1981. 'Ethnographers in their Own Cultures: Two Appalachian Cases', *Human Organization,* 40: 123–30.

Stivers, C. Richard, 1993. 'Reflections on the Role of Personal Narrative in Social Science', *Signs,* 18 (2).

Stocking, Jr., George W. (ed.), 1983. *Observers Observed: Essays on Ethnographic Fieldwork.* Madison: University of Wisconsin Press.

Strathern, M., 1987. 'An Awkward Relationship: The Case of Feminism and Anthropology', *Signs,* 12 (2).

_____, 1987a. 'Out of Context: The Persuasive Fictions of Anthropology', *Current Anthropology,* 28 (3).

Streefkerk, Hein, 1993. *On the Production of Knowledge: Fieldwork in South Gujarat 1971–1991.* Amsterdam: VU University Press, for the Centre for Asian Studies, Comparative Asian studies, 11.

Sundar, Nandini, 1997. *Subalterns and Sovereigns: An Anthropological History of Bastar.* Delhi: Oxford University Press.

Tagg, John, 1988. *The Burden of Representation: Essays on Photographies and Histories.* Basingstoke: Macmillan.

Tajfel, Henri, 1969. 'Social and Cultural Factors in Perception' in G. Lindzey and E. Aronson (eds.), *The Handbook of Psychology, Volume 3.* Reading, MA: Addison-Wesley.

Tambiah, Stanley J., 2002. *Edmund Leach: An Anthropological Life.* Cambridge: Cambridge University Press.

Tandon, Prakash,1968. *Punjabi Century.* Berkeley: University of California Press.

Taussig, Michael, 1987. *Shamanism, Colonialism and the Wild Man: A Study in Terror and Healing.* Chicago: University of Chicago Press.

Taylor, S.J. and R. Bogdan, 1984. *Introduction to Qualitative Research: The Search for Meanings.* New York: Wiley.

Thapan, Meenakshi (ed.), 1998. *Anthropological Journeys: Reflections on Fieldwork.* New Delhi: Orient Longman.

The Geeta. 1935. London: Faber and Faber.

Dutt, M.N., (ed. and tr.), 1915. *The Mahābhārata.* Kolkata: Elysium Press.

The Times Atlas of World History (1978).

Thrupp, Sylvia, 1972. 'Medieval Industry 1000–1500' in C.M. Cipolla (ed.), *The Fontana Economic History of Europe: The Middle Ages.* Collins/Fontana Books.

Timasheff, N.S., 1955. *Sociological Theory.* Garden City, New York: Doubleday Co.

Todorov, Tzvetan, 1984. *The Conquest of America: The Question of the Other.* New York: Harper and Row.

Turner, Victor, 1967. *The Forest of Symbols.* Ithaca, New York: Cornell University Press.

―――――, 1974. *Dramas, Fields and Metaphors: Symbolic Action in Human Society.* Ithaca and London: Cornell University Press.

Tylor, E.B., 1958. *The Origins of Culture.* New York: Harper Torchback.

Unnithan, T.K.N., et al. (ed.), 1967. *Sociology for India.* New Delhi: Prentice-Hall of India.

Valero, Helena, 1984. *Yo say Napëyoma: Relato de una mujer raptada por los indigenas Yanomami.* Caracas: Fundacion la Salla de Ciencias Naturales.

Van Willigen, John, 1989. *Getting Some Age on Me: The Social Organization of Older People in a Rural American Community.* Lexington: University Press of Kentucky.

Vaughan, T.R., 1967. 'Governmental Intervention in Social Research: Political and Ethical Dimensions in the Wichita Jury Recordings', in G. Sjoberg (ed.), *Ethics, Politics and Social Research.* Cambridge, Mass: Schenkman.

Vidyarthi, L.P., 1963. *The Maler: A Study in Nature-Man-Spirit Complex of a Hill Tribe.* Kolkata: Bookland Private Ltd.

Visvanathan, Susan, 1993. *The Christians of Kerala: History, Belief and Ritual among the Yakoba.* Chennai: Oxford University Press.

Visweswaran, Kamala, 1996. *Fictions of Feminist Ethnography.* Delhi: Oxford University Press.

Wadley, Susan S., 1994. *Struggling with Destiny in Karimpur, 1925–1984.* New Delhi: Vistaar Publications.

Wadley, Susan S., and Bruce W. Kerr, 1989. 'Karimpur 1925–1984: Understanding Rural India Through Restudies', in Pranab Bardhan (ed.), *Conversations Between Economists and Anthropologists: Methodological Issues in Measuring Economic Change in Rural India.* Delhi: Oxford University Press.

Ward, B.E., 1965. 'Varieties of the Conscious Models', in M. Banton (ed.), *The Relevance of Models for Social Anthropology.* London: Tavistock.

Warren, Carol A.B., 1988. *Gender Issues in Field Research.* Sage.

Watson, L.C., 1976. 'Understanding a Life History as a Subjective Document: Hermeneutical and Phenomenological Perspectives, *Ethos,* 4: 95–131.

Wax, R.H., 1971. *Doing Fieldwork: Warnings and Advice.* Chicago: University of Chicago Press.

Weber, Max, 1949. *The Methodology of the Social Sciences.* New York: The Free Press.

―――――, 1950 (1927). *General Economic History.* Glencoe: Free Press.

―――――, 1969. 'Objectivity in Social Science', in *The Methodology of the Social Sciences.* New York: Free Press.

―――――, 1976 (1904–5). *The Protestant Ethic and the Spirit of Capitalism.* London: Allen and Unwin.

―――――, 1978 (1922). *Economy and Society.* Berkeley: University of California Press.

―――――, 1988 (1924). *The Agrarian Sociology of Ancient Civilizations.* London: Verso.

Weightman, S. and S.M. Pandey, 1978. 'The Semantic Fields of *dharma* and *kartavya* in

Modern Hindi', in W.D. O'Flaherty and J.D.M. Derrett (eds), *The Concept of Duty in South Asia*. London: SOAS.

Weiner, Annette B., 1976. *Women of Value, Men of Renown: New Perspectives in Trobriand Exchange*. Austin: University of Texas Press.

White, Jr, Lynn, 1972. 'The Expansion of Technology 500–1500', in C.M.Cipolla (ed.) 1972. *The Fontana Economic History of Europe: The Middle Ages*. Collins/Fontana Books.

Whyte, William Foote, 1941. 'The Social Role of the Settlement House', *Applied Anthropology*, 1(1): 14– 19.

————, 1943 (1955). *Street Corner Society: The Social Structure of an Italian Slum*. Chicago: The University of Chicago Press.

Whyte, William Foote, 1960. 'Interviewing', in R. Adams and J. Preiss (eds) *Human Organization Research: Field Relations and Techniques*. Homewood, Ill.: Dorsey Press.

————, 1984. *Learning From the Field: A Guide from Experience*. Sage.

Wilkinson, T., and P.L. Bhandarkar, 1984. *Methodology and Techniques of Research*. Mumbai: Himalaya Publishing House.

Wilson, A.T.M., 1951. 'Introduction', in Elliott Jacques, *The Changing Culture of a Factory*. London: Tavistock.

Winch, Peter, 1958. *The Idea of a Social Science and its Relation to Philosophy*. London: Routledge & Kegan Paul.

————, 1974. 'Understanding a Primtive Society' in Bryan Wilson (ed.), *Rationality*. Oxford: Blackwell.

Wineberg, Howard, 1995. 'Censuses and Census Data', in F.N. Magill (ed.), *International Encyclopedia of Sociology*. London: Fitzroy Dearborn Publishers.

Winnicott, D.W., 1956. 'On Transference', *International Journal of Psychoanalysis*, 37.

————, 1960. 'Counter Transference', *British Journal of Medical Psychology*, 35.

Wintrop, R., 1969. 'An Inward Focus: A Consideration of Psychological Stress in Fieldwork', in F. Henry and S. Saberwal (eds), *Stress and Response in Fieldwork*. New York: Holt, Rinehart & Winston.

Wiser, C.V., and W.H. Wiser, 1930. *Behind Mud Walls*. New York: Richard R. Smith.

Wittfogel, Karl A., 1957. *Oriental Despotism: Comparative Study of Total Power*. Yale: Yale University Press.

Wolcott, Harry F., 1990. *Writing Up Qualitative Research*. Sage.

————, 1995. *The Art of Fieldwork*. AltaMira Press.

Woods, P., 1979. *The Divided School*. London: Routledge & Kegan Paul.

————, 1981. 'Understanding Through Talk', in C. Adelman (ed.), *Uttering, Muttering: Collecting, Using and Reporting Talk for Social Educational Research*. London: Grant McIntyre.

Yalman, Nur, 1967. *Under the Bo Tree: Studies of Caste, Kinship, and Marriage in the Interior of Ceylon*. Berkeley: University of California Press.

Young, Pauline V., 1968. *Scientific Social Surveys and Research*. New Delhi: Prentice-Hall of India Pvt Ltd.

Zelliot, Eleanor, 1972. 'Bibliography on Untouchability', in J.M. Mahar (ed.), *The Untouchables in Contemporary India*. Tucson: University of Arizona Press.

Additional Readings

Baker, Therese L., *Doing Social Research*. New York: McGraw-Hill (1994).

This book gives the reader a general introduction to qualitative and survey research and sampling techniques, besides a detailed account of observational studies.

Barnard, H. Russell, *Research Methods in Anthropology: Qualitative and Quantitative Approaches*. New Delhi: Sage Publications (1994).

The book renders a detailed and clear account of various techniques, both of field and survey methods, that anthropologists and sociologists use for data collection.

Barnes, John A., *The Ethics of Inquiry in Social Science: Three Lectures*. Delhi: Oxford University Press (1977).

Written by a sociologist well known for his work on the ethics and politics of research, this collection examines the nature of social enquiry in a plural society and the nature of social science in a post-imperial world.

Berreman, Gerald D., *The Politics of Truth: Essays in Critical Anthropology*. New Delhi: South Asian Publishers Pvt. Ltd. (1981).

This collection of essays, written by the author over fifteen years, deals with the ethical and political issues of research. It encourages sociologists and anthropologists to speak out on public issues and social problems when they have relevant facts, interpretations, and informed opinions.

Béteille, André, and T.N. Madan (eds), *Encounter and Experience: Personal Accounts of Fieldwork*. Delhi: Vikas Publishing House (1975).

A collection of first-hand accounts of fieldwork, this book comprises a balanced introduction to the nature of fieldwork.

Béteille, André, *Sociology: Essays on Approach and Method*. New Delhi: Oxford University Press (2002).

This book comprises essays dealing with the nature of the discipline of sociology, its relationship with social anthropology, the method sociologists adopt for the study of society, and the aspects of sociological enquiry.

Bordens, Kenneth S., and Bruce B. Abbott, *Research Design and Methods: A Process Approach*. Mountain View, California: Mayfield (1991).

This book contains well-written chapters on the construction and administration of surveys as well as techniques for appropriate sampling.

Bose, Pradip Kumar, *Research Methodology*. New Delhi: Indian Council of Social Science Research (1995).

This book contains a survey of various works done by Indian sociologists and anthropologists on research methods and methodology.

Casley, D.J., and D.A. Lury, *Data Collection in Developing Countries*. Oxford: English Language Book Society/ Clarendon Press (1981).

This book provides an introduction to the survey method, the census, and case studies. How surveys of households and household members are to be conducted and data on agricultural holdings collected are given a special treatment.

Cohn, Bernard S., 'The Census, Social Structure and Objectification in South Asia' in Bernard S. Cohn, *An Anthropologist among the Historians and Other Essays*. Delhi: Oxford University Press (1996).

A comprehensive account of the development of the census in South Asia and the use of the materials thus generated for sociological purposes.

Delanty, Gerard, *Social Science: Beyond Constructivism and Realism*. Buckingham: Open University Press (1977).

This volume contains a comprehensive account of different methodologies and paradigms employed in the social sciences.

Denzin, Norman K. and Yvonna S. Lincoln (eds), *Collecting and Interpreting Qualitative Materials*. New Delhi: Sage Publications (1998).

This volume, divided in two parts, takes up the methods of collecting and analyzing empirical materials, and the art of interpretation, evaluation, and presentation. It also has an article on the interpretation of material cultural things.

Denzin, Norman K., *The Research Act: A Theoretical Introduction to Sociological Methods*. Englewood Cliffs, New York: Prentice-Hall (1970).

This book intertwines theory and methods, arguing that theory and methods exist in a flexible and dynamic relationship.

Dooley, David, *Social Research Methods*. New Delhi: Prentice-Hall of India Pvt. Ltd. (1997).

The book offers a balanced account of theory and measurement, sampling procedures, experimental and non-experimental research designs, and a review of statistical procedures.

Ellen, R.F. (ed.), *Ethnographic Research: A Guide to General Conduct*. London: Academic Press (1984).

This book covers readings on almost all aspects of social research.

Golde, Peggy (ed.), *Women in the Field: Anthropological Experiences*. Berkeley: University of California Press (1986).

This edited volume, consisting of fourteen papers, besides an introduction, takes up the role of subjective aspects in research from the perspective of gender issues.

Grimm, Laurence G., *Statistical Applications for the Behavioural Sciences*. New York: John Wiley & Sons.

This book provides an in-depth understanding of statistical methods and their advantages and disadvantages.

Hindess, Barry, *The Use of Official Statistics in Sociology: A Critique of Positivism and Epistemology*. London: Macmillan (1973).

Besides a critical analysis of the use of official statistics, this book contains a portion on the discussion of the agrarian categories in the Census of India, 1951.

Homans, George C., *The Nature of Social Science*. New York: Harcourt, Brace & World (1967).

Discussing the characteristics of social science, this brief book argues for a more rigorous approach in social research, otherwise the various disciplines classed under the rubric of social science will remain unacceptably 'soft'.

Jacobson, David, *Reading Ethnography*. Albany: State University of New York Press (1991).

Defining ethnography as the description of behaviour in a particular culture, typically resulting from fieldwork, this book presents a succinct analysis of certain well known ethnographies and attempts their classification.

Mahajan, Gurpreet, *Explanation and Understanding in the Human Sciences*. Delhi: Oxford University Press (1992).

This text is concerned with a critical examination of the different modes of enquiry used in human sciences.

Merton, Robert. K., *Social Theory and Social Structure*. Glencoe, Ill.: Free Press (1949).

A collection of various essays, this book contains chapters that reveal the interplay between social theory and social research.

Messerschmidt, Donald (ed.), *Anthropologists at Home in North America: Methods and Issues in the Study of One's Own Society*. Cambridge: Cambridge University Press (1981).

This collection of papers critically looks at aspects of the study of one's own society, or what has come to be known as 'native anthropology'.

Moser, C.A., and G. Kelton, *Survey Methods in Social Investigation*. New York: Basic Books (1972).

Of particular use to inexperienced researchers, this book carries a thorough discussion of how to ask appropriate questions and how to refine them.

Mukherjee, Ramkrishna, *Quality of Life*. New Delhi: Sage Publications (1980).

This book shows the usefulness of scaling and statistics in qualitative research.

Mukherjee, Ramkrishna, *What Will it Be?* New Delhi: Allied Publishers (1979).

This book deals with the philosophy of social science thinking and the logic of induction.

Mukherji, Partha Nath, 'Introduction', in Partha Nath Mukherji (ed.), *Methodology in Social Research: Dilemma and Perspectives*. New Delhi: Sage Publications (2000).

This introduction to the book in honour of Ramkrishna Mukherjee provides a critical description of various methods and methodologies in sociology, including the recent ones of participatory research. Its last section offers a summary of the various works on methodological issues by Indian scholars.

Panini, M.N. (ed.), *From the Female Eye: Accounts of Women Fieldworkers Studying Their Own Communities*. Delhi: Hindustan Publishing House.

This volume provides sensitive accounts of fieldwork undertaken by female researchers.

Portrayal of People: Essays on Visual Anthropology in India. New Delhi: Anthropological Survey of India and Indian National Trust for Art and Cultural Heritage (1987).

It is a collection of essays on the anthropological and sociological value of photo-graphic and audio-visual cinematographic records.

Punch, Maurice, *The Politics and Ethics of Fieldwork*. Sage Publications (1986).

This book contrasts classical fieldwork, in which the anthropologist spent 'long, celi-bate periods' among his 'community' with contemporary researchers who study a 'bewildering variety of groups and institutions' in modern society where those being studied are critically engaged in and concerned with the research project, especially its outcome. Against this background, the author discusses the politics and ethics of research.

Sahay, K.N., *Visual Anthropology in India and its Development*. New Delhi: Gyan Publishing House (1993).

This book is a collection of articles that its author has written over a period of time on visual anthropology.

Sarantakos, Sotirios, *Social Research*. London: Macmillan Press Ltd. (1998).

The first part of this book gives a comprehensive account of the meaning of social research, the various perspectives used, types of social research, and the research process.

Silverman, David, *Interpreting Qualitative Data: Methods for Analyzing Talk, Text and Interaction*. New Delhi: Sage Publications (1993).

This book describes the essential aspects and logic of qualitative research. It deals with the techniques of analysis of texts and interview data. The question of validity and reliability has also been taken up.

Sjoberg, Gideon (ed.), *Ethics, Politics and Social Research*. London: Routledge & Kegan Paul (1967).

This is a collection of articles on the ethical and political issues encountered by dif-ferent scholars while collecting, analysing, and writing up their data.

Smelser, Neil, *Essays in Sociological Explanation*. Englewood Cliffs, New York: Prentice-Hall (1968).

This text discusses the kinds of variables and relationships that sociologists study and the methods they use to do that.

Spradley, James P., *Participant Observation*. New York: Holt, Rinehart and Winston (1980).

This is a textbook on the methodology, techniques and issues of participant observa-tion.

Thapan, Meenakshi, *Anthropological Journeys: Reflections on Fieldwork*. New Delhi: Orient Longman (1998).

This collection comprises articles that reflect upon the ethical and gender issues in social research.

'Towards an Ethics for Anthropologists', section in *Current Anthropology*, 12(3), June 1971: 321-56.

Different scholars in this section have touched upon various ethical issues.

Warren, Carol A.B., *Gender Issues in Field Research*. New Delhi: Sage Publications (1988).

This short book focuses on the role gender plays in social research, arguing that ethnography cannot be understood without explicitly taking account of the ways the gender of the researcher influences relations with the people under study and the production of the final report.

Wolcott, Harry F., *The Art of Fieldwork*. California: AltaMira Press (1995).

This book is centered on the notion and techniques of fieldwork. An important part of this book is concerned with the writing up of qualitative research.

Index